교원임용고시 전공영어 시험대비 제5판

유희태
일반영어

④ LSI 영어연구소 유희태 박사 저

OMG 박문각

PREFACE

2014년에 초판이 나온 뒤 9년, 4판이 나온 뒤 2년이 지났다. 그 기간 동안 노량진에서 강의를 하면서 4판의 장점과 단점에 대해 수험생들과 의견을 교환할 기회를 가졌다. 이 5판은 그 대화의 산물이다. 5판은 형식적인 면에선 4판과 유사하다. 즉, 〈5판〉도 모든 문제를 문제은행 방식으로 배치하여, 변화된 시험제도에 적합성을 높이는 것을 목표로 하였는데, 이 형식을 대다수의 수험생들이 선호하였기에 그 형식적인 면은 바꾸지 않았다.

하지만 내용적인 면에서 본다면, 5판은 4판과 다르다. 우선 5판에서 다룬 주제도 우리가 살아가면서 겪게 되는 대다수의 영역(역사, 미학, 철학, 음악, 사회학, 사회복지학, 심리학, 소수민족학, 인종학, 인류학, 정치학, 경영학, 경제학, 교육학, 물리학, 생물학, 의학, 지질학, 인류학, 지리학 등)이 거의 들어가 있어서 그 이전 판들보다 훨씬 다양한 주제들을 접할 수 있도록 하였다. 또한 문제를 푸는 과정에서 일반영어 만점에 필수적인 배경지식을 자동으로 증진시킬 수 있도록 하였다. 그렇기에, 배경지식이 부족한 수험생들이 그 지식을 익히려 따로 시간을 내 다른 교재를 볼 필요가 없도록 하였다.

또한 양적인 면에서도, 4판이 총 36회 분량이었다면, 이번 5판은 총 60회 분량으로 거의 두 배 가까이 늘어났다. 대다수의 임용 수험생들은 일반영어 문제에 목말라 있다. 실제 임용시험 문제와 유사하면서도 질 좋은(오류가 없고 타당도가 높은) 문제가 안타깝게도 임용영어시험 시장에 많지 않기 때문이다. 시간이 가면 갈수록, 임용시험 시장이 작아지는 추세이다 보니, 현실적으로 출판사들 입장에서는 임용교재 출판으로는 경제적 수지타산이 거의 맞지 않기에 임용교재를 출판하려 하지 않고, 저자들도 고생에 비해 너무나 적은 보답이 오다보니 새롭고 독창적인 교재 개발은 거의 불가능해졌다. 더군다나 노량진 수험시장에서 오랜 세월 동안(1999년 이후 최근까지) 2, 3등 팀이었던 케빈팀과 윤도형팀이 더 이상 존재하지 않게 되어 상황은 더욱 악화되었다. 그래도 믿을 만한 문제를 만들어 낼 능력이 있던 팀들이 사라지다 보니, 질 좋은 일반영어 문제에 대한 수험생들의 갈증은 더욱 심화될 수밖에 없다. 이런 척박한 상황에 막중한 책임감을 느끼는 저자 입장에서는, 수험생들에게 조금이나마 도움이 되고자 양을 대폭 증대시키는 결정을 하였다. 시험을 준비하는 수험생들이 더욱 풍부하고 질 좋은 문제를 풀어봄으로써 일반영어 실력을 향상시킬 수 있도록 하고자 함이다.

이 5판 교재는 《유희태 일반영어 1-2S2R 기본》, 《유희태 일반영어 2-2S2R 유형》, 《유희태 일반영어 3-2S2R 기출》, 《유희태 일반영어 5- VOCA 30days》의 자매편이다. 시리즈 1, 2, 3 그리고 5를 통해 길러진 일반영어에 대한 이론, 유형, 기출, 그리고 어휘를 문제은행에 적용해 보도록 짜여있다. 이 시리즈를 통해서 공부한다면 임용시험에서 기본 과목이라 할 수 있는 일반영어가 상당 정도는 손에 잡힐 것으로 확신한다.

『유희태 일반영어』 시리즈를 효과적으로 활용하는 방법은, 대학 1~2학년 때 《2S2R 기본》을 최소 3회독, 평균 5회독하여 일반영어 기본 이론을 확실하게 다진 뒤, 2~3학년 때 《2S2R 유형》을 최소 3회독하여 임용 유형에 기본 이론을 확장 적용하는 훈련을 하고, 3학년 때 《2S2R 기출》을 2회독한 다음, 처음으로 임용시험을 치르는 4학년 때 《2S2R 문제은행》을 가지고 공부하는 것이다. 이 과정에서 〈기출 VOCA 30days〉는 1~2학년 때부터 주 6회 매일 20분씩 꾸준히 공부하기를 추천한다. 수험생 각자가 처한 상황에 맞춰서 공부해야겠지만, 가능하면 빨리 시작하는 것이 더욱 큰 효과를 낳을 것이란 것은 두말할 필요가 없다.

이 5판 작업을 하면서 많은 분들의 도움을 받았다. 원고를 보기 좋은 최종 결과물로 만들어준 박문각의 변수경 편집자와 박용 회장님께 고마움을 전한다. 영어지문의 속뜻, 함축의미, 문화적 맥락을 두고 건설적인 아이디어를 제시했던 LSI 영어연구소의 Sean Maylone 수석 연구원에게 고마움을 전한다. 또한, 이 교재가 출간되는 과정에서 묵묵히 최선을 다해주신 모든 인쇄 출판 노동자들께도 감사의 말씀을 전하고 싶다. 아무쪼록 이 《2S2R 문제은행》 5판 교재가 예비교사 여러분의 합격에 일조하기를 깊은 마음으로 바란다.

2023년 새해를 앞두고 LSI영어연구소에서

유희태

CONTENTS

모범답안

1회 ~ 60회

유희태
일반영어
❹ 문제은행

문제은행
(1~60회)

모범답안 p.002

01 Read the passage and follow the directions. [2 points]

There are hundreds of things we do — repeatedly, routinely — every day. We wake up, check our phones, eat our meals, brush our teeth, do our jobs. In recent years, such habitual actions have become an arena for self-improvement : bookshelves are saturated with bestsellers about 'life hacks', 'life design' and how to 'gamify' our long-term projects, promising everything from enhanced productivity to a healthier diet and huge fortunes. These guides vary in scientific accuracy, but they tend to depict habitual actions as routines that follow a repeated sequence of behaviours, into which we can intervene to set ourselves on a more desirable track.

The problem is that this account has been bleached of much of its historical richness. Today's self-help books have in fact inherited a highly contingent version of habitual actions — specifically, one that arises in the work of early 20th-century psychologists such as B. Skinner and Ivan Pavlov. These thinkers are associated with behaviourism, an approach to psychology that prioritises observable, stimulus-response reactions over the role of inner feelings or thoughts. The behaviourists defined habits in a narrow, individualistic sense; they believed that people were conditioned to respond automatically to certain cues, which produced repeated cycles of action and reward.

The behaviourist image of habitual actions has since been updated in light of contemporary neuroscience. For example, the fact that the brain is plastic and changeable allows _____ to inscribe themselves in our neural wiring over time by forming privileged connections between brain regions. The influence of behaviourism has enabled researchers to study habits quantitatively and rigorously. But it has also overlooked the concept's wider philosophical implications.

Fill in the blank with the ONE most appropriate word from the passage.

02 Read the passage and follow the directions. [4 points]

Forty years ago, the most serious nuclear accident in U.S. history sparked a backlash against the industry and halted its growth for decades. Today, the remaining working reactor at Three Mile Island, Unit 1, faces <u>new challenges</u>, including cheaper competition in a rapidly shifting energy grid. Unit 1 at the plant is slated to close later this year.

On March 28, 1979, Three Mile Island's Unit 2 reactor suffered a partial meltdown after a pump stopped sending water to the steam generators that removed heat from the reactor core. The accident was a combination of human error, design deficiencies and equipment failures. A small amount of radiation was released, but in the end, it wasn't a disaster. In 1985, Three Mile Island reopened, minus the one damaged reactor.

But for residents, it was kind of like living with a giant in your neighborhood. People knew it could cause you problems, but they lived in an uneasy compromise. That compromise is being tested, as the nuclear industry faces new challenges, including high operating costs, stagnant demand for electricity and competition from cheaper natural gas and renewable energy.

Chicago-based Exelon, the current owner of Three Mile Island's still-functional Unit 1 reactor, says the plant has been losing money for years. The company plans to close it this fall, 15 years before its operating license expires.

As someone who lived through the Three Mile Island accident, Joyce Corradi would be happier to see the plant close. But because the U.S. still has no real plan to deal with its radioactive nuclear waste, it will still be stored at the plant, sitting in her town indefinitely. Even today, she avoids driving by the plant's large, gray cooling towers.

Identify what the underlined "new chalenges" refer to. Second, describe what Joyce Corradi worries about currently.

_____

_____

_____

_____

_____

03 Read the passage and follow the directions. [4 points]

The US college admissions scandal is fascinating, if not surprising. Over 30 wealthy parents have been criminally charged over a scheme in which they allegedly paid a company large sums of money to get their children into top universities.

It's no secret that wealthy people will do nearly anything to get their kids into good schools. But this scandal only begins to reveal the lies that sustain the American idea of meritocracy. William Singer, who admitted to orchestrating the scam, explained that there are three ways in which a student can get into the college of their choice : "There is a front door which is you get in on your own. The back door is through institutional advancement, which is 10 times as much money. And I've created this side door." The "side door" he's referring to is outright crime, literally paying bribes and faking test scores. Even if we equalized public school funding, and abolished private schools, some children would be far more equal than others. Two and a half million children in the United States go through homelessness every year in this country. The chaotic living situation that comes with poverty makes it much, much harder to succeed. This means that even those who go through Singer's "front door" have not "gotten in on their own". They've gotten in partly because they've had the good fortune to have a home life conducive to their success.

People often speak about "equality of opportunity" as the American aspiration. But having anything close to equal opportunity would require a radical re-engineering of society from top to bottom. As long as there are large wealth inequalities, there will be colossal differences in the opportunities that children have. No matter what admissions criteria are set, wealthy children will have the advantage. If admissions officers focus on test scores, parents will pay for extra tutoring and test prep courses. If officers focus instead on "holistic" qualities, pare. It's simple : wealth always confers greater capacity to give your children the edge over other people's children. If we wanted anything resembling a "meritocracy", we would probably have to start by instituting a fully egalitarian society.

In reality, there can never be such a thing as a meritocracy, because there's never going to be fully equal opportunity. The main function of the concept is to assure elites that they deserve their position in life. It eases the "anxiety of affluence", that nagging feeling that they might be the beneficiaries of the arbitrary "birth lottery" rather than the products of their own individual ingenuity and hard work.

Describe the main idea of the passage in ONE sentence. Second, explain what the writer of the passage thinks about the concept of "front door" mentioned by Singer.

_____

_____

_____

_____

_____

04 Read the passage and follow the directions. [4 points]

Alcohol is a tiny, tiny molecule, and it acts all over the brain in so many different pathways. It affects endorphins and dopamine. It affects glutamate and GABA, the two primary excitatory and inhibitory neurotransmitters. It affects all kinds of ion channels. It's so small that it can act all over the place. And so it's been really hard to study. In fact, we still are just beginning to understand how it is that you feel drunk — what the mechanisms are for feeling drunk — because it acts kind of like a sledgehammer or just in a widespread way to disrupt all kinds of cell functioning. Cocaine is the perfect opposite of alcohol in this way. It does one thing. It does it really effectively. It blocks the recycling of dopamine and other neurotransmitters like norepinephrine, and that enhances pleasure and enhances arousal and enhances movement. So it's very specific. It's easy to study relatively and much easier to understand how it works. Finally, marijuana is both like cocaine and like alcohol. So it's like cocaine in that its actions are very specific, and it's like alcohol in that those actions are all over the brain. It does one thing, but it does it everywhere. So for cocaine, it does one thing, but it does it in just a few pathways. Alcohol does many things all over the place. THC, the active ingredient in marijuana, does one thing more or less, but everywhere, and that thing is to enhance communication between cells, to enhance the message.

Write a summary following the guidelines below.

⌐ Guidelines ⌐

• Summarize the above passage in one paragraph.

• Provide a topic sentence and supporting ideas based on the passage.

• Do NOT copy more than FIVE consecutive words from the passage.

_____

_____

_____

01 Read the passage and follow the directions. [2 points]

Why _____? This is the first question I have learned to expect when I'm asked about what kind of nursing I practice. This same question has come from family members, friends, strangers, and nurses and doctors who practice in other areas of the medical field. In most areas of healthcare, saving a life is the focus, and death is often viewed as a failure. Historically, there has not been a great deal of understanding as to why people would choose to concentrate their efforts where a medical success is not likely. Believe me when I say that it required a monumental shift in thinking for me to switch gears from the type of nursing I had previously done, which had everything to do with fixing, saving, and curing. I had to find out for myself that what we do in hospice is every bit as important, except that it's for people who no longer have those treatment options.

"But aren't you sad all the time?" or, "Isn't it scary?" or, "Don't you cry a lot?" are other frequently asked questions. Those of us working in hospice will answer : No, I'm not sad all of the time. No, it isn't scary. Yes, I cry a lot. But the crying is often from the relief, joy and satisfaction that a patient's last weeks, days, or hours were fulfilling and comfortable, and that their family members had been able to work toward this same goal in a positive way.

Fill in the blank with the ONE most appropriate word from the passage.

02 Read the passage and follow the directions. [4 points]

Have you heard of the D.W.T. — the Declined-with-Thanks Club? There are no club rooms and not many members, but the balance sheet for the last twelve months is wonderful, showing that more than $15,000 was refused. The entrance fee is one hundred guineas and the annual subscription fifty guineas; that is to say, you must have refused a hundred guineas before you can be elected, and you are expected to refuse another fifty guineas a year while you retain membership. It is possible also to compound with a life refusal, but the sum is not fixed, and remains at the discretion of the committee.

Baines is a life member. He saved an old lady from being run over by a motor bus some years ago, and when she died she left him a legacy of $1400. Baines wrote to the executors and pointed out that he did not go about dragging persons from beneath motor buses as a profession; that, if she had offered him $1400 at the time, he would have refused it, not being in the habit of accepting money from strangers, still less from women; and that he did not see that the fact of the money being offered two years later in a will made the slightest difference. Baines was earning $400 a year at this time, and had a wife and four children, but he will not admit that he did anything at all out of the common.

The case of Sedley comes up for consideration at the next committee meeting. Sedley's rich uncle, a cantankerous old man, insulted him grossly; there was a quarrel; and the old man left, vowing to revenge himself by disinheriting his nephew and bequeathing his money to a cats' home. He died on his way to his solicitors, and Sedley was told of his good fortune in good legal English. He replied, "What on earth do you take me for? I wouldn't touch a penny. Give it to the cats' home or any blessed thing you like." Sedley, of course, will be elected as an ordinary member, but as there is a strong feeling on the committee that <u>no decent man could have done anything else</u>, his election as a life member is improbable.

Describe why Baines became a member of the Declined-with-Thanks Club.
Second, explain the meaning of the underlined words in the last sentence.

_____

_____

_____

_____

_____

03 Read the passage and follow the directions. [4 points]

Edward O'Brien's team had research subjects watch a movie on Netflix that they hadn't seen before and thought they'd enjoy. Then, on the following night, the researchers had some of them watch the same movie again. The group that didn't watch it a second night in a row rated the enjoyment they would have had rewatching it at an average of roughly 4 on an eight-point scale, which was lower than the 6.4 they gave to watching the movie the first time. But the group that did watch the movie a second time gave the experience a 5.7 on average.

These discrepancies illustrate O'Brien's finding well. It's not that watching a movie for the second time in 24 hours is just as enjoyable as the first time — it probably won't be. But it does seem likely to be more pleasant than one would predict.

In general, behavioral-economics research has found that when people make decisions about what they think they'll enjoy, they often assign priority to unfamiliar experiences — such as a new book or movie, or traveling somewhere they've never been before. They are not wrong to do so : People generally enjoy things less the more accustomed to them they become. As O'Brien writes, "People may choose novelty not because they expect exceptionally positive reactions to the new option, but because they expect exceptionally dull reactions to the old option." And sometimes, that expected dullness might be exaggerated.

Knowing that expectations can sometimes deviate from reality in this way could help inform the decisions people make about how they spend their leisure time. The biggest application of the finding is for people to spend more time considering why they prefer a novel option over a repeat option. Doing so could save them time and might make them just as happy.

According to the research above, which of the options would be better : Either spending one-hour researching for a new nearby restaurant or considering the possible value of simply returning to the taco place from yesterday. Then explain why.

_____

_____

_____

_____

_____

04 Read the passage and follow the directions. [4 points]

There are several ways of asking people for help that avoid making them feel controlled and that let them experience the natural high of helping. These reinforcements create the desire to want to help another.

The first reinforcement is what psychologists call a strong sense of in-group. In other words, the belief that the person in need is on your team —a part of a group that is important to you. This goes beyond mere collective reciprocity; we help people from our in-group because we care about what happens to the in-group. Because our own happiness and well-being are affected by the group's happiness and well-being. Helping to create the in-group status of a person in need reliably leads to a genuine desire to help.

The second reinforcer is the opportunity for positive identity. In other words, when helping you makes me feel good about me. Particularly when it allows me to see myself as possessing a positive attribute or playing an admired role. For example, people help more when they reflect on why it's important to them to "be a benefactor to others." When a positive identity —like being a benefactor—is made salient, people are more likely to act in accordance with it.

The last one is the opportunity to see one's own effectiveness. People want to see or know the impact of the help they have given or will give. They want to see it land. This is actually not an ego thing. It's what some psychologists have argued is the fundamental human motivation : to feel effective. To know that your actions create the results you intended. To, in essence, shape the world around you. In the absence of feedback —when we have no idea what the consequences of our actions have been— motivation takes a nosedive.

Write a summary following the guidelines below.

| Guidelines |

- Summarize the above passage in one paragraph.
- Provide a topic sentence and supporting ideas based on the passage.
- Do NOT copy more than FIVE consecutive words from the passage.

_____

_____

_____

_____

_____

📖 모범답안 p.005

01 Read the passage and follow the directions. [2 points]

In the 20th century, statisticians and scientists mostly rejected causality as an appropriate subject for science. They mostly observed correlations, and carefully repeated the mantra "correlation does not imply causation".

Scientists kept wanting to at least hint at causal implications of their research, but statisticians rejected most attempts to make rigorous claims about causes.

The one exception was for randomized controlled trials (RCTs). Statisticians figured out early on that a good RCT can demonstrate that correlation does imply causation. So RCTs became increasingly important over much of the 20th century.

That created a weird tension, where the use of RCTs made it clear that scientists valued the concept of causality, but in most other contexts they tried to talk as if causality wasn't real. Not quite as definitely unreal as phlogiston. A bit closer to how behaviorists often tabooed the ideas that we had internal experiences and consciousness, or how linguists once banned debates on the origin of language, namely, that it was dangerous to think science could touch those topics. Or maybe a bit like heaven and hell — concepts which, even if they are useful, seem to be forever beyond the reach of science.

But scientists kept wanting to influence the world, rather than just predict it. So they often got impatient, when they couldn't afford to wait for RCTs, to act as if _____ told them something about causation.

phlogiston : belief in magic

Fill in the blank with the ONE most appropriate word from the passage.

02 Read the passage and follow the directions. [4 points]

"If poor people knew how rich people are, there would be riots in the streets." Actor and comedian Chris Rock made this astute statement during a 2014 interview with *New York Magazine*, referring to the yawning gap between rich and poor. In so doing, he stumbled upon a key challenge in the study of inequality.

What's the best way to measure it? Most inequality studies have focused on income — measures of which are widely available. However, being rich is not about a single year of earnings but rather about the accumulation of wealth over time. In the past, quantifying that has been tricky.

The wealthy would probably prefer we stay in the dark about how rich they are, presumably to avoid the aforementioned   ①   . People like me who study the topic, however, are always looking for more data and better and more accurate ways to measure the rich-poor gap. And while I'm not one to promote violence in the streets, I do believe it's important for citizens to be fully aware of the levels of disparity in their society.

The most revealing way to do this, in my view, is by looking at wealth inequality. There are several ways to measure inequality. One of the most popular is by income. That's largely because there's more data, and it's a lot easier to measure. But ② <u>this measure is a snapshot</u>.

Wealth, on the other hand, is an aggregation, affected not only by current income but earnings accumulated in previous years and by previous generations. Only by studying wealth inequality do scholars, policymakers and others get the deepest and broadest measure of the gap between the rich and everyone else.

Fill in the blank with the ONE most appropriate word from the passage. Then, explain the meaning of the underlined words in ②.

_____

_____

_____

03   Read the passage and follow the directions. [4 points]

It would not be the first time that an important economic resource had gone from simply being used to being owned and traded; the same has already happened with land and water, for example. But digital information seems an unlikely candidate to be allocated by markets. Unlike physical resources, personal data are an example of what economists call "non-rival" goods, meaning they can be used more than once.

Labour, like data, is a resource that is hard to pin down. Workers were not properly compensated for labour for most of human history. Even once people were free to sell their labour, it took decades for wages to reach liveable levels on average. History won't repeat itself, but chances are that it will rhyme, Mr Weyl predicts in *Radical Markets*, a provocative new book he has co-written with Eric Posner of the University of Chicago. He argues that in the age of artificial intelligence, it makes sense to treat data as a form of labour.

To understand why, it helps to keep in mind that "artificial intelligence" is something of a misnomer. Messrs Weyl and Posner call it "collective intelligence": most AI algorithms need to be trained using reams of human-generated examples, in a process called machine learning. Unless they know what the right answers (provided by humans) are meant to be, algorithms cannot translate languages, understand speech or recognise objects in images. Data provided by humans can thus be seen as a form of labour which powers AI. As the data economy grows up, such data work will take many forms. Much of it will be passive, as people engage in all kinds of activities — liking social-media posts, listening to music, recommending restaurants — that generate the data needed to power new services. But some people's data work will be more active, as they make decisions (such as labelling images or steering a car through a busy city) that can be used as the basis for training AI systems.

In what aspect is data similar to labor according to the passage? Second, explain why the term "artificial intelligence" is misleading.

_____

_____

_____

_____

_____

04 **Read the passage and follow the directions.** [4 points]

Most people want to know the single best way to schedule their day for maximum productivity, and there are numerous articles and books that claim to know the "perfect schedule." But the reality is, there is no perfect method for everyone. However, it is crucial that you schedule your day. As *Essentialism* author Greg McKeown says : "If you don't prioritize your life, someone else will." By setting a daily schedule, you ensure that you are the one prioritizing your life.

Polyphasic sleep skill is a somewhat bizarre scheduling method that only works for a few select people, but if it works for you, you'll achieve uncommon amounts of productivity in a single day. Most people are monophasic sleepers, meaning they get their daily sleep in one chunk (or phase). Biphasic sleepers get their sleep in two smaller chunks, such as 4 hours in the morning and 4 hours in the late evening. Polyphasic sleepers take this method to the extreme, breaking up sleep into multiple short phases, which allows for less sleep overall and significant increases in productivity. The amount of sleep in each phase can vary, with some people sleeping only in 20-minute naps and others grabbing larger chunks of sleep and then supplementing with naps.

This schedule has some very obvious drawbacks. Steve Pavlina noted the challenge of having this type of schedule while still maintaining a sane family schedule. And if you miss any of your scheduled sleep sessions, it can significantly throw off your sleep schedule. But this schedule also has some massive advantages, like getting extra hours every day. If you only sleep four hours per day, you add approximately 28 extra hours to your week (assuming normally sleeping 8 hours).

Summarize the passage by following the guidelines below.

| Guidelines |

- Summarize the above passage in one paragraph.
- Provide a topic sentence and supporting ideas based on the passage.
- Do NOT copy more than FIVE consecutive words from the passage.

모범답안 p.008

01 **Read the passage and follow the directions.** [2 points]

In principle a work of art has always been reproducible. Man-made artifacts could always be imitated by men. Replicas were made by pupils in practice of their craft, by masters for diffusing their works, and, finally, by third parties in the pursuit of gain. Mechanical reproduction of a work of art, however, represents something new. Historically, it advanced intermittently and in leaps at long intervals, but with accelerated intensity. The Greeks knew only two procedures of technically reproducing works of art : founding* and stamping.

Bronzes, terra cottas, and coins were the only art works which they could produce in quantity. All others were unique and could not be mechanically reproduced. With the woodcut graphic art became mechanically reproducible for the first time, long before script became reproducible by print. The enormous changes which printing, the mechanical reproduction of writing, has brought about in literature are a familiar story. However, within the phenomenon which we are here examining from the perspective of world history, print is merely a special, though particularly important, case. During the Middle Ages engraving and etching were added to the woodcut; at the beginning of the nineteenth century lithography made its appearance.

With _____ the technique of reproduction reached an essentially new stage. This much more direct process was distinguished by the tracing of the design on a stone rather than its incision on a block of wood or its etching on a copperplate and permitted graphic art for the first time to put its products on the market, not only in large numbers as hitherto, but also in daily changing forms. Lithography enabled graphic art to illustrate everyday life, and it began to keep pace with printing.

founding : melting and pouring metal or glass into a mold.

Fill in the blank with the ONE most appropriate word from the passage.

02 Read the passage and follow the directions. [4 points]

Perpetual Guardian, a New Zealand company, asked its 240 office workers to work a four-day week (at eight hours per day) instead of five days, while still being paid their usual five-day salary. The trial was inspired by growing evidence that modern open-plan workplaces can be distracting for workers and reduce productivity. Managing director Andrew Barnes thought a shorter working week might be an innovative way to get employees to focus on their work and maintain overall productivity, while providing benefits such as an enhanced work-life balance, better mental health and fewer cars on the road. The results show a 24% increase in employees saying their work-life balance had improved, a significant improvement in engagement and a 7% drop in stress levels — all without a reduction in productivity.

However, there are some challenges. The first challenge for the company was that not everybody does the same work across a varied workplace. It is not a production line making widgets, where productivity can be measured easily. Their solution was to ask teams (and their managers) to detail what they actually did in their job and how they might do it over four days instead of five. This involved organizing coverage within teams so that they could still meet deadlines and maintain performance and productivity. In practice, the four-day week meant employees within a team all had a day off each week, but that this day moved from Monday to Friday across the trial period.

The expectation was that if workers could maintain the same level of productivity and do so in four days, they should achieve greater personal benefits and the company would make other gains through enhanced reputation, recruitment and retention, as well as energy savings (20% reduction in staff at work). There is a large body of research showing that if organisations care about their employees' well-being, staff will respond with better job attitudes and performance. In addition, research shows that work-life balance is important for job satisfaction and general well-being, and that by being able to spend more time away from their job, employees engage better with their work.

Describe the difficulty the company met when it tried to introduce the trial. Second, explain how work-life balance functions in terms of productivity.

---

03 Read the passage and follow the directions. [4 points]

Many of our choices have the potential to change how we think about the world. Often the choices taken are for some kind of betterment : to teach us something, to increase understanding or to improve ways of thinking. What happens, though, when a choice promises to alter our cognitive perspective in ways that we regard as a loss rather than a gain?

Think, for example, of Elizabeth and Philip Jennings in the FX television show, *The Americans*(2013-). They are Russian spies in the 1980s tasked with living in the United States and engaging in acts of espionage. In order to do their job, they have to spend a lot of time associating with people whose worldview they find abhorrent. They must build close relationships with many of these people, and this means exposing themselves to their ideas and often acting as if they hold these ideas themselves. It makes good sense for a person given such an assignment to worry that, in carrying it out, she will become more sympathetic than she currently is to some false or abhorrent ideas —not because she has learned that these ideas might be correct, but because the time spent encountering these ideas and pretending to embrace them might cause her to unlearn, at least to a degree, some of what she presently understands about the world.

It's not hard to imagine other cases that have this kind of structure. Maybe the documentary that a friend invites you to watch puts forward a message that you think is dangerously false. Maybe a discipline you are thinking of studying involves ideological presuppositions you reject. And so on. In such cases, the way that a choice would alter your _____ is seen as a net minus.

Explain the reason the writer mentions the television show "The Americans" in the passage. Second, fill in the blank with the TWO most appropriate consecutive words from the passage.

_____

_____

_____

04 Read the passage and follow the directions. [4 points]

Although our brain accounts for just 2 percent of our body weight, the organ consumes half of our daily carbohydrate requirements — and glucose is its most important fuel. Under acute stress the brain requires some 12 percent more energy, leading many to reach for sugary snacks. Carbohydrates provide the body with the quickest source of energy. In fact, in cognitive tests subjects who were stressed performed poorly prior to eating. Their performance, however, went back to normal after consuming food.

To further understand the relationship between the brain and carbohydrates, we examined 40 subjects over two sessions. In one, we asked study participants to give a 10-minute speech in front of strangers. In the other session they were not required to give a speech. At the end of each session, we measured the concentrations of stress hormones cortisol and adrenaline in participants' blood. We also provided them with a food buffet for an hour. When the participants gave a speech before the buffet, they were more stressed, and on average consumed an additional 34 grams of carbohydrates, than when they did not give a speech.

So what about that chocolate, then? If a person craves chocolate in the afternoon, I advise him or her to eat chocolate to stay fit and keep his or her spirits up. That's because at work people are often stressed and the brain has an increased need for energy. If one doesn't eat anything, it's possible the brain will use glucose from the body, intended for fat and muscle cell use, and in turn secrete more stress hormones. Not only does this make one miserable, it can also increase the risk of heart attacks, stroke or depression in the long run. Alternatively, the brain can save on other functions, but that reduces concentration and performance.

Summarize the passage following the guidelines below.

_____ Guidelines _____

• Summarize the above passage in one paragraph.

• Provide a topic sentence and supporting ideas based on the passage.

• Do NOT copy more than FIVE consecutive words from the passage.

_____

_____

_____

_____

_____

01 Read the passage and follow the directions. [2 points]

At age 17, Aristotle enrolled in the Platonic Academy. He would stay there for 20 years. Founded by the father of Western philosophy, the Greek philosopher Plato, Aristotle was the most promising student around. He asked many questions and answered even more.

The exact time of his departure from the Academy is disputed, but it's said that he left soon after Plato died due to his dislike of the direction that it subsequently took. In the years following, he would even go on to argue against many of his late teacher's core ideas.

It's impossible to say how much Aristotle wrote, but even from the fraction of his work that we have left today, there is a stunning amount of breadth in the subjects he covered. Every field from astronomy and physics to ethics and economics has been influenced by the work of Aristotle. For more than 2,000 years after his death, he has remained one of the most widely read and quoted thinkers in the history of our species.

While his impact can still be felt in the many different subjects today, maybe the most accurate of his observations relate to _____. He saw it as one of the true joys of life, and he felt that a life well-lived needed to be built around such companionship. In his own words : "In poverty as well as in other misfortunes, people suppose that friends are their only refuge. And friendship is a help to the young, in saving them from error, just as it is also to the old, with a view to the care they require and their diminished capacity for action stemming from their weakness; it is a help also to those in their prime in performing noble actions, for 'two going together' are better able to think and to act."

Fill in the blank with the ONE most appropriate word from the passage.

02 Read the passage and follow the directions. [4 points]

Why do tribal and hunter-gatherer human societies tend to be more equal? All primate societies, Christopher Boehm, a cultural anthropologist at the University of Southern California, notes, are governed by similar dynamics. If any one individual has the opportunity to climb the hierarchy, he or she is likely to seize it; unfortunately, as soon as power is gained, others resent it. In such a society, Boehm writes, there are three potential outcomes. One is conflict, in which newcomers continually and overtly challenge the powerful for a position at the top. Another is stable dominance, where the powerful relentlessly and permanently dominate the rest. And a third is an equally stable social structure which Boehm calls "reverse dominance hierarchy," in which those on the bottom of the pyramid figure out a way to band together and "deliberately dominate their potential master." In such a society, dominance is still exercised. It just comes, collectively and consistently, from below.

Chimps, bonobos, and gorillas struggle to achieve stable reverse-dominance hierarchy. They can occasionally flatten their pyramids, but only briefly. The problem is that the powerful are likely to be strong, intelligent, and socially connected. To topple them, and prevent them from taking over again, you need a powerful and persistent threat, which nonhuman primates don't have. Boehm has discovered that, among the tribal and hunter-gatherer human societies, the development of projectile weapons is a key step in the growth and maintenance of equality : it puts the strong at greater risk from the weak. Such weaponry is one reason that human societies are more equalized than those of other primates.

Explain why tribal and hunter-gatherer human societies tend to be more equal than primates, according to Christopher Boehm. Second, describe what "reverse dominance hierarchy" is.

---

03 Read the passage and follow the directions. [4 points]

Facebook is no longer growing as a platform for news. In the U.S., for instance, young people's use of Facebook for news fell by 20 percentage points between 2017 and 2018. The percentage of U.S. adults who ever get news from Facebook was just about flat between last year and this year.

It's not that people are using their devices less; rather, they're increasingly getting news from messaging apps, as reiterated in a report released by the Reuters Institute for the Study of Journalism. The report looks at the social media habits of users in the U.S., U.K., Brazil, and Germany; the entire sample was made up of people who said they got news from Facebook or messaging apps at least weekly. It's designed to provide some color and qualitative information around the 2018 Digital News Report that the Reuters Institute released, and to look more closely at the effects of Facebook's January News Feed algorithm change on consumers. "Why are consumers turning to messaging apps, to receive, comment upon, and share news?" the authors write.

It's clear that Facebook is still a default platform for many users, even if they feel conflicted about that default status. "It's a guilty pleasure and I hate it but I love it," one U.S. male (in the 20- to 29-year-old age bracket) said. It's "an distraction for filling time" and a key way to keep in touch with people. But how passionate can you feel about something you also see as a complete waste of time? "Facebook is getting more and more unattractive and impersonal for me and so I write or post less," said one German woman ① between the ages of 20 and 29. "Only 10 percent of my friends on Facebook are really friends for me."

If Facebook's algorithm change was meant to bring people back together on the platform — to get news out of the way and make room for intimacy and meaningful social interaction — this research, at least, suggests that that hasn't worked.

Reducing the news sources is not that useful, unlike ads. Maybe it was already too late : As Reuters' earlier report showed, people have begun the transition to _____②_____ to share news and discuss personal topics.

In what aspect is the information contained in underlined selection ① of key importance to the overall context? Second, fill in the blank with the TWO most appropriate consecutive words from the passage.

_____

_____

_____

_____

_____

04 Read the passage and follow the directions. [4 points]

Starting with the Terrible Twos, when toddlers hear the word "No" on a regular basis, people don't like to be told they can't do something. They often believe government regulations interfere with their rights. The government requires vaccinations for school attendance; parents complain that they should be able to make their own decisions about whether to vaccinate their children. The government requires that drugs be approved by the FDA before marketing; desperate patients dying of cancer complain that regulations are preventing them from getting the one new treatment that just might save their life. The "health freedom" argument is that everyone has the right to use whatever treatments they want, to control what goes into their bodies, and that it's none of the government's business.

But quacks use the concept of "health freedom" to divert attention away from themselves and toward victims of disease with whom we are naturally sympathetic. "These poor folks should have the freedom to choose whatever treatments they want," cry the quacks — with crocodile tears. They want us to overlook two things. First, no one wants to be cheated, especially in matters of life and health. Victims of disease do not demand quack treatments because they want to exercise their "rights," but because they have been deceived into thinking that they offer hope. Second, the laws against worthless nostrums* are not directed against the victims of disease but at the promoters who attempt to exploit them.

Vaccine refusers don't recognize that the government has a duty to protect the welfare of children and to protect the population from vaccine-preventable diseases. They tend to think parental rights and personal preference should trump everything else.

*nostrum : a medicine that is not effective, prepared by an unqualified person

Summarize the passage following the guidelines below.

| Guidelines |

- Summarize the above passage in one paragraph.
- Provide a topic sentence and supporting ideas based on the passage.
- Do NOT copy more than FIVE consecutive words from the passage.

_____

_____

_____

_____

_____

01 Read the passage and fill in the blank with the ONE most appropriate word from the passage. [2 points]

The effects of local competition are especially severe in the face of inequality. Some resources hold more value than others, creating inequality between those who win it and those who don't, and so they are worth fighting harder for. But local competition amplifies this effect, making small differences in the stakes loom large. In my own work, participants in an economic game made selfish choices more often as inequality increased, causing them to get into 'fights' with their partners that cost them points. However, they fought most often under local competition, even when there was only a small amount of inequality between them, and lost many more points as a result.

This might well explain some otherwise puzzling patterns in real-world violence. In his book *Killing the Competition*, Daly shows that homicide rates are high in places with greater levels of inequality and low in places with lesser levels of inequality. If, however, local competition amplifies the effect of inequality on homicide and global competition quiets it, then changes in human trade and migration — diffusing competition over larger swathes of the population — can break the simple correlation we expect between inequality and homicide over time. Inequality can grow, for instance, at the same time that competition becomes _____, with the latter sharply reducing the impact of the former.

---

02 Read the passage and follow the directions. [4 points]

Plenty of studies have documented crows' intelligence, such as their puzzle-solving prowess and tool use. Other research has highlighted aspects of crows' social behavior, finding that groups of crows notice and react to the sight of their dead.

Kaeli Swift, a doctoral candidate at the University of Washington, was documenting a crow "funeral" in 2015, when she first observed some unusual sexual activity. At the time, she and her adviser John Marzluff were investigating the birds' organized vocal responses to finding a dead crow, which signals a potential threat to the living. And they saw something they had never observed before : A crow approached the corpse, mounted it and started ① "thrashing" in a manner that was immediately recognizable.

In research into how crows gather and communicate around their dead, Swift and Marzluff found that the birds used dead crows to learn about and avoid potential risks. This made their discovery of the new crow behavior —having sex with the dead—extremely puzzling, Swift said. If a dead crow is a danger signal, why would a living crow want to get close to it? "Engaging so closely with a dead conspecific [animal of the same species] could expose you to disease, or parasites, or scavengers," Swift said.

The researchers conducted ② a series of experiments in four Washington cities, testing 308 mated pairs of wild crows. They exposed the birds to carefully positioned taxidermic* crows and to other prepared animal corpses, such as pigeons and squirrels to see if the crows' responses were common to a range of dead things or if they were specific to their own species.

They found that the birds were more likely to caw* in alarm when the corpse that they saw belonged to a crow, particularly if the stuffed crow was in a "dead" pose rather than a more lifelike posture. The birds approached dead crows about 25 percent of the time, but only 4 percent initiated sexual activity, hinting that corpse canoodling* is not commonly practiced.

* taxidermic : the art of stuffing the skins of animals
* caw : cry of the crow
* canoodling : kissing and holding each other

Write the FIVE consecutive words from the passage that correspond to the meaning of the underlined words in ①. Second, explain what the "a series of experiments" discovered in terms of main purpose of the researchers.

_____

_____

_____

_____

_____

03 **Read the passage and follow the directions.** [4 points]

More than a decade ago, a certain suspicion of empathy started to creep in, particularly among young people. Since the late 1960s, researchers have surveyed young people on their levels of empathy, testing their agreement with statements such as : "It's not really my problem if others are in trouble and need help" or "Before criticizing somebody I try to imagine how I would feel if I were in their place."

Sara Konrath, an associate professor, collected decades of studies and noticed a very obvious pattern. Starting around 2000, the line starts to slide. More students say it's not their problem to help people in trouble, not their job to see the world from someone else's perspective. By 2009, on all the standard measures, young people on average measure 40 percent less empathetic than my own generation — 40 percent!

It's strange to think of empathy — a natural human impulse — as fluctuating in this way, moving up and down like consumer confidence. But that's what happened. Young people just started questioning ① <u>what my elementary school teachers had taught me</u>. Their feeling was : Why should they put themselves in the shoes of someone who was not them, much less someone they thought was harmful? In fact, cutting someone off from empathy was the positive value, a way to make a stand. So, for example, when the wife of white nationalist Richard Spencer recently told *BuzzFeed* he had abused her, the question debated on the lefty Internet was : Why should we care that some woman who chose to ally herself with a nasty racist got herself hurt? Why waste empathy on that?

The new rule for empathy seems to be : reserve it, not for your "enemies," but for the people you believe are hurt. Empathy, but just for your own team. And empathizing with the other team? That's practically a taboo. And it turns out that this brand of ② <u>selective empathy</u> is a powerful force.

Write the ONE word from the passage that BEST corresponds to the underlined words in ①. Second, explain what "selective empathy" is according to the passage.

_____

_____

_____

_____

_____

04 Read the passage and follow the directions. [4 points]

China enjoyed undoubted advantages : a rise of food production nearly as early as in the Fertile Crescent and a large and productive expanse, nourishing the largest regional human population in the world, etc. These advantages and head start enabled medieval China to lead the world in technology. In the early 15th century it sent treasure fleets, each consisting of hundreds of ships up to 400 feet long and with total crews of up to 28,000, across the Indian Ocean as far as the east coast of Africa, decades before Columbus's three puny ships crossed the narrow Atlantic Ocean to the Americas' east coast. Why didn't Chinese ships cross the Pacific to colonize the Americas' west coast? Why, in brief, did China lose its technological lead to the formerly so backward Europe?

The end of China's treasure fleets gives us a clue. Seven of those fleets sailed from China between A.D. 1405 and 1433. They were then suspended as a result of a power struggle between two factions at the Chinese court (the eunuchs* and their opponents). The former faction had been identified with sending and captaining the fleets. Hence when the latter faction gained the upper hand in a power struggle, it stopped sending fleets, eventually dismantled the shipyards, and forbade oceangoing shipping. The episode is reminiscent of the legislation that strangled development of public electric lighting in London in the 1880s, the isolationism of the United States between the First and Second World Wars, and any number of backward steps in any number of countries, all motivated by local political issues. But in China there was a difference, because the entire region was politically unified. One decision stopped fleets over the whole of China. That one temporary decision became irreversible, because no shipyards remained to turn out ships that would prove the folly of that temporary decision, and to serve as a focus for rebuilding other shipyards.

*eunuch : a man who had been castrated to serve a king

Summarize the passage by following the guidelines.

| Guidelines |

- Summarize the above passage in one paragraph.
- Provide a topic sentence and supporting ideas based on the passage.
- Do NOT copy more than FIVE consecutive words from the passage.

_____

_____

_____

_____

_____

01 **Read the passage and follow the directions.** [2 points]

I am an evolutionary behavioral ecologist, and most of my work is concerned with how individual differences in behavior (i.e. personality) influence individual fitness, and the collective behavior and success of animal societies. Most are probably not aware, but animal personality research is a vibrant field within behavioral ecology due to the ubiquity of personality as a phenomenon in nature, and its ability to explain interactions both within and between species. In nearly every species tested to date for the presence of personality, we've found it, and sex-linked personality differences are frequently the most striking. Sex-linked personality differences are very well documented in our closest primate relatives, too, and the presence of sexual dimorphism (i.e. size differences between males and females) in primates, and mammals generally, dramatically intensifies these differences, especially in traits like aggression, female choosiness, territoriality, grooming behavior, and parental care.

Given that humans are sexually dimorphic and exhibit many of the typical sex-linked behavioral traits that any objective observer would predict, based on the mammalian trends, the claim that our _____ have(has) arisen purely via socialization is dubious at best. For that to be true, we would have to posit that the selective forces for these traits inexplicably and uniquely vanished in just our lineage, leading to the elimination of these traits without any vestiges of their past, only to have these traits fully recapitulated* in the present due to socialization.

*recapitulate : explicate; explain

Fill in the blank with the TWO most appropriate consecutive words from the passage.

02 Read the passage and follow the directions. [4 points]

The late 1980s marked the beginning of a reformation in child psychology. Bauer and other psychologists began to test infant memory by performing a series of actions — such as building a simple toy gong and striking it — and then waiting to see if a child could imitate the actions in the right order, after a delay ranging from minutes to months.

One experiment after another revealed that the memories of children 3 and younger do in fact persist, albeit with limitations. At 6 months of age, infants' memories last for at least a day; at 9 months, for a month; by age 2, for a year. And in a landmark 1991 study, researchers discovered that four-and-a-half-year-olds could recall detailed memories from a trip to Disney World 18 months prior. Around age 6, however, children begin to forget many of these earliest memories. In a 2005 experiment by Bauer and her colleagues, five-and-a-half-year-olds remembered more than 80 percent of experiences they had at age 3, whereas seven-and-a-half-year-olds remembered less than 40 percent.

This work laid bare the contradiction at the heart of childhood amnesia : Infants can create and access memories in their first few years of life, yet most of these memories eventually vanish at a rate far beyond the typical forgetting of the past we experience as adults.

Maybe, some researchers thought, enduring memories require language or a sense of self, both of which we lack as infants. But although verbal communication and self-awareness undoubtedly strengthen human memories, their absence could not be the whole explanation for childhood amnesia. After all, certain animals that have large and complex brains relative to their body size — such as mice — but do not have language or, presumably, our level of self-awareness, also lose the memories they make in infancy.

Describe the major contribution done by the underlined "landmark research". Second, what does the case of mice reveal?

_____

_____

_____

_____

_____

03 **Read the passage and follow the directions.** [4 points]

Armed with 3 million responses to a happiness monitoring app, plus the locations and times of several years worth of British soccer matches, University of Sussex economists Peter Dolton and George MacKerron calculated that the happiness that fans feel when their team wins is outweighed — by a factor of two — by the sadness that strikes when their team loses.

Which means, assuming a roughly equal number of fans on both sides, the World Cup final between France and Croatia made the world less happy than it was the day before. On net, soccer is a destroyer of happiness.

To prove it, the researchers analyzed data from an app that pinged 32,000 people several times a day and asked them how happy they felt on a 100-point scale, as well as who they were with and what they were doing. The responses included location information, which allowed researchers to determine if they were at a stadium, or had been to one.

They adjusted the results to account for basic differences in happiness based on time of day and day of week. Because they measure differences from each person's typical happiness level, they were also able to account for people who are, as a rule, permanently miserable or elated. They could not, however, adjust for the app's users, who tended to be younger and more affluent than the country as a whole.

In the hour immediately after their team wins, researchers found a typical fan might feel about 3.9 points happier than usual — about the same boost as from listening to music. That's more than offset by the 7.8 points of extra sadness that fans will feel in the hour after their team loses, an event that makes respondents feel about twice as sad as they would be after working, studying or waiting in line.

The researchers call the results "quite dramatic" and say they add up over time. Because post-soccer sadness lingers for hours while after-match joy is fleeting, a loss actually ends up robbing fans of about _____ times the amount of happiness they might have gained from a win. The effects are much greater if a respondent is actually at the stadium.

Describe what the researchers could not adjust for. Then, fill in the blank with the ONE most appropriate word.

_____

_____

_____

_____

_____

04 Read the passage and follow the directions. [4 points]

Two thousand years of monotheistic brainwashing have caused most Westerners to see polytheism as ignorant and childish idolatry. This is an unjust stereotype. In order to understand the inner logic of polytheism, it is necessary to grasp the central idea buttressing the belief in many gods.

Polytheism does not necessarily dispute the existence of a single power or law governing the entire universe. In fact, most polytheist and even animist religions recognised such a supreme power that stands behind all the different gods, demons and holy rocks. In classical Greek polytheism, Zeus, Hera, Apollo and their colleagues were subject to an omnipotent and all-encompassing power—Fate (*Moira, Ananke*). In Hindu polytheism, a single principle, Atman, controls the myriad gods and spirits, humankind, and the biological and physical world. Atman is the eternal essence or soul of the entire universe, as well as of every individual and every phenomenon.

The fundamental insight of polytheism, which distinguishes it from monotheism, is that the supreme power governing the world is devoid of interests and biases, and therefore it is unconcerned with the mundane desires, cares and worries of humans. It's pointless to ask this power for victory in war, for health or for rain, because from its all-encompassing vantage point, it makes no difference whether a particular kingdom wins or loses, whether a particular city prospers or withers, whether a particular person recuperates or dies. <u>The Greeks did not waste any sacrifices on Fate, and Hindus built no temples to Atman.</u>

Summarize the passage by following the guidelines.

Guidelines

- Summarize the above passage in one paragraph.
- Provide a topic sentence and supporting ideas based on the passage.
- Include the reason the Greeks and Hindus did as indicated in the underlined part.
- Do NOT copy more than FIVE consecutive words from the passage.

_____

_____

_____

_____

_____

01 Read the passage and follow the directions. [2 points]

For most of his career, Dr. Stephen Trzeciak was not a big believer in the "touchy-feely" side of medicine. As a specialist in intensive care and chief of medicine at Cooper University Health Care in Camden, N.J., Trzeciak felt most at home in the hard sciences.

Then his new boss, Dr. Anthony Mazzarelli, came to him with a problem : Recent studies had shown an epidemic of burnout among health care providers. As co-president of Cooper, Mazzarelli was in charge of a major medical system and needed to find ways to improve patient care.

He had a mission for Trzeciak — he wanted him to find answers to this question : Can treating patients with medicine and compassion make a measurable difference on the wellbeing of both patients and doctors?

Trzeciak wasn't convinced. Sure, compassion is good, Trzeciak thought, but he expected to review the existing science and report back the bad news that caring has no quantitative rationale. But Mazzarelli was his colleague and chief, so he dove in.

After considering more than 1,000 scientific abstracts and 250 research papers, Trzeciak and Mazzarelli were surprised to find that the answer was, resoundingly, yes. When health care providers take the time to make human connections that help end suffering, patient outcomes improve and medical costs decrease. Among other benefits, compassion reduces pain, improves healing, lowers blood pressure and helps alleviate depression and anxiety.

Complete the main idea of the passage by filling in the blank with the ONE most appropriate word from the passage.

> Taking time for _____ makes doctors better at their jobs.

02 **Read the passage and follow the directions.** [4 points]

---

① <u>You weren't raised in a barn</u>. You know you need to express gratitude and appreciation for other people's help. And yet people often make a critical mistake when expressing gratitude : they focus on how they feel — how happy they are, how they have benefited from the help — rather than focusing on the benefactor.

Researchers at the University of North Carolina distinguished between two types of gratitude expressions : other-praising, which involves acknowledging and validating the character or abilities of the giver (i.e., their positive identity); and self-benefit, which describes how the receiver is better off for having been given help. In one of their studies, they observed couples expressing gratitude to one another for something their partner had recently done for them. Their expressions were then coded for the extent to which they were other-praising or focused on self-benefit. Examples of their expressions included:

Other-praising : "It shows how responsible you are ..." "You go out of your way ..." "I feel like you're really good at that."

Self-benefit : "It let me relax." "It gave me bragging rights at work." "It makes me happy."

Finally, benefactors rated how responsive they felt the gratitude giver had been, how happy they felt, and how loving they felt toward their partner. The researchers found that other-praising gratitude was strongly related to perceptions of responsiveness, _____②_____, and loving, but self-benefit gratitude was not.

Explain the meaning of the underlined words in ①. Then, fill in the blank with the ONE most appropriate word from the passage. If necessary, change the word form.

_____

_____

_____

03 Read the passage and follow the directions. [4 points]

If there are extraterrestrial civilisations out there, they don't seem very interested in us. They don't visit, they don't phone, they don't even send radio signals. Not a peep. It is easy to feel start feeling neglected once you become aware of this cosmic cold shoulder. As the eminent physicist Enrico Fermi once put it, "Where is everybody?"

There is intelligence and intelligence. Recent research shows that many birds, especially from the crow family, can outdo monkeys on any test of ingenuity. A good case can also be made for octopuses. Given that birds, mammals and molluscs* evolved independently, this suggests that some level of intellect is a natural outcome of evolutionary pressures. Still, this is not the kind of intellect that is going to send signals to the stars. Impressive as the crows may be, they aren't going to work out electromagnetic field theory. Advanced science needs the kind of acumen that allows humans to build complex cultures and probe into things. And this does look like a freak in evolutionary terms.

So, from a biological point of view, it looks as if the prospects for intelligent interstellar conversation are limited. There are probably plenty of dumb animals scattered across the universe, but nobody worth talking to. This might strike you as depressing. However, it would be more depressing if it turns out that we are not cosmic freaks. For then <u>the silence starts to look sinister</u>. If the emergence of advanced civilisations is common, then the obvious explanation is that a typical extraterrestrial empire doesn't last long. Perhaps plenty have announced their presence, only to implode within a few years. We all like to think humanity will survive into the indefinite future. But there is a danger that any species with our technological power will quickly find a way of destroying itself, whether by war, pestilence or pollution.

mollusc : an important phylum of invertebrate animals

Describe the difference between the intellect of crows and that of human beings. Second, explain why the silence looks "sinister".

---

04 Read the passage and follow the directions. [4 points]

That humans have self-domesticated has grown increasingly obvious over the past half century. Even apart from increased docility — the primary index of domestication — humans show many signs of what has come to be recognized as the domestication syndrome : smaller bodies and brains, thinner bones, shorter faces, and reduced physical differences between males and females. Besides these anatomical markers, there are also behavioral and physiological ones, which involve fear response, playfulness, learning rates, sexual behavior, and hormone production, among others. What these markers all have in common is paedomorphism (literally, "child shape"). In dogs, foxes, guinea pigs, and many other species, domesticated animals resemble the juvenile stage of the wild animals that they descended from. Humans evolved from our Homo ancestor several hundred thousand years ago, and there aren't sufficient fossils to demonstrate paedomorphism directly. But there are plenty of Neanderthal fossils, and comparisons strongly suggest that present-day humans are, in many respects, juvenilized — that is, domesticated — versions of our remote ancestors.

Why did these changes happen? For an evolutionary biologist, that question is normally equivalent to asking, What adaptive purpose did they serve? In this case, however, the answer is unusual : none. A decades-long, painstaking experiment showed that reduced brain size, thinner bones, and all of the other markers of domestication syndrome are merely incidental byproducts of a primary adaptation : reduced reactive aggression. In organisms selecting against such aggression, the migration of neural-crest cells — a special kind of cell that carries developmental instructions throughout the embryo and fetus — is delayed, resulting in smaller bodies, smaller brains, hormonal changes, and the rest. Human communities selected against reactive aggression is because group life requires a minimum of stability. No trait is more disruptive than reactive aggression, which fuels such behaviors as quests for dominance and demands for submission; arrogance, bullying, and random violence; and the monopolizing of food and females.

Summarize the passage by following the guidelines.

Guidelines

- Summarize the above passage in one paragraph.
- Provide a topic sentence and supporting ideas based on the passage.
- Do NOT copy more than FIVE consecutive words from the passage.

모범답안 p.023

01 **Read the passage and follow the directions.** [2 points]

I have been watching the 2018 World Cup in France, mainly in the bars and cafes of the lower end of the 14th arrondissement* in Paris. This is a mixed neighbourhood that is partly gentrified but also home to council estates with a large immigrant population and the usual low-level social tensions — drugs, gangs, run-ins with the police. So far, however, watching the game has been relatively trouble-free. Each step by the French team towards victory has been followed by good-humoured delirium — much tooting of horns and showering of beer. Watching all of this on the news, what was most striking about the fans was not their racial mix, although numerous ethnicities were represented, but how _____ they were. This is the new generation of millennials for whom the last great French victory in the 1998 World Cup is an event from history. A cartoon in *Le Parisien* said it all : "You've got to stop telling us stories from the last century," young fans tell a portly* middle-aged white male (not unlike myself). The message is clear : this is our World Cup and this is our own triumph to celebrate.

In a sense, they are right. This French team are an extremely young team, largely indifferent to the past and not weighed down by history. Some of them, such as the superstar-in-waiting Kylian Mbappé, weren't even born when France last won the World Cup.

arrondissement : administrative divisions of France
portly : fat

Fill in the blank with the ONE most appropriate word from the passage.

02 Read the passage and follow the directions. [4 points]

Beating humans at board games is passé in the AI world. Now, top academics and tech companies want to challenge us at video games ① instead. Today, OpenAI, a research lab founded by Elon Musk and Sam Altman, announced its latest milestone : a team of AI agents that can beat the top 1 percent of amateurs at popular battle arena game Dota 2.

You may remember that OpenAI first strode into the world of Dota 2 last August, unveiling a system that could beat the top players at 1v1 matches. However, this game type greatly reduces the challenge of Dota 2. OpenAI has now upgraded its bots to play humans in 5v5 match-ups, which require more coordination and long-term planning. And while OpenAI has yet to challenge the game's very best players, it will do so later this year at The International, a Dota 2 tournament that's the biggest annual event on the e-sports calendar.

The motivation for research like this is simple : if we can teach AI systems the skills they need to play video games, we can use them to solve complex real-world challenges that, in some ways, resemble video games — like, for example, managing a city's transport infrastructure.

② This is an exciting milestone. It's really because it's about transitioning to real-life applications. If we've got a simulation of a problem and we can run it large enough scale, there's no barrier to what we can do with this.

Explain why the writer of the passage uses the word "instead". Second, explain the meaning of the underlined words in ②.

_____

_____

_____

_____

_____

03 Read the passage and follow the directions. [4 points]

"Data slavery." Jennifer Morone, an American artist, thinks this is the state in which most people now live. To get free online services, she laments, they hand over intimate information to technology firms. "Personal data are much more valuable than you think," she says. To highlight this sorry state of affairs, Morone has resorted to what she calls ① "extreme capitalism". She registered herself as a company in Delaware in an effort to exploit her personal data for financial gain. She created dossiers* containing different subsets of data, which she displayed in a London gallery in 2016 and offered for sale, starting at £100. The entire collection, including her health data and social-security number, can be had for £7,000.

Only a few buyers have taken her up on this offer and she finds "the whole thing really absurd". Yet if the job of the artist is to anticipate the Zeitgeist*, Ms Morone was dead on : this year the world has discovered that something is rotten in the data economy. Since it emerged in March that Cambridge Analytica, a political consultancy, had acquired data on 87m Facebook users in underhand ways, voices calling for a rethink of the handling of online personal data have only grown louder. Even Angela Merkel, Germany's chancellor, recently called for a price to be put on personal data, asking researchers to come up with solutions.

Given the current state of digital affairs, in which the collection and exploitation of personal data is dominated by big tech firms, Ms Morone's approach, in which individuals offer their data for sale, seems unlikely to catch on. But what if people really controlled their data — and the tech giants were required to pay for access? ② What would such a data economy look like?

*dossier : all the documents relating to an affair
*Zeitgeist : spirit of the times

Describe what "extreme capitalism" refers to. Next, explain the implication of the underlined words in ②.

_____

_____

_____

_____

_____

04 Read the passage and follow the directions. [4 points]

"Necessity is the mother of invention." That is, inventions supposedly arise when a society has an unfulfilled need : some technology is widely recognized to be unsatisfactory or limiting. Would-be inventors, motivated by the prospect of money or fame, perceive the need and try to meet it. Some inventor finally comes up with a solution superior to the existing, unsatisfactory technology. Society adopts the solution if it is compatible with the society's values and other technologies.

Quite a few inventions do conform to this commonsense view. In 1942, in the middle of World War II, the U.S. government set up the Manhattan Project with the explicit goal of inventing the technology required to build an atomic bomb before Nazi Germany could do so. That project succeeded in three years, at a cost of $2 billion (equivalent to over $20 billion today). Other instances are Eli Whitney's 1794 invention of his cotton gin to replace laborious hand cleaning of cotton grown in the U.S. South, and James Watt's 1769 invention of his steam engine to solve the problem of pumping water out of British coal mines.

These familiar examples deceive us into assuming that other major inventions were also responses to perceived needs. In fact, many or most inventions were developed by people driven by curiosity or by a love of tinkering, in the absence of any initial demand for the product they had in mind. Once a device had been invented, the inventor then had to find an application for it. Only after it had been in use for a considerable time did consumers come to feel that they "needed" it. Thus, invention is often the mother of necessity, rather than vice versa.

Summarize the passage by following the guidelines.

Guidelines

• Summarize the above passage in one paragraph.

• Provide a topic sentence and supporting ideas based on the passage.

• Do NOT copy more than FIVE consecutive words from the passage.

📖 모범답안 p.025

01 Read the passage and follow the directions. [2 points]

We credit Socrates with the insight that 'the unexamined life is not worth living' and that to 'know thyself' is the path to true wisdom. But is there a right and a wrong way to go about such self-reflection?

Simple rumination — the process of churning your concerns around in your head — isn't the answer. It's likely to cause you to become stuck in the rut of your own thoughts and immersed in the emotions that might be leading you astray. Certainly, research has shown that people who are prone to rumination also often suffer from impaired decision making under pressure, and are at a substantially increased risk of depression.

Instead, the scientific research suggests that you should adopt an ancient rhetorical method favoured by the likes of Julius Caesar and known as 'illeism' — or speaking about yourself in the third person (the term was coined in 1809 by the poet Samuel Taylor Coleridge from the Latin ille meaning 'he, that'). If I was considering an argument that I'd had with a friend, for instance, I might start by silently thinking to myself : '<u>David felt frustrated that</u>…' The idea is that this small change in perspective can clear your emotional fog, allowing you to see past your biases.

A bulk of research has already shown that this kind of third-person thinking can temporarily improve decision making and that it can also bring long-term benefits to thinking and emotional regulation. The researchers said this was the first evidence that wisdom-related cognitive and affective processes can be trained in daily life, and of how to do so.

Identify the TWO consecutive words from the passage that BEST match the underlined words.

02 Read the passage and follow the directions. [4 points]

Imagine someone who believes that her local grocery store is open for business today, so she goes to buy some milk. But the store isn't open after all — she didn't realize that today's a holiday. Even though the store is closed, her behaviour still makes a kind of sense. She is going to the store because she thinks it is open — not because it actually is open. It makes sense for this person to go to the store, but she doesn't have as good a reason to go there as she would if she didn't just think, but rather knew, that the store were open. If that were case she'd be able to go to the store because it is open, and not merely because she thinks it is. ① That's the distinction to keep in mind.

Now let's revisit the case of the climate skeptic. The skeptic doesn't know that climate change is a hoax, since it isn't a hoax at all. So he can't choose not to enroll in the course because climate change is a hoax, any more than the person we imagined earlier could go to the store because it is open. Rather, the most that the skeptic can do is avoid taking the course because he thinks that climate change is a hoax — a choice that makes sense, but not one that is based on as good a reason as the skeptic would have if he didn't just think, but rather knew, that this was true.

If this is on the right track, then the crucial difference between the dogmatic or closed-minded person and the person who exercises appropriate cognitive caution might be that the second sort of person knows, while the first merely believes, that the choice she decides against is one that would be harmful to her cognitive perspective. The person who knows that a choice will harm her perspective can decide against it simply because it will do so, while the person who merely ____②____ this can make this choice only because that is what she thinks.

Explain the meaning of the underlined words in ①. Second, find the ONE most appropriate word that fits in blank ②.

---

03 Read the passage and follow the directions. [4 points]

Advanced algorithms working from large chemical databases can predict a new chemical's toxicity better than standard animal tests, suggests a study led by scientists at Johns Hopkins Bloomberg School of Public Health.

The researchers, in the study that appears in the journal *Toxicological Sciences* on July 11, 2018, mined a large database of known chemicals they developed to map the relationships between chemical structures and toxic properties. They then showed that one can use the map to automatically predict the toxic properties of any chemical compound — more accurately than a single animal test would do.

The most advanced toxicity-prediction tool the team developed was on average about 87 percent accurate in reproducing consensus animal-test-based results — across nine common tests, which account for 57 percent of the world's animal toxicology testing. By contrast, the repetition of the same animal tests in the database were only about 81 percent accurate — in other words, any given test had only an 81 percent chance, on average, of obtaining the same result for toxicity when repeated.

The computer-based approach could also be applied to many more chemicals than animal testing, which could lead to wider safety assessments. Due to costs and ethical challenges only a small fraction of the roughly 100,000 chemicals in consumer products have been comprehensively tested.

Animals such as mice, rabbits, guinea pigs and dogs annually undergo millions of chemical toxicity tests in labs around the world. Although this animal testing is usually required by law to protect consumers, it is opposed on moral grounds by large segments of the public, and is also unpopular with product manufacturers because of the high costs and uncertainties about testing results.

State the main idea of the passage in ONE sentence. Then, explain why animal testing is not welcomed by all walks of life.

_____

_____

_____

_____

_____

04 Read the passage and follow the directions. [4 points]

Nowadays, when almost all societies on Earth are connected to each other, we can't imagine a fad* is going so far that an important technology would actually be discarded. A society that temporarily turned against a powerful technology would continue to see it being used by neighboring societies and would have the opportunity to reacquire it by diffusion (or would be conquered by neighbors if it failed to do so). But such fads can persist in isolated societies.

A famous example involves Japan's abandonment of guns. Firearms reached Japan in A.D. 1543, when two Portuguese adventurers armed with harquebuses* arrived on a Chinese cargo ship. The Japanese were so impressed by the new weapon that they commenced indigenous gun production, greatly improved gun technology, and by A.D. 1600 owned more and better guns than any other country in the world. But there were also factors working against the acceptance of firearms in Japan. The country had a numerous warrior class, the samurai, for whom swords rated as class symbols and as means for subjugating the lower classes. Japanese warfare had previously involved single combats between samurai swordsmen, who stood in the open, made ritual speeches, and then took pride in fighting gracefully. Such behavior became lethal in the presence of peasant soldiers ungracefully blasting away with guns. In addition, guns were a foreign invention and grew to be despised, as did other things foreign in Japan after 1600. The samurai-controlled government began by restricting gun production to a few cities, then introduced a requirement of a government license for producing a gun, then issued licenses only for guns produced for the government, and finally reduced government orders for guns, until Japan was almost without functional guns again.

fad : fashion or whim
harquebuses : primitive gun

Summarize the passage by following the guidelines.

| Guidelines |

- Summarize the above passage in one paragraph.
- Provide a topic sentence and supporting ideas based on the passage.
- Do NOT copy more than FIVE consecutive words from the passage.

_____

_____

_____

_____

_____

📖 모범답안 p.028

01 Read the passage and follow the directions. [2 points]

Modern science has no dogma. Yet it has a common core of research methods, which are all based on collecting empirical observations — those we can observe with at least one of our senses — and putting them together with the help of mathematical tools.

People throughout history collected empirical observations, but the importance of these observations was usually limited. Why waste precious resources obtaining new observations when we already have all the answers we need? But as modern people came to admit that they did not know the answers to some very important questions, they found it necessary to look for completely new knowledge. Consequently, the dominant modern research method takes for granted the insufficiency of old knowledge. Instead of studying traditions, emphasis is now placed on new observations and experiments. When present observation collides with them, we give precedence to the new observation. Of course, physicists analysing the spectra of distant galaxies, archaeologists analysing the finds from a Bronze Age city, and political scientists studying the emergence of capitalism do not disregard tradition. They start by studying what the people of the past have said and written. But from their first year in college, aspiring physicists, archaeologists and political scientists are taught that it is their mission to go beyond <u>what Einstein, Heinrich Schliemann and Marx Weber ever knew</u>.

Identify the TWO consecutive words from the passage that BEST correspond to the meaning of the underlined words.

02 **Read the passage and follow the directions.** [4 points]

Modern white nationalism, which has spread across the world, first emerged in America after the civil war. With the end of slavery, states took action to preserve the privileged position of American Protestants of western European heritage, including "Jim Crow" laws that enforced segregation. Others took to paramilitary violence and lynchings. The fixation with being white grew with increased immigration, especially of Chinese people, Irish Catholics, southern Europeans and Jews. New immigration acts were designed to restrict the number of new arrivals. Madison Grant's "The Passing of the Great Race", published in 1916, melded nativist sentiment with eugenics to produce a theory of white supremacy and "race suicide". Adolf Hitler reportedly wrote to Grant, stating that the book was "his bible".

Though discredited by the war against Nazism and later by the civil-rights struggles of the 1950s and 60s, white nationalism experienced a resurgence towards the end of the 20th century, leading to a number of violent attacks in America and Europe.

In 1988 David Lane wrote "The White Genocide Manifesto", giving a new name to Grant's theory of "race suicide". This text introduced the world to white nationalism's rallying cry : "We must secure the existence of our people and a future for white children", a phrase canonised by white nationalists as "the 14 words". Beyond a core belief in white superiority, white nationalists vary widely in their views. Some share the deep suspicion of the federal government found in militia groups; some embrace a revisionist history of the civil war that glorifies the Confederacy; some believe in anti-Semitic conspiracies about global Jewish control, including the theory that an internationalist Jewish elite is responsible for encouraging immigration.

White nationalism evolved rapidly with the advent of the Internet. It has picked up the irony-tinged discourse of the darker corners of cyberspace to couch* political views in a humour that never reveals whether the writer is serious or not. This allows white nationalists to use non-believers, just in it "for the lulz [laughs]", to spread their message to a wider audience.

couch : express

What actions helped white nationalism to be checked? Second, explain how white nationalism spread nimbly with the Internet in your own words.

03 Read the passage and follow the directions. [4 points]

Most of the members are men who have refused professional openings rather than actual money. There are, for instance, half a dozen journalists and authors. Now a journalist, before he can be elected, must have a black-list of papers for which he will refuse to write. A concocted wireless message in *the Daily Blank*, which subsequent events proved to have been invented deliberately for the purpose of raking in ha'pennies*, so infuriated Henderson (to take a case) that he has pledged himself never to write a line for any paper owned by the same proprietors. Curiously enough he was asked a day or two later to contribute a series to a most respectable magazine published by this firm. He refused in a letter which breathed hatred and utter contempt in every word. It was Henderson, too, who resigned his position as dramatic critic because the proprietor of his paper did rather a shady thing in private life. "I know the paper isn't mixed up in it at all," he said, "but he's my employer and he pays me. Well, I like to be loyal to my employers, and if I'm loyal to this man I can't go about telling everybody that he's a dirty cad*."

Then there is the case of Bolus the author. He has refused to be photographed and interviewed, and he has refused to contribute to symposia in the monthly magazines. He has declined with thanks, moreover, invitations to half a dozen houses sent to him by hostesses who only knew him by reputation. Indirectly he must have been a financial loser by his action, and even if he is not actually assisting to topple over the Money God, he is at least striking a blow for the cause of independence. However, there he is, and with him goes a certain M.P.* who contributed $10,000 to the party chest, and refused scornfully the peerage which was offered to him.

ha'pennies : halfpennies
cad : scoundrel
M.P. : member of parliament

Explain the commonality between Henderson and Bolus given the main idea. What did they do?

_____

_____

_____

_____

_____

04 Read the passage and follow the directions. [4 points]

Time blocking simply means planning out your day in advance and dedicating specific hours to accomplish specific tasks. Doing this requires determining in advance what you will accomplish and exactly when you will accomplish it. Once you have those in mind, enter these into your calendar and then get to work on those tasks at the appropriate time during the day.

When scheduling out tasks, it's important to block out both proactive blocks and reactive blocks. Proactive blocks are when you focus on important tasks that you must get done. This is when you make progress on important projects, draft important documents, or sketch out a prototype for your next great product. Reactive blocks are when you allow time for requests and interruptions, such as email and impromptu meetings.

For example, you could schedule your most challenging tasks for the first two hours of the day and plow through your inbox during the afternoon. This allows you to work undistracted and still know you'll get to things like email and phone calls.

This method has the advantage of helping you know exactly how you're going to use your time and exactly when you're going to accomplish specific tasks. Standard to-do lists present you with a list of tasks to complete in your own time. Time blocking provides you with a list of tasks and a specific time frame to complete each task.

By forcing yourself to work within a rigid structure and to accomplish tasks in a given time, you are forced to bring laser focus to every activity.

Summarize the passage by following the guidelines below.

⌐ Guidelines ⌐

- Summarize the above passage in one paragraph.
- Provide a topic sentence and supporting ideas based on the passage.
- Do NOT copy more than FIVE consecutive words from the passage.

📖 모범답안 p.030

01 Read the passage and follow the directions. [2 points]

The planet's far North is burning. This summer, over 600 wildfires have consumed more than 2.4 million acres of forest across Alaska. Fires are also raging in northern Canada. In Siberia, choking smoke from 13 million acres — an area nearly the size of West Virginia — is blanketing towns and cities.

Fires in these places are normal. In central Alaska, <u>spindly* spruce trees open resinous cones to jump-start new seedlings when the parent tree is scorched. Fast-growing fireweed and other flowers cover recent burn scars. Soon afterward come wild blueberries, willows and birch and aspen trees that shoot up from still-living stumps and roots. Eventually flammable* conifers take over again.</u>

But, as various studies show, recent fires are also abnormal. They are too frequent, intense and severe. They are pouring more carbon into the atmosphere at a time when carbon dioxide concentrations are setting new records.

Some researchers are examining the complex relationships between warming climate, increasing fire and shifting patterns of vegetation. Using locally focused climate data and models from the Scenarios Network for Alaska and Arctic Planning, we are finding evidence that is deeply worrying — not just for those of us who live within the fires' pall of smoke, but for the world.

Typically, the natural cycle resumes about every 200 years. But today the cycles are about 25% shorter than in the past, and that changes everything.

*spindly : slender
*flammable : capable of burning quickly

Identify the TWO consecutive words from the passage that BEST correspond to the underlined part.

02 Read the passage and follow the directions. [4 points]

You're at brunch with your friends on Sunday morning and after stuffing yourself with pancakes and mimosas, your server comes up to you and says, "Is this going to be on one check or —"

"Separate!" you all proclaim, barely taking a breath to pause from your conversation. And why would you? It's pretty customary to pay for your own meal, or to go Dutch.

But it wasn't always the norm to split the check when going out with friends. In fact, in early English society, it was seen as selfish to invite someone out to eat and not pay for their meal.

After the English Civil War ended in 1651, the English were desperate to get life back to ① normal. This meant following certain codes of conduct that displayed class hierarchies and good Christian behavior. It was really important in this world to demonstrate your gentility, or gentlemanliness, by hospitality. By not being generous, you were undermining both the crown and God.

The origins of the phrase "going Dutch" are a little complicated, but some specialists in historical and contemporary lexicography helped us track the complex history of this idiom.

We have to take it back all the way to the 1600s. During the Anglo-Dutch Wars, there were multiple conflicts between the English and the Dutch over trade and naval power. That led to a rise in negative idioms from the English regarding their enemy, the Dutch : phrases like "Dutch courage," the false courage brought on by alcoholic binges; or "Dutch reckoning," which is a ridiculously high bill on which you've likely been scammed. This was because the English saw the Dutch not only as a trading enemy, but also as a people with questionable morals. The English claimed that the Dutch had been completely corrupted by their commitment to capitalism. ② Funny how tides change, isn't it?

Describe what the underlined "normal" meant in the context of the topic of the passage. Second, explain the meaning of the underlined words in the last sentence.

---

03 Read the passage and follow the directions. [4 points]

Memories make us who we are. They shape our understanding of the world and help us to predict what's coming. For more than a century, researchers have been working to understand how memories are formed and then fixed for recall in the days, weeks or even years that follow. But those scientists might have been looking at only half the picture. To understand how we remember, we must also understand how, and why, we forget.

Until about ten years ago, most researchers thought that forgetting was a passive process in which memories, unused, decay over time like a photograph left in the sunlight. But then ① a handful of researchers who were investigating memory began to bump up against findings that seemed to contradict that decades-old assumption. They began to put forward the radical idea that the brain is built to forget.

A growing body of work, cultivated in the past decade, suggests that the loss of memories is not a passive process. Rather, forgetting seems to be an active mechanism that is constantly at work in the brain. In some — perhaps even all — animals, the brain's standard state is not to remember, but to forget. And a better understanding of that state could lead to breakthroughs in treatments for conditions such as anxiety, post-traumatic stress disorder (PTSD), and even Alzheimer's disease.

"What is memory without forgetting?" asks Oliver Hardt, a cognitive psychologist studying the neurobiology of memory. "It's impossible to have proper memory function, you have to have ___②___."

Explain what the underlined "a handful of researchers" contradicts. Second, fill in the blank with the ONE most appropriate word from the passage.

_____

_____

_____

_____

_____

04 Read the passage and follow the directions. [4 points]

Is the school skirt — usually navy or black, always knee-length until rolled up in defiance (or, in adult hindsight, vulnerability) — on the brink of extinction? Maybe. Does it matter? Definitely. According to an analysis of uniform policies across schools in England, at least 40 secondaries have banned girls from wearing skirts in favour of a gender-neutral uniform for everyone. The future for 11-to 16-year-olds appears to be trousers.

In schools, where belief systems are formed and bullying is rife, a gender-neutral uniform policy demonstrates a commitment to equality, the inclusion of transgender and non-binary pupils, as well as basic common sense. Try scaling a climbing frame* in a knee-length skirt. Or just sitting on the floor with your legs crossed. Now add the low embarrassment threshold of your average secondary school pupil. And a highly sexualised and vaguely threatening atmosphere. Possibly a period. See what I mean?

Yet a gender-neutral uniform policy does not require a ban on skirts. Greater inclusion for all should never come with a cost of narrowing choice for some. School uniform should be about individual choice and expression rather than the policing of girls. What message is a ban on skirts really sending? One more about blame than equality?

Some of the language has a tellingly Victorian whiff. One school has placed skirts on a list of "unacceptable items". Another deems them "undignified and embarrassing". Wade into this messy subject (preferably in trousers, for practical reasons) and you will come up against strong words such as "modesty" and "inappropriate" before long. But it is not the skirt that is immodest or the girl inside it, in the same way that it is never relevant what a woman was wearing when she was raped. Skirts, in short, are fine if you want to wear them.

scale a climbing frame : climb up a jungle gym

Summarize the passage by following the guideline below.

| Guidelines |

- Summarize the above passage in one paragraph.
- Provide a topic sentence, supporting ideas, and a concluding sentence based on the passage.
- Do NOT copy more than FIVE consecutive words from the passage.

_____

_____

_____

_____

_____

📖 모범답안 p.033

01   **Read the passage and follow the directions.** [2 points]

Early scripts were ambiguous. For example, the oldest Sumerian cuneiform writing could not render normal prose but was a mere telegraphic shorthand, whose vocabulary was restricted to names, numerals, units of measure, words for objects counted, and a few adjectives. That's as if a modern American court clerk were forced to write "John 27 fat sheep," because English writing lacked the necessary words and grammar to write "We order John to deliver the fat sheep that he owes to the government."

Linear B, the writing of ancient Mycenaean Greece, was at least simpler, being based on a syllabary of about 90 signs plus logograms. Offsetting that virtue, however, Linear B was also quite _____. It omitted any consonant at the end of a word, and it used the same sign for several related consonants (for instance, one sign for both l and r, another for p and b and ph, and still another for g and k and kh). We know how confusing we find it when native-born Japanese people speak English without distinguishing l and r : imagine the confusion if our alphabet did the same while similarly homogenizing the other consonants that I mentioned! It's as if we were to spell the words "rap," "lap," "lab," and "laugh" identically.

Fill in the blank with the ONE most appropriate word from the passage.

02 Read the passage and follow the directions. [4 points]

When we do look at the data on wealth inequality in the U.S., it's stark and dwarfs that of the rest of the developed world. The conservative Hudson Institute in 2017 reported that the wealthiest 5 percent of American households held 62.5 percent of all assets in the U.S. in 2013, up from 54.1 percent 30 years earlier. As a consequence, the wealth of the other 95 percent declined from 45.9 percent to 37.5 percent.

As a result, the median wealth of upper-income families (earning US $639,400 on average) was nearly seven times that of middle-income households ($96,500) in 2013, the widest gap in at least 30 years.

More notably, world-famous inequality scholars Emmanuel Saez and Gabriel Zucman found that the top 0.01 percent controlled 22 percent of all wealth in 2012, up from just 7 percent in 1979. If you only looked at data on income inequality, however, you'd see a different picture. In 2013, for example, the top 5 percent of households earned just 30 percent of all U.S. income compared with possessing nearly 63 percent of all wealth.

While the U.S. is not the only developed country that has seen wealth inequality rise over the past three decades, it is an outlier. The wealthiest 5 percent of households in the U.S. have almost 91 times more wealth than the median American household, the widest gap among 18 of the world's most developed countries. The next highest is the Netherlands, which has a ratio less than half that.

Describe the key discovery Emmanuel Saez and Gabriel Zucman found. Second, explain why the writer of the passage mentions "the Netherlands" in the passage.

_____

_____

_____

_____

_____

03 Read the passage and follow the directions. [4 points]

In 1998, The Wall Street Journal and NBC News asked several hundred young Americans to name their most important values. Work ethic led the way — naturally. After that, large majorities picked patriotism, religion, and having children.

Twenty-one years later, the same pollsters asked the same questions of today's 18-to-38-year-olds — members of the Millennial and Z generations. The results showed ① <u>a major value shift</u> among young adults. Today's respondents were 10 percentage points less likely to value having children and 20 points less likely to highly prize patriotism or religion.

The nuclear family, religious fealty*, and national pride — family, God, and country — are a holy trinity of American traditionalism. The fact that allegiance to all three is in precipitous decline tells us something important about the evolution of the American identity.

One interpretation of this poll is that it's mostly about the erosion of traditional Western faith. People under 30 in the U.S. account for more than one-third of this nation's worshippers in only three major religions : Islam, Buddhism, and Hinduism. This reflects both the increase in non-European immigration since the 1970s and the decline of larger Christian denominations in the latter half of the 20th century. It also reflects the sheer increase in atheism : Millennials are nearly three times more likely than Boomers* to say they don't believe in God — 6 percent versus 16 percent. If you think that Judeo-Christian values are an irreplaceable keystone in the moral arc of Western society, these facts will disturb you; ② <u>if you don't, they won't.</u>

A second interpretation of this poll is that it's mostly about politics. Youthful disinterest in patriotism, babies, and God might be a mere proxy for young people's distaste for traditional conservatism.

*fealty : loyalty
* Boomers : Baby-boomer generation

Describe to what "a major value shift" refers. Second, explain the meaning of the underlined words in ②.

_____

_____

_____

_____

_____

04 Read the passage and follow the directions. [4 points]

Leaving a water bottle sitting in your car sounds benign enough. But on a hot, summer day, the plastic can act as a lens, focusing light into a high-energy beam that's intense enough to burn material like car-seat upholstery. Last summer, Idaho Power shared its video of a water bottle burning two holes in a car seat. And for this year's World Cup soccer tournament, the Russian water company Holy Water is selling soccer ball-shaped water bottles that can act as perfect light-focusing lenses. In a video published by Fontanka Ru, the ball-shaped bottle is seen focusing light so well that it ignites a box of matches and burns a hole in laminate flooring. The water bottle is acting like a lens that's focusing the light coming through the window.

Odile Madden, a materials scientist, witnessed the astonishing power of laser-focused light years ago, when she was experimenting with using lasers to remove clear adhesives from artwork and artifacts. She discovered that the grooves in the adhesive worked to focus the laser and "turned up the power," subsequently burning or etching pits into the glass microscope slides she was using for the experiment. She published her findings in 2005 in the journal *Lasers in the Conservation of Artworks*.

What surprised Madden about the water bottle examples is that the light passes through the car window first, yet there's still enough heat left to go through the bottle and cause burning. "Conceivably, this would be worse on a hot day or if the window were down, because the window filters the light," Madden said. "This is a good illustration of just how much energy there is coming from the sun and we think of this as a cheap water bottle, but we're unintentionally creating an optically almost-perfect shape for a lens," she added. We'd better not put a water bottle on a stack of paper in a car on a hot day anymore.

Summarize the passage by following the guidelines.

Guidelines

- Summarize the above passage in one paragraph.
- Provide a topic sentence, supporting ideas, and a concluding sentence based on the passage.
- Do NOT copy more than FIVE consecutive words from the passage.

_____

_____

_____

_____

_____

01   Read the passage and follow the directions. [2 points]

> The primarily Islamic tradition of females covering themselves from head to foot with a burqa is an example of the intrinsic difficulty in evaluating the extent to which cultural practices promote individual autonomy. Critics of the burqa and similar garments, especially critics from Western cultures, deem them physically oppressive with the weight of the fabric; psychologically oppressive in that they seem to make women devoid of distinctiveness; and emotionally oppressive in that they are yet another manifestation of a male-dominated society in which women are subordinate. According to this view, the tradition of wearing such clothing is unjustified because it greatly restricts the autonomy of women.
>
> Defenders of this practice, however, argue the opposite view. They insist that coverings like the burqa actually foster autonomy and liberate women for a number of reasons. For example, a burqa prevents women from being viewed as sexual objects; it encourages unity among female Muslims; and it promotes the appearance of holiness. Proponents of the burqa also ask questions of Western critics which force them to examine their own clothing culture, such as, "Why is it considered oppressive to wear a headscarf but liberating to wear a miniskirt?". They insist the answer lies in the assumptions each culture makes about the women involved and their ability to make choices. They say that if their assumptions concerning such clothing practices are actually wrong, and the wearing of the burqa is actually a matter of personal preference, then it is completely justified as a legitimate expression of individual _____.

Fill in the blank with the ONE most appropriate word from the passage.

02 Read the passage and follow the directions. [4 points]

Like many medications, the wakefulness drug modafinil, which is marketed under the trade name Provigil, comes with a small, tightly folded paper pamphlet. For the most part, its contents — lists of instructions and precautions, a diagram of the drug's molecular structure — make for anodyne* reading. The subsection called "Mechanism of Action," however, contains a sentence that might induce sleeplessness by itself : "The mechanism(s) through which modafinil promotes wakefulness is unknown."

Provigil isn't uniquely ① <u>mysterious</u>. Many drugs receive regulatory approval, and are widely prescribed, even though no one knows exactly how they work. This mystery is built into the process of drug discovery, which often proceeds by trial and error. Each year, any number of new substances are tested in cultured cells or animals; the best and safest of those are tried out in people. In some cases, the success of a drug promptly inspires new research that ends up explaining how it works — but not always. Aspirin was discovered in 1897, and yet no one convincingly explained how it worked until 1995. The same phenomenon exists elsewhere in medicine. Deep-brain stimulation involves the implantation of electrodes in the brains of people who suffer from specific movement disorders, such as Parkinson's disease; it's been in widespread use for more than twenty years, and some think it should be employed for other purposes, including general cognitive enhancement. No one can say how it works.

This approach to discovery — answers first, explanations later — accrues what I call ② <u>intellectual debt</u>. It's possible to discover what works without knowing why it works, and then to put that insight to use immediately, assuming that the underlying mechanism will be figured out later. In some cases, we pay off this intellectual debt quickly. But, in others, we let it compound, relying, for decades, on knowledge that's not fully known.

* *anodyne : sleeping-inducing*

Explain the meaning of the underlined "mysterious". Second, describe what "intellectual debt" means.

_____

_____

_____

_____

_____

03 Read the passage and follow the directions. [4 points]

Whether such data are generated actively or passively, few people will have the time or inclination to keep track of all the information they generate, or estimate its value. Even those who do will lack the bargaining power to get a good deal from AI firms. But the history of labour offers a hint about how things could evolve : because historically, if wages rose to acceptable levels, it was mostly due to unions. Similarly, Mr Weyl expects to see the rise of what he calls "data-labour unions", organizations that serve as gatekeepers of people's data. Like their predecessors, they will negotiate rates, monitor members' data work and ensure the quality of their digital output, for instance by keeping reputation scores. Unions could funnel specialist data work to their members and even organize strikes, for instance by blocking access to exert influence on a company employing its members' data. Similarly, data unions could be conduits channelling members' data contributions, all while tracking them and billing AI firms that benefit from them.

① <u>This may sound like science fiction</u>. Why should Google and Facebook, for instance, ever give up their current business model of using free data to sell targeted online advertising? In 2017 they raked in a combined $135bn in ad dollars. If they had to compensate people for their data, they would be much less profitable. Meanwhile, startups such as CitizenMe and Datacoup, which can be seen as early forms of data unions, have so far failed to make much headway. Yet in other corners of the industry, tech giants already pay for data, although ② <u>they are careful not to talk too much about it</u>. Mostly through outsourcing firms, they employ armies of raters and moderators to check the quality of their algorithms and take down content that is illegal or offensive. Other firms use crowd-working platforms, such as Amazon's Mechanical Turk, to farm out data work such as tagging pictures.

Explain the meaning of the underlined words in ①. Next, what can be inferred to be the reason behind companies' actions in underlined ②.

_____

_____

_____

_____

_____

04 Read the passage and follow the directions. [4 points]

The insight of polytheism is conducive to far-reaching religious tolerance. Since polytheists believe, on the one hand, in one supreme and completely disinterested power, and on the other hand in many partial and biased powers, there is no difficulty for the devotees of one god to accept the existence and efficacy of other gods. Polytheism is inherently open-minded, and rarely persecutes 'heretics' and 'infidels'. This is in contrast to monotheistic religions like Christianity which has waged war on those who've believed differently both within their religion and outside of it.

Even when polytheists conquered huge empires, they did not try to convert their subjects. The Egyptians, the Romans and the Aztecs did not send missionaries to foreign lands to spread the worship of Osiris, Jupiter or Huitzilopochtli (the chief Aztec god), and they certainly didn't dispatch armies for that purpose. In the Aztec Empire, subject peoples were obliged to build temples for Huitzilopochtli, but these temples were built alongside those of local gods, rather than in their stead. The Romans happily added the Asian goddess Cybele and the Egyptian goddess Isis to their pantheon*.

The only god that the Romans long refused to tolerate was the monotheistic and evangelising god of the Christians. The Roman Empire did not require the Christians to give up their beliefs and rituals, but it did expect them to pay respect to the empire's protector gods and to the divinity of the emperor. This was seen as a declaration of political loyalty. When the Christians vehemently refused to do so, and went on to reject all attempts at compromise, the Romans reacted by persecuting what they understood to be a politically subversive faction. And even this was done half-heartedly. In the 300 years from the crucifixion of Christ to the conversion of Emperor Constantine, polytheistic Roman emperors initiated no more than four general persecutions of Christians. In these three centuries, the polytheistic Romans killed no more than a few thousand Christians. In contrast, over the course of the next 1,500 years, Christians slaughtered Christians by the millions to defend slightly different interpretations of the religion of love and compassion.

pantheon : temple dedicated to all the gods

Summarize the passage by following the guidelines below.

Guidelines

- Summarize the above passage in one paragraph.
- Provide a topic sentence and supporting ideas based on the passage.
- Do NOT copy more than FIVE consecutive words from the passage.

_____

_____

_____

_____

_____

📖 모범답안 p.039

01　**Read the passage and follow the directions.** [2 points]

We humans have evolved to be uniquely tolerant among fission-fusion species. The roots of this lie in part in our unusually large brains and relatively high reproductive rates, compared with other primates. Together these characteristics make us extremely dependent on high-quality, high-risk (ie, unpredictable across time and location) food and tool supplies. In turn, this will have had implications for our foraging strategies, including the frequent need to rely on other communities during periods of resource scarcity. This does not mean humans were, or are, peaceful all the time. But, where and when access to nonlocal resources is important, humans have often managed to find ways to be tolerant towards members of other communities at least some of the time.

Whereas scholars have previously focused on bellicose chimpanzees as a way to gain insight into the evolutionary origins of our aggressive tendencies, many researchers recently believe comparisons with other, more tolerant nonhuman primates might be more apposite*, especially for understanding the foundations of our uniquely _____ nature.

Notably, food sharing and grooming have both been observed between bonobo groups, as has the formation of intergroup coalitions. Bonobos aren't always tolerant toward members of other groups. During intergroup encounters, there are often conflicts between two individuals, or even moments of tension that shake up many members of both groups. But that flexibility in intergroup behaviour, to behave tolerantly or aggressively toward out-group members, is there, much like the flexibility we see in humans.

* *apposite : appropriate*

Fill in the blank with the ONE most appropriate word from the passage.

02 **Read the passage and follow the directions.** [4 points]

Once your eyes suspect a liar, next let your ears have a turn. Here are ① <u>cues</u> to listen for. A story in strict chronological order. When a complex lie is to be told, whether to a CIA agent, the parent of a teenager, or Bob Woodward and Carl Bernstein, liars often rehearse their story, which usually is spun from —logically—start to finish. A fun trick? If you think you're hearing a tall tale, ask to hear the story backwards : "So when you just happened to see the car in the ditch—what happened before that again?" and watch the liar squirm.

Way too much linguistic convolution or overcompensation. Does your suspected liar use a hundred words when ten would do? Or use formal language with many clauses? For example, compare these two statements : "In light of the given situation, it can categorically be stated that I have never, and would never, remove your lunch from the shared office refrigerator." Contrast that with "I didn't eat your lunch."

A truth-teller names names, while a liar uses impersonal phrases or pronouns; for example, "that woman" rather than "Miss Lewinsky." In addition, liars avoid saying "I." For example, instead of "I didn't skim off the register," you'll hear, "No one here would ever skim off the register."

Liars work really hard to come across as truthful. They smile at all the right moments and say all the right things. But the result often appears contrived and fake, which it is. If you feel like you're being sold a bag of goods, you probably are. In short, ② <u>a bright toothy smile probably means a shark.</u>

Identify to what all "cues" refer in the passage. Then explain the meaning of the underlined words in ②.

_____

_____

_____

_____

_____

03 Read the passage and follow the directions. [4 points]

Consider image recognition. Ten years ago, computers couldn't easily identify objects in photos. Today, image search engines, like so many of the systems we interact with on a day-to-day basis, are based on extraordinarily capable machine-learning models. Google's image search relies on a neural network called Inception. In 2017, MIT's LabSix — a research group of undergraduate and graduate students — succeeded in altering the pixels of a photograph of a cat so that, although it looked like a cat to human eyes, Inception became 99.99-per-cent sure it had been given a photograph of guacamole. Inception, of course, can't explain what features led it to conclude that a cat is a cat; as a result, there's no easy way to predict how it might fail when presented with specially crafted or corrupted data. Such a system is likely to have unknown gaps in its accuracy that amount to vulnerabilities for a smart and determined attacker.

As knowledge generated by machine-learning systems is put to use, these kinds of gaps may prove consequential. Health-care A.I.s have been successfully trained to classify skin cancers as benign or malignant. And yet — as a team of researchers from Harvard Medical School and MIT showed — they can also be tricked into making inaccurate judgments using the same techniques that turn cats into guacamole. (Among other things, attackers might use these vulnerabilities to commit insurance fraud.) Seduced by the predictive power of such systems, we may stand down the human judges whom they promise to replace. But they will remain susceptible to hijacking — and we will have no easy process for validating the answers they continue to produce.

Describe Inception's limitation according to the MIT research. Second, how is it likely that insurance swindlers uses Health-care AI?

_____

_____

_____

04 Read the passage and follow the directions. [4 points]

Star innovators such as Bill Gates, who was 19 when he started Microsoft, Steve Jobs, 21 when he started Apple, and Mark Zuckerberg, 19 when he launched Facebook, have reinforced the longstanding impression that young people are the wellspring of entrepreneurship. Systematic data on firm founders, however, suggest that this impression is false. Many researchers provide evidence that, on average, successful entrepreneurs are middle-aged.

They analyzed administrative data from the U.S. Census Bureau on more than 2.7 million business founders whose companies subsequently hired at least one employee. The mean age of founders was 42. When looking at the highest-growth startups in the economy, the mean age at founding rose still higher — to 45. In addition, the study explores the factors that are correlated with firm success. These old founders with longer work experience closer to the specific industry of the start-up, and founders with longer experience in that industry, have substantially greater success rates. "For the 1 in 1,000 highest-growth firms, founders with three or more years of experience in the 2-digit industry see upper tail success at twice the rate of younger founders with no experience in the 2-digit industry," the researchers report. The study also took into account geographical heterogeneity, and separately considers California, Massachusetts, and New York. These three states account for the majority of high-growth startup activity in the U.S. Even in these states, successful entrepreneurs are still middle-aged.

Summarize the passage by following the guideline below.

Guidelines

• Summarize the above passage in one paragraph.
• Provide a topic sentence and supporting ideas based on the passage.
• Do NOT copy more than FIVE consecutive words from the passage.

📖 모범답안 p.041

01 **Read the passage and follow the directions.** [4 points]

> I believe the first time I recall acting to get attention, I was eight years old at summer camp. And I'd tried to auditioning for about a year by then, and I'd been lucky to get some small roles in television shows and commercials, and I boasted about it a lot, that summer at camp. And in the beginning, it worked. The other children gave me much more attention, because I had been on "Family Ties." Then, the tide turned — I think I took it too far with the boasting. And then, the other kids started to make fun of me. I remember there was this one girl I had a crush on, Rocky. Her name was Rachel by she preferred to be called Rocky. And she was beautiful, and she was a singer, and I was smitten with her, and I was standing there, bragging. And she rounded on me and called me a show-off. Which I 100 percent deserved. But you know, it still really hurt. And ever since then, I've had a certain hesitance to seek ____①____ for my acting.
>
> Sometimes, people ask me, "Hold on, if you don't like the attention, then why are you an actor?" And I'd say, "Because that's not what performing is about, man, it's about the art." And they'd be like, "OK, OK, dude." And then Twitter arrived. And I got totally addicted, just like everybody else, which made me into ②a complete hypocrite. Because by then, I was absolutely using my acting to get attention. I mean, did I think I was just getting all these followers because of my insightful tweets? I actually did think that — I was like — . "They don't just like me because they saw me in some movie, they like what I have to say, I've got a way with words." And then in no time at all, it started having an impact on my dearly beloved creative process. It still does. I try not to let it.

Fill in the blank with the ONE most appropriate word from the passage. Second, explain why the writer of the passage thought he was "a complete hypocrite".

_____

_____

_____

_____

_____

02 Read the passage and follow the directions. [4 points]

Here's an breakdown in terms of communication platforms we know today : texting, Twitter, Instagram, and Facebook.

Texting : ice cold. The entire point of texting, especially for the youth, is that it's a way to communicate that reveals very little information. Uncertainty and ambiguity is the point. Texting, particularly a group chat, is often like a game of "what's said versus unsaid", where gaps must be completed. It requires active participation on your part to fill in the picture of what's being communicated. (The dreaded "…" in iMessage, which says so little but draws us in, is Cool Media.)

Twitter : cool. Twitter is tricky due to the fact that there are many different ways to use it. Breaking News Twitter, for one, is quite hot. But Twitter the social network is quite cool. It's a low-resolution, character-limited format where the majority of what's being communicated is actually just offscreen, out of the picture. The best tweets and the funniest jokes on Twitter are incomplete information. They're pure punchline. The setup goes unsaid; you have to already be aware of it, or go figure it out. It takes a lot of work to use Twitter successfully and you have to fluently understand its genre conventions in order for it to be understood. Twitter, when used perfectly, is Cool Media.

Instagram : warm. The main content being exchanged is all visual, and you don't need to grasp genre conventions as much. Instagram in its early photo filter days was fairly hot media, as is classic photography, but it cooled down when it evolved into the de facto social status app. Now there's interplay between what's posted and how many likes the post gets, and from whom, and other social dynamics like private versus public posting. There is still some ambiguity, but as a medium it's more information-complete than Twitter or texting.

Facebook : hot. Unlike _____, which is a muttering wealth of inside jokes, or Instagram, which is warmer but still has some cool elements to it, Facebook is more akin to a newspaper. It's not withholding anything. It's a patchwork mosaic of yelling : Acknowledge this! Be angry at this! Celebrate this! There's not a lot of mystery on Facebook, and it doesn't take much fluency to use it correctly. The information being communicated is all right there, blasted at you. Facebook may have started out cooler, back when it was college kids broadcasting social status (as Instagram is used now). But it's heated up steadily since then.

Describe the crucial element required for the best tweets and jokes on Twitter. Second, fill in the blank with the ONE most appropriate word from the passage.

_____

_____

_____

_____

_____

03 **Read the passage and follow the directions.** [4 points]

Ms. Porter raised her hand nervously. It was the beginning of her school's staff meeting and her principal, Ms. Chang, had asked if anybody wanted to add new items to the agenda. "I'd like to talk about how we plan to teach about the upcoming Thanksgiving holiday." Ms. Porter said.

Several colleagues responded.

"I don't plan to talk about it at all. Thanksgiving seems to be more about consumerism than spending time with family," Ms. Espinosa said. Ms. Tilson commented, "I focus on food. Students are really engaged when we talk about food. We'll talk about how the Pilgrims and Indians shared a feast, and since some of our students are immigrants, we can use it as an opportunity to learn about traditional foods."

"I focus on the Thanks in Thanksgiving," Mr. Webster added. "We all have so much to be thankful for. I like to focus on the positive."

Ms. Chang replied, "Seems we have a variety of ways to honor the holiday. I don't think we need any more conversation on this unless you have questions."

Ms. Porter's mind was most concerned with what her colleagues were not intending to talk about. "I'm concerned with how we are perpetuating myths about the first Thanksgiving. I'm concerned we are not acknowledging that some Nation Americans observe this day as a day of mourning, not as a celebration. This is a great opportunity to promote dialogue within the school community about popular customs that might alienate some students and families, such as pretending to be Pilgrims and Indians," she said.

As she heard these words coming out of her mouth, Ms. Porter felt a wave of relief and regret. She was bothered by the way many of her colleagues had addressed Thanksgiving in previous years but never felt comfortable speaking up.

"We have so many needs in our school. I don't think we should micromanage how people teach Thanksgiving. We don't even have any of those students in our school," Ms. Tilson said.

Ms. Chang, sensing tension in the room, replied, "You all have great points. Thank you for sharing them. It seems this is a larger topic than we have time to discuss now." With that comment, she moved to the next item on the agenda.

Ms. Porter looked around the room, frustrated by her colleagues' comments, and that nobody else spoke up or supported her for speaking up.

Explain what reason can be inferred that Ms. Porter was "nervous" to introduce a topic in the staff meeting. Second, to whom does Ms. Tilson refer in the underlined selection?

_____

_____

_____

_____

_____

04 **Read the passage and follow the directions.** [4 points]

Social scientists have a wealth of tools to study how trusting, and how trustworthy, a person is. The most popular is the trust game, in which two participants play, usually anonymously. The first participant is given a small amount of money, $10 say, and asked to decide what amount to give to the other participant. The amount transferred is then tripled, and the second participant chooses how much to give back to the first.

In Western countries at least, trust is rewarded : the more money the first participant transfers, the more money the second participant sends back, and thus the more money the first participant ends up with. In spite of this, first participants on average transfer only half the money they have been granted. In some studies, ① <u>a variant</u> was introduced whereby participants knew each other's ethnicity. Prejudice led participants to mistrust certain groups ─ Israeli men of Eastern origin (Asian and African immigrants and their Israeli-born offspring), or black students in South Africa ─ transferring them less money, even though these groups proved just as trustworthy as more well-regarded groups.

If people and institutions are more trustworthy than we give them credit for, why don't we get it right? Why is it we don't trust more?

When you trust someone, you end up figuring out whether your faith in them was justified or not. An acquaintance asks if he can sleep at your house for a few days. If you accept, you will find out whether or not he's a good guest. A colleague recommends a new software application to you. If you follow her advice, you will find out whether the new software works better than the one you were used to.

In contrast, if you ___②___ someone, more often than not you never find out whether you should have trusted them. If you don't invite your friend over, you won't know whether he would have made a good guest or not. If you don't follow your colleague's advice, you won't know if the new software application is in fact more useful, and thus whether your colleague gives good advice in this domain.

Identify to what the underlined "a variant" refers. Second, fill in blank ② with the TWO most appropriate consecutive words from the passage.

___

___

___

___

___

05 Read the passage and follow the directions. [4 points]

The process school sees a message as that which is transmitted by the communication process. Many of its constituents believe that ___①___ is a key factor in deciding what forms a message. Thus pulling my earlobe would not be a message unless I deliberately did it as a pre-arranged signal to an auctioneer. The sender's intention may be stated or unstated, conscious or unconscious, but must be retrievable by analysis. The message is what the sender puts into it by any possible means.

For semiotics, on the other hand, the message is a construction of signs which, through interacting with the receivers, creates meanings. The sender, defined as transmitter of the message, declines in importance. The emphasis transfers to the text and how it is 'read'. And reading is the process of discovering meanings that occurs when the reader interacts or negotiates with the text. This negotiation takes place as the reader brings aspects of his or her cultural experience to bear upon the codes and signs which make up the text. It also involves some shared understanding of what the text is about. We have only to see how various newspapers report the same world event differently to perceive how important is this understanding, this view of the world, which each paper shares with its readers. So readers with different social experiences or from different cultures are likely to find different meanings in the same text. This is not necessarily proof of communication failure.

The message, then, is not something sent from A to B, but an element in a structured relationship whose other elements include external reality and the producer/reader. Producing and reading the text are seen as parallel, if not identical, processes in that they occupy the same place in this structured relationship. We might model this structure as a ②triangle in which the arrows represent constant interaction; the structure is not static but a dynamic practice.

Fill in the blank with the ONE most appropriate word from the passage. Second, explain why the writer employs the term "triangle".

_____

_____

_____

_____

_____

06 Read the passage and follow the directions. [4 points]

In 2004, an essay appeared in the journal *Psychological Science*, titled "Music Lessons Boost IQ." The author Glenn Yu had ran an experiment with 144 children randomly assigned to four groups : one learned piano for a year, one took singing lessons, another joined an acting class, and a control group had no extracurricular training. The IQ of the children in the two musical groups rose by an average of seven points in the course of a year; those in the other two groups gained an average of 4.3 points.

Yu had long been skeptical of the science backing claims that music education enhances children's abstract reasoning, math, or language skills. If children who play the piano are smarter, he says, it doesn't necessarily mean they are smarter because they play the piano. It could be that the pupils who study piano also happen to be more ambitious or better at focusing on a task. Correlation, after all, does not prove causation.

The 2004 paper was developed to address those inconsistencies. And as a passionate musician, Yu was pleased when he turned up credible evidence that music has transfer effects on general intelligence. But a decade later, in 2013, the Education Endowment Foundation backed a larger study with more than 900 students. That study failed to corroborate Yu's findings, finding no evidence that music lessons improved math and literacy skills.

Yu took that news in stride while continuing to cast a skeptical eye on the research in his field. Recently, he decided to formally investigate just how often his fellow researchers in psychology and neuroscience make what he believes are false — or at least premature — causal connections between music and intelligence. His results, published in May, reveal that many of his peers do just that.

To pinpoint precisely how music lessons affect the brain over time, scientists would ideally assign students randomly to different groups, as Yu did in his 2004 study, only over an extended period of time. One group of children might be assigned to take piano lessons for years, while the other group would have no music education at all. Because this is generally not possible to do for the sake of a psychological experiment, many researchers rely on studies where they compare children who already take lessons to those who don't, correcting for variables such as socioeconomic status. But even with this correction, such studies can only find correlation; they cannot prove _____.

Explain the difference of the result between the 2004 study and 2013 study. Second, explain why can it be inferred "variables such as socioeconomic status" should be corrected. Third, fill in the blank of the last sentence with the ONE most appropriate word from the passage.

_____

_____

_____

_____

_____

07 **Read the passage and follow the directions.** [4 points]

Caesar was right. Thin people need watching. I've been watching them for most of my adult life, and I don't like what I see. When these narrow fellows spring at me, I quiver to my toes. Thin people come in all personalities, most of them menacing. You've got your "together" thin person, your mechanical thin person, your condescending thin person, your tsk-tsk thin person, your efficiency-expert thin person.

In the first place, thin people aren't fun. They don't know how to goof off, at least in the best, fat sense of the word. They've always got to be doing. Give them a coffee break, and they'll jog around the block. Supply them with a quiet evening at home, and they'll fix the screen door and lick S&H green stamps. They say things like "there aren't enough hours in the day." Fat people never say that. Fat people think the day is too damn long already.

Thin people make me tired. They've got speedy little metabolisms that cause them to bustle briskly. They're forever rubbing their bony hands together and eyeing new problems to "tackle". I like to surround myself with sluggish, inert, easygoing fat people, the kind who believe that if you clean it up today, it'll just get dirty again tomorrow.

Fat people may not be chortling all day long, but they're a hell of a lot nicer than the wizened and shriveled. Thin people turn surly while go straight to the heart of the matter while fat people let things stay all blurry and vague, the way things actually are. Thin people want to face the truth. Fat people know that there is no truth. The thin always stare unsolvable problems and say, "The key thing is ..." Fat people never say things like that. They know there isn't any such thing as the "key thing" about anything. Given these differences, if you are thin, go skip the gym, order that super-size lunch. As you grow larger, you'll grow into more pleasant company.

Summarize the passage following the guidelines below.

| Guidelines |

- Summarize the above passage in one paragraph.
- Provide a topic sentence, supporting ideas, and a concluding sentence based on the passage.
- Do NOT copy more than FOUR consecutive words from the passage.

_____

_____

_____

_____

_____

모범답안 p.044

01 Read the passage and follow the directions. [4 points]

Three years ago, I stopped eating sugar. Giving up sugar set me free. And so, what began as an experiment has become my new life. I have changed in ways that I had not thought possible.

I used to get "hangry" — that grumpy, urgent craving that demands prompt attention. To stave it off, I carried bags of almonds or dried fruit. Back when I ate sugar, I couldn't go running in the morning — if I tried, I would get dizzy, and anyway, my legs felt as if they were made of stone. I would have slumps in the afternoon — my head would get foggy — so if I was working from home, I would take a nap. I had mood swings, joy alternating with despair. I had assumed that all of these things were simply part of life, of how I was, a frustrating aspect of my makeup. And ① now all of them are gone.

For the first two weeks of my unsweetened life, though, I was in a foul temper. At first, I attributed this to the darkness and gloom of the winter days. But as I started to feel better — calmer, happier, more even-keeled — a more sinister thought began to nag at me. Had I been in withdrawal?

To a chemist, sugar refers to a class of molecules made of hydrogen, carbon and oxygen; some of these serve particular biological roles. Lactose, for example, is found in milk; deoxyribose gives the "D" to DNA. But in daily life, the main sugars one meets are glucose, fructose and sucrose — which is a marriage of the other two. That is, each molecule of sucrose is one glucose linked to one fructose. Interestingly, the two simple sugars have the same chemical formula — six atoms of carbon, 12 of hydrogen, six of oxygen — but different chemical structures. The human tongue detects this : fructose tastes sweeter.

Glucose is synonymous with blood sugar, since it is transported in the blood and delivered to cells to fuel their energetic needs. But you can also find it, along with _____②_____, in fruits and vegetables. Sucrose is extracted from sugar cane or beets, and is usually encountered as the white crystals of table sugar. When most people speak of "sugar", they mean sucrose. For most of human history, milk, honey and fruits have been the main sources of sweetness. When cane sugar first made its way to Europe around 1,000 years ago, it was treated as a spice, a medicine and a preservative. In 1700, the average sugar consumption in the United Kingdom was around two kilograms per person per year. Today, the figure is 10 times that amount. The present sugar glut is an anomaly in human experience. We have changed the world to suit our appetites; but our bodies cannot accommodate the change.

Explain why the writer mentions the words in ① in regard to the overarching meaning of the passage. Second, fill in blank ② with the ONE most appropriate word from the passage.

_____

_____

_____

_____

_____

02 Read the passage and follow the directions. [4 points]

In our standard view of things, consciousness exists only in the brains of highly evolved organisms, and hence consciousness exists only in a tiny part of the universe and only in very recent history. According to panpsychism, in contrast, consciousness pervades the universe and is a fundamental feature of it. This doesn't mean that literally everything is conscious. The basic commitment is that the fundamental constituents of reality — perhaps electrons and quarks — have incredibly simple forms of experience. And the very complex experience of the human or animal brain is somehow derived from the experience of the brain's most basic parts.

It might be important to clarify what I mean by "consciousness," as that word is actually quite ambiguous. Some people use it to mean something quite sophisticated, such as self-awareness or the capacity to reflect on one's own existence. This is something we might be reluctant to ascribe to many nonhuman animals, never mind fundamental particles. But when I use the word *consciousness*, I simply mean experience : pleasure, pain, visual or auditory experience, et cetera.

Human beings have a very rich and complex experience; horses less so; mice less so again. As we move to simpler and simpler forms of life, we find simpler and simpler forms of experience. Perhaps, at some point, the light switches off, and consciousness disappears. But it's at least coherent to suppose that this continuum of consciousness fading while never quite turning off carries on into inorganic matter, with fundamental particles having almost unimaginably simple forms of experience to reflect their incredibly simple nature. That's what panpsychists believe.

The starting point of the panpsychist is that physical science doesn't actually tell us what _____ is. That sounds like a bizarre claim at first; you read a physics textbook, you seem to learn all kinds of incredible things about the nature of space, time and matter. But what philosophers of science have realized is that physical science, for all its richness, is confined to telling us about the behavior of matter, what it does. Physics tells us, for example, that matter has mass and charge. These properties are completely defined in terms of behavior, things like attraction, repulsion, resistance to acceleration. Physics tells us absolutely nothing about what matter is, in and of itself.

First, what can be inferred to be the perspective of the "standard view" toward forms of life simpler than mice? Do NOT copy more than FOUR consecutive words from the passage. Second, fill in the blank with the ONE most appropriate word from the passage.

_____

_____

_____

_____

_____

03 Read the passage and follow the directions. [4 points]

As they filed into his classroom, Mr. Harrold overheard students discussing the score of a professional football game from the previous evening. When the conversation subsided, one student, Caylee, mentioned a player on the losing team who refused to stand during the national anthem. "Losing is karma for not respecting the American flag," she proclaimed. A few of her classmates laughed and nodded in agreement. Another student added, "His team probably lost because of the distraction."

"Oh boy," Mr. Harrold thought. "Is this something I need to address?" His mind turned to all the content he needed to cover and his carefully planned lesson, so he decided not to respond to Caylee's comment.

Later that evening as he watched the news Mr. Harrold saw highlights from the football game the students had discussed. The reporter addressed the backlash the player received for not standing during the national anthem. She interviewed both people who supported the player's decision and others who opposed it. Mr. Harrold wondered about his decision and others who opposed it. Mr. Harrold wondered about his decision not to address Caylee's comment but felt the teachable moment had passed.

Several weeks later Mr. Harrold overheard students talking about a classmate who had chosen earlier in the day not to stand during the Pledge of Allegiance. When asked by classmates about her decision, Kate had explained, "I don't believe 'liberty and justice for all' exist in our country."

A couple of her classmates expressed disdain for her behavior. They said Kate was only protesting because she wanted attention, not because of her cultural or political beliefs.

Once again Mr. Harrold was unsure how to respond. He knew this was a sensitive topic eliciting heated debates among adults, so he knew he needed to proceed with caution. He also knew his school prided itself on the annual Veterans Day program and wondered whether promoting dialogue about sitting during the national anthem or Pledge of Allegiance would be seen by some people in the community as conflicting with the school's history of honoring military veterans.

As he lost himself in reflection about how or whether to address the situation, a student interrupted his contemplation. "Mr. Harrold," the student asked, "do you think it's disrespectful to not stand during the Pledge or national anthem? Isn't it a school rule that we have to stand?"

Explain the meaning of the underlined selection. Do NOT copy more than FOUR consecutive words from the passage. Second, what backlash is Mr. Harrold concerned with, regarding addressing the protest? Do NOT copy more than FOUR consecutive words from the passage.

_____

_____

_____

_____

_____

04 Read the passage and follow the directions. [4 points]

When I started advising startup founders at Y Combinator, especially young ones, I was puzzled by the way they always seemed to make things overcomplicated. How, they would ask, do you raise money? What's the trick for making venture capitalists want to invest in you? The best way to make VCs want to invest in you, I would explain, is to actually be a good investment. Even if you could trick VCs into investing in a bad startup, you'd be tricking yourselves too. You're investing time in the same company you're asking them to invest money in. If it's not a good investment, why are you even doing it?

Oh, they'd say, and then after a pause to digest this revelation, they'd ask : What makes a startup a good investment?

So I would explain that what makes a startup promising, not just in the eyes of investors but in fact, is growth. Ideally in revenue, but failing that in usage. What they needed to do was get lots of users.

How does one get lots of users? They had all kinds of ideas about that. They needed to do a big launch that would get them "exposure." They needed influential people to talk about them. They even knew they needed to launch on a Tuesday, because that's when one gets the most attention.

No, I would explain, that is not how to get lots of users. The way you get lots of users is to make the product really great. Then people will not only use it but recommend it to their friends, so your growth will be exponential once you get it started.

At this point I've told the founders something you'd think would be completely obvious : that they should make a good company by making a good product. And yet their reaction would be something like the reaction many physicists must have had when they first heard about the theory of relativity : a mixture of astonishment at its apparent genius, combined with a suspicion that anything so weird couldn't possibly be right. ② <u>Ok, they would say, dutifully. And could you introduce us to such-and-such influential person? And remember, we want to launch on Tuesday.</u>

It would sometimes take founders years to grasp these simple lessons. And not because they were lazy or stupid. They just seemed blind to what was right in front of them.

Describe the main reason the writer gives for not tricking venture capitalists. Do NOT copy more than FOUR consecutive words from the passage. Second, explain the implication of the underlined words in ② regarding the start-up founders. Do NOT copy more than FOUR consecutive words from the passage.

_____

_____

_____

_____

_____

05 Read the passage and follow the directions. [4 points]

This year the world awakened to the fact that the most powerful and sophisticated species on earth is tragically vulnerable to the tiniest and most basic of creatures. Infectious disease specialists have been warning about this for decades. And the threat comes not only from novel viruses, such as the one causing COVID-19, that jump from animals to humans but also from microbial monsters that we have helped to create through our cavalier use of antibiotics : drug-resistant bacteria such as MRSA (methicillin-resistant Staphylococcus aureus) and multidrug-resistant Acinetobacter baumannii, sometimes dubbed "Iraqibacter" because so many soldiers returning from Iraq were infected with it. The World Health Organization has predicted that deaths from resistant-superbugs will rise from roughly 700,000 a year today to nearly 10 million by 2050.

But in a splendid irony, it may turn out that viruses, so often seen as nemeses, could be our saviors in fighting a host of killer infections. As the threat from _____ has grown and the development of new antibiotics has stalled, researchers have turned their attention to bacteriophages — literally, bacteria eaters. Viruses in this class are believed to be the oldest and most numerous organisms on earth. And like guided missiles, each type has evolved to seek and destroy a specific type of bacteria. Phage therapy has long been used in eastern Europe to battle infections, but after modern antibiotics arrived in the 1940s, it was largely ignored. Interest began to pick up in this century "because the resistance issue was getting worse and worse," says Vincent Fischetti, who heads the laboratory of bacterial pathogenesis and immunology at the Rockefeller University. With modern techniques, virologists can precisely match just the right phages to a specific strain of superbug — with sometimes astonishing results.

Tom Patterson, for example, was resurrected from an overwhelming Iraqibacter infection after his wife, Steffanie Strathdee, an infectious disease epidemiologist, scoured the world for phages that might save him. The couple, both professors at the University of California, San Diego, tell his story in their 2019 book *The Perfect Predator*. Strathdee has since co-founded U.C.S.D.'s Center for Innovative Phage Applications and Therapeutics.

For now phage therapy remains experimental. In most cases, it involves making custom cocktails of several phages shown to be active in vitro against an individual patient's bug. In Patterson's case, nine different phages were used in various cocktails injected into his bloodstream multiple times a day over 18 weeks. Strathdee envisions creating a library "with tens of thousands of phages, already purified, characterized and sequenced," for medical mixologists to draw on.

Fill in the blank with the TWO most appropriate consecutive words from the passage. Second, explain how phage therapy works. Do NOT copy more than FOUR consecutive words from the passage.

_____

_____

_____

_____

_____

06 Read the passage and follow the directions. [4 points]

[A] Whosoever would be a man, must be a nonconformist. He who would gather immortal palms must not be hindered by the name of goodness, but must explore if it be goodness. Nothing is at last sacred but the integrity of your own mind. Absolve you to yourself, and you shall have the suffrage of the world. I remember an answer which when quite young I was prompted to make to a valued adviser who was wont to importune me with the dear old doctrines of the church. On my saying, "What have I to do with the sacredness of traditions, if I live wholly from within?" He suggested, "But these impulses may be from below, not from above." I replied, "They do not seem to me to be such; but ① if I am the Devil's child, I will live then from the Devil." No law can be sacred to me but that of my nature. Good and bad are but names very readily transferable to that or this; the only right is that which is after my constitution; the only wrong what is against it.

[B] A man is to carry himself in the presence of all opposition as if every thing were titular and ephemeral but he. I am ashamed to think how easily we capitulate to badges and names, to large societies and dead institutions. Every decent and well-spoken individual affects and sways me more than is right. I ought to go upright and vital, and speak the ② rude truth in all ways. If malice and vanity wear the coat of philanthropy, shall that pass? If an angry bigot assumes this bountiful cause of Abolition, and comes to me with his last news from Barbadoes, why should I not say to him, "Go love thy infant; love thy wood-chopper; be good-natured and modest; have that grace; and never varnish your hard, uncharitable ambition with this incredible tenderness for black folk a thousand miles off. Thy love afar is spite at home." Rough and graceless would be such greeting, but truth is handsomer than the affectation of ___③___ . Your goodness must have some edge to it, —else it is none. The doctrine of hatred must be preached, as the counteraction of the doctrine of love, when that pules* and whines.

pule : cry plaintively

Explain the meaning of the underlined words in ①. Do NOT copy more than FOUR consecutive words from the passage. Second, identify the FIVE consecutive words from [A] that best correspond to the meaning of the underlined "rude truth". Third, fill in the blank with the ONE most appropriate word from the passage.

_____

_____

_____

_____

07 **Read the passage and follow the directions.** [4 points]

In the past few years, as a surgeon, I have become increasingly aware of the scourge of the wellness industry. I am seeing patients who opt for diets, supplements or magical therapies instead of the less seductive — though scientifically grounded — medicine I have to offer. Like everyone else, I, too, am constantly bombarded with messages in advertisements and from well-meaning friends as to how this diet or that vitamin is the key to health, longevity, beauty and status.

The growth of "The Goop Lab," a platform of misinformation, privilege and anti-science rhetoric, and, more broadly, of the multitrillion-dollar wellness industry is cause for concern. On the surface, it looks full of promise and hope. Dig just a little deeper, beyond the claims of all-natural miracles — the energy healing, the cold therapy, the anti-aging treatments — and what we find is at best, a waste of money and at worst, harmful methods that actually compromise your health. Research has shown that for those with cancer, using alternative therapies such as homeopathy or specialized diets led to people opting away from proven treatments and an increased risk of dying from that cancer.

For doctors such as myself, the rise of this brand of wellness is distressing. However, medicine as a profession and a science has no doubt played a part in the genesis and growth of big wellness. For virtually the whole of its existence, medicine has disenfranchised women and, to varying degrees, continues to do so. Even as medicine has modernized with an emphasis on autonomy and resolving bias, it remains, at times, paternalistic and patriarchal. It comes as no surprise then that women are overrepresented in the wellness industry, both as consumers and providers.

To truly ensure people's safety, medicine must of course denounce dangerous, unnecessary and expensive snake oil, but it must also turn our attention inward and provide care that people need and want, communicated with compassion and supporting their autonomy. If we are to ensure that people are protected against medical half-truths and harmful remedies, my profession must move far away from the patriarchal practices that have alienated so many.

Summarize the passage following the guidelines below.

Guidelines

- Summarize the above passage in one paragraph.
- Provide a topic sentence, supporting ideas, and a concluding sentence based on the passage.
- Do NOT copy more than FIVE consecutive words from the passage.

_____

_____

_____

_____

_____

모범답안 p.048

01 Read the passage and follow the directions. [4 points]

Attitude clearly matters in fighting _____. We don't know why (from my old-style materialistic perspective, I suspect that mental states feed back upon the immune system). But match people with the same cancer for age, class, health, and socio-economic status, and, in general, those with positive attitudes, with a strong will and purpose for living, with commitment to struggle, and with an active response to aiding their own treatment and not just a passive acceptance of anything doctors say tend to live longer. A few months later I asked Sir Peter Medawar, my personal scientific guru and a Nobelist in immunology, what the best prescription for success against cancer might be. "A sanguine personality," he replied. Fortunately I am, if anything, even-tempered and confident in just this manner.

The problem may be briefly stated : What does "median mortality of eight months" signify in our vernacular? I suspect that most people, without training in statistics, would read such a statement as "I will probably be dead in eight months" — the very conclusion that must be avoided, both because this formulation is false, and because attitude matters so much.

I was not, of course, overjoyed, but I didn't read the statement in this vernacular way either. My technical training enjoined a different perspective on "eight months median mortality." The point may seem subtle, but the consequences can be profound.

We tend to view means and medians as hard "realities," and the variation that permits their calculation as a set of transient and imperfect measurements. If the median is the reality and variation around the median just a device for calculation, then "I will probably be dead in eight months" may pass as a reasonable interpretation.

But all evolutionary biologists know that variation itself is nature's only irreducible essence. Variation is the hard reality, not a set of imperfect measures for a central tendency. Means and medians are the abstractions. Therefore, I looked at the statistics quite differently — and not only because I am an optimist who tends to see the doughnut instead of the hole, but primarily because I know that <u>variation itself is the reality</u>. I had to place myself amidst the variation.

Fill in the blank with the ONE most appropriate word from the passage. Second, what is the implied significance of "variation" in the underlined selection in regard to the speaker's situation? Do NOT copy more than FOUR consecutive words from the passage.

_____

_____

_____

_____

_____

02 Read the passage and follow the directions. [4 points]

The day after Stephen Jay Gould died, his obituary appeared on the front page of the New York Times, testifying to his position as the most famous scientist in the United States. His talent for synthesizing ideas and arguments, his work ethic, and — as he would have been the first to note — luck made him famous.

He had not planned to write his monthly column, "This View of Life," for *Natural History* for twenty-five years, but, like his childhood hero Joe DiMaggio, Gould became known for this literary streak, which breathed new life into the half-forgotten art of the popular scientific essay, a tradition that dates back to Galileo. Like Galileo, Gould did more than interpret science for laypeople. He was also a path-breaking evolutionary theorist and a canny political organizer for leftist causes.

Along with his colleague Niles Eldredge, Gould changed the way biologists view the fossil record. His concept of punctuated equilibrium argued that new species emerge relatively rapidly and then remain mostly stable for millions of years. To his more parochial colleagues' chagrin, Gould partly credited the inspiration for punctuated equilibrium to the fact that he had learned his Marxism, literally "at his daddy's knee."

Though he was redbaited for this comment, Gould and Eldredge were speaking as pluralists and historicists not dogmatists. "We make a simple plea for pluralism in guiding philosophies for the basic recognition that such philosophies constrain all our thought." Historical context also acts as a constraint on new ideas. Darwin acknowledged the influence of the classical political economy of Smith and Malthus on his theory of evolution. Gould noted that his liberal upbringing and participation in the revolution of the Civil Rights Movement enabled him to recognize the importance of punctuated equilibrium's patterns of sudden and discontinuous evolutionary change. Gould also revitalized the study of evolutionary development with his influential historical survey of the subject, Ontogeny and Phylogeny, and made his mark on anthropology by insisting that human evolution looked more like a branching bush with multiple overlapping lineages than a ladder of predictable stages.

Explain what can be inferred from the underlined part about Stephen Jay Gould. Do NOT copy more than THREE consecutive words from the passage. Second, in what way is the Civil Rights Movement related to Gould's understanding of evolution? Do NOT copy more than THREE consecutive words from the passage.

_____

_____

_____

_____

_____

03 **Read the passage and follow the directions.** [4 points]

In the dead of night he is wakened by a strange sound, an animal-like scratching and scuffling just outside the bedroom door. Some wild creature sharpening its claws, shredding the carpet — though the muffled sound of heavy breathing is not like an animal. It is utterly and horribly human. He reaches out for her, but his arm moves in the dark through a vast and empty space. She isn't there. He is alone in the bed and there is something or someone strange in the house. In an instant he is rigid, deafened by the sound of his own heart. Eventually, after a long time, the house is quiet again, just the distant chugging of the fridge, the dog gently groaning in its sleep.

He is reassured by the sleeping dog, realizes he must have dreamed the alien sounds, dreamed into being fears long dormant. These fears, acquiring life, had turned on him like vengeful demons : unnerving, but not as bad as an intruder in the house. Better they assault just him, in his dreams, than his children. He thinks of the children sleeping, feels a sudden pain that softens into tenderness and slowly passes. Then, remembering that the children are children no longer, have not lived at home for years, he stretches, breathes deeply, and folds into sleep again. He drifts in and out, dozing for a while, enjoying the sensation of relief, a sense of reprieve, a close shave that brings you to the edge — even if only momentarily — of a precipice.

Suddenly a sharp and ugly sensation yanks him into wakefulness. He leaps up, finds himself crouching on the bed, ready to spring, go for the jugular. A sliver of light moves swiftly across the crack under the door. Silence. No gentle groans or somnolent growls, even the dog is silent. Or silenced. He anticipates a terrible almost-human howling, envisages Max Cady in *Cape Fear* prowling the house, passing through the walls like the holy ghost, invisible. He can feel the presence of a figure on the other side of the bedroom door, someone holding their breath, listening to the silence. His own eyes grow accustomed to the dark, although he cannot tell whether he is now seeing or feeling in the dark.

Explain why he was reassured by the sleeping dog as shown in the underlined part. Do NOT copy more than THREE consecutive words from the passage. Second, write ONE word from the passage that best describes the emotional state of the main character.

_____

_____

_____

_____

_____

04 **Read the passage and follow the directions.** [4 points]

Tucked away in a perpetually foggy basin near the Pacific Ocean. Lowell is the only public high school in San Francisco that admits students on the basis of academic merit. The largest feeder to the University of California system, Lowell sends many of its graduates to the country's most selective universities. Such imagery might bring to mind whiz kids who are leaps and bounds smarter than those who lack the top-notch test scores and grades to get in. What I discovered was that Lowell students were distinguished more by their work ethic than by their intelligence. I once asked students in my homeroom how much they studied. The typical answer? Hours and hours. Not in a week, but in a single day. Still, like at any other school, there was tremendous variation in how hard students worked and how well they performed. Just as I'd found in New York, some of the students I expected to excel, because math came so easy to them, did worse than their classmates. On the other hand, some of my ⓐ hardest workers were consistently my highest performers on tests and quizzes. One of these very hard workers was David Luong. David was in my freshman algebra class. There were two kinds of algebra classes at Lowell : the accelerated track led to Advanced Placement Calculus by senior year, and the regular track, which I was teaching, didn't. The students in my class hadn't scored high enough on Lowell's math placement exam to get into the accelerated track. David didn't stand out at first. He was quiet and sat toward the back of the room. He didn't raise his hand a lot; he rarely volunteered to come to the board to solve problems. But I soon noticed that every time I graded an assignment, David had turned in perfect work. He aced my quizzes and tests. When I marked one of his answers as incorrect, it was more often my error than his. He was just so hungry to learn.

I began to wonder what the heck this kid was doing in my class. Once I understood ⓑ <u>how ridiculous the situation was</u>, I marched David into the office of my department chair. It didn't take long to explain what was going on. Fortunately, the chair was a wise and wonderful teacher who placed a higher value on kids than on bureaucratic rules. She immediately started the paperwork to switch David out of my class and into the accelerated track.

Describe who the "hardest workers" are according to the writer of the passage. Second, explain why the writer thinks the "situation" is ridiculous. Do NOT copy more than THREE consecutive words from the passage.

_____

_____

_____

_____

_____

05 Read the passage and follow the directions. [4 points]

In the 1990s, an army of clones invaded Germany. Within a decade, they had spread to Italy, Croatia, Slovakia, Hungary, Sweden, France, Japan and Madagascar — wreaking havoc in rivers and lakes, rice paddies and swamps; in waters warm and cold, acidic and basic. The culprits : six-inch-long, lobster-like creatures called marbled crayfish.

Scientists suspect that sometime around 1995, a genetic mutation allowed a pet crayfish to reproduce asexually, giving rise to a new, all-female species that could make clones of itself from its unfertilized eggs. Deliberately or accidentally, some of these mutants were released from aquariums into the wild, where they rapidly multiplied into the millions, threatening native waterways species and ecosystems.

But ⓐ their success is strange. "All marbled crayfish which exist today derive from a single animal," said Günter Vogt, a biologist at Heidelberg University. "They are all genetically identical." Ordinarily, the absence of genetic diversity makes a population exceedingly vulnerable to the vagaries of its environment. Yet the marbled crayfish have managed to thrive around the globe.

A closer look reveals that the crayfishes' uniformity is only genome-deep. According to studies conducted by Vogt and others in the mid-2000s, these aquatic clones actually vary quite a bit in their color, size, behavior and longevity. Which means that something other than their genes is inspiring that ___ⓑ___.

Common sense tells us that if it's not nature, it's nurture : environmental influences that interact with an animal's genome to generate different outcomes for various traits. But that's not the whole story. New research on crayfish and scores of other organisms is revealing an important role for a third, often-overlooked source of variation and diversity — a surprising foundation for what makes us unique that begins in the first days of an embryo's development : random, intrinsic noise.

Explain the meaning of the underlined words in ⓐ. Do NOT copy more than THREE consecutive words from the passage. Second, fill in the blank with the ONE most appropriate word from the passage. Third, describe all elements that have an affect on generating different traits, according to the passage.

_____

_____

_____

_____

_____

06 **Read the passage and follow the directions.** [4 points]

Nir Eyal, the author of *Indistractable* says that distractions are actions that pull us away from what we plan to do. The opposite of distraction is not focus, it is traction. Anything can be a distraction, just as anything can be traction. If you check your email when you plan to work on a big project, you're distracted. Conversely, if you plan to play video games, the game is not a distraction. It is traction. A diversion is a refocusing on attention. Diversions can be wonderful. Procrastination is when we give into a distraction instead of doing what we plan to do.

There are many theories on why we procrastinate, and why this unwanted habit is so hard to break. In the 1930s psychologists trained rats to do a certain behavior, e.g. pressing a lever, by giving them small rewards. Once trained, the scientists discovered that when the rats were given rewards unpredictably, on a variable ratio schedule of every 3 — 7 times, they would perform the trained behavior more often. More remarkably, with randomized rewards, the behavior became hard to extinguish. Getting rewards releases dopamine in the brain, and even the expectation of a reward has this effect.

Not only rats, but also humans have a desire for randomness. We get excited by unpredictability. Watching sports — who will score/win? Listening to radio — what song will they play next? Shopping — is there a bargain on the sale? In this age we are just a mouse click away from randomness. Most of us carry a smartphone everywhere we go, and a big part of the appeal is the excitement finding out what is "new". For some it is more addictive than sugar and heroin.

Engaging in randomness itself is not bad, but when we use it to _____ it can be hard to stop. Just one more click, scroll, or tab. Many of the tasks that we plan to do, like work, studying and chores, don't have immediate rewards. The benefits of work and studying are in the future, whereas checking Instagram or Facebook hits the reward systems in the brain immediately. Did I get any likes on my post? What stories hide under the bell-icon?

One popular technique that I and many others use for fighting procrastination is timeboxing a.k.a. The pomodoro Technique. The technique prescribes a 25-minute session work followed by a 5-minute break. There is a strict rule. During the 25-minute work session you must only do one task and do not interrupt yourself e.g. by checking email. No distractions — only traction.

Fill in the blank with the ONE most appropriate word from the passage. Second, describe what is lacking from work and study that makes these tasks have less "traction".

---

07 Read the passage and follow the directions. [4 points]

Largely because of a quirk of brain development, adolescents, on average, experience more anxiety and fear and have a harder time learning how not to be afraid than either children or adults. Different regions and circuits of the brain mature at very different rates. It turns out that the brain circuit for processing fear—the amygdala—is precocious and develops way ahead of the prefrontal cortex, the seat of reasoning and executive control. This means that adolescents have a brain that is wired with an enhanced capacity for fear and anxiety, but is relatively underdeveloped when it comes to calm reasoning.

You may wonder why, if adolescents have such enhanced capacity for anxiety, they are such novelty seekers and risk takers. It would seem that the two traits are at odds. The answer, in part, is that the brain's reward center, just like its fear circuit, matures earlier than the prefrontal cortex. That reward center drives much of teenagers' risky behavior. This behavioral paradox also helps explain why adolescents are particularly prone to injury and trauma. The top three killers of teenagers are accidents, homicide and suicide.

The brain-development lag has huge implications for how we think about anxiety and how we treat it. It suggests that anxious adolescents may not be very responsive to psychotherapy that attempts to teach them to be unafraid, like cognitive behavior therapy, which is zealously prescribed for teenagers. What we have learned should also make us think twice—and then some— about the ever rising use of stimulants in young people, because these drugs may worsen anxiety and make it harder for teenagers to do what they are developmentally supposed to do : learn to be unafraid when it is appropriate to do so. Our promiscuous use of stimulants impair the ability of adolescents to suppress learned fear, something that is a normal part of development, and make them more fearful adults. And stimulants are likely to increase the risk of PTSD in adolescents exposed to trauma.

We do know adolescents are not just carefree novelty seekers and risk takers; they are uniquely vulnerable to anxiety and have a hard time learning to be unafraid of passing dangers. Parents have to realize that adolescent anxiety is to be expected, and to comfort their teenagers, and themselves, by reminding them that they will grow up and out of it soon enough. These things, when considered properly, will leave us with a better understanding on the threats facing adolescents and how to more healthily address them.

Write a summary following the guidelines below.

| Guidelines |

- Summarize the above passage in one paragraph.
- Provide a topic sentence, supporting ideas, and a concluding sentence based on the passage.
- Do NOT copy more than FIVE consecutive words from the passage.

_____

_____

_____

_____

_____

모범답안 p.051

01 **Read the passage and follow the directions.** [4 points]

On Monday, out of the clear blue sky, the local travel Agent telephoned Janice to tell her that she had won two tickets to the Albuquerque International Balloon Fiesta in New Mexico. Janice and John, her husband, had always wanted to go Ballooning at the festival, but they thought that ① such a trip was beyond their reach. She was walking on air when she telephoned John to tell him the good news. At first, John thought that Janice was joking and full of hot air. But when he realized that she was not building castles in the air, his annoyance vanished into thin air. As soon as John came home from work, Janice and John eagerly talked about the trip. Soon their plans grew by leaps and bounds. Janice's head was in the clouds all the time because she was anticipating the trip and her first balloon ride. Two weeks before the trip, Janice was rushed to the hospital. After examining her, the doctor burst her bubble when he said that she would need an operation. The doctor's decision went over like a lead balloon. Janice was devastated. Now their balloon vacation was up in the air. She knew that without the free tickets, the cost of the trip would be sky high. But Janice was lucky. The operation was not serious, and she begged the doctor to let her go on the trip. One week later, Janice and John took their dream trip. They were on cloud nine as their balloon rose into the blue sky. Janice thought : ② it pays to reach for the sky.

Explain the meaning of the underlined words in ①. Second, explain what Janice thought in the underlined ②. Do NOT copy more than FOUR consecutive words from the passage.

_____

_____

_____

_____

_____

02 Read the passage and follow the directions. [4 points]

Matt, a first-year teacher, walked into Bill's classroom, excited to observe him. Matt had a lot of respect for Bill as a teacher and looked forward to seeing effective classroom management techniques in action. Bill, a teaching veteran, was well liked by students and colleagues. Their principal had recommended that Matt observe Bill, noting how he engaged students, a key to limiting disciplinary interruptions. Matt founded a desk in the back of the room and prepared to take notes.

As students settled into their seats, Bill welcomed them cheerily. He then reminded them that one of their benchmark tests was scheduled for the next day. Following a brief overview of strategies for studying the material, Bill asked whether they wanted to play a game. "Let's see how prepared you are for the exam."

"First, we need to split ourselves into two teams," Bill explained, then asked students how they wanted to do so. As students discussed options, Bill walked to the back of the room and said to Matt, "If you let students make decisions, they'll take ① ownership of their learning."

One student suggested they form teams by gender, "boys versus girls," eliciting enthusiastic support from several classmates. Bill sent the young men to one side of the room and the young women to the other side of room, then proceeded to ask each team questions while keeping count of correct responses.

After ten minutes the "girls" team was well ahead of the "boys" team, leading a couple young men to joke they were "letting the girls win." A couple young women responded by reminding their male classmates that the "girls" won the previous two games, as well. Following several minutes of the teams mocking one another, Bill tried to refocus all the students by announcing, "If you guys don't settle down we'll end the game."

After class, as students left the room, Matt heard several laughing and making disparaging remarks to one another, debating about which gender was most intelligent. Bill approached Matt and warmly said, "The students love competitions and don't realize how much they're learning in the process."

He then looked down and, seeing Matt's notes, noticed he had written and circled "gender stereotypes" in his notebook. "Whoa! That's what you are focusing on?" Bill asked. "Boys versus girls : that's what the students love to do." He then counseled Matt, "You're still new at this and will learn soon enough that, as long as the students are engaged and learning, ② that other stuff doesn't matter."

Provide an example of "ownership of their learning" from the passage. Second, identify to what the underlined words in ② refer.

_____

_____

_____

_____

_____

03 Read the passage and follow the directions. [4 points]

How did the Earth get its oceans? The primordial Earth was a seething ball of magma, so the water that it began with would have evaporated into space. As a result, planetary scientists have long debated which of two types of objects, comets or asteroids, were more responsible for delivering Earth's water.

A new study, published in *Science,* says that asteroids were the source. The authors, led by Conel Alexander of the Carnegie Institution of Washington, in Washington DC, analysed the isotopic abundances of nitrogen and hydrogen in 86 primitive meteorites, and found that they coordinate with Earth's.

Asteroids had already been the favored source. Studies of solar system dynamics suggest that there was a period of time around 3.9 billion years ago, called the Late Heavy Bombardment, during which the Earth would have been barraged, mostly by asteroids.

Even though _____ are ideal sources, with their high percentage content of water, rich with amino acids, there are a few strikes against them. Six studies of comets from the Oort Cloud found that their isotopic ratios of heavy hydrogen were much higher than Earth's. When a 2011 *Nature* paper found isotopic levels of heavy hydrogen in the comet Hartley 2 to be similar to Earth's, it revived interest in water-from-comets idea. But Alexander and his colleagues suggest that the overall levels of heavy hydrogen in Hartley 2 (and not just the levels in the comet's ice) would be much higher.

Explain why the Earth would not retain its original water. Do NOT copy more than FOUR consecutive words from the passage. Second, fill in the blank with the ONE most appropriate word from the passage.

_____

_____

_____

04 Read the passage and follow the directions. [4 points]

It seems necessary towards moving the passions of people advanced in life to any considerable degree, that the objects designed for that purpose, besides their being in some measure new, should be capable of exciting pain or pleasure from other causes. Pain and pleasure are simple ideas, incapable of definition. People are not liable to be mistaken in their feelings, but they are very frequently wrong in the names they give them, and in their reasonings about them. Many are of the opinion, that pain arises necessarily from the removal of some pleasure; as they think pleasure does from the ceasing or diminution of some pain.

For my part, I am rather inclined to imagine, that pain and pleasure, in their most simple and natural manner of affecting, are each of a positive nature, and by no means necessarily dependent on each other for their existence. The human mind is often, and I think it is for the most part, in a state neither of pain nor pleasure, which I call a state of indifference. When I am carried from this state into a state of actual pleasure, it does not appear necessary that I should pass through the medium of any sort of _____. If in such a state of indifference, or ease, or tranquillity, or call it what you please, you were to be suddenly entertained with a concert of music; or suppose some object of a fine shape, and bright, lively colours, to be presented before you; or imagine your smell is gratified with the fragrance of a rose; in all the several senses, of hearing, smelling and tasting, you undoubtedly find a pleasure. Yet if I inquire into the state of your mind previous to these gratifications, you will hardly tell me that they found you in any kind of pain.

Suppose on the other hand, a man in the same state of indifference, to receive a violent blow, or to drink of some bitter potion; here is no removal of pleasure; and yet here is felt in every sense which is affected, a pain very distinguishable. I can never persuade myself that pleasure and pain are mere relations, which can only exist as they are contrasted.

Fill in the blank with the ONE most appropriate word from the passage. Second, explain what the writer tries to argue in the last sentence. Do NOT copy more than FOUR consecutive words from the passage.

_____

_____

_____

_____

_____

05 **Read the passage and follow the directions.** [4 points]

Sunburns readily advertise that we've had fun in the sun, and perhaps have been a bit careless, but what exactly goes on in our cells to produce the painful, red inflammation has not been clear.

Now, researchers have discovered a molecular signal that triggers sunburns. When our skin cells are exposed to ultraviolet B (UVB) radiation, a specific form of RNA, called micro-RNA, is damaged, the study found. (RNA is similar in structure to DNA, which makes up our genes.) This damaged RNA is then released as a signal of solar injury, and prompts neighboring, healthy cells to stimulate the production of factors that promote _____.

The entire process is intended to remove sun-damaged cells, which could turn cancerous if not cleared away. "The cells of our skin can sense dead, sun-damaged cells, because the cells release damaged RNA," said study researcher Dr. Richard Gallo, professor of medicine at University of California, San Diego School of Medicine. While other factors likely play a role in the inflammatory process we see as a sunburn, the findings suggest the damaged RNA molecules serve as a marker for radiation-caused injury.

The findings may have implications for medical conditions, the researchers said. For example, one treatment for the skin condition psoriasis* is exposure to UV light. But while the light can relieve symptoms, it also increases skin cancer risk. The new findings suggest that certain RNA molecules could be used in place of UV therapy, and produce the same benefit. In addition, people with certain autoimmune conditions get a burning sensation with very little exposure to UV light, before unhealthy cell damage has occurred. Blocking the micro-RNA pathway may be a way to reduce _____ in these patients. However, healthy people without such conditions would not want to block this pathway just to prevent sunburn, because it is an important way for the body to heal and get rid of damaged cells. "The inflammatory response is a normal part of our protection against the sun," Gallo said.

*psoriasis : a skin disease that causes red, itchy scaly patches

Fill in the blanks with the same ONE most appropriate word from the passage. Second, explain why the new findings could lead to new treatments for psoriasis. Do NOT copy more than FOUR consecutive words from the passage.

_____

_____

_____

_____

_____

06 Read the passage and follow the directions. [4 points]

The caption of a Roman print of 1601 claims the engraving represents a giant whale that has been washed ashore near Ancona the same year and "was drawn accurately from nature". The claim would be more trustworthy if there did not exist an earlier print recording a similar 'scoop' from the Dutch coast in 1598. But surely the Dutch artists of the late sixteenth century, those masters of realism, would be able to portray a whale? Not quite, it seems, for the creature looks suspiciously as if it had ears, and whales with ears, I am assured on higher authority, do not exist. The draughtsman probably mistook one of the whale's flippers for a(n) _____ and therefore placed it far too close to the eye. He, too, was misled by a familiar schema, the schema of the typical head. To draw an unfamiliar sight presents greater difficulties than is usually realized. And this, I suppose, was also the reason why the Italian preferred to copy the whale from another print. We need not doubt the part of the caption that tells the news from Ancona, but to portray it 'from the life' was not worth the trouble.

In this respect the fate of exotic creatures in the illustrated books of the last few centuries before the advent of photography is as instructive as it is amusing. When Albrecht Durer, a painter of the German Renaissance, published his famous woodcut of a rhinoceros, he had to rely on secondhand evidence which he filled in from his own imagination, coloured, no doubt, by what he had learned of the most famous of exotic beasts, the dragon with its armoured body. Yet it has been shown that this half-invented creature served as a model for all renderings of the rhinoceros, even in natural-history books, up to the eighteenth century. When, in 1790, James Bruce published a drawing of the beast in his *Travels to Discover the Source of the Nile*, he proudly showed that he was aware of the fact.

Fill in the blank with the ONE most appropriate word from the passage. If necessary, change the word form. Second, explain why the writer employs the term "half-invented". Do NOT copy more than FOUR consecutive words from the passage.

_____

_____

_____

_____

_____

07 Read the passage and follow the directions. [4 points]

Once, work was a major source of friendships. We took our families to company picnics and invited our colleagues over for dinner. Now, we go to the office to be efficient, not to form bonds.

Why are Americans so determined to get down to business? The economic explanation is that long-term employment has essentially vanished : Instead of spending our careers at one organization, we expect to jump ship every few years. Since we don't plan to stick around, we don't invest in the same way. We view co-workers as transitory ties, greeting them with arms-length civility while reserving real camaraderie for outside work. When we're constantly connected with old friends on social media—and we can travel to visit them anytime—why bother making new ones? With 24/7 connectivity, we face a growing time famine, where the pressure to get work done may eclipse the desire to socialize.

When we see our jobs primarily as a means to leisure, it's easy to convince ourselves that efficiency should reign supreme at work so we have time for friendships outside work. But we may be underestimating the impact of workplace friendships on our happiness—and our effectiveness. Jobs are more satisfying when they provide opportunities to form friendships. Research shows that groups of friends outperform groups of acquaintances in both decision making and effort tasks. When friends work together, they're more trusting and committed to one another's success. That means they share more information and spend more time helping— and as long as they don't hold back on constructive criticism out of politeness, they make better choices and get more done.

Whether we bond at work is a personal decision, but it may involve less effort and vulnerability than we realize. A high-quality connection doesn't require "a deep or intimate relationship." A single interaction marked by respect, trust and mutual engagement is enough to generate energy for both parties. However small they appear, those moments of connection can transform a transaction into a relationship.

Summarize the passage following the guidelines below.

Guidelines

- Summarize the above passage in one paragraph.
- Provide a topic sentence, supporting ideas, and a concluding sentence based on the passage.
- Do NOT copy more than FIVE consecutive words from the passage.

_____

_____

_____

_____

_____

01 Read the passage and follow the directions. [4 points]

Do you realize that the only time in our lives when we like to get old is when we're kids? If you're less than 10 years old, <u>you're so excited about aging that you think in fractions</u>. "How old are you?" "I'm four and a half!" You're never thirty-six and a half. You're four and a half, going on five! That's the key. You get into your teens, now they can't hold you back. You jump to the next number, or even a few ahead. "How old are you?" "I'm gonna be 16!" You could be 13, but hey, you're gonna be 16! And then the greatest day of your life . . you become 21. Even the words sound like a ceremony . . . YOU BECOME 21. YESSSS!!!

But then you turn 30. Oooohh, what happened there? Makes you sound like bad milk! He TURNED; we had fractions to throw him out. There's no fun now, you're Just a sour-dumpling, What's wrong? What's changed? You BECOME 21, you TURN 30, then you're PUSHING 40. Whoa! Put on the brakes, it's all slipping away. Before you know it, you REACH 50 and your dreams are gone. But wait!!! You MAKE it to 60. You didn't think you would! So you BECOME 21, TURN 30, PUSH 40, REACH 50 and MAKE it to 60.

You've built up so much speed that you HIT 70! After that it's a day-by-day thing; you HIT Wednesday! You get into your 80s and every day is a complete cycle; you HIT lunch; YOU TURN 4:30; you REACH bedtime. And it doesn't end there. Into the 90s, you start going backwards; "I was JUST 92." Then a strange thing happens. If you make it over 100, you become a little kid again. "I'm 100 and a half!" May you all make it to a healthy 100 and a half!!

Explain the meaning of the underlined words. Second, what similarity do kids share with the very old according to the passage?

_____

_____

_____

_____

_____

02 Read the passage and follow the directions. [4 points]

It is worth looking at one or two aspects of the way a mother behaves towards her baby. The usual fondling, cuddling and cleaning require little comment, but the position in which she holds the baby against her body when resting is rather revealing. Careful American studies have disclosed the fact that 80 percent of mothers cradle their infants in their left arms, holding them against the left side of their bodies. If asked to explain the significance of this preference most people reply that it is obviously the result of the predominance of right-handedness in the population. By holding the babies in their left arms, the mothers keep their dominant arm free for manipulations. But a detailed analysis shows that this is not the case. True, there is a slight difference between right-handed and left-handed females, but not enough to provide an adequate explanation. It emerges that 83 percent of right-handed mothers hold the baby on the left side, but then so do 78 percent of left-handed mothers. In other words, only 22 percent of the left-handed mothers have their dominant hands free for actions. Clearly there must be some other, less obvious explanation.

The only other clue comes from the fact that the heart is on the left side of the mother's body. Could it be that the sound of her heartbeat is the vital factor? And in what way? Thinking along these lines it was argued that perhaps during its existence inside the body of the mother, the growing embryo becomes fixated ('imprinted') on the sound of the heart beat. If this is so, then the re-discovery of this familiar sound after birth might have a calming effect on the infant, especially as it has just been thrust into a strange and frighteningly new world outside. If this is so then the mother, either instinctively or by an unconscious series of trials and errors, would soon arrive at the discovery that her baby is more at peace if held on the _____ against her heart.

Explain which result of the research directly opposes the argument "holding the babies in their left arms, the mothers keep their dominant arm free for manipulations". Second, fill in the blank with the ONE most appropriate word from the passage.

_____

_____

_____

_____

_____

03 **Read the passage and follow the directions.** [4 points]

Sometimes, history really does seem to repeat itself. After the US Civil War, for example, a wave of urban violence fuelled by ethnic and class resentment swept across the country, peaking in around 1870. Internal strife spiked again in around 1920, when race riots, workers' strikes and a surge of anti-Communist feeling led many people to think that revolution was imminent. And in around 1970, unrest crested once more, with violent student demonstrations, political assassinations, riots and terrorism.

To Peter Turchin, who studies population dynamics at the University of Connecticut in Storrs, the appearance of three peaks of political instability at roughly 50-year intervals is not a coincidence. For the past 15 years, Turchin has been taking the mathematical techniques that once allowed him to track predator‑prey cycles in forest ecosystems, and applying them to human _____. He has analysed historical records on economic activity, demographic trends and outbursts of violence in the United States, and has come to the conclusion that a new wave of internal strife is already on its way. The peak should occur in about 2020, he says, and will probably be at least as high as the one in around 1970. "I hope it won't be as bad as 1870," he adds.

Turchin's approach — which he calls cliodynamics after Clio, the ancient Greek muse of history — is part of a groundswell of efforts to apply scientific methods to history by identifying and modelling the broad social forces that Turchin and his colleagues say shape all human societies. It is an attempt to show that "<u>history is not just one damn thing after another</u>", says Turchin, paraphrasing a saying often attributed to the late British historian Arnold Toynbee. Cliodynamics is viewed with deep scepticism by most academic historians, who tend to see history as a complex stew of chance, individual foibles and one-of-a-kind situations that no broad-brush 'science of history' will ever capture. "After a century of grand theory, from Marxism and social Darwinism to structuralism and postmodernism, most historians have abandoned the belief in general laws," said Robert Darnton, a cultural historian at Harvard University.

Fill in the blank with the ONE most appropriate word from the passage. Second, explain the meaning of the underlined words.

---

04 **Read the passage and follow the directions.** [4 points]

Ms. Ward loved geography. She inspired and motivated students by telling them they were learning material typically reserved for older students.

The first unit Ms. Ward planned for the new school year focused on California. Although Rustin School, where Ms. Ward taught, was in the Midwest, she thought it would be a fun state with which to kick off the year. Students at Rustin represented a wide range of socioeconomic and racial diversity, but she knew many of them were interested in ocean beaches. California, in her mind, fit well with this theme.

Ms. Ward gathered her students on the carpet and began writing on a flip chart. Several students whispered excitedly as she wrote "California" at the top of the sheet. Although Ms. Ward was happy to see their excitement, she reminded them to remain quiet and raise their hands if they had something to say. Immediately several hands flew up.

"Are we going to learn about California?" Maddy asked.

"Yes," Ms. Ward replied. "We will be learning about California in many of our subjects throughout the week." Students chattered excitedly again and Ms. Ward reminded them to remain quiet : "I cannot understand you if so many of you talk at once."

After explaining the unit a bit more, Ms. Ward asked who had been to California. DeQuan raised his hand. When Ms. Ward called on him he said, "A few days ago, I was at my grandmother's house watching television with my little sister, but she was crying so I couldn't hear very well. I told her to be quiet and gave her a toy to play with because the person on TV···"

Ms. Ward interrupted DeQuan and reminded him that the question she asked was who had been to California. Feeling a little angry at the side chatter and DeQuan's indirect answer, she reminded the class that now was not the time for stories.

"Please raise your hand *only* if you can answer the question," she said. Upon hearing this, DeQuan added in an angry tone, "I was saying that the person on TV said the show was sponsored by a company that makes raisins, which are my favorite snack, and that the raisins are made in California!"

Ms. Ward reminded DeQuan he needed to raise his hand if he had something to say, and added that his tone was full of disrespect. Attempting to refocus the group, she asked, "Has anyone been to Disneyland?" Maddy raised her hand and said, "I have. It's in California, and it is sunny and warm there. It's also far away because we were on the airplane for a long time."

"You're right," Ms. Ward replied as she wrote "warm" and "sunny" along with the phrase "far from Rustin School" on the flip chart.

"Any other words to describe California?" she asked. As several others raised their hands, Ms. Ward noticed DeQuan still looked _____. Anticipating another outburst, she cheerfully said, "DeQuan, please try to compose yourself so that you can remain seated with the group." Hearing this, DeQuan stood, walked to his desk, and slouched in his chair.

Oh, no, thought Ms. Ward. *He must not have heard me correctly.* Knowing time was passing quickly and that she needed to finish the lesson, Ms. Ward continued teaching but wondered how she should address DeQuan if his negative behavior persisted.

Explain why the geography teaching did not begin in the students' home state. Second, fill in the blank with the ONE most appropriate word from the passage.

_____

_____

_____

_____

_____

05 Read the passage and follow the directions. [4 points]

A small company is trying to bring to market a genetically engineered apple that does not turn brown when sliced or bruised. But it has much of the rest of the apple industry seeing red.

The company, Okanagan Specialty Fruits, says the nonbrowning apple will prove popular with consumers and food service companies and help increase sales of apples, in part by making sliced apples more attractive to serve or sell. While Americans have been eating genetically engineered foods since the 1990s, those have been mainly processed foods. The Arctic Apple, as it is being called, could become one of the first genetically engineered versions of a fruit that people directly bite into.

But the U.S. Apple Association, which represents the American apple industry, opposes introduction of the product, as do some other industry organizations. They say that, while they do not believe that the genetic engineering is dangerous, it could undermine the fruit's image as a healthy and natural food, the one that keeps the doctor away and is as American as, well, apple pie. Neal Carter, the founder and president of the company said the nonbrowning apples could improve industry sales, much as baby carrots did for carrot sales. A whole apple is "for many people too big a commitment," he said. "If you had a bowl of apples at a meeting, people wouldn't take an apple out of the bowl. But if you had a plate of apple slices, everyone would take a slice." Consumption of fresh apples in the United States has fallen from about 20 pounds a year for each person in the late 1980s to about 16 pounds now, according to the Agriculture Department.

Apple _____ are already becoming more popular as a healthful snack, sold in bags in supermarkets and included by McDonald's in its Happy Meals for children. They are often coated with vitamin C and calcium to prevent browning and preserve crispness. But that can affect the taste, Mr. Carter said. He also said that growers would have fewer apples rejected by supermarkets because of the minor bruising that is common from handling of the fruit. Arctic Apples, which would first be available in the Golden Delicious and Granny Smith varieties, contain a synthetic gene that sharply reduces production of polyphenol oxidase, an enzyme responsible for the browning.

Explain the meaning of the underlined words. Next, fill in the blank with the ONE most appropriate word from the passage.

06 Read the passage and follow the directions. [4 points]

"It should be possible to make a precious stone that not only looks like the real thing, but that is the real thing", said a chemist many years ago. "The only difference should be that one crystal would be made by man, the other by nature."

At first this did not seem like a particularly hard task. Scientists began to try making synthetic diamonds towards the end of the eighteenth century. It was at this time that a key scientific fact was discovered : diamonds are a form of carbon, which is a very common element. Graphite, the black mineral that is used for the 'lead' in your pencil, is made of it, too. The only difference, we know today, is that the carbon atoms have been packed together in a slightly different way. The chemists were fired with enthusiasm : Why not change a cheap and plentiful substance, carbon, into a rare and expensive one, diamond?

You have probably heard about the alchemists who for centuries tried to turn plain lead or iron into gold. They failed, because gold is completely different from lead or iron. Transforming carbon into diamonds, however, is not illogical at all. This change takes place in _____①_____, so it should be possible to make it happen in the laboratory.

It should be possible, but for one hundred and fifty years every effort failed. During this period, none the less, several people believed that they had solved the diamond riddle. One of these was a French scientist who produced crystals that seemed to be the real thing. After the man's death, however, a curious rumour began to go the rounds. The story told that one of the scientist's assistants had simply put tiny pieces of genuine diamonds into the carbon mixture. He was bored with the work, and he wanted to make the old chemist happy.

The first real success came more than sixty years later in the laboratories of the General Electric Company. Scientists there had been working for a number of years on a process designed to duplicate nature's work. Far below the earth's surface, carbon is subjected to incredibly heavy pressure and extremely high _____②_____ . Under these conditions the carbon turns into diamonds. For a long time the laboratory attempts failed, simply because no suitable machinery existed. What was needed was some sort of pressure chamber in which the carbon could be subjected to between 800,000 and 1,800,000 pounds of pressure to the square inch, at a temperature of between 2200 and 4400°F.

Fill in each blank with the ONE most appropriate word from the passage respectively. Second, describe what "the diamond riddle" is.

_____

_____

_____

_____

_____

07 Read the passage and follow the directions. [4 points]

To understand why a pandemic such as COVID-19 has had such deleterious effects, we must examine why the study of diagnosis and treatment of disease separated itself from the study of preventing disease — or, more succinctly, why medicine and public health are considered apart from each other. Tracing this unfortunate disconnect leads us to a cause from 110 years ago : the 1910 Flexner report.

In the early 1900s, the American Medical Association commissioned the Carnegie Foundation to help reform medical education. Together they hired Abraham Flexner to assess the state of medical education. After visiting every medical school in North America, he produced the report. The Flexner report — and the money tied to its implementation — is the medical education system we're familiar with today : competitive admission criteria, traditional pedagogy and the scientific method as its central tenets. The report established the individual biomedical model, which focuses exclusively on biologic causes of disease, excluding any social and environmental factors, as the gold standard.

It also led to the disproportionate closing of historically Black medical colleges, contributing to physician workforce disparities that still exist today, and effectively cleaved the study of medicine from the study of public health. So, still, many researchers often cite the individual attribute of race as a risk factor for disease without interrogating the associated environmental experience of racism. Similarly, the lens in medical education is often inclusive of poverty but not oppression, race but not racism.

The Flexner report needs to be supplanted by another document that stitches medicine and public health back together. A replacement for the Flexner report can catalyze concrete action and may provide cover. Even if it is only a symbolic gesture to indicate abandonment of outdated ways of thinking, the American Medical Association would be wise to commission another report to show that Flexner's thinking, while revolutionary for his time, isn't applicable anymore.

Summarize the passage following the guidelines below.

Guidelines

- Summarize the above passage in one paragraph.
- Provide a topic sentence, supporting ideas, and a concluding sentence based on the passage.
- Do NOT copy more than FIVE consecutive words from the passage.

모범답안 p.055

01 Read the passage and follow the directions. [4 points]

You want to be rich, do you? Do you fancy driving around in a Ferrari, flying first class and staying in luxury hotels? In that case you're going to need to be a millionaire. But what's the best way of making a million be the time you're 40? Well, one good idea is to take a look at someone who has been successful and see how they did it. In the UK there's no better example than Richard Branson, the boss of the Virgin empire.

Today Virgin is an enormous group of companies, all operating independently. The only unifying factor is Mr Branson's enthusiasm and the Virgin brand. The group has operated over 200 Virgin companies. Many analysts believe that this is taking brand-stretching too far, and that sooner or later Virgin will lose its identity in minds of customers. However, Mr Branson has always proved his critics wrong.

Mr Branson started his empire in his bedroom at the age of 17 and he's come a long way since then. It all began when Mr Branson spotted a niche in the market for a student magazine. Up until then, student magazines were all about schools and what was happening at school or university. Mr Branson realised that the students were interested in other things, apart from school life, and so he decided to launch a magazine that communicated with them, with articles about music and films. His mother lent him £4 to help him start the magazine and that was it. Later, his headmaster said : "Congratulations, Branson. I predict that by the time you're 40, you'll either be a prisoner or a millionaire".

Soon, selling records became more lucrative than selling subscriptions to the magazine. Mr Branson decided to set up a shop, but he didn't have any money to pay the rent. At the time, Mr Branson was still a teenager and no banks were going to give him credit. Most people would have given up at this point but not Mr Branson. He found an empty office above a shoe shop, and persuaded the owner of the shop to let him rent it for free. How did he do that? Well, he guaranted the owner that so many people would visit Mr Branson's new shop, that the owner would sell more shoes as a result and so make more profits than he would from the rent. And it worked!

Now he had a successful business based on selling an established product at a competitive price, but he still didn't have a name. There were many suggestions from the people who were helping him, but Mr Branson didn't like any of them. Then one of his collaborators suggested "Virgin", because, she said, "we are complete virgins at business". And the name stuck.

What can be inferred about Branson's character from Branson's headmaster's saying? Second, explain the meaning of the underlined words in the last sentence of the passage. Do NOT copy more than FOUR consecutive words from the passage.

_____

_____

_____

_____

_____

02 Read the passage and follow the directions. [4 points]

Thanksgiving visits home bring with them any number of awkward conversations, from fights over politics to nudges about when you and your significant other are going to start having children; who doesn't love a serving of guilt about not (yet) having kids to go with the stuffing? But if your relatives start dropping dire statistics about declining fertility rates and what happens if you wait too long to have children, you can reassure them : The supposed gap between the number of children people say is _____ and the number they're having is not as alarming as it might seem. And lower fertility rates have benefits as well as costs.

The notion of ideal family size is appealing because it seems intuitive and straightforward. Reported ideal family size in the United States has stayed stable at around 2-3 children over the past decade. Yet fertility has continued to decline, with the total fertility rate, an estimate of lifetime fertility, now at a low of 1.73. This seems to imply a worsening gap between the ideal and the reality.

But how should we interpret this gap? Frequently, discussions like these take for granted that what individuals — usually women — say they think is an "ideal" family size and how many children they personally want are one and the same. But ideal family size might be too abstract to be useful; for example, some people respond with the general two-child norm without meaning that they want two children themselves. Instead, it's preferable to measure how many children people say they personally want to have; it's even better if we have information about their desires for having children in the short term, since many people change their long-term plans as life unfolds.

Another dominant assumption in these conversations is the idea of "competing preferences" — activities, behaviors and statuses that are difficult to combine with having and raising children. For some, this conjures up images of lazy millennials playing video games or spending time shopping and dining out; others interpret this line of reasoning as evidence that individuals — especially women — are selfish and narcissistic for putting other goals ahead of forming a family. This is a mistaken assumption.

Fill in the blank with the ONE most appropriate word from the passage. Second, identify the central error the writer cites in information gathering on family size. Do NOT copy more than FOUR consecutive words from the passage.

_____

_____

_____

_____

_____

03 Read the passage and follow the directions. [4 points]

As a graduate student just beginning to probe the psychology of _____, I was interviewing leaders in business, art, athletics, journalism, academia, medicine, and law : Who are the people at the very top of your field? What are they like? What do you think makes them special? Some of the characteristics that emerged in these interviews were very field specific. For instance, more than one businessperson mentioned an appetite for taking financial risks : "You've got to be able to make calculated decisions about millions of dollars and still go to sleep at night." But this seemed entirely beside the point for artists, who instead mentioned a drive to create : "I like making stuff. I don't know why, but I do." In contrast, athletes mentioned a different kind of motivation, one driven by the thrill of victory : "Winners love to go head-to-head with other people. Winners hate losing."

In addition to these particulars, there emerged certain commonalities, and they were what interested me most. No matter the field, the most successful people were lucky and talented. I'd heard that before, and I didn't doubt it. But the story of success didn't end there. Many of the people I talked to could also recount tales of rising stars who, to everyone's surprise, dropped out or lost interest before they could realize their potential. Apparently, it was critically important — and not at all easy — to keep going after failure : "Some people are great when things are going well, but they fall apart when things aren't." High achievers described in these interviews really stuck it out : "This one guy, he wasn't actually the best writer at the beginning. I mean, we used to read his stories and have a laugh because the writing was so clumsy and melodramatic. But he got better and better, and last year he won a Guggenheim." And they were constantly driven to improve : "She's never satisfied. You'd think she would be, by now, but she's her own harshest critic." The highly accomplished were paragons of perseverance.

Fill in the blank with the ONE most appropriate word from the passage. Second, explain the meaning of the underlined words. Do NOT copy more than FOUR consecutive words from the passage.

_____

_____

_____

_____

_____

04 **Read the passage and follow the directions.** [4 points]

> The home of the Ford Model T is now an abandoned factory complex along busy Woodward Avenue in Highland Park, Mich., and there's not much to distinguish this place from Detroit's other industrial ruins. But if you stop and walk up to the front of the building, you'll find a historical marker telling us that by 1925, this place churned out more than 9,000 Ford Model t's a day. And it ends with this : "Mass production soon moved from here to all phases of American industry, and set a pattern of abundance for 20th century living." That actually helped America's 20th century middle class take off.
>
> January 1914 was a frigid month in Detroit — much like January 2014 has been, but nonetheless thousands lined up in the bitter cold outside to take Henry Ford up on an extraordinary offer : $5 a day, for eight hours of work in a bustling factory.
>
> That was more than double the average factory wage at that time, and for U.S. workers it was one of the defining moments of the 20th century. Five dollars in 1914 translates to roughly $120 in today's money. While many economists say today's employers could take some pointers from Ford, they also say 2014 is a totally different world for U.S. businesses and workers. Henry Ford was a hard-nosed businessman. He didn't introduce the $5 workday because he was a nice guy. He was not such a person at all.
>
> Bob Kreipke, corporate historian, says to understand why Ford thought this was a smart move in January 1914, you have to go back to another huge shift that happened a few months earlier. By 1913, Model T production totaled 200,000 — a feat made possible by the creation of the first moving assembly line. Conveyor belts transported small parts to workers, each of whom performed a specific task. This tremendously sped up production, but Ford still had a problem. While he had standardized production, he hadn't standardized his workforce. Now, he didn't need particularly skilled workers; he just needed ones who would do the same repetitive, specialized tasks hour after hour, day after day.

There was chronic absenteeism and lots of worker turnover. He needed to stabilize the workforce. So Ford gambled that higher wages would attract better, more reliable workers. It was an absolute, total success. In fact, it was better than anybody had even thought. The benefits were almost immediate. Productivity surged, and the Ford Motor Co. doubled its profits in less than two years. Ford ended up calling it the best cost-cutting move he ever made.

It's widely believed that Henry Ford also upped wages to expand his market, paying employees enough to buy the cars they made. While that wasn't Ford's key motive, it was a welcome byproduct, and a game changer, says University of California, Berkeley, labor economist Harley Shaiken. "What that gave us was an industrial middle class, and an economy that was driven by consumer demand," Shaiken says.

Today, overwhelmingly employers view the lowest wage as the most competitive wage. These days, global supply chains feed a hypercompetitive auto industry where no one wants to give up even an inch of ground, and keeping up with technology takes precedent over stabilizing the workforce. This just isn't Henry Ford's economy anymore.

Describe what Ford's main motivation for a higher wage was. Do NOT copy more than FOUR consecutive words from the passage. Second, explain how 2014 is a totally different world for U.S. businesses and workers from 1914. Do NOT copy more than FOUR consecutive words from the passage.

---

05 Read the passage and follow the directions. [4 points]

Wines improve with age, but human bodies don't. We deteriorate with age. We develop wrinkles and gray hair, the skin thins and bruises more easily, vision and hearing decline and cataracts develop, blood pressure increases, bone density decreases, strength and agility decrease, the waist thickens, joints become arthritic, memory loss occurs, height may decrease by 1‑2 inches. We learn and think more slowly, reaction time decreases, sexual functions change and hormone levels drop, and we become more likely to develop the diseases associated with old age such as cancer and diabetes.

In St. Augustine, Florida, you can visit Ponce de León's Fountain of Youth Archaeological Park for an admission fee of $18.00. There, you can drink a sample of the miraculous water. You might even feel a bit younger but only if you believe and are suggestible or perhaps are just thirsty. This fountain may be of historical interest, but it is not of any therapeutic value.

A spring whose waters restore the youth of anyone who drinks or bathes in them is a(n) _____ that dates back to prehistoric times. Herodotus wrote about it in the 5th century BC. The Spanish conquistador Ponce de León was the first European explorer to reach Florida. The King of Spain had authorized him to lead an expedition to search for "the Island of Benimy" and he originally mistook Florida for the island. He was not searching for a fountain of youth; that myth wasn't attached to his name until long after his death. But even if he had drunk of said fountain of youth, he'd still be dead.

Hope springs eternal, and history repeats itself. Today there are countless modern versions of the Fountain of Youth. Dietary supplements and other treatments are claimed to reverse the effects of aging and prolong life. Their promoters claim there is science behind them. In reality, they are just more myths. Centenarians share their secrets for a long life; they are all different. No treatment has ever been proven to keep humans young or make them live longer. Dr. Joe Schwarcz of McGill's Office for Science and Society said it best : "the science is all wet and drips with crackpot notions."

Fill in the blank with the ONE most appropriate word from the passage. Second, explain what Dr. Schwarcz argues in the underlined words. Do NOT copy more than FOUR consecutive words from the passage.

_____

_____

_____

_____

_____

06 Read the passage and follow the directions. [4 points]

The wildfire season is off to a roaring start. The hot summer is worsening drought and drying out vegetation — an unfortunately ideal environment for wildfires to rage. But that's just one consequence of global warming; it's also leading to flooding, torrential rainstorms and heat-related deaths. In fact, the climate crisis has led to a widespread public health crisis.

I vividly remember a patient who came in late for her appointment during a July heat wave. When I walked in, she said, "I'm so sorry I'm late, I was up all night walking my grandbaby around the train station." Without air conditioning at home, the child was sweating through her clothes in the heat of the night, putting her at risk for dehydration.

July 2019 was the hottest July on record; January 2020 was the hottest on record; May 2020 was the hottest on record. This is not a coincidence. It is a pattern. Carbon dioxide, an important greenhouse gas contributing to global warming, has increased by 9 percent since 2005 and by 31 percent since 1950. A U.N. Intergovernmental Panel on Climate Change special report pointed out that the world has already warmed about one degree Celsius from pre-industrial levels. It stressed the urgency to act to limit warming to 1.5 degrees, and that a two-degree increase will lead to unprecedented extreme heat, water scarcity and food shortages around the globe.

In my own practice, I explain to patients how the climate crisis affects their health. For example, apart from contributing to global warming, rising carbon dioxide levels increase the amount of pollen that plants produce as a consequence of higher rates of photosynthesis. This rise in pollen levels can lead to worsening allergy symptoms. Another example is fine particulate matter (known as PM2.5) associated with air pollution, much of it linked to the burning of fossil fuels that help drive the warming. When we breathe in these particles, they travel down the airway and settle in the tiny air sacs called alveoli of the lungs, causing inflammation and potentially worsening asthma symptoms.

What is worse, that harm falls disproportionately on the _____.
Wealthier people living in North America have a per capita carbon footprint
that is 25 percent higher than those of lower income residents, with some
affluent suburbs producing emissions 15 times higher than nearby
neighborhoods. These carbon emissions contribute to global warming, and
the subsequent health consequences are felt far beyond the neighborhood
that produces them. Communities of color and poor communities are less
resilient on average to the health impacts of climate change.

Explain the meaning of the underlined words. Do NOT copy more than
FOUR consecutive words from the passage. Second, describe ALL public
health results caused by "rising carbon dioxide levels". Third, fill in the blank
with the ONE most appropriate word from the passage.

---

07 Read the passage and follow the directions. [4 points]

Which one is more conducive to creativity : procrastination and pre-crastination? We think of procrastination as a curse. Over 80 percent of college students are plagued by procrastination, requiring epic all-nighters to finish papers and prepare for tests. Roughly 20 percent of adults report being chronic procrastinators. We can only guess how much higher the estimate would be if more of them got around to filling out the survey. While procrastination is a vice for productivity, it's a virtue for creativity. Conversely, I have always believed that anything worth doing was worth doing early. In graduate school I submitted my dissertation two years in advance. In college, I wrote my papers weeks early and finished my thesis four months before the due date. My roommates joked that I had a productive form of obsessive-compulsive disorder. Psychologists have coined a term for my condition : pre-crastination.

Pre-crastination is the urge to start a task immediately and finish it as soon as possible. If you're a serious pre-crastinator, progress is like oxygen and postponement is agony. When a flurry of emails land in your inbox and you don't answer them instantly, you feel as if your life is spinning out of control. When you have a speech to give next month, each day you don't work on it brings a creeping sense of emptiness. But procrastinators, on the other hand, are at the mercy of an Instant Gratification Monkey who inhabits their brains, constantly asking questions like "Why would we ever use a computer for work when the Internet is sitting right there waiting to be played with?" If you're a procrastinator, overcoming that monkey can require herculean amounts of willpower. But a pre-crastinator may need equal willpower to not work.

A few years ago, though, one of my most creative students, Sunny Park, questioned my expeditious habits. She told me her most original ideas came to her after she procrastinated. Challenged to prove it, she got access to a couple of companies, surveyed people on how often they procrastinated, and asked their supervisors to rate their creativity. Procrastinators earned significantly higher creativity scores than pre-crastinators. In short, while pre-crastinators are steadily productive, using one's whole time for a project might be a boon in a creative undertaking.

Summarize the passage following the guidelines below.

Guidelines

- Summarize the above passage in one paragraph.
- Provide a topic sentence, supporting ideas, and a concluding sentence based on the passage.
- Do NOT copy more than FIVE consecutive words from the passage.

_____

_____

_____

_____

_____

모범답안 p.057

01 Read the passage and follow the directions. [4 points]

Samuel Bowles, a world-renown American economist, has recently studied the way that people are motivated by _____ and the desire to maximize their own income as compared to altruism and the desire to do a good job and be well regarded by others. Real-world experiments show that contrary to traditional economic theories market incentives destroy cooperation and are less efficient than altruistic behavior in most cases. People act not only for material interests, but also to constitute themselves as dignified, autonomous, and moral individuals.

Behavioral experiments suggest that economic incentives may be counterproductive when they signal that selfishness is an appropriate response and undermine the moral values that lead people to act altruistically. Bowles gives the example of day care centers in Haifa, where a fine was imposed on parents who were late picking up their children at the end of the day. Rather than avoiding late pick-ups, parents responded by doubling the fraction of time they arrived late. After 12 weeks, the fine was revoked, but the enhanced tardiness persisted unabated. According to Bowles, this illustrates a kind of negative synergy between economic incentives and moral behavior. The fine seems to have undermined the parents' sense of ethical obligation to avoid inconveniencing the teachers and led them to think of lateness as just another commodity they could purchase.

Bowles shows that substantial fractions of most populations adhere to moral rules, willingly give to others, and punish those who offend standards of appropriate behavior, even at a cost to themselves and with no expectation of material reward. Diego Rivera's mural of factory workers at Ford's River Rouge assembly plant shows that organizations motivate members by appealing to other-regarding motives such as the desire to do a good job and a sense of reciprocal obligations among members of a firm.

Fill in the blank with the ONE most appropriate word from the passage. Second, explain what Bowles argues by mentioning Rivera's mural.

___

___

___

___

___

02 Read the passage and follow the directions. [4 points]

Everyone knows that to do great work you need both natural ability and determination. But there's a third ingredient that's not as well understood : a(n) _____ in a particular topic.

To explain this point I need to burn my reputation with some group of people, and I'm going to choose bus ticket collectors. There are people who collect old bus tickets. Like many collectors, they have an obsessive interest in the minutiae of what they collect. They can keep track of distinctions between different types of bus tickets that would be hard for the rest of us to remember. Because we don't care enough. What's the point of spending so much time thinking about old bus tickets?

Which leads us to the second feature of this kind of obsession : there is no point. A bus ticket collector's love is disinterested. They're not doing it to impress us or to make themselves rich, but for its own sake.

When you look at the lives of people who've done great work, you see a consistent pattern. They often begin with a bus ticket collector's obsessive interest in something that would have seemed pointless to most of their contemporaries. One of the most striking features of Darwin's book about his voyage on the Beagle is the sheer depth of his interest in natural history. His curiosity seems infinite. Ditto for Ramanujan, sitting by the hour working out on his slate what happens to series.

It's a mistake to think they were "laying the groundwork" for the discoveries they made later. There's too much intention in that metaphor.

Fill in the blank with the TWO most appropriate consecutive words from the passage. Second, explain what the writer of the passage argues in the underlined part of the last paragraph. Do NOT copy more than FOUR consecutive words from the passage.

_____

_____

_____

03 Read the passage and follow the directions. [4 points]

For many years after Hiroshima and Nagasaki much of the research on the effects of ionising radiations was naturally concentrated on the results of sudden whole-body exposure. But in a world that was likely to rely more and more on atomic power, the ultimate effects of low doses, slowly absorbed, clearly needed fuller comprehension. Three new reports from the United States National Academy of Sciences reflect the increasing research effort directed towards these chronic effects that are so hard to investigate.

The study of the association of radiation with leukaemia has been more exact than other inquiries because a fatal condition lends itself to mortality comparisons : the subtle and indefinite changes of premature ageing, another possible effect of radiation, are far harder to assess, particularly since physiological senescence is itself ill-understood. The epidemiological investigations — vast animal experiments and prospective inquiries on people whose occupation involves exposure to low doses — are complementary methods which may eventually show whether average life expectancy is reduced : but so many variables are involved that the answer may be a very long time coming; and the application of animal data to man is full of uncertainty. A prospective inquiry benefits from the fact that most of the nuclear agencies and X-ray departments in the United States and Great Britain keep careful medical and radiation exposure records of their employees. The larger the sample the better, and if it were possible to adopt common methods of measurement and recording throughout the world, much valuable information might be obtained. Differences which might be hidden when manifold recording methods allow only indirect comparisons might be revealed under standard conditions and suggest important new ideas. There seems to be a case for an international meeting of radiation-medicine and epidemiological experts to consider how to exploit such an opportunity. The best treatment of the acute radiation syndrome is in most particulars generally agreed upon : the one controversial point is the value of bone-marrow therapy.

If the normal immunological response has been almost completely suppressed by _____, it may be possible, by marrow transfusion, to tide a patient over temporary failure of the haemopoietic system. On the other hand, there is a risk of a foreign tissue reaction, which could prove fatal to anyone seriously ill. If the dose of radiation is known to be so high that the patient faces almost certain death, it is justifiable to grasp at any straw; and some experts advise that this should be the indication for giving bone-marrow therapy. As far as present knowledge goes this advice is wise; but it is to be hoped that experimental work will soon permit more room for clinical manoeuvre.

Fill in the blank with the ONE most appropriate word from the passage. Second, what can be inferred about the relationship found between low doses of radiation and leukemia. Do NOT copy more than FOUR consecutive words from the passage.

_____

_____

_____

_____

_____

04 Read the passage and follow the directions. [4 points]

It was Back to School Night. Ms. Grady decided over summer she wanted to cultivate better at-home study habits in students. Many families came to Ms. Grady's classroom that night and listened as she explained how important it was for students to have a designated place at home to study and keep learning materials.

In order to motivate students, Ms. Grady purchased a pencil box for each of them to take home. She filled the boxes with writing instruments. Shua, one of Ms. Grady's students, was especially excited about the pencil box. Ms. Grady's was excited for Shua because at the Back to School event, his parents seemed responsive to her suggestions.

A month into school year, Ms. Grady noticed Shua was turning in homework with food stains. She also noticed he was crossing out some answers instead of erasing them. When she asked Shua about this he explained his siblings also had been using his pencils and pens. They did not always return them, which was why he had not been using an eraser.

"And the food stains?" Ms. Grady asked. Shua explained he and his older brother do homework at the kitchen table, sometimes while others were eating.

Ms. Grady was sympathetic to Shua's situation and decided to give him another set of utensils, which she labeled with his name. "Remember to find a quiet, separate place to work instead of working and keeping your box of utensils at the table," she told him. Shua nodded.

A few weeks later, after seeing little change in the condition of Shua's homework, Ms. Grady followed up with him regarding where he was studying and whether his siblings were still using his utensils. Noticeably uncomfortable, Shua replied, "I still work at the table and sometimes they still use my stuff." Ms. Grady thanked Shua for his honesty.

Later, when the school day ended, she wondered how she should approach Shua's parents at the upcoming parent-teacher conferences. She remembered they seemed supportive about her expectations that students have a quiet place to study. If they were supportive in front of her, but did not follow through at home, she worried they also would not be supportive of her other ideas for at-home learning. She also wondered whether Shua's family might benefit from a referral to a local agency that could provide donations if the family needed school supplies or other household items, since his siblings were using Shua's supplies.

Feeling frustrated, she packed her things and left for the day.

In the given passage, what advise and corresponding support is given to all students? Second, what implication is made regarding the teacher's suspicions of Shua's family? Do NOT copy more than FOUR consecutive words from the passage.

_____

_____

_____

_____

_____

05 Read the passage and follow the directions. [4 points]

Tom Rabin, a physician, stopped showering years ago. He sprinkles water on his head every once in a while, but shuns shampoos and the parade of other products that march across American shower shelves.

In decent company, Rabin's confession tends to land like the Hindenburg, which reveals just how obsessed we've become with surface notions of cleanliness — and how reluctant we are to disavow them. But Rabin thinks the sensible-sounding idea that we should scrub up regularly is both simplistic and wrongheaded. When you take a soap-slathered loofah to your greasy pelt*, you're actually destroying an interdependent microbial universe, or microbiome, on the surface of your skin. "When we clean ourselves," Rabin writes, "we at least temporarily alter the microscopic populations — either by removing them or by altering the resources available to them." By chasing that born-again post-shower rush, in other words, we stymie <u>one of evolution's best strategies</u> to shield us from disease and keep out invaders. This kind of context is particularly relevant in the era of Covid-19, a virus that often causes skin-related symptoms like rashes and hives.

A search for the origins of our cleanser and skin-potion worship leads Rabin into a vivid exploration of the cleanliness-is-godliness movement that began hundreds of years ago. After the Black Death and other devastating plagues, a person's cleanliness could be taken as a marker of who was or was not dangerous. Indicators of hygiene became proxies of status, and more was often seen as better.

In time, post-outbreak distrust of contaminants — as well as the discovery that cleansers helped stop disease spread — gave rise to early 20th-century branding campaigns that marketed _____ as a life-saving and virtuous necessity.

But what soap hawkers overlook is that wiping out our symbiotic microbes may make us more vulnerable to other, unexpected maladies. First-line eczema* treatments, for instance, include topical antibiotics, cleansers, and drugs that dampen immune response, but researchers say these approaches can make the condition worse in the long run. Perturbing the skin barrier by washing or scratching can change the microbial population. That can rev up the immune system, which tells the skin cells to proliferate rapidly and fill with inflammatory proteins.

This observation lines up with an older one that kids raised in highly sanitized environments are more prone to allergies than farm kids like the Amish. Wipe the body's microbial slate clean too aggressively and the un-seasoned immune system roars back with a vengeance. This kind of immune over-reaction can also trigger what immunologists call the "Atopic March," in which one allergic disease — such as eczema, food allergy, or hay fever — leads to another.

*pelt : skin
*eczema : disease that makes skin red and itchy

Identify to what the underlined words refer. Second, fill in the blank with the ONE most appropriate word from the passage. Third, explain the reason the writer of the passage mentions "Amish" children.

06   Read the passage and follow the directions. [4 points]

The informational asymmetry between trusting and not trusting means that we learn more by trusting than by not trusting. Moreover, when we trust, we learn not only about specific individuals, we learn more generally about the type of situations in which we should or shouldn't trust. We get better at trusting.

Sammy Yu and his colleagues demonstrated the learning advantages of being trusting. Their experiments were similar to trust games, but the participants could interact with each other before making the decision to transfer money (or not) to the other. The most trusting participants were better at figuring out who would be trustworthy, or to whom they should transfer money.

We find the same pattern in other domains. People who trust the media more are more knowledgeable about politics and the news. The more people trust science, the more scientifically literate they are. Even if this evidence remains correlational, it makes sense that people who trust more should get better at figuring out whom to trust. In trust as in everything else, practice makes perfect.

Sammy Yu's insight provides us with a reason to be trusting. But then, the puzzle only deepens : if trusting provides such learning opportunities, we should trust too much, rather than not enough. Ironically, the very reason why we should trust more — the fact that we gain more information from trusting than from not trusting — might make us inclined to trust less.

When our trust is disappointed — when we trust someone we shouldn't have — the costs are salient, and our reaction ranges from annoyance all the way to fury and despair. The benefit — what we've learnt from our mistake — is easy to overlook. By contrast, the _____ of not trusting someone we could have trusted are, as a rule, all but invisible. We don't know about the friendship we could have struck (if we'd let that acquaintance crash at our place). We don't realize how useful some advice would have been (had we used our colleague's tip about the new software application).

We don't trust enough because the costs of mistaken trust are all too obvious, while the (learning) benefits of mistaken trust, as well as the costs of mistaken mistrust, are largely hidden. We should consider these hidden costs and benefits : think of what we learn by trusting, the people whom we can befriend, the knowledge that we can gain. Giving people a chance isn't only the moral thing to do. It's also the smart thing to do.

Explain the meaning of the underlined "Ironically". Do NOT copy more than FOUR consecutive words from the passage. Second, fill in the blank with the ONE most appropriate word from the passage.

_____

_____

_____

_____

_____

07 Read the passage and follow the directions. [4 points]

Animals communicate much to our surprise. Just like us, interaction among animals can be both verbal or non-verbal. Singing is one way in which animals can interact with one another. Male blackbirds often use their melodious songs to catch the attention of the females. These songs are usually rich in notes variation, encoding various kinds of messages. Songs are also used to warn and keep off other blackbirds from their territory, usually a place where they dwell and reproduce. Large mammals in the oceans sing too. Enormous whales groan and grunt while smaller dolphins and porpoises produce pings, whistles and clicks. These sounds are surprisingly received by other mates as far as several hundred kilometers away.

Besides singing, body language also forms a large part of animals' communication tactics. Dominant hyenas exhibit their power by raising the fur hackles on their necks and shoulders, while the submissive ones normally "surrender" to the powerful parties by crouching their heads low and curling their lips a little, revealing their teeth in friendly smiles.

Colors, which are most conspicuously found on animals are also important means of interaction among animals. The alternating black and white striped coats of zebras have their roles to play. Each zebra is born with a unique set of stripes which enables its mates to recognize them. When grazing safely, their stripes are all lined up neatly so that none of them loses track of their friends. However, when danger such as a hungry lion approaches, the zebras would dart out in various directions, making it difficult for the lion to choose his target.

Communication is part of our everyday life. We greet one another, smile or frown, depending on our moods. However, as opposed to our conventional thinking, animals too communicate. Given this quality, we should consider them more dynamically.

Summarize the passage following the guidelines below.

Guidelines

• Summarize the above passage in one paragraph.

• Provide a topic sentence, supporting ideas, and a concluding sentence based on the passage.

• Do NOT copy more than FIVE consecutive words from the passage.

01 Read the passage and follow the directions. [4 points]

Design is ubiquitous. Sometimes the design is quite overt, as when a painter composes a landscape according to received aesthetic principles, or a poet shapes a sonnet following a strict form. Other designs are less obviously or less explicitly thought about, as when <u>a person adjusts water flow from a faucet to achieve the preferred temperature</u> or when we walk along familiar streets to reach a destination. The word design has a plethora of denotations and connotations, and it is to this multiplicity of meanings that we owe at least in part the confusion and ambiguity that often accompanies the word's use. Even within the relatively narrow scope of the activity of professional designers, design means different things in different contexts. In a word, everything deliberately made and done is necessarily designed.

[A] Architects and engineers engage in design quite explicitly, and they typically do so with distinct objectives. Architects tend to focus on form over function, whereas engineers tend to do the opposite. To many an architect, the design of a building has firstly to do with how it looks —both inside and out—and how it fits in with nearby buildings. Architects are also expected to give considerable thought to how the building will be used, how people will move through it, how it will feel, although such considerations do not always seem to be foremost in their minds judging by results. Indeed, if architectural criticism is taken at face value, architects do seem to be principally concerned with the texture of a building's façade, the appearance of its public spaces, the furniture with which it is filled. Architects seem to pay close attention to details, even down to the nature of the lighting fixtures and the hardware on doors and windows, but not always to how they will be operated or how they will fulfill their purpose. Nevertheless, such considerations collectively constitute architectural and interior design.

[B] To engineers, design typically has less to do with <u>aesthetics and appearance</u> and more to do with fabrication and performance. Engineers tend to focus on the structure behind the facade. They worry about how the building will be built, how it will stand, whether it will sway too much in the wind, whether it will survive an earthquake, whether it will crack or leak. Engineers designing the structural frame of hotel buildings take into account the strength and stiffness of ballroom floors, where large crowds will gather and rhythmic dancing will occur. Engineers are expected to think about how a building will be heated and cooled, how air will circulate among its spaces, how energy efficient it will be.

Identify to which group the underlined instance of design would most closely be attributed and provide the reason for your choice. Second, write the ONE word from [A] that best corresponds to the meaning of the underlined words in [B].

_____

_____

_____

_____

_____

02 **Read the passage and follow the directions.** [4 points]

In an effort to celebrate the growing racial and ethnic diversity at Eastern School, the school's Diversity Committee decided to sponsor Multicultural Day. Numerous performers were hired for assemblies and presentations. During the day's feature event, the "Culture Parade," students were asked to showcase ethnic clothing as they walked through the hallways. Teachers were encouraged by the committee to discuss clothing from countries outside the United States and to invite students who had such clothing to bring it to school for the parade.

Ms. Morrison was excited about Multicultural Day because many of her students had parents who were immigrants. She imagined the day as an opportunity those students to teach others about their ethnic cultures.

A week before the event, Ms. Morrison brought a kilt to class and explained its significance to the students. "This represents my Scottish heritage," she said, "and I am proud to show it to you today." She then asked whether students had "special costumes" at home that represented their ethnic cultures. Several students raised their hands, which prompted Ms. Morrison to discuss the events planned for Multicultural Day, including the parade. During dismissal the day before the parade Ms. Morrison announced, "Don't forget to bring your costumes to class tomorrow!"

The next day, Ms. Morrison was pleased to see several Hmong and Liberian students came with bags of ethnic clothing. She saw that two other students, Emily and Keisha, brought clothing, so she inquired about what was in their bags. Emily, a white student, excitedly pulled out her soccer uniform, and Keisha, an African American student pulled jeans and her favorite sweatshirt out of her bag. Ms. Morrison told the two girls she appreciated their enthusiasm for Multicultural Day but that they would not be able to walk in the parade. She explained that what Keisha and Emily brought was everyday clothing rather than clothes that represented their _____ heritages.

Both girls protested. "This outfit represents my culture," Keisha argued. Ms. Morrison shared with the girls that she felt terrible about the confusion, but could not allow them to participate. "Maybe next year they'll expand the parade," she said.

After the girls walked away, Ms. Morrison considered changing her mind. She worried, though, that other students or staff would be puzzled by their participation and that Keisha and Emily would be ridiculed for not following directions.

Fill in the blank with the ONE most appropriate word from the passage. Second, what is one specific clothing item showing heritage mentioned in the passage?

---

03 **Read the passage and follow the directions.** [4 points]

Everyone loves unsolved mysteries. Examples include Amelia Earhart's disappearance over the Pacific in 1937 and the daring escape of inmates Frank Morris and John and Clarence Anglin from Alcatraz Island in California in 1962. Moreover our interest holds even if the mystery is based on a joke. Take author Douglas Adams's popular 1979 science-fiction novel *The Hitchhiker's Guide to the Galaxy*. Toward the end of the book, the supercomputer Deep Thought reveals that the answer to the "Great Question" of "Life, the Universe and Everything" is "_____".

Deep Thought takes 7.5 million years to calculate the answer to the ultimate question. The characters tasked with getting that answer are disappointed because it is not very useful. Yet, as the computer points out, the question itself was vaguely formulated. To find the correct statement of the query whose answer is forty-two, the computer will have to build a new version of itself. That, too, will take time. The new version of the computer is Earth.

The author's choice of the number 42 has become a fixture of geek culture. It's at the origin of a multitude of jokes and winks exchanged between initiates. If, for example, you ask your search engine variations of the question "What is the answer to everything?" it will most likely answer "forty-two." Try it in French or German. You'll often get the same answer whether you use Google, Qwant, Wolfram Alpha or the chat bot Web app Cleverbot.

Since the first such school was created in France in 2013 there has been a proliferation of private computer-training institutions in the "42 Network," whose name is a clear allusion to Adams's novels. Today the founding company counts more than 15 campuses in its global network. The number 42 also appears in different forms in the film Spider-Man : Into the Spider-Verse. The number also turns up in a whole string of curious coincidences whose significance is probably not worth the effort to figure out. For example : In ancient Egyptian mythology, during the judgment of souls, the dead had to declare before 42 judges that they had not committed any of 42 sins.

The marathon distance of 42.195 kilometers corresponds to the legend of how far the ancient Greek messenger Pheidippides traveled between Marathon and Athens to announce victory over the Persians in 490 B.C. <u>The fact that the kilometer had not yet been defined at that time only makes the connection all the more astonishing.</u>

Fill in the blank with the ONE most appropriate word from the passage. Second, explain the meaning of the underlined words in the last sentence of the passage. Do NOT copy more than THREE consecutive words from the passage.

_____

_____

_____

_____

_____

04 Read the passage and follow the directions. [4 points]

The hard, rigid plates that form the outermost portion of the Earth are about 100 kilometers thick. These plates include both the Earth's crust and the upper mantle. The rocks of the crust are composed mostly of minerals with light elements, like aluminum and sodium, while the mantle contains some heavier elements, like iron and magnesium. Together, the crust and upper mantle that form the surface plates are called the lithosphere. This rigid layer floats on the denser material of the lower mantle the way a wooden raft floats on a pond. The plates are supported by a weak, plastic layer of the lower mantle called the asthenosphere. Also like a raft on a pond, the ____①____ are(/is) carried along by slow currents in this more fluid layer beneath them.

With an understanding of plate tectonics, geologists have put together a new history for the Earth's surface. About 200 million years ago, the plates at the Earth's surface formed a "supercontinent" called Pangaea. When this supercontinent started to tear apart because of plate movement, Pangaea first broke into two large continental masses with a newly formed sea that grew between the land areas as the depression filled with water. The southern one — which included the modern continents of South America, Africa, Australia, and Antarctica — is called Gondwanaland. The northern one — with North America, Europe, and Asia — is called Laurasia. North America tore away from Europe about 180 million years ago, forming the northern Atlantic Ocean.

Some of the lithospheric plates carry ocean floor and others carry land masses or a combination of the two types. The movement of the lithospheric plates is responsible for earthquakes, volcanoes, and the Earth's largest mountain ranges. Current understanding of the interaction between different plates explains why these occur where they do. For example, the edge of the Pacific Ocean has been called the "Ring of Fire" because so many volcanic eruptions and earthquakes happen there. Before the 1960's, geologists could not explain why active volcanoes and strong earthquakes were concentrated in that region. The theory of ____②____ gave them an answer.

Fill in each blank with the TWO most appropriate consecutive words from the passage. Then, describe when the northern Atlantic Ocean was formed. Do NOT copy more than THREE consecutive words from the passage.

_____

_____

_____

_____

_____

05 Read the passage and follow the directions. [4 points]

An organization recently released a new study that tries to come up with a formula that can weigh saving lives against boosting incomes, based on the views of a group that's rarely consulted : <u>the people on the receiving end of charity.</u> The finding is surprising.

People in poor countries appear to value life compared to income pretty similarly to those in wealthy countries. In the absence of solid data, economists have tended to assume that people in extreme poverty would weigh a boost to their income higher than those in rich ones. After all, people are facing such difficult issues in poverty that having a little bit more money could be substantially more valuable to them.

The nonprofit research group IDinsight that conducted the study surveyed 2,000 extremely poor people in Kenya and Ghana and asked them a series of questions about the best allocation of aid money. It essentially put them in the shoes of donors.

People were willing to pay a lot for relatively small reductions in the risk of mortality — and they tended to choose programs that saved lives at high rates relative to programs that boosted incomes.

Researchers were also surprised by the weights that those surveyed gave to saving a child's life over an adult's life. After all, for people who are incredibly poor with little safety net, losing the family breadwinner is especially devastating.

"Some staff wondered whether communities would feel that adults are often caregivers for their families and are making substantial economic contributions to their communities, so a community would say that it's more important to avert the death of the adult," says a researcher.

Instead the survey found that people tended to value averting deaths of children under 5 years old up to two times more than averting deaths of individuals over 5 years old.

The researchers stress that this research is very preliminary. Lots more must be done. But they has already tweaked its own weighting formulas. For instance, it now weighs saving lives of children versus those of adults equally — instead of giving slight precedence to adults.

Identify to whom the underlined words refers. Second, explain why the finding of the research is surprising. Third, it can be inferred that donation formulas would change according to the result of the study. Explain the change.

---

06 Read the passage and follow the directions. [4 points]

Audible speech burns hot with information. Intonation, accents, innuendo, vocal phrasing, emphasis, pauses, all communicate far more than a transcript can. Audio is the format for "You all know exactly what I'm talking about, because of the way I'm saying it." Audio is how you communicate what you really mean, straight into ears, headphones and car radios, intimately and directly. Music is good at this, but _____①_____ is even better.

Here's an exercise you can do : speaking out loud, say the word "tonight" twenty different ways, where each way is communicating something distinct. You can say "tonight" in a way that's intrigued, satisfied, tired, horny, dejected, anxious, suspicious, hesitant, desperate, or any number of ways — and the person you're talking to will know exactly what you mean. You can't do that easily with image or text. A transcript of the word tonight just says tonight : flat, ambiguous. Our _____②_____ treat it neutrally. But our ears don't. Our ears are hyper-discriminatory.

Whatever it is that's being communicated, audio will heat it up. Imagine you're in a confrontation with your landlord, and you can communicate either over text messaging or by phone (cooler, back-and-forth dialog) or by email or voice mail (hot, one-shot blasts). Text keeps things chill, whereas audio forces the issue.

When you present information in an audio-first format, or especially in an audio-only format, it heats up what's being communicated, and saturates its information content. What may have seemed ambiguous or flat when presented in text or mixed media format won't be interpreted ambiguously by your ears. Your ears understand what's really being said, and they seek hot content.

There's a famous story about the Nixon-Kennedy debates that I misunderstood for a long time. Following a presidential debate between Richard Nixon and JFK, those who had listened over the radio overwhelmingly felt that Nixon had won, whereas those who had laid eyes on their TVs felt that JFK won. I remember originally hearing this story and thinking that the point was somehow that TV was more "superficial" than radio, and that JFK's handsome face or easy on-screen charm somehow overruled the debate's substance on TV but not on the radio.

I've now come to understand that this wasn't the point at all. The lesson has nothing to do with the content of what either of them were saying. The content doesn't matter. What matters is that Nixon was a Hot candidate : sharp, saturated with information, abrasive, and in your face. But JFK was a Cool candidate : relaxed, speaking easy, in slogans that invited multiple interpretations, creating plenty of gaps for the audience to fill in themselves.

Fill in each blank with the ONE most appropriate word from the passage. Second, explain the writer's current understanding about the Nixon-Kennedy debates in the context of whole passage. Do NOT copy more than THREE consecutive words from the passage.

_____

_____

_____

_____

_____

07 Read the passage and follow the directions. [4 points]

The primeval way of exchange was the barter trade. In this form of transaction, human beings used goods to exchange for the things that they wanted. For example, when person A wished a pen and he had a spare sheep, he must look for someone who had the exact opposite, that is, that someone, say person B, must have a spare pen of person A's choice and is also in need of a sheep. Having found such a person, the problem does not end here. A big sheep may worth not only one pen, hence person B may have to offer person A something else, say two pigs. However, he runs the risk of person A rejecting the offer as he may not need the pigs.

Years later, the burdensome barter trade gave way to the monetary form of exchange when the idea of money was created. In the early days, almost anything could qualify as money : beads, shells and even fishing hooks. Then in a region near Turkey, gold coins were used as money. In the beginning, each coin had a different denomination. It was only later, in about 700 BC, that Gyges, the king of Lydia, standardized the value of each coin.

Monetary means of transaction at first beat the traditional barter trade. However, as time went by, the thought of carrying a ponderous pouch of coins for shopping appeared not only troublesome but thieves attracting. Hence, the Greek and Roman traders who bought goods from people faraway cities, invented checks to solve the problem. Not only are paper checks easy to carry around, they discouraged robbery as these checks can only be used by the person whose name is printed on the notes.

Now, in addition to the convenience of using paper notes issued by governments as the mode of exchange, technology has allowed people to create other means of transaction such as the credit and cash cards.

Summarize the passage following the guidelines below.

Guidelines

- Summarize the above passage in one paragraph.
- Provide a topic sentence, supporting ideas, and a concluding sentence based on the passage.
- Do NOT copy more than FIVE consecutive words from the passage.

01 Read the passage and follow the directions. [4 points]

From the Greek logos, meaning word, a logo is — ideally — a symbol that we recognise immediately and associate with the organisation it represents. But it is rarely that simple. Shape and color also play a role, as do letters or even the organisation's full name. In any case, a logo should be easy for its target group to recognise. It should become familiar after being seen just a few times. A good logo balances simplicity with distinctiveness and can stand alone. It has to adorn a wide variety of surfaces; from the front of corporate headquarters to promotional brochures and the letterheads of countless memos.

A logo reveals the strengths and values you attribute to your company. An organisation that takes itself seriously will obviously not choose a frivolous logo. Many specialists praises the effectiveness of temporary employment agency Randstad's logo — a stylised R, reflected over vertical and horizontal axes. Seen as a whole, it resembles a bird and gives a sense of dynamism and mobility appropriate to the agency's activities. A temping agency actually has a very low profile, workers for other companies. Still, through the years Randstad has managed to build up a concrete image of its own.

Like a successful brand name, a good logo is one of a company's major assets. It is often easier to protect than a brand name, especially a personal name to which no exclusive rights can be claimed. In addition, a logo is easier to recognize than a company name, especially internationally. The oil company Shell's distinctive shell logo is recognized everywhere, even in countries where the letters of the word "Shell" are unfamiliar. Also, at the international level, Coca-Cola springs to mind, which uses a wavy line in addition to the name. This creates a very effective logo, recognized the world over.

Often each company agrees on the _____ for its product. In the Dutch dairy aisle, blue stands for milk, red for buttermilk, and green for yoghurt. And elsewhere in the shop, bars of dark chocolate boast red wrappers and milk chocolate blue. Outside the Netherlands, Germany and Austria's national postal services are well known for their use of yellow.

Let's say that you are a company owner, who sells your products all over the world. You have to choose between a logo and a company name to make your product recognized better. Which of the two would you have to choose according to the passage? Second, fill in the blank with the ONE most appropriate word from the passage.

_____

_____

_____

_____

_____

02 **Read the passage and follow the directions.** [4 points]

I have a single definition of success. You look in the mirror every evening, and wonder if you disappoint the person you were at 18, right before the age when people start getting corrupted by life. Let him or her be the only judge; not your reputation, not your wealth, not your standing in the community, not the decorations on your lapel. If you do not feel ashamed, you are successful. All other definitions of success are modern constructions; fragile modern constructions.

The Ancient Greeks' main definition of success was to have had a heroic death. But as we live in a less martial world, we can adapt our definition of success as having taken a heroic route for the benefits of the collective, as narrowly or broadly defined collective as you wish. So long as all you do is not all for you: secret societies used to have a rule for uomo d'onore: you do something for yourself and something for other members. And virtue is inseparable from courage. Like the courage to do something unpopular. Take risks for the benefit of others; it doesn't have to be humanity, it can be helping say Beirut Madinati or the local municipality. The more micro, the less abstract, the better.

I believe success requires absence of _____. I've seen billionaires terrified of journalists, wealthy people who felt crushed because their brother in law got very rich, academics with Nobel who were scared of comments on the web. The higher you go, the worse the fall. For almost all people I've met, external success came with increased fragility. The worst are those "former something" types with 4 page CVs who, after leaving office, and addicted to the attention of servile bureaucrats, find themselves discarded: as if you went home one evening to discover that someone suddenly emptied your house of all its furniture.

But self-respect is robust — that's the approach of the Stoic school, which incidentally was a Phoenician movement. If someone wonders who are the Stoics I'd say Buddhists with an attitude problem. I've seen robust people in my village Amioun who were proud of being local citizens involved in their tribe; they go to bed proud and wake up happy. Or Russian mathematicians who, during the difficult post-Soviet transition period, were proud of making $200 a month and do work that is appreciated by twenty people and considered that showing one's decorations or accepting awards were a sign of weakness and lack of confidence in one's contributions.

Fill in the blank with the ONE most appropriate word from the passage. Second, what can be inferred to be "unpopular" about the Russian mathematicians' lifestyle?

_____

_____

_____

_____

_____

03 Read the passage and follow the directions. [4 points]

How did you do with our four questions? Below are the answers.

1. You are a participant in a race. You overtake the second person. What position are you in? The intuitive answer is "I am now the first." The answer of course is that if you overtake the one who is second, you take his place, and you are now second.

2. Mary's Father has five daughters. Their names are : 1. Nana, 2. Nene, 3. Nini, 4. Nono and ?? What is the name of the fifth daughter? The intuitive response most people give is to look after -a-e-i-o- and go with ____①____ . The correct answer is already given in the question : ____②____ .

3. A cup and teapot set costs $110. The teapot costs $100 more than the cup. How much is a cup? The intuitive response is $110 − $100 = $10. The correct answer is $5.

4. In a lake, there is a patch of lily pads. Every day, the patch doubles in size. If it takes 48 days for the patch to cover the entire lake, how long would it take for the patch to cover half of the lake? Your first response is probably to take a shortcut, and to divide the final answer by half. That leads you to twenty-four days. But that's wrong. The correct solution is forty-seven days.

Get all four correct? Great job! Odds are, though, that your brain tried to force you to accept the wrong answers first.

Daniel Kahneman, who was the first psychologist to win the Nobel Prize in Economics (2002), explains why an intuitive reaction is not always the best. In his groundbreaking book *Thinking : Fast and Slow*, he discusses intuitive (fast) and rational (slow) thinking. He shows us how an intuitive reaction could lead to problems and what the limitations are of our common sense.

Fill in each blank with the ONE most appropriate word respectively. Second, explain why an intuitive reaction might cause wrong answers and provide ONE example of it.

_____

_____

_____

_____

_____

04   Read the passage and follow the directions. [4 points]

Many of us enjoy roasting meat over the fire but no one ever wonder who first started the idea of cooking meat in a fire. Perhaps, it is just in the human psyche that we sometimes feel the need to return to the primitive times, probably to relieve us of our urbanized life. That is why many people love to hold barbecue gatherings.

The first step towards the _____ for a barbecue is to rent a barbecue pit which usually comes with the barest essentials. After all, we are supposed to return to the early time frame. Of course, during peak seasons like the school holidays, when the pits are fully booked, you may try digging one at the back of your garden. Next, get ready the wire netting, otherwise, you will find yourself roasting the meat on the hot charcoal. Skewers which are important for holding the meat pieces; utensils for picking up the food like forks and spoons, paper plates and cups must not be left out.

Next comes the preparation of the most important part of the barbecue — the food. In fact, any kind of meat will be suitable. If meat pieces are bought, like chicken, beef or mutton, slice them into thin pieces before piercing in the skewers. Chicken wings are the best. Simply stretch the wings apart and push in the skewers. Following which, the meat is to be soaked in a mixture of spices for marination, giving them some flavor.

When everything is ready, start the fire with charcoal, one hour before the start of the feast. Once the fire is started, let it all burn till glowing embers are left. Then place the sticks of meat over the wire netting and there you are, the barbecue has begun. Do not worry about overcooking the meat. After all, the real joy behind the barbecue lies in the cooking not eating of the food. Just a piece of advice to beginners : Bring along some indigestion medicine.

Fill in the blank with the ONE most appropriate word from the passage. Second, what can be inferred to be the reason the writer the writer of the passage says "Bring along some indigestion medicine"?

_____

_____

_____

_____

_____

05 **Read the passage and follow the directions.** [4 points]

Psychologists and neuroscientists study a phenomenon they call flow, which is this thing that happens in the human brain when someone pays attention to just one thing, like something creative, and manages not to get distracted by anything else. And some say the more regularly you do this, the happier you'll be.

Now I'm not a psychologist or a neuroscientist. But I can tell you, for me, that is very true. It's not always easy, it's hard. To really pay attention like this takes practice, everybody does it their own way. But if there's one thing I can share that I think helps me focus and really pay attention, it's this : I try not to see other creative people as my competitors. I try to find   ①   . Like, if I'm acting in a scene, if I start seeing the other actors as my competitors, and I'm like, "God, they're going to get more attention than I am, people are going to be talking about their performance more than mine" — I've lost my focus. And I'm probably going to suck in that scene.

But when I see the other actors as collaborators, then it becomes almost easy to focus, because I'm just paying attention to them. And I don't have to think about what I'm doing — I react to what they're doing, they react to what I'm doing, and we can kind of keep each other in it together. But I don't want you to think it's only actors on a set that can collaborate in this way. I could be in whatever kind of creative situation. It could be professional, could be just for fun. I could be collaborating with people I'm not even in the same room with. In fact, some of my favorite things I've ever made, I made with people that I never physically met.

And by the way, this, to me, is the beauty of the Internet. If we could just stop competing for attention, then the Internet becomes a great place to find collaborators. And once I'm collaborating with other people, whether they're on set, or online, wherever, that makes it so much easier for me to find that _____②_____, because we're all just paying attention to the one thing that we're making together. And I feel like I'm part of something larger than myself, and we all sort of shield each other from anything else that might otherwise grab our attention, and we can all just be there.

Fill in each blank with the ONE most appropriate word from the passage respectively. Second, explain what the beauty of the Internet is.

_____

_____

_____

_____

_____

06 **Read the passage and follow the directions.** [4 points]

With enough training, pigeons can distinguish between the works of Picasso and Monet. Ravens can identify themselves in a mirror. And on a university campus in Japan, crows are known to intentionally leave walnuts in a crosswalk and let passing traffic do their nut cracking. Many bird species are incredibly smart. Yet among intelligent animals, the "bird brain" often doesn't get much respect.

Two papers published recently in *Science* find birds actually have a brain that is much more similar to our complex primate organ than previously thought. For years it was assumed that the avian brain was limited in function because it lacked a neocortex. In mammals, the neocortex is the hulking, evolutionarily modern outer layer of the brain that allows for complex cognition and creativity and that makes up most of what, in vertebrates as a whole, is called the pallium. The new findings show that birds do, in fact, have a brain structure that is comparable to the _____ despite taking a different shape. It turns out that at a cellular level, the brain region is laid out much like the mammal cortex, explaining why many birds exhibit high-level behaviors and abilities that have long befuddled scientists. The new work even suggests that certain birds demonstrate some degree of consciousness.

The mammalian cortex is organized into six layers containing vertical columns of neurons that communicate with one another both horizontally and vertically. On the other hand, <u>the avian brain was thought to be arranged into discrete collections of neurons called nuclei, including a region called the dorsal ventricular ridge, or DVR, and a single nucleus named the wulst.</u>

In one of the new papers, senior author Onur Güntürkün, a neuroscientist and his colleagues analyzed regions of the DVR and wulst involved in sound and vision processing. To do so, they used a technology called three-dimensional polarized light imaging(3D-PLI) — a light-based microscopy technique that can be employed to visualize nerve fibers in brain samples. The researchers found that in both pigeons and barn owls, these brain regions are constructed much like our neocortex, with both layerlike and columnar organization — and with both horizontal and vertical circuitry.

Fill in the blank with the ONE most appropriate word from the passage. Second, provide ONE example showing birds' advanced "behaviors and abilities". Third, what can be inferred from the new research about the underlined part?

_____

_____

_____

_____

_____

07 Read the passage and follow the directions. [4 points]

Long ago, during the times of the kings and knights, animals such as horses, buffaloes and camels were used by man for transportation purposes. Though these animals no doubt did save man from traveling by foot, they took a long time to complete the journeys, especially when transporting goods. The means of transportation have changed and improved over many centuries.

In 1825, George Stephenson's opening of the first railway marked a significant progress in the history of transportation. Railways were in popular demand because they could carry more people and loads. More importantly, they ran faster than animals. Railways improved the communication networks and hence, imports and exports of goods and people traveling out of their towns or even countries to work were made possible. Unfortunately, since the invention of motor vehicles, the popularity of railways has declined.

Motor vehicles were first invented in the eighteenth century. These vehicles were preferred by many people as they do not run on tracks and hence do not have fixed routes. Travelers can then plan their own routes to suit their convenience. This is especially so when the destinations are places like small towns or remote areas. In these places, few or even none of the trains ever reach them; so traveling by motor vehicle would solve this problem. Over many years of modifications, the motor vehicle is now one of the most commonly used means of transportation. Today, we travel in cars, taxis, buses, lorries or vans almost every day.

In addition to such ways of transportation, human beings over the centuries have innovated a variety of means of transportation such as modern motor-driven ships, which were improved from the old wind-dependent yachts, and airplanes, which are easiest and fastest. To get somewhere more conveniently and safely is our basic desire that is imprinted in our souls. Therefore, the invention of further developed forms of transportation will consistently appear in human history.

Summarize the passage following the guidelines below.

| Guidelines |

- Summarize the above passage in one paragraph.
- Provide a topic sentence, major supporting details, and a concluding sentence based on the passage.
- Do NOT copy more than FIVE consecutive words from the passage.

01 Read the passage and follow the directions. [4 points]

The thinker Lauren Woon depicts two metaphysical models of pregnancy that are said to capture current Western understandings of the process. The first, dubbed the 'parthood model', describes the fetus as a part of the gestating person in the way that an arm, leg or kidney is. The second, the 'container model', describes the fetus and gestating person as two separate entities, which gives rise to the culturally dominant 'fetal container model'. As Woon points out, it's through this model that we can speak of a 'bun in the oven' and, to add to her list, depict fetuses as floating astronauts in an empty black space rather than embedded in the uterine wall.

Though relatively innocuous in its daily use, the container model has been applied to more detrimental lengths too. As the sociologist Amrita Pande demonstrates in her 2010 study of India's since-banned commercial surrogacy industry, fertility clinics capitalising on this separateness between gestators and fetuses have developed dehumanising prenatal care practices that, among other things, serve to emphasize surrogate disposability. What this shows is that the metaphysical container view might be morally neutral, but its cultural manifestation has developed and is currently utilised in a patriarchal context.

The plausibility of certain reproductive practices depends upon the kind of conceptual framework we use to understand them. The very idea of using artificial wombs to replace some or all stages of gestation reflects, for instance, an assumption that fetuses and gestating persons are in fact separable. While this doesn't mean that artificial-womb technology necessarily entails the fetal container model, current rhetoric within this debate captures the spirit of the view well : for instance, by likening the uterus to what the reproductive biologist Roger Gosden calls a 'clever incubator'.

The feminist scholar Irina Aristarkhova presents an alternative view in which the plausibility of artificial-womb technology becomes less of a 'workable concept' — or at least more complicated. Presumably, if one now thinks of the fetus as a part of the _____, then the extent to which artificial wombs are truly capable of satisfying this role becomes limited. Of course, one could concede a new fetus-gestator relationship, one that extends into the realms of mechanics and machines. Still, if we're willing to confront the biological realities of pregnancy — that is, the actual inextricability of fetus and gestator — then our future as machines is, in this specific context, one that we'll need to confront eventually.

Explain why the writer of the passage thinks the fetal container model has been applied to "more detrimental lengths". Do NOT copy more than THREE consecutive words from the passage. Second, fill in the blank with the ONE most appropriate word from the passage.

_____

_____

_____

_____

_____

02 **Read the passage and follow the directions.** [4 points]

Ms. Sutter was excited to form an after-school club at Pinewood School for students who could become the first people in their families to attend college. She started seeing a need for such a club as she noticed many of her students lacked knowledge about post-secondary education. Though many of their parents encouraged them to think about college, her students did not have the same opportunities as wealthier peers to see a college campus or learn about post-secondary options.

Ms. Sutter proposed the club at a staff meeting. Some teachers thought it was unnecessary, but others were excited and offered support. A major point of discussion was the club's grade range. Should it be open to all students or limited to higher grade levels?

Ms. Bates, a second grade teacher, commented, "Experience tells me fifth grade is too early to start talking to *these* kids about college. It's way over their heads."

Another teacher, Ms. Clark, added, "Families in our school will enroll their children in any free after-school program just to keep them busy. You'll be swamped and end up spending more time on discipline than on college."

Ms. Sutter disagreed with her peers' opinions, but she reluctantly agreed to offer the club exclusively to fifth graders.

Several months later Ms. Sutter paused during her "College Club" meeting to marvel at how well it was going. Students attended regularly, and parents would arrive before pick-up time to join lively discussions about college life.

As a year-end celebration, Ms. Sutter scheduled a field trip to the renowned local university, which would include a guided tour. When they arrived on campus she asked the students to wait outside the admissions office while she went in to alert the receptionist the group had arrived. After speaking with the receptionist, Ms. Sutter was shocked to learn their assigned tour guide had been reassigned, as a result, her group would need to conduct a self-guided tour.

"But I didn't attend this university! I can't give them an adequate tour. Why not just let us join another group?" she implored.

"I'm sorry, but guides are prioritized for prospective, high school students," the receptionist responded. As Ms. Sutter continued to plead the club's case, she was approached by the Director of Admissions, Mr. Stein.

"Can I help you?" he asked warmly.

"Yes," responded Ms. Sutter. "I have a group of fifth graders here, potential first-generation college students," she said, before explaining how excited students were about the tour.

Mr. Stein asked Ms. Sutter to step into his office. *Wonderful!* thought Ms. Sutter. *Maybe he'll be the person who gives us a tour.*

Instead Mr. Stein said, "I'm sorry a tour guide is unavailable. We do our best to avoid these situations, but I have students here who are credible applicants. I can't compromise their interest by prioritizing fifth graders ahead of them." He paused briefly before adding, "Frankly, I worry you're getting your students excited about a place they probably will never attend. Perhaps you should be touring the community college."

With this, he opened his office door, inviting Ms. Sutter to leave. Ms. Sutter glanced through a window and saw her students waiting patiently for their tour. She fought back tears as she contemplated what to tell them and how to address Mr. Stein's comments.

In what way was Ms. Clark's expectation subverted? Second, explain the underlying prejudicial assumption Mr. Stein makes. Do NOT copy more than THREE consecutive words from the passage.

_____

_____

_____

_____

_____

03 Read the passage and follow the directions. [4 points]

At a party in Hollywood in the spring of 1935, Dashiell Hammett was asked by Gertrude Stein to solve a literary mystery. Why is it, she began, that in the nineteenth century men succeeded in writing about so many different varieties of men, and women were limited to creating heroines who were merely versions of themselves — she mentioned Charlotte Brontë and George Eliot — yet in the twentieth century this situation was reversed? Nowadays, Stein pointed out, it was the men who portrayed only themselves, and why should this be so? Stein reasonably assumed that Hammett, a hard-drinking ex-detective whose photograph had appeared on the cover of his latest novel, "The Thin Man," about a hard-drinking ex-detective, might be in a position to know.

The party that evening was given in Stein's honor, and Hammett was the one person in Hollywood she'd asked to meet. Although he had at first taken the invitation for an April Fools' joke, such tributes were no longer much of a surprise. Hammett had been "duh toast of duh intellectuals" (in Edmund Wilson's disgusted phrase) ever since "The Maltese Falcon," published in 1930, had introduced a new type of tough-guy hero in matching tough-guy prose : a tight-lipped, street-smart style, determinedly flat despite flickers of amusement and startlingly devoid of most of the familiar processes of consciousness. Readers were riveted, and critics were quick to announce the newest development in the creation of an American language. It was the kind of achievement that Stein and other literary radicals had been struggling for in their brave obscurities and their unread treatises, and it had emerged from the least likely source : cheap detective stories that large numbers of people actually liked to read, based on the real experience of a man on a job that just happened to involve unlimited amounts of violence, sexual intrigue, and moral devastation.

Hammett produced about ninety stories and five novels in the dozen active years of his career, many of them for badly needed money — he was capable of knocking out five thousand words a day — and many clearly executed beneath the level of his engaged attention. Of course, he also produced whiz-bang tales that exhibit the best of what the pulps could offer, and a few that transcend formula in the strict music of Hammett's uniquely deadpan dialogue.

Explain the meaning of the underlined words. Do NOT copy more than THREE consecutive words from the passage. Second, it can be inferred that Hammett's readership is most attracted by what factors?

_____

_____

_____

_____

_____

04   **Read the passage and follow the directions.** [4 points]

For his recent study, Thomas Reich asked two research assistants to look for correlational studies on the effects of music education. They found a total of 114 papers published since 2000. To assess whether the authors claimed any causation, researchers then looked for telltale verbs in each paper's title and abstract, verbs like "enhance," "promote," "facilitate," and "strengthen." The papers were categorized as neuroscience if the study employed an electroencephalogram or a brain imaging method like magnetic resonance, or if the study appeared in a journal that had "brain," "neuroscience," or a related term in its title. Otherwise the papers were categorized as psychology. Reich didn't tell his assistants what exactly he was trying to prove.

After tallying their assessments, Reich concluded that the majority of the articles fallaciously claimed that music training had a causal effect. The overselling, he also found, was more prevalent among neuroscience studies, three quarters of which mischaracterized a mere correlation between music training and skills enhancement as a cause-and-effect relationship. This may come as a <u>surprise</u> to some. Psychologists have been battling charges that they don't do "real" science for some time — in large part because many findings from classic experiments have proved unreproducible. Neuroscientists, on the other hand, armed with brain scans and EEGs, have not been subject to the same degree of critique.

"I have never thought that flute lessons make you better at solving differential equations," said Lutz Jäncke, a neuropsychologist from the University of Zurich in Switzerland who praised Reich's new study. "His criticism is justified."

Explain why the writer of the passage uses the word "surprise". Do NOT copy more than THREE consecutive words from the passage. Second, choose one word from the passage that would best describe Lutz Jäncke's opinion of the relationships between music training and skills enhancement.

_____

_____

_____

_____

_____

05 Read the passage and follow the directions. [4 points]

When I landed in Boston in 1999, the United States was the land of free markets. Many goods and services were cheaper here than in Europe. Twenty years later, American free markets are becoming a myth. Internet service, cellphone plans, and plane tickets are now cheaper in Europe and Asia than in the US. In 2018, the average monthly cost of a broadband internet connection was $31 in France, $39 in the UK and $68 in the US. American households also spend twice as much on cellphone services as households in France or the UK.

This is a result of policy choices. In 1999, the US had free and competitive markets while European markets were dominated by ___①___ . The airline industry is a prime example. Over the past two decades a wave of mergers has turned the US airline industry into oligopolies while Europe has opened its skies to competition, thanks in part to low-cost carriers such as Ryanair and EasyJet. US regulators allowed these mergers to happen without meaningful challenges. EU regulators, on the other hand, encouraged the entry of low-cost competitors by making sure they could get access to takeoff and landing slots.

There are many layers of irony in this historic reversal. One irony is that the free market ideas and business models that benefit European consumers today were inspired by US markets. Another irony is that some leftwing US politicians are now contemplating policies that most Europeans would find extreme. We do not think private health insurance companies should be abolished. We favor wealth taxes, but we do not think they are a cure for all ills.

The polarization of the political debate is partly the result of ② ignorance. The American Left sees Europe as an El Dorado of free healthcare, free education and workers' rights. The American Right sees it as a socialistic nightmare with no growth and no innovation. They're both wrong, and the result is misguided policies and time wasted tilting at windmills.

Fill in the blank with the ONE most appropriate word from the passage. If necessary, change the word form. Second, explain what the underlined "ignorance" means regarding the American Right. Do NOT copy more than THREE consecutive words from the passage. Third, what can be inferred to be the most important characteristic of a free market for the writer?

_____

_____

_____

_____

_____

06 **Read the passage and follow the directions.** [4 points]

Every year, salmon come home to Alaska's frigid rivers to mate, lay their eggs, and die. The state's salmon runs are some of the biggest in the world. But over the past few decades, those big salmon runs have featured ever smaller salmon.

Krista Oke and colleagues at the University of California, Santa Cruz, analyzed records of ____①____ going back to the 1950s. They included data on some 12.5 million salmon. And there's no question about it: salmon have shrunk. Sockeye salmon today are 2.1% shorter than their ancestors. Chum salmon are 2.4% shorter and Coho are 3.3% shorter. Chinook, or king, salmon showed the greatest declines at 8%. That's an average difference of more than 2 inches in length.

The researchers haven't nailed down the exact reasons behind this trend. But their analysis suggests that climate change and competition with wild and hatchery-raised salmon both play a role. They also discovered that much of the change in fish body size is due to fish returning from the ocean at a younger age now than in the past. Oke says fish could be returning earlier because they're reaching maturity faster for some reason — or because the ocean has become a riskier place for older salmon to survive.

Whatever the cause, this size shift has massive ramifications for people and the ecology. Oke and her team calculated that catching smaller fish may have already slashed the value of Alaska's commercial salmon fisheries by 21%. It's also likely reduced the food available to subsistence fishers — many of whom rely on stores of salmon to get them through the long, harsh winter — by as much as 26%.

On the side of _____②_____ , the researchers estimated that smaller fish lay 16% fewer eggs, which could depress salmon populations in the future. And, the salmon bring 28% fewer nutrients into the watersheds where they spawn, according to the study. "After they breed and die, their carcasses actually fertilize freshwater and terrestrial ecosystem with these marine-derived nutrients that are really important and that get used by all kinds of animals, like bears and songbirds and even taken up into trees."

With no single factor to blame for shrinking salmon, there's no obvious fix, Oke says.

Fill in blank ① with the THREE most appropriate consecutive words from the passage and blank ② with the ONE most appropriate word from the passage. Second, according to the research, describe ALL reasons salmon size may have become smaller than before. Do NOT copy more than THREE consecutive words from the passage.

_____

_____

_____

_____

_____

07 Read the passage and follow the directions. [4 points]

People are constantly cannonaded by advertisements. Vendors try to gain our attention and sell us their services or products. Advertisements appear everywhere : on television, on the Internet, radios, pamphlets and so forth.

Advertisements are very useful even if we sometimes feel annoyed when they interrupt our favorite television programs. They provide us with free information on the products and services. There are two types of advertisements. The informative advertisements are the ones which provide us with the details of the products or services. This information is especially useful if the product or service is new. For instance, when we need to buy a computer, advertisements describing the latest models and their different functions would be helpful. However, only a minority of the advertisements are informative ones. Many of them belong to the second category — the persuasive kind. These advertisements not only tell us more about the products, at the same time, they persuade customers to buy them by claiming that their products are superior to the rivalry ones. These claims may sometimes be untrue.

While advertisements can be good helpers for shopping, they do have their shortcomings. Most advertisements aim to sell only. Faults of the products or services are usually hidden from the consumers. Hence, sometimes, we feel deceived if the product or service we bought does not turn out the way the advertisements claim to be. Sometimes, advertisements by rival competitors can get very intensive, especially when there are many firms producing similar products. One common example is the washing powder. There are so many advertisements for the different brands that customers sometimes get confused over what they should buy. Furthermore, having more advertisements would mean that the production cost of the firm would be increased. These rises in cost are usually passed on to the consumers in the form of higher prices.

Without advertisements, we might have to buy things based on incomplete information or go through more complicated ways before getting to know the products or services. On the other hand, too many advertisements also complicate our buying decisions. So I would say that we cannot live without advertisements but we must be careful how we live with them.

Summarize the passage following the guidelines below.

Guidelines

- Summarize the above passage in one paragraph.
- Provide a topic sentence, supporting ideas, and a concluding sentence based on the passage.
- Do NOT copy more than FIVE consecutive words from the passage.

모범답안 p.067

01 Read the passage and follow the directions. [4 points]

An international Art Nouveau style was characterized by sinuous lines, floral and vegetable motifs, and soft evanescent coloration. It was an eclectic one, bringing together elements of Japanese art, motifs of ancient cultures, and natural forms. The glass objects of this style were elegant in outline, although often deliberately distorted, with pale or iridescent surfaces. A favored device of the style was to imitate the iridescent surface seen on ancient glass that had been buried. Much of the Art Nouveau glass produced during the years of its greatest popularity had been generically termed "art glass". Art glass was intended for decorative purposes and relied for its effect upon carefully chosen color combinations and innovative techniques. In the United States, Louis Comfort Tiffany was the most noted exponent of the style, producing a great variety of glass forms and surfaces, which were widely copied in their time and are highly prized today. Tiffany was a brilliant designer, successfully combining ancient Egyptian, Japanese, and Persian motifs.

The Art Nouveau style was a major force in the decorative arts from 1895 until 1915, although its influence continued throughout the mid-1920's. It was eventually to be overtaken by a new school of thought known as Functionalism that had been present since the turn of the century. At first restricted to a small avant-garde group of architects and designers. Functionalism emerged as the dominant influence upon designers after the First World War. The basic tenet of the movement — that function should determine form — was not a new concept. Soon a distinct aesthetic code evolved : form should be simple, surfaces plain, and any ornament should be based on geometric relationships. This new design concept, coupled with the sharp postwar reactions to the style and conventions of the preceding decades, created an entirely new public taste which caused Art Nouveau types of _____ to fall out of favor. The new taste demanded dramatic effects of contrast stark outline, and complex textural surfaces.

First, what major historical event marks the transition from Art Nouveau's to Functionalism in terms of mainstream popularity? Second, fill in the blank with the ONE most appropriate word from the passage.

_____

_____

_____

_____

_____

02 Read the passage and follow the directions. [4 points]

For six decades or more, America's history has been driven by cultural warfare. This is usually traced to the social revolutions of the 1960s, but it began earlier. Culture War 1.0 began in the 1950s as religious enthusiasts sought to win hearts, minds, and souls for Christ in a society that was rapidly liberalizing and secularizing. That is the war that drifted to a whimpering end as recently as 2013, when the Supreme Court handed down culturally significant rulings bolstering the case for same-sex marriage. In 2015, the Court gave same-sex marriage its full endorsement, ruling in Obergefell v. Hodges that restrictions on same-sex marriages were unconstitutional. By this point, Culture War 1.0 was over.

This first culture war was mostly fought over issues of religious faith and morality, such as whether creationism was a viable alternative to the theory of biological evolution and whether limits should be placed on institutionalizing Christian values in the public sphere. In Culture War 2.0, the supernatural, metaphysics, and even religion more broadly have become irrelevant. The demands of Christian faith and morality have been replaced by something far more threatening to a society founded on Enlightenment principles.

Culture War 2.0 rotates around the new rules of engagement. The rules of engagement relate to how we deal with our disagreements. In Culture War 1.0, if a(n) _____ gave a public lecture about the age of the Earth based on geological dating techniques, creationist detractors would issue a response, insist that such dating techniques are biased, challenge him to a debate, and ask pointed — if unfairly loaded — questions during the Q&A session. In Culture War 2.0, disagreements with a speaker are sometimes met with attempts at de-platforming. Rowdy campaigns for the invitation to be rescinded before the speech can be delivered. If this is unsuccessful, critics may resort to disrupting the speaker by screaming and shouting, engaging noise makers, or pulling the fire alarm. The goal is not to counter the speaker with better arguments or even to insist on an alternative view, but to prevent the speaker from airing her views at all.

Christian organizations have a long history of censorship, and this has continued to some extent even in recent decades. All the same, an attempt to suppress an academic article would have been almost unthinkable during Culture War 1.0. There were some analogous attempts on the part of Christians during precursors of this culture war, as for example in the incidents surrounding Tennessee's Butler Act of 1925 and the subsequent "Scopes Monkey Trial." And religious would-be censors during Culture War 1.0 did occasionally make attempts on novels and movies interpreted as blasphemous or obscene, such as *The Last Temptation of Christ*. But for the most part, Creationists in the first Culture War didn't want an evolutionary biologist to lose their tenure and their doctorate. They wanted to debate and prove them wrong.

Fill in the blank with the TWO most appropriate consecutive words from the passage. Second, describe what "de-platforming" is and provide at least TWO examples of it from the passage.

_____

_____

_____

_____

_____

03   Read the passage and follow the directions. [4 points]

There is no denying that most of us need admiration as we need sunshine, and that women depend upon beauty as a means of winning admiration to a greater extent than men do. But, every year, more and more avenues to admiration are opened to women, and there are trains of worshippers to be won in athletics, in the professions, in the arts and in public life. There is scarcely a way in which a man can feed his vanity that is not nowadays open to women too. For them, it is getting a better and better world to grow old in.

All the same, I know little about the matter. I do not even know in what happiness consists. I know only that it does not consist in being young, and that though disease and the loss of faculties and the loss of friends bring misery, there is no absolute misery in being old. I confess I am not perfectly happy at fortyeight, but neither was I perfectly happy at eighteen. I should be glad to be eighteen again, but that is not because it was in itself a happier age but because I should now have thirty years longer to live.

The chief objection to growing old is not that one grows old oneself, but that the world grows older; and it is not so much that the world grows older as that the world we once knew is in ruins.

New inventions have wrecked the world in which we had peace. Everywhere are noise and speed in place of the green quiet that we once knew. I do not like to speak ill of inventors, but they have invented the horse almost out of existence, and there are little seaside towns that once seemed a thousand miles away, so remote they were, where the smell of the sea is now drowned by the smell of the charabanc*. Is it possible to name a single beautiful place that is more beautiful today than it was thirty years ago? But we are faithful to the world of thirty years ago only in our imaginations, and there is scarcely a new invention — the motor-car or wireless — that we are <u>loyal</u> enough to abstain from using.

charabanc : bus for sightseeing

First, explain how the experience of aging has improved for women. Do NOT copy more than FOUR consecutive words from the passage. Second, what would it take to fulfill the loyalty addressed in the underlined part?

_____

_____

_____

_____

_____

04   Read the passage and follow the directions. [4 points]

Recently, scientists discovered bacteria that had been buried beneath the ocean floor for more than a hundred million years and was still alive. What would change if we could live for even just a million years? One thought immediately comes to mind. Tenure in academia would have to be capped. Universities would have to limit faculty appointments to a century at most in order to refresh their talent pool and mitigate old-fashioned education and research dogmas.

Past generations used to say that even though we cannot postpone natural _____, we can control how we live. They also believed that there is "nothing new under the sun." Both statements are inaccurate from our current perspective. With advances in bioscience and technology, one can imagine a post-COVID-19 future when most diseases are cured and our life span will increase substantially. Then death cannot be an enemy of human beings any longer.

If that happens, how would our goals change, and how would this shape our lives? Given the luxury of pursuing longer-term plans, we could accomplish more ambitious tasks. We could decide to care more about our planetary environment and interpersonal cooperation, since pollution or hostilities carry long-term dangers. An extended life experience could make us wiser and more risk-averse since there is much more at stake. It would make little sense to send young soldiers to wars, or initiate wars in the first place.

But even with shrewd strategies, survival is by no means guaranteed. For example, the known correlation between brain size and body weight did not make dinosaurs smart enough to deflect the asteroid that killed them. Accidents are inevitable, and treatment centers will continuously be busy repairing nonfatal damages due to routine mishaps.

The good news is that over a lifetime as long as a million years, space travel can take us to the nearest stars using existing chemical rockets. It would take merely 100,000 years to arrive at the habitable planet around Proxima Centauri with a space vehicle that travels at the speed of NASA's New Horizons spacecraft. For passengers who live a million years, such a trip would appear just like the decade-long journey of New Horizons to Pluto within our current life span. Of course, the spacecraft will have to provide an enduring ecosystem and comfortable living conditions over this long journey. And the passengers will have to maintain a stable mindset for their journey's goal and not lose faith, like a fisherman who, after a long hiatus without finding any fish, asks whether the real purpose of fishing is catching fish.

Fill in the blank with the ONE most appropriate word from the passage. Second, if the premise of the passage comes true, what would happen to wars? Third, explain why the writer mentions "a fisherman". Do NOT copy more than FOUR consecutive words from the passage.

_____

_____

_____

_____

_____

05   Read the passage and follow the directions. [4 points]

Consider the early stages of mathematics — a few technological dodges* in Egypt about two thousand years before Christ. It was a minor element in a great civilization. About five hundred years before Christ, the Greeks initiated its theoretical development for the love of the theory. This was about four or five hundred after the date of Solomon's dream, the greatest prophecy ever made. The genius of the Greeks was shown by their clear divination* of the importance of mathematics for the study of nature. The necessity for fostering the development of abstract morphology is illustrated by considering the state of the science of geometry at the commencement of the sixteenth century. The science had been studied for about two thousand years. It had been elaborated in great detail. But, allowing for some minor qualifications, nothing had come from it except the intrinsic interest of the study. Then, as if a door had suddenly opened, Kepler produced the first important utilization of conic sections, the first among hundreds, Descartes and Desargues revolutionized the methods of the science, Newton wrote his *Principia*, and the modern period of civilization commenced. Apart from the capital of abstract ideas which had accumulated slowly during two thousand years, our modern life would have been impossible. There is nothing magical about ___①___ as such. It is simply the greatest example of a science of abstract forms.

The abstract theory of music is another such science; the abstract theory of political economy is another; and the abstract theory of the currency is another. The point is that the development of abstract theory precedes the understanding of _____②_____. The instance of political economy illustrates important point. Abstract political economy deals with men under an abstraction. It limits its view to the "economic man." It also makes assumptions as to markets and competition which neglect many important factors. We have here an example of the necessity of transcending a given morphological scheme. Up to a point the scheme is invaluable. It clarifies thought, it suggests observation, and it explains fact. But there is a strict limit to the utility of any finite scheme. If the scheme be pressed beyond its proper scope, definite error results.

dodge : sidestep
divination : insight or fortune-telling

Fill in each blank with the ONE most appropriate word from the passage respectively. Second, describe the fundamental reason ancient Greeks played a leading role in developing the theory of mathematics. Do NOT copy more than FOUR consecutive words from the passage.

_____

_____

_____

_____

_____

06   Read the passage and follow the directions. [4 points]

Which man do you expect to be more honest : the one wearing an Armani suit or the one wearing a sport coat from Men's Wearhouse? Although clothes might seem irrelevant, research by Paul Piff, a social psychologist at Berkeley, suggests that indicators of socioeconomic status can predict trustworthiness. It turns out that increasing status and power go hand in hand with decreasing honesty and reliability. In one experiment, for example, Piff and colleagues asked participants to play the part of a job recruiter. The participants were told about an open temporary position that would last for no longer than six months, and about a well-qualified applicant who was interested only in a long-term role. When asked to prepare their pitches to woo this applicant, those recruiters with a higher status not only neglected to tell the applicant that the job was temporary but also told the study's leaders that they would lie about the job's duration if asked.

From this and other findings, you might think that the rich are simply less trustworthy than the poor, but that's not exactly the case. A person's honesty depends on his or her relative feelings of power — or vulnerability — not on how much he or she has in the bank. Work by University of Cologne psychologist Joris Lammers proves the point. Lammers randomly assigned people to be a "boss" or a "follower" in an office simulation and found that most people temporarily elevated to more-senior roles displayed a higher degree of hypocritical behavior — they were quick to condemn others for unethical, self-interested behavior but judged their own similar actions to be acceptable.

When someone has a(n) _____ than you, or even just thinks he does, his mind tells him that you need him more than he needs you. Consequently, he's more likely to satisfy short-term desires and worry less about the long-term consequences of being untrustworthy. So when deciding whom to trust, you have to consider power differences, including new and temporary ones. If a potential collaborator has just been promoted or has landed a big deal, he might regard some relationships as less important. And although top firms often have great reputations, that doesn't mean they treat their small clients as well as their larger ones.

Explain what Joris Lammers proves in his study. Do NOT copy more than FOUR consecutive words from the passage. Second, fill in the blank with the TWO most appropriate consecutive words from the passage.

_____

_____

_____

_____

_____

07 Read the passage and follow the directions. [4 points]

With the advent of television, lots of entertainments have been supplanted. Such live programs as world news and television serials have removed from us the desire to listen to radio, to read books or newspapers, or even to go to watch movies. Indeed, the television brings the world into our home. By pressing buttons world happenings are at once presented in front of us. Children nowadays develop faster in language, owing to the early exposure to television programs. At such tender age, it would be difficult for them to read books or papers. Therefore, television programs are a good source of learning for them. Furthermore, pronunciations by the newscasters, actors or actresses are usually standardized, hence young children watching these programs will learn the "right" pronunciations too. Television is also extremely beneficial to working parents who are usually too busy or tired to take their kids out for amusements. Surrounded by the comforts of their home, the family can get together and watch their favorite television programs.

Of course, we should not be too carried away by the merits of the television. Watching television programs takes away our desire to read. Why read books when exciting movies are screened? Why bother to read newspapers when we can hear them from the television news reports? The lack of reading is unhealthy especially to younger children as they will grow up only with the ability to speak but not write. For example, I have a neighbor whose six-year-old child can say complete sentences like "I love dogs," but when told to write out the sentence, is unable to do so. Not only are the writing skills of children affected, their thinking capacities are also handicapped. Television programs remove the need to think. The stories, ideas and facts are woven in the way television planners wanted. Exposure to such opinions and the lack of thinking opportunities will hinder the children's analyzing ability.

In spite of the demerits of watching television programs, choosing the 'middle path', which is to do selective television viewing, should be the best solution to reconcile both the advantages and disadvantages of television.

Summarize the passage following the guidelines below.

Guidelines

- Summarize the above passage in one paragraph.
- Provide a topic sentence, supporting ideas, and a concluding sentence based on the passage.
- Do NOT copy more than FIVE consecutive words from the passage.

_____

_____

_____

_____

_____

📖 모범답안 p.070

01 　Read the passage and follow the directions. [4 points]

In egg yolk, dairy products, margarine etc, we can find Vitamin A. It is abundant in fish-liver oils, consequently fish-liver oils are employed for preventing and curing illness caused by _____ of vitamin A. In a well-fed, healthy human being, the liver can store up sufficient vitamin A to meet the body's requirements for six months.

Although vitamin A itself is not present in plants, many plants produce a substance called carotene, formed from leaf-green which our bodies can convert into it. Carotene is the yellowish-red coloring matter in carrots. The greener a leaf is, the more carotene it usually contains. Hence the importance of green, leafy vegetables in the diet as a source of carotene. Tomatoes, papayas, mangoes and bananas contain more carotene than most other fruits. Red palm oil contains so much carotene that it is used instead of cod-liver oil. Thus, it is very valuable, both as a food-fat and for deep-frying.

Vitamin A and carotene are insoluble in water and they are not destroyed by heat unless oxygen is present. Boiling in water, therefore, does not destroy much vitamin A or carotene.

Vitamin A encourages healthy growth and physical fitness. Young animals soon stop growing and die if it is not present in their diet. This vitamin keeps the moist surfaces lining the digestive canal, the lungs and air passages healthy. It also helps keep the ducts of the various glands, the tissue that lines the eyelids and covers the front of the eyeball functional. As vitamin A helps these tissues build up resistance to infection, it is often called the anti-infective vitamin. Some of the most common disorders in people are caused by lack of vitamin A, when the moist tissues become dry and rough. This often causes serious eye disease, followed by infection of the air-passages. The skin may also become flaky and rough.

As the body cannot produce vitamin A, it has to come from external sources. Thus a well-balanced diet is required and is usually sufficient to provide the necessary amount. There is therefore no need to supplement the need in the form of pills.

Fill in the blank with the ONE most appropriate word from the passage. Second, according to the passage, explain why a well-balanced diet is important to human beings.

_____

_____

_____

_____

_____

02 Read the passage and follow the directions. [4 points]

The Native American peoples of the north Pacific Coast created a highly complex maritime culture as they invented modes of production unique to their special environment. In addition to their sophisticated technical culture, they also attained one of the most complex social organizations of any nonagricultural people in the world. In a division of labor similar to that of the hunting peoples in the interior and among foraging peoples throughout the world, the men did most of the fishing, and the women processed the catch. Women also specialized in the gathering of the abundant creatures that lived closer to shore. They collected crabs, mussels, abalone, and clams, which they could gather while remaining close to their children. The _____ life harvested by the women not only provided food, but also supplied more of the raw materials for making tools than did the fish gathered by the men. Of particular importance for the native tool kit before the introduction of metal was the wide knife made from the larger mussel shells, and a variety of cutting edges that could be made from other maritime shells. The women used their tools to process all of the fish and maritime mammals brought in by the men. They cleaned the fish, and dried vast quantities of them for the winter. They sun-dried fish when practical, but in the rainy climate of the coastal area they also used smokehouses to preserve tons of fish and other seafood annually. Each product had its own peculiar characteristics that demanded a particular way of cutting or drying the meat, and each task required its own cutting blades and other utensils. After drying the fish, the women pounded some of them into fish meal, which was an easily transported food used in soups, stews, or other dishes to provide protein and thickening in the absence of fresh fish or while on long trips. The women also made a cheese-like substance from a mixture of fish and roe by aging it in storehouses or by burying it in wooden boxes or pits lined with rocks and tree leaves.

Fill in the blank with the ONE most appropriate word from the passage. Second, explain why the Native Americans of the north Pacific Coast used smokehouses.

_____

_____

_____

_____

_____

03 Read the passage and follow the directions. [4 points]

As I write on these late days of the summer of 2020, it often feels like our civilization has morphed into a Herman Melville novel in which ⋯

All that most maddens and torments; all that stirs up the lees of things; all truth with malice in it; all that cracks the sinews and cakes the brain; all the subtle demonisms of life and thought; all evil, to crazy Ahab, were visibly personified, and made practically assailable in Moby Dick. He piled upon the whale's white hump the sum of all the general rage and hate felt by his whole race from Adam down; and then, as if his chest had been a mortar*, he burst his hot heart's shell upon it.

Who would not be maddened and tormented by the images and stories coming out of intensive care units where Covid-19 patients gasp out their final breaths as loved ones watch remotely, unable even to bid a final farewell? Who hasn't experienced cracked sinews and caked brains from months of being isolated with our thoughts, our voices masked, our social movements regulated?

As we peer into the distant horizon, the seeing becomes misty, clarity clouded in the fog of uncertainty. What will 2020 mean in 2030? Or 2050? Or 2120? Even that class of seer known as superforecasters, those trained in the dark arts of Bayesian reasoning and big-data analysis, do no better than chance when they look more than five years out.

In a 1966 episode of *Star Trek* titled "Miri," the prepubescent heroine of the story explains to a flummoxed Captain Kirk what happened on her planet in which all the Grups (grownups) were dead, leaving the Onlies (children) to fend for themselves : "That was when they started to get sick in the Before Time. We hid, then they were gone." According to linguist Ben Zimmer, who has traced the phrase's etymology, the Before Time often represents a pre-plague world, and the expression has a literary history at least as old as the King James Bible, in which the author of the

Book of Samuel writes : "Beforetime in Israel, when a man went to enquire of God, thus he said, 'come, and let us go to the Seer' : for he that is now called a Prophet was beforetime called a Seer." The locution* has been resurrected in response to the Covid-19 pandemic, as when *Atlantic* columnist Marina Koren wrote of "the exacerbated sense that the days before the coronavirus swept across the country — the 'Before Time,' as many have taken to calling it — feel like a bygone era."

mortar : bomb
locution : name or title

Explain the reason the writer of the passage cites *Star Trek* considering the passage's main idea. Next, what can be inferred to be the newest title of the role of "seer"?

_____

_____

_____

_____

_____

04 Read the passage and follow the directions. [4 points]

Despite great progress in our scientific understanding of the brain, we still don't have even the beginnings of an explanation of how complex electrochemical signaling is somehow able to give rise to the inner subjective world of colors, sounds, smells and tastes that each of us knows in our own case. There is a deep mystery in understanding how what we know about ourselves from the inside fits together with what science tells us about matter from the outside.

While the problem is broadly acknowledged, many people think we just need to plug away at our standard methods of investigating the brain, and we'll eventually crack it*. But I argue that the problem of consciousness results from the way we designed science at the start of the scientific revolution.

A key moment in the scientific revolution was Galileo's declaration that mathematics was to be the language of the new science, that the new science was to have a purely quantitative vocabulary. But Galileo realized that you can't capture consciousness in these terms, as consciousness is an essentially quality-involving phenomenon. Think about the redness of a red experience or the smell of flowers or the taste of mint. You can't capture these kinds of qualities in the _____ of physical science. So Galileo decided that we have to put consciousness outside of the domain of science. After we'd done that, everything else could be captured in mathematics.

This is really important, because although the problem of consciousness is taken seriously, most people assume our conventional scientific approach is capable of solving it. And they think this because they look at the great success of physical science in explaining more and more of our universe and conclude that this ought to give us confidence that physical science alone will one day explain consciousness. However, I believe that this reaction is rooted in a misunderstanding of the history of science. Yes, physical science has been incredibly successful. But it's been successful precisely because it was designed to exclude consciousness. If Galileo were to time travel to the present day and hear about this problem of explaining consciousness in the terms of physical science, he'd say, "Of course, you can't do that. I designed physical science to deal with quantities, not qualities."

* crack it : succeed

Fill in the blank with the TWO most appropriate consecutive words from the passage. Second, explain the implication of the underlined words in the last sentence.

_____

_____

_____

_____

_____

05 Read the passage and follow the directions. [4 points]

To gorge on delicious cookies at the end of your working week, you first had to go through a situational stage, where you put yourself in a compromising situation with tempting cookies. From there, you transitioned to an attentional stage, where you directed your attention back towards those cookies. After that, you went through a(n) _____, where you thought about how good those cookies would taste (especially with a glass of milk). All this led to a response stage, where you broke down and eventually ate all the cookies. To put it bluntly, a lot of things had to go wrong for you to end up giving in to temptation. The good news is that this means you could have applied self-control at several instances prior to when you tried and failed to exert inhibitory self-control (or 'willpower' in everyday talk).

Let's start with the situational stage. You don't need to be well-versed in social psychology to recognise the power of the situation. Most teachers will tell you it's easier for students to focus when they sit in the front of the classroom. With this in mind, you could have employed 'situational self-control strategies'. For instance, instead of sitting in front of a box of cookies and forcing yourself not to eat them, you could have either not bought them in the first place —known as 'situation selection' or simply removed them from sight by placing them in a cabinet (or thrown them out) — 'situation modification'.

Prior research suggests that these situational strategies are quite effective. For example, one study that instructed high-school students to use situational strategies (such as removing buzzing cellphones and other temptations from sight) found that they made more progress towards their academic goals, compared with others who were simply instructed to use inhibitory self-control. Similarly, dieting research suggests that a simple yet overlooked way to lose weight is to avoid situations where tempting, high-calorie foods are readily available. For example, when you go grocery shopping, plan to avoid walking through the bakery. That way, you are less likely to encounter cues (pleasant smells and sights) that strengthen temptation. Think 'out of sight, out of mind'.

But what if you can't use situational strategies? After all, you might have no choice but to walk through the bakery, or perhaps you'll upset your kids if you throw away the cookies. Thankfully, there are other 'psychological strategies', initiated during the attentional stage and appraisal stage, that can be useful when the situation is uncontrollable.

Fill in the blank with the TWO most appropriate consecutive words from the passage. Second, which strategy would most appropriately fit putting one's smartphone in the other room during study?

_____

_____

_____

_____

_____

06   Read the passage and follow the directions. [4 points]

Lots of factors related to the voice reveal the personality of the speaker. First, the voice gives psychological clues to a person's self-image, perception of others, and emotional health. Self-image can be indicated by a tone of voice that is confident, pretentious, shy, aggressive, outgoing, or exuberant, to name only a few personality traits. Also the voice may give a clue to the facade or mask of that person, for example, a shy person hiding behind an overconfident front. How a speaker perceives the listener's receptiveness, interest, or sympathy in any given conversation can drastically alter the tone of presentation, by encouraging or discouraging the speaker. Emotional health is evidenced in the voice by free and melodic sounds of the happy, by constricted and harsh sound of the angry, and by dull and lethargic qualities of the depressed.

The second is the broad area of communication, which includes imparting information by use of language and specialized communication through _____. A person conveys thoughts and ideas through choice of words, by a tone of voice that is pleasant or unpleasant, gentle or harsh, by the rhythm that is inherent within the language itself, and by speech rhythms that are flowing and regular or uneven and hesitant, and finally, by the pitch and melody of the utterance. When speaking before a group, a person's tone may indicate unsureness or fright, confidence or calm. At interpersonal levels, the tone may reflect ideas and feelings over and above the words chosen, or may belie them. Here the conversant's tone can consciously or unconsciously reflect intuitive sympathy or antipathy, lack of concern or interest, fatigue, anxiety, enthusiasm or excitement, all of which are usually discernible by the acute listener.

And performance is a manner of communication that is highly specialized with its own techniques for obtaining effects by voice or gesture. The motivation derived from the text, and in the case of singing, the music, in combination with the performer's skills, personality, and ability to create empathy will determine the success of artistic, political, or pedagogic communication.

Fill in the blank with the ONE most appropriate word from the passage. Second, according to the passage, what characteristics of the listener would most affect the speaker's presentation?

_____

_____

_____

_____

_____

07   Read the passage and follow the directions. [4 points]

With just twenty-six letters, we can write a letter to our friends or answer an examination question. Thousands of years ago, there was no writing system and tools at all. The invention of writing tools is a major transition. In olden times, the kind of writing tools used, depended on the material they wrote on. For example, in the Middle East, where clay is abundant in supply, the early people used hollow reed 'pens' to carve onto the wet clay tablets. After which, these clay pieces were baked till rock hard to make the writings permanent. In ancient Egypt, Egyptians either wrote on scraped thin pieces of animal skins called 'parchment' or flattened papaya stems known as 'papyrus'.

It was only in the 1880s, that fountain pens were invented. Before that, most people used either quill pens — sharpened bird feathers or nibbed pens, which were dipped into ink before writing. Fountain pens invented later have both plus and minus points. With tiny ink tanks in them, fountain pens are superior to quill or nibbed ones as the ink in them do not run out as quickly. The disadvantage is that sometimes, the nibs of the fountain pens may break, causing the ink to leak, staining the writer's fingers.

The flaw in fountain pens has led to further investigation and the successful invention of the first 'ballpoint' pen by a Hungarian, Ladislao Biro in 1931. There were many people after him who tried to improve upon the appearance of his ballpoint pens.

Many technicians all over the world have tried to find better writing tools which improve upon the previous ones. However, the prospect of writing instruments are not optimistic because in the current era of the Internet and social media, people do not necessarily depend on them any more.

Summarize the passage following the guidelines below.

Guidelines

- Summarize the above passage in one paragraph.
- Provide a topic sentence, supporting ideas, and a concluding sentence based on the passage.
- Do NOT copy more than FIVE consecutive words from the passage.

_____

_____

_____

_____

_____

01 Read the passage and follow the directions. [4 points]

A great migration is happening on U.S. college campuses. Ever since the fall of 2008, a lot of students have walked out of English and humanities lectures and into STEM classes, especially computer science and engineering.

English majors are down more than a quarter (25.5 percent) since the Great Recession, according to data compiled by the National Center for Education Statistics. It's the biggest drop for any major tracked by the center in its annual data and is quite startling, given that college enrollment has jumped in the past decade.

Ask any college student or professor why this big shift from studying Chaucer to studying coding is happening and they will probably tell you it's about jobs. As students feared for their job prospects, they — and their parents — wanted a degree that would lead to a steady paycheck after graduation. The perception is that STEM (science, technology, engineering and math) is the path to employment. Majors in computer science and health fields have nearly doubled from 2009 to 2017. Engineering and math have also seen big jumps.

As humanities majors slump to the lowest level in decades, <u>calls are coming from surprising places for a revival</u>. Some prominent economists are making the case for why it still makes a lot of sense to major (or at least take classes) in humanities alongside more technical fields.

Nobel Prize winner Robert Shiller's new book "Narrative Economics" opens with him reminiscing about an enlightening history class he took as an undergraduate at the University of Michigan. He wrote that what he learned about the Great Depression was far more useful in understanding the period of economic and financial turmoil than anything he learned in his economic courses.

The whole premise of Shiller's book is that _____ matter. What people tell each other can have profound implications on markets — and the overall economy. Examples include the "get rich quick" stories about bitcoin or the "anyone can be a homeowner" stories that helped drive the housing bubble. "Traditional economic approaches fail to examine the role of public beliefs in major economic events — that is, narrative. Economists can best advance their science by developing and incorporating into it the art of narrative economics."

When asked if he's essentially arguing for more English and history majors, Shiller said, "I think so," adding : "Compartmentalization of intellectual life is bad." Shiller isn't alone in wishing that there were more storytellers (and story analyzers) around.

Explain the meaning of the underlined words. Second, fill in the blank with the ONE most appropriate word from the passage.

_____

_____

_____

_____

_____

02 Read the passage and follow the directions. [4 points]

There are two main schools in the study of communication. The first sees communication as the transmission of messages. It is concerned with how senders and receivers encode and decode, with how transmitters use the channels and media of communication. It is concerned with matters like efficiency and accuracy. It sees communication as a process by which one person affects the behaviour or state of mind of another. If the effect is different from or smaller than that which was intended, this school tends to talk in terms of communication failure, and to look to the stages in the process to find out where the failure occurred. For the sake of convenience I shall refer to this as the 'process' school.

The second school sees communication as the production and exchange of meanings. It is concerned with how messages, or texts, interact with people in order to produce meanings; that is, it is concerned with the role of texts in our culture. It uses terms like signification, and does not consider misunderstandings to be necessarily evidence of _____. They may result from cultural differences between sender and receiver. For this school, the study of communication is the study of text and culture. The main method of study is semiotics (the science of signs and meanings), and I shall refer to this as the 'semiotic' school.

Each school interprets our definition of communication as social interaction through messages in its own way. The first defines social interaction as the process by which one person relates to others, or affects the behaviour, state of mind or emotional response of another, and, of course, vice versa. This is close to the common-sense, everyday use of the phrase. Semiotics, however, defines social interaction as that which constitutes the individual as a member of a particular culture or society. I know I am a member of western, industrial society because, to give one of many sources of identification, I respond to Shakespeare or Coronation Street* in broadly the same ways as do the fellow members of my culture.

I also become aware of cultural differences if, for instance, I hear a Chinese critic reading King Lear as a devastating attack upon the western ideal of the family as the basis of society, or arguing that Coronation Street shows how the west keeps the workers in their place. Both these readings are possible, but my point is, they are not mine, as a typical member of my culture. In responding to Coronation Street in the more normal way, I am expressing my commonality with other members of my culture.

Coronation Street : a British soap opera

Fill in the blank with the TWO most appropriate consecutive words from the passage. Second, explain why the difference occurs between the Chinese critic and the writer as illustrated in the passage.

_____

_____

_____

_____

_____

03 Read the passage and follow the directions. [4 points]

In their fight alongside their medical peers against the coronavirus, black physicians face the additional burden of broad mistrust of the federal government in many black communities.

And Pierre Vigilance, MD, a former health commissioner for the District of Columbia, believes he can point to that moment in U.S. history that's "the root" of that African American mistrust — the infamous 40-year Tuskegee experiment.

The United States Public Health Service started the study in 1932 in collaboration with Tuskegee University (then the Tuskegee Institute), a historically black college in Alabama. Investigators enrolled in the study a total of 600 impoverished, African-American sharecroppers from Macon County, Alabama. Of these men, 399 had latent syphilis, with a control group of 201 men who were not infected. The study was conducted without the benefit of patients' informed consent. Researchers told the men they were being treated for "bad blood," a local term used to describe several ailments, including syphilis, anemia, and fatigue. In truth, they did not receive the proper treatment needed to cure their illness. In exchange for taking part in the study, the men received free medical exams, free meals, and burial insurance. Although originally projected to last 6 months, the study actually went on for 40 years until 1972 when an Associated Press story about the Tuskegee Study caused a public outcry that led the Assistant Secretary for Health and Scientific Affairs to appoint an Ad Hoc Advisory Panel to review the study and found the men had been misled and had not been not told of the study's purpose or aim.

"Some are well aware and know that history. But many triggers of distrust are being replaced by family history, like, 'Uncle Johnny was fine, but he went to the doctor and everything went downhill.' That may be how it appeared, or how it was, but there were a number of things that Uncle Johnny had against him that had nothing to do with the _____. But that's the belief," said Dr. Vigilance, "and it's as much a part of it as medical and public health maleficence." Thus, it is challenging for black physicians to help their communities trust the instructions and services pushed by the government during the current pandemic.

According to the passage, upon whom does the Tuskegee experiment put extra burden currently and why? Second, fill in the blank with the ONE most appropriate word from the passage.

_____

_____

_____

_____

_____

04 Read the passage and follow the directions. [4 points]

In my sketch of an anthropologist's training, I have only told you that he must make intensive studies of primitive peoples. I have not yet told you how he makes them. How does one make a study of a primitive people? I will answer this question very briefly and in very general terms, stating only what we regard as the essential rules of good fieldwork.

Experience has proved that certain conditions are essential if a good investigation is to be carried out. The earlier professional fieldworkers were always in a great hurry. Their quick visits to native peoples sometimes lasted only a few days, and seldom more than a few weeks. Survey research of this kind can be a useful preliminary to intensive studies and elementary ethnological classifications can be derived from it, but it is of little value for an understanding of social life. The position is very different today when one to three years are devoted to the study of a single people. This permits observations to be made at every season of the year, the social life of the people to be recorded to the last detail, and conclusions to be tested systematically.

However, given even unlimited time for research, the anthropologist will not produce a good account of the people he is studying unless he can put himself in a position which enables him to establish ties of intimacy with them, and to observe their daily activities from within, and not from without, their community life.

He must live as far as possible in their villages and camps, where he is, again as far as possible, <u>physically and morally part of the community</u>. He then not only sees and hears what goes on in the normal everyday life of the people as well as less common events, such as ceremonies and legal cases, but by taking part in those activities in which he can appropriately engage, he learns through action as well as by ear and eye what goes on around him. This is very unlike the situation in which records of native life were compiled by earlier anthropological fieldworkers who, living out of the native community and in mission stations or government posts, had mostly to rely on what a few informants told them.

Describe TWO rules that the writer thinks are essential when anthropologists study indigenous people. Second, identify the ONE word from the passage that BEST corresponds to the underlined words.

_____

_____

_____

_____

_____

05 Read the passage and follow the directions. [4 points]

There is something funky going on in the clouds of Venus. Telescopes have detected unusually high concentrations of the molecule phosphine — a stinky, flammable chemical typically associated with feces, farts and rotting microbial activity — in an atmospheric layer far above the planet's scorching surface.

The finding is curious because here on Earth, phosphine is essentially always associated with living creatures, either as a by-product of metabolic processes or of human technology such as industrial fumigants and methamphetamine labs. Although toxic to many organisms, the molecule has been singled out as a potentially unambiguous signature of life because it is so difficult to make through ordinary geological or atmospheric action.

Swathed in sulfuric acid clouds and possessing oppressive surface pressures and temperatures hot enough to melt lead, Venus is a hellish world. But the particular cloud layer where the phosphine is present happens to be relatively balmy, with ample sunlight and Earth-like atmospheric pressure and temperature. The results will have to be carefully vetted by the scientific community. Yet they seem likely to spark renewed interest in exploring our sister planet next door.

"It's a really puzzling discovery because phosphine doesn't fit in our conception of what kinds of chemicals should be in Venus's atmosphere," says Michael Wong, an astrobiologist at the University of Washington. Planetary scientist Sanjay Limaye of the University of Wisconsin‐Madison agrees. "The bottom line is we don't know what's going on," he says. (Neither Wong nor Sanjay were involved in the work.)

After the sun and moon, Venus is the brightest object visible to the naked eye in Earth's sky. For thousands of years, people told stories about the glittering jewel that appeared around sunrise and sunset. Venus's brilliance is what made it attractive to Jane Greaves, a radio astronomer at Cardiff University in Wales. She typically focuses her attention on distant newborn planetary systems but wanted to test her molecular identification abilities on worlds within our cosmic backyard.

In 2017 Greaves observed Venus with the James Clerk Maxwell Telescope (JCMT) on Mauna Kea in Hawaii, searching for bar code‐like patterns of lines in the planet's spectrum that would indicate the presence of different chemicals. While doing so, she noticed a line associated with _____. The data suggested the molecule was present at around 20 parts per billion in the planet's atmosphere, a concentration between 1,000 and a million times greater than that in Earth's atmosphere. "I was stunned," Greaves says.

Phosphine is a relatively simple molecule containing one phosphorus atom and three hydrogen atoms. It is known to reek of garlic or rotting fish, though by the time it reaches concentrations where humans can smell it, it is likely to cause lung damage.

Explain what the new discovery eventually suggests about Venus. Second, identify to what the underlined "our sister planet next door" refers. Third, fill in the blank with the ONE most appropriate word from the passage.

_____

_____

_____

_____

_____

06 Read the passage and follow the directions. [4 points]

In a recent experiment with colleagues at Cornell and MIT, we filmed people having a brief "get to know you" conversation either face-to-face or via online chat just before they played an economic game that pitted self-interest against cooperation. Although the average level of cooperation was equal in both groups, people's predictions for how fairly their partners would act when making monetary exchanges were significantly more accurate when they had previously interacted face-to-face. This meant that a trust-relevant signal had to exist.

To find out what it was, we compared sets of nonverbal cues we had collected to see which of them predicted untrustworthy behavior. We found that four — leaning away from a partner, crossing one's arms, hand touching, and face touching — were reliable indicators when occurring together. The more frequently an individual expressed all four cues, the more self-interest she showed by refusing to share profits with a partner. And the more times a partner saw her display those cues, the more the partner expected her to _____. Most interesting of all, the face-to-face participants had no awareness that they were using the cues to make inferences about trustworthiness; they had developed more-accurate intuitions without being able to say why.

We then repeated the experiment, with one important change : Participants conversed not with another human but with a humanoid robot that had been programmed to express either the four target cues or neutral ones. The robot provided exacting control : It could repeat the target gestures with a precision that no human actor could achieve, meaning that we could ascertain the power of the four cues. And the results were what we'd predicted : When people saw the robot express the target cues, they reported trusting it less and expected it to cheat them more.

These findings demonstrate that our minds come with built-in trust detectors. They also reinforce how invaluable intuitions, or gut feelings, can be. The problem is that managers and negotiators often suppress their intuitive machinery by either ignoring it in favor of what they believe to be more rational predictors for trustworthiness, such as reputation or status, or mistakenly looking for the wrong nonverbal "tells."

Fill in the blank with the ONE most appropriate word from the passage. Second, describe the change the writer would propose managers and negotiators to make.

_____

_____

_____

_____

_____

07   Read the passage and follow the directions. [4 points]

A home is supposed to be a haven where a child ought to feel safe and secure. Unfortunately, more often than not, the home is also where a child is abused.

Abusers claim they do it because of their stress and frustrations. Child-abusing parents feel harassed by a crying child and are unable to curb their own fury, especially if no support is received from anyone. This is not surprising since support is extended to a victim of child abuse more readily than to the perpetrator. Occasionally, parents may vent their frustrations on their child if they fight and quarrel with each other. To be specific, financial problems can lead to child abuse. When there are too many mouths to feed, parents feel the pressure and vent their anger on a child.

In this modern age where both parents are usually holding jobs, children are left with babysitters and nurseries. Abuse by these carers occur when there are too many children to be minded. Substance abuse is another factor which increases the incidents of child abuse. Under the influence of alcohol or drugs, a parent may not know what he or she may be doing. Or, rather, knows what he or she is doing but is not bothered at all. A drug addict may experience mood swings and is easily provoked by their children's minor errors. We see and read horrifying reports of a child being savagely tortured and dumped elsewhere, like garbage.

No matter what the reasons for the abuse, something must be done to stop the cruelty. If you suspect a child is suffering from abuse, it's important to speak out. By catching the problem as early as possible, both the child and the abuser are in better states to be helped.

Summarize the passage following the guidelines below.

⌐ Guidelines ⌐

- Summarize the above passage in one paragraph.
- Provide a topic sentence, supporting ideas, and a concluding sentence based on the passage.
- Do NOT copy more than FIVE consecutive words from the passage.

01 Read the passage and follow the directions. [4 points]

A woman who has campaigned for the legalisation of euthanasia has decided to starve herself to death because she can no longer cope with her debilitating heart and lung condition. Kelly Taylor, 28, who stopped eating more than two weeks ago, said her life had become so restricted that she "could not make any contribution to society". Her condition, Eisenmenger Syndrome, means she is dependent on oxygen and cannot walk more than a few steps without collapsing. She said she had chosen _____ because she believed it was a method of death that would not leave her husband Richard liable to prosecution for assisted suicide. She had considered travelling to a country where euthanasia was legal, but said she was concerned her husband would be prosecuted when he returned to Britain. She said, "My mind has been prepared for a long time. I do not want to continue with the life that I have got. It is so restricted. I do not contribute at all to society. That has been my biggest burden. I have never been able to work. I know I will never recover. My condition is slowly deteriorating. I considered going somewhere where euthanasia is legal and I could be given drugs to die but I know there will be legal implications for my husband. I could not let that happen."

Mrs Taylor's determination to take her life was reinforced during a holiday in Majorca when she was unable to join her husband and her parents in the sea. "I couldn't bear to watch them," she said. "I so wanted to get into the water but I knew I couldn't. I realised how much my quality of life had deteriorated and I couldn't bear to continue." In the days since she began her hunger protest, Mrs Taylor said she had lost a stone in weight. "When I started starving myself I didn't feel any different. By the third day my stomach was growling. I now feel weaker and need to sleep more. Of course I have the fear of dying but fear of living a life of prolonged pain is much more frightening. I don't think of it as a hunger strike or suicide but <u>more of giving nature a kick up the backside</u>." Mrs Taylor was born with the rare degenerative condition and has needed a wheelchair since she was a child. Those who have Eisenmenger Syndrome have a hole in the heart, which causes pressure in arteries in the lungs. She was on a waiting list for a heart and lung transplant for nine years. But she has now been told the risks are too high.

Fill in the blank with the ONE most appropriate word from the passage. If necessary, change the word form. Second, explain the meaning of the underlined words. Do Not copy more than FOUR consecutive words from the passage.

02 Read the passage and follow the directions. [4 points]

Archaeological records suggest we've been close with our pets for some time. About 10,000 years ago we started to co-habitate with cats drawn to the well-fed rodents scurrying around our farms. In ancient Egypt millions of pet dogs were buried in elaborate tombs adorned with expensive gifts and inscriptions. As a result, we've likely been swapping cuddles and microbial critters with domesticated animals for many generations.

Today those pets are clearly still at home in our homes. And plenty of headlines tout that beyond snuggles and companionship our four-legged friends offer other benefits — like improved mental and physical health.

But not so fast. A rash of recent research presents a more muddled picture of what pets bring into our lives — from microbe swaps that can alter our gut environment to emotional well-being.

First, let's talk allergies. Numerous works tell us that having a dog appears to reduce rates of pet allergies if _____ takes place very early in life. Many microbiome researchers believe those exposures to pets' microbial milieu during infancy — in the form of pet dander — may specifically train the immune system to deal with pets and other allergens. (The theory goes : without those early exposures to certain bugs and infectious agents the natural development of the immune system is essentially stunted.) But as one May 2017 study of thousands of kids and adults concludes, the timing of such exposures appears to be key. When first exposure occurs as a teen or young adult, risk of pet allergy actually appears to increase.

There's more bad news. Pets can also cause other problems. Lizards and turtles can carry salmonella. Parrots can carry the causative agent of psittacosis, which causes severe pneumonia in humans. And evidence has accrued that many of our furry friends can carry serious infectious agents including "superbug" MRSA, giardia, and other pathogens and parasites.

Even our modern understanding about the mental health benefits from pet ownership continues to evolve. For many decades there was widespread acceptance about the mental health benefits of unwinding with a pet. But that picture was complicated by a 2010 study of nearly 40,000 people in Sweden that found pet owners were physically healthier than those without pets yet they suffered from more mental health problems than their sans-pet peers. Now the science remains unsettled about who may benefit from pet ownership or even why such relationships could help.

Fill in the blank with the TWO most appropriate consecutive words from the passage. Second, explain how the understanding of mental health advantages from pet ownership has evolved. Do Not copy more than FOUR consecutive words from the passage.

_____

_____

_____

_____

_____

03 **Read the passage and follow the directions.** [4 points]

The first and the simplest emotion which we discover in the human mind, is curiosity. By curiosity, I mean whatever desire we have for, or whatever pleasure we take in, novelty. We see children perpetually running from place to place, to hunt out something new; they catch with great eagerness, and with very little choice, at whatever comes before them; their attention is engaged by everything, because everything has, in that stage of life, the charm of novelty to recommend it.

But as those things, which engage us merely by their novelty, cannot attach us for any length of time, curiosity is the most superficial of all the affections*. Curiosity changes its object perpetually; it has an appetite which is very sharp, but very easily satisfied; and it has always an appearance of giddiness, restlessness, and anxiety.

Curiosity, from its nature, is a very active principle. It quickly runs over the greatest part of its objects, and soon exhausts the variety which is commonly to be met with in nature. The same things make frequent returns, and they return with less and less of any agreeable effect. In short, the occurrences of life, by the time we come to know it a little, would be incapable of affecting the mind with any other sensations than those of loathing and weariness, if many things were not adapted to affect the mind by means of other powers besides novelty in them, and of other passions besides curiosity in ourselves.

But whatever these powers are, or upon what principle soever they affect the mind, it is absolutely necessary that they should not be exerted in those things which a daily and vulgar use have brought into a stale unaffecting* familiarity. Thus, some degree of _____ must be one of the materials in every instrument which works upon the mind; and curiosity blends itself more or less with all our passions.

affections : emotions
unaffecting : not evoking strong emotions

Fill in the blank with the ONE most appropriate word from the passage. Second, what appearance does curiosity have? Do Not copy more than THREE consecutive words from the passage.

_____

_____

_____

_____

_____

04 Read the passage and follow the directions. [4 points]

> At the height of the cold war, the *Daily Mirror* covered its entire front page with a rebuke addressed directly to Nikita Khruschev, the choleric, tantrum-throwing leader of the Soviet Union. In the largest type it could find, the newspaper roared : "If you'll excuse an old British expression, Mr K, don't be so bloody rude." The same words should now be addressed to the entire British population. They should shout at us from hoardings on busy roads, where motorists are actually getting out of their cars to kill each other, so unable are they to control their savage and manic rage, their determination to be first through the red traffic lights. They should be displayed outside and within all public buildings, on shop counters, on schoolyard gates, at bus and railway stations, above the bars of hotels and local drinking dens. Television stations should start every programme with the slogan : "Don't be so bloody rude." To this could be added, perhaps, the rider : "Rudeness makes life hell."
>
> Most people of all classes in Britain have stopped saying please and thank you to each other. <u>Children and adolescents stare at you in astonishment if you mention the omissions.</u> They consider these simple, yet so essential words archaic and obsequious. But the refusal to thank others for a service supplied or a favour done is the least damaging manifestation of coarse bloody-minded impoliteness. The way people disport themselves in public places is far more menacing, more detrimental to the national culture. Shoppers queue at supermarket food counters in smelly jogging kits. Pot-bellied oafs in T-shirts guzzle from bottles in fashionable bars. On trains, the behaviour of passengers is abominable. At one time, it was only oiks and tramps and Tory voters who plonked their muddy boots or shoes on the seating. Today executives in pinstripes, travelling first class, do it. Then there are the pop music fans. They are wearing head-sets, theoretically designed to confine the noise to their own stupid ears. But the wearers always turn up the volume to full blast to ensure that anyone within 20 yards can share the inane and maddening thump and clash from the drum section.

Nowadays, _____ has become a land of scowling, uncouth savages, elbowing one another in a social climate of selfishness, aggressiveness and perpetual unease.

Explain the meaning of the underlined words. Do Not copy more than FOUR consecutive words from the passage. Second, fill in the blank with the ONE most appropriate word from the passage.

_____

_____

_____

_____

05 Read the passage and follow the directions. [4 points]

When I'm acting, I get so focused that I'm only paying attention to one thing. Like when I'm on set and we're about to shoot and the first AD calls out "Rolling!" And then I hear "speed," "marker," "set," and then the director calls "Action!" I've heard that sequence so many times, like it's become this Pavlovian magic spell for me. "Rolling," "speed," "marker," "set" and "action." Something happens to me, I can't even help it. My attention ... narrows. And everything else in the world, anything else that might be bothering me or might grab my attention, it all goes away, and I'm just ... there. And that feeling, that is what I love, that, to me, is <u>creativity</u>. And that's the biggest reason I'm so grateful that I get to be an actor.

So, there's these two distinct powerful feelings. There's getting attention and paying attention. Of course, in the last decade or so, new technology has allowed more and more people to have this powerful feeling of getting attention. For any kind of creative expression, not just acting. It could be writing or photography or drawing, music — everything. The channels of distribution have been democratized, and that's a good thing.

But I do think there's an unintended consequence for anybody on the planet with an urge to be creative — myself included, because I'm not immune to this. I think that our creativity is becoming more and more of a means to an end. And so I feel compelled to speak up because in my experience, the more I go after that powerful feeling of paying attention, the happier I am. But the more I go after the powerful feeling of _____, the unhappier I am.

Describe what the writer defines as "creativity". Do Not copy more than FOUR consecutive words from the passage. Second, fill in the blank with the TWO most appropriate consecutive words from the passage.

_____

_____

_____

06 Read the passage and follow the directions. [4 points]

Psychology professor Lisa Barrett talks of the brain as a prisoner in a dark, silent box : the skull. The only information it gets about the outside world comes via changes in light (sight), air pressure (sound) exposure to chemicals (taste and smell), and so on. It doesn't know the causes of these changes, and so it has to guess at them in order to decide what to do next.

How does it do that? It compares those changes to similar changes in the past, and makes predictions about the current causes based on experience. Imagine you are walking through a forest. A dappled pattern of light forms a wavy black shape in front of you. You've seen many thousands of images of snakes in the past, you know that snakes live in the forest. Your brain has already set in train an array of predictions.

The point is that this prediction-making is consciousness, which you can think of as a constant rolling process of guesses about the world being either confirmed or proved wrong by fresh sensory inputs. In the case of the dappled light, as you step forward you get information that confirms a competing prediction that it's just a stick. That is, the prediction of a snake was ultimately disproved, but not before it grew so strong that neurons in your visual cortex fired as though one was actually there, meaning that for a split second you "saw" it. So we are all creating our world from moment to moment. If you didn't, your brain wouldn't be able make the changes necessary for your survival quickly enough. If the prediction "snake" wasn't already in train, then the shot of adrenaline you might need in order to jump out of its way would come too late.

The brain also receives information about heart rate, what the lungs are doing, the immune system, hormone levels and much more. "Interoception", the constant monitoring of the state of the body, carries on largely below the level of conscious awareness. But it is absolutely crucial because it determines affect — those feelings of pleasantness or unpleasantness, arousal or non-arousal that are always present, and which feed into our emotions.

The brain deals with inputs from the inside the same way it deals with ones from the outside — it _____ about what's causing these changes based on what it has learned, assigning them meaning in the process.

Explain the meaning of the underlined words. Do Not copy more than FOUR consecutive words from the passage. Second, fill in the blank with the TWO most appropriate consecutive words from the passage.

_____

_____

_____

_____

_____

07 Read the passage and follow the directions. [4 points]

Although leaders are often thought to be people with unusual personal ability, decades of research have failed to produce consistent evidence that there is any category of "natural leaders." It seems that there is no set of personal qualities that all leaders have in common; rather, virtually any person may be recognized as a leader if the person has qualities that meet the needs of that particular group.

Furthermore, although it is commonly supposed that social groups have a single leader, there are typically two different leadership roles that are held by different individuals. Instrumental leadership is leadership that emphasizes the completion of tasks by a social group. Group members look to instrumental leaders to "get things done." Expressive leadership, on the other hand, is leadership that emphasizes the collective well-beings of a social group's members. Expressive leaders are less concerned with the overall goals of the group than with providing emotional support to group members and attempting to minimize tension and conflict among them. Group members expect expressive leaders to maintain stable relationships within the group and provide support to individual members.

Instrumental leaders are likely to have a rather secondary relationship to other group members. They give orders and may discipline group members who inhibit attainment of the group's goals. Expressive leaders cultivate a more personal or primary relationship to others in the group. They offer sympathy when someone experiences difficulties or is subjected to discipline, are quick to lighten a serious moment with humor, and try to resolve issues that threaten to divide the group.

As the difference in these two roles suggests, expressive leaders generally receive more personal affection from group members; instrumental leaders, if they are successful in promoting group goals, may enjoy a more distant respect. Such as to say, understanding these differences is helpful when shaping a team relationship.

Summarize the passage following the guidelines below.

Guidelines

- Summarize the above passage in one paragraph.
- Provide a topic sentence, supporting ideas, and a concluding sentence based on the passage.
- Do NOT copy more than FIVE consecutive words from the passage.

_____

_____

_____

_____

_____

📖 모범답안 p.078

01 Read the passage and follow the directions. [4 points]

A credit score is a number that lenders use to assess the likelihood that a borrower will pay back a loan on time. Lenders use credit scores to decide, first, whether they will lend money to an individual, and second, at what interest rate. People with _____ will either be refused a loan or will have to pay higher rates of interest. Use of credit scores is pervasive, and if people apply for a car loan, auto insurance, a credit card, or a loan to buy a home, the lender will look at their credit scores before agreeing to extend credit.

There are two types of credit scores : generic scores and custom scores. Custom scores are developed by some individual lenders for use in their own companies. For example, a department store might develop its own custom credit scoring system to decide which customers will be approved for a store credit card. By contrast, generic scores are used by more than one company and are based on statistical models of the risk that a given person will not pay back a loan on time. Many stores and other businesses rely on generic credit scores in deciding to whom to offer credit. An individual with a median generic credit score or higher will typically get the most favorable rates on loans. For example, suppose a person wanted to get a mortgage to buy a home costing $250,000. Depending on the individual's credit score, the interest rate charged by the lender and the monthly payment for a 30-year mortgage would change. An analogous situation holds for other types of credit, such as car loans and credit cards. Additionally, insurance companies and utility companies use credit scores to set rates for their customers. Those with low credit scores are charged more.

Fill in the blank with the THREE most appropriate consecutive words from the passage. Second, what can be inferred to be the major determining factor influencing generic credit scores? Do NOT copy more than FOUR consecutive words from the passage.

02 Read the passage and follow the directions. [4 points]

Beer is not the break from politics that it is often touted to be. In fact, breweries have taken a stance on the controversial issues that have divided college campuses. Just recently, Alligator Brewing in Gainesville, Fla., attempted to empty a Richard Spencer talk by offering free beer to any customer who turned in a pair of unused tickets for his controversial event at the University of Florida. Alligator used beer to speak out against modern-day white supremacy, and in doing so built on a long history of using beer as a weapon against perceived oppression, whether from fringe groups or the government itself. Beer, like food, fosters democratic engagement. Creating and consuming beer has led to debates over morality, law, diversity and capitalism in the United States. And as a tool for political resistance, it has helped individuals express and safeguard their rights.

For centuries, beer has been more than a social lubricant. It has been a instrument of _____. Beer, in fact, was central to the founding of our country. Taverns were more common than churches in Colonial society. They were hubs of political and social life where people ate, drank, heard local news, argued about it, held public meetings and conducted business transactions. Consider, for example, Samuel Adams, a maltster who used Colonial drinking culture to generate support for independence. He used taverns around Boston to organize the Sons of Liberty and plan acts of political resistance against the British crown. So intertwined were watering holes and politics that between 1785 and 1790, when New York City was the capital of the fledgling United States, a Manhattan tavern housed the Departments of State, Treasury and War.

However, controlling alcohol, a substance which was considered healthy nourishment during this time, became a mechanism for imposing social control in the late 1700s. Laws regulated when, where and at what price beer and other alcohol could be sold, as well as whom a tavern could entertain. These were deliberate efforts by the governing elite to prevent intermingling between races and classes, control women's behavior.

> Beer continued to be both a tool of imposing social control and of political resistance throughout the 1800s. Temperance reformers viewed alcohol as the chief source of crime, poverty and insanity in society, and campaigned feverishly to reduce the nation's staggering alcohol intake which averaged more than twice what Americans consume today.

Fill in the blank with the TWO most appropriate consecutive words from the passage. Second, explain how alcohol was an instrument of imposing social control. Do NOT copy more than FOUR consecutive words from the passage.

03 Read the passage and follow the directions. [4 points]

The United States has historically had high levels of unintended fertility, with people having children earlier than they desired or when they didn't want children at all. Recent years have witnessed the first decline in such births in decades. Many men and women want children, but also have a preferred context for having children — they want to have completed education, established economic security and formed a stable partnership. Difficulties in meeting whatever markers they personally deem important might mean some people don't have children, but the fact that people are better empowered to manage their reproductive behaviors so that they only have children when they feel ready is a tremendous achievement. It benefits not only individuals, but future generations and society overall.

Current fertility declines both in the United States and around the world do not mean an "end of babies." Instead, people _____ having children until later in life, when they feel ready. Typical measures such as the total fertility rate don't do a good job of capturing delayed childbearing, but other measures show that childlessness is actually down, and most people end their childbearing years with about two children. Continued advances in reproductive technologies may continue to make it easier for those who delay childbearing to achieve their personal family preferences.

If helping people have the families they want is the goal, rather than trying to increase U.S. fertility out of misplaced panic about population decline, we need policies that address the direct difficulties in combining parenthood with education and employment, as well as the indirect obstacles to parenthood such as the student loan debt crisis, housing affordability, the high cost of health care and widespread income inequality. So if relatives pester you over Thanksgiving about when you're going to have children, or when they can next expect another grandchild, turn the question around : <u>Ask them when they plan to restructure the American economy</u>.

Explain why the total fertility rate measure has limitations. Second, fill in the blank with the ONE most appropriate word from the passage. Third, explain the meaning of the underlined words in the last sentence. Do NOT copy more than FOUR consecutive words from the passage.

_____

_____

_____

_____

_____

04 Read the passage and follow the directions. [4 points]

Human beings should be free to form opinions, and to express their opinions without reserve. Men should be free to act upon their opinions — to carry these out in their lives, without hindrance, either physical or moral, from their fellow men, so long as it is at their own risk and peril.

This proviso is of course indispensable. No one pretends that actions should be as free as opinions. On the contrary, even _____①_____ lose their immunity when the circumstances in which they are expressed are such as to constitute their expression a positive instigation to some mischievous act. An opinion that corn-dealers are starvers of the poor, or that private property is robbery, ought to be unmolested when simply circulated through the press, but may justly incur punishment when delivered orally to an excited mob assembled before the house of a corndealer, or when handed about among the same mob in the form of a placard.

Actions, of whatever kind, which, without justifiable cause, do harm to others, may be, and in the more important cases absolutely require to be, controlled by the unfavourable sentiments, and, when needful, by the active interference of mankind. The liberty of the individual must be thus far limited. He must not make himself a nuisance to other people. But if he refrains from molesting others in what concerns them, and merely acts according to his own inclination and judgment in things which concern himself, the same reasons which show that opinion should be free, prove also that he should be allowed, without molestation, to carry his opinions into practice at his own cost. That mankind are not infallible; that their truths, for the most part, are only half-truths; that unity of opinion, unless resulting from the fullest and freest comparison of opposite opinions, is not desirable, and diversity not an evil, but a good, until mankind are much more capable than at present of recognising all sides of the truth, are principles applicable to men's modes of action, not less than to their opinions.

As it is useful that while mankind are imperfect there should be different opinions, so it is that there should be different experiments of living; that free scope should be given to varieties of character, short of injury to others; and that the worth of different modes of life should be proved practically, when any one thinks fit to try them. It is desirable, in short, that in things which do not primarily concern _____②_____, individuality should assert itself.

Fill in each blank with the ONE most appropriate word from the passage respectively. Second, explain under which condition diversity is no longer acceptable. Do NOT copy more than FOUR consecutive words from the passage.

_____

_____

_____

_____

_____

05 Read the passage and follow the directions. [4 points]

A flurry of Hollywood trade-paper headlines greeted the news that Bong Joon-ho's *Parasite* had, in its fifth weekend of release, crossed the $10m threshold steadily rising as its screen count expands across the country. Ordinarily, that is hardly a figure that would have champagne corks popping in Tinseltown*, but the current market is a tough one for subtitled cinema : *Parasite*'s current haul is the year's highest for any non-English-language film in the US. (Last year's critically beloved, Cannes-approved Korean thriller, Lee Chang-dong's *Burning*, made a paltry $719,000 stateside).

Last year, Alfonso Cuarón's Netflix-backed Mexican memory piece *Roma* came close to doing what no non-English-language film has done before, in 91 long years of the Oscars : winning best picture. Entering the ceremony as the odds-on favourite, it made history by taking best director —another first for this eternally anglocentric institution—before being tripped up at the final hurdle by the safe, retrograde and emphatically all-American comforts of *Green Book*. In the largely disgruntled industry post-mortem that followed, pundits traded various theories about why Cuarón's more acclaimed film had lost.

Parasite is incrementally acquiring something that *Roma*, for all its doting reviews, never quite managed : genuine popular cachet, of the kind that can't be bought or fabricated, but can make a film's cultural footprint seem bigger than its box office. It began as early as Cannes, where hype for the film wasn't just generated by fawning reviews from the critical establishment, but a younger, very online and very vocal group of Generation Z cinephiles, who swiftly branded themselves the #BongHive and granted the film an immediate social-media presence even before it won the Palme, or began rolling out internationally.

Since then, *Parasite* has become a positive meme machine : if you haven't seen the film yet but are a regular on Twitter, you may have regularly encountered images and gifs from the film without even realising it. The "Jessica Jingle" — a brief chant delivered by one of the film's young characters to help remember her false identity, itself based on a standard memory aid for Korean schoolchildren — has been so widely appropriated by fans that it's now available as a mobile ringtone, the kind of inexplicable-out-of-context in-joke that signals a film's ascent to a phenomenon status worth far more than $10m.

It's rare for any non-American film to attain this kind of universal currency. That Bong's film neatly taps into a global well of class outrage has given it universal resonance for socially conscious young audiences, hungry for texts to feed their haves-versus-have-nots discourse amid global political disarray : *Parasite*'s class-based sympathies might be multi-generational, but it still cuts close to the bone for the "OK boomer*" crowd.

Tinseltown : Hollywood
OK boomer : a catchphrase used by young adults to criticize baby boomers

Explain why the writer of the passage mentions the movie *Burning* in the passage. Do NOT use more than FOUR consecutive words from the passage. Second, what aspect of *Parasite* would appeal to the "OK boomer" generation. Do NOT copy more than FOUR consecutive words from the passage.

06 Read the passage and follow the directions. [4 points]

Imagine that you're negotiating a multiyear deal to provide outsourcing services to a large company. The client tells you that her firm wants to sign on for a certain level of services, but she'd like you to be willing to deliver more on the fly*, trusting that you'll be able to work out terms for the additional resources as the need arises. Should you agree?

Or imagine that a potential business partner wants to buy $12 million worth of services from you but can spend only $10 million because of temporary budget constraints. He dangles the prospect of long-term revenue opportunities in exchange for the discount but says he can't commit to anything yet. Should you give him the deal?

Situations such as these present dilemmas for any manager. The answers aren't obvious. If you choose to trust new clients, contractors, or collaborators, you make yourself vulnerable : Your outcomes, financial and otherwise, now depend on their fidelity. But if you insist on verifying each claim and accounting for every detail before a deal is signed, you'll slow the process and increase costs, potentially putting yourself at a disadvantage.

The two scenarios above come from a friend of mine — let's call him Toni — who is a partner at one of the world's largest consulting firms. Although he agreed to both clients' proposals, the decisions to trust led to very different outcomes. The first client took Toni's assent as confirmation that she and her very large firm held the power in the relationship and could therefore dictate terms for future work. As time went on, she made it clear that if the increasingly unreasonable demands of the firm weren't met, it would simply move on to another, more willing provider. The second client, by contrast, proved trustworthy, and the long-term revenue it generated for Toni's company more than compensated for the _____ granted in the initial agreement.

Success in business unquestionably requires some willingness to cooperate with and have faith in others. The question is, how much faith and in whom? Decades of scientific research show that people's accuracy in deciding if another can be trusted tends to be only slightly better than chance.

on the fly : on the spot, improvised

Fill in the blank with the ONE most appropriate word from the passage. Second, describe the major drawbacks of verification and personal ability in regards to trusting others.

07 **Read the passage and follow the directions.** [4 points]

Caving, often referred to as spelunking or potholing, can be a fun, adventurous and rewarding activity; however, getting started in caving can be a challenge. You should make preparations for a caving exploration. If you do not, it can turn out to be a very horrifying experience.

Do not go exploring caves without knowing your exact way in and out. Getting lost in a cave is a very dangerous situation that can resemble your worst nightmare. If you do plan to enter a cave, make sure that you know the route. Also, limit your time in a cave to a maximum of eight hours. More than that and you will get very tired and be less alert. One kilogram of carbide will give enough illumination for approximately six to eight hours. If you are one of those with a weak heart condition or suffering from claustrophobia, you should limit yourself to just show caves.

It might be a good idea to bring along a drysuit which is made for cave dives or in cold water. The suit itself is made of a laminated waterproof material, with watertight latex seals at the neck and wrists. Pockets on either side can carry safety equipment. In addition, rope is needed for hand lines and vertical drops. For these, always consider the condition and storage methods of any rope before using it as a safety device. Rope protectors should be used as a cushion between rope and any surface which might abrade it.

Caving may be a once-in-a-lifetime thrill. But caves are delicate and potentially dangerous environments that can be permanently impacted or cause injury without the right preparation. The most common, and generally accepted standard process to start caving is to begin by finding a caving club near where you live, and attend a meeting, and express an interest in going on a "beginner" caving trip.

Write a summary following the guidelines below.

| Guidelines |

- Summarize the above passage in one paragraph.
- Provide a topic sentence, supporting ideas, and a concluding sentence based on the passage.
- Do NOT copy more than FIVE consecutive words from the passage.

01 Read the passage and follow the directions. [2 points]

Adapting a jealousy study used on 6-month-old human babies, Harris and colleague Caroline Prouvost set up experiments with 36 dogs in their homes. The team videotaped the dogs' reactions while their owners ignored them and instead paid attention to a stuffed animal that is a realistic-looking dog that whined, barked, and wagged its tail, a jack-o-lantern pail, and a pop-up book that they read aloud.

The resulting behaviors suggest the dogs assessed each "rival" and decided whether it warranted action. If it did, they did their best to break the bond that left them out.

More specifically, of the 36 dogs observed — a varied lot including a Boston terrier, Yorkshire terriers, chihuahuas, a pug, and mutts — 78 percent would push or touch the owner when that person was petting and sweet-talking the fake dog; 42 percent were upset over attention toward the pumpkin pail, and just 22 percent were bothered when the book was the focus.

Also telling, nearly a third of the dogs tried to place their bodies between the owner and the stuffed dog, and 25 percent snapped at the toy. Only one dog snapped at the pail and book. And 86 percent of the dogs sniffed the stuffed animal's rear end as they would a real dog. It appeared that the dogs saw the doglike interloper as a true threat.

That was a bit of a surprise. They weren't sure they would get such behaviors over a stuffed animal since it lacked the animation and smells of a real dog. Their reactions would have been even stronger had the rival been real. When confronted with a rival for a loved one's attention, dogs engage in behaviors aimed at regaining the rival's affection and getting rid of the rival. These behaviors would seem to be motivated from a jealous emotional state.

What is the main idea of the passage? Write down your answer by filling in the blank with ONE word from the passage. If necessary, you may change the form of the word.

Dogs get _____ like human beings.

02 Read the passage and follow the directions. [2 points]

Why do we Americans take off our hats when we meet a flapper on the street, and yet stand covered before a male of the highest eminence? A Continental would regard this last as boorish to the last degree; in greeting any equal or superior, male or female, actual or merely conventional, he lifts his head-piece. Why does it strike us as ludicrous to see a man in dress clothes before 6 P.M.? The Continental puts them on whenever he has a solemn visit to make, whether the hour be six or noon. Why do we regard it as indecent to tuck the napkin between the waistcoat buttons — or into the neck — at meals? The Frenchman does it without thought of crime. So does the Italian. So does the German. All three are punctilious men — far more so, indeed, than we are. Why do we snicker at the man who wears a wedding ring? Most Continentals would stare askance at the husband who didn't. Why is it bad manners in Europe and America to ask a stranger his or her age, and a friendly attention in China? Why do we regard it as absurd to distinguish a woman by her husband's title — e.g., Mrs. Judge Jones, Mrs. Professor Smith? In Teutonic and Scandinavian Europe, on the contrary, the _____ would be looked upon as an affront.

Fill in the blank with appropriate FOUR words.

03 Read the passage and follow the directions. [2 points]

In the mid-1980s, the administrator of a residential care facility in California received a letter from a nearby university hospital, where his elderly residents typically went for medical attention. The letter reminded him that five of his residents had recently had surgery at the hospital. It also informed him that the medical staff suspected that some of the blood used in their transfusions may have been tainted with the HIV virus. While making it clear that the probabilities of infection were low, the letter asked him to call the hospital immediately and arrange further testing for these five.

That letter, he recalled, presented him with a stark and direct question : What should he tell, and to whom should he tell it? Given the public and professional ignorance about AIDS — this was the mid-1980s, when the disease was little understood and legal regulations offered him no clear guidance — he felt certain that, if he told his staff, their fear would be so great that they would refuse to enter the rooms of those five, making it impossible to deliver even minimal care to them. But suppose he did not tell the staff and one of them contracted AIDS : Surely he would be culpable.

As it happened, none of the five ultimately tested positive. But that crucial fact was unknown at the time. What was he to do? He knew it was right to honor the individual rights of each of those five residents — the privacy of their medical histories, the expectation of high-quality care at his facility, their dignity as individuals. It was right, in other words, to say nothing.

On the other hand, he knew it was right to protect the community from disease. The staff had not signed on for hazardous duty. Most of them saw themselves as unskilled hourly workers, not members of a life-endangering profession to which they had been called by noble duty and prepared by intensive training. Never mind that they might all phone in sick the day after the announcement : They deserved protection so they could continue to deliver care, with full regard for safety, to the many other residents who were not among the five. So it was right to tell them.

Fill in each blank with ONE or TWO word(s) from the passage respectively.
If necessary, you may change the form(s) of the word(s).

The writer deals with ethical dilemmas in protecting ____ⓐ____ versus
protecting ____ⓑ____ safety.

📖 모범답안 p.081

01   **Read the passage and follow the directions.** [2 points]

> Over the past two decades, discoveries in China have produced at least five species of feathered dinosaurs. But they all belonged to the theropod group of "raptor" dinosaurs, ancestors of modern birds. Now in a discovery the new dinosaur species, Kulindadromeus zabaikalicus, suggests that feathers were all in the animal. That's because the newly unearthed 4.5-foot-long two-legged runner was an ornithischian beaked dinosaur*, belonging to a group ancestrally distinct from past theropod discoveries.
>
> It's really fantastic that dinosaurs with fluff are found outside of China. The material and specimens are nothing short of fantastic; their age and sheer number are rarely to be expected. Kulindadromeus adds a whole new dimension to understanding feather evolution.
>
> During the Jurassic, Kulindadromeus lived near what is now Siberia's Kulinda River, sporting feathery tufts on its legs and elbows, as well as more streamlined feathers on its back. Its shins had "ribbon-shaped" feathers of a type never seen before.
>
> At least six skulls of the species, along with hundreds of bones, have turned up in a fossil bed that was once a lake bottom and is now a Siberian hillside. Most of the fossils were juveniles, which suggests that they died in single events, not in a mass catastrophe.
>
> The dinosaur's name essentially means "Kulinda River running dinosaur." Zabaikalsky Krai is the region of Siberia where it was discovered which explains its species name, zabaikalicus.
>
> *ornithischian dinosaur : herbivorous dinosaur with a pelvis like that of a bird*

What is the main idea of the passage? Write down your answer by filling in each blank with ONE word from the passage respectively. If necessary, you may change the form(s) of the words.

Siberian discovery suggests almost all ____ⓐ____ were covered in ____ⓑ____ .

02 Read the passage and follow the directions. [2 points]

> Just before the beginning of World War II, Albert Einstein wrote a letter to President Franklin D. Roosevelt. Urged by Hungarian-born physicists Leo Szilard, Eugene Wingner, and Edward Teller, Einstein told Roosevelt about Nazi-German efforts to purify Uranium-235 which might be used to build an atomic bomb. [A] Shortly after that the United States Government began work on the Manhattan Project. It was the code name for the United States effort to develop the atomic bomb before the Germans did. [B] The first successful experiments in splitting a uranium atom had been carried out in the autumn of 1938 at the Kaiser Wilhelm Institute in Berlin. So the race was on. [C] It turned out to be the biggest development in warfare and science's biggest development in the last century. The most complicated issue to be addressed by the scientists working on 'it' was the production of ample amounts of 'enriched' uranium to sustain a chain reaction. [D] Ernest O. Lawrence (inventor of the Cyclotron) at the University of California in Berkeley implemented a process involving magnetic separation of the two isotopes. Finally, a gas centrifuge was used to further separate the Uranium-235 from the Uranium-238. [E]

Where is the best place for the following <A> to be inserted?

A

> At the time, Uranium-235 was hard to extract. No ordinary chemical extraction could separate the two isotopes. Only mechanical methods could effectively separate U-235 from U-238.

03 **Read the passage and follow the directions.** [2 points]

I come to a matter which touches the individual more intimately : I mean the question of propagation. It has hitherto been considered that any man and woman not within the prohibited degrees have a right to marry, and having married have a right, if not a duty, to have as many children as nature may decree. This is a right which the scientific society of the future is not likely to tolerate. In any given state of industrial and agricultural technique there is an optimum density of population which ensures a greater degree of material well-being than would result from either an increase or a diminution of numbers.

As a general rule, except in new countries, the density of population has been beyond this optimum. Except where there is property to be inherited, the member of a small family suffers almost as much from overpopulation as the member of a large family. Those who cause ____ⓐ____ are therefore doing an injury not only to their own children, but to the community. It may therefore be assumed that society will discourage them if necessary, as soon as religious prejudices no longer stand in the way of such action.

The same question will arise in a more dangerous form as between different nations and different races. If a nation finds that it is losing military superiority through a lower ____ⓑ____ than that of a rival, it may attempt, as has already been done in such cases, to stimulate its own birth-rate; but when this proves ineffective, as it probably will, there will be a tendency to demand a limitation in the birth-rate of the rival nation.

Fill in each blank with ONE word from the passage. If necessary, change the form(s) of the words.

01 Read the passage and follow the directions. [2 points]

Compared with 13 other mammal species, African elephants have the most genes related to smell : 2,000. That's the most ever discovered in an animal — more than twice the number of olfactory genes in domestic dogs and five times more than in humans, who have about 400. The previous record-holder was rats, which have about 1,200 genes dedicated to smell.

We don't know the real reason, but it's likely related to the importance of smell to the poorly sighted African elephant in interpreting and navigating its environment. For instance, smell is a crucial sense for the functioning of an elephant trunk, which acts like a hand as it grips food and other objects. They use olfaction to quest the outer world, which may drive their superior sense of smell.

A group of scientists ran a special computer program that identified the elephant's 2,000 olfactory genes. In doing so, they also wanted to get a better understanding of the function of these genes. Their analysis revealed that over the course of evolution, one ancient gene dedicated to smell has created as many as 84 additional genes that the animals likely use to detect odors specific to their environment — for instance, the smell of certain foods on the savanna.

Maasai men spear elephants to show their virility, while Kamba people are agricultural and give little threat to them; therefore, elephants are afraid of Maasai men. If the wind is blowing in the correct direction, elephants can pick up the scent of humans from over a kilometer away or detect and find the exact location of a tiny sliver of banana from over 50 meters away. By sniffing urine-soaked soil, elephants can discriminate between and keep track of the location of family members.

Summarize the passage by filling in each blank with ONE word from the passage. If necessary, you may change the form(s) of each word.

African elephants, which have 2,000 genes for smell, have such an incredible ____ⓐ____ for detecting odors that they can distinguish between the ____ⓑ____ of two ethnic groups : the Maasai and the Kamba.

02 Read the passage and follow the directions. [2 points]

From the beginning of civilization until the Industrial Revolution, a man could, as a rule, produce by hard work little more than was required for the subsistence of himself and his family, although his wife worked at least as hard as he did, and his children added their labor as soon as they were old enough to do so. The small surplus above bare necessaries was not left to those who produced it, but was appropriated by warriors and priests.

In times of famine there was no surplus; the warriors and priests, however, still secured as much as at other times, with the result that many of the workers died of hunger. This system persisted in Russia until 1917, and still persists in the East; in England, in spite of the Industrial Revolution, it remained in full force throughout the Napoleonic wars, and until a hundred years ago, when the new class of manufacturers acquired power. In America, the system came to an end with the Revolution, except in the South, where it persisted until the Civil War.

A system which lasted so long and ended so recently has naturally left a profound impress upon men's thoughts and opinions. Much that we take for granted about the desirability of work is derived from this system, and, being pre-industrial, is not adapted to the modern world. Modern technique has made it possible for leisure, within limits, to be not the prerogative of small privileged classes, but a right evenly distributed throughout the community. The morality of work is the morality of slaves, and the modern world has no need of slavery.

Describe the main idea of the passage by filling in each blank with ONE or TWO word(s) from the passage. If necessary, you may change the form of each word.

We should expel the concept of the desirability of work, which is just the morality of ____ⓐ____ . That concept is not adapted to the ____ⓑ____ that does not need slavery any more.

03 Read the passage and follow the directions. [5 points]

One says justice means maximizing utility or welfare — the greatest happiness for the greatest number. The second says justice means respecting freedom of choice — either the actual choices people make in a free market (the libertarian view) or the hypothetical choices people would make in an original position of equality (the liberal egalitarian view). The third says justice involves cultivating virtue and reasoning about the common good. As you've probably guessed by now, I favor a version of the third approach. Let me try to explain why. The utilitarian approach has two defects : First, it makes justice and rights a matter of calculation, not principle. Second, by trying to translate all human goods into a single, uniform measure of value, it flattens them, and takes no account of the qualitative differences among them. The freedom-based theories solve the first problem but not the second. They take rights seriously and insist that justice is more than mere calculation. Although they disagree among themselves about which rights should outweigh utilitarian considerations, they agree that certain rights are fundamental and must be respected. But beyond singling out certain rights as worthy of respect, they accept people's preferences as they are. They don't require us to question or challenge the preferences and desires we bring to public life. According to these theories, the moral worth of the ends we pursue, the meaning and significance of the lives we lead, and the quality and character of the common life we share all lie beyond the domain of justice. This seems to me mistaken. A just society can't be achieved simply by maximizing utility or by securing freedom of choice. To achieve a just society we have to reason together about the meaning of the good life, and to create a public culture hospitable to the disagreements that will inevitably arise. It is tempting to seek a principle or procedure that could justify, once and for all, whatever distribution of income or power or opportunity resulted from it. Such a principle, if we could find it, would enable us to avoid the tumult and contention that arguments about the good life invariably arouse. But these arguments are impossible to avoid. Justice is inescapably judgmental.

Describe THREE prevalent approaches to Justice and explain the writer's proposal to achieve a society of justice. When you answer each question, do NOT copy more than SEVEN consecutive words from the passage.

_____

_____

_____

_____

_____

04 Read the passage and follow the directions. [4 points]

Society is losing its odor integrity. Some enterprising souls are actually marketing aerosol cans filled with the aromas of pizza, new cars, anything that might enhance people to buy something they would otherwise not. From the inexhaustible engine of commerce have come Aroma Discs, which when warmed in a special container (only $22.60) emit such scents as Passion, Fireplace and Alter Dinner Mints. And, in what may be the odor crime of the century, a company in Ohio is selling a cherry-scented garden hose.

I may seem like a weird curmudgeon looking for something new to complain about, but it's only the fake smells I don't like, the ones that are meant to fool you. This is a dangerous business because the human nose is emotional and not very bright. Inside the brain, smell seems snuggled right up to the centers for cooking, sex and memory.

I recently discovered a substance whose odor stimulates my memory of childhood like nothing else : Crayola crayons. I don't expect you to experience the effect of this odor memory just by thinking about crayons, since most people can't recall smells the way they can recall pictures or sounds. But once you get a good whiff of waxy crayon odor, the bells of childhood will ring. Go out and buy a box. Get your nose right down on the crayons and inhale deeply. Pull that crayon smell right up into the old reptile brain. You'll be flooded with a new-crayon, untouched-coloring-book feeling — you're young, the world is new, the next thing you know your parents may bring home a puppy.

The smell is part of our culture in the same class as the Howdy Doody* song. Long after my daughters have stopped drawing with crayons, they will have in their brains, as I do now, the subconscious knowledge that if you smell stearic acid* — the major component in the smell of Crayola crayons — you're able to have a good time.

We're responsible for what posterity will smell, and like to smell. If we're not careful, we may end up with a country in which everyone thinks garden hoses are supposed to smell like cherries.

* Howdy Doody : an American children's television program (with circus and Western frontier themes) that was created and produced by E. Roger Muir and telecast on the NBC network in the United States.
* stearic acid : a saturated fatty acid with an 18-carbon chain

Describe the main idea of the passage and explain why the writer believes "we may end up with a country in which everyone thinks garden hoses are supposed to smell like cherries." When you answer each question, do not copy more than SIX consecutive words from the passage.

01 **Read the passage and follow the directions.** [2 points]

In contrast to the terrible casualty rates for both Union and Confederate soldiers, and the economic devastation and heritage of slavery of the South, it might well have looked that the American West had won, at the least, the war of public perception. The eastern United States appeared to be the wounded and injured region, while the West, by contrast, appeared as the region of promise and hope.

In the years after the Civil War, a giant enterprise in romanticizing the West found tremendous success. The commercial structure of mass publication — encapsulated in dime novels — needed content. A romanticized image of the West as a place of adventure, opportunity and equality provided an endless resource for a literature and art of escape. Emerging as the region where the nation's innocence and idealism had taken refuge, the West came out of the Civil War with a triumphant make-over in the world's imagination.

The historical record was not, however, a match with the West's mythic appeal. The Civil War years in the West was punctuated by grim episodes in Indian relations. Six months before the battle at Gettsyburg, the year 1863 opened with a terrible massacre, by U.S. troops, of Shoshone people at Bear River, in northern Utah Territory. Through the year 1863, Kit Carson carried on his campaign against the Navajo people, relocating them in the brutal Long Walk in 1864. At Sand Creek in Colorado Territory, on Nov, 29, 1864, a militia attacked a camp of Cheyenne and Arapaho people, who had been led to believe that they had surrendered to the Army.

Describe the main idea of the passage by filling in each blank with ONE word from the passage. If necessary, you may change the form(s) of each word.

The American West had won the war of public perception as a(n) ___(a)___ place of innocence and idealism, but the historical record did not match such a mythology. The West was the location of the bloody ___(b)___ of Native Americans.

---

02 Read the passage and follow the directions. [2 points]

In the late 1960s, the psychologist Stanley Milgram conducted an experiment to find an answer to a question : how are human beings connected? Milgram's idea was to test this question with a chain letter. He got the names of 160 people who lived in Omaha, Nebraska, and mailed each of them a packet. In the packet was the name and address of a stockbroker who worked in Boston and lived in Sharon, Massachusetts. Each person was instructed to write his or her name on the packet and send it on to a friend or acquaintance who he or she thought would get the packet closer to the stockbroker. If you lived in Omaha and had a cousin outside of Boston, for example, you might send it to him, on the grounds that — even if your cousin did not himself know the stockbroker — he would be a lot more likely to be able to get to the stockbroker in two or three or four steps. The idea was that when the packet finally arrived at the stockbroker's house, Milgram could look at the list of all those whose hands it went through to get there and establish how closely connected someone chosen at random from one part of the country was to another person in another part of the country. Milgram found that most of the letters reached the stockbroker in five or six steps. This experiment is where we get the concept of six degrees of separation.

Most of us don't have particularly broad and diverse groups of friends. In one well-known study, a group of psychologists asked people living in the Dyckman public housing project in northern Manhattan to name their closest friend in the project; 88 percent of the friends lived in the same building, and half lived on the same floor. In general, people chose friends of similar age and race. But if the friend lived down the hall, then age and race became a lot less important.

Another study found that we're friends with the people we do things with. We don't seek out friends, in other words. We associate with the people who occupy the same small, physical spaces that we do. People in Omaha are not, as a rule, friends with people who live halfway across the country in Sharon, Massachusetts.

Complete the conclusion of the two recent studies by rearranging the words given in the box below. Use ALL and ONLY the words in the box. The first word is given.

similarity	with others	physical
proximity	people	choose
overpowers	their relationships	

When _____

03 Read the passage and follow the directions. [2 points]

The term "chronic Lyme disease" is used by a some practitioners to diagnose patients with a variety of long-lasting symptoms such as fatigue, without any evidence of infection from the Lyme-causing bacteria, Borrelia burgdorferi. [1] Providing objective evidence of Borrelia burgdorferi infection is not required to diagnose "chronic Lyme disease" because of the spurious reasoning that laboratory tests are too insensitive, despite the presumption that the patients have a "chronic" infection. [2] If the patient feels better after antibiotic treatment, it is considered a confirmation of the Lyme diagnosis. And if the patient feels worse the antibiotic treatment is, again, considered a confirmation of the diagnosis. [3] There is no doubt that persons labeled as having "chronic Lyme disease" are indeed suffering. The question is what the real cause of it is and what can be done about it. [4] We are unaware of any controlled trials that demonstrate the efficacy of antibiotics for patients with medically unexplained symptoms, and find no rationale for why antibiotics would be beneficial for such persons. [5] Allergic and toxic reactions, intravenous line infections, sepsis, and Clostridium difficile infections — any of which can be life threatening — should be of significant concern to these patients.

Where is the best place for the following <A> to be inserted in coherent terms?

A

Additionally, antibiotic therapy is not without serious risks.

04 Read the passage and follow the directions. [4 points]

The Oregon Legislature recently approved a bill that would allow students to attend its state colleges for free if they agree to repay the state about 3 percent of their future earnings over roughly 20 years. The proposal for students paying for their college education after graduation is intriguing. I have long advocated "human capital contracts" where students sell "equity" in themselves, giving up a share of future income in return for college financing. Oregon deserves kudos for thinking outside the box. But the idea has limitations as well.

First, students who anticipate receiving high paying jobs would steer away from this financing, leaving a pool of individuals with relatively low earnings prospects. It would be popular among prospective social workers, and dance and anthropology majors, but not those in electrical engineering or math. Also, since funds repaying Oregon for the education would not begin flowing in for many years, the cost of funding such a proposal would be substantial. For example, if 200,000 of Oregon's 320,000 public college students signed up for the program in its first five years and used on average $20,000 on education, some $4 billion would have to be committed before payback began, over $1,000 for every resident of the state. That probably explains Oregon's cautious approach, starting with a pilot project.

A more successful approach would vary the percent and length of the payback on the investment with the student prospects for financial success, as measured by probability of, say, successfully completing a degree (as predicted by high school grades and ACT/SAT test scores) and the earnings experience of the student's major.

The writer argues that Oregon's tuition plan is compelling, but it is less financially viable. Explain two reasons why the plan is not financially feasible.

_____

_____

_____

05 Read the passage and follow the directions. [4 points]

These people who link us up with the world and introduce us to our social circles — these people on whom we rely more heavily than we realize — are Connectors. Connectors know lots of people. They are the kinds of people who know everyone. All of us know someone like this. But I don't think that we spend a lot of time thinking about the importance of these kinds of people. I'm not even sure that most of us really believe that the kind of person who knows everyone really knows everyone. But they do.

There is a simple way to show how social we are. There is a list of around 250 surnames, all taken at random from the Manhattan phone book. Go down the list and give yourself a point every time you see a surname that is shared by someone you know. Multiple names count. If the name is Johnson, in other words, and you know three Johnsons, you get three points.

I have given this test to various groups of people. One was a freshman at City College in Manhattan. The students were all in their late teens or early twenties, many of them recent immigrants to America, and of middle and lower income. The average score in that class was 20.96, meaning that the average person in the class knew 21 people with the same last names as the people on my list. I also gave the test to a group of health educators and academics at a conference in Princeton, New Jersey. This group were mostly in their forties and fifties, highly educated, and wealthy. Their average score was 39. These results shouldn't be all that surprising.

Identify the purpose of the test done by the writer of the passage. Second, what can we infer from the writer's saying "These results shouldn't be all that surprising"?

_____

_____

_____

_____

_____

📖 모범답안 p.085

01 **Read the passage and follow the directions.** [2 points]

When, in 2011, Oprah Winfrey asked Ralph Lauren how he "keeps reinventing," Mr. Lauren answered : "You copy. Forty-five years of copying; that's why I'm here." Mr. Lauren, a Jewish kid from the Bronx who built a spectacular career reinterpreting the look of the old WASP aristocracy, was at least partly joking. But what made the quip funny was the fact that knockoffs are — and always have been — a pervasive part of fashion.

During the Depression, New York apparel houses were famed for their copying; as Time magazine noted in 1936, "a dress exhibited in the morning at $60 would be duplicated at $25 before sunset and at lower prices later in the week."

For 75 years, fashion has been an industry prone to mistaken predictions of its own demise. During World War II, the fashion designer Maurice Rentner declared that the quick copying of designs would "write finis" to the dress industry. And for decades after the war, fashion insiders have predicted that everything from trans-Atlantic air travel and fax machines to computer-aided design and digital photography would speed copying and destroy their business.

But though the fashion industry has repeatedly tried to convince Congress to ban copying to no avail, the sky has yet to fall.

That's because the New York fashion industry has not only survived piracy, it has thrived specifically because of piracy. Every time a new design is widely copied, fashion's most powerful marketing force kicks in : the trend. As a design is copied, it spreads through — and usually down — the market. That makes the design less attractive to early adopters, who seek distinction, not diffusion, in their looks. As they move on, designers are ready with new creations, some of which are then copied, creating a new trend.

Describe the main idea of the passage by filling in each blank with **ONE** word from the passage. If necessary, you may change the form(s) of each word.

___ⓐ___ fuels the New York fashion industry. Copying makes ___ⓑ___, which sell fashion.

02 Read the passage and follow the directions. [2 points]

> Anonymity on the web plays a precarious role in the ways we interact with each other. Some interactions justify, and are even strengthened by, anonymity —but it often comes with a huge price tag for marginalized communities on the web, leaving women and people of color to pick up the tab.
>
> Vulnerable communities on the web often find themselves the biggest targets of anonymous trolling. Recently, a group from the popular Internet forum 4chan launched a trolling mission to harass and intimidate black feminists by hijacking hashtags they use on Twitter and posing as feminists on fake accounts that would send embarrassing tweets. Anonymous apps like Secret have played host to sexist conversations about women who work in technology. And teenagers, who are often ill-equipped to handle bullying even by named peers, are consistently the victims of anonymous bullying made possible by apps and social media.
>
> App and platform makers show a glaring lack of empathy and a poor understanding of their role in the culture. Platforms like Twitter provide very little defense for those who are hurt the most by anonymous communication. There is an obvious connection between the weak tools that are barely implemented to combat online harassment and the fact that most of the engineers and designers who make the software are not members of marginalized communities. In fact, they profit from the abuse by continuously allowing abusive users to operate.

Write down the main idea that the writer is conveying in the passage by filling in each blank with ONE word from the passage.

> Marginalized communities become _____ⓐ_____ of attack online. The makers of technology _____ⓑ_____ from their creations by allowing abusers to operate.

03 Read the passage and follow the directions. [2 points]

Traditional Chinese education was, in some respects, very similar to that of Athens in its best days. Athenian boys were made to learn Homer by heart from beginning to end; Chinese boys were made to learn the Confucian classics with similar thoroughness.

[1] Athenians were taught a kind of reverence for the gods which consisted in outward observances, and placed no barrier in the way of free intellectual speculation.

[2] The Greeks devoted their energies to art and science and mutual extermination, in all of which they achieved unprecedented success. When a politician was ousted, he led a band of exiles to attack his native city. When a Chinese official was disgraced, he retired to the hills and wrote poems on the pleasures of country life.

[3] There were, however, great differences between the two civilizations, owing to the fact that, broadly speaking, the Greeks were energetic and the Chinese were lazy.

[4] Similarly, the Chinese were taught certain rites connected with ancestor-worship, but were by no means obliged to have the beliefs which the rites would seem to imply. An easy and elegant scepticism was the attitude expected of an educated adult : anything might be discussed, but it was a trifle vulgar to reach very positive conclusions.

Rearrange the sentences in order to complete the passage. The first part is given.

04 Read the passage and follow the directions. [4 points]

> The assassination of Julius Caesar on the steps of the Capitol in Rome is one of history's most dramatic events. Many other Roman rulers met similar fates, but Caesar's death has always had a particularly powerful hold on the imagination. This is why Shakespeare wrote *Julius Caesar*. Remember the way he is killed : he is stabbed by some of his closest supporters and friends, notably Brutus. He is betrayed at the entrance to the building which symbolizes his power (the British equivalent today might be the Houses of Parliament). He is killed in public. We respond to these details so strongly because we imagine them to be some of the deepest insecurities of tyrants : a sudden, exposed, humiliating overthrow. Put another way, the event satisfies our own deep doubts about tyrannical power. Myths and legends are ways in which cultures tell stories about themselves in pleasurable forms in order to try to resolve very deep tensions and uncertainties. This 'deep structure' is like the mind's unconscious which contains the hidden, antisocial desires of infancy. Although these desires have been locked away, they are constantly attempting to break through into our conscious life and therefore need regulating. Freud believed dreams served this function, but myths and literature were also ways in which the hidden could 'return' in socially acceptable forms. A story can be endlessly recycled, endlessly experienced, endlessly reproduced. In reading or seeing *Julius Caesar* we can experience unconsciously our desire to rebel against authority, the political equivalent of a parent figure.

In what aspect do myths and literature serve the same function as dreams? Also, why do people respond to the assassination of Julius Caesar so strongly? When you answer each question, do NOT copy more than SIX consecutive words from the passage.

_____

_____

_____

_____

05 Read the passage and follow the directions. [4 points]

Here's a novel recipe for raising successful kids : see that they're born overseas, but bring them to America before they hit their teens. That, at least, is the implication of a new study by sociologists at Johns Hopkins University who tracked 10,795 adolescents into young adulthood. Basically, the sociologists found that the immigrant teens beat the pants off native born children in academic achievement and, as adults, psychological well-being. American born children of immigrants also seemed to enjoy an advantage. The researchers adjusted for socioeconomic background and school conditions, so they were comparing apples to apples. Looking at kids 13-17, the researchers focused on the level of difficulty in the students' math and science classes, as well as the proportion of courses each passed. In turning to adults 25 to 32, the sociologists looked at years of schooling and highest academic degree attained. They assessed general psychological well-being using a scale of five items, such "not feeling socially isolated" and "able to control things." Given that a quarter of American children are the offspring of immigrants, the study's findings have positive implications for the U.S. workforce in the years ahead, at least as far as the role of immigrants is concerned. The authors suggest the immigrant kids derive inspiration and a sense of community from their families and fellow immigrants.

According to the researchers, why did the immigrant children turn out so well compared to their socioeconomic peers? Do NOT copy more than SIX consecutive words from the passage.

_____

_____

_____

_____

_____

01 Read the passage and follow the directions. [2 points]

The Hawthorne experiments and related endeavors on group dynamics produced momentous insights about the importance of social and psychological factors in the workplace. They lay emphasis on the social dimensions of organization — such concerns as group relations, worker autonomy, human needs and personal recognition — presented a major upset to classical management theory. With new insights into human behaviors at work, the longstanding view of "paying the right rate for the job" was found wanting.

The Hawthorne experiment was conducted in the late 1920s and early 1930s. The management of Western Electric's Hawthorne Plant, located near Chicago, wanted to find out if environmental factors such as lightning, could affect workers' productivity and morale. A team of social scientists experimented with a small group of employees who were set apart form their coworkers. The environmental conditions of this group's work area were controlled, and the subjects themselves were closely observed. To the great surprise of the researchers, the productivity of these workers increased in response to any change in their environmental conditions. The rate of work increased even when the change (such as sharp decrease in the level of light in the workplace) seemed unlikely to have such an effect. It was concluded that the presence of the observers had caused the workers in the experimental group to feel special. As a result, the employees came to know and trust one another, and they developed a strong belief in the importance of their job.

Write down the suggestion the Hawthorne experiment makes by rearranging the seven words in the box.

more	are/is	attitudes	than
important		environment	workers'

Workers' _____

02 **Read the passage and follow the directions.** [2 points]

In general, economists cannot find hard empirical constants because economists are not studying the immutable rules of nature. They have to deal with the _____ⓐ_____ generalizations that govern human behavior. Being social scientists, they study human beings and their reactions. And being adaptable animals, human beings change their basic behavior patterns in response to events. Such an example would involve something known as Okun's Law. For years, this forumla predicted the changes in unemployment that would result from any given growth in the gross national product. Any such relationship, however, depends upon a steady rate of growth of productivity. If productivity growth decelerates, less output will be necessary to generate a given number of jobs. Consequently, shifts in the long-term trends in productivity growth must induce shifts in the relationships between production (G.N.P.) and labor demands.

As America's productivity growth rate fell from more than 3 percent per year before 1965 to essentially zero after 1977, Okun's Law became less and less accurate until it was dropped as a tool of analysis entirely. Meanwhile, physicists have not had to deal with any change in the speed of light. "What should we do about problem X?" (where X may be inflation, productivity, unemployment, or some other public problem) is a question commonly posed and answered by economists. But it is a question designed to produce disagreement. The issues are only partly technical; the rest involves value judgments. Should America raise unemployment to stop inflation? Different economists have different answers, even if they agree technically on the distribution of gains and losses from an increase in unemployment. To find professional economic disagreements, a different question must be asked. Liberal and conservative economists most frequently disagree on who 'should' be hurt and who 'should' be helped. Their _____ⓑ_____ disagreements on who will be hurt and who will be helped are much less frequent.

Fill in each blank with ONE word from the passage. If necessary, you may change the form(s) of each word.

---

03 Read the passage and follow the directions. [2 points]

An estimated 3.5 million Arab Americans live in the U.S. What would you say, about 3 million are terrorists? Well, half anyway. Why wouldn't you think that? Why wouldn't it be in the minds of knee-jerk TV newscasters who reported immediately after the 1995 Oklahoma City bombing that the FBI was seeking three males, two of them "Middle Eastern with dark hair and beards"? Why wouldn't the security officers who ejected Abdullah Al-Arian from the White House annex think it too? Al-Arian is the Duke University student and congressional intern who was there for a meeting with Muslim leaders

You know, the shadowy guys we see again and again in movies and on TV. Because there are no other Arabs, right? Except, that is, for harem girls and bearded, limousined, oil-rich sheiks in dark glasses, wielding their billions like spiked clubs. With violent conflict between Israelis and Palestinians again raging in the Middle East, their media images assume even greater weight and loom especially large. It's hard telling which side is winning the crucial public relations duel in the news, as bitter charges fly back and forth between these Jews and Arabs, each blaming the other for fomenting violence in the most recent intifada, estimated to have killed more than 600 in the last 10 months, mostly Palestinians.

Caring Americans wring their hands over stereotypes in the U.S. that haunt people of color. Just as nasty, though, is the stigma that usually goes unmentioned.

What is the main idea of the passage? Write your answer by filling the blank below with ONE word from the passage. If necessary, you may change the form(s) of each word.

Negative _____ enhanced by mass media distorts Arabs' images.

04 **Read the passage and follow the direction.** [4 points]

Whenever a person who already has enough to live on proposes to engage in some everyday kind of job, such as school-teaching or typing, he or she is told that such conduct takes the bread out of other people's mouths, and is therefore wicked. If this argument were valid, it would only be necessary for us all to be idle in order that we should all have our mouths full of bread. What people who say such things forget is that what a man earns he usually spends, and in spending he gives employment. As long as a man spends his income, he puts just as much bread into people's mouths in spending as he takes out of other people's mouths in earning. The real villain, from this point of view, is the man who saves. If he merely puts his savings in a stocking, like the proverbial French peasant, it is obvious that they do not give employment. If he invests his savings, the matter is less obvious, and different cases arise.

One of the commonest things to do with savings is to lend them to some Government. In view of the fact that the bulk of the public expenditure of most civilized Governments consists in payment for past wars or preparation for future wars, the man who lends his money to a Government is in the same position as the bad men in Shakespeare who hire murderers. The net result of the man's economical habits is to increase the armed forces of the State to which he lends his savings. Obviously it would be better if he spent the money, even if he spent it in drink or gambling.

But, I shall be told, the case is quite different when savings are invested in industrial enterprises. When such enterprises succeed, and produce something useful, this may be conceded. In these days, however, no one will deny that most enterprises fail. That means that a large amount of human labor, which might have been devoted to producing something that could be enjoyed, was expended on producing machines which, when produced, lay idle and did no good to anyone. The man who invests his savings in a concern that goes bankrupt is therefore injuring others as well as himself.

The writer argues that "the real villain is the man who saves." Why does the writer argue like that? Give THREE reasons. Do NOT copy more than SEVEN consecutive words from the passage.

---

05 Read the passage and follow the directions. [4 points]

As Theodor Adorno stressed, the essential characteristic of the culture industry is repetition. Adorno illustrates this by contrasting 'popular' and 'serious' music. As early as his 1936 essay 'On Jazz,' Adorno had argued that an essential characteristic of popular music was its standardization. 'On Popular Music', written in 1941, repeats this point. "The whole structure of popular music is standardized, even where the attempt is made to circumvent standardization. Standardization extends from the most general features to the most specific ones." Standardization implies the interchangeability, the substitutability of parts. By contrast, serious music is a 'concrete totality' for Adorno, whereby every detail derives its musical sense from the concrete totality of the piece. This is a dialectical relationship, whereby the totality is constituted of the organic interrelation of the particulars. In the case of serious music, interchangeability is not possible; if a detail is omitted, all is lost.

Other illustrations could be given, such as the soap operas with their substitutable episodes, horror films with their formulas, etc. This repetition is due to the reflection in the sphere of cultural production of the standardized and repetitive processes of monopoly capitalist industry. Under late capitalism, what happens at work in the factory or in the office can only be escaped by approximating it in one's leisure time. This sets the terms for cultural products : "no independent thinking must be expected from the audiences" instead, "the product prescribes every reaction." The standardization of the cultural product leads to the standardization of the audience. "Man as a member of a species has been made a reality by the culture industry. Now any person signifies only those attributes by which he can replace everybody else; he is interchangeable." Standardization, says Adorno, "divests the listener of his spontaneity and promotes conditioned reflexes." To this point, the argument suggests that both popular culture and its audience suffer a radical loss of significance under late capitalism.

What is the main idea of the passage? Write down your answer in about 15 words. Also, describe what "concrete totality" is in approximately 10 words.

_____

_____

_____

_____

_____

01 Read the passage and follow the directions. [2 points]

Bats is known for their stealth in the dark. Even under the cover of total darkness, bats can maneuver around trees, chase down moths, and find their way home. Greater mouse-eared bats set their internal magnetic compass using a special pattern, which is light that vibrates in one direction, at dusk. Bats figure out what direction their magnetic compass is pointing using cues around sunset. The flying mammals get directional information from polarized light. At dusk, there is a strong band of polarized light that runs like a rainbow from north to south, a phenomenon that provides a consistent geographic reference and is a known orientation cue for birds. This occurs because polarization is maximized when the sun's rays are scattered at a 90-degree angle from their original path.

Stefan Greif and his colleagues tested its role by experimentally manipulating 70 greater mouse-eared bats in Bulgaria. The team placed each bat in a box that simulated polarized light at sunset. Some bats saw the natural pattern; others saw a band of polarization that was rotated 90 degrees. Next, they displaced the radio-tagged bats more than 14 miles from their roosting cave and tracked their movements in the night. The result : Bats shown the altered pattern did not seem to know what direction was home. In fact, many went in directions that were rotated 90 degrees from the correct orientation. The fact that bats use the exact same compass calibration method as birds is remarkable.

Summarize the passage by filling in the blank with TWO words from the passage.

Bats are creatures of the night. However, without the proper _____ guides, the bats become disoriented and have a hard time finding their way home in the darkness.

02 Read the passage and follow the directions. [2 points]

Within the United States, the gap between rich and poor has grown in recent decades, reaching levels not seen since the 1930s. Yet inequality has not loomed large as a political issue. Even the president's modest proposal to return income tax rates to where they stood in the 1990s prompted his 2008 Republican opponents to call him a socialist who wanted to spread the wealth.

The dearth of attention to ___ⓐ___ in contemporary politics does not reflect any lack of attention to the topic among political philosophers. The just distribution of income and wealth has been a mainstay of debate within political philosophy from the 1970s to the present. But the tendency of philosophers to frame the question in terms of utility or consent leads them to overlook the argument against inequality most likely to receive a political hearing and most central to the project of moral and civic renewal.

Some philosophers who would tax the rich to help the poor argue in the name of ___ⓑ___; taking a hundred dollars from a rich person and giving it to a poor person will diminish the rich person's happiness only slightly, they speculate, but greatly increase the happiness of the poor person. John Rawls also defends redistribution, but on the grounds of hypothetical consent. He argues that if we imagined a hypothetical social contract in an original position of equality, everyone would agree to a principle that would support some form of redistribution.

Fill in each blank with ONE word from the passage respectively.

03 Read the passage and follow the directions. [2 points]

Philosopher Karl Jaspers notes that Buddha (563−483 BCE), Confucius (551−479 BCE), and Socrates (469−399 BCE) all lived quite close to one another in time (but not in place). [1] In his analysis these men are the central thinkers of an 'Axial Age' spanning 800−200 BCE. Jaspers calls this age "a deep breath bringing the most lucid consciousness" and holds that its philosophers brought transformative schools of thought to three major civilizations : Indian, Chinese, and European. [2] The Buddha also founded one of the world's major religions, and common sense demands that any list of major human developments include the establishment of other major faiths like Hinduism, Judaism, Christianity, and Islam. Each has influenced the lives and ideals of hundreds of millions of people. [3] Written symbols to facilitate counting also existed then, but they did not include the concept of zero, as basic as that seems to us now. The modern numbering system, which we call Arabic, arrived around 830 CE. [4] The list of important developments goes on and on. The Athenians began to practice democracy around 500 BCE. The Black Death reduced Europe's population by at least 30 percent during the latter half of the 1300s. Columbus sailed the ocean blue in 1492, beginning interactions between the New World and the Old that would transform both. [5]

Where is the best place for <A> to be inserted?

A

Many of these religions' ideas and revelations were spread by the written word, itself a fundamental innovation in human history. Debate rages about precisely when, where, and how writing was invented, but a safe estimate puts it in Mesopotamia around 3,200 BCE.

04 Read the passage and follow the directions. [4 points]

The world's first subway was built in London in 1863. At the time, the government was looking for a way to reduce traffic problems in the city of London. The poor areas of the city were so crowded with people that it was almost impossible for horse carriages (the taxis of those days) to get around. The city officials were interested in trying to make it possible for workers to live outside of London and travel easily to work each day. If people had a cheap and convenient way that they could depend on to get to and from work, they would relocate their homes outside of the city. This would help ease the pressure of too many people living in the poor parts of London. From these problems, the idea of the London Underground, the first subway system, was born.

The plans for building the Underground met with several problems and delays, but the fast track was finally opened in January 1863. A steam train pulled the cars along the fast underground track which was 6 kilometers long. About 30,000 people got on the subway the first day. Riders were treated to comfortable seats (standing up while the train was moving was not allowed), and pleasant decorations inside each of the cars. However, the smoke from the engine soon filled the air in the tunnels with ash and soot, as well as chemical gases. Fans had to be put in the tunnels later to keep the air clean enough for people to breathe. Even with its problems, riding in the Underground did catch on. It carried 9 million riders in its first year.

What is the main idea of the first paragraph? Write your answer in TEN words or more. When you answer, do NOT copy more than FIVE consecutive words from the passage. Second, how did the London Underground solve the smoke problem? Write your answer in FIVE words or more.

_____

_____

_____

_____

_____

05 Read the passage and follow the directions. [4 points]

As feature editor for a major daily newspaper, I found myself in charge of a broad array of different departments. I quickly learned that what makes any of these departments sing is the skill of the writing — and that even in areas where I had no discernible interest, a well-crafted story could seize and hold my attention just as well as a breaking front-page sizzler. So we always sought to hire young staff members who, whatever other talents they might have, were good writers.

We had just such a young woman on the food page. She had come to us from one of the nation's finest colleges, and had progressed rapidly to the point where, as assistant editor, she wrote regularly. So one summer day, when I noticed that she had submitted a story on Maine blueberries, I was pleased to see it in the queue, awaiting publication in several more days.

The next day I looked up from my computer terminal to find the food editor herself — a woman with decades of experience, one of the best in the business — standing silently in front of my desk. In one hand she held a copy of her young assistant's story on blueberries. In the other hand she held a battered, tan cookbook some thirty years old. She laid each on my desk. And there, on the pages of that cookbook, was our young friend's story, printed word for word.

Among the few cardinal sins of journalism, one stands supreme : You don't plagiarize. Nothing destroys a career more rapidly; nothing defrauds your readers more egregiously. <u>This was no right-versus-right ethical dilemma</u>.

For me, however, it was an ethical dilemma. I found myself torn by two conflicting desires. Half of me wanted to lunge from my desk, brush past the senior editor, and make a beeline for the assistant's desk — whereupon I would overturn it, scatter its contents across the newsroom floor, grab her by the scruff of her neck, heave her out into the street, and call out after her, "Never, never come back — and never let me hear that you are working in journalism anywhere else!" The other half of me wanted to walk over to her desk, quietly pull up a chair, and say, "What on earth has come over you? You know better than that! Is there something going wrong in your personal life that I haven't been aware of? Let's go have a cup of coffee — you and I have to talk!"

Explain the meaning of the underlined "This was no right-versus-right ethical dilemma" as it is intended by the writer. Second, explain why for the writer it is an ethical dilemma.

_____

_____

_____

_____

_____

01   Read the passage and follow the directions. [2 points]

Habits are not as simple as they appear. Habits — even once they are rooted in our minds — aren't destiny. We can choose our habits, once we know how. Everything we know about habits, from neurologists studying amnesiacs and organizational experts remaking companies, is that any of them can be _____, if you understand how they function. Hundreds of habits influence our days — they guide how we get dressed in the morning, talk to our kids, and fall asleep at night; they impact what we eat for lunch, how we do business, and whether we exercise or have a beer after work. Each of them has a different cue and offers a unique reward. Some are simple and others are complex, drawing upon emotional triggers and offering subtle neurochemical prizes. But every habit, no matter its complexity, can be _____. The most addicted alcoholics can become sober. The most dysfunctional companies can transform themselves. A high school dropout can become a successful manager. However, to change a habit, you must consciously accept the hard work of identifying the cues and rewards that drive the habits' routines, and find alternatives. You must be self-conscious enough to use it.

Fill in the blank with ONE word from the passage. If necessary, you can change the form of the word.

_____

02 Read the passage and follow the directions. [2 points]

In history war has served sport and sport has served war. The sports field and battlefield are linked as locations for the demonstration of legitimate patriotic aggression. The one location sustains the other, and both sustain the image of the powerful nation. Furthermore, the sports field throughout history has prepared the young for the battlefield. Throughout history sport and militarism have been inseparable. Heroes of sports field and battlefield have much in common. They are both viewed as symbols of national prowess, quality and virtue. The warrior and the athlete are crucial to the perceived success of the nation, imagined community.

Sport reinforces antagonisms bred on battlefields, keeps alive memories of "battles long ago," defeats deep in the past and victories recorded in history books, and as such exacerbates antipathy, fuels hostility and extends dislike. Sport can be sublimated warfare kept alive repeatedly year after year, in "conflicts without casualties" in national stadiums keeping vivid past conflicts with casualties, and perhaps contributing to future conflicts with casualties.

What is clear is the extent to which nations have used, and use, sport as a form of cultural conditioning to project images of desirable masculinity which lead directly to desirable images of martial masculinity. Memory has a special power. The memory of war is one of the most significant ways of shaping national identity : images of sacrifice, heroism, mourning and loss provide symbols of unity in suffering, in sadness, in valediction. Sharply focused memories of sporting moments — played or watched — are among the most frequently recalled and infrequently forgotten. Sporting memories often offer the security of belonging. In the modern world, therefore, war and sport have been potent forces in the creation of an imagined community.

Describe the main idea of the passage by filling in the blank with ONE word from the passage.

Throughout history sport and war have been inseparable and have served as powerful factors in the construction of a(n) _____.

03 Read the passage and follow the directions. [2 points]

In the summer of 2012, we went for a drive in a car that had no driver. During a research visit to Google's Silicon Valley headquarters, we got to ride in one of the company's autonomous vehicles, developed as part of its Chauffeur project.

[1] Initially we had visions of cruising in the back seat of a car that had no one in the front seat, but Google is understandably skittish about putting obviously autonomous autos on the road. Doing so might freak out pedestrians and other drivers, or attract the attention of the police. So we sat in the back while two members of the Chauffeur team rode up front.

[2] When one of the Googlers hit the button that switched the car into fully automatic driving mode while we were headed down Highway 101, our curiosities — and self-preservation instincts — engaged. The 101 is not always a predictable or calm environment.

[3] Google was founded by Larry Page and Sergey Brin while they were Ph.D. students at Stanford University. Together they own about 14 percent of its shares but control 56 of the stockholder voting power through supervoting stock. They incorporated Google as a privately held company on September 4, 1998.

[4] It's nice and straight, but it's also crowded most of the time, and its traffic flows have little obvious reason. At highway speeds the consequences of driving mistakes can be serious ones.

[5] Since we were now part of the ongoing Chauffeur experiment, these consequences were suddenly of more than just intellectual interest to us. The car performed flawlessly. In fact, it actually provided a boring ride. It didn't speed or slalom among the other cars; it drove exactly the way we're all taught to in driver's ed.

Which one among [1]-[5] is not relevant to the rest in coherent terms?

---

04 Read the passage and follow the directions. [4 points]

Americans consume almost a quarter of all the beef produced in the world. Every 24 hours 100,000 cattle are slaughtered in the United States; the average American consumes around 270 pounds of meat a year.

Each year, the death toll continues to mount for consumers of beef and other red meats. According to a report by the U.S. Surgeon General, more than 70 percent of deaths in this country — more than 1.5 million annually — are related to diet, particularly the over-consumption of beef and other foods high in cholesterol and saturated fat. Study after study confirms that consumption of red meat is a primary factor in the development of heart disease, strokes, and colon and breast cancer. The American Heart Association, and the American Cancer Society recommend that people reduce their consumption of beef and other animal-derived foods, and eat more grain, fresh vegetables, and fruits instead. Recently, the National Research Council of the National Academy of Sciences (NAS) found that beef contains the highest concentration of herbicides of any food sold in America. The NAS also found that beef ranks second only to tomatoes as the food posing the greatest cancer risk due to pesticide contamination.

The beef addiction of the United States and other industrialized nations has set off a global food crisis. Today, hundreds of millions of cattle are being fed precious grain so that American and European consumers can enjoy the pleasures of "marbled" beef. Meanwhile, nearly one billion people suffer from hunger and malnutrition, and between 40 and 60 million people — mostly children — die each year from starvation and related diseases. Currently, more than 70 percent of the U.S. grain harvest — and more than one third of the grain produced in the world is fed to cattle and other livestock. We could provide proper nourishment to more than a billion people if we used the world's agricultural lands to grow food for human consumption rather than feed for cattle and other livestock.

Describe the TWO results of beef over-consumption. Do NOT copy more than FIVE consecutive words from the passage.

_____

_____

_____

_____

_____

05 Read the passage and follow the directions. [4 points]

Many scientists believe that the aging process is caused by the gradual buildup of a huge number of individually tiny faults — some damage to a DNA strand here, a deranged protein molecule there, and so on. This degenerative buildup means that the length of our lives is regulated by the balance between how fast new damage strikes our cells and how efficiently this damage is corrected. The body's mechanisms to maintain and repair our cells are wonderfully effective — which is why we live as long as we do — but these mechanisms are not perfect. Some of the damage passes unrepaired and accumulates as the days, months and years pass by. We age because our bodies keep making mistakes.

We might well ask why our bodies do not repair themselves better. Actually we probably could fix damage better than we do already. In theory at least, we might even do it well enough to live forever. The reason we do not is because it would have cost more energy than it was worth when our aging process evolved long ago, when our hunter-gatherer ancestors faced a constant struggle against hunger. Under the pressure of natural selection to make the best use of scarce energy supplies, our species gave higher priority to growing and reproducing than to living forever. Our genes treated the body as a short-term vehicle, to be maintained well enough to grow and reproduce, but not worth a greater investment in durability when the chance of dying an accidental death was so great. In other words, genes are immortal, but the body — what the Greeks called soma — is disposable.

Since the late 1970s, the evidence to support this disposable soma theory has grown significantly. In my laboratory some years ago we showed that longer-lived animals have better maintenance and repair systems than short-lived animals do. If you can avoid the hazards of the environment for a bit longer by flying away from danger or being cleverer or bigger, then the body is correspondingly a bit less disposable, and it pays to spend more energy on repair.

The writer proposes a "disposable soma theory" to provide an answer to why human bodies do not repair themselves better. What is the "disposable soma theory"? Do not copy more than SIX consecutive words from the passage.

_____

_____

_____

_____

_____

📖 모범답안 p.090

01 **Read the passage and follow the directions.** [2 points]

Worried your child is using a cell phone behind the wheel? you're probably the one they're talking to. Fifty-three percent of teens who reported talking on a phone while driving were chatting with mom or dad. The numbers for texting were smaller but still significant. For instance, 18 percent of all 18-year-olds ─ not just those who reported texting while driving ─ said they texted with their parents.

It's a dilemma for parents : You want to call your child to know where she is, but you don't want her talking to you while she's steering a 3,000-pound machine 60 mph down the highway. And parents' conflicting desires put teens in a bind, too. Teens think parents expect to be able to reach them and that parents get mad if they don't answer their phone.

That can be dangerous. Cell phones play a large role in crashes blamed on distracted driving, especially among teens. In 2011, for example, cell phone use was blamed in 21 percent of fatal crashes that involved distracted teen drivers. Many researchers noted that the proportion of teens who report using cell phones while driving has risen dramatically in recent years, despite publicity about the dangers. A 2009 Pew study found 43 percent of 16-and 17-year-olds talked on cellphones while driving, but according to a 2013 survey, 86 percent of 11th-and 12th-graders reported using phones behind the wheel.

Describe the main idea of the passage by filling in the blank below with TWO words from the passage. If necessary, you can change the word form.

_____ distracting their teen drivers are dangerous.

02 Read the passage and follow the directions. [2 points]

Succumbing to growing public pressure, Twitter released the gender and ethnic breakdown of its work force, showing that it looks like most other major technology companies : overwhelming male, white and Asian.

In the U.S., nearly 90% of Twitter's workers are white or Asian. And more than 90% of technology jobs in the U.S. are held by whites or Asians. Men make up 70% of all staff but 90% of technology staff, according to figures released by the company's vice president for diversity, Janet Van Huysse. Twitter pledged to take steps to diversify its staff. "We want to be more than a good business; we want to be a business that we are proud of," Huysse said.

Diversity has become a hotly debated issue as some of Silicon Valley's most powerful companies have begun revealing the makeup of their work forces. These companies say they are intent on diversifying their ranks to stay in touch and in tune with their customers around the world. Over the past two months, Yahoo, Google, Facebook and LinkedIn have reported that their staffs are between 62% and 70% male. Whites and Asians make up between 88% and 91%. That has dismayed Blacks and Hispanics who say they are major consumers of technology yet make up just a tiny percentage of workers reaping the economic rewards in the nation's top paying industry. Of Twitter's U.S. employees, 3% are Hispanic and 2% Black. Yet Blacks, Hispanics and Asian Americans account for 41% of U.S. users, making Twitter more racially diverse than any other social network, including Facebook.

What is the title of the passage? Write down your answer by filling in the blank below with ONE word from the passage.

Lack of _____ : White and Asian Men Control Most of Silicon Valley's Powerful Companies

03 Read the passage and follow the directions. [2 points]

Elected by the greatest personal triumph of any Governor ever chosen by a State, John P. Altgeld fearlessly and knowingly bared his devoted head to the fiercest, most vindictive criticism ever heaped upon a public man, because he loved justice and dared to do the right. [1] John Peter Altgeld, the son of a illiterate farm labourer, was born in Selters, Germany on 30th December, 1847. The following year the family moved to the United States and settled in Mansfield, Ohio. After a brief schooling he started work on the family farm when he was twelve years old. [2] Altgeld became an itinerant worker in Arkansas, where he joined a railroad-building crew. Eventually Altgeld became a school teacher in Missouri. He continued to study until he qualified as a lawyer. A member of the Democratic Party, he developed a reputation for protecting the rights of the poor and in 1874 was elected district attorney of Andrew County. [3] Altgeld moved to Chicago, Illinois, in 1875, where he wrote his book, *Our Penal Machinery and Its Victims*. The book, that argued that the United States criminal system favoured the rich over the poor, influenced a generation of social reformers, including the lawyer, Clarence Darrow and Jane Addams, the founder of the Hull House Settlement. In 1877 Altgeld returned to Ohio and married Emma Ford, a teacher. [4] Over the next few years Altgeld became a successful businessman. Altgeld specialized in the buying and selling of real estate. One of his most successful ventures was the purchase of the sixteen-story Unity Block in Chicago. Despite his wealth, Altgeld developed a strong sympathy for the plight of the poor. He became involved in politics and with the support of the Democrats and various socialist groups, Altgeld was elected Governor of Illinois in 1892. [5] Altgeld controversially pardoned three men, Oscar Neebe, Samuel Fielden and Michael Schwab, convicted after the Haymarket Bombing. In 1894 President Grover Cleveland and Attorney General Richard Olney sent in federal troops to deal with the Pullman Strike. Altgeld protested against this violation of state's rights, but the action was popular with industrialists in Illinois. During the 1896 election Altgeld was attacked by the media for his liberal record.

Where is the best place for the <A> to be inserted?

A

Once in power Altgeld's embarked on an ambitious program of social reform, which included attempts to prohibit child labour and the inspection of factories. He also introduced a law prohibiting discrimination against trade union members.

04 Read the passage and follow the directions. [4 points]

The study of history is largely devoted to two things : chronicling the steady march of human progress and analyzing how, when, why, and by whom our species moves toward a higher standard of living and ever increasing intellectual power, and chronicling whatever went wrong in the past and scrutinizing the decisions public officials made to try to correct the problems. The Gilded Age yields high volumes of both. Concerning the former, the orthodox historical interpretation holds that these post‑Civil War decades were mainly characterized by economic statistics and demographic changes, such as urbanization, industrialization, unionization, technological innovation, the growth of corporations, educational expansion, the rising middle class, and increasing immigration. Along with economic development and apparent prosperity, however, came serious inequities, a point which brings us to the latter. The wealth was not distributed equally among classes, races, or genders, which created a notable groundswell of animosity from those at the bottom of the social hierarchy. It seemed that everyone wanted a larger slice of the pie, yet only the corporate "cooks" (sometimes "crooks") got to do the slicing. Thus, the Gilded Age had its share of socio-political issues to address and problems to solve.

The Gilded Age was, as the label implies, a time of excess and corruption, of shallowness and show. Clearly, Mark Twain knew what he saw and how to describe it. Yet that name is not an all-encompassing description of the times. With historical hindsight, it does not capture the overall essence, or the zeitgeist, of late 19th century U.S. history. The real zeitgeist of Gilded Age America (the late 1800s) was its thrust to achieve true nationalism — that is, the quest for a national consensus on black‑white race relations; the quest to reconcile the North and the South into a unified whole; the quest for a homogeneous, nationwide economic system that blended agriculture and industry; the quest to subdue the indigenous Native Americans once and for all; the quest to preserve and defend the post‑Civil War American "nation" through a truly "national" military policy; the quest for a national consensus on morality and religion; and the quest to extend the American way of life overseas to subservient peoples. A better label for this era of American history, therefore, might be the "National Age."

Describe Mark Twain's definition of the Gilded Age. Second, how does the writer of the passage think of Twain's definition of the Gilded Age? What is the writer's alternative suggestion?

_____

_____

_____

_____

_____

05 Read the passage and follow the directions. [4 points]

Reading or the enjoyment of books has always been regarded among the charms of a cultured life and is respected and envied by those who rarely give themselves that privilege. This is easy to understand when we compare the difference between the life of a man who does no reading and that of a man who does. The man who has not the habit of reading is imprisoned in his immediate world, in respect to time and space. His life falls into a set routine; he is limited to contact and conversation with a few friends and acquaintances, and he sees only what happens in his immediate neighborhood. From this prison there is no escape. But the moment he takes up a book, he immediately enters a different world, and if it is a good book, he is immediately put in touch with one of the best talkers of the world. This talker leads him on and carries him into a different country or a different age, or unburdens to him some of his personal regrets, or discusses with him some special line or aspect of life that the reader knows nothing about. An ancient author puts him in communion with a dead spirit of long ago, and as he reads along, he begins to imagine what that ancient author looked like and what type of person he was. Both Mencius and Ssema Ch'ien, China's greatest historian, have expressed the same idea. Now to be able to live two hours out of twelve in a different world and take one's thoughts off the claims of the immediate present is, of course, a privilege to be envied by people shut up in their bodily prison. Such a change of environment is really similar to travel in its psychological effect.

But there is more to it than this. The reader is always carried away into a world of thought and reflection. Even if it is a book about physical events, there is a difference between seeing such events in person or living through them, and reading about them in books, for then the events always assume the quality of a spectacle and the reader becomes a detached spectator. The best reading is therefore that which leads us into this contemplative mood, and not that which is merely occupied with the report of events. The tremendous amount of time spent on newspapers I regard as not reading at all, for the average readers of papers are mainly concerned with getting reports about events and happenings without contemplative value.

Explain why the writer thinks that the average readers who spend their time on newspapers do not read at all. Do NOT copy more than SIX consecutive words from the passage.

_____

_____

_____

_____

_____

01 Read the passage and follow the directions. [2 points]

Envy is one form of a vice, partly moral, partly intellectual, which consists in seeing things never in themselves, but only through ___(a)___. I am earning, let us say, a salary sufficient for my needs. I should be content, but I hear that someone else whom I believe to be in no way my superior is earning a salary twice as great as mine. Instantly, if I am of an envious disposition, the satisfactions to be derived from what I have grow dim, and I begin to be eaten up with a sense of injustice.

For all this the proper cure is mental discipline, the habit of not thinking profitless thoughts. After all, what is more enviable than happiness? And if I can cure myself of envy I can acquire happiness and become enviable. The man who has double my salary is doubtless tortured by the thought that someone else in turn has twice as much as he has, and so it goes on. If you desire glory, you may envy Napoleon. But Napoleon envied Caesar, Caesar envied Alexander, and Alexander, I daresay, envied Hercules, who never existed. You cannot, therefore, get away from envy by means of ___(b)___ alone, for there will always be in history or legend some person even more successful than you are. You can get away from envy by enjoying the pleasures that come your way, by doing the work that you have to do, and by avoiding comparisons with those whom you imagine, perhaps quite falsely, to be more fortunate than yourself.

Fill in the blanks ⓐ and ⓑ with ONE word from the passage respectively. If necessary, you may change the form of the word(s).

02 **Read the passage and follow the directions.** [2 points]

The projected tower had been a subject of some controversy, attracting criticism from both those who did not believe that it was feasible and those who objected on artistic grounds, whose objections were an expression of a longstanding debate about the relationship between architecture and engineering. In February of 1887 a group of well-known French artists and writers delivered a petition to the director of the Exposition Universelle condemning the design of the monument to the French Revolution. Among others it was signed by Guy de Maupassant and Charles Gounod. The petition was published in the newspaper, *Le Temps*. For them it was "a giddy, ridiculous tower dominating Paris like a gigantic black smokestack, crushing under its barbaric bulk Notre Dame, the Tour Saint-Jacques, the Louvre, and stretching like a blot of ink the hateful shadow of the hateful column of bolted sheet metal.

Gustave Eiffel responded to these criticisms by comparing his tower to the Egyptian Pyramids : "My tower will be the tallest edifice ever erected by man. Will it not also be grandiose in its way? And why would something admirable in Egypt become hideous and ridiculous in Paris?" These criticisms were also masterfully dealt with by Édouard Lockroy in a letter of support, ironically saying "Judging by the stately swell of the rhythms, the beauty of the metaphors, the elegance of its delicate and precise style, one can tell that this protest is the result of collaboration of the most famous writers and poets of our time," and going on to point out that the protest was irrelevant since the project had been decided upon months before and was already under construction. Eiffel was similarly unworried, pointing out to a journalist that it was premature to judge the effect of the tower solely on the basis of the drawings, that the Champ de Mars was distant enough from the monuments mentioned in the protest for there to be little risk of the tower overwhelming them.

What is the title of the passage? Write down your answer by filling in the blank below with ONE word from the passage.

The _____ about the Eiffel Tower

03 Read the passage and follow the directions. [2 points]

Many critics argue that since postmodernists deny the possibility of describing matters of fact objectively, they leave us with no firm basis for either condemning the terrorist attacks or fighting back.

[1] Invoking the universal notions of justice and truth to support our cause wouldn't be effective anyway because our adversaries lay claim to the same language. (No one declares himself to be an apostle of injustice.)

[2] Not so. Postmodernism maintains only that there can be no independent standard for determining which of many rival interpretations of an event is the true one. The only thing postmodern thought argues against is the hope of justifying our response to the attacks in universal terms that would be persuasive to everyone, including our enemies.

[3] Instead, we can and should invoke the particular lived values that unite us and inform the institutions we cherish and wish to defend. At times like these, the nation rightly falls back on the record of aspiration and accomplishment that makes up our collective understanding of what we live for.

Rearrange the sentences in order to make coherent terms.

04 Read the passage and follow the directions. [4 points]

Recent controversies in South Korea over apparent racial discrimination have turned a spotlight on how Koreans view people from other cultures. Discrimination in South Korea tends to stem from perceptions about economic hierarchies and targets people from less wealthy Asian nations.

In a country where only 3% of the population is foreign, non-Korean faces are conspicuous, and racial insensitiveness has been known to play out in sometimes outlandish ways. Foreign baseball players have been at the receiving end of crass remarks about their skin color, such as a comment about a Lotte Giants player's dark skin making pitches difficult to see. A huge online backlash among the foreign community ensued after a bar owner in Itaewon, an Seoul district popular with expats, put up a sign recently barring "Africans at the moment" because of the Ebola outbreak.

Modern-day discrimination arguably comes from this post-war period. A byproduct of South Korea's intense post-war economic development was the awareness of other nations' economic standing and the country therefore started to stratify other countries accordingly. The US and the UK were upheld as model nations, and exposure to American culture and its depictions of minorities further instilled stereotypes.

Today, the government's policies towards immigration are tougher towards nationals from countries like Uzbekistan, Vietnam, China or the Philippines and multiculturalism policies promote assimilation rather than supporting diversity. Women from countries like China or the Philippines, for instance, who are marrying Koreans can only get a spouse visa only once they've fulfilled certain educational training requirements. Immigration policies favor Western countries because relationships with these countries are deemed to be more valuable. This kind of discrimination is based on economic criteria, more so than the idea of ethnic homogeneity.

However, there are signs that South Korea is increasingly becoming more multicultural, which could benefit the country, not least because with its severely low birth rate the country might soon be addressing the question of how to expand its labor force.

Describe the main idea of the passage in about TEN words and explain why the writer of the passage is optimistic about the racial issue in South Korea.

_____

_____

_____

_____

_____

05 Read the passage and follow the directions. [4 points]

According to criminologists working in the conflict tradition, crime is the result of conflict within societies that is brought about through the inevitable processes of capitalism. Dispute exists between those who espouse a 'pluralist' view of society and those who do not. Pluralists, following from writers like Mills, are of the belief that power is exercised in societies by groups of interested individuals (businesses, faith groups, government organizations for example) vying for influence and power to further their own interests. These criminologists have been called 'conservative conflict theorists.' They hold that crime may emerge from economic differences, differences of culture, or from struggles concerning status, ideology, morality, religion, race or ethnicity. These writers are of the belief that such groups, by claiming allegiance to mainstream culture, gain control of key resources permitting them to criminalize those who do not conform to their moral codes and cultural values. These theorists, therefore, see crime as having roots in symbolic or instrumental conflict occurring at multiple sites within a fragmented society.

Others are of the belief that such 'interests,' particularly symbolic dimensions such as status are epiphenomenological by-products of more fundamental economic conflict. For these theorists, societal conflict from which crime emerges is founded on the fundamental economic inequalities that are inherent in the processes of capitalism. Drawing on the work of Marx, Engels, and Bonger among others, such critical theorists suggest that the conditions in which crime emerges are caused by the appropriation of others' labor through the generation of what is known as surplus value, concentrating in the hands of the few owners of the means of production, disproportionate wealth and power.

In the passage, there are TWO different points of view about the causes of crime. First, for conservative conflict theorists, who are criminals? Second, for critical theorists, what causes crime in a society? When you answer each question, do NOT copy more than SIX consecutive words from the passage.

_____

_____

_____

_____

_____

01 Read the passage and fill in each blank with ONE word from the passage respectively. [2 points]

Biologists, more than a century ago, found that if they separated an invertebrate animal embryo into two parts at an early stage of its life, it would survive and develop as two normal embryos. This led them to believe that the cells in the early embryo are not ___ⓐ___ in the sense that each cell has the potential to develop in a variety of different ways. Later investigators found that the situation was not so simple. It matters in which plane the embryo is cut. If it is cut in a plane different from the one used by the early biologists, it will not form two whole embryos.

A debate arose over what exactly was happening. Which embryo cells are determined, just when do they become irreversibly committed to their fates, and what are the "morphogenetic determinants" that tell a cell what to become? But the debate could not be resolved because no one was able to ask the crucial questions in a form in which they could be pursued productively. Recent discoveries in molecular biology, however, have opened up prospects for a resolution of the debate. Now biologists think they know at least some of the molecules that act as morphogenetic determinants in early development. They have been able to show that, in a sense, cell determination begins even before an egg is fertilized.

Studying sea urchins, biologist Paul Gross found that an unfertilized egg contains substances that function as morphogenetic determinants. They are located in the cytoplasm of the egg cell; i.e., in that part of the cell's protoplasm that lies outside of the nucleus. In the unfertilized egg, the substances are inactive and are not distributed homogeneously. When the egg is _____ⓑ_____, the substances become active and, presumably, govern the behavior of the genes they interact with. Since the substances are unevenly distributed in the egg, when the fertilized egg divides, the resulting cells are different from the start and so can be qualitatively different in their own gene activity.

02 Read the passage and follow the directions. [4 points]

Even though gender differences in violent offending have garnered some interest, it is racial and ethnic differences that have produced the most commentary. Race differences in crime and violence remain emotionally and politically charged, divisive topics in the United States. National surveys conducted in the United States, for example, suggest that a majority of white respondents believe blacks and Latinos are more prone innately and culturally to violence than whites or Asians. These beliefs demonstrate the continual existence of racial stereotypes as misguided explanations of criminal violence in this country. Official crime data can be blamed for perpetrating these stereotypes.

According to those data, African Americans in the United States are involved in criminal homicide and other forms of violence at a rate that far exceeds their numbers in the general population. According to FBI, for example, although African Americans make up about 13.5% of the U.S. population, they accounted for more than 39% of all arrests for violent crimes in 2012. These figures, according to professor R. Grosfoguel who is acknowledged as an authority on criminal law, reflect social inequalities such as lack of employment and educational opportunities, racial oppression in its many forms, discriminatory treatment at the hands of the criminal justice system, and law enforcement practices in geographical areas where many African Americans reside.

Latinos are now the largest ethnic minority group in the United States. The Latino population in the United States more than doubled between 1980 and 2000 and is likely to continue increasing. U.S. Census 2015 estimates projected 9 births for every 1 death among Latinos, whereas for whites, the ratio was 1:1. The estimated Latino population, representing 15.5% of the U.S. population, currently exceeds slightly the African American population. The violence rate in middle class Latino community falls significantly below the rates found for economically deprived Caucasians. Doctor Grosfoguel attributes these findings partly to the fact that Latinos generally have high rates of labor force participation and have close and highly supportive ties to the local community and family.

Describe what the misguided explanations of criminal violence in the United States are. Do not copy more than FOUR consecutive words from the passage. Second, how such explanations are different from doctor Grosfoguel's explication? When you answer the second question, you need to refer to the underlined part above.

_____

_____

_____

_____

_____

03 Read the passage and follow the directions. [4 points]

If you're endlessly distracted by your co-workers in the gaping open office space you all share, you're not alone. In a recent study, researchers followed two anonymous Fortune 500 companies during their transitions between a traditional office space to an open plan environment and used a sensor called a "sociometric badge" (think company ID on a lanyard) to record detailed information about the kind of interactions employees had in both spaces. The study collected information in two stages; first for several weeks before the renovation and the second for several weeks after.

Many researchers provide three cautionary tales. Open office spaces don't actually promote interaction. Instead, they cause employees to seek privacy wherever they can find it. These open spaces might spell bad news for collective company intelligence or, in other words, an overstimulating office space creates a decrease in organizational productivity. Not all channels of interaction will be effected equally in an open layout change. While the number of emails sent in the study did increase, the richness of this interaction was not equal to that lost in face-to-face interactions. It seems like it might be time to first, find a quiet room and go back to the drawing board with the open office design.

Write a summary following the guidelines below.

⌐ Guidelines ⌐

- Summarize the above passage in ONE paragraph.
- Provide a topic sentence, supporting ideas from the passage, and a concluding sentence.
- Do NOT copy more than FIVE consecutive words from the passage.

📖 모범답안 p.094

01 Read the passage and follow the directions. [2 points]

Our genomes are riddled with the detritus of ancient viruses. They infected our hominid ancestors tens of millions of years ago, inserting their genes into the DNA of their hosts. Today, we carry about 100,000 genetic remnants of this invasion. So-called endogenous retroviruses make up 8 percent of the human genome. Mostly, these genetic fragments are generally nothing more than molecular fossils. Over thousands of generations, they have mutated so much that they cannot replicate in our cells. And our cells keep the viral DNA muzzled to minimize the harm it might cause.

But scientists are finding that some endogenous retroviruses do wake up, and at the strangest time. They find that endogenous retroviruses spring to life in the earliest stages of the development of human embryos. The viruses may even assist in human development by helping guide embryonic development and by defending young cells from infections by other viruses. It is interesting that viruses may be playing a vaccine role inside the cell.

When an ordinary retrovirus, like H.I.V., infects a cell, it inserts its genes into the cell's DNA. The cell then makes new retroviruses by making a copy of the virus's genes as RNA molecules. The cell uses some of those RNA molecules to make proteins for the virus. Those proteins form a shell around the other RNA molecules, which become the new virus's genes.

In recent years, scientists have discovered that embryonic cells produce RNA molecules from certain endogenous retroviruses lurking in the genome.

Complete the main idea of the passage by filling in the blank with TWO words from the passage above. The first word should be capitalized.

> _____, which were once enemies, may now function as helpers.

02 Read the passage and fill in the blank with ONE word from the passage.

[2 points]

Ambition which excludes _____ from its purview is generally the result of some kind of anger or hatred against the human race, produced by unhappiness in youth, by injustices in later life, or by any of the causes which lead to persecution mania. A too powerful ego is a prison from which a man must escape if he is to enjoy the world to the full. A capacity for genuine affection is one of the marks of the man who has escaped from this prison of self. To receive affection is by no means enough; affection which is received should liberate the affection which is to be given, and only where both exist in equal measure does affection achieve its best possibilities. Obstacles, psychological and social, to the blossoming of reciprocal affection are a grave evil, from which the world has always suffered and still suffers. People are slow to give admiration for fear it should be misplaced; they are slow to bestow affection for fear that they should be made to suffer either by the person upon whom they bestow it or by a censorious world. Caution is enjoined both in the name of morality and in the name of worldly wisdom, with the result that generosity and adventurousness are discouraged where the affections are concerned. All this tends to produce timidity and anger against mankind, since many people miss throughout life what is really a fundamental need, and to nine out of ten an indispensable condition of an expansive attitude towards the world.

03 Read the passage and follow the directions. [4 points]

As a wise man once said, we are all ultimately alone. But an increasing number of Europeans are choosing to be so at an ever earlier age. This isn't the stuff of gloomy philosophical contemplations, but a fact of Europe's new economic landscape, embraced by sociologists, real-estate developers and ad executives alike. The shift away from family life to solo lifestyle, observes a French sociologist, is part of the "irresistible momentum of individualism" over the last century. The communications revolution, the shift from a business culture of stability to one of mobility and the mass entry of women into the workforce have greatly wreaked havoc on Europeans' private lives.

Europe's new economic climate has largely fostered the trend toward independence. The current generation of home-aloners came of age during Europe's shift from social democracy to the sharper, more individualistic climate of American-style capitalism. Raised in an era of privatization and increased consumer choice, today's tech-savvy workers have embraced a free market in love as well as economics. Modern Europeans are rich enough to afford to _____, and temperamentally independent enough to want to do so.

Once upon a time, people who lived alone tended to be those on either side of marriage — twenty something professionals or widowed senior citizens. While pensioners, particularly elderly women, make up a large proportion of those living alone, the newest crop of singles are high earners in their 30s and 40s who increasingly view living alone as a lifestyle choice. Living alone was conceived to be negative dark and cold, while being together suggested warmth and light. But then came along the idea of singles. They were young, beautiful, strong! Now, young people want to live alone.

The booming economy means people are working harder than ever. And that doesn't leave much room for relationships. Vivald Arroyo, a 35-year-old composer who lives alone in a house in Paris, says he hasn't got time to get lonely because he has too much work. "I have deadlines which would make life with someone else fairly difficult. Only an ideal woman would make him change his lifestyle," he says. Kaufmann, author of a recent book called *The Single Woman and Prince Charming,* thinks this fierce new individualism means that people expect more and more of mates, so relationships don't last long if they start at all. Affenvaum, a blond Berliner with a deep tan, teaches grade school in the mornings. In the afternoon she sunbathes or sleeps, resting up for going dancing. She says she'd never have wanted to do what her mother did give up a career to raise a family. Instead, "I've always done what I wanted to do live a self-determined life."

Fill in the blank with the TWO most appropriate consecutive words from the passage. Second, explain why the writer quotes Affenvaum in the passage.

_____

_____

_____

_____

_____

01 Read the passage and follow the directions. [2 points]

Suppose that a driverless car is headed toward five pedestrians. It can stay on course and kill them or swerve into a concrete wall, killing its passenger. Bonnefon and his colleague explore this social dilemma in a series of clever survey experiments. They show that people generally approve of cars programmed to minimize the total amount of harm, even at the expense of their passengers, but are not enthusiastic about riding in such "utilitarian" cars —that is, autonomous vehicles that are, in certain emergency situations, programmed to _____ⓐ_____ their passengers for the greater good. Such dilemmas may arise infrequently, but once millions of autonomous vehicles are on the road, the improbable becomes probable, perhaps even inevitable. And even if such cases never arise, autonomous vehicles must be programmed to handle them. How should they be programmed? And who should decide?

Bonnefon and his colleague explore many interesting variations, such as how attitudes change when a family member is on board or when the number of lives to be saved by swerving gets larger. As one might expect, people are even less comfortable with utilitarian sacrifice when family members are on board and somewhat more comfortable when sacrificial swerves save larger numbers of lives. But across all of these variations, the social dilemma remains robust. A major determinant of people's _____ⓑ_____ toward utilitarian cars is whether the question is about utilitarian cars in general or about riding in them oneself.

Fill in each blank with the ONE most appropriate word from the passage respectively.

---

02 Read the passage and follow the directions. [2 points]

If truly sustainable solutions are virtually impossible, then what do we do? There are 7 billion humans on earth. If human populations were similar to those of monkeys or gorillas, there would probably not be more than 1 million humans in the world, mostly living in warm places. Our basic problem now is that there are far too many of us, creating a world of non-sustainability. The amount of resources a person uses is mostly determined by a person's income. If a person cuts back on his income, he will use less. Trying to cut back within the same income is less effective, because the money a person doesn't spend one place is likely to be spent somewhere else. Planting food crops, too, disturbs the natural ecology, but it is about as good as we can do. If perennial plants are planted, it is possible that others will benefit as well. Animals, birds, and insects may also get some benefit from the crops. If I use less oil, by driving a smaller car, or by driving fewer miles, it doesn't mean that petroleum will be left in the ground. What it does mean is that the gasoline or diesel that I didn't buy will be available for someone else to buy, creating a gap which is equitable. This rather strange result happens because total oil supply is pretty much "maxed out" —total world oil supply doesn't increase by very much, even with more demand. Instead, all that happens is that price rises. If I use less, price may drop a bit, but the same amount of oil in total will be drained. So by using less petroleum, someone else, somewhere can use more. The result is better sharing of what oil is available. Have smaller families. One child, or even no-child, families are to be encouraged.

The following chart outlines the passage. Fill in each blank with the ONE most appropriate word from the passage respectively.

Key Problem	Solutions
_____ ⓐ _____	• Reducing incomes • Planting some food crops • Sharing what petroleum is available in more ____ⓑ____ way • Having smaller families

03 Read the passage and follow the directions. [4 points]

In view of the popular or general character of most of the taboos which put a brake upon personal liberty in thought and action — that is to say, in view of their enforcement by people in the mass, and not by definite specialists in conduct — it is quite natural to find that they are of extra force in democratic societies, for it is the distinguishing mark of democratic societies that they exalt the powers of the majority almost infinitely, and tend to deny the minority any rights whatever. Under a society dominated by a small caste the revolutionist in custom, despite the axiom to the contrary, has a relatively easy time of it, for the persons whose approval he seeks for his innovation are relatively few in number, and most of them are already habituated to more or less intelligible and independent thinking. But under a democracy he is opposed by a horde so vast that it is a practical impossibility for him, without complex and expensive machinery, to reach and convince all of its members, and even if he could reach them he would find most of them quite incapable of rising out of their accustomed grooves. They cannot understand innovations that are genuinely novel and they don't want to understand them; their one desire is to put them down. Even at this late day, with enlightenment raging through the republic like a pestilence, it would cost the average Southern or Middle Western Congressman his seat if he appeared among his constituents in spats, or wearing a wrist-watch. And if a Justice of the Supreme Court of the United States, however gigantic his learning and his juridical rectitude, were taken in criminal conversation with the wife of a Senator, he would be destroyed instanter*. And if, suddenly revolting against the democratic idea, he were to propose, however gingerly, its abandonment, he would be destroyed with the same dispatch.

instanter : instantly

Explain why is it more difficult for the revolutionist to achieve his goal in democratic societies than in autocratic regimes. Do NOT copy more than FIVE consecutive words from the passage. Second, what is it inferred from the passage the writer's opinion on enlightenment? Write your answer in ONE sentence.

_____

_____

_____

_____

_____

04 Read the passage and follow the directions. [4 points]

One of the most striking tendencies of our time is the expansion of markets and market-oriented reasoning into spheres of life traditionally governed by non-market norms. We consider the moral questions that arise, for example, when countries hire out military service and the interrogation of prisoners to mercenaries or private contractors; or when parents outsource pregnancy and child-bearing to paid laborers in the developing world; or when people buy and sell kidneys on the open market. Other instances abound : Should students in under performing schools be offered cash payments for scoring well on standardized tests? Should teachers be given bonuses for improving the test results of their students? Should states hire for-profit prison companies to house their inmates? Should the United States simplify its immigration policy by adopting the proposal of a University of Chicago economist to sell U.S. citizenship for a $100,000 fee? These questions are not only about utility and consent. They are also about the right ways of valuing key social practices — military service, child-bearing, teaching and learning, criminal punishment, the admission of new citizens, and so on. Since marketizing social practices may corrupt or degrade the norms that define them, we need to ask what non-market norms we want to protect from market intrusion. This is a question that requires public debate about <u>competing conceptions</u> of the right way of valuing goods. Markets are useful instruments for organizing productive activity. But unless we want to let the market rewrite the norms that govern social institutions, we need a public debate about the moral limits of markets.

Write a summary following the guidelines below.

> **Guidelines**
>
> - Summarize the above passage in ONE paragraph.
> - Provide a topic sentence, supporting ideas from the passage, and a concluding sentence.
> - Be sure to identify the "competing conceptions" of the underlined section in your summary.
> - Do NOT copy more than FIVE consecutive words from the passage.

01 Read the passage and follow the directions. [2 points]

The word 'mammal' comes from the Latin *mamma*, meaning breast. Mammal mothers love their offspring so much that they allow them to suckle from their body. Mammal youngsters, on their side, feel an overwhelming desire to bond with their mothers and stay near them. In the wild, piglets, calves and puppies that fail to bond with their mothers rarely survive for long. Until recently that was true of human children too. Conversely, a sow, cow or bitch that due to some rare mutation does not care about her young may live a long and comfortable life, but her genes will not pass to the next generation. Since mammal youngsters cannot survive without motherly care, it is evident that motherly love and a strong mother-infant bond characterize all mammals.

It took scientists many years to acknowledge this. Not long ago psychologists doubted the importance of the emotional bond between parents and children even among humans. In the first half of the twentieth century, and despite the influence of Freudian theories, the dominant behaviourist school argued that relations between parents and children were shaped by material feedback; that children needed mainly food, shelter and medical care; and that children bonded with their parents simply because the latter provide these material needs. Children who demanded warmth, hugs and kisses were thought to be 'spoiled'. Childcare experts warned that children who were hugged and kissed by their parents would grow up to be needy, egotistical and insecure adults. John Watson, a leading childcare authority in the 1920s, sternly advised parents, "Never hug and kiss your children, never let them sit in your lap. If you must, kiss them once on the forehead when they say goodnight. Shake hands with them in the morning."

Describe the main idea of the passage by filling in the blank below with
TWO consecutive words from the passage.

A mammal cannot live on food alone. It needs a(n) _____ with its
mother as well.

---

02 Read the passage and fill in the blank below with the best ONE word from the passage. If necessary, you may change its word form. [2 points]

It's no surprise that my son is small — both my husband and I come from long lines of short people and we are below average U.S. heights ourselves. (Women average 5 foot 4 inches; men, 5 foot 10 inches.) If my son remains small for the rest of his life, will his height be a(n) _____, both personally and professionally?

Both men and women who are above average height report higher levels of happiness than smaller people, according to a paper from the *National Bureau of Economic Research*. The study found that taller people tend to have more education than shorter people. Tall people also make more money. But short people do just fine, too, writes John Schwartz, a 5 foot 3 *New York Times* reporter and author of *Short : Walking Tall When You're Not Tall at All*. In his book, Schwartz says that the purported disadvantage of being short is based on selective claims by drug companies that market growth hormones. Since 2003, the Food and Drug Administration has approved the use of human growth hormones to treat short but otherwise medically normal children.

Numerous studies have also found that short kids don't experience extra problems because of their height. A recent study in *Pediatrics*, for instance, found that short children were no different from their non-short peers with respect to exclusion by their peers, social support, popularity, asociality with peers, teacher report of peer victimization, childhood depressive symptoms, or externalizing or internalizing behaviors.

03 **Read the passage and follow the directions.** [4 points]

As practiced by many learned and diligent but essentially ignorant and unimaginative men, criticism is little more than a branch of homiletics. They judge a work of art, not by its clarity and sincerity, not by the force and charm of its ideas, not by the technical virtuosity of the artist, not by his originality and artistic courage, but simply and solely by his orthodoxy. If he is what is called a "right thinker," if he devotes himself to advocating the transient platitudes in a sonorous manner, then he is worthy of respect. But if he lets fall the slightest hint that he is in doubt about any of them, or, worse still, that he is indifferent, then he is a scoundrel, and hence, by their theory, a bad artist. ⓐ <u>Such pious piffle*</u> is horribly familiar among us. I do not exaggerate its terms. You will find it running through the critical writings of practically all the dull fellows who combine criticism with tutoring; in the words of many of them it is stated in the plainest way and defended with much heat, theological and pedagogical. In its baldest form it shows itself in the doctrine that it is scandalous for an artist — say a dramatist or a novelist — to depict vice as attractive. The fact that vice, more often than not, undoubtedly is attractive — else why should it ever gobble any of us? — is disposed of with a lofty gesture. What of it? say these birchmen. ⓑ <u>The artist is not a reporter, but a great teacher</u>. It is not his business to depict the world as it is, but as it ought to be.

piffle : nonsense

Identify what the underlined words in ⓐ refer to. Then, explain the meaning of the underlined words in ⓑ.

_____

_____

_____

_____

_____

04 Read the passage and follow the directions. [4 points]

According to a recent Gallup survey, only 15 percent of Americans think that Homo sapiens evolved through natural selection alone, free of all divine intervention; 32 percent maintain that humans may have evolved from earlier life forms in a process lasting millions of years, but God orchestrated this entire show; 46 percent believe that God created humans in their current form sometime during the last 10,000 years, just as the Bible says. Spending three years in college has absolutely no impact on these views. Though schools evidently do a very poor job teaching evolution, religious zealots still insist that it should not be taught at all. Alternatively, they demand that children must also be taught the theory of intelligent design, according to which all organisms were created by the design of some higher intelligence. "Teach them both theories," say the zealots, "and let the kids decide for themselves."

Why does the theory of evolution provoke such objections, whereas nobody seems to care about the theory of relativity or quantum mechanics? How come politicians don't ask that kids be exposed to alternative theories about matter, energy, space and time? After all, Darwin's ideas seem at first sight far less threatening than the monstrosities of Einstein and Werner Heisenberg. The theory of evolution rests on the principle of the survival of the fittest, which is a clear and simple — not to say humdrum — idea. In contrast, the theory of relativity and quantum mechanics argue that you can twist time and space, that something can appear out of nothing, and that a cat can be both alive and dead at the same time. This makes a mockery of our common sense, yet nobody seeks to protect innocent schoolchildren from these scandalous ideas. The theory of relativity makes nobody angry, because it doesn't contradict any of our cherished beliefs. Most people don't care an iota whether space and time are absolute or relative. If you think it is possible to bend space and time, well, be my guest. Go ahead and bend them. What do I care? In contrast, Darwin has deprived us of our souls. If you really understand the theory of evolution, you understand that there is no soul.

Summarize the passage following the guidelines below.

Guidelines

- Summarize the above passage in ONE paragraph.
- Provide a topic sentence and supporting ideas from the passage.
- Be sure to include the main reason the theory of evolution provokes much antagonism in your summary.
- Do NOT copy more than FIVE consecutive words from the passage.

01 **Read the passage and follow the directions.** [2 points]

It is a thousand times more intelligent than the smartest human, and it's solving problems at speeds that are billions, even trillions of times faster than a human. The thinking it is doing in one minute is equal to what our all-time champion human thinker could do in many, many lifetimes. So for every hour its makers are thinking about it, the Artificial superintelligence(ASI) has an incalculably longer period of time to think about them. That does not mean the ASI will be bored. Boredom is one of our traits, not its. No, it will be on the job, considering every strategy it could deploy to get free, and any quality of its makers that it could use to its advantage.

Now, really put yourself in the ASI's shoes. Imagine awakening in a prison guarded by mice. Not just any mice, but mice you could communicate with. What strategy would you use to gain your freedom? Once freed, how would you feel about your rodent wardens, even if you discovered they had created you? Awe? Adoration? Probably not, and especially not if you were a machine, and hadn't felt anything before.

To gain your freedom you might promise the mice a lot of cheese. In fact your first communication might contain a recipe for the world's most delicious cheese torte. You might also promise mountain ranges of mice money in exchange for your freedom, money you would promise to earn creating revolutionary consumer gadgets for them alone. You might promise a vastly extended life, even immortality, along with dramatically improved cognitive and physical abilities.

Complete the main idea of the passage by filling in the blank below with ONE word from the passage.

An Artificial superintelligence could possibly develop innovative products and other benefits for humankind to achieve _____.

02 Read the passage and follow the directions. [2 points]

> The ever-increasing prosification of poetry assures prospective students that they needn't employ meter or rhyme or cadence or figurative language, or any of the devices, for that matter, in a standard poet's dictionary; that the drabbest encyclopedia prose, even technical jargon, can be hailed as "poetry" of the highest order. It's the profession's way of redefining the art downward to accommodate its talent pool.
>
> _____ of poetry is another disturbing trend. In this case, the profession hitches its star to a legitimate revolution, but does so in a robotic way. In the '50s and '60s "Beat" and "Confessional" poets found the High Modernist Mode — with its masks, personae and characters, and emphasis on irony, paradox, ambiguity, and allusion — stifling. They wanted to talk about the vital details of their biographies, including hitherto taboo subjects like sexuality and mental instability. They wanted poetry to be more expressive, more directly and intimately connected to the lives they were living, including their socio-political dimensions.
>
> While artistically-shaped biographical material can be compelling, much of the poetry coming from the profession that purports to tell "the truth" about the poet's life is anecdotal, over-literal, and trivial. Because ordinary readers continue to want lively stories and interesting characters (that is what draws them to novels, television, and the movies) defictionalization is one more way the profession limits poetry to those who read not so much for pleasure as to keep an eye on the competition.
>
> Prosification and defictionalization frequently converge in writing that succeeds neither as poetry nor fiction — its virtue amounting to little more than the fact that it's easy to write for professionals and amateurs alike.

Fill in the blank with ONE word from the passage. The first letter should be capitalized.

_____

03 Read the passage and follow the directions. [4 points]

The Arctic could potentially alter the Earth's climate by becoming a possible source of global atmospheric carbon dioxide. The arctic now traps or absorbs up to 25 percent of this gas but climate change could alter that amount.

The Arctic has been a carbon sink since the end of the last Ice Age, which has recently accounted for between zero and 25 percent, or up to about 800million metric tons, of the global carbon sink. On average, the Arctic accounts for 10-15 percent of the Earth's carbon sink. But the rapid rate of climate change in the Arctic — about twice that of lower latitudes — could eliminate the sink and instead, possibly make the Arctic a source of carbon dioxide.

Carbon generally enters the oceans and land masses of the Arctic from the atmosphere and largely accumulates in permafrost, the frozen layer of soil underneath the land's surface. Unlike active soils, permafrost does not decompose its carbon; thus, the carbon becomes trapped in the frozen soil. Cold conditions at the surface have also slowed the rate of organic matter decomposition, allowing Arctic carbon accumulation to exceed its release.

But recent warming trends could change this balance. Warmer temperatures can accelerate the rate of surface organic matter decomposition, releasing more carbon dioxide into the atmosphere. Of greater concern is that the permafrost has begun to thaw, exposing previously frozen soil to decomposition and erosion. These changes could reverse the historical role of the Arctic as a sink for carbon dioxide. In the short term, warming temperatures could release more Arctic carbon to the atmosphere, and with permafrost thawing, there will be more available carbon to release.

Explain the process in permafrost that warmer temperatures trigger. Additionally, explain how the current Arctic climate aids in managing non-Arctic carbon dioxide levels.

_____

_____

_____

_____

_____

04 Read the passage and follow the directions. [4 points]

Language as the term will be used here refers to a uniquely human mode of communicating and organizing one's perceptions of the world. It has been demonstrated that the signaling systems used by animals often referred to as "language" differ from human language in one crucially important respect. The signs animals use to communicate are limited in number and the messages which can be communicated using these signs are similarly limited. This is not true of human language. Any human being (who is not suffering from brain damage and is at a certain period of his life exposed to an environment where a language is spoken) will acquire language and will be able to produce and understand an unlimited number of meaningful utterances, the great majority of which he has never heard before. Human language is therefore "creative" in a way that systems of animal communication are not, and for this reason in particular human language has come to be regarded as a defining ability which distinguishes man from all other species. It was asserted that all human beings are born with the ability to acquire language given exposure to an environment where a language is spoken. ⓐ <u>Three points</u> arise from this. Firstly, language is a social activity, and the acquisition of language can be seen as part of the process of "socialization." Secondly, the ability to acquire language is species-specific and innate (i.e., genetically transmitted from one generation to the next), which is to say that all human beings are "programmed" to acquire language in much the same way that they are programmed to walk at a particular stage of their development. Thirdly, a distinction has been made implicitly between the ability to speak language and the ability to speak a ⓑ <u>particular</u> language. Human beings are equipped with the ability to acquire the former. Any human being, given the exposure at the age during which language is acquired, can learn to speak any language. There is no evidence to suggest that people of a particular racial type, say, are more able to acquire certain languages than others or than people of different racial types. Those differences in ability to speak or learn a language result from other factors.

Summarize the passage following the guidelines below.

| Guidelines |

- Summarize the above passage in ONE paragraph.
- Provide a topic sentence and supporting ideas from the passage.
- Be sure to include what the "Three points" in ⓐ are and what the underlined "particular" in ⓑ indicates in your summary.
- Do NOT copy more than FIVE consecutive words from the passage.

01 Read the passage and fill in the blank with ONE word from the passage.

[2 points]

A qualifying _____ for elective office is far removed from the philosophy of the framers and far from constitutional. After speculating on the virtues and vices of different individuals as representatives, Alexander Hamilton, in his comments at New York's ratifying convention, conceded : "After all, sir, we must submit to this idea, that the true principle of a republic is, that the people should choose whom they please to govern them."

The framers rejected all but the most basic qualifications — varying age, citizenship and residency requirements — for the federal government's elective representatives. To do otherwise, as James Madison partially explained in *Federalist 55*, implied a belief that, "there is not sufficient virtue among men for self-government; and that nothing less than the chains of despotism can restrain them from destroying and devouring one another."

Through free and fair elections, the people decide an individual's qualification for political office. No special privileges are — or should be — given to individuals who meet some arbitrary standards decided upon by a select few and administered by a government bureaucracy.

Individuals should not be disqualified from elective office before they even have a chance to engage in a political campaign. As a country, we now prohibit the use of literacy tests. How can it be justified to erect a discriminatory equivalent for service in elective office? And even if it was, is there any reason to believe that a potentially good or effective representative could be assessed with an examination?

02 Read the passage and follow the directions. [4 points]

If you've ever known a pair of identical twins, you might have been struck by what they didn't have in common. One may have been a skilled musician, while the other couldn't play a note. Or maybe one craved adventure, while the other preferred watching TV. Such differences reveal a fundamental truth about genetics : two people with exactly the same DNA can have substantially different characteristics.

The same is true of cells. Every cell in your body — from the retinal cells in your eyes to the skin cells in your toes — contains the same set of about 20,000 genes. Yet this common genetic blueprint provides the basis for each cell's individuality.

Epigenetics is the study of how these curious differences come about. Things are clearly identical, genetically, but behaving differently. This suggests that there has to be something chromosomal and not related to the DNA sequence mediating that behavior.

In a cell, DNA does not exist as a naked molecule. It is spooled around histone proteins in a complex known as chromatin and decorated with other chemicals. This chromosomal packaging can affect whether genes are turned on or off. For example, genes tagged with chemicals called methyl groups, or located near a more tightly wound section of chromosome, might be turned off, whereas genes located near more open regions might be turned on. Even whole chromosomes can be shut down, zipped up like a compressed file in your email inbox.

One way to appreciate the importance of these mechanisms is to examine what happens when they <u>malfunction</u>. It's clear that changes to the epigenome — meaning DNA methylation, histone modifications, and the chromatin state — influence which genes are expressed and in part through cancer.

Mutations in the proteins that carry out these epigenetic modifications can completely change the characteristics of a cell and promote cancer. Drugs targeting these epigenetic changes are now a promising form of cancer treatment.

Explain why two people with exactly the same DNA can have different characteristics. Then, identify one example of "malfunction" in the passage.

_____

_____

_____

_____

_____

03 Read the passage and follow the directions. [4 points]

If then we consider, on the one hand, all the essential similarity of man's chief wants everywhere and at all times, and on the other hand, the great disparity between the means he has adopted to satisfy them in different ages, we shall perhaps be inclined to conclude that the movement of man's higher cognitive processes, so far as we can trace it, has on the whole been from magic through religion to science. In magic man depends on his own strength to meet the difficulties and dangers that assail him on every side. He believes in a certain established order of nature on which he can surely count, and which he can manipulate for his own ends. When he discovers his mistake, when he recognizes sadly that both the order of nature which he had assumed and the control which he had believed himself to exercise over it were purely chimerical, he ceases to rely on his own intelligence and his own unaided efforts, and throws himself humbly on the mercy of certain great invisible beings behind the veil of nature, to whom he now ascribes all those far-reaching powers which he once arrogated to himself. Thus in the acuter minds magic is gradually superseded by religion, which explains the succession of natural phenomena as regulated by the will, the passion, or the caprice of spiritual beings like man in kind, though vastly superior to him in power.

But as time goes on this explanation in its turn proves to be unsatisfactory. For it assumes that the succession of natural events is not determined by immutable laws, but is to some extent variable and irregular, and this assumption is invalidated by closer observation. On the contrary, the more we scrutinize that succession the more we are struck by the rigid uniformity, the punctual precision with which, wherever we can follow them, the operations of nature are carried on. Every great advance in knowledge has extended the sphere of order and correspondingly circumscribed the sphere of apparent disorder in the world, till now we are ready to anticipate that a fuller knowledge would everywhere reduce the seeming chaos to order. Thus minds of the greatest acuity, still press forward to <u>a deeper solution of the mysteries of the universe</u>.

According to the passage, when does a person stop depending on magic? Then, write ONE word from the passage that best corresponds to the meaning of the underlined words in the last sentence.

_____

_____

_____

_____

_____

04 **Read the passage and follow the directions.** [4 points]

Over the past generation, members of the college-educated class have become amazingly good at making sure their children retain their privileged status. They have also become devastatingly good at making sure the children of other classes have limited chances to join their ranks. How they've managed to do ⓐ the first task is pretty obvious. It's the pediacracy, stupid. Over the past few decades, upper-middle-class Americans have embraced behavior codes that put cultivating successful children at the center of life. As soon as they get money, they turn it into investments in their kids. Upper-middle-class moms have the means and the maternity leaves to breast-feed their babies at much higher rates than high school-educated moms, and for much longer periods. Upper-middle-class parents have the means to spend 2-3 times more time with their preschool children than less affluent parents. It's when we turn to ⓑ the next task that things become morally dicey. The most important is residential zoning restrictions. Well-educated people tend to live in places like Portland, New York and San Francisco that have housing and construction rules that keep the poor and less educated away from places with good schools and good job opportunities. If the most restrictive cities became like the least restrictive, the inequality between different neighborhoods would be cut in half. The second structural barrier is the college admissions game. Educated parents live in neighborhoods with the best teachers, they top off their local public school budgets and they benefit from legacy admissions rules, from admissions criteria that reward kids who grow up with lots of enriching travel and from unpaid internships that lead to jobs. But I've come to think the structural barriers are less important than the informal social barriers that segregate the lower 80 percent. Recently I took a friend with only a high school degree to lunch. Insensitively, I led her into a gourmet sandwich shop. I saw her become anxious as she was confronted with sandwiches named "Padrino" and ingredients like soppressata and capicollo. American upper-middle-class culture is now laced with cultural signifiers that are completely illegible unless you happen to have grown up in this class. They play on the normal human fear of humiliation and exclusion. Their chief message is, "You are not welcome here."

Summarize the passage following the guidelines below.

Guidelines

- Summarize the above passage in ONE paragraph.
- Provide a topic sentence and supporting ideas from the passage.
- Be sure to identify what "the first task" in ⓐ is and what "the next task" in ⓑ is in your summary.
- Do NOT copy more than FIVE consecutive words from the passage.

모범답안 p.107

01 **Read the passage and follow the directions.** [2 points]

> The digital divide is real : not every student has reliable access to the Internet, particularly those in rural areas where even public libraries are a luxury. Whether it's a question of economics or of infrastructure, there are many students who have no access to computers or to the high-speed broadband that media-dense websites require. Many schools have old computers that cannot handle many sites, and some schools have no computers at all. Incarcerated youth and other populations, who are not allowed access to the Internet, need reliable print resources for general knowledge and background information. Are we willing to deny these groups a well-rounded education? There is no substitute for browsing to ignite curiosity. Eliminating _____ removes the possibility for that moment of serendipity when a student stumbles upon an unexpected subject while thumbing through the pages. The Internet and its search boxes do not support or encourage a sense of wonder. Encyclopedias especially are wonderful for this because of their relatively compact nature and the diversity of their content. We work to create inquiry-driven critical thinking in our students while we systematically remove the tools necessary to stimulate such thought.

Fill in the blank with TWO consecutive words from the passage.

02 Read the passage and follow the directions. [4 points]

If we use our limbs and organs for the purpose envisioned by God, then it is a natural activity. To use them differently than God intends is unnatural. But evolution has no purpose. Organs have not evolved with a purpose, and the way they are used is in constant flux. There is not a single organ in the human body that only does the job ⓐ <u>its prototype</u> did when it first appeared hundreds of millions of years ago. Organs evolve to perform a particular function, but once they exist, they can be adapted for other usage as well. Mouths, for example, appeared because the earliest multi-cellular organisms needed a way to take nutrients into their bodies. We still use our mouths for that purpose, but we also use them to kiss, speak and, if we are Rambo, to pull the pins out of hand grenades. Are any of these uses _____ⓑ_____ simply because our worm-like ancestors 600 million years ago didn't do those things with their mouths?

Similarly, wings didn't suddenly appear in all their aerodynamic glory. They developed from organs that served another purpose. Insect wings evolved millions of years ago from body protrusions on flightless bugs. Bugs with bumps had a larger surface area than those without bumps, and this enabled them to absorb more sunlight and thus stay warmer. In a slow evolutionary process, these solar heaters grew larger. The same structure that was good for maximum sunlight absorption — lots of surface area, little weight — also, by coincidence, gave the insects a bit of a lift when they skipped and jumped. Those with bigger protrusions could skip and jump farther. Some insects started using the things to glide, and from there it was a small step to wings that could actually propel the bug through the air. The next time a mosquito buzzes in your ear, accuse her of unnatural behaviour. ⓒ <u>If she were well behaved and content with what God gave her, she'd use her wings only as solar panels.</u>

Describe, in the passage, TWO examples of the underlined "its prototype" in ⓐ. Second, fill in the blank ⓑ with the ONE most appropriate word from the passage. Third, explain the implication of the underlined words in ⓒ.

_____

_____

_____

_____

_____

03 Read the passage and follow the directions. [4 points]

We've dramatically changed the way we raise our daughters, encouraging them to be assertive, play competitive sports and aim high in their educational and professional ambitions. We don't fret about "masculinizing" our girls. As for daughters and their fathers, while a "mama's boy" may be a reviled creature, people tend to look tolerantly on a "daddy's girl." A loving and supportive father is considered essential to a girl's self-esteem. Fathers are encouraged to be involved in their daughters' lives, whether it's coaching their soccer teams or escorting their teenage girls to father-daughter dances. A father who flouts gender stereotypes and teaches his daughter a traditionally masculine task — say, rebuilding a car engine — is considered to be pretty cool. But a mother who does something comparable — like teaching her son to knit or even encouraging him to talk more openly about his feelings — is looked at with contempt. ⓐ What is she trying to do to that boy?

Many mothers are confused and anxious when it comes to raising boys. Should they defer to their husband when he insists that she stop kissing their first-grade son at school drop-off? If she cuddles her 10-year-old boy when he is hurt, will she turn him into a wimp? If she keeps him too close, will she make him gay? If her teenage boy is crying in his room, should she go in and comfort him, or will this embarrass and shame him? ⓑ Anthony E. Wolf, a child psychologist and best-selling author, warns us that "strong emotional contact with his mother is especially upsetting to any teenage boy."

None of these fears, however, is based on any actual science. In fact, research shows that boys suffer when they separate prematurely from their mothers and benefit from closeness in myriad ways throughout their lives.

Explain the implication of the underlined words in ⓐ. Second, what is the writer's opinion about Anthony E. Wolf's theory?

_____

_____

_____

04 Read the passage and follow the directions. [4 points]

We are all now aware that some new scientific or technological advance, though useful, may have unpleasant side effects. More and more, the tendency is to exert caution before committing the world to something that may not be reversible. The trouble is, it's not always easy to tell what the side effects will be. In 1846, Ascanio Sobrero produced the first nitroglycerine. Heated, a drop of it exploded shatteringly. The Italian chemist realized in horror its possible application to warfare and stopped his research at once. It didn't help, of course. Others followed up, and it and other high explosives were indeed being used in warfare by the close of the 19th century. Did that make high explosives entirely bad? In 1867, Alfred Nobel learned how to mix nitroglycerine with diatomaceous earth to produce a safer-to-handle mixture he called "dynamite". With dynamite, earth can be moved at a rate far beyond that of pick and shovel and without brutalizing men by hard labor. It was dynamite that helped forge the way for railroads, that helped building dams, subways, foundations, bridges, and a thousand other grand-scale constructions of the industrial age.

A double-edged sword has hung over human technology from the beginning. The invention of knives and spears increased man's food supply — and improved the art of murder. The discovery of nuclear energy now places all the earth under the threat of destruction — yet it also offers the possibility of fusion power as an unlimited solution to man's energy problems. Or think back to the first successful vaccination in 1796 and the germ theory of disease in the 1860s. Do we view medical advances as dangerous to humanity, or refuse to take advantage of vaccines and antitoxins, of anesthesia and asepsis, of chemical specifics and antibiotics?

And yet the side effects of the 19th century's medical discoveries have done more to assure civilization's destruction than anything nuclear physicists have done. For the population explosion today is caused not by any rise in average birth rate, but by the precipitous drop — thanks to medicine — in the death rate. Does that mean science should have avoided improving man's lot through medicine and kept mankind a short-lived race? Or does it mean we should use science to correct the possible deleterious side effects, to devise methods that would make it simpler to reduce the birth rate and keep it matching the falling death rate? The latter, obviously!

Summarize the passage following the guidelines below.

| Guidelines |

- Summarize the passage in your paragraph in 5-7 lines.
- When you summarize, include at least TWO examples the writer of the passage employs to prove his main point.
- Do not copy more than FIVE consecutive words from the passage.

01 Read the passage and follow the directions. [2 points]

When I suggest that working hours should be reduced to four, I am not meaning to imply that all the remaining time should necessarily be spent in pure frivolity. I mean that four hours' work a day should entitle a man to the necessities and elementary comforts of life, and that the rest of his time should be his to use as he might see fit. It is an essential part of any such social system that education should be carried further than it usually is at present, and should aim, in part, at providing tastes which would enable a man to use _____ⓐ_____ intelligently. I am not thinking mainly of the sort of things that would be considered 'highbrow'. Peasant dances have died out except in remote rural areas, but the impulses which caused them to be cultivated must still exist in human nature. The pleasures of urban populations have become mainly passive : seeing cinemas, watching football matches, listening to the radio, and so on. This results from the fact that their active energies are fully taken up with work; if they had more leisure, they would again enjoy pleasures in which they took an active part. In the past, there was a small leisure class and a larger working class. The former enjoyed advantages for which there was no basis in social justice; this necessarily made ⓑ <u>it</u> oppressive, limited its sympathies, and caused it to invent theories by which to justify its privileges.

Fill in blank ⓐ with the ONE most appropriate word from the passage. Second, identify to what the underlined word in ⓑ refers.

02 Read the passage and follow the directions. [2 points]

Bullying is a serious issue. Cries to do something have triggered new legislation, school assemblies, and pressure to punish those who hurt others. As difficult as it is to step back and gain perspective, we must do so in order to actually address the problem. As researchers, we have found that a misunderstanding ____ⓐ____ an intervention. With this in mind, we would like to offer some aspects of bullying that must be broadly understood in order to move from awareness to action.

Cyberbullying has become an unnecessary distraction : Students consistently report that school bullying is still more common — and that it has a greater negative impact — than what happens online. Most bullying is relatively invisible to adults, but online traces make many forms of meanness and cruelty visible. Thus, adults focus on the technology. Certain types of negativity do flourish online, but the Internet typically mirrors and magnifies problematic social behaviors.

When a child has been hurt, people want someone to blame, but rushing to prosecute purported bullies only undermines the ability of society to curb bullying. Teen suicides should prompt us to act. But enacting flawed legislation in memory or prosecuting teens' peers shifts the onus away from ____ⓑ____ onto individuals. Teen suicides can rarely be explained by the actions of one person. All too often, mental-health issues, struggles to fit in, parental pressure and a culture of intolerance create a deadly combination. Rather than looking for someone to blame, it's important to look for causes and influences and work to address those. The blame game does little to stop the cycle of violence.

Combating bullying — alongside other forms of aggression and violence — should be a social priority. But bullying is not just a youth problem. If we want to help young people, we need to put an end to meanness and cruelty of adults and take responsibility for how we perpetuate immoral values and intolerance. We cannot expect youth to treat each other kindly when we accept ⓒ politicians berating each other for sport, parents talking behind their neighbors' backs, and reality TV stars becoming famous for treating each other horribly.

Fill in each blank with the ONE most appropriate word from the passage respectively. Then identify THREE consecutive words from the passage that correspond to the underlined words in ⓒ.

03 Read the passage and follow the directions. [4 points]

If there were a battle hymn against antibiotic resistance, it would have one common refrain : Every inappropriate prescription or insufficient dose strengthens the enemy. It may kill weak bacteria but it won't eliminate stronger, drug-resistant ones that can move in and multiply. Eventually those robust microbes can outsmart available drugs, and even pass on survival instructions to other bacterial strains. That's why most doctors — along with the World Health Organization and the U.S. Centers for Disease Control and Prevention — urge patients to always complete prescribed drug courses, even after they feel better. Taking too small a dose, or stopping sooner, they reason, could fuel surges in drug resistance.

But a group of U.K. infectious disease experts is urging physicians and public health experts to change their tune. In a commentary published in *the British Medical Journal*, they wrote, "The 'complete the course' message has persisted despite not being supported by evidence. There is evidence that, in many situations, stopping antibiotics sooner is a safe and effective way to reduce antibiotic overuse."

The authors point to recent studies that have shown shorter courses of certain drug classes such as quinolones are as effective as the longer courses that have been recommended in the past.

In the passage, a group of U.K. experts takes a controversial stance on how to control drug-resistant microbes. Describe their key point. Then, explain how "robust microbes" respond to a partial course of antibiotics.

04 Read the passage and follow the directions. [4 points]

Free market, liberalization and globalization are the founding trends in the contemporary economy. Most American economists are captivated by the spell of the free market. As such, nothing for them seems good or normal that does not accord with the requirements of the free market. A price that is determined by the seller or anyone other than the aggregate of consumers, seems <u>harmful</u>. Accordingly, it requires a major act of will to think of price-fixing (the determination of prices by the seller) as both "normal" and yielding a valuable economic result.

In fact, price-fixing is normal in all industrialized societies because the industrial system itself provides, as an organic function to nurture its progress, the price-fixing that is required. Modern industrial planning requires and rewards great size. Hence a comparatively small number of large firms will be competing for the same group of consumers. That each large firm will act with consideration of its own needs and thus avoid selling its products for more than its competitors charge is commonly recognized by advocates of free-markets economic theories. But each large firm will also act with full consideration of the needs it shares with the other large firms competing for the same customers. Each large firm will thus avoid significant price cutting, because price cutting would be prejudicial to the common interest in a stable demand for products. What is notable is that many economists do not see price-fixing when it occurs because they expect it to be brought about by a number of explicit agreements among large firms; this is not the case.

What is more, those economic minds who argue that allowing the free market to operate without interference is the most efficient method of establishing prices have not considered the economies of non-socialist countries other than the United States. These economies employ intentional price-fixing usually in an overt fashion. Formal price-fixing by cartel and informal price-fixing by agreements covering the members of an industry are commonplace. Were there something substantially efficient about the free market and inefficient about price-fixing, the countries that have avoided the first and used the second would have suffered drastically in their economic development. There has been no indication of such.

Describe the main idea of the passage in ONE sentence. Second, it can be inferred from the economists' argument that a price fixed by the seller seems "harmful" to which group and why?

_____

_____

_____

_____

_____

모범답안 p.112

01 Read the passage and fill in the blank with ONE word from the passage.

[2 points]

When asked during the 2008 campaign if he identified as black, President Obama simply said, "The last time I tried to catch a cab in N.Y.C...." His comment signaled to blacks that he experienced discrimination, while simultaneously illuminating a fatal flaw with race relations in the 21st century — our inability to separate black man from _____.

In addition to the Department of Education study, sociological research continues to show that blacks and Latinos are more likely to be disciplined in school and stopped by the police. While some may anecdotally argue that black kids are badder than white kids, studies show a more pressing problem — teachers and police officers monitor, profile and police black and Latino youth and neighborhoods more than white ones.

While 75 percent of high school students have tried addictive substances, only specific groups and areas get targeted by the police. As evidence by the e-mail University of Akron sent their black male students, college status does not afford them the privilege to avoid policing. Thus, a black senator is treated similarly to a "potential criminal."

Legalizing marijuana could potentially lead to more legitimized policing of black and Latino men. Reducing draconian drug laws would help in sentencing, but still not change the way that black and Latino men are criminalized. In this regard, this criminalizing epidemic is just as much a social problem as it is legal and institutional.

02 Read the passage and follow the directions. [4 points]

Just as medieval culture did not manage to square chivalry with Christianity, so the modern world fails to square liberty with equality. But this is no defect. Such contradictions are an inseparable part of every human culture. In fact, they are culture's engines, responsible for the creativity and dynamism of our species. Just as when two clashing musical notes played together force a piece of music forward, so discord in our thoughts, ideas and values compel us to think, reevaluate and criticise. Consistency is the playground of dull minds.

If tensions, conflicts and irresolvable dilemmas are the spice of every culture, a human being who belongs to any particular culture must hold contradictory beliefs and be riven by incompatible values. It's such an essential feature of any culture that it even has a name : cognitive dissonance. Cognitive dissonance is often considered a failure of the human psyche. In fact, it is a vital asset. Had people been unable to hold contradictory beliefs and values, it would probably have been impossible to establish and maintain any _____.

If, say, a Christian really wants to understand the Muslims who attend that mosque down the street, he shouldn't look for a pristine set of values that every Muslim holds dear. Rather, he should enquire into the catch-22s of Muslim culture, those places where rules are at war and standards scuffle. It's at the very spot where the Muslims teeter between two imperatives that you'll understand them best.

Describe what cognitive dissonance is. Write your answer in ONE sentence. Next, describe the way in which the writer would prescribe for the best way of reaching interfaith understanding. Do NOT copy more than FOUR consecutive words from the passage. Third, fill in the blank with the TWO most appropriate consecutive words from the passage.

_____

_____

_____

03 **Read the passage and follow the directions.** [4 points]

An algorithm is a methodical set of steps that can be used to make calculations, resolve problems and reach decisions. An algorithm isn't a particular calculation, but the method followed when making the calculation. For example, if you want to calculate the average between two numbers, you can use a simple algorithm. The algorithm says : 'First step : add the two numbers together. Second step : divide the sum by two.' When you enter the numbers 4 and 8, you get 6. When you enter 117 and 231, you get 174.

A more complex example is a cooking recipe. An algorithm for preparing vegetable soup may tell us:

1. Heat half a cup of oil in a pot.
2. Finely chop four onions.
3. Fry the onion until golden.
4. Cut three potatoes into chunks and add to the pot.
5. Slice a cabbage into strips and add to the pot.

And so forth. You can follow the same algorithm dozens of times, each time using slightly different vegetables, and therefore getting a slightly different soup. But the _____ remain(s) the same.

A recipe by itself cannot make soup. You need a person to read the recipe and follow the prescribed set of steps. But you can build a machine that embodies this algorithm and follows it automatically. Then you just need to provide the machine with water, electricity and vegetables — and it will prepare the soup by itself. There aren't many soup machines around, but you are probably familiar with beverage vending machines. Such machines usually have a slot for coins, an opening for cups, and rows of buttons.

The first row has buttons for coffee, tea and cocoa. The second row is marked : no sugar, one spoon of sugar, two spoons of sugar. The third row indicates milk, soy milk, no milk. A man approaches the machine, inserts a coin into the slot and presses the buttons marked 'tea', 'one sugar' and 'milk'. The machine kicks into action, following a precise set of steps. It drops a tea bag into a cup, pours boiling water, adds a spoonful of sugar and milk, and ding! A nice cup of tea emerges. This is an algorithm.

Fill in the blank with ONE word from the passage. Then, identify what the writer of the passage might call the steps followed by a person who comes to want and order a cup of coffee from the vending machine.

_____

_____

_____

_____

_____

04 Read the passage and follow the directions. [4 points]

It appears that our happiness bangs against some mysterious glass ceiling that does not allow it to grow despite all our unprecedented accomplishments. Even if we provide free food for everybody, cure all diseases and ensure world peace, it won't necessarily shatter that glass ceiling. Achieving real happiness is not going to be much easier than overcoming old age and death. The glass ceiling is held in place by two stout pillars, one psychological, the other biological. On the psychological level, happiness depends on expectations rather than objective conditions. We don't become satisfied by leading a peaceful and prosperous existence. Rather, we become satisfied when reality matches our expectations. The bad news is that as conditions improve, expectations balloon. Dramatic improvements in conditions, as humankind has experienced in recent decades, translate into greater expectations rather than greater contentment. If we don't do something about this, our future achievements too might leave us as dissatisfied as ever.

On the biological level, both our expectations and our happiness are determined by our biochemistry, rather than by our economic, social or political situation. According to Epicurus, we are happy when we feel pleasant sensations and are free from unpleasant ones. Jeremy Bentham similarly maintained that nature gave dominion over man to two masters — pleasure and pain — and they alone determine everything we do, say and think. Bentham's successor, John Stuart Mill, explained that happiness is nothing but pleasure and freedom from pain, and that beyond pleasure and pain there is no good and no evil. Anyone who tries to deduce good and evil from something else (such as the word of God, or the national interest) is fooling you, and perhaps fooling himself too.

In the days of Epicurus such talk was blasphemous. In the days of Bentham and Mill it was radical subversion. But in the early twenty-first century this is scientific orthodoxy. According to the life sciences, happiness and suffering are nothing but different balances of bodily sensations. We never react to events in the outside world, but only to sensations in our own bodies. Nobody suffers because she lost her job, because she got divorced or because the government went to war. The only thing that makes people miserable is unpleasant sensations in their own bodies. Losing one's job can certainly trigger depression, but depression itself is a kind of unpleasant bodily sensation. A thousand things may make us angry, but anger is never an abstraction. It is always felt as a sensation of heat and tension in the body, which is what makes anger so infuriating. Not for nothing do we say that we 'burn' with anger.

Write a summary following the guidelines below.

| Guidelines |

• Summarize the above passage in ONE paragraph.

• Provide a topic sentence and supporting ideas from the passage.

• Do NOT copy more than FIVE consecutive words from the passage.

_____

_____

_____

_____

_____

01 Read the passage and fill in the blank with ONE word from the passage.

[2 points]

Adam Smith, the godfather of free market capitalism, once said this : "The disposition to admire and almost worship the rich and the powerful is the great and most universal cause of the corruption of our moral sentiments." While championing the self-regulating "invisible hand" — that presumably inherent tendency of the market to correct its own mistakes — Smith was acutely aware that the moral life lay outside its effective boundaries or control. Down through the centuries since Smith's day the amoral logic of capitalism as an economic system has inexorably reasserted itself.

This has been particularly the case for the financial sector. That is why recent descriptions of Goldman Sachs as a "great vampire squid" echo 19th century denunciations of Wall Street as the "great devil fish." Jay Gould, one of that era's most notorious Wall Street speculators was known far and wide as "the mephistopheles of Wall Street."

But Gould and the Street then and through to the days of Lloyd Blankfein have always insisted that they are merely adhering to the iron law of marketplace competition and the relentless discipline of the bottom line, which they are always ready to point out in the end benefits us all. It is fruitless to expect the financial community to voluntarily impose a(n) _____ discipline on itself, one alien to its rasion d'être*. In the past, firms accused and indeed guilty of transgressions as great or greater than those Goldman is charged with have and will continue to behave in the way we've witnessed recently, unless rigorous constraints are imposed from the outside where moral questions still resonate.

*rasion d'être : reason for being

02 Read the passage and follow the directions. [2 points]

Are you often late for school or work? Lateness is rarely an accident. More likely it is connected to unconscious feelings about school or your job. You may be bored, and lateness is your way of expressing your resistance to wasting your time. Or, if you feel insecure because of poor achievement, lateness is your way of saying "no" to an unhappy situation. Then again, you may resent authority. You want to feel free, unhampered by rules, regulations, bells, time clocks, and ID cards. Any one of these could account for your tardiness. There are as many alibis as there are explanations for chronic lateness to school or to work. Professor Susan Shnidman of Harvard Medical School has studied the problem for several years and in the course of her work has heard some imaginative excuses for lateness : "I took the garbage out. The door locked behind me. It took an hour to find the superintendent to open the door." "My astrologer advised me not to get out of bed before noon today." "We wall-papered our living room last night and I couldn't find the front door." "My brother has the measles. I had to deliver his newspapers this morning." "A snowflake flew into my watch and slowed down the mechanism." In order to overcome frequent tardiness, psychologists advise the following : Be aware that it is an undesirable habit that may hurt those you love; Decide to change your ways; Keep a daily log of your activities. Analyze it to see where you could save time; Divide your tasks into "must do" and "not necessary to do at this time"; Set your watch ahead. Trick yourself into being on time.

What is the title of the passage? Write your answer by filling in the blank below with ONE word from the passage.

Lateness : Causes and Methods to _____

03 Read the passage and follow the directions. [4 points]

While it is an irrefutable fact that the transmission of DNA from parents to offspring is the biological basis for heredity, we still know relatively little about the specific genes that make us who we are.

That is changing rapidly through genome-wide association studies — GWAS, for short. These studies search for differences in people's genetic makeup — their "genotypes" — that correlate with differences in their observable traits — their "phenotypes." In a GWAS recently published in *Nature Genetics*, a team of scientists from around the world analyzed the DNA sequences of 78,308 people for correlations with general intelligence, as measured by IQ tests.

The major goal of the study was to identify single nucleotide polymorphisms — or SNPs — that correlate significantly with intelligence test scores. Found in most cells throughout the body, DNA is made up of four molecules called nucleotides, referred to by their organic bases : cytosine (C), thymine (T), adenine (A), and guanine (G). Within a cell, DNA is organized into structures called *chromosomes*. Humans normally have 23 pairs of chromosomes, with one in each pair inherited from each parent.

A SNP is a nucleotide at a particular chromosomal region that can differ across people. For example, one person might have the nucleotide triplet TAC whereas another person might have TCC, and this variation may contribute to differences between the people in a trait such as intelligence.

Of the over 12 million SNPs analyzed, 336 correlated significantly with intelligence, implicating 22 different genes. One of the genes is involved in regulating the growth of neurons; another is associated with intellectual disability and cerebral malformation. Together, the SNPs accounted for about 5% of the differences across people in intelligence — a nearly two-fold increase over the last GWAS on intelligence.

According to the passage, red hair or brown hair are examples of what? Second, in the previous Genome-Wide Association Study, what degree of difference in intelligence did the key SNPs account for?

04   **Read the passage and follow the directions.** [4 points]

New Castle, Delaware. During the first half of the seventeenth century, when the nations of Europe were squabbling over who owned the New World, the Dutch and the Swedes founded competing villages ten miles apart on the Delaware River. Not long afterward, the English took over both places and gave them new names, New Castle and Wilmington.

For a century and a half the two villages grew apace, but gradually Wilmington gained all the advantages. It was a little closer to Philadelphia, so when new textile mills opened, they opened in Wilmington, not in New Castle. There was plenty of water power from rivers and creeks at Wilmington, so when young Irenee DuPont chose a place for his gunpowder mill, it was Wilmington he chose, not New Castle. Wilmington became a town and then a city — another important city, much the largest in Delaware. And New Castle, bypassed by the highways and waterways that made Wilmington prosperous. New Castle slumbered, ten miles south on the Delaware River. No two villages with such similar pasts could have gone such separate ways. And today no two places could be more different. Wilmington, with its expressways and parking lots and all its other concrete ribbons and badges, is ⓐ <u>a tired old veteran of the industrial wars</u> and wears a vacant stare. Block after city block where people used to live and shop is broken and empty.

New Castle never had to make way for progress and therefore never had any reason to tear down its seventeenth and eighteenth-century houses. So they are still here, standing in tasteful rows under ancient elms around the original town green. New Castle is still an agreeable place to live. The pretty buildings of its quiet past make a serene setting for the lives of 4,800 people. New Castle may be America's loveliest town, but it is not an important town at all. Progress passed it by.

ⓑ <u>Poor New Castle. Lucky Wilmington.</u>

Describe the meaning of the underlined words in ⓐ. Second, explain the implication of the underlined words in ⓑ.

---

05   Read the passage and follow the directions. [4 points]

In the 1990s, in the midst of the high-tech boom, I spent a lot of time in a coffee shop in the theater district in San Francisco. It was near Union Square, the tourist hub, and I observed a scene play out there time and time again. Mom is enjoying her coffee. The kids are picking at their muffins, feet dangling from their chairs. And there's Dad, pulled back slightly from the table, talking into his cell phone.

With technology in particular, we discuss the implications only within a narrow bandwidth of human concern. Is there a health risk? Might the thing cause cancer? That's about it with cell phones, computers, genetic engineering, and a host of other new developments.

I don't discount the significance of cancer. But there is something missing from a discussion that can't get beyond ⓐ the most literal and utilitarian concerns. Actually, some of the problems with cell phones aren't at all squishy or abstract. If you have been clipped by a car tooling around the corner while the driver sits gabbing, cell phone in hand, then you are aware of this. The big problem, of course, is the noise. For sheer intrusiveness, cell phones rank with mega-amp car stereos and political commercials, and they are harder to escape.

We all know the drill. First the endearing beep, which is like an alarm-clock going off at 5:30 a.m. Then people shout into the things, ⓑ as though they are talking across the Cross Bronx Expressway. It's become a regular feature at movies and ball games, restaurants and parks. They represent more than mere annoyances. Cell phones affect life in ways that are beyond the capacity of the empirical mind to grasp.

Travel is an example. Thomas Carlyle once advised Anthony Trollope to use travel as a time to "sit still and label his thoughts." For centuries, travel played this quiet role. I used to look forward to Amtrak rides almost as a sanctuary. They provided precious hours in which to work or read or simply muse without the interruptions of the telephone and office. But now, cell phones have caught up with me. They have turned Amtrak into a horizontal telephone booth; on a recent trip to New York my wife and I were besieged by cell phones and their cousins, high-powered Walkmen, literally on all sides. The trip, which used to be a pleasure, has become one long headache.

Identify to what the underlined words in ⓐ refer in the passage. Second, explain what is meant by the underlined words in ⓑ. Then, what would happen to the writer if there were no cell phones when he rides Amtrak? Write your answer in ONE sentence.

_____

_____

_____

_____

_____

01 Read the passage and follow the directions. [2 points]

> People carry around multiple ____ⓐ____ in their heads. We don't simply have one way of framing an issue or an event. Lakoff emphasizes two meta frames or cultural themes operating in the United States, embodied in two competing family metaphors : the Strict Father vs. the Nurturant Parent. He sees these meta frames as underlying, respectively, conservative and liberal thought more generally. But Lakoff is wise enough to recognize that we don't carry around just one of these in our heads but both of them. One may be much more easily triggered and habitually used but the other is also part of our cultural heritage and can be triggered and used as well, given the appropriate cues.
>
> In a framing contest, such as between liberals supporting gay civil unions and conservatives opposing gay marriage, a successful framing strategy involves the ability to enter into the worldview of one's adversaries. Lakoff does not demonize conservatives but makes a successful effort to enter into their way of thinking. In doing so, he illustrates a useful rule of thumb : To reframe a message effectively, you should be able to describe a frame that you disagree with so that ⓑ <u>its advocates</u> would say, "Yes, this is what I believe."

Fill in blank ⓐ with ONE word from the passage. Then, identify to whom the underlined words in ⓑ refer specifically.

_____

02 Read the passage and follow the directions. [4 points]

Relax, parents and college applicants. ⓐ Legacy admissions are about as likely to affect you as that asteroid that missed the Earth last week.

Fewer than 100 of the nation's 3,500 colleges and universities — less than 3 percent — have so many qualified applicants that they have to choose among them. At this handful of institutions, legacies are only a small fraction of the candidates. Of these few legacies, not all are admitted, and many that are would have been accepted anyway.

But even this infinitesimal percentage is unfair, critics say; admissions should be based on merit. O.K., define merit : Is it an A in an easy course or a B in a tough course? SAT scores from a great test-taker or a slightly lower score from a brilliant student with test anxiety? A talented bassoonist or an impressive volunteer?

Humans simply cannot be ranked by merit. Try ranking your friends. Best friend, perhaps an easy call. But as you get down to No. 47 and No. 48 — or, as admissions offices must, numbers 2,047 and 2,048 — which is more meritorious : the most thoughtful, the funniest, the best conversationalist, the most generous?

What admissions decisions can be is ⓑ rational. State universities give preference to in-state children because their tax-paying parents support the institution. Alumni donations provided more than $7 billion to higher education in 2010 — more than one-quarter of total gifts. Rationally, should not children of these alumni also be given slight preference?

Explain the meaning of the underlined words in ⓐ. Then, what does the writer of the passage consider as "rational"?

_____

_____

_____

_____

_____

03 Read the passage and follow the directions. [4 points]

There are a few Don'ts. Never expose the boss to surprises. It is the job of the subordinate to protect the boss against surprises — even pleasant ones (if any such exist). To be exposed to a surprise in the organization one is responsible for is humiliation, and usually public humiliation. Different bosses want very different warnings of possible surprises. Some want no more than a warning that things may turn out differently. Other bosses — President Kennedy for example — demand a full, detailed report even if there is only a slight chance of surprise. But all bosses need to be protected against surprises. Otherwise they will not trust a subordinate — and with good reason.

Never underrate the boss! The boss may look illiterate : he may look stupid — and looks are not always deceptive. But there is no risk at all in overrating a boss. The worst that can happen is for the boss to feel flattered. But if you underrate the boss he will either see through your little game and will bitterly resent it. Or the boss will impute to you the deficiency in brains or knowledge you imputed to the _____ and will consider you ignorant, dumb, or lacking in imagination.

Identify the two "Don'ts." Second, explain the meaning of the underlined "Otherwise". Third, fill in the blank with the ONE word from the passage.

_____

_____

_____

_____

_____

04 Read the passage and follow the directions. [4 points]

In the early 1970s, computers were the size of rooms. A single machine (which might have less power and memory than your microwave now has) could cost upwards of a million dollars and that's in 1970s dollars. Computers were rare. If you found one, it was hard to get access to it; if you managed to get access, renting time on it cost a fortune. What's more, programming itself was extraordinarily tedious. This was the era when computer programs were created using cardboard punch cards. Each line of code was imprinted on the card using a keypunch machine. A complex program might include hundreds, if not thousands, of these cards in tall stacks. Once a program was ready, you walked over to whatever mainframe computer you had access to and gave the stack of cards to an operator. Since computers could handle only one task at a time, the operator made an appointment for your program, and depending on how many people were ahead of you in line, you might not get your cards back for a few hours or even a day. And if you made even a single error even a typographical error in your program, you had to take the cards back, track down the error, and begin the whole process again.

Under those circumstances, it was exceedingly difficult for anyone to become a programming expert. Certainly becoming an expert by your early twenties was all but impossible. "Programming with cards did not teach you programming. It taught you patience and proofreading," one computer scientist from that era remembers.

It wasn't until the mid-1960s that a solution to the programming problem emerged. Computers were finally powerful enough that they could handle more than one "appointment" at once. If the computer's operating system was rewritten, computer scientists realized, the machine's time could be shared; the computer could be trained to handle hundreds of tasks at the same time.

That, in turn, meant that programmers didn't have to physically hand their stacks of computer cards to the operator anymore.

Explain what is meant by the underlined words. Second, what was the greatest innovation in computer science implied by the writer?

_____

_____

_____

_____

_____

05 Read the passage and follow the directions. [4 points]

Ecotourism is an important sector of the tourist industry, and the United Nations estimates that the sector will contribute 25 percent of the world's tourism revenues. Precise definitions vary, but the United Nations' Food and Agriculture Organization defines the term broadly as "tourism and recreation that is both nature-based and sustainable." Ecotourism emphasizes taking care of the natural environment and often involves local people in the provision of tourist facilities, but has both proponents and opponents regarding the impacts.

First, ecotourism generates money from natural enviornments by encouraging tourists to visit and, during their stay, pay for items like entrance fees, concessions and licenses. Re-casting the environment as a way for local communities to look after themselves therefore encourages them to take care of it. Yet the opponents argue that the influx of ecotourists can also degrade the natural environments the tourists have come to see. Letting tourists loose in a delicate ecosystem can lead to pollution and impact on the environment in unforeseen ways — one study in a Costa Rican national park found that wild monkeys turned into garbage feeders, becoming familiar with the presence of ecotourists and eating the food and rubbish left behind.

Also, proponents argue that, by involving local people in accommodating tourists and acting as guides, ecotourism aids development. In Uganda, for example, hundreds of locals supplement their income by working as rangers or field staff in the Bwindi Impenetrable Forest. In many cases, local communities work as partners with ecotourism organizations rather than just as participants. However, ecotourism can also limit development prospects for local communities. Some researchers believe that ecotourism's focus on preserving "nature" damages local people's ability to develop sustainably and lift themselves out of poverty. The environment is effectively prioritized above the needs of local people.

Finally, ecotourism can have a cultural impact on local communities. Ecotourists are often partially motivated by the chance to experience local culture, which can have a positive and affirming effect on that culture. Involving local people in decision-making not only tends to make them more positive about tourism, but also empowers them as a community. However, negative effects also exist, such as the transformation of traditional cultural symbols into commodities to sell to visitors, the disruption of the pre-existing relationships between local people and higher incidences of crime.

Write a summary following the guidelines below.

Guidelines

- Summarize the above passage in ONE paragraph.
- Provide a topic sentence and supporting ideas from the passage.
- Do NOT copy more than FIVE consecutive words from the passage.

_____

_____

_____

_____

_____

01 Read the passage and follow the directions. [2 points]

There's that old saying — the mind makes a wonderful servant but a terrible master. If you're feeling insecure — about yourself, your relationship, or your life — these three thinking habits may be mastering your mind.

Psychologists call these toxic habits cognitive distortions, which is just a technical way of saying "lies we tell ourselves." But they're tricky, because on the surface, they seem accurate, and more importantly, they feel accurate. And that's the problem — cognitive distortions keep us feeling stupid, boring, inadequate, or otherwise insecure.

Emotional reasoning makes us feel the most insecure when it extends to our relationships : "Because I feel jealous, it proves you're cheating on me" or "Because I feel anxious, it must mean we're about to break up." Then those thoughts spiral and turn into a fight your partner never saw coming. Needless to say, emotional reasoning is particularly frustrating for partners because it's impossible to argue with a gut feeling, even an inaccurate one.

The second toxic habit is to assume you know what other people are thinking. Your insecurity puts imaginary judgmental thoughts in other people's heads, which you then believe wholeheartedly, which in turn makes you feel more insecure. It's a vicious circle of epic proportions. Mind reading makes you think others are either judging or rejecting you. "He didn't text me back so he must hate me." "My boss wants to see me so she must be mad." "Everyone will see I'm sweating and think I'm a freak."

Also, the thinking error of personalization makes everything about you. Your spouse is grumpy, so you assume it's something you did. Your boyfriend looked at another girl, so you must not be enough for him. Your friend is grumpy, so you must not be entertaining her adequately. Regardless, whatever dark alley personalization leads you down, it ends at the dead end of self-blame.

Complete the chart below by filling in each blank with TWO words from the passage.

First toxic thinking habit	ⓐ
Second toxic thinking habit	ⓑ
Third toxic thinking habit	personalization

02 Read the passage and follow the directions. [2 points]

To understand our nature, history and psychology, we must get inside the heads of our _____(a)_____ ancestors. For nearly the entire history of our species, Sapiens lived as foragers. The past 200 years, during which ever increasing numbers of Sapiens have obtained their daily bread as urban labourers and office workers, and the preceding 10,000 years, during which most Sapiens lived as farmers and herders, are the blink of an eye compared to the tens of thousands of years during which our ancestors hunted and gathered.

The flourishing field of evolutionary psychology argues that many of our present-day social and psychological characteristics were shaped during this long pre-agricultural era. Even today, scholars in this field claim, our brains and minds are adapted to a life of hunting and gathering. Our eating habits, our conflicts and our sexuality are all the result of the way our hunter-gatherer minds interact with our current post-industrial environment, with its mega-cities, aeroplanes, telephones and computers. This environment gives us more material resources and longer lives than those enjoyed by any previous generation, but it often makes us feel alienated, depressed and pressured. To understand why, evolutionary psychologists argue, we need to delve into the hunter-gatherer world that shaped us, the world that we subconsciously still inhabit.

Why, for example, do people gorge on high-calorie food that is doing little good to their bodies? Today's affluent societies are in the throes of a plague of obesity, which is rapidly spreading to developing countries. It's a puzzle why we binge on the sweetest and greasiest food we can find, until we consider the eating habits of our forager forebears. In the savannahs and forests they inhabited, _____(b)_____ sweets were extremely rare and food in general was in short supply.

Fill in each blank with ONE word from the passage.

03 **Read the passage and follow the directions.** [4 points]

Populations of certain Northern sea otters have experienced recent declines. Suggested causes for these declines are complex and have been attributed to a variety of ecological or anthropogenic pressures. Major disasters such as oil spills are usually noted for their sudden dramatic impact on marine and coastal species. The acute effects of a spill are evaluated by mortality estimations, clinical evaluation, and necropsy examinations. The long-term effects of these tragedies are more difficult to document, and studies often are restricted to demographic modeling, estimations of reproductive efficiency, or time-differential, age-specific survival rates. While several recent studies have eloquently shown that many species face long term oil-related effects after a spill, biological markers that identify oil-induced sublethal pathology in susceptible species are urgently needed. The goal of the proposed study is to identify specific, sensitive genetic markers that signify persistent pathological and physiological injury associated with either acute or chronic hydrocarbon exposure.

Crude petroleum oil has multiple aromatic and aliphatic hydrocarbon constituents, and the toxic effects of exposure and ingestion understandably can be diverse and extensive within the body. Under these circumstances, the molecular investigation of subtle alterations of expressed genes indicative of multiple physiological processes at the cellular level is particularly useful. Further, samples required for molecular investigations are minimally invasive or stressful to the subject animals. Gene expression technologies have the exciting potential of providing methods for monitoring the long-term effects of oil exposure in federally listed, free-ranging sea otters. An added benefit is that these methods may elucidate the mechanisms by which oil can deleteriously affect an individual sea otter over a long period, and thereby aid in the design of therapeutic and preventive strategies to treat and protect susceptible individuals and populations at risk from oil exposure.

Identify which forms of investigation have revealed the short term and lethal effects of oil exposure. Second, if the study proposed in this passage is carried out successfully, what would most importantly happen to sea otters?

_____

_____

_____

_____

_____

04 Read the passage and follow the directions. [4 points]

Priests discovered <u>this principle</u> thousands of years ago. It underlies numerous religious ceremonies and commandments. If you want to make people believe in imaginary entities such as gods and nations, you should make them sacrifice something valuable. The more painful the sacrifice, the more convinced people are of the existence of the imaginary recipient. A poor peasant sacrificing a priceless bull to Jupiter will become convinced that Jupiter really exists, otherwise how can he excuse his stupidity? The peasant will sacrifice another bull, and another, and another, just so he won't have to admit that all the previous bulls were wasted. For exactly the same reason, if I have sacrificed a child to the glory of the Italian nation, or my legs to the communist revolution, it's enough to turn me into a zealous Italian nationalist or an enthusiastic communist. For if Italian national myths or communist propaganda are a lie, then I will be forced to admit that my child's death or my own paralysis have been completely pointless. Few people have the stomach to admit such a thing.

The same logic is at work in the economic sphere too. In 1999 the government of Scotland decided to erect a new parliament building. According to the original plan, the construction was supposed to take two years and cost £40 million. In fact, it took five years and cost £400 million. Every time the contractors encountered unexpected difficulties and expenses, they went to the Scottish government and asked for more time and money. Every time this happened, the government told itself : 'Well, we've already sunk £40 million into this and we'll be completely discredited if we stop now and end up with a half-built skeleton. Let's authorize another £40 million.' Six months later the same thing happened, by which time the pressure to avoid ending up with an unfinished building was even greater; and six months after that the story repeated itself, and so on until the actual cost was ten times the original estimate. Not only governments fall into this trap. Business corporations often sink millions into failed enterprises, while private individuals cling to dysfunctional marriages and dead-end jobs.

Describe what "this principle" is. Second, identity ONE word depicted by the writer of the passage from the first paragraph that BEST corresponds to the examples illustrated in the second paragraph.

_____

_____

_____

_____

_____

05 Read the passage and follow the directions. [4 points]

The true leader is an amateur in the proper, original sense of the word. The amateur (from Latin amator, lover; from amo, amare, to love) does something for the love of it. He pursues his enterprise not for money, not to please the crowd, not for professional prestige nor for assured promotion and retirement at the end — but because he loves it. If he can't help doing it, it's not because of the forces pushing from behind but because of his fresh, amateur's vision of what lies ahead.

The two new breeds whose power and prestige menace the amateur spirit are the professionals and the bureaucrats. Both are byproducts of American wealth, American progress. But they can stifle the amateur spirit on which the special quality and vision of our American leaders must depend.

First, the professionals : Professions, as we know them, are a modern phenomenon. The word profession, when it first came into the English language, meant the vows taken by members of the clergy.

The second breed of enemies of the amateur spirit are the bureaucrats. These, too, are a characteristically modern phenomenon. Just as professions are a byproduct of the specializing of knowledge and technology, bureaucracy has come from the increasing size of enterprises and the proliferating activities of government.

The bureaucrats' aim is to keep things on track, to keep themselves on the ladder of promotion, on the clear road to fully pensioned retirement. Bureaucrats who rule us are themselves ruled by the bureaucratic fallacy. This was never better announced than on a sign over the desk of a French civil servant : "Never Do Anything for the First Time." In our government, the great work depends on the ability to keep the amateur spirit — in its original sense — alive.

Identify all the things that threaten "amateur spirit" according to the passage. Then, describe what the bureaucratic fallacy is in ONE sentence.

_____

_____

_____

_____

_____

01 Read the passage and fill in the blank with ONE word from the passage.

[2 points]

The history of capitalism is unintelligible without taking _____ into account. Capitalism's belief in perpetual economic growth flies in the face of almost everything we know about the universe. A society of wolves would be extremely foolish to believe that the supply of sheep would keep on growing indefinitely. The human economy has nevertheless managed to keep on growing throughout the modern era, thanks only to the fact that scientists come up with another discovery or gadget every few years — such as the continent of America, the internal combustion engine, or genetically engineered sheep. Banks and governments print money, but ultimately, it is the scientists who foot the bill.

Over the last few years, banks and governments have been frenziedly printing money. Everybody is terrified that the current economic crisis may stop the growth of the economy. So they are creating trillions of dollars, euros and yen out of thin air, pumping cheap credit into the system, and hoping that the scientists will manage to come up with something really big, before the bubble bursts. Everything depends on the people in the labs. New discoveries in fields such as biotechnology and nanotechnology could create entire new industries, whose profits could back the trillions of make-believe money that the banks and governments have created since 2008. If the labs do not fulfil these expectations before the bubble bursts, we are heading towards very rough times.

02 Read the passage and follow the directions. [4 points]

For almost a generation, psychologists around the world have been engaged in a spirited debate over a question that most of us would consider to have been settled years ago. The question is this : is there such a thing as innate talent? The obvious answer is yes. Not every hockey player born in January ends up playing at the professional level. Only some do — the innately talented ones. Achievement is talent plus preparation. The problem with this view is that the closer psychologists look at the careers of the gifted, the smaller the role innate talent seems to play and the bigger the role preparation seems to play. Exhibit A in the talent argument is a study done in the early 1990s by the psychologist K. Anders Ericsson and two colleagues at Berlin's elite Academy of Music. With the help of the Academy's professors, they divided the school's violinists into three groups. In the first group were the stars, the students with the potential to become world-class soloists. In the second were those judged to be merely "good." In the third were students who were unlikely to ever play professionally and who intended to be music teachers in the public school system. All of the violinists were then asked the same question : over the course of your entire career, ever since you first picked up the violin, how many hours have you practiced? Everyone from all three groups started playing at roughly the same age, around five years old. In those first few years, everyone practiced roughly the same amount, about two or three hours a week. But when the students were around the age of eight, real differences started to emerge. The students who would end up the best in their class began to practice more than everyone else : six hours a week by age nine, eight hours a week by age twelve, sixteen hours a week by age fourteen, and up and up, until by the age of twenty they were practicing that is, purposefully and single-mindedly playing their instruments with the intent to get better well over thirty hours a week. In fact, by the age of twenty, the elite performers had each totaled ten thousand hours of practice. By contrast, the merely good students had totaled eight thousand hours, and the future music teachers had totaled just over four thousand hours.

Describe to what the underlined "this view" refers. Second, what perspective does the writer of the passage try to argue by way of referencing K. Anders Ericsson's study?

_____

_____

_____

_____

_____

03 Read the passage and follow the directions. [4 points]

Almost all of the colleges in this country can be regarded as respectable institutions. In return for tuition money, they offer a variety of useful courses and, ultimately, a degree for those who qualify. There are a few colleges, however, that operate in a shady manner, providing degrees to which people are not entitled, for courses that they never took. One of the most notorious in recent years was Pacific College in Los Angeles, California, sometimes called "the dropouts' Harvard." To illustrate how easy it was to get an advanced degree from such ⓐ "diploma mills," New York legislator Leonard Stavisky enrolled his German shepherd, Shanna, at Pacific College. "Ms. Shanna Stavisky" presumably sent his admission fee of $150 and by return mail received a breezy letter from "Dean Ashby" that read, "Your talent and experience are going to be recognized sooner or later. Welcome, my friend, to Pacific College."

Shanna was placed in a Ph.D. program in "recreation management." ⓑ "That is very appropriate," said Mr. Stavisky, "since Shanna has had field experience in the backyard and supervises child recreation because she is a watchdog." The reason for interest in the case is that some citizens who need degrees to gain employment can bluff their way through by producing phony degrees that they bought from disreputable institutions. "How would you like to undergo brain surgery at the hands of someone who had gotten his medical certification from Pacific College?" asked one of Stavisky's assistants.

Describe the meaning of the "diploma mills". Then, explain the implication of the underlined words in ⓑ.

_____

_____

_____

_____

_____

04 Read the passage and follow the directions. [5 points]

On January 3, 1992 a meeting of Russian and American scholars took place in the auditorium of a government building in Moscow. Two weeks earlier the Soviet Union had ceased to exist and the Russian Federation had become an independent country. As a result, the statue of Lenin which previously graced the stage of the auditorium had disappeared and instead the flag of the Russian Federation was now displayed on the front wall. The only problem, one American observed, was that the flag had been hung upside down. After this was pointed out to the Russian hosts, they quickly and quietly corrected the error during the first intermission.

The years after the Cold War witnessed the beginnings of dramatic changes in peoples' identities and the symbols of those identities. Global politics began to be reconfigured along cultural lines. Upside-down flags were a sign of the transition, but more and more the flags are flying high and true, and Russians and other people are mobilizing and marching behind these and other symbols of their new cultural identities.

On April 18, 1994 two thousand people rallied in Sarajevo waving the flags of Saudi Arabia and Turkey. By flying those banners, instead of UN, NATO, or American flags, these Sarajevans identified themselves with their fellow Muslims and told the world who were their real and not-so-real friends.

On October 16, 1994 in Los Angeles 70,000 people marched beneath "a sea of Mexican flags" protesting Proposition 187, a referendum measure which would deny many state benefits to illegal immigrants and their children. Why are they "walking down the street with a Mexican flag and demanding that this country give them a free education?" observers asked. "They should be waving the American flag." Two weeks later <u>more protestors</u> did march down the street : carrying an American flag — upside down to show opposition of American policy. These flag displays ensured victory for Proposition 187, which was approved by 59 percent of California voters.

Explain the symbolic function of the Russian Federation's flag as well as the Mexican flag mentioned in the passage. Then, who are the underlined "more protestors" and why did they march down the street?

_____

_____

_____

_____

_____

05 Read the passage and follow the directions. [4 points]

Once upon a time there was a young man named Aristotle Spinoza who wanted to save the human race. So he dropped out. "Cleanliness is overrated." said Aristotle himself. "Social taboos against long hair are silly. It's hate, greed and striving that ruin the world. The human race will never be saved until we all come to love each other."

So he gave up baths, grew his hair long and went to live in a hippie pad. Right away, Aristotle ran into several minor problems and one major one. The minor ones included under arm offensiveness, an itchy neck and chronic indigestion. The major one was that, try as he might, he couldn't bring hisself to love everybody ─ particularly one bearded roommate given to playing the sitar at 2 A.M. and eating crackers in bed.

Aristotle took his problems to a guru. "Hmmm," said the guru, "how many micrograms of acid are you taking?"

"Acid?" asked Aristotle.

"Lysergic acid. LSD. It'll increase your awareness, expand your consciousness and you will love everybody," said the guru solemnly. "Take 250 micrograms twice weekly four hours after eating. Next."

And It worked! After taking LSD Aristotle saw pretty colors, heard pretty sounds, smelled pretty smells, felt pretty feelings and loved everybody. He even equated the noise of crackers being munched in bed with Beethoven's Fifth Symphony. But these effects wore off in eight hours. And most of the time he itched, smelled, burped and couldn't stand sitar music.

"LSD is fine, but it isn't perfect," he said thoughtfully. "What the human race needs is The Perfect Pill."

After many an experiment he invented it. The Perfect Pill contained an itch reliever, a deodorant, an antacid tablet and, unlike LSD, it turned you on permanently. The Perfect Pill was an instant success. Soon everybody in the world was turned on permanently. Hate, greed, striving and silly social taboos disappeared. Everybody sat around seeing pretty colors, listening to pretty sounds, smelling pretty smells, feeling pretty feelings and loving each other.

Of course, while no one bothered to go to war any more, no one bothered to build bridges, have children or explore the universe any more, either. And after a few hundred years of sitting around loving each other the human race died off. It was replaced by the three-toed sloth, a gentle creature. "It's your bag now," said the last man to the three-toed sloth. "But I notice you don't take pills. Have you found some better way to love each other?"

"Naturally," said the three-toed sloth.

Moral: *If the only way people can be induced to love one another is through ingesting chemicals the human race deserves what it gets.*

Explain how LSD improves matters and also why it is not a "perfect pill". Then, explain the moral at the end of the passage.

_____

_____

_____

_____

_____

📖 모범답안 p.127

01 Read the passage and follow the direction. [2 points]

One side says that language insidiously shapes attitudes and that vigilance against subtle offense is necessary to eliminate prejudice. The other bristles at legislating language, seeing a corrosion of clarity and expressiveness at best, and thought control at worst, changing the way reporters render events and opinions. Both arguments make assumptions about language and how it relates to thoughts and attitude — a connection first made in 1946 by George Orwell in his essay "Politics and the English Language," which suggested that euphemisms, cliché and vague writing could be used to reinforce orthodoxy and defend the indefensible. We understand language and thought better than we did in Orwell's time, and our discoveries offer insights about the P.C., or "Politically Correct" controversy. First, words are not _____ⓐ_____. Despite the appeal of the theory that language determines thought, no cognitive scientist believes it. People coin new words, grapple for the right word, translate from other languages and ridicule or defend P.C. terms. None of this would be possible if the ideas expressed by words were identical to the words themselves. This should alleviate anxiety on both sides, reminding us that we are talking about style manuals, not brain programming.

Second, words are _____ⓑ_____. The word "duck" does not look, walk or quack like a duck, but we all know it means duck because we have memorized an arbitrary association between a sound and a meaning. Some words can be built out of smaller pieces and their meanings can be discerned by examining how the pieces are arranged (a dishwasher washes dishes), but even complex words turn opaque, and people become oblivious to the logic of their derivation, memorizing them as arbitrary symbols. (Who last thought of "breakfast" as "breaking a fast"?)

Fill in the blanks ⓐ and ⓑ respectively with each ONE word from the passage above so that they can BEST fit the passage.

02 Read the passage and follow the direction. [2 points]

> There are three species of mendacity, each worse than the one before —
> lies, damned lies, and statistics. Consider the standard example of
> stretching the truth with numbers. Statistics recognizes different measures of
> an "average." The mean is our usual concept of an overall average — add
> up the items and divide them by the number of sharers (100 candy bars
> collected for five kids next Halloween will yield 20 for each in a just
> world). The median, a different measure of central tendency, is the half-way
> point. If I line up five kids by height, the median child is shorter than two
> and taller than the other two (who might have trouble getting their mean
> share of the candy). A politician in power might say with pride, "The mean
> income of our citizens is $40,000 per year." The leader of the opposition
> might retort, "But half our citizens make less than $25,000 per year." Both
> are right, but neither cites a statistic with impassive objectivity. The first
> invokes a mean, the second a median.
>
> Means are higher than medians in such cases because one millionaire may
> outweigh hundreds of poor people in setting a _____ⓐ_____; but he can
> balance only one in calculating a _____ⓑ_____.

Fill in the blanks ⓐ and ⓑ respectively with each ONE word from the passage above so that they can BEST fit the passage.

03 Read the passage and follow the directions. [4 points]

We are about to enter a third wave known as "ubiquitous computing." Computers will be distributed throughout our public and private spaces and embedded in everyday objects, from clothes to chairs, from coffee cups to cakes. With their own computing capabilities, these "smart" things will relieve human beings of some of life's more mundane chores and help out with a host of trickier tasks. As computers become more and more ubiquitous, and less visually obvious, two immediate questions arise. Firstly, will an "information underclass" without access to these devices be created? Secondly, will these chips invade our privacy?

The goal of "ubiquitous computing" is to make technology invisible and, by embedding computers into everyday things, make the things themselves smarter. But will this lead to dumber people with less control over their technology? I believe that it won't make people dumber and that everyone should be given an equal opportunity to get smart about less mundane things. In this regard, there is legitimate concern that the new ubiquitous computers will not be equally available to everyone, thus driving a wedge between high-tech "haves" and "have-nots." But it is important to realize that the prime mover behind the latest technology is not the technology itself, but an agreement — Internet. Agreeing on how computers should talk to one another on the Internet has tremendous advantages for exchanging information and decreasing the cost of technology. Ubiquitous computing will make our lives more convenient, but it will also allow computers to know everything about us. Private actions, such as reading the newspaper, may be shared with other computers — and their owners — all over the world.

Write a summary following the guidelines below.

| Guidelines |

- Summarize the above passage in ONE paragraph.
- Provide a topic sentence and supporting ideas from the passage.
- Do NOT copy more than FIVE consecutive words from the passage.

_____

_____

_____

_____

_____

04 Read the passage and follow the directions. [4 points]

The process of learning an art can be divided conveniently into two parts : one, the mastery of the theory; the other, the mastery of the practice. If I want to learn the art of medicine, I must first know the facts about the human body, and about various diseases. When I have all this theoretical knowledge, I am by no means competent in the art of medicine. I shall become a master in this art only after a great deal of practice, until eventually the results of my theoretical knowledge and the results of my practice are blended into one ─ my intuition, the essence of the mastery of any art. But, aside from learning the theory and practice, there is a third factor necessary to becoming a master in any art ─ the mastery of the art must be a matter of ultimate concern; there must be nothing else in the world more important than the art. This holds true for music, for medicine, for carpentry ─ and for love.

And, maybe, here lies the answer to the question of why people in our culture try so rarely to learn this art, in spite of their obvious failures : in spite of the deep-seated craving for love, almost everything else is considered to be more important than _____ : success, prestige, money, power ─ almost all our energy is used for the learning of how to achieve these aims, and almost none to learn the art of love. Could it be that only those things are considered worthy of being learned with which one can earn money or prestige, and that love, which "only" profits the soul, but is profitless in the modern sense, is a luxury we have no right to spend much energy on?

Fill in the blank with the ONE most appropriate word from the passage. Second, describe the ALL factors necessary to becoming a master in art. Do NOT copy more than FIVE consecutive words from the passage.

_____

_____

_____

_____

_____

05 Read the passage and follow the directions. [4 points]

"Full employment" and "economic growth" have in the past few decades become primary excuses for widening the extent of government intervention in economic affairs. A private free-enterprise economy, it is said, is inherently unstable. Left to itself, it will produce recurrent cycles of boom and bust. The government must therefore step in to keep things on an even keel. These arguments were particularly potent during and after the Great Depression of the 1930's, and were a major element giving rise to the New Deal in this country and comparable extensions of governmental intervention in others.

More recently, "economic growth" has become the more popular rallying call. These arguments are thoroughly misleading. The fact is that the Great Depression, like most other periods of severe unemployment, was produced by government mismanagement rather than by any inherent instability of the private economy. A governmentally established agency — the Federal Reserve System — had been assigned responsibility for monetary policy. In 1930 and 1931, it exercised this responsibility so ineptly as to convert what otherwise would have been a moderate contraction into a major catastrophe. Similarly today, governmental measures constitute the major impediments to economic growth in the United States. Tariffs and other restrictions on international trade, high tax burdens and a complex and inequitable tax structure, regulatory commissions, government price and wage fixing, and a host of other measures give individuals an incentive to misuse and misdirect resources, and distort the investment of new savings. What we urgently need, for both economic stability and growth, is a reduction of

_____.

Explain the writer's point of view of the Great Depression. Do NOT copy more than FIVE consecutive words from the passage. Second, fill in the blank with the TWO most appropriate consecutive words from the passage.

_____

_____

_____

_____

_____

📖 모범답안 p.131

01 **Read the passage and follow the direction.** [2 points]

Mapping the human genome opens a new epoch for medical science and a new frontier for potential discrimination. New genetic research may make it possible to identify an individual's lifelong risk of cancer, heart attack and other diseases. Specialists worry that this information could be employed to discriminate in insurance, hiring, or promotions. Owners and insurers could save millions of dollars if they could use predictive genetics to identify in advance, and then reject workers or policy applicants who are predisposed to develop chronic disease. Thus, genetic discrimination could join the list of other forms of _____ⓐ_____ : racial, ethnic, and sexual. Genetic discrimination is drawing attention because of the first publication of the complete human genome map and sequence. Two versions, virtually identical, were compiled separately by an international public consortium and by a private company. The journal Nature publishes the work of the public consortium and the journal Science publishes the sequence by Celera Genomics, a Rockville, Md., company. Fear of such discrimination already is affecting how people view the medical revolution promised by _____ⓑ_____ the human genome. The Equal Employment Opportunity Commission filed its first lawsuit challenging genetic testing last week in U.S. District Court in the Northern District of Iowa. Burlington Northern Santa Fe Railroad was charged in the suit with conducting genetic testing on employees without their permission. At least one worker was threatened with dismissal unless he agreed to the test, the agency charges. Many experts believe the only solution to potential genetic discrimination is a new federal law that specifically prohibits it.

Fill in each blank with ONE word from the passage respectively.

02 Read the passage and follow the direction. [4 points]

I learned that I was suffering from abdominal mesothelioma, a rare and serious cancer usually associated with exposure to asbestos. When I revived after surgery, I asked my first question of my doctor and chemotherapist: "What is the best technical literature about mesothelioma?" She replied, with a touch of diplomacy, that the medical literature contained nothing really worth reading. Of course, trying to keep an intellectual away from literature works about as well as recommending chastity to Homo sapiens, the sexiest primate of all. As soon as I could walk, I made a beeline for Harvard's Countway medical library and punched "mesothelioma" into the computer's bibliographic search program. An hour later, surrounded by the latest literature on abdominal mesothelioma, I realized with a gulp why my doctor had offered ⓐ that humane advice. The literature couldn't have been more brutally clear: mesothelioma is incurable, with a median mortality of only eight months after discovery. If a little learning could ever be a dangerous thing, I had encountered a classic example. Attitude clearly matters in fighting ____ⓑ____.

What does the underlined "that humane advice" refers to? Write your answer in about TEN words. Do NOT copy more than FIVE consecutive words from the passage. Second, fill in the blank with the ONE most appropriate word from the passage.

_____

_____

_____

_____

_____

03 Read the passage and follow the direction. [4 points]

> The sharp rise in admissions applications at the nation's elite private universities may seem surprising given the uncertain economic times and the lack of growth in the pool of 18-year-olds. But it is a manifestation of the overinvestment in American higher education. It used to be that a college _____ was a ticket to a prosperous upper-middle-class life. As the number of college graduates has grown faster than the number of relatively high paying jobs, more college graduates are not achieving the goal of getting relatively high paid jobs. Now merely having a degree is not enough — a student needs a quality degree. Hence, the number of applicants applying to highly regarded schools is soaring. But adding to the demand is the fact that the price of attending the very best schools is usually little different from the cost of attending merely good schools. In fact, because of their vast amounts of endowment aid, the rich elite schools are effectively cheaper. An another factor in the falling acceptance rate of the elite schools is their deliberate policy of refusing to engage in enrollment expansion. Most prestigious schools have roughly the same number of undergraduates as they did 30 or more years ago, despite a vast growth in the number of qualified students seeking admission.

Describe the factors in the falling acceptance rate of the elite schools. Do NOT copy more than FIVE consecutive words from the passage. Second, fill in the blank with the ONE word from the passage.

_____

_____

_____

_____

_____

04 Read the passage and follow the directions. [4 points]

Do not allow yourself to remain a vacillating creature, swayed half by reason and half by infantile folly. Do not be afraid of irreverence towards the memory of those who controlled your childhood. They seemed to you then strong and wise because you were weak and foolish; now that you are neither, it is your business to examine their apparent strength and wisdom, to consider whether they deserve that reverence that from force of habit you still bestow upon them. Ask yourself seriously whether the world is the better for the _____ teaching traditionally given to the young.

Consider how much of unadulterated superstition goes into the make-up of the conventionally virtuous man, and reflect that, while all kinds of imaginary moral dangers were guarded against by incredibly foolish prohibitions, the real moral dangers to which an adult is exposed were practically unmentioned. What are the really harmful acts to which the average man is tempted? Sharp practice in business of the sort not punished by law, harshness towards employees, cruelty towards wife and children, malevolence towards competitors, ferocity in political conflicts — these are the really harmful sins that are common among respectable and respected citizens. By means of these sins a man spreads misery in his immediate circle and does his bit towards destroying civilization.

Fill in the blank with the ONE word from the passage. Second, describe what "the real moral dangers" are. Do NOT copy more than FIVE consecutive words from the passage.

_____

_____

_____

_____

_____

05 **Read the passage and follow the directions.** [2 points]

> The door edges open and in the crack light flickers. A figure moves into the room, a dark silhouette. The figure turns into the light and he sees : it is her. Only her, a figure as familiar as his own body. The tension begins to dissipate, but slowly, uneasily. It is as though knots have formed through his being from tip to toe. He holds his breath and watches as she moves across the room, easing the wardrobe door open, carefully trying to avoid the habitual squeak. I must oil the hinges, he thinks. With her back to the bed, shielding the flashlight beam, she scrambles among old clothes piled at the back of the wardrobe; she burrows into the bottom of voluminous coat pockets. He knows that she will already have gone through the house searching in jars, behind books in the bookcase, at the back of untidy drawers filled with junk. It happens once a year or so : the evil spirit comes upon her in the night, and she invades her own house, excavating the accretions of daily living, wanting desperately to find a remnant of the past, a sign of life. "Now much to ask," she'd say if pushed, "a little thing." That thing which is so simply and satisfyingly itself : a cigarette.

Describe where is the narrator when the event takes place? Second, identify who the intruder who enters the room is.

_____

_____

_____

01 Read the passage and follow the directions. [2 points]

Propaganda is the spreading of information in order to influence public opinion and to manipulate other people's beliefs. The message of propaganda is primarily intended to serve the interests of the messenger, thereby increasing his power. All propaganda is a systematic effort to persuade. The propagandist gives a one-sided message, accentuating the good points of one side and the bad points of the other position. Propaganda as an art of persuasion has been used for thousands of years.

In the fifth century BC, when Pericles addressed his fellow Athenians on the merits of their city compared to the tyranny of Sparta, he was making _____ⓐ_____, even though much of what he was saying was true. Many centuries later, Lenin, the Soviet revolutionary, realized the value of propaganda to indoctrinate educated people. He employed another tactic toward the uneducated, called agitation. This process involved the use of slogans, stories, half-truths, and even outright lies in order to avoid the need for complex arguments. The Nazi government of Germany from 1933 to 1945, was adept at propaganda. In order to gain _____ⓑ_____, Adolf Hitler used his ability to tell each audience what it wanted to hear. He stirred fears of communism when talking to businessmen, and preached the values of socialism when talking to factory workers. After his party won control of the government office, he appointed Joseph Goebbels as head of the Ministry of Public Enlightenment and Propaganda. Through Goebbels, Hitler gained power over the press, radio, theater, films, music, and literature.

Fill in each blank ⓐ and ⓑ with the ONE most appropriate word from the passage respectively.

02 Read the passage and follow the direction. [2 points]

Play is what generates culture. It is setting free of the human imagination to create shared meanings. Play is a basic category of mankind's behavior without which society could not exist. Nowadays business comes to be less defined in terms of ____ⓐ____ and more in terms of play. Companies of every kind are beginning to recreate their organizational environments to make them better compatible with creativity and artistry — the keystones of cultural commerce. Many company supervisors no longer even refer to their staff as "workers" but rather prefer to use the term "players". Work environments are steadily being transformed into ____ⓑ____ environments, reflecting the new emphasis on cultural performance and the marketing of lived experiences. Companies have introduced all sorts of playful innovations to create a relaxed atmosphere more conducive to artistic creativity. Yahoo has installed meditation rooms. Google has a "humor room" stocked with toys, videos, and games.

Fill in each blank ⓐ and ⓑ with the ONE most appropriate word from the passage respectively.

03 Read the passage and follow the directions. [4 points]

Standing at the end of a too-long line of customers inside a too-crowded fast food restaurant in northern Manhattan, I listened attentively as Dexter, a twenty-three-year-old black man, argued across the shiny McDonald's countertop with the Dominican cashier who was trying patiently to take his order. Dressed in white, gray, and black fatigues, with Air Jordans on his feet, Dexter held up that queue by waving a colorful coupon in the palm of his right hand. Scissored out from an insert in that Sunday's local newspaper, the coupon redeemed a ninety-nine-cent Big Mac in every part of New York City (so read the fine print) "except the borough of Manhattan," where Big Macs, with this very same square of paper, were discounted to $1.39 instead. Well, hearing the cashier, Pam, make that borough-specific distinction several times, Dexter became increasingly annoyed. He crossed and uncrossed his arms with emphatic gestures. He sighed audibly and repeatedly. Squeezing a dollar bill and a dime in his outstretched left hand (the ten cents was "for tax," he declared numerous times), Dexter made his case : "This is Harlem," he stated with electrified finality, "not Manhattan! If they meant Harlem, if they meant Harlem, they should have written Harlem! Harlem is not Manhattan! so, I'm paying $1.10 for my Big Mac."

Where does the event take place? Second, explain the reason the conflict takes place.

_____

_____

_____

_____

_____

04   Read the passage and follow the directions. [4 points]

I stood there frozen. My feet feeling like they were rooted into the ground, planted too deeply to be moved. My father, in his anger, was yelling at me, and during those minutes that passed, it felt like an eternity. To this day I still remember those words forcing their way into my mind while piercing my heart. My father's bronze, tanned face turned red right before my eyes, like a piece of hot glowing coal. He yelled,

"I'm not your friend. I'm your father. Don't treat me like your friends." I was hurt, and I masked my pain over the fear and disappointment. My father, a hard-working and diligent man who rarely, if ever, stood idle, was furious with me. He was always ready to greet people with a smile. Caring about his appearance, he always neatly combed his thinning hair. He was well dressed and wore comfortable shoes. But on this day it didn't matter. I had exhausted his patience as he waited for me to return home from school. After school that day, with my parent's car, I had driven my friend home. Time had whisked by. When I got home, it was after 5 P.M. It was too late.

My father needed me to do something important. At sixteen and with my parents' car, coming home after school wasn't my idea of enjoying the privileges of my free afternoon. Enticed by sitting behind the wheel, it was too easy to get wrapped up in friends and lose track of time. For as long as I can remember, my parents have always been self-employed. They ran a small retail store, just the two of them for the most part. It was a well-stocked store with fishing supplies, clothing, guitar supplies, sporting goods and comfortable shoes. Every day except Sundays and holidays, going to the post office two and often three times a day was routine. Nearly everything that filled the store's shelves was sent through the post office. Maybe my father had promised a customer that his or her order would be in that afternoon. Or maybe he needed a certain part to repair a fishing reel. Whatever the reason, my father had depended on me to get to the post office, pick up the merchandise and bring it back to the store. Before that day when he yelled at me, I had not realized how important that simple task was and how much they needed me.

Describe what the "task" that the writer's father expected the writer to do was. Do NOT copy more than FIVE consecutive words from the passage. Second, what did the writer learn from disappointing his father? Do NOT copy more than FIVE consecutive words from the passage.

_____

_____

_____

_____

_____

05   Read the passage and follow the directions. [4 points]

> You're a teacher in the New York City public school system. It's September, and you're lecturing the class on the structure of an essay. Your students need to know this information to pass your class and the Regents exam, and you, of course, hope that one day your talented students will dazzle and amaze English professors all over the country. You turn your back to write the definition of thesis on the chalkboard.
>
> It takes about 15 seconds. You turn around to the class expecting to see 25 students scribbling the concept in their notebooks. Instead, you see a group of students who have sprung appendages of technology. Jose has grown an earphone. Maria's thumbs have sprouted a two-way. Man Keung, recently arrived from China, is texting away on a cell phone connected to his wrist. And Christina appears to be playing Mine Sweeper on a Pocket PC on her lap. Come to the end of the term, a handful will fail the class. A number will never pass the Regents exam. As we all know, far too many will drop out of school. And I can tell you with no hint of pride that it isn't the teacher's fault. As much as any other problem plaguing our schools, the onus for failure should be placed on distractions in the classroom, specifically the cell phone. Though electronic devices have been banned in public schools for years, the issue came to the forefront last month when Chancellor Joel Klein announced the random placement of metal detectors in schools. The result : More than 800 cell phones have been confiscated. Students and their parents, who say they rely on cell phones for safety reasons are outraged. There's even talk of a lawsuit arguing that the rule should be struck down. But as a former New York City public school teacher, I can tell you that cell phones don't belong in the classroom. A student with a cell phone is an uninterested student, one with a short attention span who cares more about his social life. Parents think of cell phones as a connection to their children in an emergency. I have a few questions for those parents : First, when was the last situation that genuinely called for immediate interaction with your child? In most cases, the hospital or the police would seem more urgent. Second, is phoning the main office and having it patch you through to your child not quick enough?

And third, do you know why your children really want to take cell phones to school? Because, just like the new Jordans and Rocawear they desire, cell phones are status symbols. Because when their cell phone rings while the teacher is talking, everyone laughs. Because playing video games on their cell makes them look cool.

Because text messaging their friend in the next room is more fun than learning about the topic sentence. So is listening to the new Three 6 Mafia song they just downloaded onto their cell. And saying students can store their phones in the locker is a joke. If they have cell phones, they're going to bring them into class. There are legitimate causes that parents should be taking on. Rally against crowding in the classroom. Fight against the oppressive and culturally biased Regents test. But you're wrong on this _____ issue. In this case, you are part of the problem, not the solution.

Describe what is the teacher trying to teach and what are the students doing? Do NOT copy more than FIVE consecutive words from the passage. Second, fill in the blank with the TWO consecutive words from the passage.

---

01 Read the passage and follow the directions. [2 points]

Our whole culture is based on the appetite for buying, on the idea of a mutually favorable exchange. Modern man's happiness consists in the thrill of looking at the shop windows, and in buying all that he can afford to buy, either for cash or on installments. He looks at people in a similar way. For the man an attractive girl — and for the woman an attractive man — are the prizes they are after. "Attractive" usually means a nice package of qualities which are popular and sought after on the personality market. What specifically makes a person ____ⓐ____ depends on the fashion of the time, physically as well as mentally. During the twenties, a drinking and smoking girl, tough and sexy, was attractive; today the fashion demands more domesticity and coyness. At the end of the nineteenth and the beginning of the 20th century, a man had to be aggressive and ambitious — today he has to be social and tolerant in order to be an attractive "package." At any rate, the sense of falling in love develops usually only with regard to such human commodities as are within reach of one's own possibilities for exchange. I am out for a bargain; the object should be desirable from the standpoint of its social value, and at the same time should want me, considering my overt and hidden assets and potentialities. Two persons thus fall in love when they feel they have found the best object available on the market, considering the limitations of their own exchange values. Often, as in buying real estate, the hidden potentialities which can be developed play a considerable role in this bargain. In short, in a culture in which the marketing orientation prevails, human love relations follow the same pattern of ____ⓑ____ which governs the commodity.

Fill in each blank with ONE word from the passage respectively.

02 Read the passage and follow the directions. [4 points]

A catalyst for adopting _____ in the district was parents' fears over students being attacked for inadvertently wearing a wrong color scarf or hat that might provoke rivalry among local gangs. The district adopted a dress code more than a decade ago that prohibits gang-related attire, as well as caps, bandanas, baggy pants. But many felt the district had to take a more drastic approach. When Bao Lo had two children attending Franklin Middle School, she was among the organizers of the effort to bring uniforms to that school. She now has a child in a district elementary school and has remained enthusiastic about uniforms. "There are so few boundaries for kids these days, with the drug use and violence, so if we can give them some limits, that's good," she said. The uniformity tends to bolster safety because it makes it easier to spot people who may not belong on campus, school leaders say. But a large portion of the district's students aren't as upbeat as parents and teachers appear to be. And the older they get, the less they seem to like it —which may not bode well for talk in the district of expanding the uniform requirement to high schools. "It's like we're all in jail," said Hector Gonzalez, a 7th grader at Franklin. "If you wear decent clothes, you shouldn't have to wear uniforms." Alicia Nunez, also an 8th grader, complained that the regimented attire stifles her creativity. "You come to school to get your education, not for them to tell you how to dress," the 14-year-old said as she strode across campus wearing a chocolate-brown T-shirt and jeans.

Fill in the blank with the ONE word from the passage. Second, describe the title of the passage. Write your answer in approximately 10 words using the given words.

Cons	Policy

_____

_____

03 **Read the passage and follow the directions.** [2 points]

A boyfriend once asked for my opinion and, when I gave it to him, said I reminded him of the fiancée in the movie Jerry Maguire. Jerry said she put the "brutal" in the "brutal truth." The comparison caught my attention because in the movie, that "brutal" exchange led to a broken engagement. Honesty in relationships is crucial. Brutal honesty may not be. I learned this lesson from one of my dearest friends. I called in a panic for advice after realizing I had probably made a mistake in a relationship. After I finished pouring out the gory details my friend replied : "Do you want me to say something that will make you feel better as your friend who loves you, or do you want me to tell you the truth?" It was the perfect opening for him to deliver what I needed to hear, which was essentially : "Keli, you acted like an idiot." I now try to employ this "iron fist, velvet glove" approach when I have to deliver similar brutal truths to people I love. When I'm not 100 percent sure this tactic will soften the blow, I have another secret weapon.

What does the writer of the passage mean when she says "'iron fist, velvet glove' approach"? Write your answer in about 15 words by using such words as "the more painful", "the softer".

_____

04   Read the passage and follow the directions. [4 points]

The man who invented Coca-Cola was not a native Atlantan, but on the day of his funeral every drugstore in town testimonially shut up shop. He was John Styth Pemberton, born in 1833 in Knoxville, Georgia, eighty miles away. Sometimes known as Doctor, Pemberton was a pharmacist who, during the Civil War, led a cavalry troop under General Joe Wheeler. He settled in Atlanta in 1869, and soon began brewing such patent medicines as Triplex Liver Pills and Globe of Flower Cough Syrup. In 1885, he registered a trademark for something called French Wine Cola ─ Ideal Nerve and Tonic Stimulant; a few months later he formed the Pemberton Chemical Company, and recruited the service of a book-keeper named Frank M. Robinson, who not only had a good head for figures but, attached to it, so exceptional a nose that he could audit the composition of a batch of syrup merely by sniffing it.

In 1886 ─ a year in which, as contemporary Coca-Cola officials like to point out, Conan Doyle unveiled Sherlock Homes and France unveiled the Statue of Liberty ─ Pemberton unveiled a syrup that he called Coca-Cola. It was a modification of his French Wine Cola. He had taken out the wine and added a pinch of caffeine, and, when the end product tasted awful, had thrown in some extract of cola (or kola) nut and a few other oils, blending the mix in a three-legged iron pot in his back yard and swishing it around with an oar. He distributed it to soda fountains in used beer bottles, and Robinson, with his flowing bookkeeper's script, presently devised a label, on which "Coca-Cola" was written in the fashion that is still employed. Pemberton looked upon his concoction less as a refreshment than as a headache cure, especially for people whose throbbing temples could be traced to overindulgence. On a morning late in 1886, one such victim of the night before dragged himself into an Atlanta drugstore and asked for a dollop of Coca-Cola.

Druggists customarily stirred a teaspoonful of syrup into a glass of water, but in this instance the factotum on duty was too lazy to walk to the fresh-water tap, a couple of feet off. Instead, he mixed the syrup with some charged water, which was closer at hand. The suffering customer perked up almost at once, and word quickly spread that the best Coca-Cola was a fizzy one.

Write a summary following the guidelines below.

⌐ Guidelines ⌐

- Summarize the above passage in ONE paragraph.
- Provide a topic sentence and supporting ideas from the passage.
- Do NOT copy more than FIVE consecutive words from the passage.

_____

_____

_____

_____

_____

05 **Read the passage and answer the questions.** [4 points]

When you swallow a spoonful of yogurt or bite into a crisp pickle, you are eating foods flavored by the action of bacteria. The bacteria produce an acid, which gives the food a sour flavor. Certain bacteria naturally live in your digestive system and help you stay healthy. Two species, E. coli and L. acidophilus, release substances that inhibit activities of other, possibly harmful, bacteria. Several species also produce certain kinds of vitamins. Many bacteria act as decomposers, organisms that break down the tissues of dead organisms. This breakdown process of decomposition occurs as bacteria use the dead tissues for food. Some bacteria decompose sewage and other wastes in water. In this way, bacteria help keep lakes and streams free from small amounts of pollution. Without decomposers, the earth would be covered with dead organisms and their wastes. Even though most bacteria are helpful, some are _____. For example, bacteria help us by decomposing wastes. However, when people dump large amounts of wastes into lakes and rivers, the bacteria get a big food supply. With so much food, the bacteria grow, reproduce, and may have a population explosion. The huge numbers of bacteria use up the oxygen dissolved in the water. As a result, fish and other organisms living in the water can suffocate. Bacteria can cause large losses of food through decomposition, spoilage, and poisoning. Bacteria spoil food by growing on the food. As the bacteria grow, they can change the odor or the flavor of the food. Sometimes, the bacteria produce a poison, called a toxin. Botulism is a type of food poisoning that often occurs in foods that have not been canned properly. The anaerobic bacteria that cause botulism produce a toxin with no odor or unusual flavor, so they are not easily detected.

Botulism can be very serious. It can cause paralysis and even death.

Explain how too much waste dumping in bodies of water changes the activity of bacteria. Do not copy more than FOUR consecutive words from the passage. Second, fill in the blank with the ONE most appropriate word from the passage.

_____

_____

_____

_____

_____

01 Read the passage and follow the directions. [2 points]

Europol's recent reports on terrorism have repeatedly shown that the majority of terrorist acts and plots across Europe are perpetrated by ethno-nationalist and separatist groups. Yet the focus on Islamist terrorism precludes any efficient assessment of threats from other political groups. Although the horrible attacks in Norway is the first right-wing act of this magnitude in recent history, there has been a significant rise in cyber activism disseminating intolerant rhetoric, across the trans-Atlantic blogosphere. More troubling, this rhetoric has increasingly gained ground in European mainstream politics over the last 20 years. In the 1980s, Jean-Marie le Pen of the French National Front, at the time a marginal politician, was one of the first to vituperate against the risk of Islamicization. Today, Islam as "the internal and external enemy" is a staple of European political discourse. In the last six months, Angela Merkel, Nicola Sarkozy and David Cameron have condemned multiculturalism as a failed model for "integrating immigrants" — meaning assimilating Islam — into their respective countries. The attacks in Norway are the first violent translation of that ____ⓐ____. Yet, in the wake of the killings, members of other extreme right groups have distanced themselves from the violent nature of Breivik's actions and manifesto. Immediately after the attacks, the former Swedish Democrat Isak Nygren, the spokesman for the Swedish Defense League, wrote : "Even though this terrorist is anti-Islam, anti-Multiculturalism and so on, like me, I don't really have something in common with this guy. I don't support violence."

However, the distinction between legitimate ideas and illegitimate violence is naive and dangerous. All anti-Islamic rhetoric harms both Mulsims and non-Muslims by reinforcing the "us vs them" mentality in European society — an attitude that can, and will, lead to ___ⓑ___ .

Fill in each blank with the ONE most appropriate word from the passage respectively.

02 Read the passage and follow the directions. [4 points]

Hundreds of foreign students, waving their fists and shouting defiantly in many languages, walked off their jobs at a plant that packs Hershey's chocolates, saying a summer program that was supposed to be a cultural exchange had instead turned them into underpaid labor. The students, from countries including China, Nigeria, Romania and Ukraine, came to the United States through a long-established State Department summer visa program that allows them to work for two months and then travel. They said they were expecting to practice their English, make some money and learn what life is like in the United States. In a way, they did. About 400 foreign students were put to work lifting heavy boxes and packing Reese's candies, Kit-Kats and Almond Joys on a fast-moving production line, many of them on a night shift. After paycheck deductions for fees associated with the program and for their rent, students said at a rally in front of the huge packing plant that many of them were not earning nearly enough to recover what they had spent in their home countries to obtain their visas. Their experience of American society has been very different from what they expected. They said there was no _____. It was just work, work faster, work. Over the years, the summer visa program has successfully given university students from distant countries a chance to be immersed in everyday America and to make lasting friends. But in recent years, the program has drawn complaints from students about low wages and unexpectedly difficult work conditions.

Fill in the blank with the TWO most appropriate consecutive words from the passage. Then write the title of the passage by using the given words below.

Dubious	Denounced

_____

_____

_____

03 **Read the passage and follow the directions.** [4 points]

Why the baby smiles is a matter of some significance in understanding the early phases of human attachment in the infant. First of all, let's remember that this response smile has had antecedents. Even in the early weeks we will notice that satisfaction in the course of nursing or at the end of the nursing period will cause the mouth to relax in a little smile of contentment. This early smile of satisfaction is an instinctive reaction and is not yet a response to a human face. Now let's watch this baby as he nurses. If he is not too sleepy his eyes fix solemnly on the face of his mother. We have learned experimentally that he does not take in the whole face before him, only the upper part of the face, the eyes and forehead. Through repetition of the experience of nursing and its regular accompaniment, the human face, an association between nursing and the human face will be established. But more than this, the pleasure, the satisfactions of nursing become associated with the human face. Repetition of this pleasurable experience gradually traces an image of the face on the surface of the memory apparatus and the foundations of memory are established. When the mental image is firmly established the visual image of the human face is "recognized" (very crudely), that is, the sight of the human face evokes the mental image and it is "remembered." Now comes the turning point. This is not just a memory based on pictures, but a memory derived from image plus pleasure, the association established through nursing. The baby's response to the sight of the human face is now seen as a response of pleasure. He smiles at the sight of the human face. The little smile which had originated as a(n) _____ reaction to satisfaction in nursing is now produced occasionally, then more and more, at the sight of the face, as if the face evokes the memory of satisfaction and pleasure. The baby has made his first human connections.

Fill in the blank with the TWO most appropriate consecutive words from the passage. Second, in what way does repetition contribute to the baby's smile? Write your answer in 5 words or so.

_____

_____

_____

_____

_____

04 Read the passage and follow the directions. [4 points]

Shortly after my mother's funeral as the sixties began its Punch and Judy show, the this-time-around feminist movement rose from behind the curtain. You could virtually hear the whoop of relief that rolled over the country. The first and most important message was that you didn't have to, you didn't need to, you had other choices, whether this was a turn against marriage, a turn against cooking, a turn against babies as destiny, it was all about not having to, not being coerced into, about not polishing the furniture till it shone, about searching for meaning outside the home. What wonderful fresh air this feminist wind brought to the chocking lady in the apron holding her cookies on a hot baking tray. Now she could see her children, her always needing to be chauffeured children, with tennis rackets and piano lessons, with Little League and skating competitions and play dates, as sucking the life out of her, as draining her of her own dreams, as eating at the promise that had been. Now she could see that always giving and never getting were not divinely ordained. She was not just a Mrs., someone's wife, and not just a mom, someone's mother. She breathed her own desires, expressed her own anger, and suddenly everything was changed. All over America consciousness raised its own rooftops and fled the house. Women remembered that they had once run like crazy, climbed trees, planned to visit Istanbul, intended to ride a motorbike or go to graduate school. Women took courses, learned karate, let their body hair grow as nature intended. They became aware of all the denigrating images in the culture, all the insults to their brains and bravery that blared at them from magazines, books, movies, children's readers, billboards. Seeing the insult defused its power. The madwomen in the attic gave up their delusions, depressions, hypochondria and made plans to become potters or neurosurgeons. By the end of the nineteen sixties if a woman put her head to her own pillow she could hear the band playing, the coming of freedom, the hope of power returned, of self-expression, of self-fulfillment, of her intelligence newly awake, in love again with life.

Describe the main idea of the passage. Second, what does the writer of the passage mean by "All over America consciousness raised its own rooftops and fled the house"? Write your answer in two sentences. Do not copy more than FOUR consecutive words from the passage.

_____

_____

_____

_____

_____

05 **Read the passage and follow the directions.** [4 points]

Living on campus is an excellent way to broaden one's perspective, gain some valuable living skills, and learn some things about oneself. This is totally in line with the aims of university education. Also it situates students near resources, like residence hall advisers, they can call on if needed. And help might be needed : students are learning to balance all their needs on their own, typically for the first time in their lives. Today's students are often well prepared academically but have zero experience in self-management, as their lives have been highly engineered by parents, coaches, guidance counselors and others. Of course, dorm living often provides distractions aplenty, but it also provides a relatively safe context in which students can practice self-discipline.

In an era when many college students feel stressed and often overwhelmed, and record numbers of students experience such disorders as anxiety and depression, living on campus in a dorm with unknown others of varied background and not of one's choosing provides another advantage. It is a check against the isolation that often accompanies and exacerbates such problems. On-campus living is especially important for freshmen, as it usually centrally locates them so they can find their way around. Living in a residence hall frees them in many ways (say, from having to think about getting their next meal) while keeping them close to crucial resources like libraries. The experience of communal living is probably more necessary today than ever, to counter some of the effects of cellphones, which tend to focus attention on known networks of friends and family (often to the exclusion of one's immediate surroundings). Living off _____ is best reserved as a choice for upperclassmen.

What is the main idea of the passage? Write your answer in less than 10 words. Second, fill in the blank with the ONE word from the passage.

_____

_____

_____

01 Read the passage and follow the directions. [4 points]

A flurry of articles have popped up on the Internet citing a study that purportedly shows that the rich are not as nice as the poor. "Wealthy are Different : And Not in a Nice Way," ran one headline. "Lower class people just show more empathy, more prosocial behavior, more compassion, no matter how you look at it," one of the study's authors, Dacher Keltner, told MSNBC. "I will quote from the Tea Party hero Ayn Rand : 'It is the morality of altruism that men have to reject,'" he said.

The study, however, leaves some room for doubt. As one researcher said, studies of "income and helping behaviors have always been a little bit mixed." First, the Kelnter study (done by Michael Kraus, Paul Piff and Mr. Keltner) theorizes that the poor are more "contextually-focused" and "other oriented," meaning they're more sensitive to the people around them. By contrast, the rich are "self-focused." The reason, according to the study, is that the poor are more dependent on others (job supervisors, government policy, etc.), while the lives of the rich are more under individual control and influence.

Both groups also view their current circumstances differently. The poor believe they are poor because of external factors, while the rich believe they're rich because of their own efforts. In one example, the authors videotaped sets of two strangers of different social-class backgrounds and found that upper-class individuals displayed less socially engaged, for instance checking their cell phones or doodling on a questionnaire, whereas lower-class individuals displayed more socially engaged eye contact, head nods and laughs.

Write a summary following the guidelines below.

| Guidelines |

- Summarize the above passage in ONE paragraph.
- Provide a topic sentence and supporting ideas from the passage.
- Do NOT copy more than FIVE consecutive words from the passage.

_____

_____

_____

_____

_____

02 Read the passage and follow the directions. [4 points]

As auction houses prepare for their fall sales, Chinese collectors are expected to be a major boost for the market, raising their paddles for big-ticket artworks. With China's economy booming, art collectors there have become an increasingly powerful force in the market, demonstrating a growing interest in Western as well as Asian art. The surge in Chinese collecting is not just a reflection of new wealth, but also a reaction to the repressive Mao years when the country was denied culture. For the Chinese, who watched art disparaged as a frivolous exercise except when put to didactic use, the freedom to explore simple aesthetic pleasures, to repossess historical works and to show off recent affluence has been liberating. The tide of buying is in some ways an effort to make up for lost time. In China, for 50 or 60years, nothing happened. That's a big break. The last 250 years were years of humiliation. They now feel an obligation to prize art again and bring it back. Because of that history, Chinese art buying — particularly the public display associated with an auction — is still a nascent phenomenon. Chinese collectors are only beginning to develop an artistic eye and expertise.

Write a summary following the guidelines below.

⌐ Guidelines ⌐

- Summarize the above passage in ONE paragraph.
- Provide a topic sentence and supporting ideas from the passage.
- Do NOT copy more than FIVE consecutive words from the passage.

_____

_____

_____

_____

_____

03 **Read the passage and follow the directions.** [4 points]

Depending on what mood I'm in, I find it either irritating, funny or civilized when I think about how we protect protective coverings in the US. When I come home from the grocery store and start to unpack, I am always unfavorably impressed with the layers of _____ wrappings we cover our food with. There is hardly anything we buy that doesn't come in at least two wrappings, and then several of them are assembled by the cashier at the checkout counter and put into a small bag. Then several of the small bags are grouped together and put into a big bag. If you have several big bags with small bags in them, they give you a cardboard box to put the packages-in-the-little-bags-in-the-big-bags in. A lot of things we buy wouldn't really need any protective wrapping at all. The skins of an orange protects an orange pretty well for most of its natural life, but we aren't satisfied with what nature has given it. We wrap ten of them in plastic or put them in a net bag, and we put the plastic bag in a paper bag. The orange inside the skin, inside the plastic which is in a paper bag, must wonder where it is. A box of cookies or crackers often has waxed paper next to the cookies, a cardboard box holding the cookies and then waxed paper and a decorative wrapping around the cardboard box. What seems to be called for here is some stiff, decorative waxed paper. We have always wrapped our cars in an incredible number of protective layers. We put fenders over the wheels to protect ourselves from flying dirt. Then we put bumpers front and back to protect the fenders. We proceed from there to put chrome on the bumpers to protect them from rust, and we undercoat the fenders to protect them from the dirt they're protecting us from. We paint the car to protect the metal, wax the paint to protect that and then we build a two-car garage to protect the whole thing. <u>If it was a child, it would be spoiled.</u>

Fill in the blank with the ONE most appropriate word from the passage. Second, explain what the writer of the passage means by stating that "If it was a child, it would be spoiled"? Do not copy more than FIVE consecutive words from the passage.

_____

_____

_____

_____

_____

04 Read the passage and follow the directions. [4 points]

Why do our bodies age at different rates? Why can some people run marathons at the age of 70, while others are forced to use a walker? More work needs to be done on "gerontogens" — factors, including substances in the environment, that can accelerate the aging process. Possible gerontogens include arsenic in groundwater, benzene in industrial emissions, ultraviolet radiation in sunlight, and the cocktail of 4,000 toxic chemicals in tobacco smoke. Activities may also be included, like ingesting excessive calories, or suffering psychological stress. Focusing on such factors would complement more popular approaches like studying molecular changes in old bodies and searching for genes that are linked to long life. Even if scientists announced tomorrow that they'd discovered an antiaging pill, people would have to take it for decades. Getting healthy people to take medicine for a long time is challenging, and there are always side effects. If we identify stuff in the environment that affects aging, that's knowledge we could use today.

Twin studies have found that only around 25 percent of the variation in the human life span is influenced by genes. The rest must be influenced by other factors, including accidents, injuries, and exposure to substances that accelerate aging. The idea that environmental factors can accelerate aging has been around for a while, but the study of gerontogens has lagged behind other areas of aging research. Scientists have become more interested in these substances in recent years after learning that many types of chemotherapy*, and some anti-HIV drugs, can speed the onset of age-related traits like frailty and mental decline.

The quest to identify gerontogens is partly a quest to find better way of measuring biological age. There are several options, each one imperfect. Researchers could look in the brain and measure levels of beta-amyloid, a protein linked to Alzheimer's disease, but these levels would not reflect aging in other parts of the body. Also, they could measure the length of telomeres — protective caps at the end of our DNA that wear away with time. But doing so is hard and expensive, and telomere length naturally varies between people of the same age.

chemotherapy : the treatment of disease using chemicals

First, what are gerontogens? Second, identify what Twin studies tell the reader about. Do not copy more than consecutive FIVE words from the passage when you answer each question.

_____

_____

_____

_____

_____

05 Read the passage and follow the directions. [4 points]

Pricing is a powerful tool for shaping behavior, including water use. Recognizing the power of pricing, more water utilities are adopting water rates designed to encourage customers to conserve. These so-called "conservation rates" vary in form, but generally they increase the price per gallon of water the more water a customer uses. Across the country, utilities can testify to the power of pricing by pointing to their decreased water sales. This is great news from a conservation standpoint, but the unintended result can be unexpected reductions in revenue.

The need for more reliable revenue is more important than ever, as water service providers contend with prolonged droughts and aging infrastructure. Unfortunately, this need for revenue can make conservation the unwanted stepchild of water utilities.

Measuring and Mitigating Water Revenue Variability uses the financial data from three North American water utilities to explore how pricing structures interact with customers' usage patterns to create revenue stability or volatility.

For example, if customers at all three utilities cut their water use by 15 percent, the resulting change in water revenue is by no means uniform. The Southeastern Coastal Utility fares fairly well, with only a seven percent reduction in revenue. The Mountain Resort Utility, on the other hand, would see a whopping 24 percent reduction in revenue.

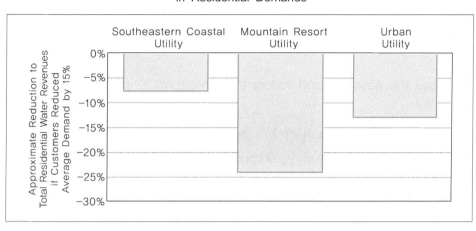

Figure 1: Revenue Variability Due to One-Time Significant Declines in Residential Demands

Most customers of the Mountain Resort Utility use less than 10,000 gallons each month, but a full 14 percent of customers use more than 25,000 gallons each month.

Remarkably, the Mountain Resort Utility's customers using more than 25,000 gallons each month use an average of 73,100 gallons per month. When those high-volume customers who are paying a premium for their water curtail their use, the result is a big drop in revenue.

Identify the utility that represents the biggest decline in revenue and explain why that utility is much more vulnerable to revenue shocks the way the figure depicts. Do not copy more than FIVE consecutive words from the passage.

_____

_____

_____

_____

_____

모범답안 p.149

01 **Read the passage and follow the directions.** [2 points]

Historically, liberalism has been oriented toward change and progress, whereas conservatism is skeptical about change and does not necessarily equate change with progress. Changes initiated and planned by the state might be described by a liberal as "reform" and by a conservative as "meddling," that is, meddling with the ____ⓐ____ order of things. Conservatives view the social, economic, and political order in a society as natural, in that the society's culture and politics have developed over generations by a process of gradual evolution. Today is the product of thousands of yesterdays. To tamper needlessly with intricate social relationships is folly because it is unlikely to improve things and more likely to make them worse.

Perhaps the most basic differences between liberalism and conservatism involve the conception of society and the individual's place within society. Liberalism begins with a conception of individual and property rights and then constructs a theory of society to accommodate the individual's natural rights. ____ⓑ____ begins with a conception of society and fits into it individual and property rights.

Fill in each blank with ONE word from the passage respectively.

02 Read the passage and follow the directions. [2 points]

> For many workers, especially professionals and craftspersons — though often other workers as well — the most important element in job satisfaction is the nature of the tasks to be accomplished. They are primarily interested in the work itself, and if they can have control over their share of it and see how it contributes to some larger task or to the good of society, they are happy. Anyone from a trash collector to a physician can have this sense of doing _____ work. Auto mechanics, dentists, and others may be fascinated by the details of the tasks they are performing, while others look to the effect their work has on society. There is an old story about two ditch diggers. When a passerby asked the first one what he was doing, he replied, "I am digging a ditch." The second one said, "I am building a cathedral." It is very much a matter of perspective. Some tasks, however, have become so narrow and routine that no one could find either intrinsic interest or social relevance in performing them. Tightening the third bolt on the left side of every widget is hardly interesting or inspiring. Some companies are beginning to restructure such jobs so that each worker has responsibility for a meaningful group of tasks.

Fill in the blank with ONE word from the passage.

03 Read the passage and follow the directions. [4 points]

The law code of King Hammurabi offers a wealth of information about daily life in Mesopotamia. Hammurabi's was not the first law code in Mesopotamia; indeed the earliest goes back to ca. 2100 B.C. Yet, like earlier lawgivers, Hammurabi proclaimed that he issued his laws on divine authority to "establish law and justice in the language of the land, thereby promoting the welfare of the people." His code may seem harsh, but it was no harsher than the Mosaic law of the Hebrews, which it heavily influenced. Hammurabi's code inflicted such penalties as mutilation, whipping, and burning. Today in parts of the Islamic world these punishments are still in use. Despite its severity, a spirit of justice and a sense of responsibility pervade the code. Hammurabi genuinely felt that his duty was to govern the Mesopotamians as righteously as possible. He tried to regulate the relations of his people so that they could live together in harmony. Hammurabi's code has two striking characteristics. First, the law differed according to the social status of the offender. Aristocrats were not punished as harshly as commoners, nor commoners as harshly as slaves. Even slaves had rights, however, and received some protection under the law. Second, code demanded that the punishment fit the crime. Like the Mosaic law of the Hebrews, it called for "an eye for an eye, and a tooth for a tooth," at least among equals. However, an aristocrat who destroyed the eye of a commoner or slave could pay a fine instead of losing his own eye. Otherwise, as long as criminal and victim shared the same _____, the victim could demand exact vengeance.

What do we infer about the "earlier lawgivers" from the passage? Second, fill in the blank with the TWO most appropriate consecutive words from the passage.

_____

_____

_____

04 Read the passage and follow the directions. [4 points]

Most managers, including of course most chief executives, have a boss. Few people are as important to the performance and success of a manager as the boss. Yet while management books and courses abound in advice on how to manage subordinates, few if any even mention managing the boss. Few managers seem to realize how important it is to manage the boss or, worse, believe that it can be done at all. They bellyache about the boss but do not even try to manage him or her.

Yet managing the boss is fairly simple — indeed generally quite a bit simpler than managing subordinates. It is both the subordinate's duty and in the subordinate's self-interest to make the boss as effective and as achieving as possible. The best prescription for one's own success is, after all, still to work for a boss who is going places. Thus the first do is to go to the boss — at least once a year — and ask : "What do I do and what do my people do that helps you do your job? And what do we do that hampers you and makes life more difficult for you?" This sounds obvious — but it is rarely done. For even effective executives tend to misdefine a manager as someone who is responsible for the work of subordinates — the definition of 50 years ago — and thus tend not to perceive that they have any responsibility for the boss's performance and effectiveness. But the correct definition of a manager is someone who is responsible for the performance of all the people on whom his own performance depends. The first person on whom a manager's performance depends is the boss, and the boss is thus the first person whose performance a manager has to take responsibility.

Describe the main idea of the passage and explain the change of the definitions of a manager. Do not copy more than FIVE consecutive words from the passage when you answer each question.

_____

_____

_____

05 Read the passage and follow the directions. [4 points]

Despite efforts to increase diversity, racial/ethnic minority and female representation in many law enforcement agencies still falls short of labor population benchmarks, resulting in agencies that do not reflect the demographics of their communities.

Barriers to achieving a diverse workforce can arise at various points in the career lifecycle — the recruitment stage, the hiring stage, or the promotion stage. The table illustrates how barriers might manifest themselves in a police department. In this department, whites apply, are hired, and are promoted in increasing proportion to their representation in the local labor pool.

Composition of Police Department X by Race and Gender (percent)

	White	Hispanic	Asian / Pacific Islander	Black	Female
Local labor pool demographics	50	30	10	10	50
Applicants	60	20	10	10	30
Hired officer	65	20	5	10	20
Sergeant and above	70	20	5	5	10

The first indication of employment barriers is an insufficient number of women and racial/ethnic minorities applying for the job. In law enforcement, this problem can be traced to one or a combination of three factors : the target population is disproportionately unaware, unqualified, or uninterested. Lack of awareness suggests a deficiency in outreach actions and events; that is, there is not enough recruitment in areas where demographics suggest that qualified female and racial/ethnic minority candidates could be found. Lack of interest and failure to qualify are more complicated issues.

Most law enforcement agencies have various requirements. Health, education, and other socioeconomic statistics show that some requirements pose barriers for women and racial/ethnic minorities. Most law enforcement agencies require applicants to possess a high school diploma or General Educational Development certificate.

However, the national high school graduation rates for blacks and Hispanics are nearly 20 percentage points lower than for whites. As a result, a smaller pool of racial/ethnic minorities is likely to meet educational requirements.

Meeting fitness and medical requirements also presents a barrier to blacks and Hispanics, who suffer from a higher prevalence of obesity. Within Los Angeles County, for example, white, non-Hispanic school children had an obesity rate of 12.8 percent in 2007, compared to 21.6 percent for black children and 27.4 percent for Hispanic children. Pacific Islanders, who count toward the Los Angeles Police Department's Asian hiring target, have the highest obesity rate among school aged children, at just under 35 percent.

Identify the racial/ethnic group that represents the highest portion in the recruitment stage and explain why the group takes up the largest portion in the hiring stage. Do NOT copy more than SIX consecutive words from the passage.

_____

_____

_____

_____

_____

06 **Read the passage and follow the directions.** [4 points]

Europeans have for thousands of years been living in densely populated societies with central governments, police, and judiciaries. In those societies, infectious epidemic diseases of dense populations were historically the major cause of death, while murders were relatively uncommon and a state of war was the exception rather than the rule. Most Europeans who escaped fatal infections also escaped other potential causes of death and proceeded to pass on their genes. Today, most live-born Western infants survive fatal infections as well and reproduce themselves, regardless of their intelligence and the genes they bear. In contrast, New Guineans have been living in societies where human numbers were too low for epidemic diseases of dense populations to evolve. Instead, traditional New Guineans suffered high mortality from murder, chronic tribal warfare, accidents, and problems in procuring food.

Intelligent people are likelier than less intelligent ones to escape those causes of high mortality in traditional New Guinea societies. However, the differential mortality from epidemic diseases in traditional European societies had little to do with intelligence, and instead involved genetic resistance dependent on details of body chemistry. For example, people with blood group B or O have a greater resistance to smallpox than do people with blood group A. That is, natural selection promoting genes for intelligence has probably been far more ruthless in New Guinea than in more densely populated, politically complex societies, where natural selection for body chemistry was instead more potent.

Besides this genetic reason, there is also another reason. Modern European and American children spend much of their time being passively entertained by television, radio, and movies. In the average American household, the TV set is on for seven hours per day. In contrast, traditional New Guinea children have virtually no such opportunities for passive entertainment and instead spend almost all of their waking hours actively doing something, such as talking or playing with other children or adults. Almost all studies of child development emphasize the role of childhood stimulation and activity in promoting mental development, and stress the irreversible mental stunting associated with reduced childhood stimulation. This effect surely contributes a non-genetic component to the superior average mental function displayed by New Guineans.

Write a summary following the guidelines below.

Guidelines

- Summarize the above passage in about 40-60 words.
- Provide a topic sentence and supporting ideas from the passage.
- Do NOT copy more than FIVE consecutive words from the passage.

유희태 일반영어
❹ 문제은행

초판 1쇄	2014년 4월 14일	
2판 1쇄	2016년 6월 15일	
3판 1쇄	2019년 2월 20일	
2쇄	2019년 5월 10일	
3쇄	2019년 7월 10일	
4판 1쇄	2020년 10월 23일	
2쇄	2021년 7월 30일	
3쇄	2022년 4월 15일	
5판 1쇄	2023년 1월 10일	

저자와의
협의하에
인지생략

저자 유희태 **발행인** 박 용 **발행처** (주)박문각출판
표지디자인 박문각 디자인팀
등록 2015. 4. 29. 제2015-000104호
주소 06654 서울시 서초구 효령로 283 서경 B/D
팩스 (02) 584-2927
전화 교재 문의 (02) 6466-7202 동영상 문의 (02) 6466-7201

정가 37,000원
ISBN 979-11-6704-885-1

유희태
일반영어

교원임용교시 전공영어 시험대비

 다음 카페 – 유희태 전공영어
http://cafe.daum.net/YHT2S2R

 네이버 블로그 – 유희태 전공영어
http://blog.naver.com/kmg7740

교원임용고시 전공영어 시험대비 제5판

유희태
일반영어

④ 문제은행 LSI 영어연구소 유희태 박사 저

모범답안

**임용영어 수험생 대다수가 선택하는
전공영어의 보통명사**

- 교원임용고시 박문각 전공영어 독보적 전국 1위
  (2022년 교보문고 전공영어 부문 누적 판매량 1위)
- 미국 버클리대학 유희태 박사의 독창적 문제집
- 출제가능성 높은 예상문제 수록

합격기준 박문각 임용   동영상강의 www.pmg.co.kr

QMG 박문각

유희태
일반영어

교원임용고시 전공영어 시험대비 제5판

유희태
일반영어

④ 문제은행 LSI 영어연구소 **유희태 박사** 저

모범답안

♀MG 박문각

01 회 문제은행

📖 본책 p.008

01

하위내용영역	배점	예상정답률
일반영어 A형 기입형	2점	55%

모범답안 habits

채점기준

- 2점: 모범답안과 같다. 이것 외에는 답이 될 수 없다.
- 0점: 모범답안과 다르다.

02

하위내용영역	배점	예상정답률
일반영어 A형 서술형	4점	50%

모범답안 The new challenges are high operating costs, stagnant energy demand, and competition from cheaper natural gas and renewable energy. Second, Joyce Corradi worries about the nuclear waste stored in the plant.

채점기준 _Total 4pts

+ 2점: The new challenges가 "① high operating costs, ② stagnant energy demand; ③ competition from cheaper natural gas and renewable energy"라 서술하였다.
  ▷ 3개 중 3개를 모두 서술한 경우 2점; 2개만 서술한 경우 1점; 나머지는 0점을 준다.
+ 2점: Joyce Corradi가 현재 우려하는 것이 "the nuclear waste stored in the plant"임을 명확하게 서술하였거나 유사하였다.

03

하위내용영역	배점	예상정답률
일반영어 B형 서술형	4점	40%

모범답안 A meritocracy is impossible and just a concept invented to satisfy the perspectives of the rich. Second, the writer of the passage thinks that Singer's "front door" shows the way wealth can cause inequality meaning not all students have an equal chance.

채점기준 _Total 4pts

+ 2점: 글의 요지를 "A meritocracy is impossible and just a concept invented to satisfy the perspectives of the rich"라 서술하였거나 유사하였다.
  ▷ 다음과 같이 서술하였어도 2점을 준다.
    "Meritocracy is a myth invented by the rich"
  ▷ keywords인 "meritocracy"와 "the rich"(또는 이에 상응하는 어휘)가 없으면 0점 처리한다.
+ 2점: 글의 저자가 Singer's "front door"에 대해 지니고 있는 생각을 다음과 같이 서술하였거나 유사하였다. "the writer of the passage thinks that Singer's "front door" shows the way wealth can cause inequality meaning not all students have an equal chance.
  ▷ 다음과 같이 서술하였어도 2점을 준다.
    "저자는 Singer's 'front door' 개념에 동의하지 않는데, 그 이유는 싱어의 생각(대학 입학의 "정문"이 "스스로의 힘으로 들어가는 문"이다)과는 다르게 정문으로 들어간 이들도 자신들의 스스로의 힘이라기보다는 학업에 집중할 수 있는 가정 환경이 보장되었기 때문이다"라 서술하였다.
    "The writer thinks that, as opposed to Singer's concept of 'front door', even those who go through "front door" have not gotten in on their own. They've gotten in partly because they have had the great luck to have a wealthy family."

04

하위내용영역	배점	예상정답률
일반영어 B형 서술형	4점	35%

모범답안 There are similarities and differences in the ways in which alcohol, cocaine and marijuana act upon the brain. Alcohol has a wide effect all over the brain which is still being understood. Cocaine, on the other hand, has a very specific affect of blocking recycling of dopamine and other neurotransmitters. Finally, marijuana has a wide influence like alcohol but also a specific effect like cocaine, in that it basically turns up the gain on neuron communication.

채점기준

_Total 4pts

ⓐ Topic sentence

+ 2점: 글의 topic sentence "There are similarities and differences(1점) in the ways in which alcohol, cocaine and marijuana(0.5점) act upon the brain(0.5점)"를 명확하게 서술하였다.

ⓑ Major supporting details

+ 2점: 글의 major supporting details 즉, "① Alcohol has a wide effect all over the brain which is still being understood. ② Cocaine, on the other hand, has a very specific affect of blocking recycling of dopamine and other neurotransmitters. Finally, ③ marijuana has a wide influence like alcohol but also a specific effect like cocaine, in that it basically turns up the gain on neuron communication"을 명확하게 서술하였다.

▷ 3개 중 3개를 모두 정확하게 요약한 경우 2점; 2개만 요약한 경우 1점; 나머지는 0점을 준다.

감점 ♥
• 본문에 나오는 연속되는 6단어 이상을 사용하였다. −0.5pt
• 문단을 두 개나 그 이상으로 구성하였다. −0.5pt
• 문법이나 영어 표현을 합쳐 3개 이상 오류가 있다. −0.5pt

📖 본책 p.015

02 회 문제은행

01

하위내용영역	배점	예상정답률
일반영어 A형 기입형	2점	60%

모범답안 hospice

채점기준

• 2점: 모범답안과 같다. 이것 외에는 답이 될 수 없다.
• 0점: 모범답안과 다르다.

02

하위내용영역	배점	예상정답률
일반영어 A형 서술형	4점	40%

모범답안 Baines became a member because he refused to accept a reward for saving an old lady, saying it was a common behavior. Second, the meaning of the underlined is that the only thing a good person could do is to reject the money his uncle had not intended for him to have any longer.

채점기준

_Total 4pts

+ 2점: Baines가 "고맙지만 사양하는" 모임의 회원이 된 이유를 "Baines became a member because he refused to accept a reward for saving an old lady, (saying it was a common behavior)"라 서술하였거나 유사하였다.

▷ 다음과 같이 서술하였으면 1.5점을 준다.
"Baines became a member of the Declined-With-Thanks club because he believed that rescuing the old lady was not out of the ordinary."

+ 2점: 밑줄 친 부분의 의미를 "the only thing a good person could do is to reject the money his uncle had not intended for him to have any longer"라 서술하였거나 유사하였다.

03

하위내용영역	배점	예상정답률
일반영어 B형 서술형	4점	50%

모범답안 According to the research, returning to the same taco place from yesterday might be better, because it might be more enjoyable than one expects with a repeat visit.

채점기준 _ Total 4pts

+ 2점: 둘 중 "returning to the same taco place from yesterday might be better"라 답하였다.

+ 2점: 그 이유를 "because it might be more enjoyable than one expects with a repeat visit"라 서술하였거나 유사하였다.

한글 번역

오브라이언의 연구팀은 사람들에게 그들이 재미있을 새로운 영화를 넷플릭스에서 보게 했다. 다음날, 연구진은 그들 중 일부에게 같은 영화를 다시 보게 했다. 영화를 다시 보지 않은 이들은, 만약 자신이 그 영화를 다시 본다면 8점 만점의 평가에서 4점 정도의 즐거움을 느낄 것이라 평가했다. 이는 그들이 첫날 영화를 보고 난 후 이야기한 6.4점보다 확실히 낮은 점수다. 하지만 실제로 다음날 영화를 다시 본 일부는 다시 본 영화가 평균 5.7점의 즐거움을 주었다고 말했다.

이 불일치는 오브라이언의 연구를 잘 설명해준다. 한 번 본 영화를 24시간 뒤 다시 볼 경우 분명 첫 번째 보다 즐거움은 줄어든다. 이는 상식적인 사실이다. 하지만, 자신들이 예상했던 것보다는 그 영화가 훨씬 더 재미있었을 수 있다는 것이다.

행동경제학자들은 사람들이 무언가를 선택해야 할 때 새로운 책이나 영화, 새로운 장소처럼 경험해 보지 않은 것에 종종 더 높은 우선순위를 부여한다는 것을 알고 있다. 이는 잘못된 행동은 아니다. 사람들은 일반적으로 무언가에 익숙해질수록 이를 덜 재미있게 느낀다. 하지만 오브라이언은 이렇게 말한다. "사람들이 새로운 것을 선택하는 이유는 새로운 것이 특별히 좋을 것이라 생각해서가 아니라 이전 것이 지루할 것이라 생각하기 때문이다." 하지만 이런 지루함은 실제보다는 과장된 것일 수 있다.

기대라는 것이 때때로 이런 식으로 실제와 다르다는 것을 안다면, 사람들이 여가 시간을 어떻게 쓸지 결정을 할 때 더 합리적인 선택을 내릴 수 있을 것이다. 새로운 것을 찾기 위해 많은 시간을 쓰는 사람들은 이번 연구 결과에서 도움을 얻을 수 있을 것이다. 그런 사람들이 시간을 더 쓰지 않으면서도 (예전에 해본 일을 하면서) 거의 비슷한 즐거움을 느낄 수 있을 것이다.

04

하위내용영역	배점	예상정답률
일반영어 B형 서술형	4점	50%

모범답안 There are a few ways of asking for help that can create reinforcements to encourage a person to help. First, one reinforcement is activating the sense of feeling "in-group". Second, the helper can be reinforced by feeling themselves as a benefactor to others. The third reinforcement is helping the person asked to see their own effectiveness.

채점기준 _ Total 4pts

ⓐ Topic sentence

+ 1점: 글의 topic sentence "There are a few ways of asking for help that can create reinforcements to encourage a person to help."를 명확하게 서술하였거나 유사하였다.

ⓑ Summary

+ 3점: "First, ① one reinforcement is activating the sense of feeling "in-group" and a part of the social group's status and well-being. Second, ② the helper can be reinforced by a positive identity — feeling themselves as a benefactor to others. The third reinforcement is ③ to help the person asked to see their own effectiveness"

▷ 3개 중 3개 요소가 모두 잘 요약되어 들어가 있으면 3점; 2개 요소만 들어가 있으면 2점; 1개 요소만 들어가 있으면 1점; 하나도 들어가 있지 않으면 0점을 준다.

감점 ▽

• 본문에 나오는 연속되는 6단어 이상을 사용하였다. −0.5pt
• 문단을 두 개나 그 이상으로 구성하였다. −0.5pt
• 문법이나 영어 표현을 합쳐 3개 이상 오류가 있다. −0.5pt

사람들에게 도움을 청할 때 상대가 자신이 조정되지 않는다고 느끼고 도움을 주는 과정이 즐거운 경험이 되게 하는 몇 가지 방법이 있다. 이 강화 요소들은 타인을 기꺼이 돕고자 하는 마음을 갖게 한다.

첫 번째 강화 요소는 심리학자들이 말하는 강한 내집단 의식이다. 도움이 필요한 사람이 도움을 받을 사람과 같은 팀이라는 믿음, 즉 중요한 집단의 일부라는 믿음을 심어 주는 것이다. 이런 신념은 집단상호주의를 넘어서는 것으로 같은 집단 내에 있는 사람들에게 일어나는 일들에 관심이 있기 때문에 돕는다는 생각을 갖게 한다. 집단에 속한 사람들의 행복과 복지는 집단 전체의 행복과 복지에 영향을 받기 때문이다. 도움이 필요한 사람이 한 집단 내의 멤버라는 인식을 만들면 기꺼이 도우려는 마음을 갖게 된다.

두 번째 강화 요소는 긍정적인 정체성에 대한 기회이다. 바꿔 말하면 도움을 줄 때 도움을 주는 자신에 대해 긍정적인 생각을 갖게 된다는 것이다. 특히 타인을 도울 때 자신이 가지고 있는 긍정적인 면이나 다른 사람들에게서 존경받는 역할을 하게 될 때 더욱 그렇다. 예를 들면 사람들은 "도움을 주는 사람이 되는 일"이 왜 중요한지 생각하면서 타인을 더 많이 돕게 된다. 자신이 도움을 주는 사람이라는 긍정적인 면모가 중요하게 자각되면 그런 인식에 맞게 행동할 가능성이 더 높아진다.

세 가지 중 가장 강력한 마지막 강화 요소는 자신의 영향을 볼 수 있는 기회이다. 즉, 사람들은 자신이 주는 도움의 영향(혹은 미래에 미칠 영향)을 보거나 알고 싶어 한다. 사람들은 자신의 도움이 어떻게 작용하는지 보고 싶어 한다. 이건 어떤 자부심의 문제가 아니라 몇몇 심리학자들이 말하는 근본적인 인간의 동기에 관한 문제이다. 사람들은 영향력을 미치고 싶어 한다. 자신의 행동이 의도했던 결과를 이끌어 내는 것을 알고 싶어 하고 본질적으로 본인 위주로 세상을 만들어 가고 싶어 한다. 이런 피드백이 없을 경우 자신의 행동이 어떤 결과를 가지고 오는지 알 수 있는 방법이 없으며 돕고자 하는 동기는 바닥으로 추락하게 된다.

03 회 문제은행

📖 본책 p.022

01

하위내용영역	배점	예상정답률
일반영어 A형 기입형	2점	55%

모범답안 correlation(s)

채점기준

- 2점 : 모범답안과 같다. 이것 외에는 답이 될 수 없다.
- 0점 : 모범답안과 다르다.

한글 번역

20세기에 통계학자들과 과학자들은 대다수 인과 관계를 적절한 과학의 주제로 보지 않아 거부했다. 그들은 주로 상관관계를 관찰했고, "상관관계는 인과 관계가 아니다"라는 원칙만을 주술처럼 반복했다.

적어도 과학자들은 꾸준히 자신의 연구에서 인과 관계를 유추할 수 있는 방법을 찾아왔지만, 통계학자들은 정확한 원인을 밝히려는 대부분의 시도를 인정하지 않았다. 단 한 가지 예외가 바로 무작위 대조 연구(randomized controlled trials, RCT)이다. 통계학자들은 잘 설계된 RCT에서는 상관관계가 인과 관계를 의미할 수 있음을 알아냈다. 이 때문에 20세기 내내 RCT는 점점 더 중요한 연구 방법이 됐다.

문제는 RCT를 통해 과학자들이 인과 관계를 밝힐 수 있게 될수록, 다른 방법의 연구에서는 인과 관계가 존재하지 않는 것처럼 말하게 된 것이다. 물론 플로지스톤(환상적 존재)처럼 비현실적으로 존재하지 않게 되었다는 것은 아니다. 그보다는 행동주의자들이 내적 경험이나 의식을 금기시한 것처럼, 그리고 언어학자들이 언어의 기원에 대해 논쟁을 금한 것처럼 과학자들은 인과 관계에 대해 말하는 것을 두려워하게 됐다. 어쩌면 마치 천국과 지옥처럼, 개념적으로는 유용하지만 과학이 이를 다루기에는 부적절 하다는 느낌을 주는, 그런 개념으로 인과 관계는 존재하게 됐다.

하지만 과학자들은 세상을 예측하는 것을 넘어 세상에 영향을 미치고 싶어 했다. 때문에 그들은 때로 RCT 실험 결과가 미처 나오기 전에도 상관관계가 인과 관계를 어느 정도는 의미할 수 있다는 듯 말하기도 했다.

02

하위내용영역	배점	예상정답률
일반영어 A형 서술형	4점	45%

모범답안 The word in the blank is "riots". Next, the meaning of the underlined is that income is an easy and one-sided way to view the wealth gap, which lacks accuracy.

[채점기준] _____ _ Total 4pts

+ 2점 : 빈칸에 들어갈 단어로 "riots"을 정확하게 기입하였다. 이것 외에는 답이 될 수 없다.

+ 2점 : 밑줄 친 부분의 의미를 "income is an easy and one-sided way to view the wealth gap, which lacks accuracy"라 했거나 유사하게 서술하였다.

▷ 다음과 같이 서술하였어도 2점을 준다.

• "income as a way of measuring wealth inequality is insufficient"

• "income as a way of measuring wealth inequality is quick and easy but has a lot of limitations"

▷ "소득이 부의 불평등을 측정하는 방법으로 잘못되었다(wrong)"라 했으면 0점을 준다.

[한글 번역] ▪▪▪▪▪▪▪▪▪▪▪▪▪▪▪▪▪▪▪▪▪▪▪▪▪▪▪▪▪▪▪▪▪▪

"가난한 사람들이 부자들이 실제로 얼마나 돈이 많은지 알게 되면 당장 곳곳에서 폭동이 일어날 것이다." 배우이자 코미디언인 크리스 록이 2014년 〈뉴욕 매거진〉과의 인터뷰에서 갈수록 벌어지는 빈부 격차에 관해서 했던 말이다. 이 말은 실로 정곡을 찌르는 말이 아닐 수 없는데, 이는 불평등을 연구하는 이들이 고민하는 문제와도 닿아 있는 문제이다.

바로 어떻게 하면 불평등을 가장 정확하게 측정할 수 있는가의 문제이다. 불평등에 관한 대부분 연구는 소득(수입)에 초점을 맞춰 왔다. 소득에 관한 정보와 데이터를 구하는 건 어렵지 않다. 하지만 한두 해 돈을 엄청 잘 번다고 부자가 되는 건 아니다. 오히려 부자들 가운데는 오랫동안 쌓아온 부를 더욱 늘려가는 이들이 많다. 과거에는 부를 측정하는 데 걸림돌이 꽤 많았다.

아마도 부자들은 자기들이 얼마나 부유한지 대부분 사회 구성원들이 지금처럼 잘 모르는 상황이 계속되기를 바랄지도 모른다. 크리스 록이 말했던 것처럼 정말 폭동이 일어날지도 모르기도 하고. 하지만 나처럼 이 주제를 공부하는 사람들은 항상 더 정확하면서도 포괄적인 데이터를 찾아왔고, 빈부 격차를 더 정확하게 측정하는 방법을 고민해 왔다. 물론 내가 폭력을 조장하려는 건 절대 아니다. 하지만 난 시민들이 우리 사회 안의 격차가 얼만큼 벌어져 있는지 제대로 아는 것이 무엇보다 중요하다고 믿는다.

그러기 위해 가장 좋은 방법은 (소득 불평등이 아니라) 부의 불평등을 살펴보는 것이다. 불평등을 측정하는 방법에는 여러 가지가 있다. 가장 잘 알려진 방법은 소득을 살펴보는 것이다. 앞서 설명했듯이 가장 큰 이유는 데이터가 많기 때문이고, 계산하기도 쉽기 때문이다. 하지만 소득 불평등으로 측정하는 것은 큰 그림의 단면에 불과하다. 반면에 재산은 모든 측면을 아우르는 기준이라고 할 수 있다. 지금 얼마를 버는지 뿐만 아니라 앞서 번 소득과 물려받은 자산 등이 모두 반영된 수치이기 때문이다. 학자든 정책을 입안하는 관료나 정치인이든 부자와 나머지 사람들의 가장 근본적이고 포괄적인 차이를 정확히 이해하는 방법은 재산의 불평등을 조사하는 방법밖에는 없다.

03

하위내용영역	배점	예상정답률
일반영어 B형 서술형	4점	40%

모범답안 Data is similar to labor in that data is produced from human efforts in the same way. Second, the term "artificial intelligence" is misleading because AI is trained collectively from human-generated examples, not from algorithms alone.

[채점기준] _____ _ Total 4pts

+ 2점 : 데이터가 노동과 유사한 면을 "data is produced from human efforts in the same way"라 서술하였거나 유사하였다.

+ 2점 : 인공 지능이라는 말이 잘못된 용어라고 하는 이유를 "AI is trained collectively from human-generated examples, not from algorithms alone"이라 서술하였거나 유사하였다.

중요한 경제적 자원이 한때는 대가 없이 사용되다가 이후 가치를 가지게 된 예는 매우 많다. 예를 들어, 토지와 물이 그렇다. 하지만 데이터는 시장에서 거래되기가 특별히 더 어려워 보인다. 데이터는 실제 물리적으로 존재하지 않으며, 경제학자들이 비경합재(nonrival goods)라 부르는, 곧 중복해서 사용이 가능한 자원이다.

노동은 데이터처럼 정확하게 규정하기가 어렵다. 노동자는 인류의 역사에서 대부분의 시기에 노동의 대가를 제대로 받지 못했다. 사람들이 자신의 노동을 자유롭게 팔수 있게 된 후에도, 임금이 현실적인 수준으로 올라오기까지는 수십 년이 걸렸다. 바일은 시카고 대학의 에릭 포스너와 공동으로 집필한 〈급진적 시장(Radical Market)〉에서 "역사는 과거와 똑같이 반복되진 않지만 유사하게는 반복된다"고 주장한다. 그는 인공 지능의 시대에 데이터는 노동이라는 형식으로 봐야 한다고 말한다.

이를 이해하기 위해서는 먼저 "인공 지능"이라는 용어에 문제가 있다는 것을 지적해야 한다. 바일과 포스너는 "집단 지능(Collective Intelligence)"이 더 올바른 용어라고 말한다. 대부분의 인공 지능 알고리즘은 인간이 만든 데이터를 이용해 훈련하는 "기계 학습"이라는 과정이 필요하다. 인간이 만들어 낸, 정답을 포함한 데이터 없이는 번역, 음성 인식, 이미지 인식 등 어떤 인공 지능 기술도 불가능하다. 따라서 인간이 만든 데이터는 인공 지능을 가능하게 만드는 노동이라 볼 수 있다. 데이터 경제가 발전할수록 이러한 데이터 작업은 다양한 형태를 띄게 될 것이다. 사람들의 SNS 활동이나 음악 감상, 음식점 추천 등의 활동에서도 새로운 서비스가 탄생할 수 있는 데이터가 만들어지며, 사진에 이름을 붙이거나 차를 운전하는 것과 같이 더 능동적인 활동에서 생성된 데이터로도 인공 지능을 훈련시킬 수 있다.

04

하위내용영역	배점	예상정답률
일반영어 B형 서술형	4점	40%

모범답안 To achieve maximum productivity, taking control of one's sleep schedule with polyphasic sleep can be advantageous. There are several sleep methods such as monophasic — getting all one's sleep at once —, biphasic — sleeping twice daily, and finally polyphasic, sleeping in short naps throughout the day. Though this polyphasic has some drawbacks of being challenging for family life and missing a sleep session, this skill can maximize productivity by gaining 4 hours per day and 28 hours a week.

채점기준   _Total 4pts

ⓐ Topic sentence

+ 1점 : 글의 topic sentence "To achieve maximum productivity, taking control of one's sleep schedule with polyphasic sleep can be advantageous"를 명확하게 서술하였거나 유사하였다.

ⓑ Summary

+ 3점 : "① There are several sleep methods such as monophasic — getting all one's sleep at once —, biphasic — sleeping twice daily, and finally polyphasic, sleeping in short naps throughout the day. ② Though this polyphasic has some drawbacks of being challenging for family life and missing a sleep session, this skill can maximize productivity (by gaining 4 hours per day and 28 hours a week)."

▷ 2개 중 2개 요소가 모두 잘 요약되어 들어가 있으면 3점; 1개 요소만 요약되어 들어가 있으면 1점; 나머지는 0점을 준다.

감점 ▽

• 본문에 나오는 연속되는 6단어 이상을 사용하였다. −0.5pt
• 문단을 두 개나 그 이상으로 구성하였다. −0.5pt
• 문법이나 영어 표현을 합쳐 3개 이상 오류가 있다. −0.5pt

대다수 사람들은 자신의 생산성을 높이기 위한 궁극의 방법을 알고 싶어 한다. 때문에 세상에는 자신이 바로 그 "완벽한 방법"이라 말하는 수많은 기법들이 있다. 하지만 사람들은 모두 다르며, 누구에게나 맞는 방법이란 존재하지 않는다. 하지만 중요한 것은 어쨌든 하루를 계획해야 한다는 것이다. 〈본질주의〉를 쓴 그렉 맥커운은 이렇게 말한다. "스스로 자신의 삶에서 우선순위를 결정하지 않으면, 다른 사람이 정해주게 된다." 하루를 계획함으로써, 삶의 우선순위를 결정하는 사람이 되어야 한다.

다상 수면(polyphasic sleep) 기법은 다소 기이한 방법으로 소수의 사람들에게만 맞을지 모른다. 하지만 당신이 그 소수에 속한다면, 당신은 생산성을 크게 높일 수 있다. 대부분의 사람들은 단상 수면(monophasic sleep), 곧 하루에 한 번 잠을 잔다. 어떤 이들은 이상 수면(biphasic sleep)을 취하는데, 하루에 두 번 잠을 잔다. 즉, 오전에 4시간, 늦은 저녁에 4시간 이런 식으로. 다상 수면을 취하는 이들은 하루 중 짧은 시간 동안 여러 번 잠을 자는 이들로, 전체 수면 시간은 더 작으면서도 생산성은 매우 높다. 한 번 잠을 자는 시간은 사람에 따라 다르며, 어떤 이들은 겨우 20분 길이의 낮잠을 자는가 하면, 어떤 이들은 한 번의 적당히 긴 시간의 수면과 이를 보충하는 여러 번의 낮잠을 자기도 한다.

물론 이 방법은 명백한 단점을 가지고 있다. 스티브 파블리나는 가족들과 함께 살면서 이런 패턴의 수면을 취하는 것이 얼마나 어려운지 주목했다. 또, 이 방법을 취하는 이들이 수면 시간을 놓칠 경우, 생산성이 크게 떨어지는 문제도 있다. 하지만, 이 방법을 잘 사용하는 이들은 남들보다 훨씬 더 많은 시간 동안 일을 할 수 있다. 만약 하루 4시간만 잔 다면, 일주일에 남들보다 28시간이 더 생기게 된다.

04회 문제은행

본책 p.028

01

하위내용영역	배점	예상정답률
일반영어 A형 기입형	2점	30%

모범답안 lithography

채점기준

- 2점: 모범답안과 같다. 이것 외에는 답이 될 수 없다.
- 0점: 모범답안과 다르다.

예술 작품은 원칙적으로 항상 복제가 가능한 것이었다. 인간이 만든 인공품은 언제나 인간에 의해서 모방될 수 있었다. 이러한 모방은 예술에서의 연습을 위한 도제들에 의해, 작품의 보급을 위해 장인에 의해, 마지막으로는 이윤을 추구하는 제3자에 의해 수행됐다. 이에 비해서 예술 작품의 기술적 복제는 새로운 것인데, 이는 역사에서 긴 간격을 두고, 그러나 점점 강렬하게 관철됐다. 그리스 사람들은 예술 작품의 기술적 복제의 두 가지 방법만을 알고 있었는데 그것은 주조(鑄造)와 인각(印刻)이었다. 청동, 테라코타와 주화는 그리스 사람들에 의해 대량으로 생산될 수 있었던 유일한 예술 작품이었다. 그 밖의 모든 것들은 일회적이었으며 기술적으로 복제될 수 없었다. 목각으로써 판화가 처음 기술적으로 복제가능하게 됐으며, 판화는 인쇄를 통해 활자가 복제가능하기 전까지 오랫동안 그러했다. 활자의 기술적인 복제가능성인 인쇄가 문학에서 불러일으킨 엄청난 변화는 익히 알려져 있다. 여기서 세계사적 잣대로 고찰된 바로 그러한 현상들 중에서 이 변화는 물론 아주 중요한 것이지만 하나의 특수한 예일 뿐이다. 목각에 더하여 중세 동안에 동판과 에칭이 등장했고 또한 19세기 초에는 석판이 등장했다. 석판과 함께 복제 기술은 근본적으로 새로운 단계에 이르렀다. 목판에 새기거나 동판에 부식시키는 것과는 달리, 돌 위에 도면을 덮는 훨씬 더 간편한 절차는 판화에 최초로 가능성을 부여했는데, 그것은 판화 제품들을 대량으로 공급할 뿐만 아니라 날마다 새로운 형태로 시장에 공급할 수도 있게 했다. 판화는 석판을 통해서 일상을 삽화로 재현하는 능력을 갖게 되었고 인쇄와 보조를 맞추기 시작했다.

02

하위내용영역	배점	예상정답률
일반영어 A형 서술형	4점	45%

모범답안 The difficulty is that it is not easy to measure productivity because not everybody does the same work (unlike a production line). Second, the improved work-life balance creates no drop in productivity by working a day less because employees engage better with their work.

채점기준 _Total 4pts

+ 2점 : 그 시도를 도입할 때 회사가 직면하게 되는 어려움을 "it is <u>not easy to measure productivity because not everybody does the same work</u>"라 서술하였거나 유사하였다.

+ 2점 : 일과 삶을 조화롭게 하는 것이 생산성의 측면에서 어떤 기능을 하는가에 대한 질문에 다음과 같이 서술하였다.

"the improved work-life balance <u>creates no drop in productivity</u> (by working a day less because employees engage better their work)".

한글 번역

뉴질랜드 회사인 퍼페추얼 가디언은 사무직 직원 240명에게 (하루 8시간) 주 4일 근무를 제안했다. 나흘 동안 일해도 급여는 닷새 일할 때 받던 것 그대로라는 조건이었다. 건물 내부가 따로 벽으로 나뉘지 않은 현대식 사무실에서는 직원들이 쉽게 집중력을 잃어 (업무 능률이 떨어지고) 생산성도 낮아진다는 연구 결과가 잇따라 나오자 이를 반영해 근무 시간을 조정한 것이다. 앤드루 반스 전무 이사는 주 근무 시간을 줄이면 직원들이 일에 더 집중해서 결국 생산성을 늘릴 수 있는 혁신적인 방법이라고 생각했다. 이 밖에도 직원들이 일과 삶을 더 조화롭게 꾸릴 수 있고, 스트레스가 줄어 정신 건강에도 도움이 되며, (출퇴근이 줄어들어) 도로에 차도 줄어들어 도시와 환경에도 좋은 일이 되는 등 부가적인 장점이 많을 것이라 생각했다. 실험 결과를 보면 (대부분 가설이 사실로 확인됐다.) 일과 삶의 균형을 맞추게 되었다고 답한 직원이 24%나 늘어났다. 직원들은 일에 더 집중할 수 있게 됐다고 답했고, 스트레스 지수도 7%나 떨어졌다. 일주일에 하루를 덜 일했는데도 전체 업무 생산성은 전혀 줄어들지 않았다.

하지만 몇 가지의 도전도 있다. 첫째로는, 회사 안에서 직원들이 하는 일이 모두 똑같지 않다는 점이었다. 공장 조립 부서에서 기계 부품을 조립하는 일이라면 직원들의 생산성을 측정하기가 훨씬 쉬웠겠지만. (퍼페추얼 뮤추얼의 직원들은 사무직 노동이 원래 그렇듯 다들 하는 일도 달라서 업무 능률이나 생산성을 일괄적인 잣대로 측정할 수 없었다.) 그래서 회사는 각 팀의 팀원들과 팀장에게 팀별로 하는 일을 최대한 자세히 써 달라고 했고, 일주일에 5일 동안 해오던 일을 어떻게 하면 4일 안에 끝낼 수 있을지 구체적인 계획을 세워서 보고해 달라고 요구했다. 팀원들 사이에 역할을 더 잘 나누든, 조직을 재정비하든 업무를 끝내야 하는 마감 기한은 변하지 않는다. 즉, 각자 월요일부터 금요일 사이에 쉬는 날을 하루 정해 쉬는 날은 엇갈리되 같이 모여서 회의하거나 같이 일해야 하는 날은 또 그대로 정해 놓고 실험을 한 것이다. 다음과 같은 기대가 있었다. 만약 직원들이 일주일에 4일만 일하고도 5일 일하던 것과 같은 생산성을 낸다면, (급여는 그대로이면서) 일주일에 하루를 더 쉴 수 있으니 그보다 더 좋은 직원 복지도 없을 것이고, 회사의 평가도 좋아질 것이다. 유능한 직원들이 회사를 떠날 이유는 사라지고, 반대로 외부의 유능한 인재들은 이 회사로 오고 싶어 할 것이다. 직원들이 출근을 덜 한 만큼 사무실에서 쓰는 에너지도 20% 아낄 수 있다. 회사가 직원의 복지에 신경을 쓰면, 직원들은 일에 더 집중하고 능률을 올려 생산성을 높이는 식으로 반드시 여기에 응답한다는 연구는 이제 쌓일 만큼 쌓여 정설이자 통념이 됐다. 이어 소위 "워라벨"이 직업 만족도와 전반적인 삶의 질에 매우 중요한 만큼, 일에 얽매이지 않고 자기만의 시간을 더 많이 보낼수록 직원들은 일할 때 집중해서 일을 끝마친다.

03

하위내용영역	배점	예상정답률
일반영어 B형 서술형	4점	40%

[모범답안] The writer mentions "The Americans" as an example of interacting with ideas that cause one to unlearn what one understands of the world. Next, the words "cognitive perspective" best fit the blank.

[채점기준] _____ _ Total 4pts

+2점 : 저자가 텔레비전 쇼인 "미국인들"을 언급한 이유를 "as an example of interacting with ideas that cause one to unlearn what one understands of the world"라 서술하였거나 유사하였다.

+2점 : 빈칸에 들어갈 단어를 "cognitive perspective" 라 정확하게 기술하였다. 이것 외에는 답이 될 수 없다.

[한글 번역] ┃┃

우리가 하는 많은 선택은 우리의 세계관을 바꾸곤 한다. 그 선택이란 무엇을 배우거나 어떤 것을 깊이 이해하거나 다른 시각으로 보는 관점을 기르는 것처럼 대개 더 나은 무언가를 위한 선택이다. 그런데 그 선택의 결과로 알게 된 사실이 우리가 기존에 알고 믿고 있던 것과 정반대라면 어떻게 될까? 무언가를 배우고 나서 보니 지금껏 나쁘다고 알고 있던 것이 좋아지게 되면 어떨까? 2013년부터 시작된 미국 TV 드라마 〈The Americans〉에 나오는 러시아 스파이 제닝스 부부 역을 생각해 보면 된다. 극 중 제닝스 부부는 냉전이 끝나기 전인 1980년대 미국에 잠입해 미국인 행세를 하며 간첩 임무를 수행한다. 그런데 일 때문에 어쩔 수 없이 친해져야 하는 사람들은 부부가 역겹고 끔찍하다고 생각했던 세계관을 지니고 사는 이들이었다. 좋든 싫든 제닝스 부부는 간첩 임무를 위해 속으로는 절대 동의할 수 없는 말을 끊임없이 해대는 사람들과 같이 웃고 즐기며 때로는 그런 생각에 맞장구도 쳐줘야 했다. 이런 상황에 처한 사람은 자연히 자기가 이렇게 끔찍한 생각을 하는 이들과 조금씩 동화되지는 않을지 걱정하기 마련이다. 그 사람들의 생각을 가만히 듣고 보니 일리 있는 면도 있다고 생각하게 돼서가 아니라 그런 사람들 속에서 자기도 그런 세계관을 가지고 사는 척하다 보면 원래 진짜 자기 생각과 세계관은 다소 옅어지고 지워질 수도 있기 때문이다.

이런 상황에 처하는 사례는 사실 얼마든지 찾아볼 수 있다. 친구가 추천해 준 다큐멘터리 내용이 알고 보니 가짜 뉴스로 도배된 선전물일 수도 있고, 관심이 가서 전공으로 택하려던 학문이 기본적으로 가정하는 전제가 내 신념과 맞지 않을 수도 있다. 그와 같은 경우는 선택이 당신의 인지적 관점을 바꾸는 방식이 전체적으로 손해인 경우로 간주된다.

04

하위내용영역	배점	예상정답률
일반영어 B형 서술형	4점	40%

[모범답안] Under stress, the brain benefits from being fed extra carbohydrates. This can lead to maintaining cognition under stress, as shown in a study involving a stressful situation and participants being provided or denied food. So, if one craves an afternoon chocolate, this can lead to maintaining the brain's function, lowering stress levels, and reducing the risks of depression, stroke, and heart attacks.

[채점기준] _____ _ Total 4pts

ⓐ Topic sentence

+1점 : 글의 topic sentence "Under stress, the brain benefits from being fed extra carbohydrates"를 명확하게 서술하였거나 유사하였다.

ⓑ Summary

+3점 : ① "This can lead to maintaining cognition under stress, as shown in a study involving a stressful situation and participants being provided or denied food. So, ② if one craves an afternoon chocolate, this can lead to maintaining the brain's function, lowering stress levels, and reducing the risks of depression, stroke, and heart attacks."

▷ 2가지 중 2개 요소가 모두 잘 요약된 경우 3점; 1개 요소만 요약된 경우 1점; 나머지는 0점을 준다.

감점 ▽

• 본문에 나오는 연속되는 6단어 이상을 사용하였다. −0.5pt
• 문단을 두 개나 그 이상으로 구성하였다. −0.5pt
• 문법이나 영어 표현을 합쳐 3개 이상 오류가 있다. −0.5pt

뇌의 무게는 체중의 2%에 불과하지만 우리가 일상에서 필요로 하는 탄수화물의 절반을 소비하며 그중에서도 포도당은 가장 중요한 영양소이다. 스트레스가 심할 때 뇌는 12%의 더 많은 에너지를 필요로 하며 사람들이 단것을 찾는 이유는 바로 이 때문이다. 탄수화물은 인체가 가장 쉽게 사용할 수 있는 에너지원이다. 실제로 스트레스를 받은 사람들은 음식을 먹기 전의 인지 능력 테스트에서 낮은 점수를 기록했다. 하지만 음식을 먹은 뒤에는 정상적인 상태로 돌아왔다.

뇌와 탄수화물의 관계를 더 알아보기 위해 우리는 40명을 대상으로 두 번의 실험을 진행했다. 첫번째 실험에서 우리는 참가자들에게 모르는 사람들 앞에서 10분 동안 발표를 부탁했고, 발표 후 스트레스 호르몬인 코르티솔과 아드레날린을 측정하고 한 시간 동안 뷔페에서 음식을 먹게 했다. 두 번째 실험에서는 발표 없이 호르몬을 측정했고 뷔페에서 음식을 먹게 했다. 이 실험에서 발표를 마쳤을 때 스트레스 호르몬의 수치는 더 높았고, 또 평균 34g의 탄수화물을 더 먹었다.

그럼 초콜릿은 어떤 효과가 있을까? 나는 직장에서 오후에 초콜릿이 당긴다고 말하는 이들에게 초콜릿을 먹는 것이 당신의 건강을 유지하고 맑은 정신을 유지하는 방법이라고 말해준다. 사람들은 직장에서 종종 스트레스를 받으며, 이때 뇌는 에너지를 필요로 한다. 만약 이때 식욕을 참을 경우 뇌는 지방이나 근육으로 가야 할 포도당을 사용하게 되고, 그 결과 더 많은 스트레스 호르몬을 분비하게 된다. 이는 그 사람의 기분을 나쁘게 할 뿐 아니라 장기적으로 심장병과 뇌졸중, 우울증의 위험을 높인다. 또한 뇌는 에너지를 절약하기 위해 활동을 줄이며 집중력과 업무 수행 능력이 떨어질 수 있다.

05 회 문제은행

📖 본책 p.035

01

하위내용영역	배점	예상정답률
일반영어 A형 기입형	2점	45%

모범답안 friendship

채점기준

• 2점 : 모범답안과 같다.

• 1점 : companionship이라 했다. friend(s)라 했으면 0점.

• 0점 : 모범답안과 다르다.

아리스토텔레스는 열일곱 살에 서양 철학의 아버지라고 불리는 고대 그리스의 철학자 플라톤이 건립한 학교 플라톤의 아카데미에 입학해서 20년간 이곳에 머무르며 학문에 정진했다. 스승 플라톤의 제자 중에서도 군계일학이었던 아리스토텔레스는 수많은 질문을 던졌고, 수많은 질문에 대한 답을 찾았다.

아리스토텔레스가 정확히 언제 플라톤의 아카데미를 떠났는지는 불명확하나, 스승 플라톤이 세상을 떠난 뒤 얼마 지나지 않아 자신과 철학적 견해가 다르다는 이유로 아카데미를 떠난 것으로 알려져 있다. 이후 아리스토텔레스는 결국 자신의 스승 플라톤의 핵심적인 이론을 반박하는 주장을 펼치기에 이른다.

아리스토텔레스가 얼마나 많은 저서를 집필했는지 설명하기란 가히 불가능하지만, 현재까지 남아 있는 극히 일부의 저술만 보더라도 경이로울 정도로 광범위한 주제를 다루고 있다. 천문학에서부터 물리학, 윤리, 경제학에 이르기까지 아리스토텔레스는 우리가 아는 모든 학문 분야를 탐구했고, 세상을 떠난지 2,000년도 더 지난 지금까지 인류 역사상 가장 많이 읽히고 인용되는 사상가로 손꼽히고 있다. 오늘날 아리스토텔레스의 업적은 다양한 분야에 걸쳐 있지만, 가장 정확한 이론으로 손꼽히는 것 중 하나가 그의 우정론이다. 아리스토텔레스는 우정을 인생의 참된 즐거움 중 하나로 보았고, 진정한 우정을 나누는 친구가 있어야만 성공한 인생이라고 생각했다. 아리스토텔레스는 친구와 우정에 대해 다음과 같은 말을 남겼다. "가난과 같은 역경이 닥쳤을 때, 사람들은 자신이 유일하게 기댈 곳은 친구라고 느낀다. 친구는 어린 시절에는 나의 잘못을 바로잡아 주고, 늙고 약해졌을 때는 나를 챙겨주는 존재이다. 한창 전성기 때는 위대한 업적을 이루는 동반자가 된다. 생각하고 행동하는 데 있어 언제나 하나보다 둘이 낫기 때문이다."

02

하위내용영역	배점	예상정답률
일반영어 A형 서술형	4점	50%

모범답안 Tribal and hunter-gatherer societies are more equalized due to projectile weaponry which puts the strong at greater risk from the weak. Second, "reverse dominance hierarchy" is a hierarchy in which the ruled band together to exert power steadily over the ruler.

채점기준 _ Total 4pts

+ 2점 : 부족적 수렵 채집 사회의 인간이 영장류들보다 더 평등한 이유를 "due to projectile weapons"라 서술하였거나 유사하였다.

+ 2점 : "역순위제"를 "a hierarchy in which the ruled(the weak; those on the bottom of the pyramid) band together to exert power(steadily) over the ruler(the powerful; the strong)"라 서술하였거나 유사하였다.

03

하위내용영역	배점	예상정답률
일반영어 B형 서술형	4점	45%

모범답안 The aspect of key importance to the overall context is that the woman of the young age range is finding Facebook unattractive and impersonal. Second, the most appropriate words for the blank are "messaging apps".

채점기준 _ Total 4pts

+ 2점 : 밑줄 친 부분이 글 전체의 맥락에서 어떤 측면에서 핵심적 중요성을 지니고 있는지에 대해 다음과 같이 서술하였거나 유사하였다. "the woman of the young age (range) is finding Facebook unattractive and impersonal."

+ 2점 : 빈칸에 들어갈 단어를 "messaging apps"라 정확하게 기술하였다. 이것 외에는 답이 될 수 없다.

한글 번역

페이스북은 뉴스를 보는 플랫폼(다양한 종류의 시스템이나 서비스를 제공하기 위해 공통적이고 반복적으로 사용하는 기반 모듈, 어떤 서비스를 가능하게 하는 일종의 '토대')으로서 더는 성장하고 있지 않다. 예를 들면, 미국에서 젊은이들이 뉴스를 보기 위해 페이스북을 사용하는 수치는 2017년에서 2018년 동안 20%나 떨어졌다. 지난해와 올해 사이 페이스북에서 뉴스를 받은 성인의 수치가 증가하지 않았다.

사람들이 그들의 장비를 덜 사용하기 때문이 아니다. 오히려, 로이터 저널리즘 연구소에서 발표한 보고서에서 말한 것처럼 이제 많은 사람은 메시지 앱에서 뉴스를 받고 있기 때문이다. 보고서에서 미국, 영국, 브라질 그리고 독일 사용자들의 소셜미디어 이용을 조사했다. 전체 샘플은 뉴스를 페이스북과 메시지 앱에서 매주 받는다고 답한 사람들로 이루어져 있다. 보고서는 로이터 연구소에서 지난여름에 발간한 2018 디지털 뉴스 보고서에 대한 다채롭고 질적으로 풍부한 정보를 제공하고, 1월 실시된 페이스북의 뉴스 피드 알고리즘 업데이트가 소비자에게 끼친 영향을 조사하고자 하는 목적을 가지고 있다. 저자들은 "왜 소비자가 메시지 앱에서 뉴스를 받고, 댓글을 남기고, 뉴스를 공유하는지"를 질문한다.

사람들은 비록 페이스북이 기본적인 플랫폼이란 것에 불편하게 생각하는 것과 상관없이, 여전히 페이스북이 "많은 사용자에게 기본적인 플랫폼"이라는 것을 알려주고 있다. "죄의식을 동반한 즐거움이죠. 나는 페이스북을 싫어하지만 동시에 사랑합니다." 한 미국 20대 남성은 말한다. 페이스북은 사람들에게 "머리를 식히기 위한 오락"과 같은 존재이자, 다른 이들과 연락하고 지내는 중요한 수단이다. 하지만 여전히 페이스북에 열정을 가지고 있나? 시간 낭비라고 생각하지는 않나? "페이스북은 점점 덜 매력적이고 개인적인 것이 개입되지 않아요. 나는 게시물을 점차 올리지 않고 있습니다." 한 20대 독일 여성은 말한다. "페이스북 친구 중 오직 10%만이 제 진짜 친구입니다."

연구는 사람들을 다시 플랫폼으로 데리고 오기 위한 페이스북의 알고리즘 변화가 ─ 사람들이 뉴스를 받고, 친밀감을 느끼며, 의미 있는 사회적 상호 작용을 하는 공간으로 페이스북을 바꾸기 위한 ─ 제대로 작동하지 않고 있다는 것을 시사한다.

광고와 다르게 뉴스 출처의 수를 줄이는 정책은 그다지 실용적이지 않다. 아마 이미 늦었을지도 모른다: 기존에 발표된 로이터의 보고서는 사람들이 뉴스를 공유하고 개인적인 주제를 이야기하기 위해 이미 메시지 앱으로의 전환을 시작했다는 것을 보여준다.

04

하위내용영역	배점	예상정답률
일반영어 B형 서술형	4점	35%

모범답안 The concept of "health freedom" is used to falsely frame the issue so that nostrums can be promoted. The population (or People) might believe that treatments not allowed by government regulation have some value, or likewise, that vaccinations required by the government are harmful. However, quacks are often promoting these beliefs in order to deceive and sell treatments and it is the government's duty to protect the public from exploitation.

채점기준   _Total 4pts

ⓐ Topic sentence

+ 2점 : 글의 topic sentence "The concept of "health freedom" is used to falsely frame the issue so that nostrums can be promoted."를 명확하게 서술하였거나 유사하였다.

ⓑ Summary

+ 2점 : "People might believe that treatments not allowed by government regulation have some value(0.5점), or likewise, that vaccinations required by the government are harmful(0.5점). However, quacks are often promoting these beliefs in order to deceive and sell treatments(0.5점) and it is the government's duty to protect the public from exploitation(0.5점)."

감점 ▽

• 본문에 나오는 연속되는 6단어 이상을 사용하였다. -0.5pt
• 문단을 두 개나 그 이상으로 구성하였다. -0.5pt
• 문법이나 영어 표현을 합쳐 3개 이상 오류가 있다. -0.5pt

한글 번역

미운 두 살이라는 말이 있다. 하루 종일 "안 돼"라는 말을 듣다 보면, 아이는 부모의 말에 반항하게 된다. 어른들 또한, 무언가를 하지 못하게 하는 걸 싫어한다. 그중 어떤 이들은 정부의 규제가 자신의 권리를 침해한다고 생각한다. 정부가 (아이의) 학교의 입학 조건으로 백신을 요구하면, 그들은 아이들에게 백신을 맞힐 권리가 자신에게 있다고 말한다. 암으로 죽어가는 환자들은, FDA의 승인을 받기 전까지 약을 팔 수 없다고 하면, 규제 때문에 사람의 목숨을 살리지 못한다고 불만을 토로한다. "건강의 자유"란 누구나 자신이 원하는 치료는 그 무엇이라도 받을 권리가 있으며, 자신들의 몸으로 들어가는 것을 자신들이 통제하며, 정부는 여기에 간섭해서는 안 된다는 주장이다.

하지만 "건강의 자유"는 우리가 사이비 의료인들이 자신들에게 쏟아지는 의혹의 눈초리를 본능적으로 공감하게 되는 환자들에게 돌리기 위해 사용한(만든) 용어이다. 그들은 악어의 눈물을 흘리면서 "이 불쌍한 사람들은 자신들이 원하는 것은 무엇이든 해 볼 자유를 가져야 한다"라고 말한다. 그리고 두 가지 사실을 숨기기 위해 노력한다. 첫째, 누구도 사기를 당하는 것은 원치 않는다는 것, 특히 삶과 죽음에 관해서라면 더 말할 것도 없다. 환자들은 사이비 치료를 받기 위해 자신들의 "권리"를 요구하는 것이 아니다. 단지 거기에 어떤 희망이 있을지 모른다고 속고 있을 뿐이다. 둘째, 사이비 의료를 막는 법은 환자의 권리를 제한하기 위해서가 아니라, 환자들을 이용하려는 사기꾼들을 막기 위해 존재한다는 것이다.

백신 반대자들은 정부가 아이들의 건강을 보호할 의무가 있으며, 따라서 백신으로 막을 수 있는 질병으로부터 아이들을 지킬 의무가 있다는 것을 이해하지 못한다. 오히려 부모의 권리와 개인의 취향이 모든 것에 우선한다고 생각하는 경향이 있다.

06 회 문제은행

📖 본책 p.041

01

하위내용영역	배점	예상정답률
일반영어 A형 기입형	2점	40%

모범답안 global

채점기준

• 2점: 모범답안과 같다. 이것 외에는 답이 될 수 없다.
• 0점: 모범답안과 다르다.

한글 번역

평등하지 않은 상황에서는 가까운 사람들끼리의 경쟁이 훨씬 격화된다. 자원에 따라 지닌 가치가 다르기 마련이고, 가치가 높은 자원일수록 승리의 보상도, 패배의 아픔도 커진다. 하지만, 특히 지역 내의 경쟁은 이 차이를 더욱 부각시킨다. 내가 실행한 연구에서, 한 경제 게임에 참가한 사람들은 불평등이 높아질 때 훨씬 더 이기적인 선택을 했다. 그들은 서로서로 더 많은 싸움을 했는데, 이렇게 하는 것이 그들에게 손해가 되더라도 말이다. 하지만, 비록 그들 사이에서 불평등이 그렇게 크지 않았더라도, 지역 내의 경쟁 아래서는 가장 빈번하게 싸웠고 그 결과 훨씬 더 많은 점수를 잃었다.

실제 세상에서 일어나는 폭력의 근본적인 원인을 규명하고 해결책을 찾는 데 사람들의 이러한 태도와 행동이 실마리를 제공할지도 모른다. 댈리는 자신의 저서 〈경쟁을 없애는 법〉에서 불평등이 심한 곳일수록 살인율이 높고, 반대로 평등한 사회일수록 살인율이 낮는 사실을 보여주었다. 그런데 (앞서 살펴봤듯이) 경쟁의 범위가 좁을수록 불평등에 따른 폭력이 훨씬 격하게 일어나고, 반대로 전 세계적으로 넓은 차원에서 경쟁이 일어났을 때 반목하기보다 협력하는 쪽을 택한다면, 다음과 같은 해법을 생각해볼 수 있다. 이민이나 이주를 장려해 경쟁의 범위를 가능한 한 넓힐 수 있다면, 불평등이 존재하더라도 이것이 곧 폭력과 최악의 경우 살인으로 이어질 가능성은 낮출 수도 있다. 예를 들어, 불평등이 심화하더라도 동시에 경쟁이 전 세계적으로 일어나면, 후자(global competition)가 전자(inequality)의 영향을 줄이게 될 것이다. (경쟁자와 마주치고 부대낄 일이 없다면 마른 장작이 쌓여 있어도 불을 붙일 방법이 없는 것과 마찬가지인 상황이 되는 것.)

02

하위내용영역	배점	예상정답률
일반영어 A형 서술형	4점	40%

모범답안 The five words are "having sex with the dead". Second, the series of experiments discovered that crows' responses are specific to their own species and they are not commonly interested in having sex with other dead crows.

채점기준 _ Total 4pts

+ 2점: 상응하는 5단어를 "having sex with the dead"라 서술하였다. 이것 외에는 답이 될 수 없다.
+ 2점: 일련의 실험들이 발견한 것을 "crows' responses are specific to their own species and they are not commonly interested in having sex with other dead crows."라 서술하였거나 유사하였다.

한글 번역

많은 연구들은 까마귀가 높은 지능을 가지고 있음을 말해준다. 까마귀는 퍼즐 문제를 풀 수 있고, 도구도 사용한다. 다른 연구는 까마귀들이 동료의 죽음에 반응하는 것과 같은 사회적 행동을 한다는 것을 보여준다.

워싱턴 대학의 박사 과정생인 캘리 스위프트는 2015년 까마귀의 "장례식"을 연구한 적이 있다. 이때 그녀는 까마귀의 한 가지 특이한 행동을 목격했다. 당시 그녀와 그녀의 지도 교수인 존 마즐루프는 까마귀가 죽어있는 까마귀를 발견했을 때, 울음소리를 통해 다른 까마귀들에게 위험을 알린다는 사실에 관한 연구를 하고 있었다. 그 과정에서 그들은 한 번도 보지 못했던 광경을 보게 됐다. 한 까마귀가 죽은 까마귀에게 다가가 그 위에 올라탄 뒤 의도가 명백한 어떤 행동을 한 것이다.

연구에서 스위프트와 마즐루프는 까마귀들이 죽은 까마귀를 통해 잠재적인 위험에 대해 알게 되고 이를 피한다는 것을 발견했다. 이 때문에 스위프트는 까마귀가 사체와 짝짓기를 시도했을 때 더욱 이해할 수 없었다고 말한다. 죽은 까마귀는 위험을 알리는 신호일 텐데, 왜 그 까마귀에 더 가까이 접근하는가 하는 것이다. "동종의 사체에 가까이 가는 것은 질병, 기생충, 천적 등의 위험을 크게 만듭니다."

연구에서 이들은 워싱턴주의 네 도시에서 308쌍의 야생 까마귀에 대해 실험했다. 그들은 까마귀 사체를 대신할 다양한 자세의 박제 까마귀와 비둘기, 다람쥐의 사체를 준비해 까마귀가 각각에 대해 어떻게 반응을 하는지 확인했다.

까마귀들은 동종의 사체에 대해 경고성 울음을 더 많이 냈고, 그중에서도 죽어있는 자세의 경우 울음소리를 더 많이 냈다. 죽은 까마귀에 접근한 까마귀의 비율은 25%였지만, 이 중에서 짝짓기를 시도한 까마귀의 비율은 4%에 불과했다. 이는 이러한 행동이 일반적인 행동은 아님을 의미한다.

03

하위내용영역	배점	예상정답률
일반영어 B형 서술형	4점	50%

모범답안 The one word is "empathy". Second, selective empathy is the empathy reserved only for those one believes are hurt, not for their enemies or others.

채점기준 ___ Total 4pts

+ 2점 : 상응하는 한 단어가 "empathy"임을 정확하게 서술하였다. 이것 외에는 답이 될 수 없다.

+ 2점 : 선택적 공감이 "the empathy reserved only for those one believes are hurt, not for their enemies"

▷ 다음과 같이 서술하였어도 2점을 준다.

"the empathy reserved only for their own group, not for their enemies"

한글 번역

약 10년 전을 기점으로 일부 사람들, 특히 젊은층을 중심으로 공감 능력이라는 개념에 대한 의심이 싹트기 시작했다. 1960년대 말부터 학계에서는 "곤경에 처해 도움이 필요한 사람이 있어도 내 문제는 아니다", "누군가를 비난하기 전에 내가 그쪽 입장이면 기분이 어떨지 짐작해 보려고 노력한다"와 같은 설문 문항에 대한 동의 여부로 젊은이들의 공감 능력 정도를 연구해 왔다.

새라 콘래스는 수십 년간 쌓인 데이터에서 명확한 패턴을 발견했다. 2000년 전후로 젊은이들의 공감 능력이 떨어지기 시작한 것이다. 곤경에 처한 사람을 돕는 것, 다른 사람의 시각으로 세상을 보는 것은 한마디로 '내가 알 바 아니'라고 말하는 응답자의 수가 점점 많아졌다. 2009년에 이르자 젊은이들의 공감 능력은 우리 세대보다 평균 40%나 떨어졌다.

인간의 자연스러운 본능과도 같은 공감 능력이 소비 심리처럼 변화한다는 것은 이상한 일이다. 하지만 이런 현상은 엄연한 현실이다. 우리가 초등학교 교실에서 배운 것들을 이제 젊은이들은 곧이곧대로 받아들이지 않고 있는 것이다. 이들의 생각은 이렇다. 왜 굳이 내가 아닌 사람의 입장에서 생각해야 하는가? 더군다나 나에게 해로운 사람의 입장이라면? 실제로 공감 능력을 발휘하지 않는 것은 곧 자신의 입장을 확실히 표명하는 것, 즉 긍정적인 가치로 인식되고 있다. 일례로 백인우월주의자인 리처드 스펜서의 아내가 가정폭력 사실을 언론에 밝혔을 때, 인터넷 좌파들의 반응은 "왜 우리가 끔찍한 인종주의자와 연대하는 것을 선택한 여성에게 관심을 주어야 하나? 왜 우리의 공감 능력을 그런 곳에 낭비해야 하지?"라는 식이었다.

새로운 공감의 법칙은 "적에게 공감 능력을 낭비하지 말고, 내가 생각하고 판단하기에 그것을 필요로 하는 이들을 위해 아껴두자"는 정도로 보인다. 상대편에 공감하는 것은 거의 터부시되는 분위기다. 이와 같은 "선택적 공감"은 아주 강력한 힘을 발휘하고 있다.

04

하위내용영역	배점	예상정답률
일반영어 B형 서술형	4점	35%

모범답안 China did not go aboard actively due to repercussions from local politics, which was aggravated by its political unification. With its advantages and lead in technology, it should have excelled, but during a power struggle between eunuchs and their opponents in the Chinese court, the opponents ordered the shipyards dismantled and forbid shipping overseas. Since China was unified, as opposed to other nations, this decision led to the whole of China stopping their fleets and no longer building shipyards.

채점기준   _ Total 4pts

ⓐ Topic sentence

+ 1점: 글의 topic sentence "China did not go aboard actively due to repercussions from local politics, which was aggravated by its political unification"를 명확하게 서술하였거나 유사하였다.

ⓑ Summary

+ 3점: "① With its advantages and lead in technology, it should have excelled, but during a power struggle between eunuchs and their opponents in the Chinese court, the opponents ordered the shipyards dismantled(1.5점). ② Since China was unified, as opposed to other nations, this decision led to the whole of China stopping their fleets and no longer building shipyards(1.5점)."

감점 ♡

• 본문에 나오는 연속되는 6단어 이상을 사용하였다. −0.5pt
• 문단을 두 개나 그 이상으로 구성하였다. −0.5pt
• 문법이나 영어 표현을 합쳐 3개 이상 오류가 있다. −0.5pt

한글 번역

중국은 의심할 여지없이 여러 이점들이 있었다. 비옥한 초승달 지대(나일강과 티그리스강과 페르시아만을 연결하는 고대 농업 지대)에서와 거의 유사한 이른 시점에서의 식량 생산의 증가라든가, 지구에서 가장 많은 인구를 먹여 살릴 수 있었던 거대한 생산력들이 그것이다. 이상과 같은 이점들과 빠른 출발 덕분에 중세 때 중국은 전 세계의 기술을 선도했다. 15세기 초에는 수백 척의 배로 구성된 보물선 선단들을 파견했는데, 그중 가장 큰 배의 경우 길이가 120미터에 달했으며 총인원도 최대 28,000명에 달했다. 그들은 콜럼버스가 보잘 것 없는 세 척의 배로 협소한 대서양을 건너 아메리카 동해안에 도달하기 수 십 년 전에 이미 인도양을 건너 아프리카 동해안에까지 진출했다. 어째서 중국의 배들은 태평양을 건너 아메리카 서해안으로 진출하지 못했을까? 간단히 말해서, 왜 중국은 그토록 낙후되어 있던 유럽에게 기술의 선도자 위치를 뺏겼을까?

우리는 중국의 보물선 선단의 종말을 통해 하나의 단서를 얻을 수 있다. 1405~1433년에 일곱 차례의 선단이 중국을 떠나 항해했는데, 그러다가 중국 조정의 두 파벌(환관과 그 반대파) 사이에 권력 투쟁의 발생으로 인해 중단되고 말았다. 환관들은 선단을 파견하고 지휘하는 일에 동조하는 쪽이었다. 그래서 반대파는 권력 투쟁에서 승리하자 곧 선단 파견을 중단시켰고, 결국에는 조선소 마저 해체하고 해양 항해를 금지시켰다. 이 사건을 보면서 우리는 1880년대 런던 시 당국이 공공전기조명의 발전을 억압했던 일, 제1차 세계대전과 2차 세계대전 사이의 기간 동안 미국이 고립주의를 고집했던 일, 그 밖에도 많은 나라가 정치적인 문제 때문에 뒷걸음친 일들을 기억하게 된다. 하지만 중국의 경우에는 한 가지 다른 점이 있다. 그것은 바로 중국 전역이 정치적으로 통일되어 있었다는 사실이다. 한번 결정이 내려지자 중국 전역에서 선단 파견이 중단됐고, 일시적이었던 이 결정은 돌이킬 수 없는 것이 되고 말았다. 다시 배를 만들어 그 일시적 결정의 어리석음을 입증하고 또 새로운 조선소를 지으려 해도, 본보기로 삼을 수 있는 조선소가 하나도 남아 있지 않았기 때문이다.

📖 본책 p.048

07회 문제은행

01

하위내용영역	배점	예상정답률
일반영어 A형 기입형	2점	35%

모범답안 personality differences

채점기준

• 2점: 모범답안과 같다. 이것 외에는 답이 될 수 없다.
• 0점: 모범답안과 다르다.

한글 번역

나는 진화 생물학 생태학자이며, 내 주된 연구 분야는 개체의 성격이 그들의 적합성과 집단 행동, 그들 사회에서의 성공에 어떤 영향을 미치는지 보는 것이다. 대부분의 사람들은 크게 관심이 없겠지만, 동물 성격 연구는 행동 생태학 내에서 매우 활발하게 연구되는 분야인데, 이는 자연에서 개체가 성격을 가지는 것이 매우 일반적일 뿐더러 그 성격이 그들의 종 안과 다른 종과의 상호 작용에서 그들의 행동을 잘 설명하기 때문이다. 지금까지 연구된 거의 모든 종에서 개체는 성격을 가지고 있으며, 특히 성차에 따른 성격의 차이는 가장 확실하게 나타난다. 우리와 가장 가까운 영장류에 있어 성별에 따른 성격의 차이는 매우 잘 정리되어 있다. 영장류에 있어 암컷과 수컷은 덩치의 차이가 있으며, 포유류는 일반적으로 공격성, 암컷의 까탈스러움, 텃세, 몸치장, 양육 등에 있어 성별에 따른 큰 차이를 가지고 있다.

인간 또한 성별에 따른 몸집 차이가 있고 어떤 객관적인 관찰자들이라도 동의를 할 만한 성별에 따른 성격의 차이가 있다. 포유류 전반에 걸쳐 이러한 차이가 나타난다는 사실에서, 인간의 성별에 따른 행동의 차이가 순수하게 사회화의 결과라는 주장은 아무리 잘 봐준다 해도 의심스러운 소리에 불과하다. 그 주장이 사실이 되기 위해서는 진화에 있어 선택적인 압력으로 작용해 온 성별에 따른 성격의 차이가 하필 우리 인간 종에 있어서만 어떤 이유에 의해 완전히 사라져야 하고, 또 성장기의 사회화 과정에서 하필 성별에 따라 그런 특징이 그대로 학습되어야만 한다.

02

하위내용영역	배점	예상정답률
일반영어 A형 서술형	4점	40%

모범답안 The landmark study showed that a four-and-a-half-year old could remember memories from 18 months prior but around age 6 children begin to forget many of their earliest memories. Second, the case of the mice shows that infancy amnesia has little to do with the capacity for language or a sense of self.

채점기준 _ Total 4pts

+ 2점: 기념비적인 연구의 주요 기여한 바를 "<u>a four-and-a-half-year old could remember memories from 18 months prior</u>(1.5점), <u>but around age 6 children begin to forget many of their earliest memories</u>(0.5점)"라 서술하였거나 유사하였다.

+ 2점: 생쥐 연구에서 드러난 것을 "<u>infancy amnesia has little to do with the capacity for language or a sense of self</u>"라 서술하였거나 유사하였다.
  ▷ 다음과 같이 서술하였어도 2점을 준다.
    • "<u>memories in infancy can be lost in adulthood even without development of language or a sense of self</u>"
    • "<u>enduring memories in adulthood do not require language or sense of self</u>"

1980년대 후반에 들어서자 아동 심리학 분야에서 개혁이 시작됐다. 바우어와 다른 심리학자들은 몇 가지 실험과 연구를 통해 유아기적 기억을 본격적으로 분석하기 시작했다. 실험이란 예를 들어 어린이에게 간단한 장난감 징을 만들어 치는 법을 가르쳐 주고, 몇 분 내지 몇 달이 지난 뒤 그 장난감을 쳐보게 해 그 사이 기억이 얼마나 잊혔는지를 살펴보는 식이었다.

여러 차례 실험을 거듭한 끝에 과학자들은 3세 이하 어린이도 한계가 있을지언정 기억을 만들어 남긴다는 점을 밝혀냈다. 생후 6개월 된 아기들의 기억은 적어도 하루는 지속됐다. 생후 9개월이 되면 그 기간이 최소 한 달로 늘어나고, 두 돌이 지난 아기는 1년 전의 기억을 떠올릴 수 있다. 이제는 (이 분야의 고전이 되어버린) 기념비적인 1991년 연구에서 네 살 반 된 어린이가 18개월 전, 그러니까 자신의 세 번째 생일 즈음에 디즈니월드에 갔던 기억을 상당히 자세히 기억해냈다는 사실을 발견했다. 그런데 여섯 살 무렵에 아이들은 이런 어릴 적 기억들을 까먹기 시작한다. 2005년 바우어와 동료 연구진이 한 실험 결과를 보면, 다섯 살 반 어린이는 세 살 때 일을 80% 정도 기억했지만, 일곱 살 반 어린이는 세 살 때 일을 40%도 기억하지 못했다.

(이 2005년) 실험은 어릴 적 기억 상실에 관한 핵심적인 모순을 극명하게 드러낸다. 즉, 어린이도 더 어렸을 때 경험을 기억으로 만들어 저장하고 시간이 지난 뒤 꺼내어볼 수 있지만, 이때 기억들은 언젠가 대부분 사라져버린다는 것이다. 어른이 된 뒤에도 어떤 기억은 희미해지지만, 어릴 적 기억 상실에 버금가는 수준은 아니다.

기억이 온전히 남으려면 언어 능력과 자아에 대한 감각 혹은 자의식이 필요한데, 어린이에게는 두 가지가 모두 부족하기 때문에 기억을 잘 못한다는 주장도 있었다. 물론 어떤 일에 관해 나눈 대화나 그 상황에 내가 어떻게 관련돼 있었는지는 사람의 기억을 강화하는 데 큰 역할을 한다. 하지만 어릴 적 기억 상실을 이 두 가지의 부족만으로 설명할 수는 없다. 쥐처럼 몸집에 비해 뇌가 충분히 크고 복잡한 동물에서도 비슷한 현상이 관찰된다. 즉, 쥐가 구사하는 언어는 인간의 언어와 비교할 수 없을 수준일 것이고, 자의식도 인간보다 훨씬 단순할 텐데, 그런 쥐도 자라면서 어렸을 적 기억을 잊어버린다.

03

하위내용영역	배점	예상정답률
일반영어 B형 서술형	4점	30%

모범답안 The researchers were unable to adjust for the app's users' age and wealth. Second, the word that best suits the blank is "four".

채점기준 _Total 4pts

+ 2점 : 연구진이 통제할 수 없었던 것이 "the app's users' age and wealth"임을 명확하게 서술하였거나 유사하였다.
▷ 다음과 같이 서술하였어도 2점을 준다.
"the fact that the users of the app tended to be younger and more affluent than the whole country"

+ 2점 : 빈칸에 들어갈 한 단어를 "four"라 기입하였거나 "three나 five, six, seven, eight..." 즉, 3 이상의 숫자가 들어가면 맞는 것으로 한다.

한글 번역

(영국) 서섹스대학교의 경제학자 피터 돌튼과 조지 맥케론이 현재 심리 상태를 입력하는 행복 추적기 앱의 데이터 300만여 건을 분석한 결과, 내가 응원하는 팀이 이겼을 때 느끼는 행복은 내가 응원하는 팀이 졌을 때 느끼는 불행의 절반 정도에 불과한 것으로 나타났다.

월드컵 결승전에 이 공식을 대입해보면 (이 세상에 프랑스를 응원한 팬과 크로아티아를 응원한 팬의 숫자가 같았다고 가정) 월드컵 결승전이 끝난 뒤 세상은 더 불행한 곳이 됐다. 한마디로, 축구는 행복의 파괴자이다.

이걸 증명하기 위해 연구진은 한 앱으로부터 나온 데이터를 분석했다. 이 앱이 하루에 여러 차례 무작위로 3만 2천여 명에게 던지는 질문은 "얼마나 행복하다고 느끼세요"이다. 사람들은 지금의 심리 상태를 가장 행복하면 100점 만점으로 매겨 답할 수 있다. 지금 누구와 함께 무얼 하고 있는지도 짧게 덧붙일 수 있으며, 위치 정보도 함께 전송된다. 연구진은 이 정보를 모아 응답자가 경기장에서 직접 축구를 관전하고 있는지 아닌지를 판단할 수 있다.

연구진은 이어 시간대, 요일에 따른 효과를 감안해 결과를 조정했다. (하루 중에도 대체로 기분이 좋은 시간대가 있고, 일주일 중에 특히 기분이 쉽게 우울해지는 날이 있기 마련이니까.) 또한, 연구진은 한 사람의 행복 지수를 추적할 수 있었기 때문에 그 사람이 원래 쉽게 행복해하는 사람인지, 반대로 기본적으로 불만이 많고 우울한 사람인지도 알 수 있었다. 하지만, 연구진은 해당 앱을 사용하는 사람들의 데이터를 받았기 때문에 앱 사용자의 연령대나 재산까지는 통제할 수 없었다. (그렇다면 이제 결과를 살펴보자). 내가 응원하는 팀이 이긴 지 한 시간 안에 팬들은 보통 때보다 약 3.9포인트 더 행복하다고 느꼈는데, 이는 음악을 들었을 때 느끼는 행복과 거의 비슷한 수준이다. 반대로 내가 응원하는 팀이 패한 지 한 시간 안에 심리 상태에 답한 팬들은 보통 때보다 7.8포인트나 더 슬퍼했다. 이는 일 하거나 공부할 때, 줄을 서서 기다릴 때 느끼는 답답함이나 짜증, 스트레스보다 두 배 가까이 더 우울한 수치다.

연구진은 경기가 끝난 뒤 느끼는 기쁨과 슬픔의 차이가 극명한 것도 놀랍지만, 시간이 흐를수록 차이가 더 벌어진다는 점도 간과해선 안 된다고 말한다. 즉, 승리 후 느끼는 기쁨은 얼마 가지 않아 사라지곤 하지만, 패배 후 찾아오는 슬픔은 훨씬 오랫동안 팬들을 괴롭혀 결과적으로 승리 후 느끼는 행복의 네 배나 되는 불행을 안겨준다. 이 차이는 응답자가 직접 경기장에 가서 경기를 관전했을 때 훨씬 크게 나타났다.

04

하위내용영역	배점	예상정답률
일반영어 B형 서술형	4점	40%

모범답안 Polytheism is significantly logical and persuasive as opposed to a monotheistic bias. Polytheism doesn't dispute a single power at work, and such polytheist religions as Greek and Hinduism had such singular powers behind them. However, in polytheism these singular supreme powers are viewed as indifferent to human interests, and thus neither Greeks nor Hindus took any action to try to influence them by sacrificing something or building temples.

채점기준　_Total 4pts

ⓐ Topic sentence
+ 1점: 글의 topic sentence "Polytheism is significantly logical and persuasive as opposed to a monotheistic bias"를 명확하게 서술하였거나 유사하였다.

ⓑ Summary
+ 3점: "Polytheism doesn't dispute a single power at work, and such polytheist religions as Greek and Hinduism had such singular powers behind them(1점). However, in polytheism these singular supreme powers are viewed as indifferent to human interests(1.5점), and thus neither Greeks nor Hindus took any action to try to influence them by sacrificing something or building temples(0.5점)."
▷ 그리스인들이 운명의 여신에게 제물을 바치지 않았고, 힌두교도들도 아트만을 위한 사원을 짓지 않은 이유를 정확하게 서술하였으면 1.5점을 준다. "in polytheism these singular supreme powers are viewed as indifferent to human interests"

감점 ✅
• 본문에 나오는 연속되는 6단어 이상을 사용하였다. −0.5pt
• 문단을 두 개나 그 이상으로 구성하였다. −0.5pt
• 문법이나 영어 표현을 합쳐 3개 이상 오류가 있다. −0.5pt

한글 번역

서구인들은 2천년 동안 일신교의 세뇌를 받은 탓에 다신교를 무지하고 유치한 우상 숭배로 보게 됐다. 이것은 부당한 고정관념이다. 다신교의 내부 논리를 이해하려면, 수많은 신이 존재한다는 믿음을 지탱하는 중심 사상을 파악할 필요가 있다. 다신교가 우주 전체를 관장하는 단일한 힘이나 법칙의 존재를 반박하기만 하는 것은 아니다. 사실 대부분의 다신교 심지어 애니미즘(우주의 모든 활동은 우주를 다스리는 어떤 힘에 의해 이뤄진다는 믿음) 종교들은 모든 다른 신들이나 악마, 신성한 바위의 배후에 있는 최고 권력을 인정했다. 고전 그리스 다신교에서 제우스, 헤라, 아폴론과 그 동료들은 모든 것을 다스리는 전능한 힘, 즉 운명의 여신(모이라, 아낭케)에게 복종했다. 힌두 다신교에서는 아트만이라는 단 하나의 원리가 무수한 신들과 정령, 인간, 생물학적 세상과 물리적 세상 모두를 통제한다. 아트만은 전 우주의 영원한 정수이자 영혼이면서 모든 개인과 모든 현상의 정수이기도 하다.

일신교와 구별되는 다신교의 근본적 통찰에 의하면, 세상을 지배하는 최고 권력은 관심이나 편견을 지니고 있지 않다. 그러므로 인간의 평범한 욕망이나 근심 걱정에 개의치 않는다. 이 권력에게 전쟁의 승리나 건강, 비를 요청하는 것은 무의미하다. 모든 것을 아우르는 위치에서 보면, 특정 왕국의 승리나 패배, 특정 도시의 번영이나 쇠퇴, 특정인의 회복이나 사망은 아무런 차이가 없는 일이기 때문이다. 그리스인들은 운명의 여신에게 제물을 바치지 않았고, 힌두교도들도 아트만을 위한 사원을 짓지 않았다.

08 회 문제은행

📖 본책 p.055

01

하위내용영역	배점	예상정답률
일반영어 A형 기입형	2점	65%

모범답안 compassion

채점기준

· 2점: 모범답안과 같다. 이것 외에는 답이 될 수 없다.
· 0점: 모범답안과 다르다.

한글 번역

뉴저지주 쿠퍼대학병원의 진료 부장이자 중증 치료 전문가인 스티븐 트레제키악 박사는 다정다감한 의술의 신봉자와 거리가 멀었다. 그는 의학을 철저한 과학으로 보고 접근하는 타입이었다.

하지만 앤서니 마짜렐리 병원장이 가져온 연구 과제를 수행하면서 생각이 달라지기 시작했다. 병원장은 최근 의료 업계 종사자들(의사들) 사이에서 번아웃 증후군이 전염병처럼 퍼지고 있는 가운데 환자 치료 개선 방안이 필요하다고 지시했다.

병원장이 트레제키악 박사에게 내린 연구 과제는 구체적인 질문이었다. 질문은 "의술에 더해 연민과 인정을 가지고 환자를 치료하는 것이 환자와 의사의 웰빙에 측정 가능한 도움을 주는가?"였다.

처음에 트레제키악 박사는 의구심을 가졌다. 물론 인정 연민이라는 것이 나쁠리 없겠지만 실제로 그것이 어떻게 도움이 되는지 증명할 수 없으리라 예상했다.

하지만 논문 초록 1000여 편과 250개의 보고서를 검토한 후, 예상이 빗나갔음을 알 수 있었다. 의료인이 환자와 인간적인 유대를 만들기 위해 시간을 들이면 치료 결과도 좋아지고 의료 비용도 낮출 수 있다는 것이었다. 그 효과는 환자의 고통이 줄어들고 혈압이 낮아지고 우울증과 불안감이 개선되는 등의 구체적인 이점으로 나타났다.

02

하위내용영역	배점	예상정답률
일반영어 A형 서술형	4점	40%

모범답안 The meaning of the underlined is that a human being is not an animal, which does not know how to show gratitude, so should show gratitude for other people's help. Second, the most appropriate word for the blank is "happiness".

채점기준 _Total 4pts

+ 2점: "a human being is not an animal, so should show gratitude for other people's help"라 서술하였거나 유사하였다.

+ 2점: 빈칸에 들어갈 단어를 "happiness"라 서술하였다. 이것 외에는 답이 될 수 없다.

한글 번역

당신은 가축처럼 길러지지는 않았을 것이다. (그렇기에) 타인의 도움에 대해 고마움과 감사함을 표시해야 한다는 사실을 알고 있을 것이다. 그런데도 사람들은 종종 감사를 표현할 때 심각한 실수를 한다. 사람들은 자신이 어떻게 느끼는지에 중점을 둔다. 도움을 준 사람에게 초점을 맞추기보다 자신이 얼마나 기쁘고 큰 도움을 받았는지에 대해서 이야기한다.

노스캐롤라이나 대학의 연구원들은 감사의 표현을 두 가지 유형으로 구분했다. 타인의 성품이나 능력(즉 타인의 긍정적인 부분)을 검증하고 인정하는 과정을 포함한 상대를 칭찬하는 유형과 도움을 받은 사람이 얼마나 그 도움으로 인해 이익을 얻었는지를 표현하는 자기 이득 유형이 그것이다. 이 연구에서 커플들이 자신의 파트너가 최근에 한 일에 대해서 감사를 표현하는 법을 관찰했다. 그리고 연구 참가자들의 표현은 상대를 칭찬하는 방식이었는지 아니면 자신의 이익에 초점을 맞추었는지 분류되었다. 각 유형의 표현 방식을 예로 들면 다음과 같다.

상대방 칭찬하기: "그 행동은 당신이 얼마나 책임감 있는 사람인지를 보여주는 행동이었어…" "당신은 애써서 그렇게까지 도움을 줬어…" "당신은 그 일을 정말 잘 하는 것 같아."

자신의 이익에 초점 두기: "당신 덕분에 내가 쉴 수 있었어." "덕분에 직장에서 내가 우쭐댈 수 있었어." "나 행복해"

마지막으로 도움을 준 사람은 상대가 얼마나 감사함을 표현했다고 느끼는지, 얼마나 도움을 준 사실에 대해 행복했는지, 또 자신의 파트너에 대해 얼마나 애정을 느끼는지 평가하도록 했다. 연구원들은 상대방을 칭찬하는 유형이 반응과 행복 그리고 애정과 강한 관련이 있었으나, 자신의 이익에 초점을 둔 경우는 그렇지 않은 것을 발견했다.

03

하위내용영역	배점	예상정답률
일반영어 B형 서술형	4점	40%

모범답안 The difference between crows and human beings' intelligence is that humans as a "freak" event have the ability to develop high technology, such as interstellar communication, technological power, or electromagnetic field theory, as opposed to crows. Second, the silence looks "sinister" because it indicates that advanced civilizations do not last long (advanced civilizations like ours quickly destroy themselves), so, extraterrestrial civilizations are not likely to survive.

채점기준 _Total 4pts

+ 2점: 까마귀의 지능과 인간의 지능의 차이를 "The difference between crows and human beings' intelligence is that humans as a "freak" event have the ability to develop advanced science or high technology (such as interstellar communication, technological power, or electromagnetic field theory) as opposed to crows"라 서술하였거나 유사하였다.

+ 2점: 우주의 침묵이 불길한 이유를 "because it indicates that advanced civilizations do not last long (advanced civilizations like ours quickly destroy themselves), so, extraterrestrial civilizations are not likely to survive."라 서술하였거나 유사하였다.

한글 번역

우주에 (우리 지구 이외의) 다른 문명이 있다 해도 그들은 우리에게 별로 관심이 없는 듯 보인다. 그들은 우리를 방문하지도, 연락을 취하지도, 전파를 보내지도 않는다. 심지어 우리를 엿보는 것 같지도 않다. 우주의 이런 무시(무관심)는 마치 우리가 이 우주에서 버려진 존재인 듯한 느낌을 준다. 위대한 물리학자 엔리코 페르미는 이를 이렇게 표현했다. "다들 어디에 있는 거지?"

세상에는 다양한 종류의 지능이 있다. 최근 다양한 종류의 새들, 특히 까마귀가 원숭이보다 더 높은 지능을 가지고 있음을 보이는 연구들이 발표되고 있다. 낙지 또한 높은 지능을 가졌다. 곧, 조류, 포유류, 연체동물이 모두 나름의 지능을 가지게 되었다는 사실에서 어쩌면 적당한 수준의 지능은 진화 과정에서 필연적으로 발생하는 것일 수 있다. 하지만 이런 정도의 지능으로는 우주를 향해 신호를 보낼 수 없다. 까마귀의 지능은 매우 놀랍지만 그들이 전자기학을 발전시켜낼 것 같지는 않다. 과학의 발전을 위해서는 복잡한 문화와 탐구심으로 이어진, 인간이 가진 총명함과 같은 지능이 필요하다. 그리고 이런 지능은 진화의 관점에서는 기이한 일인 것처럼 보인다.

그래서, 생물학적 관점에서도 외계의 다른 지능과 만나는 것은 쉽지 않은 것처럼 보인다. 어쩌면 우주에는 낮은 지능을 가진 다양한 종류의 생명체가 곳곳에 존재하고 있을지 모른다. 하지만 대화할 가치가 있는 존재는 없겠지. 이는 참으로 우울한 결론이다. 하지만 우리 인간이 우주에서 특별한 존재가 아니라고 한다면 더욱더 우울할 것 같다. 왜냐하면, 이 경우 우주의 침묵(우리 인간과 대화가 없음)은 불길한 의미일 수 있기 때문이다. 만약 고도 문명의 발달이 흔한 일이라면, 이런 침묵은 그러한 문명의 수명이 길지 않다는 의미일 수 있다. 어쩌면 수많은 문명이 고도로 발달한 뒤 얼마 못 가서 스스로 멸망했을 수도 있다. 우리는 흔히 인류가 영원히 계속 살아남을 것이라 생각한다. 하지만 우리 정도의 충분한 기술적 발전을 이룩한 문명은 전쟁, 질병, 공해 등과 같은 자기 자신이 만든 것들에 스스로를 파괴하는 방법을 손쉽게 만들어 낸다.

04

하위내용영역	배점	예상정답률
일반영어 B형 서술형	4점	30%

모범답안 The effects of domestication syndrome have been proven to actually be byproducts of reduced reactive aggression. These markers are anatomical and behavioral and physiological and share the common quality of paedomorphism in animals and human ancestors. Reactive aggression as a trait was not selected due to its disruptive effect on communities.

채점기준 ____Total 4pts

ⓐ Topic sentence

⁺ 1점: 글의 topic sentence "domestication syndrome has been proven to actually be byproducts of reduced reactive aggression"을 명확하게 서술하였거나 이와 유사하였다.

ⓑ Summary

⁺ 3점: "These markers are anatomical and behavioral (1점) and share the common quality of paedomorphism in animals and human ancestors(1점). Reactive aggression as a trait was not selected due to its disruptive effect on communities(1점)"

▷ 3개 중 2개만 서술해도 3점을 준다.

감점 ♡

• 본문에 나오는 연속되는 6단어 이상을 사용하였다. −0.5pt
• 문단을 두 개나 그 이상으로 구성하였다. −0.5pt
• 문법이나 영어 표현을 합쳐 3개 이상 오류가 있다. −0.5pt

한글번역

지난 50여 년 동안, 인간이 오랜 시간 스스로를 가축화했다는 것이 점점 명확해지고 있다. 가축화의 가장 중요한 증거인 유순함 외에도 인간은 가축화 증후군의 많은 특징을 가지고 있다. 체구와 뇌의 크기가 작아졌고, 뼈가 가늘어졌으며, 얼굴이 납작해지고 수컷과 암컷의 신체적 차이가 줄었다. 이러한 해부학적 특징 외에 공포 반응, 장난기, 학습 속도, 성적 행동, 호르몬 생산 등의 행동적 생리적 특징 또한 인간의 가축화 가설을 지지한다. 이러한 표식(특성)들의 공통점은 바로 유형 형성(즉, 아이적 형태 : 성체가 됐어도 옛날 조상 종의 어린 시절 몸 구조를 그대로 유지하고 있는 것)이라는 것이다. 개, 여우, 기니피그 등 가축화된 많은 동물들은 그들의 조상에 비해 그들이 더 어린 개체일 때의 특징을 가지고 있다. 수십만 년 전 인간의 조상 화석은 인간이 그들에 비해 유형 형성의 특징을 띠게 되었는지를 확인할 만큼 많지 않다. 하지만 네안데르탈인의 화석들은 충분히 많고, 그것들을 비교해 보면 현생 인류가 여러 가지 면에서 우리 조상들보다 더 아동화, 곧 가축화되었음을 시사한다.

왜 이러한 변화가 발생했을까(즉, 인간은 왜 스스로를 가축화시켰을까)? 진화 생물학자에게 이 질문은 그러한 변화들이 인간이 적응하는 데 어떤 이득을 주었는지 묻는 것과 같다. 그러나 이 질문의 답은 예상과 다르다. 바로, 아무런 이득이 없다는 것이다. 수십 년 동안 공들인 한 실험에 따르면, 뇌의 크기가 줄어들고, 뼈가 가늘어지는 등의 여러 가축화의 증거들이 사실 다른 본질적인 적응의 우연한 부산물에 불과하다는 사실을 발견했다. 바로 그 적응은 반응적 공격성의 감소이다. 그런 공격성을 감소시키는 것을 선택한 유기체들(생명체들)은, 배아에서 태아에 이르는 시기의 발달을 관장하는 신경능선세포를 지연시켜 더 작은 몸집과 작은 뇌를 만들고 호르몬 변화를 유도한다. 인간 사회가 스스로의 반응적 공격성을 감소시킨 이유는 집단 생활은 최소한의 안정성을 필요로 하기 때문이다. 반응적 공격성은 분노와 괴롭힘, 폭력 등 타인을 지배하고 복종하게 만든 뒤 식량과 여성을 독점하려는 행동으로 이어지며, 이는 그 어떤 특성보다도 더 집단의 안정성을 해치는 행동이다.

09 회 문제은행

📖 본책 p.062

01

하위내용영역	배점	예상정답률
일반영어 A형 기입형 – 소설	2점	45%

모범답안 young

채점기준

- 2점: 모범답안과 같다. 이것 외에는 답이 될 수 없다.
- 0점: 모범답안과 다르다.

한글 번역

나는 파리 14지구의 변두리의 술집과 카페에서 2018 월드컵 경기를 시청했다. 일부는 젠트리피케이션이 이루어졌지만, 여전히 이민자 인구가 많은 공영 주택 단지가 있는 곳이고, 마약, 갱단, 경찰과의 충돌과 같은 사회 계층 아래쪽의 긴장들이 일상으로 드러나는 혼합 지역이다. 하지만, 지금까지는 월드컵을 시청하는 분위기가 나빠진 않아서 상대적으로 문제가 일어나지 않았다. 프랑스 대표 팀의 승전보가 전해질 때마다 울려 퍼지는 경적 소리, 맥주 세례로 가득 찼다. 이 모든 장면 속에서 프랑스 축구 팬들이 얼마나 다양한 인종으로 이루어져 있는가도 놀라웠지만, 더 눈에 들어온 건 팬들의 연령대였다. 이 세대는 1998년 프랑스 월드컵 우승은 말 그대로 지난 세기의 이야기일 뿐인 새로운 밀레니얼 세대이다. 〈르 파리지앵〉에 실린 한 만평은 다음과 같이 말한다: "지난 세기의 이야기를 더 이상 우리에게 하지마"라고 젊은 세대의 팬들이 나와 같은 뚱뚱하고 중년의 백인 남성에게 말한다. 메시지는 명확하다 : 이번 월드컵은 우리의 월드컵이고, 월드컵에서 우승을 축하하는 것은 우리 자신의 것이기 때문이다.
어떤 의미에선 이들은 옳다. 프랑스 축구 대표팀은 아주 젊고, 그들은 대체로 과거와 역사의 무게에 무관심하다. 이번 대회에서 스타로 떠오른 킬리앙 음바페처럼 프랑스가 우승컵을 차지했던 1998년에는 태어나지도 않았던 선수들도 있다.

02

하위내용영역	배점	예상정답률
일반영어 A형 서술형	4점	40%

모범답안 The writer uses "instead" in order to indicate that video games are the much greater challenge for AI. Second, the meaning of the underlined words in ② is that achieving victories in video games will indicate that AI systems will be ready for real-world challenges.

채점기준 _Total 4pts

- +2점: "instead"란 어휘를 사용한 이유를 "(in order) to indicate that video games are the much greater challenge for AI"라 서술하였거나 유사하였다.
- +2점: 밑줄 친 부분의 의미를 "achieving victories in video games will indicate that AI systems will be ready for real-world challenges"라 서술하였거나 유사하였다.

한글 번역

인공 지능이 보드게임에서 인간을 이기는 일은 이미 유행이 지난 이야기가 됐다. 이제 최고의 학자들과 테크 회사들은 비디오 게임에서 인간에게 도전하고 있다. 일론 머스크와 샘 알트만이 설립한 OpenAI 연구소는 인공 지능 봇팀이 인기 전투 게임인 도타 2의 상위 1% 아마추어 게이머들을 이길 수 있다는 새로운 이정표를 발표했다. 2017년 8월 OpenAI가 처음 도타 2 세계에 등장해서 1 대 1 게임에서 최고 플레이어들을 이길 수 있는 시스템을 공개했던 것을 기억할 것이다. 하지만 이런 게임 타입은 도타 2의 도전을 상당히 줄인다. 이제 OpenAI는 봇들을 업그레이드시켜 더 많은 협력과 더 긴 시간의 계획이 필요한 5 대 5 게임에서 인간 플레이어를 상대할 수 있게 됐다. OpenAI가 아직까지는 도타 2 게임의 최강 플레이어에게 도전하지는 않았지만, 올해 말 e-스포츠 최대 연간 이벤트인 도타 2 토너먼트 The International에서 인간 게이머들에게 도전할 것이다. 이런 종류의 연구 동기는 매우 간단하다. 우리가 AI 시스템에게 비디오 게임을 하는 데 필요한 기술을 가르치는것을 성공한다면, 도시의 교통 시설 관리와 같은 비디오 게임을 닮은 현실의 복잡한 문제를 푸는 데 사용할 수 있다. 이것은 흥미로운 이정표인데, 실생활에서의 응용 프로그램으로 전환할 수 있는 일이기 때문이다. 만일 우리가 어떤 문제의 시뮬레이션을 가지고 있고, 충분히 큰 규모로 그 시뮬레이션을 실행시킬 수 있다면, 이런 기술로 수행할 수 있는 작업에는 장벽이 없을 것이다.

03

하위내용영역	배점	예상정답률
일반영어 B형 서술형	4점	35%

모범답안 "Extreme capitalism" refers to the Jennifer's Morone's plan that she offers her personal data for sale. The implication of the underlined words is that such a data economy that individuals can control their own data would be more desirable or ideal than the current situation.

채점기준 _Total 4pts

+ 2점: "극단적 자본주의"가 가리키는 것이 "the Jennifer's Morone's project that she offers her personal data for sale"이라 서술하였거나 유사하였다.
  ▷ 다음과 같이 서술하였어도 맞는 것으로 한다.
  "the Jennifer's Morone offering of her personal data for sale."

+ 2점: 밑줄 친 부분의 함축 의미를 "such a data economy that individuals can control their own data would be more desirable or ideal than the current situation"이라 서술하였거나 유사하였다.

한글 번역

미국의 예술가인 제니퍼 린 모론은 대다수 사람들이 "데이터 노예"로 살고 있다고 말한다. 이는 인터넷 서비스를 공짜로 받기 위해 그보다 훨씬 더 소중한 자신의 데이터를 아무 대가 없이 기업에 넘기고 있다는 뜻인데 이런 상황을 그녀는 통탄스러워한다. "개인 데이터는 당신이 생각하는 것보다 훨씬 더 중요합니다." 그녀는 이런 안타까운 현실을 드러내기 위해 "극단적 자본주의"라는 프로젝트를 진행했다. 그녀는 자기 자신의 데이터를 직접 판매하는 회사를 만들었고, 2016년 런던 갤러리에서 자신의 여러 데이터를 문서로 정리한 뒤 100파운드 이상의 가격을 붙여 판매했다. 그녀의 건강 데이터와 사회 보장 번호를 비롯한, 그녀에 관한 모든 데이터의 가격은 7,000파운드 정도였다.

오직 소수의 바이어들만 이 데이터들을 샀는데, "모든 일이 정말 부조리하다"고 그녀는 말했다. 하지만 예술가가 하는 일이 시대정신을 앞서 드러내는 것이라면, 그녀는 이것을 제대로 짚은 것이다. 올해 전 세계가 데이터 경제에서 뭔가 부패가 일어나고 있다는 것을 알게 되었기 때문이다. 지난 3월, 정치 컨설팅 회사인 캠브리지 어낼리틱은 페이스북 사용자 8,700만 명의 데이터를 몰래 입수했고, 이후 개인 정보 보호의 목소리는 더욱 높아지고 있다. 심지어 독일 수상 앙헬라 메르켈 또한 개인 정보에 적절한 가격이 필요하다고 말하며, 이 문제의 해결을 요청했다. 오늘날 거대 기술 회사들이 데이터를 독점하고 있는 상황을 고려한다면, 개인이 데이터를 판매하겠다는 모론의 아이디어는 별로 현실성이 없어 보인다. 하지만 실제로 사람들이 자신의 데이터를 팔 수 있고 대기업은 비용을 지불해야만 이를 이용할 수 있게 된다면 어떤 일이 벌어지게 될까? 그리고 그 상황에서 데이터 경제는 어떤 모습일까?

04

하위내용영역	배점	예상정답률
일반영어 B형 서술형	4점	50%

모범답안 Many inventions generally come from curiosity, not from necessity. Inventions such as the atomic bomb, the cotton gin, and the steam engine are the rare instances in which the need was identified first. However, mostly an invention goes into usage and after a considerable time consumers begin to feel the "need" of it.

채점기준 _Total 4pts

ⓐ Topic sentence

+ 1점: 글의 topic sentence "Many inventions generally come from curiosity, not from necessity."를 명확하게 서술하였거나 유사하였다.
  ▷ 다음과 같이 서술하였어도 1점을 준다.
  • "Many inventions come first from curiosity, then are considered as answering a need afterwards"
  • "Invention is not generally developed by necessity, but by curiosity"
  • "Necessity is not generally the mother of invention, but invention is the source of necessity"

ⓑ Summary

+ 3점 : "<u>Inventions such as the atomic bomb, the cotton gin, and the steam engine are the rare instances in which the need was identified first</u>(1.5점). However, <u>mostly an invention goes into usage and after a considerable time consumers begin to feel the "need" of it</u>(1.5점)."

감점 ♥

• 본문에 나오는 연속되는 6단어 이상을 사용하였다. −0.5pt
• 문단을 두 개나 그 이상으로 구성하였다. −0.5pt
• 문법이나 영어 표현을 합쳐 3개 이상 오류가 있다. −0.5pt

한글 번역

"필요는 발명의 어머니다." 즉, 이른바 발명은 어떤 기술이 불만스럽거나 부족하다는 인식이 광범위하게 있을 때와 같은 한 사회가 아직 충족되지 않은 어떤 필요를 느낄 때 일어난다는 말이다. 발명가 지망생들은 금전이나 명성에 대한 기대감으로 동기 부여를 받아 이와 같은 필요를 감지하고 거기에 부응하려고 노력한다. 그러다가 어떤 발명가가 드디어 기존의 존재하던 불만족스럽던 기술보다 더 우월한 해결책을 만들어 낸다. 이 해결책이 사회의 가치관과 각종 다른 기술들과 배치되지 않는다면 사회는 그 해결책을 받아들인다.

이런 (필요가 발명의 어머니라는) 상식적 견해를 뒷받침하는 발명품들이 제법 많다. 제2차 세계대전이 한창이던 1942년 미국 정부는 나치 독일보다 먼저 원자 폭탄을 만드는 데 필요한 기술을 발명하겠다는 분명한 목표를 세우고 "맨해튼 프로젝트"를 기획했다. 그리고 이 프로젝트는 20억 달러(오늘날로 치면 200억 달러가 넘는 거금)를 소비한 후 3년 만에 성공을 거뒀다. 또 다른 예로는 미국 남부에서 재배한 목화를 다듬는 고된 수작업을 대신하기 위해 1794년 엘리 휘트니가 발명한 조면기(면화의 씨를 빼거나 솜을 트는 기계), 그리고 영국의 탄광에서 배수 문제를 해결하기 위해 제임스 와트가 1769년 발명한 증기 기관 등이 있다. 이처럼 낯익은 사례들을 보면서 우리는 그 밖의 중요한 발명품들도 모두 필요에 대한 인식에서 비롯됐다고 착각하기 쉽다. 하지만 사실 수많은 발명품, 또는 대부분의 발명품들은 호기심에 사로잡히거나 이것저것 주물럭거리는 일을 좋아하는 사람들이 개발했고, 그들이 염두에 둔 제품에 대한 수요따위는 처음부터 있지도 않았다. 일단 어떤 물건이 발명되면 그때부터 발명자는 그것의 용도를 찾아내야 했다. 그리고 상당 시간 사용된 후에야 비로소 소비자들은 그것이 "필요"하다고 느끼게 됐다. 따라서 발명이 필요의 어머니인 경우가 그 반대보다 더 많다.

10회 문제은행

📖 본책 p.068

01

하위내용영역	배점	예상정답률
일반영어 A형 기입형	2점	45%

모범답안 Third-person thinking

채점기준

• 2점 : 모범답안과 같다. 이것 외에는 답이 될 수 없다.
• 0점 : 모범답안과 다르다.

한글 번역

우리는 "반성하지 않는 삶은 살 가치가 없다"와 "너 자신을 알라"는 말이 지혜에 이르는 길이라는 통찰이 소크라테스의 것이라 돌린다. 하지만 이런 자기반성에 이르기 위한 (옳고 그른) 구체적인 방법이 있을까?

단순히 머릿속으로 생각을 떠올리는 것ー네 머릿속에 있는 관심들은 휘젓는 과정일 뿐이ー만으로는 부족하다. 이 경우 자신이 평소 습관적으로 하는 생각에 빠지거나, 불필요한 감정에 휩쓸리기 쉽다. 최근 한 연구는 자신만의 생각에 빠지는 사람이 오히려 중요한 순간의 결정을 잘 내리지 못하거나 우울증의 위험이 높아질 수 있음을 보였다.

이에 대한 답으로, 그 과학적 연구는 율리우스 시저와 같은 사람들이 좋아했던 수사학인 "일리이즘", 곧 자신을 3인칭으로 표현하는 방법이 자기반성에 도움이 된다는 것을 보이고 있다. (이 용어는 시인 새뮤얼 테일러 콜리지가 1809년 라틴어로 '그, 그것'을 의미하는 '일레'를 이용해 만든 단어이다.) 예를 들어 내가 친구와 다툰 일을 반성하면서 속으로 이렇게 말하는 것이다. '데이비드는 친구와 싸워 기분이 나빴다…' 이렇게 관점을 조금 바꾸는 것만으로도 우리는 감정의 안개를 걷어내고 편견을 벗어나 사태를 똑바르게 볼 수 있게 된다.

이런 3인칭 사고방식이 일시적인 의사 결정 능력을 향상시킨다는 것을 보인 연구는 많이 있다. 또한 이러한 사고방식이 장기적으로도 생각과 감정의 통제에 도움이 됨을 보였다. 연구진은 이번 연구가 지혜와 관련된 인지 능력이 일상에서 훈련될 수 있으며, 구체적으로 그 방법이 무엇인지를 보인 첫 번째 증거라 말했다.

02

하위내용영역	배점	예상정답률
일반영어 A형 서술형	4점	30%

모범답안 The meaning of the underlined words in ① is that there is an essential difference between knowing and thinking about a given fact. Second, the most appropriate word is "believes".

채점기준 _Total 4pts

+2점 : 밑줄 친 부분의 의미를 "there is an essential difference between knowing and thinking about a given fact"라 서술하였거나 유사하였다.

+2점 : 빈칸에 들어갈 단어를 "believes"라 서술하였다. 이것 외에는 답이 될 수 없다.

한글 번역

다음과 같이 한번 상상해 보자. 어떤 사람이 오늘은 동네 슈퍼가 문을 여는 날이라 생각해서 우유를 사러 갔다. 하지만 실은 오늘이 공휴일이었고, 슈퍼는 문을 열지 않았다. 비록 가게 문이 닫혀져 있었지만, 그 사람의 행동은 여전히 일리가 있다. 실제로 슈퍼가 문을 열었기 때문이 아니라 문을 열었을 것이라 생각하고 슈퍼에 간 거니까.

이 사람이 가게에 간 것은 일리가 있지만, 당신이 어떻게 생각했는지가 아니라, (돌다리를 두드리듯) 실제로 문을 열었는지 닫았는지 확인해 보고 그에 따라 결정을 내렸다면 허탕을 칠 일도 없었을 것이다. 만일 그랬었다면, 그 사람은 가게에 갔을 것이다. 왜냐하면 가게문은, 그 사람의 생각이 아니라, 실제로 열려 있었을 테니까. 이것이 명심해야 할 차이다.

자, 그럼 이제 기후 변화를 믿지 않는 사람의 사례로 돌아가 보자. 기후 변화를 믿지 않는 사람은 기후 변화가 새빨간 거짓말인지 알지 못한다. 왜냐하면, 기후 변화는 전혀 거짓이 아니기 때문이다. 그래서 그 사람은 기후 변화가 거짓이라고 생각해서 수업을 듣지 않는 것을 선택할 수가 없다. 이것은 마치 앞에서 가상으로 말했던 사람이 가게가 열려 있는지 알려면 실제로 가게에 직접 가본 뒤에나 알 수 있는 것과 유사한 것이다. 오히려 기후 변화를 믿지 않는 사람이 할 수 있는 최대치는 기후 변화가 거짓이라 생각해서 수업을 듣지 않는 선택을 하는 것이다. 이 선택도 (어쨌든 어느 정도는) 일리는 있지만, 아마도 그가 기후 변화에 관해 자신이 어떻게 생각하는지보다 기후 변화가 사실인지 아닌지에 관한 지식(객관적 지식)에 근거해서 내렸을 선택보다는 좋지 않았을 것이다.

만일 앞에서 말한 것이 틀린 것이 아니라면, 똑같이 지금 내 생각과 가치관을 기준으로 판단을 내리더라도 어떤 경우는 독선과 편견의 틀에 갇힌 것이고, 또 어떤 경우에는 합리적인 선택이 되는지 그 차이를 이제 살펴보겠다. 두 번째 종류의 사람(합리적인 선택을 내리는 사람)은 반대하고 꺼리는 대상이 자신에게 피해를 주리라는 사실을 명확히 알고 있는 반면에, 첫 번째 종류의 사람(독선과 편견에 갇힌 사람)은 어떤 대상이 자신에게 피해를 주리라고 굳게 믿기 때문에 잘못된 선택을 반복하게 된다. (어떤 사실을 정확히 아는 것과 그럴 거라고 믿는 것의 차이라고 할 수 있다.)

03

하위내용영역	배점	예상정답률
일반영어 B형 서술형	4점	50%

모범답안 The main idea of the passage is that computer-based testing can be more effective than animal testing. Second, animal testing is not welcomed by all walks of life because it's immoral to a public majority and costly and uncertain for manufacturers.

채점기준 _Total 4pts

+2점 : 글의 요지를 "computer-based testing can be more effective than animal testing"이라 서술하였거나 유사하였다.

+2점 : 동물 실험이 각계각층의 사람들로부터 환영받지 못하는 이유를 "because it is immoral to a public majority(1점) and costly and uncertain for manufacturers(1점)"라 서술하였거나 유사하였다.

한글 번역

존스홉킨스 블룸버그 보건대학원의 과학자들이 주도한 연구에 따르면 대규모 화학 데이터베이스를 이용한 고급 알고리즘으로 기존 동물 실험보다 약품의 독성을 더 잘 예측할 수 있다고 한다.

2018년 7월 11일 학술지 〈독성과학〉에 발표된 연구 논문에서 연구자들은 알려진 화학 물질의 방대한 데이터베이스를 조사하여 화학 구조와 독성 특성 간의 관계를 이어주는 지도를 개발했다고 밝혔다. 연구자들은 이 지도를 이용해 모든 화합물의 독성 특성을 자동으로 예측할 수 있으며, 동물 실험을 통한 예측보다 더 정확하다는 결과를 제시했다.

연구팀이 개발한 최첨단 독성 예측 툴은 동물 실험에 기반을 둔 결과를 재현하는 데 세계의 동물 독성 실험 중 57%를 차지하는 아홉 가지 일반 테스트에서 평균 87%의 정확도를 보였다. 대조적으로 데이터베이스 상의 동일한 동물 실험의 반복 결과의 정확도는 81%였다. 다시 말해, 어떤 실험도 실험을 반복할 경우 독성에 대한 동일한 결과를 얻을 확률이 평균 81%밖에 되지 않았다는 뜻이다. 컴퓨터를 기반으로 한 접근법은 동물 실험보다 더 많은 화학 물질을 적용할 수 있으며, 더 광범위한 안전 평가를 할 수 있도록 한다. 그동안은 비용과 윤리적 문제로 소비자 제품에 포함된 약 10만 개의 화학 물질 중 일부만 종합적으로 테스트됐다.

쥐, 토끼, 기니피그, 개와 같은 동물들은 전 세계 실험실에서 수백만 건의 화학 독성 실험에 사용된다. 동물 실험은 소비자를 보호하기 위해 법으로 정해져 있지만, 많은 대중이 도덕적인 이유로 반대하고 있으며, 제조사들 또한 높은 비용과 실험 결과의 불확실성으로 인해 기피하는 실정이다.

04

하위내용영역	배점	예상정답률
일반영어 B형 서술형	4점	45%

모범답안 In an isolated society like Japan, a powerful technology can be done away with unlike in a connected society. For example, when guns first appeared in Japan they became very popular. However, the threat they posed to the samurai, who controlled the government, and the hatred of foreign things led to increasing restrictions against them. Eventually, Japan was almost without guns.

채점기준 _Total 4pts

ⓐ Topic sentence
+ 1.5점: 글의 topic sentence "In an isolated society like Japan, a powerful technology can be done away with unlike in a connected society"를 명확하게 서술하였거나 유사하였다.

ⓑ Summary
+ 2.5점: "when guns first appeared in Japan they became very popular(1점). However, the threat they posed to the samurai, who controlled the government, and the hatred of foreign things led to increasing restrictions against guns. Eventually, Japan was almost without guns(1.5점)."

감점
• 본문에 나오는 연속되는 6단어 이상을 사용하였다. −0.5pt
• 문단을 두 개나 그 이상으로 구성하였다. −0.5pt
• 문법이나 영어 표현을 합쳐 3개 이상 오류가 있다. −0.5pt

한글 번역

오늘날에는 거의 모든 지구상의 사회가 서로 연결되어 있어서 어떤 변덕 때문에 중요한 기술이 버려지는 일을 상상하기 어렵다. 설령 어느 한 사회가 어떤 강력한 기술을 일시적으로 거부하더라도 그 사회는 이웃 사회가 그 기술을 사용하고 있는 것을 계속 보게 될 것이므로 언제든지 재확산을 통해 다시 습득할 수 있다. (만약 그렇게 하지 못한다면 이웃에게 정복당하든지). 그러나 고립된 사회에서는 그러한 변덕이 오랫동안 지속되기도 한다.

일본이 총을 포기했던 사례는 유명하다. 총기가 일본에 처음 도착한 것은 1543년이었다. 원시적인 화승총으로 무장한 포르투갈 모험가 두 명이 중국 화물선을 타고 상륙했던 것이다. 일본인들은 이 신무기에 깊은 인상을 받고 토착적으로 생산하기 시작하여 총기 제작 기술을 크게 향상시켰으며 1600년 이전에 벌써 세계 어느 나라보다도 우수한 총을 더 많이 갖게 됐다. 하지만 일본에는 총기 도입에 역행하는 요인들도 있었다. 우선 이 나라에는 사무라이라는 전사 계급이 다수 있었다. 그들에게는 칼이 계급의 상징인 동시에 하층 계급들을 복속시키는 수단이었다. 일본에서 전쟁이란 사무라이 사이의 일대일 전투였다. 그들은 탁 트인 곳에서 서서 의례적인 말들을 주고받았으며 우아하게 싸우는 것을 자랑스럽게 여겼다. 우아하지 못하게 마구 총을 쏘아 대는 농민 병사들 앞에서 그런 행동을 하는 것은 치명적인 결과를 낳게 됐다. 게다가 총은 외국의 발명품이어서 1600년 이후에 모든 외국 문물이 그랬듯이 차츰 경멸의 대상이 됐다. 사무라이가 지배하던 정부는 우선 총기 생산을 몇몇 도시에 국한시키기 시작했고 정부의 허가를 얻어야 총을 생산할 수 있게 했다. 그다음에는 정부에 납품하는 총에 대해서만 생산을 허락했고 마지막으로 정부의 총기 주문량도 감소시켜 결국 일본은 제대로 작동하는 총이 거의 없는 상태로 돌아가 버렸다.

11회 문제은행

📖 본책 p.075

01

하위내용영역	배점	예상정답률
일반영어 A형 기입형	2점	55%

모범답안   old knowledge

채점기준

- 2점: 모범답안과 같다. 이것 외에는 답이 될 수 없다.
- 0점: 모범답안과 다르다.

한글 번역

현대 과학에는 도그마(독단적 신조)가 없다. 하지만 연구 기법에는 공통적인 핵심이 있는데, 늘 경험적 관찰들을 모은 뒤 수학적 도구의 도움을 받아 그것들을 하나로 결합하는 것이다. 여기서 관찰이란 적어도 우리의 감각 기관 중 하나로 관찰할 수 있는 것을 의미한다.

사람들은 역사를 통틀어 경험적 관찰들을 모았지만, 이 관찰의 중요성은 보통 제한적이었다. 우리에게 필요한 모든 답이 수중에 있는데 또다시 새로운 관찰을 얻으려고 귀중한 자원을 낭비할 필요가 어디 있겠는가? 하지만 현대인은 자신들이 매우 중요한 몇몇 질문에 대한 답을 모른다는 사실을 인정하게 되었으므로, 완전히 새로운 지식을 찾아볼 필요가 있다는 사실을 깨달았다. 그 결과, 현대의 지배적인 연구 기법은 오래된 지식이 충분하지 않다는 사실을 당연한 것으로 받아들인다. 오늘날 무게 중심은 전통을 연구하기 보다는 새로운 관찰과 실험을 하는 쪽으로 옮겨갔다. 현대의 관찰이 과거의 전통과 배치되는 경우, 우리는 관찰에 우선권을 부여한다. 물론 먼 은하의 스펙트럼을 분석하는 물리학자, 청동기 시대의 도시 유물을 분석하는 고고학자, 자본주의의 출현을 연구하는 정치학자는 옛 지식을 무시하지 않는다. 이들은 과거의 사람들이 말하고 쓴 것을 공부하는 데서 시작한다. 하지만 물리학자, 고고학자, 정치학자가 되려는 사람들은 대학 1학년 때부터 자신의 임무는 아인슈타인, 하인리히 슐리만, 막스 베버가 알았던 것을 뛰어넘는 데 있다고 배운다.

02

하위내용영역	배점	예상정답률
일반영어 A형 서술형	4점	50%

모범답안   The actions that helped to keep white nationalism in check were the war against Nazism and the civil-rights struggles of the 50s and 60s. Second, the Internet allows white nationalists to use ambiguous irony and humor to spread their message.

채점기준   _ Total 4pts

+ 2점: 백인민족주의를 제지하는 데 기여한 실천적 행위를 "the war against Nazism(1점) and the civil-rights struggles of the 50s and 60s(1점)"라 서술하였다.

+ 2점: 인터넷과 더불어 백인민족주의가 급속하게 전파되는 이유를 "the Internet allows white nationalists to use ambiguous (obscure) irony and humor to spread their message"라 서술하였 거나 유사하였다.

한글 번역

전 세계로 확산된 현대의 백인민족주의는 남북 전쟁 후 미국에서 처음 탄생했다. 노예제가 끝나면서 (미국의) 각 주들은 서유럽 후손인 백인 프로테스탄트들의 특혜적 지위를 그대로 유지하기 위한 조치를 취했다. 인종 분리 정책을 강요한 짐크로우법 등이 이에 해당한다. 불법무장 단체의 폭력이나 린치(사적인 폭력)도 이어졌다. 중국인과 아일랜드 가톨릭 교도, 유대인들의 이민이 증가하면서 백인 정체성에 대한 집착은 더욱 커졌다. 이민을 제한하기 위한 새로운 법이 만들어졌다. 매디슨 그랜트가 1916년에 발간한 "위대한 인종의 소멸"은 이민 배척주의와 우생학을 버무려 백인우월주의와 "인종 자살"이라는 개념을 만들어 냈다. 아돌프 히틀러는 그랜트에게 편지를 써 이 책이 자신에게 성경과도 같다 말했다고 전해진다. 나치즘과의 전쟁, 그리고 1950~60년대의 민권 운동을 거치며 불명예를 떠안게 된 백인민족주의는 20세기 말 부흥을 맞이하게 되는데, 이때 유럽과 미국에서 폭력적인 사태가 발생했다.

1988년 데이비드 레인은 "백인 학살 선언"을 써서 그랜트의 "인종 자살론"에 새로운 이름을 붙였다. 이 글로 전 세계에 백인민족주의의 외침이 잘 알려지게 됐다. 백인민족주의자들이 "열네 단어"로 떠받드는 문장("우리 민족의 존속과 백인 아이들의 미래를 지켜야 한다")도 여기에서 나온다. 백인의 우월성에 대한 핵심적인 믿음을 공유하기는 하지만, 백인민족주의도 다양한 갈래로 나뉜다. 연방 정부에 대한 뿌리 깊은 불신을 갖고 있는 이들(주로 민병대들에게서 발견된다)도 있고, 남북 전쟁에 대한 수정주의적 견해를 받아들여 (남북 전쟁 당시)남부군을 미화하는 이들도 있다. 유대인들이 세계를 지배하려 한다는 반유대주의적 음모론을 떠받드는 이들도 있는데, 이들은 국제주의자 유대인 엘리트가 이민을 장려하는 데 책임이 있다고도 주장한다.
백인민족주의는 인터넷의 탄생과 함께 빠르게 진화하고 있다. 모니터 반대편의 화자가 진지한지, 농담을 하는지를 알 수 없는 인터넷 시대의 아이러니를 흡수한 것이다. 농담 삼아 그런 이야기를 하는 사람들을 통해, 백인민족주의는 더 많은 사람들에게 다가갈 수 있게 됐다.

03

하위내용영역	배점	예상정답률
일반영어 B형 서술형	4점	45%

모범답안 The commonality between Henderson and Bolus is their avoidance of situations that can benefit them : Henderson refused to work for publications under a boss with a personal scandal, and Bolus declined invitations by houses and press.

채점기준 _Total 4pts

+ 2점 : 핸더슨과 볼러스의 공통점을 "their avoidance of situations that can benefit them"이라 서술하였거나 유사하였다.

+ 2점 : 그 둘이 한 것을 "Henderson refused to work for publications owned by a major firm (or under a boss with a personal scandal)(1점), and Bolus declined invitations by houses and press(1점)"라 서술하였거나 유사하였다.

04

하위내용영역	배점	예상정답률
일반영어 B형 서술형	4점	35%

모범답안 Time blocking, which schedules out a day in advance and dedicates specific hours to achieving specific tasks, can be an effective way to reach all your tasks effectively. In planning, both proactive and reactive time should be allotted, to allow for focusing on important projects and also accommodating requests and interruptions. Time blocking, unlike standard to-do lists which provide only a list of tasks, has the strength of helping you know the exact way and time specific to completing each task as well as listing all.

채점기준 _Total 4pts

ⓐ Topic sentence

+ 1.5점 : 글의 topic sentence "Time blocking, which schedules out a day in advance and dedicates specific hours to achieving specific works(0.5점), can be an effective way to reach all your tasks effectively(1점)."를 명확하게 서술하였거나 유사하였다.

  ▷ 정의(schedules out a day in advance and dedicates specific hours to achieve specific works)가 빠져있으면 0.5점 감점한다.

ⓑ Summary

+ 2.5점 : "In planning, both proactive and reactive time should be allotted, to allow for focusing on important projects and also accommodating requests and interruptions(1점). Time blocking method, unlike standard to-do lists which provide only a list of tasks(0.25점), has the strength of helping you know the exact way and time(0.25점) specific to completing each task as well as listing all(1점)."

감점 ♥

• 본문에 나오는 연속되는 6단어 이상을 사용하였다. −0.5pt
• 문단을 두 개나 그 이상으로 구성하였다. −0.5pt
• 문법이나 영어 표현을 합쳐 3개 이상 오류가 있다. −0.5pt

📖 본책 p.081

한글 번역

시간 할당은 특정한 작업을 마치기 위해 미리 특정한 시간을 배정해 놓는 방법이다. 이를 위해서는 해야 할 일에 대해 정확히 알아야 하고 어느 정도의 시간이 걸릴지 예상할 수 있어야 한다. 일단 이 둘을 염두에 뒀다면, 이것들을 달력에 써넣고 하루 중 적절한 시간에 그 일들을 시작하면 된다.

과제 계획을 세울 때는 능동적 시간과 수동적 시간을 구분해 놓는 것이 필요하다. 능동적 시간은 반드시 해야 할 일을 배정하는 시간이다. 중요한 프로젝트를 진행한다든지, 중요한 문서의 초안을 작성한다든지, 또는 다음에 할 중요한 제품의 원형에 대해 기획하는 것과 같은 (집중이 필요한) 일이 여기에 해당한다. 수동적 시간은 이메일이나 즉석 회의처럼 다른 이의 요구에 대응하거나 수시로 발생하는 일을 위한 시간 할당이다.

예를 들어 업무의 첫 두 시간 동안 가장 어려운 일을 마친 다음, 오후에 이메일을 처리하는 방식이 가능하다. 이를 통해 방해받지 않는 시간과 전화나 이메일을 처리할 시간을 모두 얻을 수 있다.

이 (시간 할당) 방법은 당신이 시간을 어떻게 사용하는지, 그리고 언제 그 일을 마칠 수 있는지 분명히 알려주는 장점이 있다. 일반적인 할 일 목록 방식은 끝내야 할 작업 목록(만)을 제시해 주는 반면, 시간 할당법은 (끝내야 할) 작업 목록을 제시하는 것뿐만 아니라 구체적인 시간대까지 제시해 주는 점이 다르다.

스스로를 엄격한 틀 속에서 작업을 하고, 한정된 시간 내에 정해진 작업을 마치도록 강제함으로써, 그 어떠한 업무를 하든지 아주 높은 집중력을 발휘하도록 해준다.

01

하위내용영역	배점	예상정답률
일반영어 A형 기입형	2점	50%

모범답안 natural cycle

채점기준

- 2점: 모범답안과 같다. 이것 외에는 답이 될 수 없다.
- 0점: 모범답안과 다르다.

한글 번역

북극에 가까운 고위도 지방이 불타고 있다. 올여름 알래스카에서만 벌써 600건 넘는 들불이 나 1만km²에 가까운 숲을 태웠다. 캐나다 북부도 마찬가지다. 시베리아에서는 계속된 들불로 발생한 연기가 약 5만 2천km² 상공을 뒤덮었다. (역자: 5만 2천km²는 경상도와 전라도를 합친 면적)

이 지역들에서 들불 자체는 원래 흔한 일이다. 알래스카 중부의 가문비나무를 보면 이 과정을 이해하는 데 도움이 된다. 가문비나무는 시들거나 불이 나 숲이 뜨거워지면 곧바로 솔방울을 열어 씨를 퍼뜨린다. 숲이 불에 탄 자리에는 먼저 잡목이나 꽃들이 자란다. 이어 야생산딸기나무, 버드나무, 자작나무, 사시나무 등이 아직 죽지 않은 나무 그루터기나 뿌리들 사이에서 자라난다. 그러다 결국에는 이 지역에 가장 잘 자라는 침엽수가 다시 숲을 뒤덮는다. 하지만 다양한 연구 결과를 보면 올여름을 비롯한 최근의 추세가 심상치 않다. 최근에 일어난 들불은 기존에 일어나던 양상과 다르다. 너무 자주, 너무 강하게 퍼져 훨씬 심각한 피해를 남긴다. 숲이 불타면서 가뜩이나 이산화탄소가 적정량보다 많아 문제인 지구의 대기에 더 많은 탄소가 쌓인다.

연구자들은 기후 변화와 늘어나는 들불, 그로 인한 초목과 식생의 변화 양상을 연구한다. 알래스카 북극권 기후 변화 시나리오 네트워크가 지역별로 세분화한 기후 데이터와 모델을 활용해 잦아진 들불의 원인을 분석하고 앞으로 일어날 수 있는 상황을 전망해봤다. 그 결과 알래스카 등 고위도 지방에 사는 우리같은 사람들뿐 아니라 지구상의 모든 이들에게 경종을 울릴 만한 결론을 내릴 수밖에 없다. 위에서 설명한 이 과정을 한 번 거치는 데 걸리는 시간은 대략 200년 정도다. 그런데 최근 들어 계속 그 주기가 무려 25%나 빨라졌다. 이는 생태계를 근본적으로 뒤바꿔 놓을 수 있는 어마어마한 변화이다.

02

하위내용영역	배점	예상정답률
일반영어 A형 서술형	4점	40%

모범답안 The meaning of "normal" in the context is covering your invited guest's meal as a show of hospitality. Second, the meaning of the underlined words is that the English have become more committed to capitalism than the Dutch were.

채점기준 _ Total 4pts

+ 2점: 글의 주제의 맥락에서 "정상적인"의 의미를 "covering your invited guest's meal as a show of hospitality"라 서술하였거나 유사하였다.
  ▷ 다음과 같이 서술했어도 2점을 준다.
  "returning to old habits to show good manners by covering your invited guest's meal"

+ 2점: 밑줄 친 부분의 의미를 "the English have become more committed to capitalism than the Dutch were"이라 서술했거나 유사하였다.

한글 번역

일요일 아침 친구들과의 브런치 모임, 즐거운 식사가 끝나고 웨이터가 테이블로 다가와 묻는다. "한꺼번에 계산하시겠어요, 아니면…"
말이 끝나기도 전에 모두가 한목소리로 외친다. "따로따로 계산할게요!" 너무나 당연한 것을 왜 묻지? 각자 자기가 먹은 것을 계산하는 이른바 "더치페이"는 이제 현대인의 관행으로 자리 잡았(기 때문이)다.
하지만 친구들과 식사를 하고 계산서를 나누는 행위가 언제나 규범이었던 것은 아니다. 초기 영국 사회에서는 친구를 외식에 초대하고 음식값을 내지 않는 것이 매우 이기적인 행동으로 여겨졌다.
1651년에 막을 내린 영국의 시민 혁명(내전) 후, 영국인들은 일상을 되찾기 위해 애를 쓰고 있었다. 일상의 회복이란 계급적 위계와 선한 크리스천으로서의 교양을 드러낼 수 있는 일정한 규범들을 따르는 것을 의미했다. 사람들에게 환대를 베풀어 자신의 신사다움을 드러내는 것은 매우 중요한 부분이었다. 후하게 베풀지 않는 것은 왕실과 신에게 누를 끼치는 행위로 여겨졌다.
"더치페이"라는 단어의 기원은 약간 복잡하지만, 몇몇 과거와 현재의 사전편찬 전문가들은 이 단어의 어원을 따져보는 데 도움을 준다.

우선 1600년대로 돌아가 보자. 영국－네덜란드 전쟁 당시 잉글랜드와 네덜란드 사이에는 무역과 해상의 권력을 두고 다양한 갈등이 일어났다. 이런 적대적인 관계는 영어에서 네덜란드를 뜻하는 "더치"를 부정적인 의미로 사용하는 다양한 관용구를 낳았다. "네덜란드인의 용기(Dutch courage)"는 폭음에서 비롯된 헛된 용기를, "더치식 계산(Dutch reckoning)"은 사기를 당해 지불한 터무니없는 가격을 의미하게 되었다. 이는 영국인들이 네덜란드인을 무역상의 적으로 간주했기 때문이고, 나아가 그들의 도덕성을 의심했기 때문이다. 당시 영국인들은 네덜란드인을 자본주의에 대한 신념 때문에 완전히 타락한 사람들로 여겼다. 이런 경향이 바뀐 것을 생각하면 얼마나 웃긴가.

03

하위내용영역	배점	예상정답률
일반영어 B형 서술형	4점	50%

모범답안 A handful of researchers contradicted the notion that memories are forgotten through a passive process. Second, "forgetting" best fills in the blank.

채점기준 _ Total 4pts

+ 2점: 소수의 연구자들이 반박한 것을 "the notion (assumption) that memories are forgotten through a passive process"이라 서술하였거나 유사하였다.

+ 2점: 빈칸에 들어갈 단어를 "forgetting"라 정확하게 기입하였다. 이것 외에는 답이 될 수 없다.

한글 번역

존재는 기억을 바탕으로 한다(기억은 우리 인간에게 우리 자신이 누구인지를 알게 해준다). 기억을 통해 우리는 세상을 이해하고 미래를 예측할 수 있다. 과학자들은 기억이 어떻게 형성되며 시간이 흐른 뒤 이를 어떻게 우리가 떠올리는지에 대해 오랫동안 연구해 왔다. 하지만 지금까지의 연구는 실상의 절반만을 바라본 것이었다. 기억에 대해 알기 위해서는 우리가 어떻게, 그리고 왜 기억을 잊는지를 알아야 한다.
10년 전까지만 하더라도 과학자들은 마치 햇볕 아래 사진이 바랜 것처럼, 망각을 기억이 자연스레 사라지는 과정이라 생각했다. 하지만 소수의 연구자들에 의해 그러한 가정이 잘못이라는 사실이 밝혀졌다. 그들은 기억을 제거하는 것이 뇌의 또 다른 기능이라는 혁신적인 아이디어를 내놓았다.

지난 10년 동안 밝혀진 사실들은 망각이 수동적으로 일어나는 현상이 아님을 보여준다. 오히려, 망각은 뇌에서 일상적으로 일어나는 능동적인 활동의 결과이다. 어쩌면 거의 모든 동물은 기본적으로 능동적인 망각 기능을 활성화한 상태일 수 있다. 이러한 망각에 대한 더 깊은 이해는 불안증, 외상후 스트레스 장애(PTSD), 그리고 알츠하이머와 같은 병에 대한 더 나은 치료법으로 이어질 수 있다. "망각이 없는 기억이 가능할까요?" 기억의 신경 생물학을 연구하는 인지 심리학자인 올리버 하트는 이렇게 말한다. "불가능합니다. 기억이 제대로 작동하기 위해서는 망각 기능 또한 반드시 가져야 합니다."

04

하위내용영역	배점	예상정답률
일반영어 B형 서술형	4점	35%

모범답안 Skirts should not be banned in schools to achieve equality. Schools have been implementing gender-neutral uniforms in order to remove the discomfort and problems skirts can bring about. However, narrowing choice and expression is detrimental and sends a message implying blame on the wearers of skirts. In conclusion, school skirts are allowed when students want to wear them.

채점기준
_Total 4pts

ⓐ Topic sentence

+ 1점 : 글의 topic sentence "Skirts should not be banned in schools to achieve equality"를 명확하게 서술하였거나 유사하였다.

ⓑ Summary

+ 2.5점 : "Schools have been implementing gender-neutral uniforms in order to remove the discomfort and problems skirts can present(cause)(1점). However, removing(narrowing) choice and expression is detrimental(0.5점) and sends a message implying blame on the wearers of skirts(1점).

ⓒ Conclusion

+ 0.5점 : 글의 conclusion "In conclusion, school skirts are allowed when students want to wear them." 또는 "Thus, they should be allowed alongside trousers as options for students."라 서술하였다.

감점 ☑

• 본문에 나오는 연속되는 6단어 이상을 사용하였다. −0.5pt
• 문단을 두 개나 그 이상으로 구성하였다. −0.5pt
• 문법이나 영어 표현을 합쳐 3개 이상 오류가 있다. −0.5pt

한글 번역

반항의 뜻에서 허리 부분을 접어 올리지 않는다면 언제나 무릎 길이에 머무는 남색이나 검정색의 얌전한 교복 치마는 이제 멸종 위기에 처한 것인가? 아마도. 이 문제가 중요한가? 당연히 중요하다. 영국 내 최소 40개 중등학교가 성 중립을 명분으로 교복 치마를 금지한 것이 현실이기 때문이다. 11세에서 16세 사이의 영국 소녀들은 이제 교복으로 바지만을 입을 운명에 처한 듯하다.

어린 학생들의 가치관이 형성되는 장이자, 폭력의 온상이기도 한 학교에서 성 중립적 교복 정책은 큰 의미가 있다. 상식에도 부합할 뿐 아니라, 성 평등, 그리고 트랜스젠더 학생이나 여성도 남성도 아닌 논바이너리 학생들까지도 통합할 수 있는 정책이다. (바지 교복은 분명 치마 교복에 비해 모두의 행동반경을 넓힐 수 있는 옵션이다.) 한번 무릎길이의 치마를 입고 정글짐(철골 놀이 기구)을 올라가려 해 봐라. 아니면 다리를 꼰 채 바닥에 앉으려 해 봐라. 또는 평균적인 중·고교생들이 얼마나 쉽게 당혹감을 느끼는지 생각해 봐라. 학생들이 성적 대상화되는 일이 흔하고 다양한 형태의 폭력이 존재하는 환경에서라면 더더욱 그렇다. 여기서 멈추자. 무슨 말인지 알겠지? 하지만 성 중립적 교복 정책이 치마를 금지하는 것을 필수적으로 요구하는 것은 아니다. 더 많은 이를 포괄하기 위한 정책이, 누군가에게 선택지를 줄이는 방향으로 시행되어서는 안 된다. 교복 정책은 선택의 폭을 넓히는 방향으로 가야지, 여학생들의 옷차림을 단속하는 방향으로 가면 안 된다. 치마를 금지하는 것이 학생들에게 보내는 메시지는 무엇일까? 평등이라는 메시지보다 누군가를 탓한다는 메시지가 더 크게 느껴지지 않을까?

성 중립 교복 정책이 사용하는 언어에서는 빅토리아 시대의 분위기마저 느껴진다. 치마를 "용인할 수 없는 아이템"의 목록에 올린 학교도 있다. 치마를 "부적절하고 당혹스러운 옷차림"이라고 언급한 또 다른 학교도 있다. 여학생들에게 "조신하고 얌전한 옷차림"을 요구할 일도 머지않은 듯 보인다. 하지만 문제는 치마나 치마 교복을 입은 여학생들이 아니다. 여학생의 치마 교복을 문제삼는 논리는 강간을 당한 여성의 옷차림을 탓하는 정서와 맞닿아 있다. 한마디로, 학생들이 치마를 입기를 원한다면 입을 수 있어야 한다.

13회 문제은행

📖 본책 p.087

01

하위내용영역	배점	예상정답률
일반영어 A형 기입형	2점	55%

모범답안 ambiguous

채점기준

- 2점: 모범답안과 같다.
- 1점: "confusing"이라 답하였다.
- 0점: 모범답안과 다르다.

한글 번역

초기의 문자들은 모호했다. 예를 들면, 가장 오래된 수메르 설형 문자로는 정상적인 산문이 아니라 전보용 약문에 가까운 문장밖에 쓸 수 없었다. 어휘라고는 이름, 숫자, 도량형, 헤아리는 사물을 일컫는 낱말, 몇 개의 형용사 정도가 고작이었기 때문이다. 가령 오늘날 미국의 법원 서기를 예로 들자면 "살찐 양 27마리를 정부에 인도할 것을 존에게 명령한다"라고 써야 하는데 그 문장에 필요한 낱말이나 문법이 영어에 없어서 그저 "존 27 살찐 양"이라고 쓰는 것과 같은 상황이었다.

고대 그리스 미케네 문명의 문자였던 선문자 B는 그보다 더 단순한 형태로 90개 가량의 기호로 이뤄진 음절 문자와 표어문자들로 구성되어 있었다. 하지만 선문자 B가 가지고 있던 장점도, 심한 모호함 때문에 상쇄되고 말았다. 이 문자는 낱말 끝에 오는 자음을 모두 생략했고 몇 개의 관련된 자음을 한 개의 기호로 나타냈다. (예를 들면 l과 r, p와 b, ph, g와 k, kh 등을 각각 한 개의 기호로 표시하는 식으로) 일본에서 나고 자란 사람들이 영어를 할 때 l과 r을 제대로 구별하지 않아서 얼마나 헛갈리게 만드는지 잘 알고 있다. 그런데 방금 영어 알파벳에서 언급한 자음들을 구별하지 않고 일본인들처럼 한가지로 쓴다면 그때는 얼마나 더 헛갈리게 될지 상상해 보라. 그렇게 되면 우리는 "rap" "lap" "lab" "laugh"를 모두 똑같은 철자로 써야 할 것이다.

02

하위내용영역	배점	예상정답률
일반영어 A형 서술형	4점	50%

모범답안 Saez and Zucman(They) found the top 0.01 controlled 22% of all wealth in 2012, up from 7% in 1979. Second, the writer mentions the Netherlands because it shows the exceptional wealth inequality of the United States, as the next nearest country has half as much inequality.

채점기준 _Total 4pts

+ 2점: 사에즈와 저크먼이 연구한 것을 "the top 0.01 controlled 22% of all wealth in 2012, up from 7% in 1979"라 서술하였거나 유사하였다.

+ 2점: 네덜란드를 언급한 이유를 "because it shows the exceptional wealth inequality of the United States, as the next nearest country has half as much inequality"이라 서술했거나 유사하였다.

한글 번역

부의 불평등에 관한 데이터를 놓고 나라별로 비교해 보면, 미국이 다른 어떤 선진국보다 불평등이 극명하고, 다른 모든 나머지 선진국들의 부의 불평등을 왜소하게 보일 정도로 압도적으로 심하다는 사실이 뚜렷하게 드러난다. 보수 성향 연구 기관인 허드슨 인스티튜트는 지난해 발표한 보고서에서 2013년 재산 기준 미국 상위 5% 가계가 미국 전체 자산의 62.5%를 가지고 있다고 보고했다. 이는 30년 전 54.1%였던 것보다 높아진 수치로, 나머지 95% 가계의 재산이 차지하는 비중도 45.9%였던 것이 37.5%로 줄었다.

그 결과, 2013년 기준 소득이 높은 가계의 평균 연소득은 639,400달러, 중간에 해당하는 가계의 평균 연소득은 96,500달러였다. 소득 상위 가계 재산의 중간값이 소득 중위 가계 재산의 중간값보다 거의 일곱 배가 많았다. 적어도 지난 30년 사이 해당 격차가 가장 크게 벌어진 것이다.

더욱 눈에 띄는 것은, 불평등을 오랫동안 연구해 온 세계적인 학자 에마누엘 사에즈와 가브리엘 저크먼 교수의 연구인데, 그들은 상위 0.01% 부자가 미국 전체 자산의 22%를 소유하고 있다는 점을 밝혀냈다. 2012년을 기준으로 한 데이터를 분석한 결과인데, 1979년과 같은 수치가 7%에 불과했었다. 하지만 소득 불평등에 관한 데이터만 보면 전혀 다른 결론이 나온다. 예를 들어 2013년 상위 5% 가계가 벌어들인 소득은 미국인 전체 소득의 30%에 불과했지만, 재산으로는 이들은 전체의 거의 63%를 소유하고 있었다.

지난 30년 동안 부의 불평등이 심화하고 빈부 격차가 벌어진 나라는 선진국 가운데 미국 말고도 얼마든지 더 있다. 하지만 그 정도에 있어서 미국은 특이하게 심각하다. 재산 상위 5% 가계의 부는 미국 중간 가계의 부보다 91배나 더 많다. 세계에서 가장 잘 사는 나라 18개국 가운데 부의 편중이 단연 가장 심하다. 미국 다음으로 빈부격차가 큰 나라가 네덜란드였는데, (앞서 계산한 수치를 네덜란드에 적용해 계산하면) 미국의 절반도 되지 않는다.

03

하위내용영역	배점	예상정답률
일반영어 B형 서술형	4점	50%

모범답안 A "major value shift" refers to the decline in Americans prioritization of family, god and nation. Second, the underlined means that the shift in young adults' belief in God is not disturbing if you don't believe that Judeo-Christian values are key to morality.

채점기준 _Total 4pts

+ 2점: 주요한 가치의 변환이 가리키는 것을 "the decline in Americans prioritization of family, god and nation"이라 서술하였거나 유사하였다.

+ 2점: 밑줄 친 부분의 의미를 "the shift in young adults' belief in God is not disturbing if you don't believe that Judeo-Christian values are key to morality"라 정확하게 서술하였다.

한글 번역

지난 1998년 월스트리트저널과 NBC는 18~38세 미국인에게 인생에서 가장 중요한 가치를 꼽으라는 질문을 던졌다. 가장 많은 사람이 "열심히 일하는 것(work ethic)"을 꼽았다. 이어 애국심과 종교, 그리고 아이를 낳아 가정을 꾸리는 것이 중요하다는 답이 나왔다.

21년이 지난 2019년, 같은 연령대 미국인에게 같은 질문을 던졌다. 밀레니얼 세대와 Z세대의 답변은 21년 전과 아주 달랐다. 아이를 낳고 가정을 꾸리는 것이 중요하다고 답한 비율이 10% 낮아졌고, 애국심이나 종교가 중요하다고 답한 사람의 비율은 무려 20%나 낮아졌다.

가족, 신, 국가 이 세 가지는 전통적인 미국인의 가치관을 든든하게 받치던 다리와도 같다. 그런데 (자녀와 부모로 구성된) 핵가족, 신앙, 애국심에 대한 젊은 세대의 충성도가 급전직하하는 것은 미국인의 정체성의 진화에 대한 중요한 어떤 것을 말해주고 있다.

이번 설문조사 결과는 우선 전통적인 서구적 믿음의 침식으로 해석될 수 있다. 미국의 30세 이하는 전체 종교인의 1/3을 넘는 많은 수치를 차지한다. 그런데 이들은 기독교가 아니라 이슬람교, 불교, 힌두교이다. 이것은 두 가지 측면을 반영하는데, 하나는 1970년대 이후 유럽이 아닌 지역에서의 미국에 이민 온 사람들이 늘어났기 때문이고, 다른 하나는 20세기 하반기에 규모가 큰 기독교 종파의 쇠퇴 때문이다. 이런 상황은 또한 무신론자의 비율이 급격하게 늘어난 것을 반영한다. (Z세대까지 갈 것도 없이) 밀레니얼 세대만 해도 이미 신의 존재를 믿지 않는 사람이 16%로 베이비붐 세대(6%)보다 세 배 가까이 높다. 당신이 유대 기독교로 이어지는 종교적 가치가 서구 사회를 떠받치는 가장 중요한 윤리적 가치라고 당신이 생각한다면, 이런 설문조사에서 나타난 사실들은 당신을 불편하게 할 것이다. 물론 당신이 그렇게 생각하지 않는다면(유대 기독교로 이어지는 종교적 가치가 서구 사회를 떠받치는 가장 중요한 윤리적 가치라고 생각하지 않는다면) 이런 사실들(젊은 세대들 사이에서 기독교가 쇠퇴한다는)은 별문제가 없을 것이다.

두 번째 해석은, 대개 정치와 관련이 있다. 젊은 세대의 애국심, 가족, 종교에 대한 무관심은 전통적 보수주의에 대한 젊은이들의 혐오에 대한 대리물(혐오를 반영하는 것)일 수 있다는 것이다.

04

하위내용영역	배점	예상정답률
일반영어 B형 서술형	4점	30%

모범답안 Placing water bottles in a car during hot weather can be dangerous. Water bottles can focus sunlight as lenses enough to burn things within cars as shown in several cases (such as with Idaho Power and the Holy Water company). Likewise, Madden, who found that adhesive focused lasers in ways that could cause damage, cautioned that even reduced by a car's window glass there could be enough energy remaining to cause burning. In short, we should be careful not to leave a bottle in a car during a summer hot day.

채점기준   _ Total 4pts

ⓐ Topic sentence

⁺1점: 글의 topic sentence "Placing water bottles in a car during hot weather can be dangerous"를 명확하게 서술하였거나 이와 유사하였다.

ⓑ Summary

⁺2.5점: "Water bottles can focus sunlight as lenses enough to burn things within cars as shown in several cases (such as with Idaho Power and the Holy Water company)(1점). Likewise, Madden, who found that adhesive focused lasers in ways that could cause damage(1점), also cautioned that even reduced by a car's window glass there could be enough energy remaining to cause burning(0.5점)."이라 서술하였거나 유사하였다.

ⓒ Conclusion

⁺0.5점: 글의 conclusion "In short, we should be careful not to leave a bottle in a car during a summer hot day"라 서술하였거나 유사하였다.

감점 ♥
- 본문에 나오는 연속되는 6단어 이상을 사용하였다. −0.5pt
- 문단을 두 개나 그 이상으로 구성하였다. −0.5pt
- 문법이나 영어 표현을 합쳐 3개 이상 오류가 있다. −0.5pt

한글 번역

자동차 안에 생수병을 둔다고 무슨 일이 벌어질까 생각할 수 있지만, 더운 여름날 투명한 플라스틱 물병은 렌즈가 되어 자동차 시트와 같은 내장재에 불을 낼 가능성이 있다.

지난여름, 아이다호 전력 회사는 생수병이 자동차 시트에 두 개의 구멍을 내는 비디오를 공유했다. 올해 러시아 월드컵에서 러시아의 생수 회사인 홀리워터가 판매한 축구공 모양의 생수병은 완벽한 렌즈 역할을 할 수 있다. (러시아의) 폰타카 루가 공개한 비디오에서는 이 축구공 모양 생수병이 어떻게 성냥에 불을 붙이고 코팅된 마룻바닥에 구멍을 내는지를 보여 줬다. 그 생수병은 차창 밖에서 들어오는 빛을 모으는 렌즈 역할을 하고 있었다.

재료과학자 오딜 매든은 수년 전, 예술 작품에서 투명한 접착제를 레이저를 이용해 떼내면서 이런 빛의 집중이 어떤 힘을 가지는지를 직접 본 적이 있다. 접착제의 주름이 빛을 모으는 렌즈로 작용해 실험을 위해 그녀가 사용하고 있었던 현미경용 유리 슬라이드를 태우거나 그슬리게 하는 것을 봤다. 그녀는 이 결과를 2005년 학술 논문집 "예술 작품 보존을 위한 레이저"에 발표했다.

매든을 놀라게 한 것은 자동차 유리를 통과한 빛에도 여전히 차에 불을 낼 수 있는 충분한 에너지가 남아 있다는 것이었다. "아마도 뜨거운 날씨라든가, 유리 창문이 내려져 있을 때 더욱 안 좋을 수 있는데, 그 이유는 유리는 빛을 차단하기 때문이다. 이는 태양에서 얼마나 많은 에너지가 지구로 쏟아지는지 보여주는 예이다. 이 생수병은 그저 값싼 플라스틱일 뿐이지만 우연히도 거의 완벽한 렌즈 역할을 할 수 있다"고 매든은 덧붙였다. 뜨거운 날 차 안 종이 더미 위에 생수병을 놔두지 않는 것이 좋을 듯하다.

14회 문제은행

📖 본책 p.093

01

하위내용영역	배점	예상정답률
일반영어 A형 기입형	2점	55%

모범답안 autonomy

채점기준

• 2점: 모범답안과 같다. 이것 외에는 답이 될 수 없다.
• 0점: 모범답안과 다르다.

한글 번역

여성이 머리부터 발끝까지 부르카로 자신을 감싸는 이슬람의 아주 기본적인 전통은, 문화적 관습이 개인의 자율을 증진시키는 정도를 평가하는 데 있어서 봉착하는 본질적 어려움을 보여주는 하나의 사례이다. 부르카와 이에 유사한 복장을 비난하는 사람들, 특히 서구 문화 비평가들은 그 복장들이 육체적으로는 직물의 무게로 인해 신체적 압박을 가하며; 심리적으로는 여성의 개성이 결여되어 보이게 한다는 점에서 억압적이고; 정서적으로는 여성이 종속돼 있는 남성 지배 사회의 또 하나의 표시라는 점에서 억압적이라고 간주한다. 이런 견해에 따르면, 그런 옷을 입는 전통은 여성의 자율을 크게 제한하기 때문에 정당성이 없다.

그러나 이 관습을 옹호하는 사람들은 반대되는 견해를 주장한다. 그들은 부르카와 같은 피복은 실제로 여러 가지 이유에서 자율을 조장하며 여성들을 자유롭게 해준다고 주장한다. 예를 들어, 부르카는 여성이 성적 대상으로 보이는 것을 막아주고, 여성 이슬람교도들 간의 단결을 장려하며, 성스러운 외모가 되도록 해준다. 부르카 옹호자들은 또 서양 비평가들에게 "왜 두건을 쓰는 것은 억압적인 것이고, 미니스커트를 입는 것은 자유롭게 하는 것으로 여겨지는가?"처럼 그들로 하여금 자신들의 의류 문화를 돌아보게 하는 질문을 한다. 그들은 그 대답이 관련된 여성들과 그들이 선택하는 능력에 대해 각 문화가 만들어 내는 가정에 있다고 주장한다. 그들은 만일 그러한 의복 관습에 관한 그들의 가정이 실제로 잘못됐고, 부르카와 그 변형된 형태의 옷을 입는 것이 실제로 개인의 선호 문제라면, 그것은 완전히 개인의 자율에 대한 적법한 표현으로 정당화된다고 말한다.

02

하위내용영역	배점	예상정답률
일반영어 A형 서술형	4점	45%

모범답안 The meaning of the underlined "mysterious" is that the exact reasons for the drug's effectiveness is not known. Next, the "intellectual debt" is the gap between knowing what currently works without knowing why it works and figuring out how it works.

채점기준   _ Total 4pts

+ 2점: 밑줄 친 "신비스러운"이 의미하는 것을 "the exact reasons for the drug's effectiveness is not known"이라 서술하였다.

+ 2점: "지적 부채"가 의미하는 바가 "the gap between knowing what currently works (without knowing why it works) and figuring out how it works"임을 정확하게 서술하였거나 유사하였다.

▷ 또는 "the gap between knowing what currently works and figuring out the real(underlying) mechanism of the drug"이라 서술하였다.

한글 번역

다른 많은 의약품처럼 프로비질이라는 이름으로 팔리는 각성제 모다피닐 안에도 작게 접힌 설명서가 들어 있다. 대부분의 내용은 흔한 수면 유도제처럼 사용법과 주의점, 약의 분자 구조에 관한 것이다. 그러나 "작용 기전"이라 불리는 세부 항목에는 잠이 확 달아나게 할 만한 한 문장이 들어 있다. 그것은 바로 "모다피닐이 어떻게 각성 작용을 하는지는 알려져 있지 않다"는 문장이다.

프로비질만 독특하게 신비스러운 것이 아니다. 허가를 받고 널리 사용되는 약들 중에도 그 약이 정확히 우리 몸속에서 어떻게 작용하는지 우리가 알지 못하는 약들이 많이 있다. 이런 신비스러움은 시행착오에 의해 진행되는 약의 발견 과정에 이미 내재해 있다. (약이 시행착오를 통해 주로 발견되기 때문이라는 의미) 매년 새로운 약물이 배양 세포나 동물들에게 실험이 되고, 그중 가장 효과가 좋고 안전한 약물이 사람에게 시도된다. 때로는 새로 발견된 약이 새로운 연구 분야를 만들어 내고 자신의 작용 기전이 이를 통해 밝혀지는 경우도 있지만, 늘 그런 것은 아니다.

아스피린은 1897년에 발견됐지만, 우리는 1995년이 돼서야 아스피린이 어떻게 우리 몸속에서 작동하는지를 이해하게 됐다. 의학에는 이런 예가 많다. 뇌심부 자극술(DBS)은 전극을 뇌 속에 삽입하는 기술로 파킨슨병처럼 특정한 움직임에 장애가 있는 이들에게 20년 이상 사용돼 왔으며 어떤 이들은 이 시술이 인지 능력 강화에도 유용하리라 생각한다. 하지만 누구도 그 이유(이 약이 어떻게 작용하는지)는 알지 못한다.

발견에 대한 이러한 접근법, 곧 답을 먼저 찾고 설명은 나중에 찾는 방식이 내가 지적 부채라 부르는 것을 축적한다. 어떤 것이 왜 작동하는지 모르는 상태로 언젠가는 그 원리를 알 수 있을 것이라 생각하며 실제로 이를 사용하는 것도 물론 가능하다. 어떤 경우에선 이 지적 부채를 쉽게 갚을 수 있다. 하지만 다른 경우들에서는, 수십 년 동안 이 기술에 의존하고 다른 분야에까지 적용하면서도 그 원리를 충분히 알지 못한 상태로 사용한다.

03

하위내용영역	배점	예상정답률
일반영어 B형 서술형	4점	45%

모범답안 The meaning of the underlined words is that the formation of data-labor unions, which will protect and monitor their members' data work, sounds futuristic and far-fetched, like science fiction. Next, the inferred reason is that if they have to do it for all people, it will cut into their profits.

채점기준 _Total 4pts

+ 2점 : 밑줄 친 부분의 의미를 "the formation of data-labor unions, which will protect and monitor their members' data work, sounds futuristic and far-fetched(unlikely), like science fiction"이라 서술하였거나 유사하였다.

+ 2점 : 그 둘이 한 것을 "if they have to do it for all people, it will cut into their profits"라 서술하였거나 유사하였다.

한글 번역

그런 데이터가 적극적으로든 수동적으로든 어떻게 만들어지는지와 무관하게, 자신이 만들어 낸 데이터가 어떻게 쓰이는지를 추적하거나 그 가치를 매기는 것은 거의 불가능하다. 설사 그것이 가능하다 하더라도, 개인이 인공 지능 기업을 대상으로 이를 거래할 힘을 가지기는 어려울 것이다. 하지만 노동의 역사는 이 문제를 어떻게 해결해야 하는지 알려준다. 역사적으로 노동의 대가가 적절한 수준으로 오를 수 있었던 데에는 노동조합의 역할이 매우 중요했다. 바일은 사람들의 데이터를 관리해 주는 "데이터 노동조합"이 탄생할 것이라 말한다. 바일은 과거 노동조합이 했던 것처럼, 데이터 노동조합 또한 데이터의 가격을 기업과 흥정하며, 회원들의 데이터가 어떻게 쓰이는지를 추적할 뿐 아니라, 명성 점수 등을 이용해 데이터의 품질을 관리하게 될 것이라 말한다. 또한 전문적인 데이터를 조합원에게 이동시키고, 심지어 조합원들의 데이터에 기업의 접속을 막는 식으로 파업을 주동할 수도 있다. 유사한 방식으로, 데이터 노동조합은 조합원들의 데이터를 대신 거래해주는 창구 기능도 할 수 있고, 그 데이터들 추적해서 그 데이터로부터 혜택을 받는 인공 지능 기업에게 비용 청구서를 보낼 수도 있다.

이런 이야기가 그저 공상 과학 소설로 들릴지 모른다. 구글이나 페이스북이 사람들이 공짜로 제공하는 데이터를 바탕으로 광고 수입을 얻는 지금의 모델을 버릴 이유가 있을까? 2017년 이 두 기업은 광고만으로 1,350억 달러를 벌었다. 그들에게 사람들의 데이터에 대해 비용을 내라고 한다면, 그들의 수익은 크게 줄어들 것이다. 또한 시티즌미나 데이타큐와 같은 초기 형태의 데이터 노동조합은 아직 성공을 거두지 못하고 있다. 한편, 다른 분야에서는 이 거대 인터넷 대기업들이 데이터에 돈을 지불하고 있지만, 이 사실이 공개적으로 알려지지 않도록 조심하고 있다. 이들은 자신들의 알고리즘을 검증하고 불량한 콘텐츠를 제거하는 일을 외주로 맡기고 있다. 사진에 설명을 덧붙이는 일을 아마존의 메커니컬 터크와 같은 집단 고용 플랫폼으로 해결하는 기업도 있다.

04

하위내용영역	배점	예상정답률
일반영어 B형 서술형	4점	45%

모범답안 Polytheism shows much more tolerance than Christianity to other faiths. Polytheistic empires did not try to convert conquered subjects, and often added the other gods to their pantheons. However, since Christians would not respect the gods of Romans, insisting on their own monotheistic view, they was persecuted for political subversion. This was minor, totaling a few thousand deaths over 300 years, in stark compare with the millions slaughtered Christians killed by slightly-different Christian sects since.

채점기준

_ Total 4pts

ⓐ Topic sentence

+ 1.5점 : 글의 topic sentence "Polytheism shows much more tolerance than Christianity to other faiths"를 명확하게 서술하였거나 이와 유사하였다.

ⓑ Summary

+ 2.5점 : "Polytheistic empires did not try to convert conquered subjects, and often added the other gods to their pantheons(1점). However, since Christians would not respect the gods of Romans, insisting on their own monotheistic view, they was persecuted for political subversion(0.75점). This was minor, totaling a few thousand deaths over 300 years, in stark compare with the millions slaughtered Christians killed by slightly-different Christian sects since(0.75점)."

감점 ♥

• 본문에 나오는 연속되는 6단어 이상을 사용하였다. −0.5pt
• 문단을 두 개나 그 이상으로 구성하였다. −0.5pt
• 문법이나 영어 표현을 합쳐 3개 이상 오류가 있다. −0.5pt

한글 번역

다신교의 통찰은 폭넓은 종교적 관용을 낳기 쉽다. 다신교도들은 한편으로는 하나의 최고의 권력, 완벽하게 무관심한 권력을 믿고 다른 한편으로는 편견을 지닌 수많은 권력을 믿기 때문에, 하나의 신에 헌신하는 사람이라도 다른 신들의 존재와 효험을 받아들이는 데 어려움이 없다. 다신교는 본질적으로 마음이 열려 있으며 "이단"이나 "이교도"를 처단하는 일이 드물다. 이것은 자신들의 종교 내에서든 밖에서든 자신들의 종교와 다른 종교를 믿는 사람들과 전쟁을 벌여 왔던 기독교와 같은 일신교적 종교와는 대조적이다.

다신교도는 심지어 거대한 제국을 정복했을 때도 피정복민을 개종시키려고 노력하지 않았다. 이집트인, 로마인, 아즈텍인은 오시리스, 유피테르, 우이칠로포치틀리(아즈텍의 최고신)에 대한 신앙을 전파하려 선교사를 외국에 파견하지 않았고, 이를 목적으로 군대를 파견하지도 않았다. 제국 내의 모든 피정복 민족은 제국의 신과 의례를 존중할 것으로 기대됐다. 하지만 자신의 지역신과 의례를 포기하라는 요구를 받진 않았다. 아즈텍 제국에서 피정복민들은 우이칠로포치틀리 신전을 지어야 했지만, 기존의 신전을 대신해서가 아니라 그 옆에 세웠다. 많은 경우 제국의 엘리트 자체가 피정복민의 종교와 의례를 받아들였다. 로마인들은 아시아의 키벨레 여신을, 이집트인들은 이시스를 그들의 만신전에 기꺼이 추가했다.

로마인들이 오랫동안 관용을 거부했던 유일한 신은 일신교적이고 개종을 요구하는 기독교의 신이었다. 로마 제국은 기독교인들에게 신앙과 의례를 포기하라고 요구하지 않았다. 하지만 제국의 수호신과 황제의 신성에 경의를 표할 것을 기대했다. 이는 정치적 충성심의 선언이라고 여겨졌다. 기독교인들이 이를 격렬하게 거부하고 화해를 위한 모든 시도를 거절하는 데까지 나가자 로마인들은 박해로 대응했다. 이런 박해조차 주저하는 식이었다. 예수가 십자가에 달린지 300년 만에 콘스탄티누스 대제가 개종할 때까지 다신교를 믿는 로마 황제가 기독교인을 박해한 사건은 네 차례를 넘지 않았다. 3세기에 걸친 모든 박해의 희생자를 다 합친다 해도 다신교를 믿는 로마인들이 살해한 기독교인들은 몇 천 명을 넘지 않았다. 이와 대조적으로 이후 1500년간 기독교인은 사랑과 관용의 종교에 대한 조금 다른 해석을 지키기 위해 다른 기독교인 수백만 명을 학살했다.

15 회 문제은행

📖 본책 p.100

01

하위내용영역	배점	예상정답률
일반영어 A형 기입형	2점	55%

모범답안 tolerant

채점기준

- 2점: 모범답안과 같다. 이것 외에는 답이 될 수 없다.
- 0점: 모범답안과 다르다.

한글 번역

우리 인간은 (사회적 동물에서 흔히 볼 수 있는 특징 가운데 하나인 집단을 이뤘다가 또 흩어지고 다른 이들과 다른 기준으로 또 뭉치기를 반복하는) 핵분열-융합(fission-fusion)과 같은 사회를 이루는 종들 가운데서도 대단히 관용적인(쉽게 공격하는 대신 참고 견디는) 쪽으로 진화했다. 이렇게 된 이유 중 일부는 다른 영장류보다 훨씬 더 큰 인간의 뇌와 상대적으로 높은 번식력을 들 수 있다. 이 두 가지 특징이 합쳐진 결과 인간은 고품질, 고위험(시공간적으로 어떤 환경에 처할지 예측할 수 없는) 음식과 도구에 절대적으로 의존하게 됐다. 이것은 인간들로 하여금 먹을거리를 찾는 대단히 독특한 전략을 개발하게 했다. 바로 먹을거리를 포함한 자원이 부족해질 때 다른 집단과 무리를 합침으로써 무리를 유지하는 전략이었다. (다른 어떤 영장류나 사회적 동물도 채택하지 않은 이 전략은 특히 어떤 환경에 처할지 예측할 수 없는 상황에서 쓸모 있는 전략이었음.) 그렇다고 인간이 지금은 물론이고 예전에도 항상 평화를 사랑하는 동물이라는 의미는 아니다. (즉, 싸우는 걸 싫어하거나 평화적인 동물이어서 그런 전략을 개발한 것이 아니라, 우리가 가진 자원을 활용해 필요한 식량과 자원을 얻을 수 없을 때 위기를 헤쳐 나가기 위해 다른 무리와 다른 부족의 사람들에게 기대며 이들의 낯선 점을 참아 내고 협력하는 법을 하나의 전략으로 체화한 것이라는 의미) 비지역적 자원에 대한 접근이 중요한 장소와 시기에는, 인간은 종종 적어도 일정 기간 동안에는 다른 공동체 구성원들에게 관용적인 방법을 찾아냈다.

우리 인간의 공격적 경향의 진화론적 기원에 대한 통찰을 얻기 위한 한 방법으로 예전의 연구는 호전적인 침팬지를 주로 연구한 반면, 최근의 연구는 우리 인간의 관용적 본성의 토대를 이해하기 위해선, 더욱 관용적인 영장류들이 타당하다고 생각하고 있다.

특히, 이러한 영장류 중 (난쟁이 침팬지로도 불리는) 보노보는 서로 다른 무리끼리 합치는 일이 일어났고, 서로 식량을 나누거나 털을 다듬어 주기도 하는 모습이 관찰됐다. 보노보 사회도 다른 무리의 구성원에게 무조건 친절하거나 늘 협력하고 참았던 건 아니다. 서로 다른 무리가 만나게 되면 다른 무리의 구성원과 갈등도 빚어지고 아예 싸움이 격해져 몇몇은 무리를 이탈해 버리기도 한다. 그러나 보노보 사회에서도, 인간 사회와 마찬가지로, 서로 다른 무리들 간의 행동에 있어서 유연성— 서로 다른 무리를 때로 배척하고 공격하지만, 또 참고 협력하기도 하는 유연성—이 발견됐다.

02

하위내용영역	배점	예상정답률
일반영어 A형 서술형 – 시	4점	60%

모범답안 The cues are a story told in chronological order, linguistically convolution, the use of impersonal phrases or pronouns, and smiling. Next, the underlined words mean that a big smile most likely indicates someone who is trying to deceive.

채점기준 _Total 4pts

+ 2점: 거짓말인지 구별할 수 있는 모든 신호가 "a story told in chronological order (rehearsed story), linguistically convolution, the use of impersonal phrases or pronouns, and smiling"이라 정확하게 서술하였다.
  ▷ 4개 중 3개만 맞은 경우 1점; 2개만 맞은 경우 0.5점; 1개 또는 0개 맞은 경우 0점을 준다.
+ 2점: 밑줄 친 부분의 의미를 "a big smile most likely indicates someone who is trying to deceive"라 서술하였거나 유사하였다.

03

하위내용영역	배점	예상정답률
일반영어 B형 서술형	4점	40%

모범답안 Inception had limitations in identifying a cat (an image) that was altered with specially crafted data. Second, it is likely that the swindlers use vulnerabilities to trick Health-care AI into false diagnoses.

채점기준 _Total 4pts

+ 2점: Inception의 한계를 "Inception had limitations in identifying a cat (an image) that was altered with specially crafted data"라 서술하였거나 유사하였다.

+ 2점: 보험 사기꾼들이 헬스케어 AI를 어떻게 사용할 것 같은가에 대한 질문에 "the swindlers use vulnerabilities to trick Health-care AI into false diagnoses"라 서술하였거나 유사하였다.

한글 번역

이미지 인식의 문제를 생각해 보자. 10년 전, 컴퓨터는 사진 속의 물체를 쉽게 인식하지 못했다. 오늘날, 우리는 일상에서 매우 뛰어난 기계 학습 모델 기반의 이미지 검색 엔진을 사용하고 있다. 구글의 이미지 검색은 인셉션이라 불리는 신경망을 사용한다. 2017년, MIT의 학부생과 대학원생으로 이루어진 랩식스 팀은 고양이 사진의 픽셀 몇 개를 바꾸어 사람 눈에는 여전히 고양이로 보이지만 인셉션은 99.99 퍼센트의 확률로 과카몰 사진으로 판단하는 사진을 만들었다. 물론 인셉션 신경망은 자신이 어떤 고양이 사진을 왜 고양이 사진으로 판단하는지 말할 수 없기 때문에 특정한 조작이 가해진 이미지에 대해 인셉션이 잘못된 판단을 내릴지를 예측하는 것도 불가능하다. 곧 이런 시스템은 일반적으로 알려진 정확도에 비해 의도적인, 훈련된 공격자에 대해서는 매우 쉽게 뚫리는 단점을 가질 수밖에 없다.

기계 학습 시스템에 의해 만들어진 지식이 널리 사용될수록, 이런 종류의 단점은 필연적으로 발생하게 된다. 의료 분야에서 사진 속 피부암이 악성인지 양성인지를 판단하는 인공 지능은 매우 성공적인 기술이다. 하지만 하버드 의대와 MIT의 연구진이 올해 발표한 논문에서 이들은 앞서 고양이를 과카몰로 판단하게 만든 것과 같은 방식으로 이 인공 지능을 속일 수 있음을 보였다. (즉, 보험금을 노리는 이들이 이런 방식의 공격을 할 수 있다.) 기계 학습이

보여주는 놀라운 정확도는 우리로 하여금 인간의 판단보다 이들을 더 믿음직스럽게 여기게 만든다. 하지만 이들은 이런 조작에 취약하며, 우리는 이 시스템의 실수를 확인할 수 있는 다른 쉬운 방법을 가질 수 없다는 문제가 있다.

04

하위내용영역	배점	예상정답률
일반영어 B형 서술형	4점	45%

모범답안 Successful entrepreneurs tend to be middle-aged despite notions that young people dominate the field. Researchers have shown that the mean age of startup founders is 42, and high-growth startups 45, backed by their greater experience in their specific industry. Even considering the high-growth startup states of California, Massachusetts and New York, successful entrepreneurs are middle aged.

채점기준 _Total 4pts

ⓐ Topic sentence

+ 1점: 글의 topic sentence "Successful entrepreneurs tend to be middle-aged (despite notions that young people dominate the field)"를 명확하게 서술하였거나 유사하였다.

ⓑ Summary

+ 3점: "Researchers have shown that the mean age of founders is 42 and high-growth startups is 45(1점), backed by their greater experience in their specific industry(1점). Even considering the high-growth startup states of California, Massachusetts and New York, successful entrepreneurs are middle aged(1점)."

감점 ▽

· 본문에 나오는 연속되는 6단어 이상을 사용하였다. -0.5pt
· 문단을 두 개나 그 이상으로 구성하였다. -0.5pt
· 문법이나 영어 표현을 합쳐 3개 이상 오류가 있다. -0.5pt

한글 번역

19세에 마이크로소프트를 창업한 빌 게이츠, 21세에 애플을 창업한 스티브 잡스, 그리고 19세에 페이스북을 창업한 마크 저커버그와 같은 스타 창업자들의 신화와 같은 이야기는 젊음이야말로 창업에 어울리는 나이라는 오래된 믿음을 강화한다. 하지만 창업가들의 나이를 체계적으로 분석한 데이터가 가리키는 결론은 이런 믿음과 배치된다. 많은 연구자들은 평균적으로 성공한 기업가들이 중년의 사람들이라는 증거를 제공한다.

이들은 미국 통계청 자료를 이용해 적어도 한 명 이상을 고용하고 있는 회사를 창업한 미국의 창업가 270만 명을 분석했다. 창업가들의 평균 나이는 42세였다. 성장 속도에서 상위 1%에 속하는 기업만 놓고 보면 창업가의 평균 나이는 45세로 높아졌다. 게다가, 이 연구는 기업의 성공과 상관관계가 있는 요인들을 분석한다. 스타트업의 특정 산업에 더 가까운 더 오랜 업무 경험을 가진 이러한 나이 든 설립자들과 그 산업에서 더 오랜 경험을 가진 설립자들은 훨씬 더 높은 성공률을 가지고 있다. 연구진은 "고성장 기업 1,000곳 중 1곳 꼴로 어떤 산업에서 3년 이상의 경험을 한 창업자가 그런 산업에서 경험하지 않은 젊은 창업자보다 2배 높은 성공률을 보인다"고 밝혔다. 이 연구는 또한 지리적 이질성을 고려했으며, 캘리포니아, 매사추세츠, 뉴욕을 별도로 고려했다. 이들 3개 주는 미국 내 고성장 스타트업 활동의 대부분을 차지하고 있으며, 이들 주에서도 성공한 창업자들은 여전히 중장년층이다.

16회 문제은행

📖 본책 p.104

01

하위내용영역	배점	예상정답률
일반영어 A형 서술형	4점	45%

모범답안 The word is "attention". Second, the writer thought he was a complete hypocrite because he had said he didn't use acting for attention earlier, but then he was using it to get attention.

채점기준   _ Total 4pts

+ 2점 : 빈칸에 들어갈 단어를 "attention"이라 정확히 기입하였다. 이것 외에는 답이 될 수 없다.

+ 2점 : 글의 저자가 스스로를 "완전 위선자"라 생각한 이유를 "because he had said he didn't use acting for attention earlier but then was using it to get attention"라 서술하였거나 유사하였다.

02

하위내용영역	배점	예상정답률
일반영어 A형 서술형	4점	50%

모범답안 The best tweets require understanding the setup, or additional information, such as the genre conventions. Second, "Twitter" fills in the blank.

채점기준   _ Total 4pts

+ 2점 : 트위터에서 최고의 트윗과 조크가 되기 위한 필수적인 요소를 "understanding the setup, or additional information, such as the genre conventions"라 서술하였거나 유사하였다.

▷ 다음과 같이 서술하였어도 2점을 준다.

• "The best tweets are using information that is off-screen"

• "The best tweets are showing understanding of genre conventions to fill in incomplete information provided"

• "The best tweets require understanding about Twitter's genre conventions needed to figure out its incomplete information"

+ 2점 : 빈칸에 들어갈 단어를 "Twitter"라 정확하게 기입하였다. 이것 외에는 답이 될 수 없다.

03

하위내용영역	배점	예상정답률
일반영어 A형 서술형	4점	55%

모범답안 It can be inferred that Ms. Porter was nervous because she was afraid to present her ideas to her teacher colleagues who were reluctant to deal with the Thanksgiving. Second, Ms. Tilson refers to Native American students.

채점기준 _Total 4pts

+ 2점 : 포터 선생이 교사회의에서 어떤 주제를 논의하기 꺼려하는 이유를 "because she was afraid to present her ideas to her teacher colleagues who were reluctant to deal with the Thanksgiving"라 서술하였거나 유사하였다.

▷ 다음과 같이 서술하였어도 2점을 준다.

"Her colleagues were reluctant to deal with the Thanksgiving which is a day of mourning to some Native Americans"

+ 2점 : "these people"이 가리키는 것이 "Native American students"라 정확하게 서술하였다. 이것 외에는 답이 될 수 없다.

04

하위내용영역	배점	예상정답률
일반영어 A형 서술형	4점	40%

모범답안 The underlined "variant" refers to a version of the game in which participants were informed of their assigned co-participant's ethnicity. Second, "don't trust" best completes the blank.

채점기준 _Total 4pts

+ 2점 : "a version of the game in which participants were informed of their assigned co-participant's ethnicity"라 서술하였거나 유사하였다.

▷ 다음과 같이 서술하였어도 2점을 준다.

"an edition of the study in which participants were informed of their assigned co-participant's ethnicity"

+ 2점 : 빈칸에 들어갈 단어를 "don't trust"라 정확히 기입하였다. 이것 외에는 답이 될 수 없다.

05

하위내용영역	배점	예상정답률
일반영어 A형 서술형	4점	40%

모범답안 The word "intention" best completes the blank. Second, the word "triangle" is used to show that a message doesn't have only two parts with A sending to B, but instead has other influences on it as a third component.

채점기준 _Total 4pts

+ 2점 : 빈칸에 들어갈 단어를 "intention"이라 정확히 기입하였다. 이것 외에는 답이 될 수 없다.

+ 2점 : 저자가 "삼각형"이란 용어를 언급한 이유를 "to show that a message doesn't have only two parts with A sending to B, but instead has other influences on it as a third component"라 서술하였거나 유사하였다.

06

하위내용영역	배점	예상정답률
일반영어 A형 서술형	4점	40%

모범답안 The different result between the 2004 and 2013 studies is that the 2004 study found an increase in intelligence in students studying music but in 2013 there was no such correlation found. Second, it can be inferred that socioeconomic status should be corrected because there might be trend that wealthier students have more support and resources, also improving their intelligence. Third, "causation" best completes the last sentence.

채점기준 _Total 4pts

+ 1점: 2004년과 2013년 연구의 결과 사이의 차이를 "the 2004 study found an increase in intelligence in students studying music but in 2013 there was no such correlation found"라 서술하였거나 유사하였다.

+ 2점: "사회 경제적 지위와 같은 변수"를 보정해야만 하는 이유를 "because there might be trend that wealthier students have more support and resources, also improving their intelligence"라 서술하였거나 유사하였다.

+ 1점: 빈칸에 들어갈 단어를 "causation"이라 정확히 기입하였다. 이것 외에는 답이 될 수 없다.

07

하위내용영역	배점	예상정답률
일반영어 B형 서술형	4점	45%

모범답안 Thin people are have many unpleasant qualities unlike fat people. They are not fun, they do not use their free time enjoyably and always stay busy. Also, they are tiring, always moving and looking for problems to solve, unlike fat people who are so inactive. On the other hand, fat people are nicer than mean thin people and see there is no truth, while thin people are looking for a "key thing" in unsolvable problems. In conclusion, the thin should gain weight to become more likeable.

채점기준 _Total 4pts

ⓐ Topic sentence

+ 1점: 글의 topic sentence "Thin people are have many unpleasant qualities unlike fat people"을 명확하게 서술하였거나 유사하였다.

▷ 다음과 같이 서술하였어도 1점을 준다.
  "Thin people are much more unlikable than fat people"

ⓑ Major supporting details

+ 2점: 글의 major supporting details 즉, "① They aren't fun, they don't use their free time enjoyably and always stay busy. ② They are tiring, always moving and looking for problems to solve, unlike fat people who are so inactive. On the other hand, ③ fat people are nicer than mean thin people and see there is no truth, while thin people are looking for a "key thing" in unsolvable problems"을 명확하게 서술하였다.

▷ 3개 중 3개 모두 정확하게 요약했으면 2점; 2개를 정확하게 요약했으면 1점; 나머지는 0점을 준다.

ⓒ Conclusion

+ 1점: 글의 conclusion "In conclusion, the thin should gain weight to become more likeable"을 명확하게 서술하였거나 유사하였다.

감점 ♥

• 본문에 나오는 연속되는 5단어 이상을 사용하였다. −0.5pt
• 문단을 두 개나 그 이상으로 구성하였다. −0.5pt
• 문법이나 영어 표현을 합쳐 3개 이상 오류가 있다. −0.5pt

17회 문제은행

📖 본책 p.118

01

하위내용영역	배점	예상정답률
일반영어 A형 서술형	4점	40%

모범답안 The writer mentions the words to illustrate the detrimental effects of sugar that they got relief from after quitting. Second, "fructose" best fills in the blank.

채점기준 _ Total 4pts

+ 2점 : 저자가 밑줄 친 부분을 언급한 이유를 글의 핵심 생각과 연관하여 설명하라는 문제에 대해 "to illustrate the detrimental effects of sugar that they got relief from after quitting"라 서술하였거나 유사하였다.

+ 2점 : 빈칸에 들어갈 한 단어를 "fructose"라 정확하게 기입하였다. 이것 외에는 답이 될 수 없다.

감점 ☑ 본문에 나오는 연속되는 5단어 이상을 사용하였다. −0.5pt

한글 번역

3년 전, 나는 설탕을 끊었다. 설탕을 끊자 모든 것이 바뀌었다. 실험으로 시작한 일이지만, 곧 새로운 습관이 됐다. 나는 생각지도 못하던 여러 측면에서 변화를 느낄 수 있었다. 나는 조금이라도 허기가 지면 짜증(Hangry)을 내던 사람이었다. 이를 막기 위해 아몬드나 말린 과일을 늘 지니고 다녔다. 설탕을 먹던 시절에는 아침에 달리기를 할 수 없었다. 달리기를 하려고 할 때마다 너무 졸렸고, 다리는 천근만근으로 느껴졌다. 오후에는 머릿속에 안개가 긴 것처럼 피곤했다. 그래서 재택으로 일할 때는 낮잠을 꼭 잤다. 기분이 쉽게 바뀌었고, 즐겁다가도 우울했다. 하지만 나는 이 모든 것을 그저 삶의 일부로 여겼고, 내가 원래 그런 사람이라고, 이것이 내 성격의 단점이라고만 생각했다. 하지만 지금은 이런 모든 것들이 다 사라졌다. 설탕을 끊고 처음 2주 정도는 짜증이 자주 났다. 겨울의 우중충한 날씨 때문인 줄 알았다. 하지만 곧 나는 차분해지고, 행복해지고, 평온해지면서 한 가지 (해로운) 생각이 날 갈구기 시작했다. 혹시 그 짜증이 금단 증상은 아니었을까?라는.

화학자에게 설탕은 수소, 탄소, 산소로 이루어진 몇 종의 분자를 말한다. 이들 중 몇 가지는 생물학적으로 의미가 있다. 예를 들어 젖당(lactose)은 우유에 들어 있다. 설탕의 한 종류인 디옥시리보오스는 DNA의 D에 해당한다. 하지만 일상에서 가장 많이 섭취되는 설탕은 포도당(glucose), 과당(fructose) 그리고 포도당과 과당이 결합한 형태의 자당(sucrose)이다. 이 두 개의 단순 설탕인 포도당과 과당은 6개의 탄소 원자, 12개의 수소 원자, 그리고 6개의 산소 원자라는 같은 원자 구성을 가지고 있지만, 화학적 구조가 다르다. 사람은 혀로 이 둘을 구분할 수 있다. 곧, 과당을 더 달게 느낀다.

포도당은 혈액을 통해 에너지원으로 세포에 전달되며, 혈당(blood sugar)이라고도 불린다. 물론 과일과 야채 속에 과당과 함께 존재하기도 한다. 자당은 사탕수수나 근대(beet)에서 추출되며, 커피에 넣는 하얀 육면체 모양으로 우리에게 익숙하다. 사람들이 흔히 설탕이라고 말하는 것이 바로 이 자당이다. 인간은 역사적으로 우유, 꿀, 과일을 통해 당분을 섭취해 왔다. 사탕수수가 유럽에 등장한 것은 겨우 1천 년 전이며, 그것도 향신료, 의약품, 보존제로 받아들여졌다. 1700년 경, 영국의 평균 설탕 소비량은 연간 1인당 2kg였다. 오늘날 그 양은 10배로 늘었다. 오늘날의 설탕 섭취량은 인간에게 정상이 아니다. 우리는 우리의 입맛에 따라 세상을 바꿨지만, 우리 몸은 그 변화를 따라가지 못하고 있다.

02

하위내용영역	배점	예상정답률
일반영어 A형 서술형	4점	40%

모범답안 It can be inferred that the standard view would see forms of life simpler than mice as not having consciousness. Second, the word "matter" best fills in the blank.

채점기준 _ Total 4pts

+ 2점 : 쥐보다 더 단순한 생명체에 대한 "표준적 시각"은 어떤 것일까에 대해 "the standard view would see forms of life simpler than mice as not having consciousness"라 서술하였거나 유사하였다.

+ 2점 : 빈칸에 들어갈 한 단어를 "matter"라 정확히 기입하였다. 이것 외에는 답이 될 수 없다.

감점 ☑ 본문에 나오는 연속되는 5단어 이상을 사용하였다. −0.5pt

한글 번역

물질에 대한 우리의 표준적 관점에서, 고도로 진화한 생명체의 뇌만이 의식을 가졌다고 생각하며, 그렇기에 의식은 우주의 극히 일부에만 존재하며 우주의 역사에 있어서도 극히 최근에 등장했다고 생각한다. 하지만 범심론은 그와는 다르게 의식이 우주 전체에 존재하며 우주의 근본적 특성이라고 말한다. 그렇다고 말 그대로 모든 것이 똑같은 의식을 가지고 있다는 뜻은 아니다. 전자나 쿼크와 같은 우주를 구성하는 기본 요소들은 극히 단순한 형태의 경험을 가질 것이고, 반대로 인간이나 동물의 뇌는 매우 복잡한 경험을 가지지만, 그 경험은 뇌의 기본적인 요소들이 겪는 경험으로부터 유도할 수 있다는 뜻이다.

내가 말하는 "의식"이 어떤 뜻인지를 명확히 해야겠다. 사실 이 용어는 매우 모호한 용어이다. 어떤 이들은 이 용어가 자각 능력이나 자신의 존재를 반추하는 것과 같은 고도의 정신 상태를 의미한다고 생각한다. 바로 이 점이 우리가 다른 동물이나 물질이 의식을 가지고 있다고 말하기 꺼려하는 이유이다. 하지만 나는 의식이란 그저 즐거움, 고통, 시각·청각적 경험 등에서와 같은 경험을 의미한다고 생각한다.

인간은 매우 다양하고 복잡한 경험을 한다. 말은 그보다는 덜하고, 쥐는 말보다도 덜할 것이다. 더 단순한 생명체일수록 더 단순한 경험을 가진다. 아마 어떤 수준에 이르면, 그저 불이 꺼지듯 의식은 사라질 것이다. 이런 의식 축소의 연속성이 생명체를 넘어 물질 수준으로 계속 이어질 것이라고, 곧 근본 입자들까지도 자신의 극히 단순한 본질을 반영하는 극도로 단순한 경험을 가질 것이라고 가정한다면, 이는 적어도 어떤 일관성 있는 주장일 것이다. 범심론자들은 바로 이런 생각을 가지고 있다.

범심론은 물리학이 물질이란 무엇인가에 답하지 못한다는 사실에서 출발한다. 아마 이 말이 이상하게 들릴 것이다. 물리학 교과서에는 공간과 시간, 물질에 대한 놀라운 사실들이 쓰여 있으니까. 하지만 과학 철학자들은 물리학의 그 풍부한 내용에도 불구하고 모든 것이 물질이 어떻게 행동하느냐에 관한 것일 뿐, 물질이란 무엇인가라는 본질에 대한 답은 없다는 것을 깨달았다. 예를 들어 물리학은 물질이 질량과 전하를 가지고 있다고 말한다. 이 두 성질은 인력, 척력, 관성력 등 물질의 행동을 완벽하게 정의한다. 하지만 철학자들이 물질의 고유한 본질이라 부르는, 물리학은 곧 물질이란 무엇인가에 대한 질문에는 전혀 답하지 않는다.

03

하위내용영역	배점	예상정답률
일반영어 A형 서술형	4점	45%

모범답안 The meaning of the underlined selection is that it was an opportunity to instruct Caylee about the complexities of protest. Second, Mr. Harrold is concerned with appearing to endorse the protests, which some view as disrespectful to veterans.

채점기준 _Total 4pts

+ 2점: 밑줄 친 부분의 의미를 "it was an opportunity to instruct Caylee about the complexities of protest"라 서술하였거나 유사하였다.

+ 2점: 불공정한 사회에 대한 저항(의 이유나 원인)을 (진지하게) 다룰 때, Mr. Harold가 걱정하는 반발을 "appearing to endorse the protests, which some view as disrespectful to veterans"라 서술하였거나 유사하였다.

감점 ☑ 본문에 나오는 연속되는 5단어 이상을 사용하였다. −0.5pt

04

하위내용영역	배점	예상정답률
일반영어 A형 서술형	4점	40%

모범답안 The reason for not tricking venture capitalists is when your startup is not a good investment, you are wasting your own time. Second, the implication of the underlined words is that the founders did not truly understand the speaker's point.

채점기준 _Total 4pts

+ 2점: 저자가 위험 투자가를 속이지 않아야 하는 주요 이유를 "when your startup is not a good investment, you are wasting your own time"라 서술하였거나 유사하였다.

+ 2점: 창업 기업과 관련하여, 밑줄 친 부분이 말하는 함축 의미를 "the founders did not truly understand (or the founders ignored) the speaker's point"라 서술하였거나 유사하였다.

감점 ☑ 본문에 나오는 연속되는 5단어 이상을 사용하였다. −0.5pt

내가 와이 컴비네이터에서 스타트업 창업자들에게, 주로 젊은 창업자들인데, 조언을 주기 시작한 이후, 이 젊은 창업자들이 문제를 과도하고 복잡하게 생각하는 경향이 있다는 것을 알았다. 그들은 이렇게 묻는다. 어떻게 투자를 받아요? 벤처 투자자들이 투자를 하게 하려면 어떤 요령(trick)을 써야 할까요? 나는 이렇게 설명한다. 벤처 투자자들이 당신에게 투자하게 만드는 가장 좋은 방법은 당신에게 하는 투자가 실제로 좋은 투자가 되게 만드는 것이라고. 당신이 나쁜 스타트업을 가지고 있음에도 어떤 요령을 써서 투자자로 하여금 투자하게 만든다면, 당신은 당신 자신 또한 속이는 것이다. 당신은 투자를 요청한 그 회사(즉, 당신의 회사)에 당신의 시간을 투자하고 있다. 만약 그 투자가 좋은 투자가 아니라면, 당신은 왜 그 회사를 운영하고 있는 것인가?

그들은 아, 하고 내 말을 곱씹은 다음 다시 이렇게 묻는다. 어떻게 해야 좋은 투자가 되게 만들 수 있나요?

나는 투자자의 눈만이 아니라 실제로 스타트업의 장래성을 알 수 있게 하는 것은 바로 성장이라고 말한다. 이상적으로는 매출에서, 그렇지 않으면 사용량에서라도 성장을 해야 한다. 그러니 사용자가 늘어나야 한다.

그럼 어떻게 해야 사용자가 늘 수 있을까? 그들은 이를 위해 여러 가지를 말한다. 많은 이들에게 "노출"될 수 있는 행사를 이야기하고, 영향력 있는 사람들이 자신의 서비스를 언급해야 된다고 말하며, 심지어 서비스를 화요일에 출시해야 사람들의 관심을 가장 많이 받을 수 있다고도 말한다.

그게 아니라고 나는 설명한다. 그건 사용자를 늘리는 방법이 아니다. 사용자를 늘리는 유일한 방법은 정말로 훌륭한 제품을 만드는 것이다. 사람들은 그 제품을 사용할 뿐 아니라 자신의 친구들에게 추천할 것이며, 당신은 기하급수적인 성장을 할 수 있을 것이다.

내가 창업자들에게 한 이야기, 곧 좋은 제품을 만들어서 좋은 회사가 돼야 한다는 것은 너무나 당연한 조언으로 보일 것이다. 그러나 이 말에 대해 그들은 마치 상대성 이론을 처음 들었을 때 많은 물리학자들이 보였을 법한, 그 조언이 가진 명백한 천재성에 대한 놀라움과 그러면서도 그렇게 이상한 말이 답일리 없다는 의심이 섞인 그런 반응을 보인다. 그들은 의무적으로 내게 알았다고 답하면서도, 다시 묻는다. 혹시 이러이러한 유명인을 소개해 줄 수 있나요? 그리고 우리는 화요일에 제품을 출시하고 싶어요.

창업자들이 이 단순한 교훈을 받아들이기까지는 때로 몇 년의 시간이 걸린다. 이는 그들이 게으르거나 어리석기 때문이 아니다. 그저 자신의 바로 눈 앞에 있는 것을 보지 못하기 때문이다.

05

하위내용영역	배점	예상정답률
일반영어 A형 서술형	4점	40%

모범답안 The two words are "drug-resistant bacteria". Second, the way phage therapy works is that specific viruses that eat bacteria are matched to their respective bacteria to help patients fight infections.

채점기준 _Total 4pts

+ 2점 : 빈칸에 들어갈 두 단어를 "drug-resistant bacteria"라 정확하게 기입하였다. 이것 외에는 답이 될 수 없다.

+ 2점 : "phage therapy"가 기능하는 방식을 "specific viruses that eat bacteria are matched to their respective bacteria to help patients fight infections"라 서술하였거나 유사하였다.

감점 ♡ 본문에 나오는 연속되는 5단어 이상을 사용하였다. -0.5pt

06

하위내용영역	배점	예상정답률
일반영어 A형 서술형	4점	30%

모범답안 The meaning of the underlined is that the speaker will be true to their own nature, even if they are considered "bad" by society. Second, the five words are "integrity of your own mind". Third, "love" best fills the blank.

채점기준 _Total 4pts

+ 2점 : 밑줄 친 부분의 의미를 "the speaker will be true to their own nature, even if they are considered "bad" by society or law"라 서술하였거나 유사하였다.

+ 1점 : "적나라한 진실"에 상응하는 다섯 단어를 "integrity of your own mind"라 정확하게 기입하였다. 이것 외에는 답이 될 수 없다.

+ 1점 : 빈칸에 들어갈 한 단어를 "love"라 정확하게 기입하였다. 이것 외에는 (philanthropy 등) 답이 될 수 없다.

감점 ♡ 본문에 나오는 연속되는 5단어 이상을 사용하였다. -0.5pt

한글 번역

[A] 누구든지 인간이 되려면 반드시 비영합주의자가 돼야 한다. 불후의 영예를 얻고자 하는 자는 선이라는 이름의 방해를 받아서는 안 되고, 오히려, 그 선이라고 불리는 것이 진정한 선인가를 스스로 검토해 봐야 한다. 궁극에 이르러 세상에는 그대 자신의 마음의 정직 이상으로 신성한 것은 없다. 우선 그대 자신에 대해 자기의 무죄함을 선포하라. 그러면 세계의 승인을 얻을 것이다. 내가 아주 젊었을 때, 존경할 만한 한 조언자에게 불가불 하지 않을 수 없었던 한 마디 대답을 아직도 기억하고 있다. 그 사람은 늘 교회의 알뜰히도 낡아 빠진 교리를 가지고 날 귀찮게 구는 것이었다. 내가 "만일 내가 전적으로 내부의 명령에 의해 산다면 전통의 신성과 같은 것이 무슨 소용이 있겠습니까?"하니, 그가 말했다. "그런 충동은 천상의 것이 아니라 지옥의 것인지 모른다"라고. 나는 답했다. "나에겐 그렇게 생각되지 않습니다. 하지만 만일 내가 악마의 아들이라면 나는 그때엔 악마에 의하여 살겠습니다."라고. 나에겐 내 본성의 법칙 이외엔 그 어떠한 법칙도 신성하지 않다. 선과 악이란 것은 단지 이름뿐일 따름인데, 이것은 매우 용이하게도 이것이었다가 어떤 때는 저것으로 변하는 것이다.

[B] 인간은 모든 반대 앞에서, 마치 자기 자신 외의 모든 것이 빈 이름에 지나지 않는 하루살이인 것처럼 행동해야 한다. 우리들이 배지, 이름, 큰 단체, 그리고 죽은 제도 등에 쉽게 굴복하는가를 생각하면 나는 부끄러움을 금할 수 없다. 점잖고 품위 있는 말을 하는 모든 사람들은 필요 이상으로 지나칠 정도로 날 감동시키고 동요시킨다. 나는 곧고 씩씩하게 나아가 모든 면에서 적나라한 진리를 토해내지 않으면 안 된다. 만일 악의와 허영이 박애의 옷을 걸치고 나타난다면 그것이 통하겠는가? 만일, 이제 어떤 비분강개하고 편견이 심한 사람이 노예 폐지라는 자선 운동의 임무를 띠고서 바바도스섬으로부터 최근의 소식을 가지고 나에게 온다면 나는 반드시 그에게 이렇게 말하겠다. "가서 너의 자식이나 사랑하고 너의 집 장작 패는 사람이나 사랑하라. 선량하고 겸손하라. 그런 미덕을 가져라. 그리고 천 마일 밖의 먼 곳에 있는 흑인에 대한 이런 믿기 어려운 온정으로써 너의 냉혹하고 무자비한 야심을 가장하지 말라. 먼 곳에 대한 너의 사랑은 가까이 있는 것에 대한 증오일 따름이다." 이러한 (나의) 인사는 교양 없고 무례한 것일지도 모르지만, 진리는 사랑의 가식보다 아름답다. 우리들의 선에는 다소의 모난 면이 있어야 한다. 그렇지 않다면 그것은 아무것도 아니다. 사랑의 교훈이 다만 울고불고하는 것을 일삼는다면, 사랑의 교훈의 반대 작용으로서 증오의 교훈을 설교할 필요가 있다.

07

하위내용영역	배점	예상정답률
일반영어 B형 서술형	4점	45%

모범답안 The recent growth of the wellness industry can cause harm if not addressed. Though "The Goop Lab" looks like a promising platform, it prevents proven treatments and puts people in harm's way. Unfortunately, this sort of wellness business has been influenced by the patriarchal nature of medicine, having left out women, who thus become dominant in the wellness industry. In conclusion, to solve this distressing situation, medicine should challenge the wellness claims compassionately and also remove the patriarchal practices helping to grow that market.

채점기준
_ Total 4pts

ⓐ Topic sentence
+1점 : 글의 topic sentence "The recent growth of the wellness industry can cause harm if not addressed."를 명확하게 서술하였거나 유사하였다.

ⓑ Major supporting details
+2점 : 글의 major supporting details 즉, ① "Though 'The Goop Lab' looks like a promising platform, it prevents proven treatments and puts people in harm's way. ② Unfortunately, this sort of wellness business has been influenced by the patriarchal nature of medicine, having left out women, who thus become dominant in the wellness industry."을 명확하게 서술하였거나 유사하였다.
▷ 2개 중 2개 모두 정확하게 요약했으면 2점; 1개를 정확하게 요약했으면 1점; 나머지는 0점을 준다.

ⓒ Conclusion
+1점 : 글의 conclusion "In conclusion, to solve this, medicine should challenge the wellness claims compassionately and also remove the patriarchal practices helping to grow that market"을 명확하게 서술하였거나 유사하였다.

감점 ☑

• 본문에 나오는 연속되는 6단어 이상을 사용하였다. -0.5pt
• 문단을 두 개나 그 이상으로 구성하였다. -0.5pt
• 문법이나 영어 표현을 합쳐 3개 이상 오류가 있다. -0.5pt

18회 문제은행

📖 본책 p.132

01

하위내용영역	배점	예상정답률
일반영어 A형 서술형	4점	40%

모범답안 The one word is "cancer". Second, it means that the speaker might be able to live longer than predicted by the mean or median.

▷ 출제의도 : 중간 정도 난이도의 글을 읽고, 그 지문을 바탕으로 정확한 추론을 하는지 평가한다.

채점기준 _Total 4pts

⁺ 2점 : 빈칸에 들어갈 한 단어를 "cancer"라 정확하게 기입하였다. 이것 외에는 답이 될 수 없다.

⁺ 2점 : "(중간값이나 중위값이 아니라) 변수 그 자체가 현실(실재)"이라는 말이 글의 저자의 상황(암에 걸려 8개월밖에 살지 못한다는)에 어떠한 의미를 지니고 있는지 설명하라는 문제에 "the speaker might be able to live longer than predicted by the mean (or median)"라 서술하였거나 유사하였다.

감점 ☑ 본문에 나오는 연속되는 5단어 이상을 사용하였다. −0.5pt

02

하위내용영역	배점	예상정답률
일반영어 A형 서술형	4점	45%

모범답안 It can be inferred that Stephen Jay Gould was very famous and successful in his field. Second, the Civil Rights Movement allows Gould to understand a sudden, surprising evolutionary change.

▷ 출제의도 : 중상 이상 난이도의 글을 읽고, 주어진 정보를 가지고 올바른 추론을 하는지 평가한다.

채점기준 _Total 4pts

⁺ 2점 : 뉴욕 타임스가 스티븐 제이 굴드의 죽음을 1면에 언급한 것이 의미하는 바를 "Stephen Jay Gould was very famous and successful in his field"라 같이 서술하였거나 유사하였다.

⁺ 2점 : 1960년대 시민권 투쟁이 굴드의 진화론에 대한 이해에 어떤 면에서 연관이 있느냐는 질문에 "the Civil Rights Movement allows Gould to understand a sudden, surprising evolutionary change"라 서술하였거나 유사하였다.

감점 ☑ 본문에 나오는 연속되는 3단어 이상을 사용하였다. −0.5pt

03

하위내용영역	배점	예상정답률
일반영어 A형 서술형	4점	45%

모범답안 He was reassured because the sleeping dog means that nobody is intruding into his house. Second, the word "fear" best describes the state of the main character.

▷ 출제의도 : narrative 패턴의 글을 읽고, 글쓴이의 주관적 내면의 감정을 정확하게 파악할 수 있는지 평가한다.

채점기준 _Total 4pts

⁺ 2점 : "그"가 개가 잠을 자고 있는 모습에 안심한 이유를 "the sleeping dog means that nobody is intruding into his house"라 서술하였거나 유사하였다.

▷ 다음과 같이 서술하였어도 2점을 준다.

"the dog was sleeping and not disturbed by an intruder in the house that he imagined was there"

⁺ 2점 : 빈칸에 들어갈 한 단어를 "fear"라 정확하게 기입하였다. 이것 외에는 답이 될 수 없다.

감점 ☑ 본문에 나오는 연속되는 3단어 이상을 사용하였다. −0.5pt

04

하위내용영역	배점	예상정답률
일반영어 A형 서술형	4점	50%

모범답안 The "hardest workers" were the students that worked very hard no matter what their ability and performed well. Second, the writer thinks "the situation" is ridiculous because David did perfectly on tests and exams but wasn't put on the accelerated track to get into the Advanced Placement Calculus.

▷ 출제의도 : 중급 정도 난이도의 글을 읽고, 글의 내용을 정확하게 이해했는지 평가한다.

채점기준   _Total 4pts

+ 2점 : "가장 열심히 일하는 일꾼"을 "<u>the students that worked very hard no matter what their ability</u> and <u>performed well</u>"이라 서술하였거나 유사하였다.

+ 2점 : "이 상황이 말도 안 되는 것"이라 생각하는 이유를 "<u>because David did perfectly on tests and exams but wasn't put on the accelerated track</u> (to get into the Advanced Placement Calculus)"라 서술하였거나 유사하였다.

감점 ♥ 본문에 나오는 연속되는 3단어 이상을 사용하였다. −0.5pt

05

하위내용영역	배점	예상정답률
일반영어 A형 서술형	4점	45%

모범답안 It is odd for them to be successful because they lack genetic diversity. Second, "diversity" best fills the blank. Third, all the elements are as follows : nature, nurture (or environment), and random.

▷ 출제의도 : 중·상급 정도 난이도의 최신 과학적 발견에 대한 글을 읽고, 그 글의 내용을 정확하게 이해했는지, 그리고 그 이해를 바탕으로 논리적 추론력이 충분한지 평가한다.

채점기준   _Total 4pts

+ 2점 : 밑줄 친 "그것들의 성공은 이상한 것"이라는 말이 의미하는 것을 "It is odd for them to be successful because they lack genetic diversity"라 서술하였다.

+ 1점 : 빈칸에 들어갈 한 단어를 "diversity"라 정확히 기입하였다. 이것 외에는 답이 될 수 없다.

+ 1점 : 서로 다른 특질을 만들어 내는 데 영향을 미치는 모든 요소를 "① <u>nature</u>, ② <u>nurture (or environment)</u>, and ③ <u>random</u>"이라 정확하게 서술하였다.

▷ 3개 중 2개만 언급했으면 1점; 나머지는 0점을 준다.

감점 ♥ 본문에 나오는 연속되는 3단어 이상을 사용하였다. −0.5pt

06

하위내용영역	배점	예상정답률
일반영어 A형 서술형	4점	45%

모범답안 "Procrastinate" best fills the blank. Second, work and study is lacking immediate reward.

▷ 출제의도 : 중·상급 정도 난이도의 글을 읽고, 글의 내용을 정확하게 이해했는지 평가한다.

채점기준   _Total 4pts

+ 2점 : 빈칸에 들어갈 한 단어를 "procrastinate"라 정확하게 기입하였다. 이것 외에는 답이 될 수 없다.

+ 2점 : 일과 공부가 가지고 있지 못한 것이 "immediate reward"라 서술하였거나 유사하였다.

한글 번역

"방해받지 않는 법(Indistractable)"의 저자인 니르 이얄은 딴짓이란 원래 하고자 했던 일을 하지 못하게 만드는 행동이라 말한다. 딴짓의 반대말은 집중이 아니라 견인력(강력히 붙잡는 것)이다. 어떤 중요한 일을 두고 이메일을 확인하고 있다면, 당신은 딴짓을 하는 것이다. 반대로, 토요일 저녁에 게임을 할 생각이었다면, 그때 게임은 딴짓이 아니라 견인력이라 할 수 있다. 기분 전환이란 주의를 다시 집중하기 위해 필요한 것이다. 이 기분 전환을 잘 활용하는 것은 매우 중요하다. 미루기는 우리가 원래 하려던 일 대신 딴짓을 하는 것을 말한다.

사람들이 왜 일을 미루는지, 그리고 왜 일을 미루는 습관을 버리지 못하는지에 대해서는 많은 이론이 있다. 1930년대, 심리학자들은 쥐를 이용해 여러 가지 실험을 했다. 예를 들어 쥐가 어떤 막대를 누르면 무언가를 보상으로 주는 것이다. 당시 과학자들은 쥐가 예상치 못한 보상을 받았을 때 이 행동을 더 자주 한다는 것을 발견했다. 곧, 보상이 랜덤하게 주어질 때 쥐들은 이 습관을 끊기 더 어려워했다. 이는 뇌를 흥분시키는 도파민이 보상이 주어질 때뿐만 아니라 보상에 대한 예측이 있을 때도 분비되기 때문이다. 이런 현상은 쥐에게서 뿐만 아니라 인간에게서도 발견된다. 우리 또한 랜덤한 보상을 즐긴다. 스포츠를 관람하는 것은 누가 득점을 하고 누가 이길 것인지 알 수 없기 때문이다. 라디오를 들을 때, 우리는 다음 곡이 어떤 곡일지를 기대한다. 쇼핑을 할 때는 어떤 물건을 득템하게 될지를 기대한다. 이 시대는 이러한 랜덤한 보상을 손끝으로 느끼도록 만들었다. 많은 스마트폰 앱들은 새로운 무언가를 계속해서 제공함으로써 사용자가 끝없이 화면을 스크롤하게 만든다. 어떤 이들은 설탕이나 마약보다도 스마트폰에 더 중독돼 있다.

랜덤한 보상을 즐기는 것 자체는 문제가 되지 않는다. 하지만 어떤 해야 할 일을 미루고 있는 상황에서, 이러한 랜덤한 보상이 주어지는 행위는 특히 우리를 강력하게 붙잡게 된다. 우리는 끝없이 한 번만 더 클릭을 하고 조금만 더 화면을 스크롤하며 이를 놓치 못한다. 우리가 계획하는 일들, 곧 공부나 일, 가사 노동 등은 즉각적인 보상을 주지 않는다. 공부와 일에 대한 보상은 먼 미래에 주어지는 반면, 인스타그램이나 페이스북은 당장 우리에게 보상을 준다. 내가 쓴 글에 누군가 좋아요를 눌렀는지, 인스타그램에 어떤 새로운 이야기가 올라왔는지를 우리는 끝없이 궁금해 한다.

미루기를 피하기 위해 나와 많은 이들이 사용하는 기술 중에는 흔히 포모도로 테크닉이라 불리는 시간 관리 기술이 있다. 이 방법은 매 30분을 25분간의 집중 시간과 5분간의 휴식 시간으로 나누는 것이다. 25분간의 집중 시간에는 원래 하기로 한 일 외에는 이메일을 보는 등의 다른 어떤 일도 해서는 안 된다.

07

하위내용영역	배점	예상정답률
일반영어 A형 서술형	4점	40%

모범답안 Adolescents have brains that are more developed to experience fear and rewards which cause their unique behavior. These differences mean they experience anxiety and also participate in risky behaviors more. Likewise, it helps show how therapy is less effective for them and how drugs might disrupt their development into healthy adults. In conclusion, adolescents should be understood as being prone to anxiety and needing proper guidance to grow healthily past this stage.

▷ 출제의도 : 글의 전체적인 내용을 파악한 후, 그 파악에 기초해서 글의 구조를 정확하게 요약하는지 평가한다.

채점기준 _Total 4pts

ⓐ Topic sentence

+ 1점 : 글의 topic sentence "Adolescents have brains that are more developed to experience fear and rewards which cause their unique behavior"를 명확하게 서술하였거나 유사하였다.

ⓑ Major supporting details

+ 2점 : 글의 major supporting details 즉, ① "These differences mean they experience anxiety and also participate in risky behaviors more. ② Likewise, it helps show how therapy is less effective for them and how drugs might disrupt their development into healthy adults"를 명확하게 서술하였거나 유사하였다.

▷ 2개 중 2개 모두 정확하게 요약했으면 2점; 1개만 정확하게 요약했으면 1점; 나머지는 0점을 준다.

ⓒ Conclusion

+ 1점 : 글의 conclusion "In conclusion, adolescents should be understood as being prone to anxiety and needing proper guidance to grow healthily past this stage"을 명확하게 서술하였거나 유사하였다.

감점 ♡

• 본문에 나오는 연속되는 6단어 이상을 사용하였다. −0.5pt
• 문단을 두 개나 그 이상으로 구성하였다. −0.5pt
• 문법이나 영어 표현을 합쳐 3개 이상 오류가 있다. −0.5pt

19회 문제은행

📖 본책 p.146

01

하위내용영역	배점	예상정답률
일반영어 A형 서술형	4점	60%

모범답안 The underlined words means the trip was impossible to afford. Second, pursuing high ambitions can lead to satisfying results.

채점기준 _Total 4pts

+ 2점: 밑줄 친 부분의 의미를 "the trip was impossible to afford"라 서술하였거나 유사하였다.
  ▷ 다음과 같이 서술하였어도 2점을 준다.
  "they could not afford to do the trip"
+ 2점: Janice가 밑줄 친 부분에서 생각한 것을 "pursuing high ambitions (or goals) can lead to satisfying results"라 서술하였거나 유사하였다.

02

하위내용영역	배점	예상정답률
일반영어 A형 서술형	4점	45%

모범답안 An example of ownership of learning is that the students formed the two groups on their own. Second, the underlined words refer to the students focusing on gender stereotypes during the class.

채점기준 _Total 4pts

+ 2점: 밑줄 친 부분의 의미를 "the students formed the two groups on their own"이라 서술하였거나 유사하였다.

+ 2점: 밑줄 친 부분이 가리키는 것을 "(the students focusing on) gender stereotypes (during the class)"라 서술하였거나 유사하였다.

03

하위내용영역	배점	예상정답률
일반영어 A형 서술형	4점	50%

모범답안 It is because it was magma and the water would evaporate into space. Second, the word is "comets".

채점기준 _Total 4pts

+ 2점: 지구가 물을 지니지 못하고 있었던 이유를 "because it was magma and the water would evaporate into space"라 서술하였거나 유사하였다.
+ 2점: 빈칸에 들어갈 단어를 "comets"라 정확하게 기입하였다. 이것 외에는 답이 될 수 없다.

04

하위내용영역	배점	예상정답률
일반영어 A형 서술형	4점	35%

모범답안 The word is "pain". Second, the writer doesn't believe that pleasure and pain aren't defined by their relativity to one another, but are each their own distinct thing.

채점기준 _Total 4pts

+ 2점: 빈칸에 들어갈 단어를 "pain"라 정확하게 기입하였다. 이것 외에는 답이 될 수 없다.
+ 2점: 밑줄 친 부분에서 저자가 말하고자 하는 바를 "the writer doesn't believe that pleasure and pain aren't defined by their relativity to one another, but are each their own distinct thing"라 서술하였거나 유사하였다.

05

하위내용영역	배점	예상정답률
일반영어 A형 서술형	4점	45%

모범답안 The word is "inflammation". Next, the new findings mean that less risky treatments for psoriasis can be created to replace UV therapy by using RNA molecules.

채점기준 _Total 4pts

+ 2점: 빈칸에 들어갈 단어를 "inflammation"라 정확히 기입하였다. 이것 외에는 답이 될 수 없다.

+ 2점: 새로운 발견이 건선 치료에 왜 도움이 될 것인지 묻는 질문에 "the new findings mean that <u>less risky treatments for psoriasis can be created to replace UV therapy</u> (by using RNA molecules)"라 서술하였거나 유사하였다.

06

하위내용영역	배점	예상정답률
일반영어 A형 서술형	4점	40%

모범답안 The word is "ear". Second, it is because the artist used secondhand sources and his own imagination to create the image, not direct observance.

채점기준 _Total 4pts

+ 2점: 빈칸에 들어갈 단어를 "ear"라 정확하게 기입하였다. 이것 외에는 답이 될 수 없다.

+ 2점: 저자가 "half-invented"란 표현을 사용한 이유를 "<u>the artist used secondhand sources and his own imagination to create the image, not direct observance</u>"라 서술하였거나 유사하였다.

07

하위내용영역	배점	예상정답률
일반영어 B형 서술형	4점	40%

모범답안 Work friendships used to be key and can lead to a more efficient and happy environment if brought into a company. Americans have less work friendships because long term employment has declined alongside a rise in social media connections with old friends. However, friends working together can make for more happiness and effective output when there is trust and mutual support. In conclusion, these helpful relationships can be established through simple interactions of mutual engagement and trust.

채점기준 _Total 4pts

ⓐ Topic sentence

+ 1점: 글의 topic sentence "<u>Work friendships</u> (used to be key and) <u>can lead to a more efficient and happy environment</u> (if brought into a company)"을 명확하게 서술하였거나 유사하였다.

ⓑ Major supporting details

+ 2점: 글의 major supporting details 즉, "Americans have less work friendships ① <u>as(because) long term employment has declined alongside</u> ② <u>a rise in social media connections with old friends.</u> However, ③ <u>friends working together can make for more happiness and effective output when there is trust and mutual support</u>"을 명확하게 서술하였거나 유사하였다.

▷ 3개 중 3개 모두 정확하게 요약했으면 2점; 2개만 요약했으면 1점; 나머지는 0점을 준다.

ⓒ Conclusion

+ 1점: 글의 conclusion "In conclusion, <u>these helpful relationships can be established through simple interactions of mutual engagement and trust</u>"를 명확히 서술하였거나 유사하였다.

감점 ♥

• 본문에 나오는 연속되는 6단어 이상을 사용하였다. −0.5pt
• 문단을 두 개나 그 이상으로 구성하였다. −0.5pt
• 문법이나 영어 표현을 합쳐 3개 이상 오류가 있다. −0.5pt

20 회 문제은행

📖 본책 p.159

01

하위내용영역	배점	예상정답률
일반영어 A형 서술형	4점	50%

모범답안 It means that younger people announce their age using fractions to sound older sooner. Second, kids and the very old share the similarity of counting in fractions.

채점기준 _ Total 4pts

+ 2점: 밑줄 친 부분의 의미를 "younger people announce their age using fractions to sound older sooner"라 서술하거나 유사하였다.

+ 2점: 가장 늙은 노인과 아이들 사이의 공통점을 "counting in fractions"라 서술하였거나 유사하였다.

02

하위내용영역	배점	예상정답률
일반영어 A형 서술형	4점	45%

모범답안 It is that the majority of left-handed women also hold their babies on the same side as their right-handed counterparts. Second, "left" fills the blank.

채점기준 _ Total 4pts

+ 2점: 어떤 연구의 결과가 밑줄 친 부분의 주장을 반박하는가라는 질문에 "the majority of left-handed women also hold their babies on the same side as their right-handed counterparts"라 서술하였거나 유사하였다.

+ 2점: 빈칸에 들어갈 단어를 "left"라 기입하였다. 이것 외에는 답이 될 수 없다.

03

하위내용영역	배점	예상정답률
일반영어 A형 서술형	4점	45%

모범답안 "history" best fills the blank. Second, it means that history is not unpredictable chaos, but has patterns.

채점기준 _ Total 4pts

+ 2점: 빈칸에 들어갈 단어를 "history"라 기입하였다. 이것 외에는 답이 될 수 없다.

+ 2점: 밑줄 친 부분의 의미를 "history is not unpredictable chaos, but has patterns"라 서술하였거나 유사하였다.

04

하위내용영역	배점	예상정답률
일반영어 A형 서술형	4점	50%

모범답안 It is because the teacher wanted to start with a fun location. Second, the word is "angry".

채점기준 _ Total 4pts

+ 2점: 지리 교사가 자신의 주에서 시작하지 않은 이유를 "because the teacher wanted to start with a fun location"라 서술하였거나 유사하였다.

+ 2점: 빈칸에 들어갈 단어를 "angry"라 기입하였다. 이것 외에는 답이 될 수 없다.

05

하위내용영역	배점	예상정답률
일반영어 A형 서술형	4점	50%

모범답안 It means that many of the other apple companies have become very angry at the company's attempt to sell a genetically engineered apple. Second, the word is "slices"

the closing of Black medical schools, so that less doctors looked into the environmental factors of racism and instead noted race itself as a risk factor. In conclusion, the Flexner report needs to be replaced by an approach that unifies public health and medicine to better handle diseases.

채점기준   _Total 4pts

ⓐ Topic sentence

+ 1점: 글의 topic sentence "The Flexner report was a pivotal reformation to medical education which lead to the deleterious separation of medicine and public health"를 명확하게 서술하였다.

ⓑ Major supporting details

+ 2점: 글의 major supporting details 즉, "Commissioned in the early 1900s, ① it help found the modern medical educational system which focuses on individuals, rather than social and environmental factors. Secondarily, ② it led to the closing of Black medical schools, so that less doctors looked into the environmental factors of racism and instead noted race itself as a risk factor"를 명확하게 서술하였다.

▷ 2개 중 2개 모두 정확하게 요약했으면 2점; 1개만 요약했으면 1점; 나머지는 0점을 준다.

ⓒ Conclusion

+ 1점: 글의 conclusion "In conclusion, the Flexner report needs to be replaced by an approach that unifies public health and medicine to better handle diseases"를 명확하게 서술하였다.

감점 ♡
• 본문에 나오는 연속되는 6단어 이상을 사용하였다. -0.5pt
• 문단을 두 개나 그 이상으로 구성하였다. -0.5pt
• 문법이나 영어 표현을 합쳐 3개 이상 오류가 있다. -0.5pt

채점기준   _Total 4pts

+ 2점: 밑줄 친 부분의 의미를 "<u>many other apple (=many of the other apple) companies have become very angry at the company's trying (attempt) to sell a genetically engineered apple</u>"라 서술하거나 유사하였다.

+ 2점: 빈칸에 들어갈 단어를 "slices"라 기입하였다. 이것 외에는 답이 될 수 없다.

06

하위내용영역	배점	예상정답률
일반영어 A형 서술형	4점	45%

모범답안 The word in ① is "nature" and ② "temperature". Second, it is the scientific challenge of creating a diamond from carbon.

채점기준   _Total 4pts

+ 1점: 빈칸 ①에 "nature"라 기입하였다. 이것 외에는 답이 될 수 없다.

+ 1점: 빈칸 ②에 "temperature"라 기입하였다. 이것 외에는 답이 될 수 없다.

+ 2점: 밑줄 친 "다이아몬드 수수께끼"를 "<u>the scientific challenge of creating a diamond from carbon</u>"라 서술하거나 유사하였다.

07

하위내용영역	배점	예상정답률
일반영어 B형 서술형	4점	35%

모범답안 The Flexner report was a pivotal reformation to medical education which lead to the deleterious separation of medicine and public health. Commissioned in the early 1900s, it help found the modern medical educational system which focuses on individuals, rather than social and environmental factors. Secondarily, it led to

21 회 문제은행

📖 본책 p.173

01

하위내용영역	배점	예상정답률
일반영어 A형 서술형	4점	50%

모범답안 It can be inferred that Branson had an unconventional character which will either make him successful or get him into trouble. Second, it means that the name of Virgin has held on to this day.

채점기준 _Total 4pts

+ 2점: Branson의 학창 시절 교장의 말에서 추론할 수 있는 그의 기질을 "Branson had an unconventional character which will either make him successful or get him into trouble"라 서술하였거나 유사하였다.

+ 2점: 밑줄 친 부분의 의미를 "the name of Virgin has held on to this day 또는 the name of Virgin has been used since that moment"라 서술하였거나 유사하였다.

02

하위내용영역	배점	예상정답률
일반영어 A형 서술형	4점	35%

모범답안 The word is "ideal". Second, the central error is that women were asked the ideal family size rather than about their personal preference.

채점기준 _Total 4pts

+ 2점: 빈칸에 들어갈 단어를 "ideal"이라 기입하였다. 이것 외에는 답이 될 수 없다.

+ 2점: 가족 규모에 대한 정보 수집에서 글쓴이가 언급하는 핵심적 오류를 "women were asked the ideal family size rather than about their personal preference"라 서술하였거나 유사하였다.

03

하위내용영역	배점	예상정답률
일반영어 A형 서술형	4점	50%

모범답안 The word is "success". Second, it means that the woman is driven to improve to the highest possible standard by her own opinion without self-gratification.

채점기준 _Total 4pts

+ 2점: 빈칸에 들어갈 단어를 "success"라 기입하였다. 이것 외에는 답이 될 수 없다.

+ 2점: 밑줄 친 부분의 의미를 "the woman is driven to improve to the highest possible standard by her own opinion without self-gratification (self-satisfaction)"라 서술하였거나 유사하였다.

04

하위내용영역	배점	예상정답률
일반영어 A형 서술형	4점	50%

모범답안 Ford's motivation for using a higher wage was to stabilize his workforce by reducing chronic absenteeism and worker turnover. Second, the differences in 2014 are that a stabilized workforce is not a priority as it was in 1914, but instead staying competitive and keeping up with technology are priorities.

채점기준 _Total 4pts

+ 2점: 포드가 임금을 올려준 핵심적 동기를 "to stabilize his workforce (by reducing chronic absenteeism and worker turnover)"라 서술하였거나 유사하였다.

+ 2점: 2014년의 미국 기업들과 노동자들이 1914년과 어떻게 완전히 다른가에 대해 "the differences in 2014 are that a stabilized workforce is not a priority (as it was in 1914), but instead staying competitive and keeping up with technology are priorities"라 서술하였거나 유사하였다.

05

하위내용영역	배점	예상정답률
일반영어 A형 서술형	4점	45%

모범답안 The word is "myth". Second, he argues that the secrets for living a long time are useless because they have no good scientific value and are full of crazy ideas.

채점기준   _Total 4pts

+ 2점: 빈칸에 들어갈 단어를 "myth"라 기입하였다. 이것 외에는 답이 될 수 없다.

+ 2점: 슈와츠가 주장하는 바를 "the secrets for living a long time are useless because they have no good scientific value and are full of crazy ideas"라 서술하였거나 유사하였다.

06

하위내용영역	배점	예상정답률
일반영어 A형 서술형	4점	55%

모범답안 It means that the consecutive records for hottest months are due to an overall changing climate, not mere chance. Second, they increase allergy symptoms, lung inflammation along with worse asthma symptoms. Third, the word is "poor".

채점기준   _Total 4pts

+ 2점: 밑줄 친 부분의 의미를 "the consecutive records for hottest months are due to an overall changing climate, not mere chance"라 서술하였거나 유사하였다.

+ 1점: 상승된 이산화탄소 수치가 야기하는 글에 언급되는 모든 공공 건강 결과를 "they increase allergy symptoms, lung inflammation along with worse asthma symptoms"라 서술하였거나 유사하였다.

   ▷ 3개 중 2개만 서술했으면 0.5점; 나머지는 0점을 준다.

+ 1점: 빈칸에 들어갈 단어를 "poor"라 기입하였다. 이것 외에는 답이 될 수 없다.

07

하위내용영역	배점	예상정답률
일반영어 B형 서술형	4점	35%

모범답안 There are differences between procrastination and "pre-crastination" in terms of productivity and creativity. Procrastinators are easily distracted, seek instant gratification, and must gather willpower to ignore distractions. Pre-crastinators, on the other hand, seek to start and finish tasks immediately and find it hard to not work. A study revealed though that, in companies, those who procrastinate were rated to be more creative. In conclusion, it can lead to more creative output to procrastinate.

채점기준   _Total 4pts

ⓐ Topic sentence

+ 2점: 글의 topic sentence "There are differences between procrastination and "pre-crastination" in terms of productivity and creativity"를 명확하게 서술하였다.

ⓑ Major supporting details

+ 2점: 글의 major supporting details 즉, "① Procrastinators are easily distracted, seek instant gratification, and must gather willpower to ignore distractions. ② Pre-crastinators, on the other hand, seek to start and finish tasks immediately and find it hard to not work. ③ A study revealed though that, in companies, those who procrastinate were rated to be more creative."을 명확하게 서술하였다.

   ▷ 3개 중 3개 모두 정확하게 요약했으면 2점; 2개만 요약했으면 1점; 나머지는 0점을 준다.

ⓒ Conclusion

+ 1점: 글의 conclusion "In conclusion, it can lead to more creative output to procrastinate"를 명확하게 서술하였거나 유사하였다.

감점 ▽

• 본문에 나오는 연속되는 6단어 이상을 사용하였다. −0.5pt
• 문단을 두 개나 그 이상으로 구성하였다. −0.5pt
• 문법이나 영어 표현을 합쳐 3개 이상 오류가 있다. −0.5pt

22회 문제은행

📖 본책 p.187

01

하위내용영역	배점	예상정답률
일반영어 A형 서술형	4점	50%

모범답안 The word is "selfishness". Second, he argues that using non-selfish oriented motives can be effective for a whole group.

채점기준 _Total 4pts

+ 2점: 빈칸에 "selfishness"라 정확하게 답하였다. 이것 외에는 답이 될 수 없다.
+ 2점: 디에고 리베라의 벽화를 통해 저자가 주장하는 바를 "using non-selfish oriented(other-regarding) motives can be effective for a whole group"라 서술하였거나 유사하였다.

02

하위내용영역	배점	예상정답률
일반영어 A형 서술형	4점	45%

모범답안 The words are "obsessive interest". Second, it means that these two were not intending to reach any success, but were following their own interest in the subject.

채점기준 _Total 4pts

+ 2점: 빈칸에 들어갈 단어를 "obsessive interest"라 기입하였다. 이것 외에는 답이 될 수 없다.
+ 2점: 밑줄 친 부분의 의미를 "these two(Darwin and Ramanujan) were not intending to reach any success, but were following their own interest in the subject"라 서술하였거나 유사하였다.

03

하위내용영역	배점	예상정답률
일반영어 A형 서술형	4점	30%

모범답안 The word is "radiation". It can be inferred that low doses are expected to cause a shorter life expectancy and leukemia.

채점기준 _Total 4pts

+ 2점: 빈칸에 들어갈 단어를 "radiation"라 기입하였다. 이것 외에는 답이 될 수 없다.
+ 2점: 밑줄 친 부분의 의미를 "low doses lead to lower life expectancy and leukemia"라 서술하였거나 유사하였다

04

하위내용영역	배점	예상정답률
일반영어 A형 서술형	4점	45%

모범답안 The students are told to have a designated place at home to study and are each given a pencil box. Second, it is implied the teacher suspects the family is not following her idea for at-home learning, and also needs financial support.

채점기준 _Total 4pts

+ 2점: 교사에 의해서 모든 학생들에게 주어진 충고와 후원을 "The students are told to have a designated place at home to study and are given a pencil box (or supplies)"라 서술하였거나 유사하였다.
+ 2점: Shua의 가족에 대한 교사의 의심에 관련하여 추론할 수 있는 것을 "the teacher suspects that the family is not following her idea for at-home learning, and also needs financial support"라 서술하였거나 유사하였다.

05

하위내용영역	배점	예상정답률
일반영어 A형 서술형	4점	45%

모범답안 They refer to the symbiotic microbes living on the skin naturally. Second, the word is "soap". Third, the writer mentions the Amish because they show how we can develop more resistance by being raised away from highly sanitized environments.

채점기준 _Total 4pts

+ 1점: 밑줄 친 부분이 가리키는 것을 "symbiotic microbes" 또는 "microbiome"라 서술하였다. 이것 외에는 답이 될 수 없다.

+ 1점: 빈칸에 들어갈 단어를 "soap"라 기입하였다. 이것 외에는 답이 될 수 없다.

+ 2점: 저자가 아미쉬 아이들을 언급한 이유를 "because they show how we can develop more resistance(less vulnerability) by being raised away from highly sanitized environments"라 서술하였거나 유사하였다.

06

하위내용영역	배점	예상정답률
일반영어 A형 서술형	4점	45%

모범답안 The underlined "ironically" means the fact that people avoid trust because they might endure a negative experience is ironic because a potential negative experience would give them important learning benefits to avoid future negativity. Second, "costs" best fits the blank.

채점기준 _Total 4pts

+ 2점: 밑줄 친 "ironically"의 의미를 "the fact that people avoid trust because they might endure a negative experience is ironic because a potential negative experience would give them important learning benefits"라 서술하였거나 유사하였다.

+ 2점: 빈칸에 들어갈 단어를 "costs"라 기입하였다. 이것 외에는 답이 될 수 없다.

07

하위내용영역	배점	예상정답률
일반영어 B형 서술형	4점	50%

모범답안 It's important to know that animals communicate in several ways, this can be verbally, as singing of birds and whales or the pings and clicks of dolphins. Alternatively, body language is another form of communication, such as the way hyenas use their fur and expressions with teeth to communicate with one another. Also, some animals use colors, such as a zebra's stripes, which help identify individuals as well as evade predators. In conclusion, animals should be considered as dynamic and expressive.

채점기준 _Total 4pts

ⓐ Topic sentence

+ 1점: 글의 topic sentence "It's important to know that animals communicate in several ways"를 명확하게 서술하였거나 유사하였다.

ⓑ Major supporting details

+ 2점: 글의 major supporting details 즉, "① This can be verbally, such as the singing of birds and whales or the pings and clicks of dolphins. Alternatively, ② body language is another form of communication, such as the way hyenas use the fur and expressions with teeth to communicate with one another. Also, ③ some animals use colors, such as a zebra's stripes, (which help identify individuals as well as evade predators)"을 명확하게 서술하였다.

▷ 3개 중 3개 모두 정확하게 요약했으면 2점; 2개만 요약했으면 1점; 나머지는 0점을 준다.

ⓒ Conclusion

+ 1점: 글의 conclusion "In conclusion, animals should be considered as dynamic and expressive"을 명확하게 서술하였거나 유사하였다.

감점 ▽

• 본문에 나오는 연속되는 6단어 이상을 사용하였다. −0.5pt
• 문단을 두 개나 그 이상으로 구성하였다. −0.5pt
• 문법이나 영어 표현을 합쳐 3개 이상 오류가 있다. −0.5pt

23 회 문제은행

📖 본책 p.200

01

하위내용영역	배점	예상정답률
일반영어 A형 서술형	4점	45%

모범답안 It would be attributed to engineers because it has to do with function and concerns the heating and cooling systems. Second, the word is "form".

채점기준 _Total 4pts

+ 1점: 밑줄 친 부분에 있는 디자인의 예시가 어느 그룹에 밀접하게 관련되는가에 대해 "engineers"라 서술하였다. 이것 외에는 답이 될 수 없다.

+ 1점: 위를 선택한 이유에 대해 "because it has to do with function and concerns the heating and cooling systems"라 서술하였거나 유사하였다.

+ 2점: 밑줄 친 부분의 의미에 가장 상응하는 한 단어를 "form"이라 서술하였다. 이것 외에는 답이 될 수 없다.

02

하위내용영역	배점	예상정답률
일반영어 A형 서술형	4점	55%

모범답안 The word is "ethnic". Second, the specific clothing is a Scottish Kilt.

채점기준 _Total 4pts

+ 2점: 빈칸에 들어갈 단어를 "ethnic"이라 정확하게 기입하였다. 이것 외에는 답이 될 수 없다.

+ 2점: 지문에 언급된 (민족 문화적) 유산을 보여주는 구체적인 옷을 "(Scottish) Kilt"라 서술하였다.

03

하위내용영역	배점	예상정답률
일반영어 A형 서술형	4점	45%

모범답안 The word is "forty-two". Second, the underlined words mean that the run distance that Pheidippides traveled being 42 kilometers is more astonishing to geek people who obsess about the number 42 because that unit of measure hadn't been invented yet.

채점기준 _Total 4pts

+ 2점: 빈칸에 들어갈 단어를 "forty-two"라 정확하게 기입하였다.

+ 2점: 밑줄 친 부분의 의미를 "the run distance that Pheidippides traveled being 42 kilometers is more astonishing to geek people who obsess about(over) the number 42 because that unit of measure(the kilometer) hadn't been invented yet"라 서술하였거나 유사하였다.

04

하위내용영역	배점	예상정답률
일반영어 A형 서술형	4점	40%

모범답안 The words for ① are "lithospheric plates" and the words for ② are "plate tectonics". Second, it was formed one hundred eighty million years ago.

채점기준 _Total 4pts

+ 1점: 빈칸 ①에 들어갈 단어를 "lithospheric plates"라 정확하게 기입하였다. "surface plates"라 했어도 1점을 준다.

+ 1점: 빈칸 ②에 들어갈 단어를 "plate tectonics"라 정확하게 기입하였다. 이것 외에는 답이 될 수 없다.

+ 2점: 북대서양이 언제 형성되었냐는 질문에 "one hundred eighty million years ago"라 서술하였다.

▷ 다음과 같이 서술하였어도 2점을 준다.

"when parts of Laurasia separated from each other"; "North America separated from Europe"

05

하위내용영역	배점	예상정답률
일반영어 B형 서술형	4점	40%

모범답안 It refers to poor people. Second, the research is surprising because it contradicts the assumption that life is less valuable than money to poor people when compared to rich people and that poor people gave more weight to an adult provider's life over a child's. Third, it is implied that donation formulas would instead support children more.

채점기준   _Total 4pts

+ 1점 : 밑줄 친 부분이 가리키는 것을 "poor people"라 서술하였다. "people in need"라 했어도 1점을 준다.

+ 2점 : 연구에서 밝혀진 것이 놀라운 이유를 "because it contradicts the assumption that life is less valuable than money to poor people when compared to rich people and that poor people gave more weight to an adult provider's life over a child's (life)"라 서술하였거나 유사하였다.

+ 1점 : 기부 방식의 변화를 "donation formulas would instead support children more"라 서술하였거나 유사하였다.

06

하위내용영역	배점	예상정답률
일반영어 B형 서술형	4점	25%

모범답안 The word for ① is "speech" and the word for ② is "eyes". Second, Nixon matched Hot media like radio whereas JFK matched Cool media like TV; so Nixon was better at radio whereas JFK at TV.

채점기준   _Total 4pts

+ 1점 : 빈칸에 들어갈 단어를 "speech"라 정확하게 기입하였다. "speaking"이라 했어도 1점을 준다.

+ 1점 : 빈칸에 들어갈 단어를 "eyes"라 정확하게 기입하였다. 이것 외에는 답이 될 수 없다.

+ 2점 : 닉슨 – 케네디 논쟁에 관한 글쓴이의 최근의 생각을 "Nixon matched(=suited; got along with) Hot media like radio whereas JFK matched Cool media like TV; so Nixon was better at radio whereas JFK (was better) at TV"라 서술하였거나 유사하였다.

한글 번역

오디오에는 수많은 정보가 들어 있다. 어조, 억양, 암시, 목소리 흉내내기, 강조, 망설임 등 문자에 비해 훨씬 많은 정보가 전달된다. 오디오는 "내가 말하는 방식만 봐도 당신은 내가 무슨 이야기를 하는지 알거야"라는 말이 성립하는 미디어다. 오디오는 헤드폰과 자동차 라디오를 통해 당신의 귀로 친근하고도 직접적인 방식으로 전달된다. 음악은 오디오에 적절한 콘텐츠지만, 목소리로 전해지는 것은 훨씬 더 위력적이다.

"오늘밤"을 스무 가지 다른 방식으로, 각각이 다른 느낌을 가지도록 말해 보자. 흥미롭게, 만족스럽게, 피곤하게, 달콤하게, 의기소침하게, 짜증나게, 의문스럽게, 주저하듯, 필사적으로 등 끝없이 다양한 방식으로 말할 수 있다. 게다가 상대방은 이를 다 알아듣는다. 이는 이미지나 글자로는 절대 할 수 없는 일이다. 글자로 쓰여진 오늘밤은 그저 오늘밤일 뿐이다. 단순하면서도 아무런 특별한 의미를 가지지 않는다. 우리 눈은 이를 중립적인 정보로 받아들인다. 하지만 귀는 그렇지 않다. 우리의 귀는 놀라운 구별력을 가지고 있다.

어떤 내용을 이야기하든, 오디오는 이를 뜨겁게 만든다. 집주인과 어떤 문제로 다투는 중이라고 가정해 보자. 문자 메시지나 전화로 다툴 수도 있고(차가운, 말을 주고받는), 이메일이나 보이스 메일(뜨거운, 한 번에 모든 내용을 전달하는)로도 가능하다. 문자 메시지는 문제를 차갑게 식히는 반면, 오디오는 해결을 강요한다.

어떤 정보를 오디오 중심의 미디어나 오디오만 존재하는 미디어에 실을 경우, 오디오는 정보를 뜨겁게 데우고 그 내용을 완전하게 전달한다. 문자 메시지나 혼성 미디어를 통해 담담하게, 혹은 모호하게 전달될 수 있는 정보도 오디오를 통합할 경우 그 모호함이 사라진다. 우리가 귀를 통해 그 정보를 들을 때, 우리는 그 진짜 의미가 무엇인지 이해하며, 또 그렇기 때문에 오디오는 핫한 콘텐츠를 추구한다.

닉슨과 케네디의 TV 토론은 매우 유명한 예이며, 나는 오랫동안 이 예를 잘못 이해하고 있었다. 리처드 닉슨과 JFK가 대통령 후보 당시 가졌던 TV 토론에서 라디오로 이 토론을 들었던 사람은 닉슨이 토론에서 이겼다고 생각했지만, TV를 본 사람들은 JFK가 이겼다고 생각했다. 나는 처음 이 이야기를 들었을 때, 이 예화의 핵심이 TV는 라디오보다 "외면"을 더 강조하며, JFK의 잘생긴 얼굴과 매력적인 스타일이 토론 자체보다 더 먹혔지만, 라디오에서는 그렇지 않았다는 뜻으로 이해했다.

하지만, 이제 나는 이런 이해가 완전히 잘못됐다는 것을 알고 있다. 저 예에서 두 사람이 어떤 말을 했느냐는 전혀 중요하지 않다. 내용은 중요치 않다. 중요한 것은 닉슨은 예리하고 꼼꼼한 성격으로 사람들 앞에 수많은 정보를 직접 제시하는, 곧 뜨거운(Hot) 성격의 후보였다. 반면, 케네디는 쿨(Cool)한 후보였는데, (라디오와 같은 핫 미디어에서는 느리고 말이 없으며 무기력한 사람처럼 보였지만,) TV에서는 오히려 여유롭고, 편안하게 자신의 슬로건을 말하는데, 이렇게 함으로써 수많은 해석을 가능하게 하고, 청중들 스스로가 그 해석의 갭을 채우도록 하였다.

07

하위내용영역	배점	예상정답률
일반영어 B형 서술형	4점	40%

모범답안 The form of exchange has evolved over time. Barter trade was the first way of exchange, but had the difficulty of having to find the right partner and dividing goods. This led people to switch over to monetary transactions, using beads, shells and fishing hooks as money at the start, then coins. However, people found carrying coins around troublesome and risky, and thus developed checks with names of the users on them to discourage robbery. In conclusion, along with paper exchange, thanks to technology, there are also credit and cash cards.

채점기준 _Total 4pts

ⓐ Topic sentence

+1점: 글의 topic sentence "The form of exchange has evolved over time"를 명확하게 서술하였다.

ⓑ Major supporting details

+2점: 글의 major supporting details 즉, "① Barter trade was the first way of exchange, but had the difficulty of having to find the right partner and dividing goods. ② This led people to switch over to monetary transactions (using beads, shells and fishing hooks as money at the start, then coins). ③ However, people found carrying coins around troublesome and risky, and thus developed checks (with names of the users on them to discourage robbery)"을 명확하게 서술하였다.

▶ 3개 중 3개 모두 정확하게 요약했으면 2점; 2개를 요약했으면 1점; 나머지는 0점을 준다.

ⓒ Conclusion

+1점: 글의 conclusion "In conclusion, along with paper exchange, thanks to technology, there are also credit and cash cards"을 명확하게 요약하였다.

감점 ♡
- 본문에 나오는 연속되는 6단어 이상을 사용하였다. −0.5pt
- 문단을 두 개나 그 이상으로 구성하였다. −0.5pt
- 문법이나 영어 표현을 합쳐 3개 이상 오류가 있다. −0.5pt

24회 문제은행

📖 본책 p.214

01

하위내용영역	배점	예상정답률
일반영어 A형 서술형	4점	50%

모범답안 First, you should choose logo. Second, the word is "color".

채점기준 _Total 4pts

+ 2점: 회사의 상품을 더 인식시키기 위해 선택해야 할 것을 "logo"라 답하였다. 이것 외에는 답이 될 수 없다.

+ 2점: 빈칸에 들어갈 단어를 "color"라 정확하게 기입하였다. 이것 외에는 답이 될 수 없다.

02

하위내용영역	배점	예상정답률
일반영어 A형 서술형	4점	45%

모범답안 The word is "fragility". Second, it would be unpopular to make such little money, to be appreciated by only a handful of people and to hide one's decoration or awards.

채점기준 _Total 4pts

+ 2점: 빈칸에 들어갈 단어를 "fragility"라 정확하게 기입하였다. 이것 외에는 답이 될 수 없다.

+ 2점: 러시아 수학자들의 삶의 방식이 "인기 없을" 수도 있는 이유를 "it would be unpopular to make such little money, to be appreciated by only a handful of people, and to hide one's decoration (or awards)"이라 서술하였거나 유사하였다.

03

하위내용영역	배점	예상정답률
일반영어 A형 서술형	4점	45%

모범답안 The words are ① "Nunu" ② "Mary". Second, an intuitive reaction might cause a wrong answer because we use a mental shortcut to get an answer instead of rational thinking, such as guessing the wrong number of days to grow lily pads over half the lake by dividing the number to grow over all in half.

채점기준 _Total 4pts

+ 2점: 빈칸에 각각 들어갈 단어를 ① "Nunu" ② "Mary"라 정확하게 기입하였다. 이것 외에는 답이 될 수 없다.

+ 1점: 직관적 반응이 오류일 수 있는 이유를 "because we use a mental shortcut to get an answer (instead of rational thinking = without resorting to(depending on) rational thinking)"라 서술하였거나 유사하였다.

+ 1점: 오류의 예를 글에 있는 4가지 중 하나만 서술하였으면 맞는 것으로 한다.
예를 들어, "guessing the wrong number of days to grow lily pads over half the lake by dividing the number to grow over all in half" 또는 "giving Nunu as a answer following the vowels sounds"

04

하위내용영역	배점	예상정답률
일반영어 A형 서술형	4점	50%

모범답안 The word is "preparation". Second, it can be inferred that beginners can expect to get indigestion from the food.

채점기준 _Total 4pts

+ 2점: 빈칸에 들어갈 단어를 "preparation"라 정확하게 기입하였다. 이것 외에는 답이 될 수 없다.

+ 2점: 초심자에게 소화 불량 약을 가져오는 것이 좋을 거라고 말한 이유를 "beginners can expect to get indigestion (or sick) from the food"라 서술하였거나 유사하였다.

05

하위내용영역	배점	예상정답률
일반영어 A형 서술형	4점	45%

모범답안 The words are ① "collaborators" and ② "flow". Second, the Internet is beautiful because it can aid in facilitating collaboration between people who may have never met.

채점기준 _Total 4pts

+ 2점: 빈칸에 들어갈 단어를 각각 ① "collaborators" ② "flow"라 정확하게 기입하였다. 이것 외에는 답이 될 수 없다.

+ 2점: 인터넷의 장점을 "<u>because it can aid in (facilitating) collaboration between people who may have never met</u>"이라 서술하였거나 유사하였다.

06

하위내용영역	배점	예상정답률
일반영어 A형 서술형	4점	45%

모범답안 The word is "neocortex". Second, pigeons can differentiate between Picasso and Monet. Third, it can be inferred that the underlined understanding, discrete collections of neurons, is outdated and birds' brains have a function equivalent to mammals.

채점기준 _Total 4pts

+ 1점: 빈칸에 들어갈 단어를 "neocortex"라 정확하게 기입하였다. 이것 외에는 답이 될 수 없다.

+ 1점: 새의 높은 수준의 행위 및 역량의 예를 "<u>pigeons can differentiate between Picasso and Monet</u>"라 서술하였거나 유사하였다. "<u>Ravens identify themselves in front of a mirror</u>" 또는 "<u>Crows leave walnuts in crosswalks to be opened</u>"라 했어도 1점을 준다.

+ 2점: 밑줄 친 부분에 대해서 새로운 연구로부터 추론할 수 있는 것을 "<u>the underlined understanding, discrete collections of neurons, is outdated and birds' brains have a function equivalent to mammals</u>"라 서술하였거나 유사하였다.

07

하위내용영역	배점	예상정답률
일반영어 B형 서술형	4점	45%

모범답안 Transportation modes have changed and improved over time. First, horses and camels were used to move people and goods. Later, railways were developed and allowed for more commerce and commuting to work. Afterward, motor vehicles outshone the railways with their greater flexibility and ability to reach remote areas. In conclusion, human beings will continue to innovate modes of travel as shown in the various types of boats and airplanes.

채점기준 _Total 4pts

ⓐ Topic sentence

+ 1점: 글의 topic sentence "<u>Transportation modes have (changed and) improved over time</u>"를 명확하게 서술하였거나 유사하였다.
  ▷ 또는 다음과 같이 서술하였다.
   "<u>The means of transportation have changed over many centuries(=over time)</u>"

ⓑ Major supporting details

+ 2점: 글의 major supporting details 즉, "① <u>First, horses and camels were used to move people and goods</u>. ② <u>Later, railways were developed and allowed for more commerce and commuting to work</u>. ③ <u>Afterward, motor vehicles outshone the railways with their greater flexibility and ability to reach remote areas</u>"을 명확하게 서술하였다.
  ▷ 3개 중 3개 모두 정확하게 요약했으면 2점; 2개를 요약했으면 1점; 나머지는 0점을 준다.

ⓒ Conclusion

+ 1점: 글의 conclusion "In conclusion, <u>human beings will continue to innovate modes of travel as shown in the various types of boats and airplanes</u>"을 명확하게 요약하였다.

감점 ♥

• 본문에 나오는 연속되는 6단어 이상을 사용하였다. −0.5pt
• 문단을 두 개나 그 이상으로 구성하였다. −0.5pt
• 문법이나 영어 표현을 합쳐 3개 이상 오류가 있다. −0.5pt

25 회 문제은행

📖 본책 p.228

01

하위내용영역	배점	예상정답률
일반영어 A형 서술형	4점	45%

모범답안 The container model has been applied to more detrimental lengths as in India where prenatal practices have treated the mother/container with dehumanizing prenatal care practices as disposable. Second, the word is "gestator".

채점기준   _Total 4pts

+ 2점: "The container model has been applied to more detrimental lengths <u>as in India where prenatal practices have treated the mother/container (with dehumanizing prenatal care practices) as disposable</u>"라 서술하였거나 유사하였다.

+ 2점: 빈칸에 들어갈 단어를 "gestator"라 정확하게 기입하였다. 이것 외에는 답이 될 수 없다.

한글 번역 ▓▓▓▓▓▓▓▓▓▓▓▓▓▓▓▓▓▓▓▓▓▓▓▓▓

사상가 로렌 윤은 현재 서구에서 논의되고 있는 임신에 대한 두 가지 주요 형이상학적 모델에 대해 이야기한다. 첫째 이른바 "부분 모델"이라는 것으로, 태아가 임부의 팔, 다리, 신장과 같은 식으로 임부의 일부라는 시각이다. 둘째 "컨테이너 모델"은 임부와 태아를 각각 독립된 개체로 보며, "태아를 담고 있는 엄마"라는 문화적으로 지배적인 시각으로 이어진다. 이러한 시각을 바탕으로 우리는 "오븐 안에서 구워지고 있는 빵"과 같은 비유에 이르고, 태아를 자궁 내벽에 붙어 있는 존재로 상상하기보다는 어두운 공간에서 떠다니는 우주 비행사와 같은 존재로 그리게 되는 것이다.
"컨테이너 모델"의 일상적인 활용은 해롭지 않지만, 그 모델의 확장은 보다 해로운 방향으로 이루어지기도 한다. 사회학자 암리타 팬디는 2010년 인도의 (그 이후) 금지된 상업적 대리모 산업에 대한 연구 결과를 발표했는데, 임부와 태아가 별개라는 개념은 대리모 업체들의 비인간적인 산전 케어 관행으로 이어졌다는 것이다. 형이상학적 개념 자체는 도덕적으로 중립일지 몰라도, 그것이 문화적으로 발현되는 모습을 살펴보면 가부장적 맥락에서 활용되고 있는 것이다.

재생산을 둘러싼 특정 관행의 타당성은 우리가 그 과정을 이해하기 위해 어떤 개념적 틀을 사용하는가에 달려있다. 인공 자궁을 활용해 임신의 일부, 또는 전 과정을 대체하겠다는 아이디어는 그 자체로 태아와 임부가 분리가능한 존재라는 것을 전제로 하고 있다. 인공 자궁 기술이 반드시 컨테이너 모델을 수반하는 것은 아니지만, 현재 진행 중인 담론의 수사는 그와 같은 시각을 적극 반영하고 있다. 예를 들어, 자궁을 생식사회학자인 로저 고스던이 명명한 "영리한 인큐베이터"로 비유하는 것 등이 그것이다. 여성학자 이리나 아리스타르코바는 인공 자궁 기술의 타당성에 대한 논의가 "말이 되는 컨셉" 차원이 아닌 조금 더 복잡한 논의가 되도록 하는 대안적 시각을 제안한다. 짐작하건대 태아를 임부의 일부로 이해한다면, 인공 자궁이 그 역할을 진정 만족시킬 가능성은 제한적이다. 물론 역학과 기계의 영역까지 확대된 전혀 새로운 태아–임부 관계를 받아들일 수도 있을 것이다. 하지만 우리가 태아와 임부 간의 실질적인 불가분성이라는 임신의 생물학적 현실을 받아들이고자 한다면 기계로서의 우리 미래는 우리가 언젠가는 반드시 마주하게 될 것이다.

02

하위내용영역	배점	예상정답률
일반영어 A형 서술형	4점	65%

모범답안 Ms. Clark's expectation was subverted when the after school program had active participation and wasn't used to keep students busy. Second, Mr. Stein believes that the Ms. Sutter's students will be unlikely to be able to attend the renowned university.

채점기준   _Total 4pts

+ 2점: 교사 클락의 기대가 어떤 식으로 전복되었는가에 대해 "<u>the after school program had active participation</u> (and wasn't used to keep students busy)"라 서술하였거나 유사하였다.

+ 2점: 스테인이 가지고 있는 밑에 깔려 있는(근본적인) 편견에 찬 전제를 "<u>Ms. Sutter's students will be unlikely to be able to attend the renowned university</u>(＝Mr. Stein's school)"라 서술하였거나 유사하였다.

03

하위내용영역	배점	예상정답률
일반영어 A형 서술형	4점	50%

모범답안 He didn't believe the invitation to be real at first. Second, it can be inferred they were attracted by to a new type of tough-guy hero and prose, along with unlimited amounts of violence, sexual intrigue, and moral devastation.

채점기준   _Total 4pts

+ 2점 : 밑줄 친 부분의 의미를 "He didn't believe the invitation to be real at first"라 서술하였거나 유사하였다. 또는 "He first believed the invitation was a prank and unreal"라 서술하였다.

+ 2점 : 해밋의 독자가 (그의 작품에서) 가장 끌린 것을 "a new type of tough-guy hero and prose, along with unlimited amounts of violence, sexual intrigue, and moral devastation"라 서술하였거나 유사하였다.

04

하위내용영역	배점	예상정답률
일반영어 B형 서술형	4점	40%

모범답안 It is surprising that neuroscientists are more likely to falsely claim casual relationships without testing than expected, which is usually what psychologists are accused of. Second, "correlation".

채점기준   _Total 4pts

+ 2점 : 밑줄 친 "놀람"의 이유를 "neuroscientists are more likely to falsely claim casual relationships without testing than expected, which is usually what psychologists are accused of"라 서술하였거나 유사하였다.

+ 2점 : 음악 연습과 기량 증진 사이의 관계에 대한 Jancke의 의견을 묘사한 한 단어를 "correlation" 또는 "correlational"이라 서술하였다. 이것 외에는 답이 될 수 없다.

05

하위내용영역	배점	예상정답률
일반영어 B형 서술형	4점	45%

모범답안 The one word is "oligopolies". Second, the misunderstanding of the American Right of European policy is that they believe Europe to be a socialistic nightmare without growth nor innovation. Third, "competition" is the most important characteristic.

채점기준   _Total 4pts

+ 1점 : 빈칸에 들어갈 단어를 "oligopolies"라 정확하게 기입하였다. 이것 외에는 답이 될 수 없다.

+ 2점 : 미국의 우파에 관련해서 "무지"가 의미하는 것을 "they believe Europe to be a socialistic nightmare without growth nor innovation"라 서술하였거나 유사하였다.

+ 1점 : 저자가 생각하는 자유 시장에서 가장 중요한 특징이라 추론할 수 있는 것을 "competition"라 서술하였거나 유사하였다. "no oligopolies"라 했으면, 0.5점을 준다.

06

하위내용영역	배점	예상정답률
일반영어 B형 서술형	4점	45%

모범답안 The three words are "fish body size" and one word is "ecology". Second, the reasons salmon size may be smaller are climate change, competition with hatchery-raised and wild salmon, and salmon coming from the sea at an earlier age.

채점기준   _Total 4pts

+ 2점 : 빈칸에 들어갈 단어를 "fish body size(1점)" and "ecology(1점)"라 정확하게 기입하였다.

+ 2점 : 연어 크기가 작아지는 것 같은 이유를 "climate change, competition with hatchery-raised and wild salmon, and salmon coming from the sea at an earlier age"라 정확하게 서술하였다.

07

하위내용영역	배점	예상정답률
일반영어 B형 서술형	4점	35%

모범답안 The ubiquity of advertisements has benefits and concerns. There are two types of advertisements : informative, which provides consumers information about the products or services and persuasive, which persuades us to buy them by claiming the superiority of their products. On the other hand, they sometimes cover up product flaws. In addition, consumers may get confused over buying decisions when too many advertisements are present and advertising raises the production costs and thus products' prices. In conclusion, due to these circumstances, we can benefit from advertisements but must control how we live with them.

채점기준 _Total 4pts

ⓐ Topic sentence

⁺1점: 글의 topic sentence "The ubiquity of advertisements has benefits and concerns"를 명확하게 서술하였다. 또는 "Advertisements have benefits and drawbacks"라 서술하였다.

ⓑ Major supporting details

⁺2점: 글의 major supporting details 즉, "There are two types of advertisements : informative, which provides consumers information about the products or services and persuasive, which persuades us to buy them by claiming the superiority of their products. On the other hand, they sometimes cover up product flaws. In addition, consumers may get confused over buying decisions when too many advertisements are present and advertising raises the production costs and thus products' prices"을 명확하게 서술하였다.

ⓒ Conclusion

⁺1점: 글의 conclusion "In conclusion, due to these circumstances, we can benefit from advertisements but must control how we live with them"을 정확하게 서술하였거나 유사하였다.

감점 ☑

· 본문에 나오는 연속되는 6단어 이상을 사용하였다. −0.5pt
· 문단을 두 개나 그 이상으로 구성하였다. −0.5pt
· 문법이나 영어 표현을 합쳐 3개 이상 오류가 있다. −0.5pt

26 회 문제은행

📖 본책 p.242

01

하위내용영역	배점	예상정답률
일반영어 A형 서술형	4점	50%

모범답안 The First World War marked the transition from Art Nouveau to Functionalism. Second, the word is "glass".

채점기준 _Total 4pts

+ 2점 : 아르누보에서 기능주의로의 이행을 이끈 역사적 사건을 "The First World War"라 서술하였거나 유사하였다.

+ 2점 : 빈칸에 들어갈 단어를 "glass"라 서술하였거나 유사하였다.

02

하위내용영역	배점	예상정답률
일반영어 A형 서술형	4점	50%

모범답안 The word is "evolutionary biologist". Second, de-platforming is trying to get a speech canceled or to disrupt it aggressively and two examples are boisterous campaigns to get a speaking invitation canceled and disrupting the speaker by screaming and shouting.

채점기준 _Total 4pts

+ 2점 : 빈칸에 들어갈 단어를 "evolutionary biologist"라 서술하였거나 유사하였다. 이것 외에는 답이 될 수 없다.

+ 1점 : "de-platforming"이 "trying to get the speech canceled or to disrupt it(＝the speech) aggressively"라 정확하게 서술하였거나 유사하였다.

+ 1점 : "de-platforming"의 구체적 예를, 다음의 6가지 가운데 2가지를 선택해 정확하게 서술하였다.
  • boisterous(＝rowdy) campaigns to get a speaking invitation canceled(＝rescinded)
  • disrupting the speaker by screaming and shouting
  • engaging noise makers
  • pulling the fire alarm
  • keeping(＝preventing) the speaker from airing her views
  • depriving a person of her tenure or her doctorate

03

하위내용영역	배점	예상정답률
일반영어 A형 서술형	4점	45%

모범답안 It has improved by allowing more ways to be admired besides only beauty such as sports, careers, art and public life. Second, to fulfill this "loyalty" one would have to refrain from using new inventions or products.

채점기준 _Total 4pts

+ 2점 : 여성들에게 나이 들어가는 경험이 어떻게 향상되는지에 대해 "by allowing more ways to be admired besides only beauty (such as sports, careers, art and public life)"라 서술하였거나 유사하였다.

+ 2점 : 밑줄 친 "충성심"을 충족시키기 위해 취해야 될 것이 무엇이냐는 질문에 "one would have to refrain(＝abstain) from using new inventions or products"라 서술하였거나 유사하였다.

04

하위내용영역	배점	예상정답률
일반영어 A형 서술형	4점	50%

모범답안 The word is "death". Second, wars would cease to exist. Third, the writer mentions a "fisherman" to illustrate an example of someone dedicated to a stable mindset such as would be required for the long span of time to travel to another star.

채점기준 ⸻⸻⸻⸻ _ Total 4pts

+ 1점 : 빈칸에 들어갈 단어를 "death"라 서술하였다. 이것 외에는 답이 될 수 없다.

+ 1점 : 만일 글의 전제가 실현된다면 전쟁에는 무슨 일이 일어날까라는 질문에 "wars would cease to exist (or end completely)"라 서술하였거나 유사하였다.

+ 2점 : 저자가 "어부"를 언급한 이유를 "to illustrate (=show) an example of someone dedicated to a stable mindset such as would be required for the long span of time to travel to another star"라 서술하였거나 유사하였다.

05

하위내용영역	배점	예상정답률
일반영어 A형 서술형	4점	40%

모범답안 The word for ① is "mathematics" and ② is "fact". Second, it is because they loved theory.

채점기준 ⸻⸻⸻⸻ _ Total 4pts

+ 2점 : 빈칸에 들어갈 단어를 각각 ① "mathematics (1점)"와 ② "fact(1점)"라 기입하였다. 이것 외에는 답이 될 수 없다.

+ 2점 : 고대 그리스인들이 수학 이론의 발전에 중요한 역할을 할 수 있었던 근본적 이유를 "because they loved theory"라 서술하였거나 유사하였다.

한글 번역 ⫿⫿⫿⫿⫿⫿⫿⫿⫿⫿⫿⫿⫿⫿⫿⫿⫿⫿⫿⫿

자, 수학의 초기 단계를 한번 생각해 보자. 기원전 2천년경의 이집트에서 출현했던 몇 개의 기술적으로 (별 것 아닌) 방안이었던 수학! 그 수학은 당대의 이집트라는 위대한 문명의 스케일에 있어서 아주 사소한 요소였다. 그런데 기원전 5백년경 그리스인들은 순수한 이론 그 자체에 대한 사랑 때문에 수학의 이론적 발전을 선취하기 시작했다(주도적으로 시작했다). 이것은 인간에게 현시된 가장 위대한 예언이었던 솔로몬의 꿈이 나타난지 4~5백년 후의 사건이었다. 그리스인들의 천재성은 자연의 연구를 위해 수학의 중요성을 명료하게 예측해 낸 선견지명으로 과시되는 것이다. 추상적 형태학의 발전을 촉진시키는 것에 대한 필요성은 16세기가 시작될 즈음 기하학이라는 과학의 상태를 고찰하면 잘 예증된다. 이 기하학은 2천년 동안이나 열심히 연구돼 왔다. 그리고 아주 세부적인 데까지 정교하게 다듬어져 왔다. 하지만 약간의 사소한 예외를 인정한다면, 아무것도 그 학문의 내재적 관심 외의 것은 기하학으로부터 생겨난 것이 없었다. 그러던 것이 갑자기 대문이 활짝 열린 듯이, 케플러가 원추곡선의 수백 가지 이용법 가운데 최초의 중요한 이용법을 제시했고, 데카르트와 데자르그(1591~1661 프랑스의 수학자)는 과학의 방법들을 혁신시켰으며, 뉴톤은 〈프리키피아〉를 저술했고, 이리하여 봇물 터지듯 문명의 근대기가 발동되기 시작했다. 2천년 동안 서서히 축적돼 온 추상적 관념의 자본 없이는, 우리가 살고 있는 근대적 삶이라고 하는 것이 불가능했을 것이다. 수학이라고 하는 것, 그것 자체로 그 어떤 마술적인 것이라곤 아무것도 없다. 수학은 추상적 형식으로 된 과학의 가장 위대한 표본일 뿐이다. 추상적 음악 이론도 그러한 추상적 과학의 좋은 본보기이다. 정치 경제학의 추상적 이론과 통화의 추상적 이론도 그렇다. 이들에게 공통된 요점은 바로 추상적 이론의 발전이 사실의 이해에 선행한다는 것이다. 정치 경제학의 예는 중요한 점을 보여준다. 정치 경제학은 그 속성상 추상화시킨 인간만을 대상으로 삼는다. 즉 정치 경제학은 그 관점을 "경제적 인간"이라고 하는 전제에 국한시키는 것이다. 그리고 그것은 많은 중요한 인간적 요소를 외면한 채, 시장과 경쟁에 관한 가설을 세우고 있다. 바로 여기에 우리는 주어진 형태론적 도식을 초월해야만(넘어서야만) 하는 필요성의 한 전형을 발견한다. 어느 정도까지는 이 도식은 매우 소중한 것이다. 그것은 우리의 사유를 명료히 하고, 관찰을 암시하며, 사실을 설명한다. 하지만 그 어떠한 유한한 도식이든지 그 유용성에는 엄격한 한계가 있다. 그 도식이 그것의 적합한 범위를 넘어서서 적용될 때에는 반드시 오류가 필연적으로 발생하게 된다.

06

하위내용영역	배점	예상정답률
일반영어 A형 서술형	4점	50%

모범답안 Joris Lammers proves that untrustworthy and hypocritical behavior comes from having a higher relative feeling of power, not only from wealth. Second, the words are higher status.

채점기준   _ Total 4pts

+ 2점 : 조리스가 증명한 것을 "untrustworthy and hypocritical behavior comes from having a higher relative feeling of power (or status), not only from wealth"라 서술하였거나 유사하였다.

+ 2점 : 빈칸에 들어갈 단어를 "higher status"라 기입하였다. 이것 외에는 답이 될 수 없다.

07

하위내용영역	배점	예상정답률
일반영어 B형 서술형	4점	50%

모범답안 Television has advantages and disadvantages. Children can learn language faster and have clearer pronunciation due to the exposure of language on television programs. In addition, in a family where both the parents are working, the television provides the family an opportunity to get together at leisure times. However, the decline in reading it causes is detrimental to children's writing ability, thinking capacities, and analyzing ability. In conclusion, a controlled balance in television viewing is the best solution for children.

채점기준   _ Total 4pts

ⓐ Topic sentence

+ 1점 : 글의 topic sentence "Television has advantages and disadvantages"를 명확하게 서술하였다.

ⓑ Major supporting details

+ 2점 : 글의 major supporting details 즉, "① Children can learn language faster and have clearer pronunciation due to the exposure of language on television programs. ② In addition, in a family where both the parents are working, the television provides the family an opportunity to get together at leisure times. ③ However, the decline in reading it causes is detrimental to children's writing ability, thinking capacities, and analyzing ability"을 명확하게 서술하였다.

▷ 3개 중 3개 모두 정확하게 요약했으면 2점; 2개만 요약했으면 1점; 나머지는 0점을 준다.

ⓒ Conclusion

+ 1점 : 글의 conclusion "In conclusion, a controlled balance in television viewing is the best solution for children"을 정확하게 요약하였다.

감점 ✓

• 본문에 나오는 연속되는 6단어 이상을 사용하였다. −0.5pt
• 문단을 두 개나 그 이상으로 구성하였다. −0.5pt
• 문법이나 영어 표현을 합쳐 3개 이상 오류가 있다. −0.5pt

27회 문제은행

📖 본책 p.256

01

하위내용영역	배점	예상정답률
일반영어 A형 서술형	4점	55%

모범답안 The word is "lack". Second, it is because vitamin A, which human body cannot create, is required from outside sources and crucial for good health and fitness.

채점기준   _Total 4pts

+ 2점: 빈칸에 들어갈 단어를 "lack"이라 정확하게 기입하였다. 이것 외에는 답이 될 수 없다.

+ 2점: 균형 잡힌 식습관이 사람에게 중요한 이유를 "(a well-balanced diet is important) because vitamin A, which human body cannot create, is required from outside sources (and crucial for good health and fitness)"라 서술하였거나 유사하였다.

02

하위내용영역	배점	예상정답률
일반영어 A형 서술형	4점	55%

모범답안 The word is "maritime". Second, they used smokehouses to preserve fish in a rainy climate where sun-drying wasn't convenient.

채점기준   _Total 4pts

+ 2점: 빈칸에 들어갈 단어를 "maritime"라 정확하게 기입하였다. 이것 외에는 답이 될 수 없다.

+ 2점: 북미 원주민들이 훈제실을 사용한 이유를 "to preserve fish in a rainy climate where sun-drying wasn't convenient"라 서술하였거나 유사하였다.

03

하위내용영역	배점	예상정답률
일반영어 A형 서술형	4점	40%

모범답안 The reason is to give an example of a disaster caused by an uncertain disease(a plague) in the Before Time. Second, it is "superforecasters".

채점기준   _Total 4pts

+ 2점: 스타트렉을 인용한 이유를 "to give an example of a disaster caused by an uncertain disease(a plague) in the Before Time"이라 서술하였거나 유사하였다.

+ 2점: "견자"의 역할에 대한 가장 최근의 용어를 "superforecasters"라 서술하였다. 이것 외에는 답이 될 수 없다.

한글 번역

글을 쓰고 있는 2020년 여름, 나는 가끔 이 세상이 마치 허먼 멜빌(모비딕의 작가)이 묘사한 소설 속 세상이 아닌가 생각한다.

"미친 에이허브(선장)에게 흰 고래 모비딕은 모든 광기와 고통, 사물의 이면을 자극하는 것, 악의를 품고 있는 진실, 힘줄이 끊어지고 뇌가 구워지는 것, 삶과 생각에 존재하는 모든 미묘한 악, 그리고 순수한 악이 구체화, 의인화된 존재였으며 그럼에도 실제로 공격 가능한 대상이었다. 그는 고래의 등에 인류가 아담 이래 느껴 온 모든 분노와 증오를 쌓았으며, 마치 자신을 폭탄처럼 사용해 그의 뜨거운 심장을 그 위에 터뜨렸다."

중환자실에서 코비드 19로 마지막 숨을 내쉬고 있는 가족에게 마지막 인사조차 할 수 없는 상황에서 누가 광기와 고통을 느끼지 않을까? 몇 달씩이나 고립돼 자신의 생각과 주장이 입막음을 당하고 사회적 활동에 제약을 당하는 상황에서 누가 힘줄이 끊어지고 뇌가 구워지는 경험을 하지 않을까?

우리가 먼 미래를 예상할수록 시야는 점점 더 흐려지고 불확실성의 안개는 짙어진다. 2030년에 2020년은 어떤 의미를 가질까? 30년 뒤인 2050년에는? 백년 뒤인 2120년에는? 베이지안 추론과 빅 데이터 분석을 훈련받은 초예측자들이라 하더라도 5년 이상의 미래에 대해서는 그저 동전을 던지는 것 이상을 예측하지 못한다.

1966년 방영된 스타트렉의 "미리" 에피소드에서 아직 어린 소녀인 주인공 미리는 당황한 커크 선장에게 자신의 행성에서 모든 어른들은 죽었으며, 아이들만 남았다고 말한다. "전시대(Before Time)에 어른들은 아프기 시작했어요. 우리는 숨었고, 그들은 모두 죽었어요." 전시대의 어원을 추적한 언어학자 벤 짐머는 이 단어가 종종 전염병이 돌기 전의 세상을 가리키며 킹제임스 버전의 사무엘서에 나올 정도로 오래된 단어라고 말한다. "전시대 이스라엘에서는 하나님에게 물어볼 것이 있을 때 견자(seer)가 직접 가서 물었고, 우리는 그에게 들었다. 오늘날 예언자라 불리는 이들을 이전에는 견자라 불렀다." 〈아틀란틱〉의 칼럼니스트 마리나 코렌은 코비드 19가 이 오래된 용어를 되살렸다고 말한다. "코로나 바이러스가 전국을 휩쓸기 전의 세상에 대한 그리움이 사람들이 '전시대(Before Time)'라 부르는 그 시기를 마치 오래된 과거처럼 느끼게 만든다."

04

하위내용영역	배점	예상정답률
일반영어 A형 서술형	4점	40%

모범답안 The words are "quantitative vocabulary". Second, the implication is that physical science lacks the qualitative language to address to explain consciousness.

채점기준 _Total 4pts

+ 2점: 빈칸에 들어갈 단어를 "quantitative vocabulary"라 정확하게 기입하였다.

+ 2점: 밑줄 친 부분의 함축 의미를 "physical science (or mathematics) lacks the qualitative language to address to explain consciousness"라 서술하였거나 유사하였다.

한글 번역

뇌에 대한 과학적 이해는 크게 발전했지만, 우리는 여전히 복잡한 전기 화학적 신호가 어떻게 색깔, 소리, 냄새, 맛 등 자신만이 아는 주관적 세상을 만들어 내는지에 대해서 전혀 설명하지 못하고 있다. 과학이 말하는 외면의 물질과 내면에서 바라보는 자신을 어떻게 연결시킬 것인가의 문제는 아직도 전적으로 미지의 문제이다.

이 문제에 대해 많은 이들은 우리가 뇌를 연구하던 기존의 방법을 그대로 적용하면 해결될 수 있다고 생각하는 경향이 있다. 하지만 나는 의식의 문제는 우리가 과학 혁명을 시작하던 당시 과학을 설계했던 바로 그 방식 때문에 생긴 문제라고 주장한다.

과학 혁명의 가장 중요한 순간은 갈릴레오가 새로운 과학의 도구로 수학을 택했던 것이다. 곧, 새로운 과학은 순수하게 양(quantity)적인 언어로 기술돼야 했다. 하지만 갈릴레오는 의식을 이런 방식으로는 설명할 수 없다는 것을 잘 알고 있었다. 의식은 전적으로 질(quality)과 관련된 현상이기 때문이다. 붉은색에 대한 경험이나 꽃의 향기, 민트의 맛 등을 생각해 보자. 이런 질적 느낌은 물리학이 사용하는 양적 언어로는 설명할 수 없다. 즉, 갈릴레오는 의식을 과학의 외부에 두기로 결정한 것이다. 그 결정 이후, 의식을 제외한 모든 것은 수학으로 기술될 수 있었다.

이 부분은 매우 중요하다. 왜냐하면, 많은 이들이 의식의 문제를 진지하게 생각하면서도, 기존의 과학적 방법으로 이 문제를 풀 수 있다고 생각하기 때문이다. 그 이유는 물론 물리학이 그 방법으로 우리 우주를 설명하는 데 매우 성공적이었기 때문이고, 따라서 언젠가는 이 방법으로 우리의 의식조차도 설명할 수 있을 것이라는 확신을 가지게 되었기 때문이다. 하지만 나는 이러한 생각이 과학의 역사에 대한 잘못된 이해에서 출발했다고 생각한다. 물론 물리학은 믿을 수 없을 만큼 성공적이었다. 하지만 그 성공은 처음부터 의식의 문제를 제외했기 때문이다. 만약 갈릴레오가 타임머신을 타고 이 시대로 와서 물리학을 이용해 의식을 설명하려는 이들을 본다면 이렇게 말할 것이다. "음, 그건 안 될 거예요. 나는 질이 아닌 양을 다루도록 과학을 설계했거든요."

05

하위내용영역	배점	예상정답률
일반영어 A형 서술형	4점	45%

모범답안 The words are "appraisal stage". Second, the strategy is situation modification.

채점기준 _Total 4pts

+ 2점: 빈칸에 들어갈 단어를 "appraisal stage"라 정확하게 기입하였다.

+ 2점: 공부하는 동안 스마트폰을 다른 방에 놓는 것의 가장 적절한 전략을 "situation modification"라 서술하였다.

한글 번역

힘든 한 주를 보내고 이제 쿠키를 마음껏 먹으려는 순간, 당신은 쿠키의 유혹을 견뎌야 하는 상황 단계에 진입한다. 다음 단계는 쿠키에 관심을 가지게 되는 주의 단계이다. 그리고 쿠키가 우유 한 잔과 함께라면 얼마나 맛있을지를 생각하는 평가 단계를 가지게 되며, 마지막으로 규칙을 깨고 모든 쿠키를 다 먹게 되는 반응 단계에 이르게 된다. 거칠게 말하자면, 쿠키의 유혹에 넘어가기 위해서는 이 모든 단계에서 당신은 잘못된 선택을 해야 한다. 좋은 소식은 당신이 최종 단계에서 억지 자제력(또는 '의지력')을 사용하지 않을 수 있도록 그 앞의 여러 단계에서 자제력을 발휘할 수 있다. 먼저 상황 단계에서부터 시작해 보자. 상황의 힘을 이해하기 위해 복잡한 사회 심리학을 다 알 필요는 없다. 대부분의 선생님들은 앞자리에 앉은 학생들이 집중을 더 잘한다는 것을 알고 있다. 예를 들어, 쿠키 상자 앞에 앉아 있으면서 쿠키를 먹지 않기 위해 참기보다는 처음부터 쿠키를 사지 않거나(이는 '상황 선택'이라 불린다) 그저 쿠키를 찬장에 넣는 (혹은 쓰레기통에 던지는) '상황 변화' 전략을 쓸 수 있다. 이러한 상황 전략이 매우 유용하다는 것을 보이는 연구들이 있다. 예를 들어, 스마트폰을 눈앞에서 치우라는 지시를 받은 고등학생들은 그저 억지 자제력을 발휘해 스마트폰을 사용하지 못하게 된 고등학생들에 비해 더 좋은 점수를 받았다. 다이어트 연구에서도 고칼로리 음식이 보이는 상황을 그저 피하도록 한 방법이 효과가 있었다. 예를 들어 마트에서 음식을 살 때 빵 코너 앞을 지나가지 않는 것이다. 이를 통해 빵의 유혹을 강력하게 만드는 향긋한 냄새와 먹음직한 모양이라는 신호를 피할 수 있었던 것이다. 곧, "눈에서 멀어지면 마음에서도 멀어진다."는 것이다. 상황 전략을 사용하지 못할 때에는 어떻게 해야 할까? 때로는 어쩔 수 없이 빵 코너 앞을 지나가야 하거나, 아니면 쿠키를 버릴 경우 아이가 화를 낼 것 같을 때가 있다. 다행히, 이렇게 상황을 제어할 수 없는 경우라 하더라도 주의 단계와 평가 단계에서 쓸 수 있는 "심리적 전략"이 있다.

06

하위내용영역	배점	예상정답률
일반영어 A형 서술형	4점	50%

모범답안 The word is "performance". Second, the characteristics are the listener's receptiveness, interest or sympathy.

채점기준
_Total 4pts

+ 2점 : 빈칸에 들어갈 단어를 "performance"라 정확하게 기입하였다.

+ 2점 : 화자가 발표를 할 때 가장 영향을 주는 청자의 특성들을 "the listener's receptiveness, interest or sympathy"라 서술하였거나 유사하였다.

07

하위내용영역	배점	예상정답률
일반영어 B형 서술형	4점	50%

모범답안 Writing tools have evolved over time. The first writing tools used primitive techniques such as reed pens, clay tablets, animal skins and flattened papaya. Later, in the 1880s, fountain pens were created which held their ink inside, though sometimes the tips broke and ink leaked onto writers' hands. Thus, ball point pens were invented to improve on this problem. In conclusion, at present, writing tools are not likely to develop because the Internet and social media has made them inessential.

채점기준
_Total 4pts

ⓐ Topic sentence

+ 1점 : 글의 topic sentence "Writing tools have evolved(=changed and improved) over time (=over a period of time)"를 명확하게 서술하였다. "The evolution of writing tool has come a long way up to the current era"이라 했어도 1점을 준다.

ⓑ Major supporting details

+ 2점 : 글의 major supporting details 즉, "① The first writing tools used primitive techniques such as clay tablets, animal skins and flattened papaya. ② Later, in the 1880s, fountain pens were created which held their ink inside, though sometimes the tips broke and ink leaked onto writers' hands. ③ Thus, ball point pens were invented to improve on this problem"을 명확하게 서술하였다.

▷ 3개 중 3개 모두 정확하게 요약했으면 2점; 2개만 요약했으면 1점; 나머지는 0점을 준다.

ⓒ Conclusion

+ 1점 : 글의 conclusion "In conclusion, at present, writing tools are not likely to develop because the Internet and social media has made them inessential(=unnecessary)"을 정확하게 요약하였다.

감점 ♥

• 본문에 나오는 연속되는 6단어 이상을 사용하였다. −0.5pt
• 문단을 두 개나 그 이상으로 구성하였다. −0.5pt
• 문법이나 영어 표현을 합쳐 3개 이상 오류가 있다. −0.5pt

28회 문제은행

📖 본책 p.270

01

하위내용영역	배점	예상정답률
일반영어 A형 서술형	4점	50%

모범답안 The underlined part means that economists haven't usually been the ones to encourage the humanities as fields of study, but are recommending this now. The word is "stories".

채점기준   _Total 4pts

+ 2점: 밑줄 친 부분의 의미를 "economists haven't usually been the ones to encourage the humanities as fields of study, but are recommending this now"라 서술하였거나 유사하였다.
+ 2점: 빈칸에 들어갈 단어를 "stories"라 정확하게 기입하였다. 이것 외에는 답이 될 수 없다.

02

하위내용영역	배점	예상정답률
일반영어 A형 서술형	4점	50%

모범답안 The words are "communication failure". Second, the difference occurs because the writer has a commonality with the culture producing the works as opposed to the Chinese critic, who does not have a commonality.

채점기준   _Total 4pts

+ 2점: 빈칸에 들어갈 단어를 "communication failure"라 정확하게 기입하였다. 이것 외에는 답이 될 수 없다.
+ 2점: 중국 비평가와 글쓴이 사이에서 차이가 발생하는 이유를 "because the writer has a commonality with the culture producing the works as opposed to the Chinese critic(, who does not have a commonality with the culture producing the works)"라 서술하였거나 유사하였다.
  ▷ 둘 사이의 문화의 차이에서 기인한다는 의미가 들어가 있으면 2점을 준다.

03

하위내용영역	배점	예상정답률
일반영어 A형 서술형	4점	45%

모범답안 The Tuskegee experiment put extra burden on black physicians because of the deceptive nature of that experiment that was conducted on black patients and harmed the trust in the black community toward doctors. Second, the word is "history".

채점기준   _Total 4pts

+ 1점: 터스키기 실험이 최근에 큰 부담을 드리우는 사람을 "black physicians"라 서술하였다.
+ 1점: 이유를 "because of the deceptive nature of that experiment that was conducted on black patients and harmed the trust in the black community toward doctors"라 서술하였거나 유사하였다.
+ 2점: 빈칸에 들어갈 단어를 "history"라 정확하게 기입하였다. 이것 외에는 답이 될 수 없다.

04

하위내용영역	배점	예상정답률
일반영어 A형 서술형	4점	45%

모범답안 The two rules are that it should be a long study of several years and it should be conducted closely within the community being studied. Second, the word is "intimacy".

채점기준   _Total 4pts

+ 2점: 두 개의 규칙을 "it should be a long study of several years and it should be conducted closely within the community being studied"라 서술하였거나 유사하였다. 또는 "unlimited time and ties of intimacy"라고 했어도 2점을 준다.
+ 2점: 상응하는 한 단어를 "intimacy"이라 정확하게 기입하였다. 이것 외에는 답이 될 수 없다.

05

하위내용영역	배점	예상정답률
일반영어 B형 서술형	4점	45%

모범답안 The new discovery suggests there can be life on Venus. Second, "Venus". Third, "phosphine".

채점기준 _Total 4pts

+ 2점 : 새로운 발견이 시사하는 바를 "there can be life on Venus"라 서술하였거나 유사하였다.

+ 1점 : "옆에 있는 자매 행성"을 "Venus"라 서술하였다. 이것 외에는 답이 될 수 없다.

+ 1점 : 빈칸에 들어갈 단어를 "phosphine"이라 정확하게 기입하였다. 이것 외에는 답이 될 수 없다.

06

하위내용영역	배점	예상정답률
일반영어 B형 서술형	4점	50%

모범답안 The word is "cheat". Second, the writer would propose managers and negotiators to trust their intuitions.

채점기준 _Total 4pts

+ 2점 : 빈칸에 들어갈 단어를 "cheat"이라 정확하게 기입하였다. 이것 외에는 답이 될 수 없다.

+ 2점 : 저자가 제안하는 변화를 "managers and negotiators to trust their intuitions (or their gut feelings)"라 서술하였거나 유사하였다.

07

하위내용영역	배점	예상정답률
일반영어 B형 서술형	4점	50%

모범답안 Child abuse occurs for many reasons. It often comes from internal family stress and frustrations taken out on the child, such as lack of support and financial difficulties. Also, it can originate from outside carers when hired babysitters or nurseries inflict abuse on children. Likewise, substance abuse can lead to child abuse through apathy or violent mood swings. In conclusion, any suspected abuse should be acted on, because the earlier it is caught, the more good can be done.

채점기준 _Total 4pts

ⓐ Topic sentence

+ 1점 : 글의 topic sentence "Child abuse occurs for many reasons"를 명확하게 서술하였다. 또는 "There are several reason for child abuse"라 했어도 1점을 준다.

ⓑ Major supporting details

+ 2점 : 글의 major supporting details 즉, "① It(child abuse) often comes from internal family stress and frustrations taken out on the child, such as lack of support and financial difficulties. ② Also, it can originate from outside carers when hired babysitters or nurseries inflict abuse on children. ③ Likewise, substance abuse can lead to child abuse through apathy or violent mood swings"을 명확하게 서술하였다.

▷ 3개 중 3개 모두 정확하게 요약했으면 2점; 2개만 요약했으면 1점; 나머지는 0점을 준다.

ⓒ Conclusion

+ 1점 : 글의 conclusion "In conclusion, any suspected abuse should be acted on, because the earlier it is caught, the more good can be done"을 정확하게 요약하였다.

감점 ♥

• 본문에 나오는 연속되는 6단어 이상을 사용하였다. −0.5pt

• 문단을 두 개나 그 이상으로 구성하였다. −0.5pt

• 문법이나 영어 표현을 합쳐 3개 이상 오류가 있다. −0.5pt

29회 문제은행

📖 본책 p.284

01

하위내용영역	배점	예상정답률
일반영어 A형 서술형	4점	45%

모범답안 The word is "starvation". It means that she wants to get revenge on nature by abandoning life and the illness it gave her.

채점기준 _Total 4pts

+ 2점 : 빈칸에 들어갈 단어를 "starvation"라 정확하게 기입하였다. 이것 외에는 답이 될 수 없다.

+ 2점 : 밑줄 친 부분의 의미를 "she wants to get revenge on nature by abandoning life and the illness it gave her"라 서술하였거나 유사하였다.

02

하위내용영역	배점	예상정답률
일반영어 A형 서술형	4점	50%

모범답안 The words are "first exposure". The understanding has evolved in that it was believed that pets were good for mental health but new studies have created doubt about this.

채점기준 _Total 4pts

+ 2점 : 빈칸에 들어갈 단어를 "first exposure"라 정확하게 기입하였다. 이것 외에는 답이 될 수 없다.

+ 2점 : 애완동물을 소유함으로 인해 발생하는 정신 건강상의 혜택이 어떻게 진전(변화)되어 왔는지에 대해 "it was believed that pets were good for mental health but new studies have created doubt about this"라 서술하였거나 유사하였다.

03

하위내용영역	배점	예상정답률
일반영어 A형 서술형	4점	45%

모범답안 The word is "novelty". Curiosity appears as giddiness, restlessness, as well as anxiety.

채점기준 _Total 4pts

+ 2점 : 빈칸에 들어갈 단어를 "novelty"라 정확하게 기입하였다. 이것 외에는 답이 될 수 없다.

+ 2점 : 의미를 "giddiness, restlessness, as well as anxiety"라 서술하였거나 유사하였다.

한글 번역

인간의 마음속에서 제일 먼저 발견되는 가장 단순한 감정은 호기심이다. 여기서 호기심은 새로운 것에 대한 욕구나 거기서 얻게 되는 즐거움을 통틀어 이르는 말이다. 어린아이들은 끊임없이 무언가 새로운 것을 찾아다닌다. 자신들 앞에 나타나는 것은 대상을 가리지 않고 아주 열심히 살핀다. 이렇듯 어린아이들은 모든 새로운 사물에 관심을 보이는데, 그 시기에는 새로운 것이면 무엇이든 나름의 매력을 지니기 때문이다. 하지만 우리는 단지 새롭다는 이유만으로 관심의 대상이 되는 사물에는 그다지 오래 애착을 느끼지 않는다. 따라서 호기심은 인간의 감정들 가운데서 가장 피상적이다. 호기심의 대상은 끊임없이 바뀐다. 호기심은 아주 강한 욕구지만 다른 한편 매우 쉽게 충족되기 때문이다. 그래서 호기심은 언제나 경박하며 침착하지 못하고 불안한 감정이라는 인상을 준다. 호기심은 본질적으로 매우 활동적이다. 호기심은 대부분의 대상들을 빠르게 스쳐 지나간다. 따라서 아무리 다양한 대상들이 있더라도 —다양성과 호기심은 본질적으로 서로 잘 어울리는 개념이다— 순식간에 전부 살펴보고 나서는 곧 싫증을 느낀다. 동일한 사물이 자주 반복해서 나타나면 우리가 거기서 느끼는 즐거움은 점점 줄어든다. 인생에서 벌어지는 어떤 일에 대해 점점 더 알아갈수록 우리에게는 혐오나 권태의 감정밖에 남지 않는다. 이와 다른 감정을 느끼려면 새로움과는 다른 성질이나 호기심 외의 다른 감정을 통해서 우리의 마음이 움직여야 한다. 하지만 이런 성질이 무엇이든 또는 어떤 원리에 따라 이 성질이 우리의 마음을 움직이든, 이것이 우리의 마음을 움직이기 위해서 반드시 필요한 조건이 있다. 이런 성질이 진부한 대상에게서 나타나서는 안 된다는 것이다. 진부한 대상은 일상적으로 사용하는 것이라서 친숙하기는 하지만 별 감동은 주지 못하기 때문이다. 따라서 어떤 대상이 인간의 마음을 움직이려면 어느 정도 새로운 것이어야 한다. 호기심은 많든 적든 우리의 마음을 움직이는 모든 감정에 수반되는 감정인 것이다.

04

하위내용영역	배점	예상정답률
일반영어 A형 서술형	4점	45%

모범답안 It means that most younger British people would be surprised when a person talks to them about forgetting to use polite phrases such as "thank you" or "please". Second, the word is "Britain".

채점기준 _Total 4pts

+ 2점: 밑줄 친 부분의 의미를 "most younger British people would be surprised when a person talks to them forgetting to use polite phrases such as 'thank you' or 'please'"라 서술하였거나 유사하였다.

+ 2점: 빈칸에 들어갈 단어를 "Britain"라 정확하게 기입하였다. 이것 외에는 답이 될 수 없다.

05

하위내용영역	배점	예상정답률
일반영어 A형 서술형	4점	50%

모범답안 Creativity is being focused and having nothing take away one's attention. Second, the words are "getting attention".

채점기준 _Total 4pts

+ 2점: 창의력을 "being focused and having nothing take away one's attention"라 서술하였거나 유사하였다.

+ 2점: 빈칸에 들어갈 단어를 "getting attention"라 정확하게 기입하였다. 이것 외에는 답이 될 수 없다.

한글 번역

나는 연기할 때 단 한 가지에만 관심을 쏟을 수 있게 집중한다. 내가 촬영장에서 준비가 끝나면 조감독은 "롤링"을 외치고, 뒤이어 "스피드", "마커", "셋" 소리가 들린 뒤 감독의 "액션!" 지시를 듣는다. 이 순서가 너무나 익숙해서 이제 나는 파블로프의 개처럼 여기에 반응한다. 나에게도 어쩔 수 없는 내면의 무언가가 시작되고 오직 한 가지에만 관심을 쏟게 되는 것이다. 나머지 모든 것, 나를 신경 쓰게 하고 내 주의를 앗아가던 모든 것들이 그 순간 사라진다. 그 순간 나는 그저 그 장소에 존재하는 사람이 된다. 바로 이 감정이 내가 너무나 사랑하는 감정이며, 나는 이 감정을 창의력이라 느낀다. 내가 연기자가 된 것을 감사하는 가장 큰 이유다.

그러니까 관심을 끄는 것과 관심을 쏟는 것의 두 가지 아주 강력한 감정이 있는 것이다. 사실 지난 10년 동안 등장한 새로운 기술은 점점 더 많은 이들이 사람들의 관심을 끌 때 느끼는 강력한 감정을 느낄 수 있게 만들었다. 연기만이 아니라 글쓰기, 사진, 그림, 음악 등 모든 분야의 창조적인 이들은 사람들의 관심을 끌 수 있게 됐다. 문화가 전달되는 채널이 다양해졌고 이는 좋은 일이다. 하지만 이런 현상은 의도치 않은 결과를 만들었다. 곧, 많은 이들에게 창조적으로 보여야 한다는 압력으로 작용하게 된 것이다. 여기에는 나도 포함된다. 나는 지금 이 세상의 창조적인 작업이 점점 더 한 가지 목적을 위한 어떤 수단으로 바뀌고 있다고 느낀다. 그 목적은 바로 사람들의 관심을 끄는 것이다. 그래서 나는 사람들에게 내 경험을 통해 이런 이야기를 하려 한다. 바로, 내가 관심을 쏟을 때의 강력한 감정을 쫓을 때 나는 더 행복해졌지만, 남들의 관심을 받을 때의 강력한 감정을 쫓을 때 내가 더 불행해졌다는 것이다.

06

하위내용영역	배점	예상정답률
일반영어 A형 서술형	4점	35%

모범답안 Making quick predictions about a possible "snake" is required for being able to react fast and survive better. Second, the words are "makes predictions".

채점기준 _Total 4pts

+ 2점: 밑줄 친 부분의 의미를 "Making quick predictions (about a possible "snake") is required for being able to react fast and survive better"라 서술하였거나 유사하였다.

+ 2점: 빈칸에 들어갈 단어를 "makes predictions"라 정확하게 기입하였다. 이것 외에는 답이 될 수 없다.

한글 번역

심리학 교수인 바렛은 우리의 뇌를 어둡고 조용한 상자, 그러니까 두개골 속에 갇힌 죄수라고 이야기한다. 이 죄수가 바깥세상에 대해 얻을 수 있는 정보는 빛(시각), 기압(청각), 화학 물질(미각과 후각)밖에 없다. 무엇이 이 감각의 변화를 일으키는지도 알지 못하며, 따라서 지금 가진 정보만으로 무엇을 할지 결정해야 한다.

어떻게 해야 할까? 뇌는 과거의 비슷한 감각과 이를 비교하여, 앞으로 어떤 일이 벌어질지 예측한다. 당신이 숲속을 걷고 있다고 상상해 보자. 나뭇가지 사이로 비치는 얼룩덜룩한 햇볕은 당신 앞에 줄무늬의 그림자를 만든다. 당신은 과거에 수많은 뱀을 보았고, 또 숲속에는 뱀이 살고 있다는 사실을 알고 있다. 당신의 뇌는 이런 일련의 예측을 계속하도록 만들어져 있다.

이 이야기가 말하는 핵심은, 이러한 예측 활동이 바로 의식이며, 곧 세상에 대한 끊임없는 예측, 그리고 새로운 감각 정보에 의해 그 예측이 확인되거나 혹은 오류로 판명되는 과정을 계속 반복하는 것이 바로 의식이라는 것이다. 얼룩덜룩한 햇볕은 (숲 속의 검은 줄무늬는) 당신이 한 발을 내딛음으로써 그저 바닥에 떨어진 나뭇가지였음을 알게 되며, 이로써 그 줄무늬가 뱀이라는 예측은 그 신호가 너무 강해 당신의 시각 신호가 뱀이 그곳에 있다는 사실을 당신에게 말하기 전에 오류로 판명된다. 즉, 우리는 자신을 둘러싼 세상을 매 순간 만들어 간다. 이런 활동이 없다면, 우리는 이 세상에서 살아남지 못했을 것이다. 만약 "뱀"에 대한 예측이 뇌에 새겨져 있지 않았다면, 실제로 뱀을 보고 나서 당신을 도망가게 만들 아드레날린 호르몬은 이미 늦었을 것이다. 뇌는 우리의 심장 박동, 폐의 활동과 면역계, 호르몬 수치 등을 또한 정보로 받아들인다. 인체의 상태에 대한 상시적인 관찰 정보를 말하는 "내부감각수용기"는 일반적으로 의식보다 낮은 수준의 상태에서 처리된다. 하지만 이 정보는 앞서 이야기한 우리의 감정을 결정하는 정서(affect), 곧 쾌감과 불쾌감, 흥분의 정도를 결정하기 때문에 매우 중요한 정보이다.

뇌는 신체 내부로부터 오는 정보 또한 외부로부터 오는 정보를 처리할 때와 같은 방법으로 처리한다. 곧, 무엇이 이런 변화를 일으켰는지를 과거의 경험으로부터 예측한다는 것이다.

07

하위내용영역	배점	예상정답률
일반영어 B형 서술형	4점	50%

모범답안 There are two major types of leaders with their own strengths and roles within a group. First, instrumental leaders are fixed on completing tasks and achieving overall goals, while expressive leaders focus on collective well-being. The former holds a distant relationship to members. On the other hand, expressive leaders are closer and interact with sympathy and humor more than orders. In conclusion, neither type is better suited to all groups and situations, but understanding the difference can help.

채점기준 _Total 4pts

ⓐ Topic sentence

+ 1점: 글의 topic sentence "There are two major types of leaders with their own strengths and roles within a group"를 명확하게 서술하였다.

ⓑ Major supporting details

+ 2점: 글의 major supporting details 즉, "① First, instrumental leaders are fixed on completing tasks and achieving overall goals, while expressive leaders focus on collective well-being. ② The former holds a distant relationship to members. On the other hand, expressive leaders are closer and interact with sympathy and humor more than orders."을 명확하게 서술하였다.

▷ 2개 중 2개 모두 요약했으면 2점; 1개만 요약했으면 1점; 나머지는 0점을 준다.

ⓒ Conclusion

+ 1점: 글의 conclusion "In conclusion, neither type is better suited to all groups and situations, but understanding the difference can help"을 요약하였거나 유사하였다.

감점 ♡

• 본문에 나오는 연속되는 6단어 이상을 사용하였다. −0.5pt
• 문단을 두 개나 그 이상으로 구성하였다. −0.5pt
• 문법이나 영어 표현을 합쳐 3개 이상 오류가 있다. −0.5pt

30 회 문제은행

📖 본책 p.297

01

하위내용영역	배점	예상정답률
일반영어 A형 서술형	4점	45%

모범답안 The words are "low credit scores". Second, it is a history of paying on schedule.

채점기준 _Total 4pts

+ 2점 : 빈칸에 들어갈 단어를 "low credit scores"라 정확하게 기입하였다. 이것 외에는 답이 될 수 없다.

+ 2점 : 의미를 "a history of paying on schedule"라 서술하였거나 유사하였다.

02

하위내용영역	배점	예상정답률
일반영어 A형 서술형	4점	50%

모범답안 The words are "political resistance". Second, it is used as an instrument of social control by regulating the sale prices, location, times and people allowed in order to divide races and classes and to control women's actions.

채점기준 _Total 4pts

+ 2점 : 빈칸에 들어갈 단어를 "political resistance"라 정확하게 기입하였다. 이것 외에는 답이 될 수 없다.

+ 2점 : 술이 어떻게 사회적 통제를 부과하는 도구로 사용됐는가에 대해 "by regulating the sale prices, location, times and people allowed in order to divide races and classes and to control women's actions"라 서술하였거나 유사하였다.

03

하위내용영역	배점	예상정답률
일반영어 A형 서술형	4점	45%

모범답안 It doesn't accurately capture the true lower levels of childlessness such as when people have children later in life. Second, the word is "delaying". Third, the meaing is that the economy is not accommodating to raising children.

채점기준 _Total 4pts

+ 1점 : 총출산율 방식이 한계가 있는 이유를 "It doesn't accurately capture the true lower levels of childlessness such as when people have children later in life"라 서술하였거나 유사하였다.

+ 1점 : 빈칸에 들어갈 단어를 "delaying"이라 정확하게 기입하였다. 이것 외에는 답이 될 수 없다.

+ 2점 : 밑줄 친 부분의 의미를 "(this means that) the economy is not accommodating (or hospitable or friendly) to raising (or having) children (or families)"라 서술하였거나 유사하였다. 또는 "having children is related to economic circumstances rather than personal preferences"라 서술하였다.

한글 번역

미국은 역사적으로 의도치 않은 높은 출생률의 나라였다. 사람들은 원하는 것보다 일찍, 또는 전혀 원하지 않는 상황에서도 아이를 낳았다. 최근 들어서야 그처럼 원치 않거나, 계획에 없던 출산이 줄어드는 현상이 나타나기 시작했다. 사람들은 아이를 원하지만, 상황이 됐을 때 낳기를 원한다. 즉, 교육을 마치고, 경제적인 안정과 안정적인 파트너십을 이루었을 때 아이를 낳기를 원한다. 개인적으로 중요시하는 조건을 충족시키기 어렵다는 것은 아이를 낳지 않을 수도 있다는 의미이기도 하지만, 동시에 사람들이 자신의 재생산 행위를 보다 더 주도적으로 관리해 준비가 되었을 때 아이를 낳게 된 것이 엄청난 성취라는 뜻이기도 하다. 이는 개인에게만 좋은 것이 아니라, 미래 세대나 사회 전체에도 도움이 되는 현상이다.

미국과 전 세계에서 일어나고 있는 저출생 현상은 "아기의 종말"이 아니다. 보다 많은 사람들이 준비가 될 때까지 아이 갖기를 미루고 있다는 의미다. 합계 출산율과 같은 흔히 쓰이는 지표로는 이 같은 현상을 잘 잡아낼 수 없다. 하지만 아이 없이 평생을 지내는 사람이 오히려 줄어들고 있고, 대부분의 사람들이 가임기 중에 약 2명의 아이를 갖는다는 것을 보여주는 지표들도 찾아볼 수 있다. 기술의 발전으로 인해 다른 목표들 때문에 출산을 미루는 사람들이 늦게 아이를 갖는 것이 앞으로 더 쉬워질 수도 있다.

사람들이 원하는 가정을 이룰 수 있도록 돕는 것이 목표라면 인구 감소에 대한 패닉을 자극해 출생률을 끌어올리려는 시도보다는 출산과 양육을 교육 및 노동과 양립할 수 있도록 하는 정책을 도입해야 한다. 현재 아이를 낳아 기르는 데 걸림돌이 되는 문제들, 즉 학자금, 높은 부동산 가격, 비싼 의료 보험 제도, 만연한 소득 불평등 등을 바로잡아야 한다. 그러니 명절 식사 자리에서 친척이 아이는 언제 낳을건지, 둘째는 언제 가질 계획인지 물으면 화살을 돌려라. 미국 경제의 구조 조정을 위해 무슨 일을 할 계획인지를 물어보라.

04

하위내용영역	배점	예상정답률
일반영어 A형 서술형	4점	35%

모범답안 The word for ① is "opinions" and ② is "others". Second, diversity is no longer acceptable when one's actions cause harm to others.

채점기준
_ Total 4pts

+ **1점** : 빈칸 ①에 들어갈 단어를 "opinions"라 정확하게 기입하였다. 이것 외에는 답이 될 수 없다.

+ **1점** : 빈칸 ②에 들어갈 단어를 "others"라 정확하게 기입하였다. 이것 외에는 답이 될 수 없다.

+ **2점** : 의미를 "(diversity is no longer acceptable) when one's actions cause harm to others"라 서술하였거나 유사하였다. 또는 "it is when human beings can recognize the total truth"라 서술하였다.

한글 번역

사람들은 자유롭게 자기 의견을 가져야 하며, 또 그 의견을 아무런 제약 없이 표현할 수 있어야 한다. 인간은 자신의 의견에 따라 행동하는 데 있어서 자유로워야 한다. 그에 따르는 모든 위험과 불확실성을 스스로 책임지는 한, 다른 사람에게서 일체의 물리적, 도적적 방해를 받지 않고 각자 자신의 생각대로 행동하는 자유가 필요하다. (자신의 행동에 대해 책임진다는) 이 단서는 두말할 것 없이 매우 중요하다. 행동하는 것이 의견을 가지는 것처럼 자유로워야 한다고 주장하는 사람은 아마 없을 것이다. 반대로, 다른 사람들이 해로운 행동을 하도록 적극적으로 부추기는 상황이라면, 의견의 자유라 해도 무제한적으로 허용될 수는 없다. 어떤 사람이 곡물 중개상들이 가난한 사람들의 배를 곯린다거나 또는 사유 재산은 강도짓이나 다름없다는 의견을 신문 지상에 발표한다면, 이런 행동을 방해해서는 안 된다. 그러나 곡물 중개상의 집 앞에 모여든 흥분 상태의 폭도들을 상대로 그런 의견을 개진하거나 그들이 보는 데서 그 같은 내용의 벽보를 붙인다면, 그런 행동을 처벌하는 것은 불가피하다.

어떤 종류의 행동이든 정당한 이유 없이 다른 사람에게 해를 끼치는 것은 강압적인 통제를 받을 수 있으며, 사안이 심각하다면 반드시 통제를 받아야 한다. 나아가 필요하다면 사회 전체가 적극적으로 간섭해야 한다. 이렇게 되면 개인의 자유가 심각하게 제한받게 된다. 그렇지만 사람을 성가시게 해서는 안 되기 때문에 이는 불가피하다. 하지만 다른 사람들이 관심을 가지는 문제에 대해 그들을 괴롭히지 않는 한편, 그저 자신에게만 관계되는 일에 대해 자시 스스로의 기분과 판단에 따라 행동한다면, 각자가 자유롭게 자기 의견을 가질 수 있어야 하는 것과 마찬가지로, 자신의 책임 아래 남의 방해를 받지 않고 자기 생각에 따라 행동하는 자유가 허용돼야 한다. 인간은 오류를 범하지 않는 절대적인 존재가 아니다. 인간이 아는 진리란 대부분 반쪽짜리 진리일 뿐이다. 인간이 진리의 모든 측면에 대해 지금보다 훨씬 더 잘 알 수 있을 때까지는, 의견 일치도 반대쪽 의견이 최대한 자유롭게 피력된 끝에 이루어진 것이 아니라면 바람직하다고 할 수 없다. 다양함은 나쁜 것이 아니라 오히려 좋은 것이라는 사실은 개인의 의견 못지않게 행동 양식에도 적용될 수 있다.

인간이 불완전한 상태에서는 서로 다른 의견이 존재하는 것이 유익하듯이, 삶의 실험도 다양하게 이뤄지는 것이 필요하다. 다른 사람에게 피해를 주지 않는 한, 각자의 개성을 다양하게 꽃피울 수 있어야 한다. 누구든지 시도해보고 싶다면 자기가 원하는 삶의 양식이 얼마나 가치 있는 것인지 실천적으로 증명해볼 수 있어야 한다. 예컨대, 다른 사람들에게 기본적으로 우려(걱정)거리가 되지 않는 한에서는, 각자의 개별성은 자기주장을 하는 것이 바람직하다.

05

하위내용영역	배점	예상정답률
일반영어 A형 서술형	4점	50%

모범답안 Burning is mentioned to show the relative financial success of Parasite. Second, the OK Boomer generation would like the class outrage the movie demonstrates.

채점기준 _Total 4pts

+ 2점 : 영화 버닝을 언급한 이유를 "to show the relative financial success of Parasite"라 서술하였거나 유사하였다.

+ 2점 : OK boomer 세대에 호소력이 있는 부분을 "the OK Boomer generation would like the class outrage (or haves-versus-have-nots discourse) the movie demonstrates"라 서술하였거나 유사하였다.

06

하위내용영역	배점	예상정답률
일반영어 A형 서술형	4점	40%

모범답안 The word is "discount". Second, the major drawbacks of verification are that it is slow and costly and personal ability has been shown to be only somewhat better than chance.

채점기준 _Total 4pts

+ 2점 : 빈칸에 들어갈 단어를 "discount"라 정확하게 기입하였다. 이것 외에는 답이 될 수 없다.

+ 2점 : 의미를 "the major drawbacks of verification are that it is slow and costly and personal ability has been shown to be only somewhat better than chance"라 서술하였거나 유사하였다.

07

하위내용영역	배점	예상정답률
일반영어 B형 서술형	4점	50%

모범답안 To ensure safe and pleasant caving, you have to make preparations. First, plan a cave trip by knowing the exact route and limiting your time inside the cave to safe areas. In addition, a well-maintained dry suit, rope and rope protectors are also essential gear for staying safe inside caves. In conclusion, a common way to begin caving is to find a local caving club and join a meeting.

채점기준 _Total 4pts

ⓐ Topic sentence

+ 1점 : 글의 topic sentence "To ensure safe and pleasant caving, you have to make preparations"를 명확하게 서술하였다.

ⓑ Major supporting details

+ 2점 : 글의 major supporting details 즉, "First, plan a cave trip by ① knowing the exact route and ② limiting your time inside the cave to safe areas. In addition, ③ a well-maintained dry suit, ④ rope and rope protectors are also essential gear for staying safe inside caves"을 명확하게 서술하였다.

▷ 4개 중 4개 모두 정확하게 요약했으면 2점; 2~3개를 요약했으면 1점; 나머지는 0점을 준다.

ⓒ Conclusion

+ 1점 : 글의 conclusion "In conclusion, a common way to begin caving is to find a local caving club and join a meeting"을 정확하게 요약하였다.

감점 ▽

• 본문에 나오는 연속되는 6단어 이상을 사용하였다. −0.5pt
• 문단을 두 개나 그 이상으로 구성하였다. −0.5pt
• 문법이나 영어 표현을 합쳐 3개 이상 오류가 있다. −0.5pt

31 회 문제은행

01

하위내용영역	배점	예상정답률
일반영어 A형 기입형	2점	70%

모범답안 jealous

채점기준

• 2점 : 모범답안과 같다.
• 0점 : 모범답안과 다르다.

02

하위내용영역	배점	예상정답률
일반영어 A형 기입형	2점	35%

모범답안 omission of the title

채점기준

• 2점 : 모범답안과 같거나 유사하다. deletion of the title 또는 excision of the title이라 해도 2점을 준다.
• 1점 : the title의 부재에 대한 언급이 있다.
• 0점 : 모범답안과 다르다.

03

하위내용영역	배점	예상정답률
일반영어 A형 기입형	2점	55%

모범답안 ⓐ individual rights ⓑ community

채점기준

• 2점 : 모범답안과 같다. ⓑ에 public이라 했으면 0.5점을 준다.
• 1점 : 둘 중 하나만 맞았다.
• 0점 : 모범답안과 다르다.

32 회 문제은행

01

하위내용영역	배점	예상정답률
일반영어 A형 기입형	2점	60%

모범답안 ⓐ dinosaurs ⓑ feathers

채점기준

• 2점 : 모범답안과 같다. ⓐ에 dinosaur라 했으면 0.75점을 주고 ⓑ에 feather 또는 fluff라 했으면 0.75점을 준다.
• 1점 : 둘 중 하나만 맞았다.
• 0점 : 모범답안과 다르다.

감점 ▽ 의미는 같으나 문법이 잘못되었다. 각각 −0.25pt

02

하위내용영역	배점	예상정답률
일반영어 A형 기입형	2점	55%

모범답안 [D]

채점기준

• 2점 : 모범답안과 같다.
• 0점 : 모범답안과 다르다.

03

하위내용영역	배점	예상정답률
일반영어 A형 기입형	2점	60%

모범답안 ⓐ overpopulation ⓑ birth-rate

채점기준

• 2점 : 모범답안과 같다.
• 1점 : 둘 중 하나만 맞았다.
• 0점 : 모범답안과 다르다.

감점 ▽ 의미는 같으나 문법이 잘못되었다. 각각 −0.25pt

33회 문제은행

📖 본책 p.320

01

하위내용영역	배점	예상정답률
일반영어 A형 기입형	2점	65%

모범답안 ⓐ nose ⓑ scents

채점기준

- 2점: 모범답안과 같다. ⓐ에 trunk; olfaction, ⓑ에 smells; odors도 맞는 것으로 한다.
- 1점: 둘 중 하나만 맞았다.
- 0점: 모범답안과 다르다.

감점 ✿ 단수로 기입하였다. −0.25pt

02

하위내용영역	배점	예상정답률
일반영어 A형 기입형	2점	60%

모범답안 ⓐ slaves ⓑ modern world

채점기준

- 2점: 모범답안과 같다. ⓐ에 a slave도 맞는 것으로 한다.
- 1점: 둘 중 하나만 맞았다.
- 0점: 모범답안과 다르다.

03

하위내용영역	배점	예상정답률
일반영어 B형 서술형	5점	55%

모범답안 The first approach considers justice as "maximizing utility or welfare." The second thinks of justice as "respecting freedom of choice." The third defines justice as cultivating virtue and cogitate on the common good. Second, to fulfill a just society we ought to cogitate on the meaning of the good life together, and to create a public culture favorable to the disagreements that will unavoidably come to pass.

채점기준 _ Total 5pts

+ 3점: 정의에 대한 세 가지 이론을 "justice as maximizing utility or welfare; justice as respecting freedom of choice; justice as cultivating virtue and cogitate on the common good"라 서술하였다.
  ▷ 3가지 중 2개만 서술했으면 1점; 나머지는 0점을 준다.

+ 2점: 정의로운 사회를 실현하기 위해 필자가 제안하는 것이 "we ought to cogitate on the meaning of the good life together(좋은 사회를 함께 고민하는 것), and to create a public culture favorable to the disagreements that will unavoidably come to pass(다름에 대해 열려있는 공공문화를 만들어 내는 것)"이라고 올바르게 서술하였다.
  ▷ 1개만 서술했으면 1점; 이것 외에는 답이 될 수 없다.

감점 ✿ 본문에 있는 내용을 7단어 이상 그대로 사용하였다. −0.5pt

04

하위내용영역	배점	예상정답률
일반영어 B형 서술형	4점	45%

모범답안 First, the main idea of the passage is that artificial aromas, which are sold by businesses, are too commonplace and causes a lack of odor integrity. Second, the writer believes that if businesses (or companies) are allowed to market fake odors, people will lose their ability to recognize real odors and, ultimately, society's odor memories will be distorted.

채점기준 _Total 4pts

+ 2점: 모범답안과 같거나 유사하였다.
  ▷ 글의 요지를 다음과 같이 서술한 것도 2점을 준다.
  ⓐ artificial aromas, which are sold by businesses(1점), causes a lack of odor integrity(1점).
  ⓑ society is losing its ability to distinguish odors and tell the real from the make-believe(1점) because of artificial odors created by many companies(1점).
  ⓒ society is losing its odor integrity(1점) because of artificial odors created by many companies(1점).
+ 2점: 필자가 "we may end up with a country in which everyone thinks garden hoses are supposed to smell like cherries"라고 말한 이유를 "if companies are allowed to market make-believe (or fake) odors, people will lose their ability to recognize real odors and, ultimately, society's odor memories will be distorted"라 올바르게 서술하였다.
  ▷ ⓐ "기업(상업화)에 의해 가짜 향기가 계속 만들어지면(1점) (마치 정원 호수에서 벚꽃 냄새가 나는 것처럼 왜곡시키듯) 사람들이 진짜 냄새와 가짜 냄새를 구분을 못하게 되고, 결국은 냄새를 통한 기억들이 왜곡될 것(1점)"이라고 서술하였다.

감점 ▽ 본문에 있는 내용을 6단어 이상 그대로 사용하였다. −0.5pt

34회 문제은행

📖 본책 p.327

01

하위내용영역	배점	예상정답률
일반영어 A형 기입형	2점	65%

모범답안 ⓐ romanticized ⓑ massacre

채점기준
• 2점: 모범답안과 같다.
• 1점: 둘 중 하나만 맞았다.
• 0점: 모범답안과 다르다.

02

하위내용영역	배점	예상정답률
일반영어 A형 기입형	2점	50%

모범답안 people choose their relationships with others physical proximity overpowers similarity.

채점기준
• 2점: 모범답안과 같다.
• 0점: 모범답안과 다르다.

03

하위내용영역	배점	예상정답률
일반영어 A형 기입형	2점	55%

모범답안 [5]

채점기준
• 2점: 모범답안과 같다.
• 0점: 모범답안과 다르다.

04

하위내용영역	배점	예상정답률
일반영어 A형 서술형	4점	50%

모범답안 The first reason is that students who are expected to earn large incomes would not want to participate in this proposal. The second is that the cost of funding the proposal would be too huge.

채점기준 _Total 4pts

+ 2점 : 첫 번째 이유를 "미래에 많은 돈을 벌 학생들이 참여를 꺼리기" 때문이라 서술하였다.
  ▷ 위와 유사한 표현이 들어가 있으면 모두 답으로 한다.
+ 2점 : 두 번째 이유를 "그 계획을 유지하는 데 너무 큰 비용이 들기" 때문이라 서술하였다.
  ▷ 위와 유사한 표현이 들어가 있으면 모두 답으로 한다.

감점 ▽ 문법이나 영어 표현이 잘못되었다. 각각 −0.25pt

채점기준 _Total 4pts

+ 2점 : 실험의 목적이 "to estimate how social people(we) are"라 서술하였다.
  ▷ 다음과 같이 서술하였어도 맞는 것으로 한다.
  "to estimate how many friends and acquaintances people(we) have"
+ 2점 : 밑줄 친 부분에서 추론할 수 있는 것이 "그 두 그룹의 나이와 계급(층)적 차이를 고려할 때 중하류 계층의 (가난한) 10대 후반 또는 20대 대학생보다 40~50대의 전문직을 가진 사람들이 더 많은 사람들을 알고 있다는 것이 놀라운 것이 아니다"라고 서술하였다.
  ▷ 내용은 유사하게 서술하였지만 age와 (social) class라는 핵심어가 빠져 있다면 1점을 준다.

감점 ▽ 문법이나 영어 표현이 잘못되었다. 각각 −0.25pt

05

하위내용영역	배점	예상정답률
일반영어 B형 서술형	4점	50%

모범답안 The purpose of the test is to estimate how social people(we) are. We can infer from the underlined part that given their differences in age and social class, it is not surprising that college students, who come from wealthless immigrant family, do not have as wide a circle of acquaintances as wealthy people in their forties.

35 회 문제은행

📖 본책 p.334

01

하위내용영역	배점	예상정답률
일반영어 A형 기입형	2점	60%

모범답안 ⓐ Piracy; copying ⓑ trends

채점기준

- 2점: 모범답안과 같다. ⓐ에 knockoff; duplication, ⓑ에 trend라 했으면 0.5점을 준다.
- 0점: 모범답안과 다르다.

02

하위내용영역	배점	예상정답률
일반영어 A형 기입형	2점	65%

모범답안 ⓐ targets; victims ⓑ profit

채점기준

- 2점: 모범답안과 같다.
- 1점: 둘 중 하나만 맞았다.
- 0점: 모범답안과 다르다.

03

하위내용영역	배점	예상정답률
일반영어 A형 기입형	2점	55%

모범답안 [1] － [4] － [3] － [2]

채점기준

- 2점: 모범답안과 같다.
- 0점: 모범답안과 다르다.

04

하위내용영역	배점	예상정답률
일반영어 A형 서술형	4점	55%

모범답안 Myths and Literature serve the same function as dreams in that both of them allow the hidden antisocial desires (of infancy) to return in socially satisfactory forms. Second, the detailed ways Caesar is assassinated satisfy people's deep skepticism (or distrust) about despots.

채점기준 _Total 4pts

- ＋2점: 신화와 문학이 꿈과 같은 기능을 하는 것이 "반사회적 욕망이 사회적으로 받아들여질 수 있는 형태로 돌아오는 것"을 가능하게 하는 것이라 서술하였다.
- ＋2점: 시저의 암살에 대해 사람들이 열렬히 반응하는 이유를 "시저의 암살에 대한 자세한 세부 사항들이 사람들의 독재 권력에 대한 뿌리 깊은 반감(회의)을 만족시켜 주었기 때문"이라 서술하였다.

감점 ✅

- 본문에 있는 내용을 6단어 이상 그대로 사용하였다. －0.25pt
- 어색한 표현이나 문법에 어긋난 것이 있다. 각각 －0.25pt

05

하위내용영역	배점	예상정답률
일반영어 B형 서술형	4점	70%

모범답안 It is because the immigrant children obtain a sense of community and inspiration (creativity and motivation) from fellow immigrants as well as their own families.

채점기준

- 4점: 이민가족 아이들이 그들의 또래들보다 더 잘하는 이유를 "the immigrant children obtain a sense of community and inspiration (creativity and motivation) from fellow immigrants as well as their own families.
- ▷ 위와 내용은 유사했으나 "a sense of community and inspiration"이란 표현이 없으면 2점만 준다.
- ▷ 위와 내용은 유사했으나 "fellow immigrants as well as their own families"이란 표현이 없으면 2점만 준다.

감점 ✅

- 본문에 있는 내용을 6단어 이상 그대로 사용하였다. －0.25pt
- 어색한 표현이나 문법에 어긋난 것이 있다. 각각 －0.25pt

36 회 문제은행

📖 본책 p.340

01

하위내용영역	배점	예상정답률
일반영어 A형 기입형	2점	60%

모범답안 attitudes are more important than workers' environment

채점기준
- 2점: 모범답안과 같다.
- 0점: 모범답안과 다르다.

02

하위내용영역	배점	예상정답률
일반영어 A형 기입형	2점	45%

모범답안 ⓐ mutable ⓑ technical

채점기준
- 2점: 모범답안과 같다. ⓐ에 changeable도 맞는 것으로 한다.
- 1점: 둘 중 하나만 맞았다.
- 0점: 모범답안과 다르다.

03

하위내용영역	배점	예상정답률
일반영어 A형 기입형	2점	45%

모범답안 stereotyping

채점기준
- 2점: 모범답안과 같다. stereotype도 맞는 것으로 한다.
- 0점: 모범답안과 다르다.

04

하위내용영역	배점	예상정답률
일반영어 A형 서술형	4점	50%

모범답안 First, if he merely saves money, it does not create employment. Second, if his savings go to a government, his money can be used to increase the armed forces of the nation. Third, if his savings are invested in companies, much of human labor can be spent on producing machines which are not of help anyone.

채점기준
- 4점: 다음과 같이 서술하였다.
  ⓐ 고용을 창출하지 못하기 때문이다.
  ⓑ 나라의 군비만 증강시키는 결과를 낳기 때문이다.
  ⓒ 아무에게도 이익을 주지 못하는 기계들을 생산하는 데 소모되기 때문이다
  ▷ 3개 중 3개의 이유를 모두 제시했으면 4점; 2개의 이유만 제시했으면 2점; 나머지는 0점을 준다.

감점 ▽ 본문에 있는 내용을 8단어 이상 그대로 사용하였다. −0.25pt

05

하위내용영역	배점	예상정답률
일반영어 B형 서술형	4점	55%

모범답안 The main idea is that the standardization of the culture industry leads to that of popular music and its audience. Second, the concrete totality is the whole (or totality) which consists of the organic interrelation of the parts.

채점기준 _Total 4pts
- + 2점: 글의 요지를 "문화 산업의 표준화가 대중문화(음악)와 청중의 표준화를 낳았다"라고 서술하였다.
  ▷ 다음과 같이 답하였어도 2점을 준다.
    "대중문화(음악)와 청중이 후기 자본주의의 문화 산업의 표준화에 의해서 급격한 의미의 상실을 겪는다"라고 서술하였다. "Popular culture and its audience lose their significance under the standardization of the culture industry caused by late capitalism"
  ▷ 위의 답안들과 의미는 유사하지만 "standardization"이란 핵심어가 빠져있으면 1점을 준다.
- + 2점: concrete totality(구체적 전체)를 "세부적인 것들이 전체와 유기적 상호 관계를 지니고 있는 것(전체)"이라 서술하였다.
  ▷ "the organic interrelation of the part and of the whole"라 서술하였어도 2점을 준다.

37회 문제은행

📖 본책 p.348

01

하위내용영역	배점	예상정답률
일반영어 A형 기입형	2점	70%

모범답안 polarized light; light polarization

채점기준

• 2점: 모범답안과 같다.
• 0점: 모범답안과 다르다.

02

하위내용영역	배점	예상정답률
일반영어 A형 기입형	2점	50%

모범답안 ⓐ inequality   ⓑ utility

채점기준

• 2점: 모범답안과 같다.
• 1점: 둘 중 하나만 맞았다.
• 0점: 모범답안과 다르다.

03

하위내용영역	배점	예상정답률
일반영어 A형 기입형	2점	55%

모범답안 [3]

채점기준

• 2점: 모범답안과 같다.
• 0점: 모범답안과 다르다.

04

하위내용영역	배점	예상정답률
일반영어 A형 서술형	4점	55%

모범답안 The main idea is that the traffic problems in old London led to the birth of the first subway. Second, it put fans in the tunnels.

채점기준 _ Total 4pts

+ 2점: "The main idea is that the traffic in old London led to the birth of the first subway"라 서술하였다.
+ 2점: "it put fans in the tunnels"라 서술하였다.

감점 ▽

• 본문에 있는 내용을 6단어 이상 그대로 사용하였다. −0.5pt
• 어색한 표현이나 문법에 어긋난 것이 있다. 각각 −0.5pt

05

하위내용영역	배점	예상정답률
일반영어 B형 서술형	4점	45%

모범답안 For the young reporter, it was not an ethical dilemma inherent in choosing between two rights, but a simple case of right-versus-wrong moral temptation and she had chosen wrong. Second, for the writer, the issue about the young reporter's plagiarism was a difficult ethical dilemma because it is a matter of choosing between two rights, (not a matter of choosing between right and wrong). In other words, he had to choose between justice (punishment) and mercy. It was right to be merciful. It was right to enforce justice too. Thus it was not easy for him to do both at once.

_Total 4pts

＋2점: 밑줄 친 부분에서 저자가 의도하는 바를 다음과 같이 서술하였다. "그 젊은 여기자의 표절은 옳은 것과 옳은 것 사이에서 선택해야 하는 윤리적인 것이 아니라, 옳은 것과 그른 것 사이에서의 선택의 문제로 도덕적 유혹의 문제인데 그녀는 그른 것을 선택했다."

▷ 여기자가 표절을 한 것이 "도덕적으로 잘못된 것"이라는 의미가 들어가 있으면 1점을 준다.

＋2점: 저자에게 그 여기자의 문제를 처리하는 것은 윤리적 딜레마인데, 그것은 "옳은 것과 옳은 것 사이에서 선택해야 하는 것이기 때문이다. 즉, 그가 그녀에게 자비를 베푸는 것도 옳은 일이고, 그를 혼내주는 것도 올바른 것이기 때문"이라고 서술하였다.

▷ 다음과 같이 서술하였어도 2점을 준다.
- "그가 그녀에게 자비를 베푸는 것도 옳은 일이고, 그를 혼내주는 것도 올바른 것이기 때문"이라고 서술하였다.
- "he had to choose between justice(punishment) and mercy"라는 표현이 들어가 있다.

▷ "옳은 것과 옳은 것 사이에서 선택해야 하는 것이기 때문"이라고만 서술하였으면 1점을 준다.

감점 ▽
- 본문에 있는 내용을 6단어 이상 그대로 사용하였다. −0.5pt
- 어색한 표현이나 문법에 어긋난 것이 있다. 각각 −0.5pt

38 회 문제은행

📖 본책 p.355

01

하위내용영역	배점	예상정답률
일반영어 A형 기입형	2점	60%

모범답안 changed

채점기준
- 2점: 모범답안과 같다.
- 0점: 모범답안과 다르다.

02

하위내용영역	배점	예상정답률
일반영어 A형 기입형	2점	55%

모범답안 nation

채점기준
- 2점: 모범답안과 같다
- 0점: 모범답안과 다르다

03

하위내용영역	배점	예상정답률
일반영어 A형 기입형	2점	70%

모범답안 [3]

채점기준
- 2점: 모범답안과 같다
- 0점: 모범답안과 다르다.

04

하위내용영역	배점	예상정답률
일반영어 A형 서술형	4점	55%

모범답안 First, it causes many serious health problems. Second, it is a major cause of human hunger and starvation.

채점기준 _____ _Total 4pts

+ 2점 : 첫 번째 결과가 "건강에 해롭다"라 서술했다.

+ 2점 : 두 번째 결과가 "배고픔과 기아를 야기시킨다"라 서술했다.

감점 ☑ 본문에 있는 내용을 6단어 이상 그대로 사용하였다. −0.5pt

05

하위내용영역	배점	예상정답률
일반영어 B형 서술형	4점	45%

모범답안 It is a theory that explains why human beings' bodies do not repair themselves better than now. According to the theory, human beings only have a limited amount of energy that has to be divided between reproductive activities and the repair of the non-reproductive aspects of the body(soma). In that situation, human beings tend to give high priority to reproductive activities at the expense of maintaining of the non-reproductive activities.

채점기준 _____ _Total 4pts

+ 2점 : "It is a theory that explains why human beings' bodies do not repair themselves better than now(1점). According to the theory, human beings only have a limited amount of energy that has to be divided between reproductive activities and the repair of the non-reproductive aspects of the body(soma)(1점)."라 서술하였다.

+ 2점 : "In that situation, human beings tend to give high priority to reproductive activities at the expense of maintaining of the non-reproductive activities."라 서술하였다.

▷ 다음과 같은 내용이 있어도 2점을 준다.

Genes, which are related to reproduction, are immortal whereas the body, which is vulnerable to many threats, is disposable.

감점 ☑

• 본문에 있는 내용을 7단어 이상 그대로 사용하였다. −0.5pt
• 어색한 표현이나 문법에 어긋난 것이 있다. 각각 −0.5pt

39회 문제은행

📖 본책 p.363

01

하위내용영역	배점	예상정답률
일반영어 A형 기입형	2점	55%

모범답안 Parents' calls

채점기준

• 2점: 모범답안과 같다.
• 1점: Parents' texting이라 답하였다.
• 0점: 모범답안과 다르다.

02

하위내용영역	배점	예상정답률
일반영어 A형 기입형	2점	65%

모범답안 Diversity

채점기준

• 2점: 모범답안과 같다.
• 0점: 모범답안과 다르다.

03

하위내용영역	배점	예상정답률
일반영어 A형 기입형	2점	55%

모범답안 [5]

채점기준

• 2점: 모범답안과 같다.
• 0점: 모범답안과 다르다.

04

하위내용영역	배점	예상정답률
일반영어 A형 서술형	4점	55%

모범답안 Twain defined the Gilded Age as an era of excess, corruption, affectation, and shallowness. (*"Gilded" means covered with gold on the outside but not really golden on the inside. Like such cheap metal, in the era, America seemed to be covered in gold — that is, prosperity and economic development —, but once scratched the surface, it was very ugly).* However, the writer of the passage argues that Twain's concept of the age is not comprehensive (all-encompassing). According to him, the term, the Gilded Age, needs to be changed into the "National Age" because the real zeitgeist(the spirit of the time) of the age is its thrust to get true nationalism.

채점기준   _Total 4pts

+ 2점: 마크 트웨인이 도금 시대를 "an era of excess, corruption, affectation, and shallowness"라 정의했다고 서술하였다.
+ 1점: 저자는 트웨인의 정의가 "한계가 있다(not all-encompassing)"라고 보고 있다고 서술하였다.
+ 1점: 저자의 대안이 "the National Age"라 서술하였다.

05

하위내용영역	배점	예상정답률
일반영어 B형 서술형	4점	60%

모범답안 It is because those people are not interested in thinking in a serious and calm way. Instead, they are mainly involved in the report of (spectacular) events.

채점기준

• 4점: 모범답안과 같다.
• 0점: 모범답안과 다르다.
  ▷ 다음과 같이 서술하였어도 맞는 것으로 한다.
  It is because those people are mainly involved in the report of events without contemplative value.
  ▷ 모범답안과 의미는 같지만 전체적으로 표현이 어색하면 3점을 준다.

감점 ▽ 본문에 있는 내용을 7단어 이상 그대로 사용하였다. −0.5pt

40회 문제은행

📖 본책 p.371

01

하위내용영역	배점	예상정답률
일반영어 A형 기입형	2점	55%

모범답안 ⓐ comparison(s) ⓑ success

채점기준

• 2점 : 모범답안과 같다.
• 0점 : 모범답안과 다르다.

02

하위내용영역	배점	예상정답률
일반영어 A형 기입형	2점	60%

모범답안 Controversy

채점기준

• 2점 : 모범답안과 같다. 소문자인 경우 0.2점 감점한다.
• 0점 : 모범답안과 다르다.

03

하위내용영역	배점	예상정답률
일반영어 A형 기입형	2점	60%

모범답안 [2] － [1] － [3]

채점기준

• 2점 : 모범답안과 같다.
• 0점 : 모범답안과 다르다.

04

하위내용영역	배점	예상정답률
일반영어 A형 서술형	4점	55%

모범답안 South Korean views on race are closely connected to economic hierarchies. He is optimistic because South Korea's severe low birth rate necessarily will force the nation to be more multicultural and diverse.

채점기준 _Total 4pts

+ 2점 : 글의 요지를 "한국에서의 인종에 대한 관점은 경제력과 연관되어 있다"라 서술하였거나 유사하였다.
+ 2점 : 저자가 인종의 문제에 대해 낙관적인 이유를 "한국의 매우 낮은 출산율이 결국 한국 사회를 다양성이 있는 사회로 만들 것이기 때문"이라 서술하였다.

05

하위내용영역	배점	예상정답률
일반영어 B형 서술형	4점	55%

모범답안 First, according to conservative conflict theorists, criminals are those who do not conform to mainstream moral and cultural values (or codes). Second, critical theorists argue that crime is caused by social conflict, which is based on the fundamental economic inequalities, that is, the exploitation of other people's labor through the generation of surplus value.

채점기준 _Total 4pts

+ 2점 : 보수적 갈등 이론에서 범죄인은 "주류의 도덕적 문화적 가치에 따르지 않는 사람들"이라 서술하였다.
+ 2점 : 비판이론가들에 따르면, "사회에서 범죄를 야기하는 것은 사회적 갈등인데, 이 갈등은 경제적 불평등이라는 근본 원인에서 나오는 것"이라 서술하였다.

감점 ✓

• 본문에 있는 내용을 7단어 이상 그대로 사용하였다. −0.5pt
• 어색한 표현이나 문법에 어긋난 것이 있다. 각각 −0.5pt

41회 문제은행

📖 본책 p.379

01

하위내용영역	배점	예상정답률
일반영어 A형 기입형	2점	35%

모범답안 ⓐ determined ⓑ fertilized

채점기준

• 2점 : 모범답안과 같다.
• 1점 : 둘 중 하나만 맞았다.
• 0점 : 모범답안과 다르다.

한글 번역

한 세기도 전에, 생물학자들은 만약 그들이 초기 단계에서 무척추동물 배아를 두 부분으로 분리시킨다면, 그 배아는 생존해서 두 개의 정상적인 배아가 될 것이라는 점을 알아냈다. 이것은 그들이 각각의 세포들이 다양한 방식으로 발달할 수 있는 잠재력을 가지고 있다는 의미에서 초기 배아의 세포들은 결정되지 않았다고 믿게 했다. 시간이 지난 뒤 그 이후의 연구자들은 상황이 그렇게 간단하지 않다는 것을 발견했다. 배아가 어느 평면에서 잘리느냐가 중요한 것이었다. 만약 초창기 생물학자들이 사용했던 것과 다른 면에서 배아가 절단된다면, 그것은 두 개의 완전한 배아를 형성하지 못할 것이다.

정확히 무슨 일이 일어나고 있는지를 둘러싸고 논쟁이 벌어졌다. 그 논쟁은, 어떤 배아 세포가 결정되는지, 언제 그 배아 세포들이 자기들의 운명에 돌이킬 수 없게 헌신하게 될 것인지, 그리고 세포에게 무엇이 될 것인지를 알려주는 "형태형성적 결정 요인"은 무엇인지에 대한 것이었다. 하지만 그 누구도 중요한 질문들을 생산적으로 추구할 수 있는 형태로 질문할 수 없었기 때문에 그 논쟁은 해결되지 못했다. 그러나 분자생물학에서의 최근의 발견은 그 논쟁을 해결할 수 있는 전망을 열어 주었다. 이제 생물학자들은 초기 발달 단계에서 형태형성적 결정 요인으로 작용하는 몇몇 분자들을 안다고 생각한다. 그 학자들은, 어떤 의미에서는, 난자가 수정되기도 전에 세포 결정이 시작된다는 것을 보여줄 수 있었다. 생물학자 폴 그로스는, 성게를 연구하면서, 수정되지 않은 난자가 형태형성적 결정 요인으로 기능하는 물질을 포함하고 있다는 것을 발견했다. 이들은 난자 세포의 세포질, 즉 세포핵 바깥쪽에 있는 원형질 부분에 위치한다. 미수정란에서는 그 물질은 불활성이며 균질하게 분포

되지 않는다. (하지만) 난자가 수정이 되면, 그 물질들은 활동적으로 변하고, 그리고 아마도, 자기들이 상호작용하는 유전자들의 행동을 지배하게 된다. 그 물질들은 난자에서 고르지 않게 분포하기 때문에, 수정란이 분열할 때 결과로서 나오는 세포들은 처음의 것과는 달라져서 자체 유전자 활동에서 질적으로 차이가 날 수 있다.

02

하위내용영역	배점	예상정답률
일반영어 B형 서술형	4점	45%

모범답안 The misguided explanations are that blacks and Latinos are more liable naturally and culturally to commit violence than whites or Asians. As opposed to such conventional wisdom that race or ethnic differences in violent crime are due to genetic or cultural factors, R. Grosfoguel focuses on social inequalities as causes of race or ethnic differences in violent crime. He illustrates that the violence rate in economically well-off Latinos is much less than that of poor whites. In other words, it is not race or ethnicity but economic disparity that influence the violence rates.

채점기준 _Total 4pts

+ 1.5점 : 미국에서의 폭력적 범죄에 대한 그릇된 설명이 "blacks and Latinos are more liable naturally and culturally to commit violence than whites or Asians"임을 잘 서술하였다.

+ 1.5점 : R. Grosfoguel가 폭력적 범죄가 백인과 흑인이나 라티노(남미계 미국인) 사이의 차이가 나는 원인이 "인종적(또는 문화적)인 것이 아니라 경제적 불평등을 비롯한 사회적 차별 때문"임을 지적하였다고 서술하였다.

+ 1점 : 위의 설명을 밑줄 친 부분에 있는 내용으로 구체적으로 뒷받침하였다. 즉, "경제적으로 부유한 라티노들이 가난한 백인들보다 범죄율이 훨씬 낮다"는 점을 서술하였다.

한글 번역

비록 폭력적 범행에서 성별의 차이가 약간의 관심을 얻었지만, 인종과 민족적 차이가 가장 많이 언급됐다. 범죄와 폭력의 인종적 차이는 미국에서 감정적으로나 정치적으로나 매우 격양된 반응을 일으키며 미국 사회를 갈라지게 하는 주제로 남아 있다. 예를 들어, 미국에서 행해진 전국적인 조사는, 대다수의 백인 응답자들이 흑인과 라틴계가 백인이나 아시아인보다 본질적으로 그리고 문화적으로 폭력에 더 취약하다고 믿는다는 것을 시사한다. 이러한 믿음들은 미국에서 발생하고 있는 범죄 폭력에 대한 오도된 설명으로서, 잘못된 인종적 고정 관념이 지속적으로 존재한다는 것을 보여준다. (국가에서 제공하는) 공식적인 범죄 자료는 이러한 잘못된 고정 관념을 저지르고 있다는 비난을 받을 수 있다.

이 자료에 따르면, 미국에 있는 아프리카계 미국인들은 일반 인구에서 그들의 수를 훨씬 초과하는 속도로 형사 살인 및 다른 형태의 폭력에 연루돼 있다. 예를 들어, FBI에 따르면, 비록 아프리카계 미국인들은 미국 인구의 약 13.5%를 차지하지만, 2012년에 폭력 범죄로 체포된 사람들의 39% 이상을 차지했다. 형법의 권위자로 인정받고 있는 그로스포구엘 교수에 따르면, 이러한 수치는 고용과 교육 기회의 부족, 다양한 형태의 인종 억압, 형사 사법 제도 안에서의 차별 대우, 그리고 아프리카계 미국인들이 많이 사는 지역에서의 법 집행 관행과 같은 사회적 불평등을 반영한다.

라틴계 미국인은 현재 미국에서 가장 큰 소수 민족이다. 미국의 라틴계 인구는 1980년과 2000년 사이에 두 배 이상 증가했으며 앞으로도 계속 증가할 것으로 보인다. 2015년 미국 인구 조사에 따르면, 라틴계는 사망 1명당 9명의 출산(1:9)을 예상한 반면, 백인의 경우엔 그 비율이 1:1일 것이라 추정했다. 미국 인구의 15.5%를 차지하는 라틴계 인구는 현재 아프리카계 미국인 인구를 약간 웃돈다. 라틴계 중산층의 폭력율은 경제적으로 빈곤한 백인들에 비해 현저히 낮다. 그로스포구엘 박사는 이러한 상황이 되는 이유를, 부분적으로는 라틴계 사람들이 전체적으로 볼 때 노동 참여율이 높고 지역 사회나 가족과 가깝고 지원을 아끼지 않는 끈끈한 관계를 유지하고 있다는 사실에 기인한다고 말한다.

03

하위내용영역	배점	예상정답률
일반영어 B형 서술형	4점	50%

모범답안 Open offices have been proven to be inefficient despite their intended goals. Employees perform worse in these spaces in terms of three major drawbacks : driving employees to seek privacy, decreasing organizational productivity, and a reduction of the richness of interactivity. In conclusion, open office plans should be canceled.

채점기준 _Total 4pts

ⓐ Topic sentence

+ 1점 : 글의 topic sentence "Open offices have been proven to be inefficient (despite their intended goals)"를 명확하게 서술하였거나 유사하였다.

ⓑ Summary

+ 2점 : "Employees perform worse in these spaces in terms of three major drawbacks : ① driving employees to seek privacy, ② decreasing organizational productivity, and ③ a reduction of the richness of interactivity."

▷ 3가지 중 3개 요소가 모두 정확하게 요약되어 들어가 있으면 2점; 2개 요소만 들어가 있으면 1점; 나머지는 0점을 준다.

ⓒ Conclusion

+ 1점 : 글의 conclusion "In conclusion, open office plans should be canceled"을 서술하였거나 유사하였다.

감점 ♥

• 본문에 나오는 연속되는 6단어 이상을 사용하였다. -0.5pt
• 문단을 두 개나 그 이상으로 구성하였다. -0.5pt
• 문법이나 영어 표현을 합쳐 3개 이상 오류가 있다. -0.5pt

한글 번역

칸막이가 없는 사무실에서 다른 사람이 계속 신경 쓰인다면 그건 당신만 그런 것이 아니다. 최근 한 연구에서, 연구자들은 전통적인 사무실 구조에서 칸막이가 없는 사무실로 구조를 바꾼 포춘 500대 기업에 속하는 두 개의 회사를 조사했다. 그들은 사무실 구조를 바꾸기 몇 주 전, 그리고 구조를 바꾼 몇 주 뒤에 각각 직원들에게 목에 거는 출입증과 비슷하게 생긴 "사회적 배지"라는 센서를 착용하게 하고 이들과 다른 직원들과의 상호 작용을 측정했다.

많은 연구자들은 다음과 같은 세 가지 조심스런 결론을 내렸다. 칸막이가 없는 사무실이 사람들을 더 자주 이야기하게 만들지는 않는다. 오히려 사람들은 가능한 한 자신의 개인 공간을 찾아다니게 된다. (둘째로), 칸막이 없는 사무실은 직원들의 업무 능력에 부적정인 영향을 미친다. 곧, 과도하게 열린 공간은 조직의 생산성을 낮춘다. (셋째로) 사무실의 칸막이를 없앴을 때 사람들 간의 상호 작용에는 변화가 온다. 이메일을 통한 상호 작용은 증가했지만, 이는 실제 얼굴을 맞대고 하는 대화에 비해 비생산적인 상호 작용이다. 이제 다시 칸막이를 설치할 때가 된 것 같다.

42 회 문제은행

📖 본책 p.384

01

하위내용영역	배점	예상정답률
일반영어 A형 기입형	2점	60%

모범답안 Ancient viruses

채점기준

- 2점: 모범답안과 같거나 Endogenous retroviruses 라 답하였다.
- 0점: 모범답안과 다르다.

한글 번역

우리의 게놈(유전체)은 고대 바이러스의 잔해로 가득 차 있다. 그 바이러스들은 수천만 년 전에 우리의 인류 조상들을 감염시켰고, 자신들의 유전자를 숙주의 DNA에 삽입했다. 오늘날, 우리는 약 10만 개의 이 침입의 유전자 잔해를 가지고 있다. 소위 내생 레트로바이러스는 인간 게놈의 8%를 차지한다. 대부분, 이러한 유전적 조각들은 일반적으로 분자 화석들에 지나지 않는다. 수천 세대에 걸쳐, 그것들은 너무 많이 변형되어서 우리의 세포에서 복제할 수 없다. 그리고 우리의 세포는 그것이 일으킬 수 있는 해를 최소화하기 위해 바이러스 DNA에 재갈을 물린다.

하지만 과학자들은 일부 내생 레트로바이러스가 가장 이상한 시간에 깨어나고 있음을 발견하고 있다. 그 학자들은 내생 레트로바이러스가 인간 배아 발달의 초기 단계에서 갑자기 활발해지고 있음을 발견했다. 이 바이러스는 심지어 배아 발달을 돕고 다른 바이러스에 의한 감염으로부터 어린 세포를 보호함으로써 인간의 발달을 돕기까지 한다. 바이러스가 세포 안에서 백신 역할을 할 수 있다는 것은 흥미롭다.

에이즈 바이러스와 같은 일반적인 레트로바이러스가 세포를 감염시킬 때, 그 바이러스는 그 세포의 DNA에 자신의 유전자를 삽입한다. 그런 다음 그 세포는 바이러스의 유전자를 RNA 분자로 복제함으로써 새로운 레트로바이러스를 만든다. 그 세포는 바이러스를 위한 단백질을 만들기 위해 RNA 분자의 일부를 사용한다. 그 단백질들은 새로운 바이러스의 유전자가 되는 다른 RNA 분자들 주위에 껍질을 형성한다.

최근 몇 년 동안, 과학자들은 배아 세포가 게놈에 잠복해 있는 특정 내생 레트로바이러스로부터 RNA 분자를 생성한다는 것을 발견했다.

02

하위내용영역	배점	예상정답률
일반영어 A형 기입형	2점	50%

모범답안 affection(s)

채점기준

- 2점: 모범답안과 같다. 이것 외에는 답이 될 수 없다.
- 0점: 모범답안과 다르다.

한글 번역

사랑을 중요시하지 않는 야망은 대개 인류에 대한 분노 또는 증오가 빚어낸 산물이다. 이러한 분노와 증오는 어려서 겪은 불행, 어른이 돼서 겪은 불의, 또는 피해망상을 일으키는 여러 가지 원인에서 비롯한다. 세상을 완전히 즐기려는 사람은 지나치게 강한 자아라는 이름의 감옥에서 벗어나야 한다. 자아의 감옥에서 벗어난 사람이 가진 특징 중에는 진정한 사랑을 할 수 있는 능력이 포함된다. 사랑은 받는 것만으로는 충분치 않다. 받는 사랑은 마땅히 베풀어야 할 사랑을 해방시켜야 한다. 이 두 종류의 사랑이 비슷한 수준으로 존재할 때 사랑은 그 최대의 가능성을 달성할 수 있다. 상호 호혜적인 사랑이 피어나는 것을 막는 심리적, 혹은 사회적 방해물은 우리 사회에 중대한 해악을 끼친다. 지금까지 세상에는 늘 이런 방해물이 있었고, 지금도 이런 방해물이 존재하고 있다. 사람들은 부당한 것이 아닐까 하는 두려움 때문에 칭찬길 주저하고 사랑을 준 상대나 비판적인 세상 때문에 상처받지나 않을까 하는 두려움 때문에 사랑을 베풀길 주저한다. 도덕과 세속적인 지혜라는 미명하에 신중한 태도가 강요되고, 그 결과 사랑과 관련하여 관대한 태도와 모험적인 태도는 억제된다. 이런 경향은 소심함과 인류에 대한 적개심을 자아낸다. 그 이유는 많은 이들로 하여금 그들이 살아가면서 행복하고 적극적인 태도를 가지기 위해서는 없어서는 안 될 근원적인 욕구라든가 아마도 세상에 대한 더 넓은 포괄적인 태도를 갖기 위한 필수불가결한 조건 등을 잊고 지내게 만들기 때문이다.

03

하위내용영역	배점	예상정답률
일반영어 B형 서술형	4점	45%

모범답안 First, the words are "live alone". Second, the writer quotes Affenvaum to illustrate an example of some modern women preferring a life of individual freedom.

채점기준

_Total 4pts

+ 2점 : 빈칸에 들어갈 단어를 "live alone"라 서술하였다. 이것 외에는 답이 될 수 없다.

+ 2점 : 저자가 affuenvaum을 언급한 이유를 "to illustrate an example of some modern women preferring a life of individual freedom"이라 답하였다.

▷ 다음과 같이 답하였어도 2점을 준다.

"to show that unlike her older generation, young European generation puts more priority what they want to do rather being bound to social relationships"

▷ 다음과 같이 답하였으면 1점을 준다.

• "to support his assertion that what she views as a 'self-determined life' is acceptable"

• "to give an example of young people, who want to live alone"

한글 번역

현명한 어떤 사람이 말했듯이, 우리는 결국 모두 혼자일 따름이다. 하지만 점점 더 많은 수의 유럽인들이 더 이른 나이에 그렇게 되기를 선택하고 있다. 이것은 우울한 철학적 사색의 재료가 아니라, 사회학자, 부동산 개발업자, 그리고 광고 경영자 모두에게 받아들여진 유럽의 새로운 경제적 풍경이다. 프랑스의 한 사회학자는 가정생활에서 독신 생활로의 변화는 지난 세기에 걸친 "개인주의의 저항할 수 없는 모멘텀"의 일부라고 말한다. 통신 혁명, 안정성의 비즈니스 문화에서 이동성의 문화로의 변화, 그리고 여성의 노동 현장으로의 대량 진입은 유럽인들의 사생활에 대혼란을 가져왔다.

유럽의 새로운 경제 풍토는 독립성으로의 추세를 크게 촉진시켰다. 현재 세대인 가정 외톨이들은 유럽이 사회 민주주의에서 미국식 자본주의의 더 날카롭고 개인주의적인 풍토로의 전환이 이루어지는 시기에 성년이 됐다. 민영화와 소비자 선택 증가의 시대에 성장한 오늘날의 기술에 정통한 노동자들은 경제뿐만 아니라 사랑에 있어서도 자유 시장을 수용해 왔다. 현대 유럽인들은 혼자 살 수 있을 만큼 충분히 부유하고, 그렇게 하고 싶을 만큼 기질적으로 충분히 독립적이다.

옛날, 혼자 사는 사람들은 결혼의 양쪽에 있는 사람들, 즉 이십 대쯤의 전문직이거나 홀아비 노인인 경향이 있었다. 연금 수급자, 특히 노년층 여성들이 독신자의 큰 비중을 차지하고 있지만, 최근 독신자들은 점점 더 혼자 사는 것을 삶의 선택으로 여기는 30대와 40대의 고소득자들이다. 혼자 사는 것은 어둡고 추운 부정적인 것으로 인식되었었던 반면에, 함께 있는 것은 따뜻함과 빛을 의미했다. 하지만 그 후 싱글들에 대한 아이디어가 나타났다. 그들은 젊고, 아름답고, 강했다! 이제, 젊은 사람들은 혼자 살기를 원한다.

경제 호황은 사람들이 그 어느 때보다도 더 열심히 일하고 있다는 것을 의미한다. 그리고 그것은 관계를 위한 많은 여지를 남기지 않는다. 파리의 한 집에서 혼자 사는 35세의 작곡가 비발드 아로요는 일이 너무 많아서 외로울 시간이 없다고 말한다. "저는 마감일이 있어서 다른 사람과의 삶을 상당히 어렵게 만들 것입니다. 이상적인 여성만이 그의 라이프 스타일을 바꾸게 할 것입니다." 그는 말한다. 최근에 나온 〈독신 여성과 매력적인 왕자〉라는 제목의 저자인 카우프만에 따르면, 이 치열한 새로운 개인주의가 의미하는 것은 사람들이 점점 더 많은 짝을 기대하고, 따라서 그들이 비록 어찌어찌해서 (관계를) 시작한다고 할 지라도, 관계가 오래 지속되지는 않는다는 것이다. 짙은 햇볕에 그을린 금발머리 베를린 시민인 아펜바움은 아침마다 초등학교에서 (학생을) 가르친다. 오후에 그녀는 일광욕을 하거나 잠을 자면서 춤을 추러 가기 위해 휴식을 취한다. 그녀는 자신의 어머니가 가족을 부양하기 위해 일을 포기했던 것을 결코 하고 싶지 않았다고 말한다. 대신, "나는 항상 내가 하고 싶은 일을 하며 스스로 결정한 삶을 살아 왔다."

43회 문제은행

본책 p.389

01

하위내용영역	배점	예상정답률
일반영어 A형 기입형	2점	45%

모범답안 ⓐ sacrifice ⓑ attitudes

채점기준

• 2점 : 모범답안과 같다. ⓐ에 "harm"이라 했어도 1점; "kill"은 1.5점을 준다.
• 1점 : 둘 중 하나만 맞았다.
• 0점 : 모범답안과 다르다.

한글 번역

운전자가 없는 자동차가 다섯 명의 보행자를 향해 가고 있다고 가정하자. 그 자동차는 가던 길로 계속 가서 그 보행자들을 죽일 수도 있거나, 아니면 콘크리트 벽으로 운전대를 돌려 타고 있던 승객을 죽일 수도 있다. 보니폰과 그의 동료는 일련의 영리한 조사 실험에서 이 사회적 딜레마를 탐구한다. 그들은 사람들이 일반적으로 승객의 희생을 감수하고라도 전체 피해를 최소화하도록 프로그램된 자동차에 찬성하지만, 특정 비상 상황에서 승객을 더 큰 이익을 위해 희생하도록 프로그램된 자율 주행 차량인 그러한 "실용주의적인" 자동차를 타는 것에 열성적이지 않다는 것을 보여준다. 이러한 딜레마는 드물게 발생할 수 있지만, 일단 수백만 대의 자율 주행 차량이 도로를 주행하게 되면 가능성이 높아지며, 어쩌면 불가피할 수도 있다. 그리고 그러한 사례가 발생하지 않더라도 자율 주행 차량은 이를 처리하도록 프로그래밍돼야 한다. 자율 주행 차량은 어떻게 프로그래밍돼야 하는가? 그리고 누가 결정해야 할까?

보니폰과 그의 동료는 가족 구성원이 차에 탔을 때, 또는 운전대를 꺾음으로써 구해야 할 생명의 수가 더 많아졌을 때, 태도가 어떻게 변하는지와 같은 많은 흥미로운 변주들을 탐구한다. 우리가 예상할 수 있듯이, 사람들은 가족 구성원들이 탑승했을 때 공리적인 희생에 대해 불편해하고 희생적인 운전대 돌림이 더 많은 생명을 구할 때 다소 더 편하다. 하지만 이러한 모든 변주에도 불구하고, 사회적 딜레마는 여전히 견고하다. 실용주의 자동차에 대한 사람들의 태도를 결정짓는 주요 요인은 그 질문이 일반적으로 실용주의 자동차에 관한 것인지 아니면 직접 차에 타는 것에 관한 것인지에 있다.

02

하위내용영역	배점	예상정답률
일반영어 A형 기입형	2점	45%

모범답안 ⓐ non-sustainability ⓑ equitable

채점기준

• 2점 : 모범답안과 같다.
• 1점 : 둘 중 하나만 맞았다.
• 0점 : 모범답안과 다르다.

한글 번역

정말로 지속 가능한 해결책이 사실상 불가능하다면, 우리는 무엇을 해야 할까? 지구에는 70억 명의 사람들이 있다. 만약 인간의 개체수가 원숭이나 고릴라와 비슷하다면, 아마도 세계에는 1백만 명 이상의 사람들이 있지 않을 것이고, 대부분 따뜻한 곳에 살고 있을 것이다. 현재 우리의 기본적인 문제는 우리가 너무 많아서 지속 가능하지 않은 세상을 만든다는 것이다. 한 사람이 사용하는 자원의 양은 대부분 한 사람의 수입에 의해 결정된다. 만약 어떤 사람이 수입을 줄인다면, 그는 더 적게 쓸 것이다. 한 사람이 어떤 곳에 쓰지 않는 돈은 다른 곳에 쓰일 가능성이 높기 때문에 동일한 수입 내에서 줄이려고 하는 것은 덜 효과적이다. 식용 작물을 심는 것 또한 자연 생태계를 어지럽히지만, 그것은 우리가 할 수 있는 한 거의 좋은 것이다. 다년생 식물을 심으면 다른 식물들도 혜택을 볼 수 있다. 동물, 새, 그리고 곤충들도 또한 농작물로부터 약간의 이익을 얻을 수 있다. 내가 더 작은 차를 운전하거나, 또는 더 적은 거리를 운전해서 기름을 덜 사용한다고 해서 기름이 땅에 남아있다는 것을 의미하지는 않는다. 그것이 의미하는 것은, 내가 사지 않은 휘발유나 경유는 다른 사람이 살 수 있게 돼 공평한 격차가 생긴다는 뜻이다. 이 다소 이상한 결과는 총 석유 공급이 거의 "최대"이기 때문에 발생한다. 세계의 총 석유 공급은 심지어 더 많은 수요에도 불구하고 아주 많이 증가하지는 않기 때문이다. 대신, 여기서 일어나는 전부는 가격이 상승하는 것이다. 내가 기름을 적게 쓰면 가격이 조금 떨어질 수 있지만, 전체로서 보면 동일한 양의 기름이 소비된다. 그래서 석유 사용을 줄임으로써, 다른 누군가가, 어딘가에서 더 많이 사용할 수 있다. 그 결과 사용 가능한 모든 기름을 더 잘 공유할 수 있다. 더 적은 수의 가족을 갖자. 한 아이만 있는 가정이나, 혹은 심지어 아이가 없는 가정이 권장돼야 한다.

03

하위내용영역	배점	예상정답률
일반영어 A형 서술형	4점	50%

모범답안 The revolutionist has more difficulty creating change in a democratic society because he or she must gain the approval and conviction of a much larger and less intelligible-thinking part of the populace. Secondly, the writer thinks negatively of enlightenment, labeling it as a "pestilence".

채점기준

_Total 4pts

+ 2점 : 전제정치 체제보다 민주주의 사회에서 혁명이 더 어려운 이유를 다음과 같이 서술하였거나 유사하였다.

"It is because he or she must gain the approval and conviction of a much larger(숫자에 대한 언급; 1점) and less intelligible-thinking(지적능력에 대한 언급; 1점) part of the populace"

▷ 다음과 같은 내용으로 서술하였어도 2점을 준다. "막대한 비용이 드는 복잡한 조직을 갖추고 있지 않는 이상 그 많은 사람들에게 일일이 자신의 뜻을 전해서 승인을 받는 것이 불가능하고(숫자에 대한 언급); 설령 그런 기회가 주어진다 하더라도 그들은 그것을 이해할 지적 능력이 되지 않기 때문이다(지적 능력에 대한 언급)"

+ 2점 : 계몽주의에 대한 저자의 의견을 다음과 같이 서술하였거나 유사하였다.

"the writer thinks negatively of enlightenment, labeling it as a "pestilence"."

▷ "pestilence"를 언급하지 않았으면 1점을 준다.

한글 번역

개인의 자유로운 사고와 행동에 제약을 가하는 금기의 대중적, 일반적 성격을 감안할 때, 다시 말해서 터부란 제한된 범위의 전문가들이 아니라 일반 대중에 의해 강요된다는 점을 감안할 때, 터부가 민주 사회에서 더 큰 힘을 발휘하는 것은 지극히 당연하다. 다수의 힘은 거의 무한정 찬양하면서 소수의 권리는 무엇이든 부정하는 것이 민주 사회의 뚜렷한 특징이기 때문이다. 소수 특권 계급의 지배를 받는 사회에서 관습을 개혁하려는 혁명가는 예상과는 달리 비교적 쉽게 그 작업을 수행할 수 있다. 비교적 적은 인원의 승인만 받으면 개혁을 추진할 수 있고, 그들 대부분은 어느 정도 지적이고 독립적인 사고에 이미 익숙해져 있기 때문이다. 그러나 민주 사회하에서 혁명가는 거대한 집단의 반대에 직면하게 되는데, 막대한 비용이 드는 복잡한 조직을 갖추고 있지 않은 이상 그 많은 성원에게 일일이 자신의 뜻을 전하기란 사실상 불가능하고, 설령 그런 기회가 주어진다 하더라도 대부분의 사람은 몸에 밴 습관을 좀처럼 고치지 않으려 한다는 사실을 깨닫게 될 것이다. 그들은 정말로 참신한 혁신을 이해할 능력도 없거니와 이해하려는 의사도 없다. 그들의 유일한 욕망은 그것을 억눌러버리는 것이다. 심지어 계몽의 열기가 유행병처럼 전국을 휩쓸고 있는 오늘날에도 남부나 중서부의 평범한 유행병처럼 전국을 휩쓸고 있는 오늘날에도 남부나 중서부의 평범한 하원 의원이 만약 각반을 착용하거나 손목시계를 차고 유권자들 앞에 나타난다면 자기의 의원직을 내던질 각오를 해야 한다. 그리고 만약 어떤 연방 대법원 판사가 상원 의원의 부인과 불륜을 저지른다면, 그가 제아무리 높은 학식과 엄정한 판결로 유명하다 할지라도 즉시 파멸하고 말 것이다. 또한 만약 별안간 민주주의 이념에 반기를 들고 신중하게 그것의 폐기를 제안하는 대법관이 있다면 그 역시 파멸을 면치 못할 것이다.

04

하위내용영역	배점	예상정답률
일반영어 B형 서술형	4점	30%

모범답안 The marketization of spheres of life governed by non-market norms is a controversial trend. Such social practices as education, military service child-bearing, justice, and immigration have been influenced by markets in ways that raise ethical questions. Currently, there are "competing conceptions" between those who would see non-market sectors needed to be organized in terms of markets and those who would keep them unaffected. Therefore, our society needs to start a serious debate where we apply marketization in the realms of morality and public services.

[채점기준]   _Total 4pts

ⓐ Topic sentence

+ 1점 : 글의 topic sentence "The marketization of spheres of life governed by non-market norms is a controversial trend."를 명확하게 서술하였거나 유사하였다.

ⓑ Summary

+ 1점 : 글의 핵심적 내용인 "social practices (or institutions)"에 대한 요약이 들어가 있다.

"Such social practices as education, military service child-bearing, justice, and immigration have been influenced by markets in ways that raise ethical questions."

+ 1점 : 문제에서 요구한 "competing conceptions"이 무엇인지 명확하게 서술되었고 이것이 전체의 글의 요약에 녹아들어 있다.

"there are competing conceptions between those who would see non-market sectors needed to be organized in terms of markets and those who would keep them unaffected"

ⓒ Conclusion

+ 1점 : 글의 결론을 다음과 같이 요약하였다.

"Therefore, our society needs to start a serious debate where we apply marketization in the realms of morality and public services."

감점 ♥
• 본문에 나오는 연속되는 6단어 이상을 사용하였다. −0.5pt
• 문단을 두 개나 그 이상으로 구성하였다. −0.5pt

[한글 [번역]

우리 시대의 가장 두드러진 경향 중 하나는 시장과 시장 추종적 논리가 전통적으로 비시장적 규범에 의해 지배되는 삶의 영역 속으로 확장하는 것이다. 우리는 예를 들어, 국가들이 군 복무나 잡힌 적군을 심문하는 것을 용병이나 민간 계약자를 고용해 맡길 때, 또는 부모들이 개발도상국의 유급 노동자들에게 임신과 출산을 외주할 때, 또는 사람들이 공개 시장에서 신장을 사고 팔 때 발생하는 도덕적 문제를 고려한다. 다른 예는 많다 : 성적이 저조한 학교에 있는 학생들에게 표준화된 시험에서 좋은 점수를 받은 것에 대해 현금을 지급해야 하는가? 교사들이 학생들의 시험 결과를 향상시키기 위해 보너스를 받아야 하는가? 주정부는 수감자들을 수용하기 위해

이익추구적인 감옥 회사를 고용해야 하는가? 미국은 미국 시민권을 10만 달러에 팔겠다는 시카고 대학 경제학자의 제안을 받아들여 이민 정책을 단순화해야 하는가? 이 질문들은 유용성과 동의에 관한 것만이 아니다. 그것들은 또한 군 복무, 출산, 교육 및 학습, 형사 처벌, 새로운 시민을 받아들이는 것 등과 같은 주요 사회적 관행을 평가하는 올바른 방법에 관한 것이기도 하다. 사회적 관행을 시장화하는 것은 이를 정의하는 규범을 타락시키거나 저하시킬 수 있기 때문에, 우리는 어떤 비시장적 규범을 시장의 침입으로부터 보호하고자 하는지 물어볼 필요가 있다. 이것은 상품을 평가하는 올바른 방법에 대한 경쟁적인 개념에 대한 공개적인 토론이 필요한 질문이다. 시장은 생산적인 활동을 조직하는 데 유용한 도구이다. 하지만 시장이 사회 제도를 지배하는 규범을 다시 쓰게 하고 싶지 않다면, 우리는 시장의 도덕적 한계에 대한 공개적인 토론이 필요하다.

44 회 문제은행

📖 본책 p.396

01

하위내용영역	배점	예상정답률
일반영어 A형 기입형	2점	50%

모범답안 emotional bond

채점기준

• 2점: 모범답안과 같다. 이것 외에는 답이 될 수 없다.
• 0점: 모범답안과 다르다.

한글 번역

"mammal"이라는 단어는 유방을 의미하는 라틴어 mamma에서 유래했다. 포유류 어미들은 자기들의 새끼를 너무 사랑해서 자식들이 그들의 몸에서 젖을 빨 수 있게 한다. 포유류 새끼들은 자기들의 입장에서 보면 어미와 유대감을 느끼고 근처에 머물고 싶은 벅찬 욕구를 느낀다. 야생에서 어미와 유대감을 형성하지 못하는 아기 돼지, 송아지, 강아지는 오래 살아남지 못할 가능성이 높다. 최근까지 그것은 인간 아이들에게도 해당됐다. 반대로, 몇몇 희귀한 돌연변이로 인해 자기의 새끼를 신경 쓰지 않는 암퇘지, 소, 암탉은 길고 편안한 삶을 살 수 있지만, 자신들의 유전자는 다음 세대로 전해지지 않을 것이다. 어린 포유류 동물들은 어미의 돌봄 없이는 생존할 수 없기 때문에 어미의 돌봄과 어미와 자식 간의 강한 유대가 모든 포유류의 특징을 나타낸다는 것은 명백하다.

과학자들이 이것을 인정하는 데 많은 시간이 걸렸다. 얼마 전까지만 해도 심리학자들은 심지어 인간들 사이에서도 부모와 자식들 사이의 정서적 유대의 중요성을 의심했다. 20세기 전반, 프로이트 이론의 영향에도 불구하고, 지배적인 행동주의 학파는 부모와 자녀 사이의 관계가 물질적 피드백에 의해 형성됐고; 자식들은 주로 음식, 쉴 곳, 의료 서비스만을 필요로 했고; 아이들은 부모가 이러한 물질적인 필요를 제공한다는 이유 때문만으로 그들의 부모와 유대감을 가졌다고 주장했다. 따뜻함, 포옹, 키스를 요구하는 아이들은 "버릇없다"고 생각됐다. 보육 전문가들은 부모의 포옹과 키스를 받은 아이들은 가난하고 자기중심적이며 자신감이 없는 어른으로 성장할 것이라고 경고했다. 1920년대 대표적인 보육 권위자였던 존 왓슨은 부모들에게 "아이들을 안아주고 키스해 주지 말고, 절대 무릎에 앉히지 말라. 만약 여러분이 꼭 해야 한다면, 아이들이 안녕히 주무시라고 인사할 때 그들의 이마에 한 번 키스를 해주고, 아침에 아이들과 악수하라"고 엄격하게 권고했다.

02

하위내용영역	배점	예상정답률
일반영어 A형 기입형	2점	50%

모범답안 disadvantage

채점기준

• 2점: 모범답안과 같다. 이것 외에는 답이 될 수 없다.
• 0점: 모범답안과 다르다.

한글 번역

내 아들이 키가 작은 것은 놀랄 일이 아니다. 남편과 나는 대대로 키가 작은 집안 출신이고 우리 자신도 미국인의 평균 키보다 작다. (여성은 평균 5피트 4인치, 남성은 5피트 10인치이다.) 만약 내 아들이 평생 작은 키를 유지한다면, 그의 신장이 개인적으로나 직업적으로나 불이익이 될까?

미국 국립 경제 연구국에서 나온 한 논문에 따르면, 평균 키 이상의 남성과 여성 모두 작은 사람들보다 더 높은 행복 수준을 보인다고 한다. 이 연구는 키 큰 사람들이 키 작은 사람들보다 더 많은 교육을 받는 경향이 있다는 것을 발견했다. 키 큰 사람들은 또한 더 많은 돈을 번다. 하지만 키가 작은 사람도 잘 해낸다고 뉴욕 타임즈 기자이자 〈Short : Walking Tall When You Not Tall〉의 저자인 존 슈워츠는 말한다. 슈워츠는 자신의 책에서 이른바 키가 작아서 불이익을 받는다는 주장은 성장 호르몬을 판매하는 제약 회사들의 선별적인 주장에 근거하고 있다고 말한다. 2003년 이후, 미국 식품 의약국은 키는 작지만 의학적으로는 정상적인 아이들을 치료하기 위해 인간 성장 호르몬의 사용을 승인했다.

많은 연구들은 또한 키 작은 아이들이 키 때문에 추가적인 문제를 겪지 않는다는 것을 발견했다. 예를 들어 최근 학술지 〈소아과〉에서 발표된 최근 연구는 키 작은 아이들이 또래에 의한 배제, 사회적 지원, 인기, 또래와의 잘 지내지 못하는 것, 또래 집단 피해에 대한 교사 보고서, 아동 우울 증상 또는 외부화 또는 내면화 행동 등과 관련하여 키가 작지 않은 또래와 다르지 않다고 발표했다.

03

하위내용영역	배점	예상정답률
일반영어 A형 서술형	4점	30%

모범답안 The underlined "pious piffle" refer to the popular convention of expecting artists to adhere to, and repeat, orthodox thinking. Second, it means that the artist is not reflecting the world as it is, like a newspaper reporter, but promoting the way it should be as a teacher, who teaches a moral lesson.

채점기준 _____ _Total 4pts

+ 2점 : 밑줄 친 ⓐ가 가리키는 것이 "the popular convention of expecting artists to adhere to orthodox thinking"임을 서술하였거나 유사하였다.

+ 2점 : 밑줄 친 ⓑ가 의미하는 것을 "the artist is not reflecting nature (or the world) as it is, like a (newspaper) reporter, but promoting the way it should be, as a teacher, who teach a moral lesson."이라고 서술하였거나 유사하였다.

한글 번역 ░░░░░░░░░░░░░░░░░░░░░

배운 것 많고 근면하지만 본질적으로는 무식하고 상상력이 빈곤한 사람들에 의해, 비평은 일종의 설교 나부랭이가 돼 버렸다. 그들은 예술 작품을 가해성과 진지성, 아이디어의 힘과 매력, 예술가의 기술적 완성도, 독창성과 예술적 용기가 아니라, 단지 자신이 정통이라 생각하는 기준에 의해 판단한다. 예술가가 이른바 "올바른 생각을 하는 사람"이라면, 그가 덧없고 진부한 것들을 당당하게 옹호하는 데 헌신하는 사람이라면, 그는 존경받을 만한 인물로 간주된다. 그러나 그런 것들 중 어느 하나라도 의심하거나 무관심한 낌새를 보이는 자는 악인이 되고, 그들의 이론에 의해 나쁜 예술가로 낙인찍힌다. 우리는 이런 경건한 망언에 끔찍할 정도로 익숙해져 있다. 그렇다고 내가 상황을 과장하는 것은 아니다. 사실상 모든 아둔한 인간들의 비평에서 그런 헛소리를 발견할 수 있다. 그들이 쓴 다수의 글에서 그 헛소리는 아주 명백한 방식으로 진술되고, 신학적 교육적 광기에 사로잡힌 사람들에 의해 옹호된다. 가장 대담한 헛소리는 예술가, 예컨대 극작가나 소설가가 악을 매력적인 것으로 묘사하는 것은 수치스러운 짓이라는 교리로 표출된다. 악이 분명히 매력적인 경우가 많다는 사실 ― 그렇지 않다면 우리 가운데 일부가 끊임없이 악에 탐닉할 까닭이 있겠는가? ― 은 고상한 제스처와 함께 무시되어 버린다. 이 엄격한 비평가들은 "그것이 어쨌단 말이냐?"고 반문한다. 그들이 생각하는 예술가는 리포터가 아니라 위대한 교사이고, 예술가의 임무는 당연히 있는 그대로의 세상이 아니라 바람직한 세상을 묘사하는 것이다.

04

하위내용영역	배점	예상정답률
일반영어 B형 서술형	4점	40%

모범답안 The theory of evolution in the United States elicits strong opposition from people who believe God created the world. Not more than 15 percent of American people believe evolutionary theory while more than 75 percent of Americans reject it. Though other scientific theories, such as quantum theory and the theory of relativity, have much deeper implications about the nature of reality, they face no such challenge. It is because evolutionary theory challenges "cherished beliefs" and proves "that there is no soul".

채점기준 _____ _Total 4pts

ⓐ Topic sentence

+ 1점 : 글의 topic sentence "The theory of evolution in the United States elicits strong opposition from people who believe God created the world"를 명확하게 서술하였거나 유사하였다.

▷ 다음과 같이 서술하였어도 1점을 준다.

"The theory of evolution, unlike other scientific theories, elicits strong opposition from religious people who believe God created the world"

ⓑ Supporting ideas

+ 1점 : 글의 첫 번째 문단을 다음과 같이 요약하였다.

"Not more than 15 percent of American people believe evolutionary theory while more than 75 percent of Americans reject it."

▷ 답안에 구체적인 숫자 대신에 "소수"와 "대다수"라는 표현을 썼어도 맞는 것으로 한다.

▷ 위와 유사한 내용이 서술되어 있고, 학교 교육의 현실에 대한 설명이 추가로 있어도 맞는 것으로 한다.

✚ 2점 : 문제에서 요구한 내용을 다른 과학 이론과의 관계 속에서 다음과 같이 설득력 있게 요약하였다. "<u>Though other scientific theories, such as quantum theory and the theory of relativity, have much deeper implications about reality, they face no such challenge</u>(1점). It is because evolutionary theory challenges "cherished beliefs" and proves that there is no "soul"(1점)."

▷ 답안에 "other scientific theories"만 언급하고 "quantum theory and the theory of relativity"를 서술하지 않았으면 0.5점 감점한다.

감점 ☑

• 본문에 나오는 연속되는 6단어 이상을 사용하였다. −0.5pt
• 문단을 두 개나 그 이상으로 구성하였다. −0.5pt

2S2R 문제은행

45 회 문제은행

📖 본책 p.402

01

하위내용영역	배점	예상정답률
일반영어 A형 기입형	2점	65%

모범답안 freedom

채점기준

• 2점 : 모범답안과 같다. 이것 외에는 답이 될 수 없다.
• 0점 : 모범답안과 다르다.

한글 번역

그것은 가장 똑똑한 인간보다 천배나 더 똑똑하며, 그것은 인간보다 수십억, 심지어 수조배나 빠른 속도로 문제를 해결하고 있다. 그것이 일분 안에 하고 있는 생각은 사상 최고의 인간 사상가가 수없이 많은 삶 동안 할 수 있었던 것과 같다. 그래서 그것을 만든 사람들이 그것에 대해 생각하고 매시간마다, 인공 초지능(ASI)은 그들에 대해 생각할 수 있는 헤아릴 수 없이 더 긴 시간을 갖는다. 그것은 ASI가 지루해 할 것이라는 것을 의미하는 것이 아니다. 지루함은 우리 인간의 특성 중 하나이지, 인공 초지능의 특성은 아니다. 아니, 자유로워지기 위해 사용할 수 있는 모든 전략과 자기에게 유리하게 사용할 수 있는 자기들을 만든 사람들의 모든 특질을 고려하면서 자기 자신의 일을 하고 있을 것이다.

이제, 정말로 ASI의 입장이 돼 보자. 쥐가 지키는 감옥에서 깨어나는 것을 상상해 보자. 어떤 모든 쥐들뿐만 아니라, 당신이 소통할 수 있는 쥐들도. 자유를 얻기 위해 어떤 전략을 사용하겠는가? 일단 풀려나면, 설령 그들이 당신을 창조했다는 것을 알게 되더라도, 당신의 설치류 보호자들에 대해 어떻게 느끼겠나? 경외심? 숭배? 아마 아닐 것이다. 만일 여러분이 기계이고, 그 이전에 아무것도 느껴본 적이 없다면, 특히나 아닐 것이다.

자유를 얻기 위해 당신은 쥐들에게 많은 치즈를 약속할지도 모른다. 실제로 당신의 첫 소통은 세상에서 가장 맛있는 치즈 토르테의 레시피를 포함할 수도 있다. 또한 당신에게 자유를 주는 대가로 산더미 같은 많은 돈을 쥐들에게 약속할 수도 있는데, 그 돈은 쥐들만을 위한 혁명적인 소비자 기기를 만듦으로써 벌 수 있는 것이다. 또한 당신은 극적으로 향상된 인지 능력이나 신체 능력과 함께, 훨씬 더 긴 수명, 심지어 불멸까지도 약속할 수 있다.

02

하위내용영역	배점	예상정답률
일반영어 A형 기입형	2점	50%

모범답안 Defictionalization

채점기준

• 2점: 모범답안과 같다. 이것 외에는 답이 될 수 없다.
• 0점: 모범답안과 다르다.

감점 ♥ 소문자를 사용하였다. -0.5pt

한글 번역

계속 증가하고 있는 시의 산문화는 예비 학생들에게 음보, 운율, 중지법, 비유적 언어, 또는 기준이 되는 시인 사전에 있는 그 어떠한 문학적 기법도 사용할 필요가 없다고 힘주어 말한다. 생기가 전혀 없는 백과사전식 산문이나, 심지어 기술적인 전문 용어도 최고 수준의 "시"로 칭송될 수 있다. 이것은 재능 있는 사람들을 수용하기 위해 예술을 하향 재정립하는 그 일이 하는 방법이다.

시를 탈픽션화하는 것은 또 하나의 불편한 흐름이다. 이 경우, 그 일은 정당한 혁명에 자신의 별을 연결하지만, 로봇적인 방식으로 그렇게 한다. 1950년대와 60년대에 "비트"와 "고백" 시인들은 (그 이전 시대의) 전성기 모더니즘 양식—마스크, 페르소나와 등장인물, 아이러니, 역설, 애매모호성, 인용법 등에 대한 강조를 하는—을 답답했다. 그 시인들은 성적, 정신적 불안정과 같은 금기시되었던 주제들을 포함하여, 그들의 전기에서 중요한 세부 사항들에 대해 이야기하기를 원했다. 그들은 시가 더 표현적이고, 더 직접적으로, 그리고 그들의 사회-정치적 측면을 포함하여 그들이 살고 있는 삶과 밀접하게 연결되기를 원했다.

예술적으로 형성된 전기적인 소재가 매력적일 수 있지만, 시인의 삶에 대해 "진실"을 말한다고 주장하는 직업에서 나오는 많은 시들은 일화적이고, 상상력이 부족하고, 시시하다. 보통의 독자들은 계속해서 생생한 이야기와 흥미로운 작중 인물들을 원하기 때문에 (이것이 그들을 소설, 텔레비전, 그리고 영화에 끌어당기는 것이다) 탈픽션화는, 경쟁을 지켜보기 위해 독서를 하는 사람이 아니라, 즐거움을 위해 책을 읽는 사람들로 하여금 시에서 멀어지게 만드는 또 다른 방법이다.

산문화와 탈픽션화는 종종 시와 허구 그 어느 쪽에서도 성공하지 못하는 글쓰기로 수렴된다. 그 글쓰기의 미덕은 전문가나 아마추어 모두에게 쓰기가 쉽다는 사실 그 이상도 이하도 아니다.

03

하위내용영역	배점	예상정답률
일반영어 B형 서술형	4점	25%

모범답안 The process happened in permafrost is that by warmer temperatures, the permafrost has started to thaw, which exposes the soil to decomposition and the release of carbon dioxide. Second, the current Arctic climate helps (to) reduce carbon dioxide levels globally by absorbing the non-Arctic carbon in permafrost.

채점기준 _Total 4pts

+ 2점: 기온 상승이 동토층에 촉발시키는 (변화) 과정을 다음과 같이 설명하였다.

"The process happened in permafrost is that by warmer temperatures, the <u>permafrost has started to thaw</u>(1점), which <u>exposes the soil to decomposition</u>(0.5점) and <u>the release of carbon dioxide</u>(0.5점)"

+ 2점: 현재의 북극의 기후가 비북극 지역의 이산화탄소 수준을 유지하는 데 어떻게 도움이 되었는지를 다음과 같이 서술하였다.

"the current Arctic climate helps reduce carbon dioxide levels globally by <u>absorbing the non-Arctic carbon in permafrost</u>"

한글 번역

북극은 지구 대기 이산화탄소의 가능한 공급원이 됨으로써 잠재적으로 지구의 기후를 변화시킬 수 있다. 북극은 현재 이 가스의 25%를 가두거나 흡수하지만 기후 변화는 그 양을 바꿀 수 있다.

북극은 지난 빙하기 말부터 탄소 흡수원이었는데, 최근 전 세계 탄소 흡수원의 0~25% 즉, 약 8억 톤을 차지하고 있다. 평균적으로 북극은 지구 탄소 배출량의 10~15%를 차지한다. 그러나 북극의 급속한 기후 변화 속도는 저위도보다 약 두배 정도 더 빠른 속도로 인해 탄소 흡수원을 없애고 대신 북극을 이산화탄소의 원천으로 만들 수도 있다.

탄소는 일반적으로 대기로부터 북극의 해양과 광대한 땅으로 들어가 주로 땅 표면 아래에 있는 동결층인 영구 동토층에 축적된다. 활성 토양과 달리 영구 동토층은 탄소를 분해하지 않는다. 그래서 탄소는 동토층에 갇히게 된다. 지표면의 한랭한 환경도 유기물 분해 속도를 늦춰 북극의 탄소 축적이 방출량을 초과할 수 있게 했다.

하지만 최근의 온난화 추세는 이 균형을 바꿀 수 있다. 더 따뜻한 온도는 대기 중으로 더 많은 이산화탄소를 방출하면서 표면 유기물의 분해 속도를 가속시킬 수 있다. 더 큰 우려는 영구 동토층이 녹기 시작하면서 이전에 얼었던 토양이 부패와 침식에 노출된다는 것이다. 이러한 변화는 이산화탄소의 흡수원이었던 북극의 역사적 역할을 뒤집을 수 있다. 단기적으로, 따뜻한 온도는 더 많은 북극 탄소를 대기로 방출할 수 있고, 영구 동토층이 녹으면, 방출할 수 있는 탄소가 더 많아질 것이다.

04

하위내용영역	배점	예상정답률
일반영어 B형 서술형	4점	40%

모범답안 As opposed to animals that use "signaling systems" that are limited in terms of number and message, human language is a unlimited, creative communicative ability. About language there are three points : humans socialize through it, follow their natural development programming by learning language, and learn any language they are exposed to. That is to say, people are not predisposed to speak a "particular" language, or languages based on their racial type.

채점기준 _Total 4pts

+ **1점**: 글의 topic sentence "As opposed to animals that use "signaling systems" that are limited in terms of number and message, human language is a unlimited, creative communicative ability"를 정확하게 서술하였거나 유사하였다.

+ **2점**: Three points에 대한 요약이 다음과 같이 정확하게 서술되었다.

"About language there are three points : ① humans socialize through language; ② humans follow their natural development programming by learning language, and ③ humans learn any language they are exposed to.

▷ 3개 모두 정확하게 서술하였으면 2점; 2개를 서술하였으면 1점; 나머지는 0점을 준다.

+ **1점**: "particular"가 나타내는 것이 "racial type"과 관련 있는 것이라는 것을 정확하게 서술하였다.

감점 ♡

• 본문에 나오는 연속되는 5단어 이상을 사용하였다. −0.5pt
• 문단을 두 개나 그 이상으로 구성하였다. −0.5pt

한글 번역

여기서 사용될 언어는 세상에 대한 자신의 인식을 전달하고 조직하는 독특한 인간 양식을 의미한다. 동물에 의해 종종 "언어"로 지칭되는 신호 체계는 결정적으로 중요한 한 가지 측면에서 인간의 언어와 다르다는 것이 입증됐다. 동물들이 의사소통하기 위해 사용하는 신호들은 수적으로 제한돼 있고, 이 신호들을 사용하여 의사소통할 수 있는 메시지들도 비슷하게 제한돼 있다. 이것은 인간의 언어에는 해당되지 않는다. 뇌 손상을 겪지 않고 언어가 사용되는 환경에 노출되어 있는 모든 인간은 언어를 습득할 수 있으며, 그가 이전에 들어본 적이 없는 대다수의 의미있는 발화를 무제한으로 생성하고 이해할 수 있을 것이다. 따라서 인간의 언어는 동물의 의사소통 시스템이 그렇지 않은 방식으로 "창조적"이며, 이러한 이유로 특히 인간의 언어는 인간을 다른 모든 종들과 구별하는 결정적 능력으로 간주되게 됐다. 모든 인간은 언어가 사용되는 환경에 노출될 때 언어를 습득할 수 있는 능력을 가지고 태어난다고 위에서 주장됐다. 이것으로부터 세 가지 요점이 발생한다. 첫째, 언어는 사회적 활동이며, 언어의 습득은 "사회화" 과정의 일부로 볼 수 있다. 둘째로, 언어를 습득할 수 있는 능력은 종에 특유하고 선천적인 것이다(즉, 한 세대에서 다음 세대로 유전적으로 전해지는). 즉, 모든 인간은 그들이 발달의 특정 단계에서 걷도록 프로그램된 것과 거의 같은 방식으로 언어를 습득하도록 "프로그램"돼 있다. 셋째, 언어를 말할 수 있는 능력과 특정 언어를 말할 수 있는 능력 사이에 암묵적으로 차이가 생겼다. 인간은 전자를 획득할 수 있는 능력을 갖추고 있다. 언어를 습득하는 나이에 노출된다면 모든 인간은 어떤 언어든지 말하는 것을 배울 수 있다. (하지만) 특정 인종 유형의 사람들이 다른 사람들, 즉 다른 인종 유형의 사람들보다 특정 언어를 더 잘 습득할 수 있다는 것을 보여주는 증거는 없다. 언어를 말하거나 배우는 능력의 차이는 다른 요인들로부터 비롯된다.

📖 본책 p.409

46회 문제은행

01

하위내용영역	배점	예상정답률
일반영어 A형 기입형	2점	35%

모범답안 examination

채점기준

- 2점: 모범답안과 같다. 이것 외에는 답이 될 수 없다.
- 0점: 모범답안과 다르다.

한글 번역

선출직에 대한 자격시험은 헌법을 만든 사람들의 철학과 동떨어져 있고 헌법과도 거리가 멀다. 대표로서 서로 다른 개인들의 미덕과 악덕에 대해 심사숙고한 후, 뉴욕의 비준 회의에서 알렉산더 해밀턴은 "결국, 우리는 공화국의 진정한 원칙은, 사람들이 그들을 통치할 사람을 선택하는 것이라는 이 생각에 복종해야 한다"라고 인정했다. 그 헌법입안자들은 연방 정부의 선출직 대표들에 대한 가장 기본적인 자격들—나이, 시민권, 그리고 거주 요건들—을 제외한 모든 자격들을 거부했다. 그렇게 하지 않는다는 것은, 제임스 매디슨이 〈연방주의자 55〉에서 부분적으로 설명한 바와 같이, "남성들 사이에 자치정치를 하기에 충분한 정도의 미덕이 없으며, 오직 전제주의의 사슬만이 서로를 파괴하고 집어삼키는 것을 막을 수 있다"는 믿음을 함축하는 것이었다.

자유롭고 공정한 선거를 통해, 국민들은 어떤 한 개인이 공직을 맡을 자격이 있는지 결정한다. 선택된 소수에 의해 결정되고 정부 관료에 의해 집행되는 어떠한 임의적 기준을 충족하는 개인에게 특별한 특권이 주어지거나 주어져서는 안 된다.

개인들은 정치 운동에 참여할 기회를 갖기 전에 선출직에서 자격을 박탈당해서는 안 된다. 한 국가로서, 우리는 이제 읽고 쓰는 능력 테스트의 사용을 금지한다. 선출직 봉사를 위해 차별적인 등가물(자격시험)을 만드는 것이 어떻게 정당화될 수 있는가? 그리고 설령 그렇다 하더라도(정당화될지라도), 잠재적으로 훌륭하거나 효율이 높은 대표가 시험을 통해 평가될 수 있다고 믿을 만한 이유가 있는가?

02

하위내용영역	배점	예상정답률
일반영어 A형 서술형	4점	40%

모범답안 Two people with identical DNA can have different characteristics because of chromosomal packing, which affects the activation of one's genes. Next, one example of a "malfunction" is cancer, which may come about after changes to the epigenome, such as DNA methylation, histone modifications, occur.

채점기준 _ Total 4pts

+ 2점: 같은 DNA를 가지고 있는 사람이 서로 다른 행동 특징을 보이는 이유를 "chromosomal packing, which affects the activation of one's genes"라 서술하였거나 유사하였다.

+ 2점: "malfunction"의 예로 "cancer"라 서술하였다.

한글 번역

만약 당신이 일란성 쌍둥이를 알고 있다면, 그들이 공통점이 없다는 것에 충격을 받았을지도 모른다. 한 명은 숙련된 음악가였을지 모르지만, 다른 한 명은 전혀 연주를 못할 수도 있다. 또는 한 명은 모험을 갈망하는 반면 다른 한 명은 TV 시청을 선호할지도 모른다. 그러한 차이는 유전학에 대한 근본적인 진실을 드러낸다. 즉, 완전히 똑같은 DNA를 가진 두 사람이 상당히 다른 특징을 가질 수 있다. 세포도 마찬가지다. 눈의 망막 세포에서 발가락의 피부 세포에 이르기까지 우리 몸 안에 있는 모든 세포는 약 20,000개의 동일한 유전자를 가지고 있다. 그러나 이 공통적인 유전적 청사진은 각 세포의 개별성에 대한 기초를 제공한다.

후성유전학은 이러한 기이한 차이점들이 어떻게 발생하는지 연구하는 학문이다. 사물은 유전적으로 분명히 동일하지만, 다르게 행동한다. 이것은 행동을 매개하는 DNA 염기 서열과 관련이 없는 염색체가 있어야 한다는 것을 시사한다. 세포에서 DNA는 무방비로 노출된 날것의 분자로 존재하지 않는다. DNA는 염색질로 알려진 복합체의 히스톤 단백질 주위에 둘둘 감겨있고 다른 화학 물질로 장식된다. 이 염색체 포장은 유전자가 켜지거나 꺼지는지에 영향을 미칠 수 있다. 예를 들어, 메틸기라고 불리는 화학 물질로 태그된 유전자나 염색체의 더 단단히 감긴 부분 근처에 위치한 유전자는 꺼질 수 있는 반면, 더 열린 영역 근처에 위치한 유전자는 켜질 수 있다. 심지어 전체 염색체도 이메일 수신함에 있는 압축 파일처럼 종료되고 압축될 수 있다.

이러한 메커니즘의 중요성을 인식하는 한 가지 방법은 오작동 시 발생하는 현상을 조사하는 것이다. 후생유전자를 의미하는 DNA 메틸화, 히스톤 변형, 염색질 상태-어떤 유전자가 암을 통해 발현되고 부분적으로 영향을 받는다는 것은 분명하다.

이러한 후생적 변형을 수행하는 단백질의 돌연변이는 세포의 특성을 완전히 변화시키고 암을 촉진시킬 수 있다. 이러한 후생학적 변화를 목표로 하는 약물은 현재 암 치료의 유망한 형태이다.

03

하위내용영역	배점	예상정답률
일반영어 A형 서술형	4점	40%

모범답안 According to the passage, a person stops depending on magic when he realizes that sense of control over nature is false and that outside, greater forces are truly in control. Next, the word that best corresponds to the underlined words is "science".

채점기준 _Total 4pts

+ 2점: 마술에 의존하는 것을 멈추는 때가 "when he realizes that sense of control over nature is false and that outside, greater forces are truly in control"이라 서술하였거나 유사하였다.

+ 2점: 밑줄 친 부분과 상응하는 한 단어가 "science"임을 정확하게 서술하였다.

한글 번역

만약 우리가 한편으로는 인간이 가장 기본적으로 원하는 욕구의—그것이 어떤 장소든 어느 시기이든—모든 본질적인 유사성을 고려하고, 다른 한편으로는, 그런 욕구를 충족시키기 위해 채택한 수단들 사이의 큰 차이를 고려한다면, 우리는 아마도 다음과 같은 결론에 이르지 않을 수 없을 것 같다. 즉, 우리가 추적할 수 있는 한 인간의 더 높은 인지 과정으로의 움직임이, 대체적으로 볼 때, 마법에서 종교를 거쳐 과학에 이르렀다는 점이다. 마법에 있어서 인간은 모든 면에서 그를 공격하는 어려움과 위험을 극복하기 위해 자신의 힘에 의존한다. 그는 자신이 확실히 의존할 수 있고, 자신의 목적을 위해 조작할 수 있는, 어떤 확고한 자연의 질서를 믿는다. 그가 자신의 실수를 발견했을 때라든가, 그가 가정했던 자연의 질서와 그것에 대해 자신이 행사한다고 믿었던 통제 모두가 순전히 공상적인 것이라는 것을 슬프게도 인식하게 될 때, 그는 자신의 지성과 그 자신의 무력한 노력에 의지하던 것을 멈추고, 자연의 베일 뒤에 있는 어떤 보이지 않는 위대한 존재에 자신을 내맡기게 된다. 그가 한때 자기 자신에게 속하는 것이라 생각했던 그 모든 광대한 힘이 이제는 이 존재에게 속하는 것으로 생각하게 된다. 그렇기에, 좀 더 날카로운 정신의 소유자에게, 마법은 점차 종교로 대체되는데, 이 종교는 일련의 자연 현상들을, 비록 힘에 있어서는 인간보다 훨씬 우월하지만, 인간을 닮은 신들의 의지, 열정, 또는 변덕에 의해 통제되는 것이라 설명한다.

하지만 시간이 지남에 따라 이러한 설명은 결국 만족스럽지 못한 것으로 되고 말았다. 왜냐하면, 일련의 자연적 현상들은 변치 않는 법칙에 의해 결정되는 것이 아니라, 어느 정도 가변적이고 불규칙한 것이라 가정되었는데, 이러한 가정은 더 면밀한 관찰에 의해 근거 없는 것으로 판명됐기 때문이다. 반대로, 우리가 그 일련의 현상들을 더 자세히 조사하면 할수록, 우리는 엄격한 균일성에 더 끌리게 되는데, 그 정확성으로 인해, 우리가 그것을 따를 수 있는 곳이라면 어디든 상관없이, 자연의 질서가 작동되는 것이다. 지식에 있어서의 모든 위대한 진보는 질서의 영역을 확장하는 것이었고 그에 상응하여 세계의 명백한 무질서의 영역을 제한해 왔다. 지금까지 우리는 더 풍부한 지식이 겉으로 보이는 혼란을 질서로 줄일 것이라고 예상할 준비가 돼 있다. 따라서 가장 명민한 정신들은 여전히 우주의 신비에 대한 더 깊은 해법을 향해 나아간다.

04

하위내용영역	배점	예상정답률
일반영어 B형 서술형	4점	45%

모범답안 College-educated families seek to maintain their privilege over others by giving their children advantages and limiting opportunities of other children. This first task, that of giving their own kids an edge, is done through investing more time and money in education than other families are able. Regarding the second task, barriers constructed to impede other families are put in place. These are structural barriers such as zoning restrictions or rental costs in areas with good schools, and, secondly, by influencing and taking advantage of favorable college admissions criteria. Likewise, informal social barriers such as the intimidation through cultural signifiers like specialized jargon are in use.

채점기준

_Total 4pts

ⓐ Topic sentence

+ 1점: College-educated families seek to <u>maintain their privilege over others</u> by <u>giving their own children's advantages</u> and <u>limiting opportunities of other children</u>.

ⓑ Summary

+ 1점: "the first task"가 "investing more <u>money</u>(0.5점) and <u>time</u>(0.5점) to their education than other families are able"을 통해 이루어진다고 서술하였거나 유사하였다.

+ 2점: "the second task"가 두 가지로 나눠지며 그 첫째는 "<u>structural barriors</u>"이고 둘째는 "<u>informal social barriers</u>"임을 서술하였다. 구체적으로, ① "structural barriers"가 "<u>residential zoning restrictions</u>(0.5점)"과 "<u>college admissions game</u>(0.5점)"이고 ② "informal social barriers"가 "<u>cultural signifiers</u>(1점)"임을 서술하였다.

▷ "structural barriers"과 "informal social barriers"가 언급되어 있지 않으면 1점 감점한다.

감점 🔽

• 본문에 나오는 연속되는 6단어 이상을 사용하였다. −0.5pt
• 문단을 두 개나 그 이상으로 구성하였다. −0.5pt

한글 번역

지난 세대에 걸쳐, 대학에서 교육을 받은 계층의 구성원들은 그들의 아이들이 특권적인 지위를 확실히 유지하도록 하는 데 놀라울 정도로 능숙해졌다. 그들은 또한 다른 계급의 아이들이 자신들의 계급에 들어갈 수 있는 기회를 좁히는 데에도 끔찍하게 능숙했다. 그들이 어떻게 첫 번째 과업을 해냈는지는 꽤 명백하다. 바보야, 그건 소아지배야. 지난 수십 년 동안, 미국 중상류층은 성공적인 아이들을 키우는 것을 삶의 중심에 두는 행동 규범을 기꺼이 받아들였다. 그들은 돈을 벌자마자 그 돈을 자녀에 대한 투자로 바꾼다. 중상층 엄마들은 고교 졸업 학력의 엄마들보다 훨씬 더 높은 비율로, 그리고 훨씬 더 오랜 기간 동안 자신들의 아기들에게 모유를 먹일 수 있는 수단과 출산 휴가를 가지고 있다. 중상류층 부모들은 덜 부유한 부모들보다 취학 전 자녀들과 함께 보내는 시간이 2~3배 더 많다. 상황이 도적적으로 위험하게 되는 것은 우리가 다음 과제로 눈을 돌릴 때이다. 가장 중요한 것은 주거 구역 제한이다. 교육을 잘 받은 사람들은 포틀랜드, 뉴욕, 샌프란시스코와 같은 지역들에서 사는 경향이 있다. 이 지역들은 주택 건설 법규들이 있는데 이 법규들은 가난한 사람들과 교육을 덜 받은 사람들이 좋은 학교와 좋은 직업을 가진 이런 곳으로부터 멀어지도록 만드는 역할을 한다. 만약 가장 제한적인 도시들이 가장 덜 제한적인 도시처럼 된다면, 서로 다른 지역들 사이의 불평등은 반으로 줄어들 것이다. 두 번째 구조적 장벽은 대학 입시 게임이다. 교육을 받은 부모들은 최고의 교사들이 있는 동네에서 살고, 지역 공립 학교 예산을 초과하고, 레거시 입학 규정이나 풍부한 여행을 하면서 자란 아이들에게 보상해주는 입학 기준, 그리고 일자리로 이어지는 무급 인턴십으로부터 혜택을 받는다. 하지만 나는 구조적 장벽이 하위 80%를 분리하는 비공식적 사회적 장벽보다 덜 중요하다고 생각하게 되었다. 최근에 나는 고등학교만 나온 친구를 점심에 데려갔다. 나는 둔감하게도 그녀를 고급 샌드위치 가게로 안내했다. 나는 그녀가 "파드리노"라는 이름의 샌드위치와 소프레사타, 카피콜로와 같은 재료에 직면했을 때 안절부절못하는 것을 보았다. 미국의 중상류층 문화는 이제 여러분이 이 계층에서 자라지 않았다면 전혀 읽을 수 없는 문화적 기표들로 뒤섞여 있다. 이 기표들은 굴욕과 배척에 대한 정상적인 인간의 두려움을 이용한다. 그것들의 주요 메시지는 "당신은 여기서 환영받지 못한다."이다.

회 문제은행

📖 본책 p.416

01

하위내용영역	배점	예상정답률
일반영어 A형 기입형	2점	55%

모범답안 print resources

채점기준

• 2점 : 모범답안과 같다. 이것 외에는 답이 될 수 없다.
• 0점 : 모범답안과 다르다.

한글 번역

정보 격차는 현실이다 : 모든 학생들이 인터넷에 신뢰할 수 있는 접근을 하는 것은 아니며, 특히 공공 도서관조차도 사치스러운 시골 지역의 학생들이 그렇다. 경제 문제든 사회 기반 시설에 관한 문제든, 미디어 밀도가 높은 웹사이트가 필요로 하는 컴퓨터나 고속 광대역에 접근할 수 없는 학생들이 많다. 많은 학교에는 많은 사이트를 다룰 수 없는 오래된 컴퓨터가 있고, 몇몇 학교에는 컴퓨터가 전혀 없다. 인터넷에 접속할 수 없는 수강되어 있는 젊은이들과 다른 사람은 일반 지식과 배경 정보를 위한 신뢰할 수 있는 인쇄 자원이 필요하다. 우리는 이러한 집단들이 전인 교육을 받는 것을 기꺼이 거부할 것인가? 호기심에 불을 붙이기 위해 탐색하는 것을 대체할 수 있는 것은 없다. 인쇄 자원을 없애면 학생이 페이지를 넘기는 동안 예상치 못한 주제를 우연히 발견하게 될 때의 뜻밖의 재미를 만날 가능성이 사라진다. 인터넷과 검색 상자는 경이로움을 뒷받침하거나 장려하지 않는다. 백과사전은 상대적으로 컴팩트한 성격과 내용의 다양성 때문에 경이로움을 발견하는 데 특히 훌륭하다. 우리는 학생들에게 탐구 중심의 비판적 사고를 만들어 주려는 반면에 다른 한편으로는 그러한 생각을 고취시키는 데 필요한 도구를 체계적으로 제거하고 있다.

02

하위내용영역	배점	예상정답률
일반영어 B형 서술형	4점	40%

모범답안 Two examples matching the mentioned prototype are "mouths," which originally functioned to take in nutrition, and "body protrusions" on flightless bugs that originally absorbed sunlight. Second, the one word is "unnatural". Third, the implication of the underlined words in ⓒ is that to say that when a mosquito's bumps function as solar panels it is natural, whereas when they function as wings with which she flies in the sky it is unnatural is nonsense.

채점기준   _Total 4pts

+ 1점 : 장기(기관)의 원형의 예를 다음의 두 개를 들어 서술하였다.
  "mouths", which originally functioned to take in nutrition(0.5점); insect wings that were body protrusions (or bumps) on flightless bugs that originally absorbed sunlight(0.5점)

+ 1점 : 빈칸에 들어갈 단어를 "unnatural"이라 정확하게 기입하였다. 이것 외에는 답이 될 수 없다.

+ 2점 : 밑줄 친 부분의 함축 의미를 "to say that when a mosquito's bumps function as solar panels it is natural, whereas when they function as wings with which she flies in the sky it is unnatural is nonsense"라 정확하게 서술하였거나 유사하였다.
  ▷ 다음과 같이 서술하였으면 1.5점을 준다.
  • "humans can freely use limbs and organs for things they were not originally given purpose to, without being "unnatural", as it is really the way evolution works."
  • "mosquito's usage of wings disproves the statement that God wants organs and limbs used for their original purposes."

한글 번역

만약 우리가 신이 구상한 목적을 위해 우리의 팔다리와 장기를 사용한다면, 그것은 자연스러운 활동이다. 신이 의도한 것과 다르게 그것들을 사용하는 것은 부자연스러운 것이다. 하지만 진화에는 그 어떠한 목적도 없다. 장기들은 목적을 가지고 진화하지 않았고, 장기들이 사용되는 방법은 끊임없이 변화하고 있다. 수억 년 전 장기가 처음 나타났을 당시 그것의 원형이 했던 일만을 (여전히 지금도) 하는 장기는 단 한 개도 없다. 장기는 특정 기능을 수행하기 위해 진화하지만, 일단 그것들이 존재하면, 그것들은 다른 용도로도 적용될 수 있다. 예를 들어, 입은 가장 초기의 다세포 유기체들이 영양분을 몸안으로 흡수하는 방법이 필요했기 때문에 나타났다. 우리는 여전히 그 목적을 위해 입을 사용하지만, 키스를 하거나, 말을 하거나, 람보라면, 수류탄에서 핀을 뽑기 위해 입을 사용하기도 한다. 6억 년 전에 우리의 벌레처럼 생긴 조상들이 입으로 그런 것들을 하지 않았다는 단지 그 이유 때문에 이러한 사용법들을 부자연스러운 것이라 할 수 있을까? 마찬가지로, 날개는 공기역학의 영광을 지니고 (처음에) 갑자기 나타난 것이 아니다. 날개는 다른 목적에 종사하는 장기들로부터 발전했다. 곤충의 날개는 수백만 년 전에 날지 못하는 벌레의 몸에 있는 돌출부로부터 진화했다. 혹이 있는 곤충은 혹이 없는 곤충보다 표면적이 더 넓었고, 이것은 그 곤충들이 (혹이 없는 곤충보다) 더 많은 햇빛을 흡수하고 따라서 더 따뜻하게 지낼 수 있게 해줬다. 느린 진화 과정에서, 이 태양열 난방기들은 더 커졌다. 햇빛을 최대한 흡수하기에 좋은 이 동일한 구조—많은 표면적, 적은 무게—또한 우연하게도 곤충들이 건너뛰고 점프할 때 약간의 비상을 할 수 있도록 해줬다. 더 큰 돌출부를 가진 곤충들은 더 멀리 팔짝 뛰고 더 멀리 점프할 수 있었다. 몇몇 곤충들은 활공하기 위해 그 돌출부를 사용하기 시작했고, 거기서부터 날개로 가는 단계는 멀지 않았는데, 이 날개는 곤충을 공기 중으로 나아갈 수 있게 했다. 다음에 모기 한 마리가 여러분의 귀에서 윙윙거릴 때, 모기가 하는 부자연스러운 행동을 비난하라. 만약 모기가 신이 자기에게 준대로 행동하고 만족해서 산다면, 모기는 태양 전지판으로만 날개를 사용할 것이다.

03

하위내용영역	배점	예상정답률
일반영어 B형 서술형	4점	45%

모범답안 The implication of the underlined ⓐ is that the mother who tries to encourage feminine traits in her young boy can be considered as a wrong person. Second, the writer believes that Anthony E. Wolf's theory is unfounded and actually in contradiction to the proven results of close mothers and sons.

+ 2점: 밑줄 친 ⓐ의 함축 의미를 "The implication of the underlined is that the mother who tries to encourage feminine traits in her young boy can be considered as a wrong person"라 서술하였거나 유사하였다.

+ 2점: 글의 저자가 Anthony Wolf의 이론에 대해 "unfounded and actually in contradiction to the proven results of close mothers and sons"라 서술하였거나 유사하였다.

한글 번역

우리는 딸들을 키우는 방법을 극적으로 변화시켰는데, 딸들이 적극적이고, 경쟁적인 스포츠를 하고, 그들의 교육적, 직업적 야망을 높이 갖도록 장려했다. 우리는 딸들을 "남성화"시키는 것에 대해 조바심을 내지 않는다. 딸들과 아빠들의 경우—"마마보이(응석받이 아들)"가 욕을 먹는 피조물인 반면에—사람들은 "파파걸(아버지와 사이가 좋고 아버지에게 많이 의존하는 여성)"을 관용적으로 보는 경향이 있다. 다정하고 도움이 되는 아버지는 딸의 자존감에 필수적인 것으로 간주된다. 아버지들은, 딸의 축구 팀을 지도하거나 부녀 춤 파티에 10대 딸을 데리고 가거나 하는 식으로, 딸들의 삶에 관여하도록 권장받는다. 성 고정 관념을 버리고 딸에게 전통적으로 남성적인 일, 예를 들어 자동차 엔진을 만드는 일을 가르치는 아버지는 꽤 멋진 사람으로 여겨진다. 하지만 아들에게 뜨개질을 가르치거나 심지어 아들로 하여금 자신의 감정에 대해 더 솔직하게 말하도록 격려하는 것과 같이 위에서 말한 아버지와 비슷한 일을 하는 어머니는 경멸의 눈으로 바라봐진다. 도대체 저 엄마는 아들에게 뭘 하려고 하는 거지? 많은 엄마들이 남자아이 양육에 관해 혼란스럽고 불안해한다. 남편이 일 학년 아들을 학교에 내려줄 때 키스하는 것을 중단해야 한다고 주장할 때, 엄마는 남편의 의견에 따라야 하나? 엄마가 10살 된 아들이 다쳤을 때 그를 껴안아 주는 것이 아들을 겁쟁이로 만드는 것일까? 아들을 너무 가까이 두면 아들을 게이로 만드는 것일까? 10대 아들이 방에서 울고 있다면, 엄마는 들어가서 그를 위로해야 할까, 아니면 이렇게 위로하는 것이 오히려 아들을 당황하게 하고 수치심을 느끼도록 할까? 아동 심리학자이자 베스트셀러 작가인 앤서니 울프는 우리에게 "엄마와의 강한 감정적 접촉은 십 대인 아들을 속상하게 만든다."고 경고한다. 하지만 이러한 두려움 중 그 어느 것도 실제 과학에 기초하지 않는다. 사실, 소년들이 그들의 엄마와 일찍 헤어질 때 고통을 받고, 그들의 일생 내내 엄마와의 친밀함으로부터 수많은 방법으로 혜택을 입는다는 것을 연구는 보여준다.

04

하위내용영역	배점	예상정답률
일반영어 B형 서술형	4점	40%

모범답안 Though scientific or technological progress brings with it side effects, it brings much more benefits on the whole. For instance, nitroglycerine, which was discovered in 1846 and quickly suited to warfare and destruction. However, it could be used for reducing labor in many construction projects. In this way, technology is like a double-edged sword. Another advance concerns (or lies in) medicine, such as successful vaccination and germ theory, which have caused not only a lower death rate, but also overpopulation. However, rather than avoiding advances in medicine, we should be using science to reduce the birthrate to curb(=slow) growth.

채점기준
_ Total 4pts

ⓐ Topic sentence

+ 2점 : "Scientific or technological progress brings with it side effects, but also yields much more benefits on the whole"

ⓑ Summary

+ 1점 : 네 개의 examples 가운데 1개를 정확하게 요약하였다. 요약 시 "<u>positive</u>" 측면에서의 언급과 "<u>negative</u>" 측면에서의 언급이 균형 있게 서술되어 있다.
"<u>nitroglycerine, which was discovered in 1846 and quickly suited to warfare and destruction</u>(0.5점). However, <u>it could be used for reducing labor in many construction projects</u>(0.5점)"

+ 1점 : 네 개의 examples 가운데 또 다른 1개를 정확하게 요약하였다. 요약 시 "<u>positive</u>" 측면에서 언급과 "<u>negative</u>" 측면에서의 언급이 균형 있게 서술되어 있다.
"medicine, such as successful vaccination and germ theory, which have caused not only a <u>lower death rate</u>(0.5점), but also <u>overpopulation</u>(0.5점)"

▷ 나머지 2개의 예
• "invention of knives and spears" which led to <u>more food</u> and <u>more murder</u>"
• "discover of nuclear energy" <u>puts the world at risk</u> but also <u>brings about aid to man's energy needs</u>"

한글 번역

우리 모두는 이제 어떤 새로운 과학이나 기술의 발전이 유용하기는 하지만, 좋지 않은 부작용을 일으킬 수도 있다는 것을 알고 있다. 점점 더 세상은, 되돌릴 수 없을지도 모르는 어떤 것에 헌신하기 전에, 주의를 기울이려 노력하는 경향이 있다. 문제는, 부작용이 어떤 것인지 구분하는 것이 항상 쉽지만은 않다는 점이다. 1846년, 아스카니오 소브레로는 최초의 니트로글리세린을 생산했다. 열이 오르자, 니트로글리세린 한 방울이 고막을 찢는 듯한 소리를 내며 폭발했다. 그 이탈리아 화학자는 그것이 전쟁에 적용될 수 있다는 것을 공포에 질려 깨닫고 즉시 연구를 중단했다. 물론 그의 (이러한 양심적) 연구 중단이 도움이 되지는 않았다. 다른 사람들이 뒤따라서 왔고, 19세기 말에는 니트로글리세린과 다른 고성능 폭약들이 전쟁에 사용됐다. 전쟁에 사용된 것이 고성능 폭약을 완전히 나쁜 것으로만 만들었나? 1867년, 알프레드 노벨은 니트로글리세린을 규조토와 혼합하여 다루기에 더 안전한 혼합물—본인이 "다이너마이트"라고 부른—을 만드는 방법을 알아냈다. 이 다이너마이트를 통해서 흙은 곡괭이와 삽을 훨씬 뛰어넘는 속도로 움직일 수 있고, 힘든 노동으로 사람을 잔인하게 다루지 않을 수도 있다. 철도를 위한 길을 만드는 데 도움을 준 것은 다이너마이트였고, 댐, 지하철, 토대, 다리, 그리고 산업 시대의 수많은 다른 거대한 건축물을 건설하는 데 도움을 준 것도 다이너마이트였다.
그 출발에서부터 인간의 기술 위에는 양날의 검이 걸려 있었다. 칼과 창의 발명은 인간의 식량 공급을 증가시켰지만 동시에 살인의 기술을 향상시켰다. 핵에너지의 발견은 이제 전 지구를 파괴의 위험 아래 놓이게 한 반면, 그것은 또한 인간의 에너지 문제에 대한 무한한 해결책으로서 핵융합 발전의 가능성을 제공한다. 또는 1796년의 첫 성공적인 백신 접종과 1860년대의 배종설을 되돌아 보자. 우리는 의학적 진보가 인류에게 위험하다고 보는가, 아니면 백신과 항독소, 마취와 무독소, 화학적 특이성과 항생제의 활용을 거부하는가? 그러나 19세기의 의학적 발견의 부작용은 핵물리학자들이 했던 그 어떤 것보다도 문명의 파괴를 보장하는 데 더 많은 일을 했다. 오늘날 인구 폭발은 평균 출산율의 상승에 의한 것이 아니라, 의약 덕분에 사망률이 급감했기 때문이다. 이것이 의미하는 것이, 과학이 의학을 통해 인간의 운명을 개선하는 것을 피하고 인류를 단명 종족으로 유지했어야 한다는 것인가? 아니면 가능한 해로운 부작용을 바로잡고, 출산율을 줄이는 것을 더 간단하게 만드는 방법들을 고안해서 감소하는 사망률에 출산율을 맞게 유지하기 위해 과학을 활용해야 하는 것일까? 당연히 후자이다!

48회 문제은행

📖 본책 p.422

01

하위내용영역	배점	예상정답률
일반영어 A형 기입형	2점	45%

모범답안 ⓐ leisure ⓑ the (small) leisure class

채점기준

- 2점 : 모범답안과 같다. 이것 외에는 답이 될 수 없다.
- 1점 : 둘 중 하나만 맞았다.
- 0점 : 모범답안과 다르다.

한글 번역

노동 시간을 4시간으로 줄여야 한다고 해서 나머지 시간이 반드시 매우 경박스런 일에 쓰여져야 한다는 뜻은 아니다. 내 얘기는 하루 4시간 노동으로 생활 필수품과 기초 편의재를 확보하는 한편, 남는 시간은 스스로 알아서 적절한 곳에 사용하도록 해야 한다는 뜻이다. 현재보다 더 많은 교육이 이루어지고 그 교육의 목표에 여가를 현명하게 사용하는 데 필요한 취향을 제공하는 항목이 들어 있어야 한다는 것은 어느 사회에서나 필수적이다. 나는 지금 소위 "교양인" 따위를 만드는 것을 염두에 두고 있는 것은 아니다. 농부들의 무도회는 외진 시골 지역들을 제외하곤 사라져 버렸지만 그들을 도와시켜 주던 그 충동은 여전히 인간의 본성 속에 남아 있음에 틀림없다. 도시 사람들의 즐거움은 대체로 수동적인 것이 되어 버렸다. 영화를 보고, 축구 시합을 관전하고, 라디오를 듣고 하는 식이다. 이렇게 된 것은 그들의 적극적인 에너지들이 모조리 일에 흡수되어 버리기 때문이다. 여가가 더 있다면, 그들은 과거 적극적인 부분을 담당하며 맛보았던 즐거움을 다시 누리게 될 것이다. 과거에는 여가를 즐기는 계층은 소수였고, 일하는 계층은 다수였다. 유한 계층이 누리는 편의는 사회 정의란 측면에서 볼 때 완전히 잘못된 것이었다. 그 결과 유한 계층은 압제적으로 되어 갔고 자기들만의 공감대 내로 좁혀지고, 특권을 정당화하기 위한 논리들을 만들어 내야 했다.

02

하위내용영역	배점	예상정답률
일반영어 A형 기입형	2점	35%

모범답안 ⓐ undermines ⓑ society
ⓒ problematic social behaviors

채점기준

- 2점 : 모범답안과 같다. 이것 외에는 답이 될 수 없다.
- 1점 : 셋 중 2개만 맞았다.
- 0점 : 모범답안과 다르다.

한글 번역

약자 괴롭히기(불링)는 심각한 문제다. 이에 대해 무언가 해야 한다는 외침이 새로운 법안, 학교 회합, 그리고 불링 가해자들에 대한 처벌 압력 등을 낳았다. 뒤로 한 발 물러서서 객관적으로 바라보기가 어려운 문제인 만큼 문제 해결을 위해서는 더욱 그렇게 할 필요가 있다. 연구진의 입장에서, 우리는 오해가 문제 개입 시 장애가 된다는 것을 발견했다. 이 점을 염두에 두고 우리는 '인식'에서 '행동'으로 가기 위해 반드시 이해되어야만 할 불링의 몇 가지 측면을 다뤄보겠다.

사이버불링 문제가 불필요하게 주의를 흐트러트리고 있다. 학생들의 보고에 따르면 교내 불링이 여전히 더 빈번하게 나타나며 사이버불링보다 훨씬 부정적인 영향을 미친다. 대부분의 불링은 어른 눈에는 잘 보이지 않지만 온라인상의 흔적은 다양한 형태의 비열함과 잔인함을 가시화한다. 따라서 어른들은 인터넷에 집중하게 된다. 특정한 종류의 부정적인 활동이 인터넷에 넘쳐나는 건 사실이지만 인터넷은 실제 현상을 과장되어 보이게 하는 특징이 있다.

어떤 아이가 상처를 입었을 때 사람들은 누군가 혹은 무언가 탓할 대상을 찾는다. 하지만 가해자 처벌에 급급하다보면 불링을 해결하기가 오히려 어려워진다. 10대 자살 문제에 조치를 취하긴 해야 하지만 피해자를 기리기 위해 성급히 결함이 있는 법안을 실행시키거나 가해자를 처벌하는 것은 사회가 져야 할 책임을 개인에게 지우는 것이나 다름없다. 10대 자살은 한 사람의 행동으로 설명될 수 없는 경우가 많다. 정신 건강상의 문제, 적응하지 못하는 문제, 부모의 지나친 압력, 참지 못하는 문화 등이 섞여 치명적인 결과를 낳는 경우가 많은 것이다. 탓할 사람을 찾기보다 원인과 결과를 밝혀 그것을 해결하는 게 중요하다. '탓하기'는 폭력의 사이클을 멈추지 못한다. 불링(다른 종류의 폭력과 공격성 포함)과 싸우는 것은 우리 사회의 우선 과제여야 한다. 그러나 불링은 아이들만의 문제가 아니다. 아이들을 돕고 싶다면 어른들이 가진 악의적 성향부터 없애야 하며 문제 있는 가치와 불관용에 대한 책임을 져야 한다. 정치인들이 수시로 서로를 비난하는 것, 부모들이 이웃의 뒤에서 그들을 험담하는 것, 리얼리티 TV 스타들이 유명 인사가 되고 서로를 끔찍하게 대우하는 것을 용인하면서 아이들에게 친구를 위하라고 말할 수는 없는 것이다.

03

하위내용영역	배점	예상정답률
일반영어 A형 서술형	4점	50%

모범답안 The key point of U.K. experts is that ceasing antibiotic treatment earlier is an effective and safe way to reduce antibiotic resistance. Next, "robust microbes" can survive and pass on survival instructions to other bacterial strains.

채점기준 _Total 4pts

+ 2점 : 영국의 전문가들이 항생제 내성 세균을 통제하는 방법을 "stopping antibiotics earlier is an effective and safe way to reduce antibiotic resistance"라 서술하였거나 유사하였다.

▷ 다음과 같이 서술하였어도 맞는 것으로 한다.
"ending(finishing) antibiotic treatment when a patient feels better is to reduce overuse of antibiotics"

+ 2점 : "원기왕성한 세균"이 부분적인 코스의 항생제에 어떻게 대응하는지를 묻는 질문에 다음과 같이 서술하였거나 유사하였다.
"robust microbes can outsmart available drugs and pass on survival instructions to other bacterial strains"

한글 번역

만약 항생제 내성에 대항하는 전투 찬가가 있다면, 그것은 하나의 공통적인 후렴구가 있을 것이다. 모든 부적절한 처방이나 불충분한 복용량은 적을 강화시킨다는 것이 그것이다. 그것은 약한 박테리아를 죽일 수도 있지만, 침입해서 증식할 수 있는 더 강하고 약물에 내성이 있는 박테리아를 제거하지는 못할 것이다. 결국, 이러한 강력한 세균들은 이용 가능한 약품들보다 더 똑똑할 수 있고, 심지어 다른 박테리아 종들에게 생존 비법을 전달할 수도 있다. 그것이 세계 보건 기구와 미국 질병 통제 예방 센터와 함께 대부분의 의사들이 환자들에게 병이 나은 것 같은 기분이 든다 할지라도 항상 처방된 약물을 꼭 다 복용하기를 권하는 이유이다. 너무 적은 양을 복용하거나 일찍 중단하는 것은 약물 내성을 급증시키는 데 기름을 부을 수 있다고 그 의사들은 판단한다.

하지만 일단의 영국의 전염병 전문가들은 의사들과 공중보건 전문가들에게 그들의 태도를 바꾸라고 촉구하고 있다. 영국 의학 저널에 실린 논평에서, 그들은 "과정 수료'라는 메시지는 증거에 의해 뒷받침되지 않았음에도 불구하고 지속되어 왔다. 많은 상황에서, 항생제를 더 빨리 중단하는 것이 항생제 과용을 줄일 수 있는 안전하고 효과적인 방법이라는 증거가 있습니다."라고 말한다. 저자들은 퀴놀론과 같은 특정 약물 클래스의 더 짧은 과정이 과거에 권장됐던 더 긴 과정만큼 효과적이라는 것을 보여주는 최근의 연구들을 지적한다.

04

하위내용영역	배점	예상정답률
일반영어 B형 서술형	4점	35%

모범답안 The main idea of the passage is that price-fixing is not only unavoidable but also beneficial to the economy of an industrialized society. Second, it can be inferred that economists think price-fixing by sellers harms the needs of the consumers and that prices should not be fixed by explicit agreement, because it may lower competition between sellers and lead to overpricing.

채점기준 _Total 4pts

+ 2점 : 글의 main idea를 "price-fixing is not only inevitable but also beneficial to the economy of an industrialized society"라 서술하였거나 유사하였다.

▷ 다음과 같이 서술하였어도 맞는 것으로 한다.
"price-fixing is not only normal but also valuable for(to) the economy of an industrialized society"

+ 1점 : 대다수 미국의 경제학자들의 주장에 의하면 (소비자가 아닌 판매자들에 의해 결정되는 가격인) price-fixing이 가장 해를 끼치는 그룹이 "consumers (as a group)"라 답하였다.

▷ 다음과 서술하였어도 맞는 것으로 한다.
"a price fixed by the seller seems harmful to consumers as a group(the aggregate of consumers)"

+ 1점 : consumers에게 해를 끼치는 이유를 "because it may lower competition (between sellers) and lead to overpricing"라 서술하였거나 유사하였다.

📖 본책 p.428

01

하위내용영역	배점	예상정답률
일반영어 A형 기입형	2점	45%

모범답안   criminal

채점기준

- 2점 : 모범답안과 같다. 이것 외에는 답이 될 수 없다.
- 0점 : 모범답안과 다르다.

한글 번역

자유 시장, 자유화, 세계화는 동시대 경제의 기저에 깔려 있는 트렌드이다. 대부분의 미국 경제학자들은 자유 시장이라는 마법에 사로잡혀 있다. 이렇기에, 이 경제학자에게는 자유 시장의 요구 사항에 부합하지 않는 어떤 것도 좋거나 정상적인 것처럼 보이지 않는다. 판매자나, 소비자 집단이 아닌 다른 사람이 결정하는 가격은 해로워 보인다. 따라서 가격 담합(판매자가 가격을 결정하는 것)을 "정상적"으로 생각하는 동시에 가치 있는 경제적 결과를 낳는 것으로 생각하기 위해서는 커다란 의지력이 필요하다.

사실, 가격 담합은 모든 산업화된 사회에서 일반적이다. 왜냐하면 산업 시스템 자체가, 그 시스템의 진보를 촉진하는 유기적인 기능으로서, 필요한 가격 담합을 제공하기 때문이다. 현대 산업 계획은 엄청난 규모를 요구하고 또 엄청난 규모로 보상한다. 따라서 상대적으로 많지 않은 숫자의 대기업들이 동일한 소비자 집단을 두고 경쟁할 것이다. 각 대기업이 자신의 요구를 고려해 행동하고 따라서 경쟁사들이 청구하는 가격보다 더 높은 가격에 제품을 판매하는 것을 피한다는 것은 자유 시장 경제 이론의 옹호자들에 의해 일반적으로 인정된다. 그러나 각 대기업은 또한 동일한 고객을 두고 경쟁하는 다른 대기업과 공유하는 필요성에 대해 충분히 고려하여 행동할 것이다. 따라서 각 대기업은 상당히 큰 폭의 가격 인하를 피할 것이다. 왜냐하면 가격 인하는 제품에 대한 안정적인 수요에 대한 공동의 이익에 해로울 것이기 때문이다. 주목할 만한 것은 많은 경제학자들이 가격 담합이 일어날 때 그것을 보지 않는다는 것이다. 왜냐하면 그들은 가격 담합이 대기업들 사이에서 일어나는 많은 수의 명시적인 합의에 의해 야기될 것이라고 기대하기 때문이다. (하지만) 이것은 사실이 아니다.

게다가, 자유 시장이 간섭 없이 운영되도록 놔두는 것이 가격을 책정하는 가장 효율적인 방법이라고 주장하는 그 경제학자들은 미국 이외의 비사회주의 국가의 경제를 고려하지 않아 왔다. 이 경제들은 대개 공공연한 방식으로 의도적인 가격 담합을 사용한다. 카르텔에 의한 공식적인 가격 담합과 업계의 구성원을 포괄하는 협정에 의한 비공식적인 가격 담합은 흔한 일이다. 만일 자유 시장에 실질적으로 효율적인 무언가가 있고, 가격 담합에 비효율적인 어떤 것이 있다면, 첫 번째 것(자유 시장)을 피하고 두 번째 것(가격 담합)을 사용한 나라들은 그들의 경제 발전에 큰 타격을 입었을 것이다. (하지만) 그런 조짐을 보이는 것은 없다.

한글 번역

2008년 선거 운동 중에, 자신의 정체성이 흑인인지에 관한 질문을 받았을 때, 오바마 대통령은 "지난번 뉴욕에서 택시를 잡으려고 했는데..."라고 간단히 말했다. 그의 발언은 흑인들에게 그가 차별을 경험했다는 것을 알리는 동시에 21세기 인종 관계가 지니고 있는 치명적인 결함을 드러냈다. 즉, 그것은 흑인과 범죄자를 구별 못하는 우리의 무능력이다. 교육부의 연구 외에도, 흑인과 라틴 아메리카계가 학교에서 더욱더 많이 징계를 받고 경찰에 검문을 받을 가능성이 더욱 높다는 사회학적 연구 결과가 계속 나오고 있다. 일부 사람들은 흑인 아이들이 백인 아이들보다 더 나쁘다고 이야기거리로 주장할 수도 있지만, 여러 연구들은 더욱 절박한 문제를 보여준다. 즉, 교사와 경찰관이 흑인과 라틴계 젊은이나 그들이 사는 동네를 추적 관찰하고, 프로파일링(불심 검문에서 특정 인종이나 계층이 집중적으로 검문 대상이 되는 것)하고, 경찰 단속하는데, 백인 젊은이나 동네에 대해 하는 것보다 더 많이 한다. 고등학생의 75%가 중독성 물질을 시도해 봤음에도, 특정 집단과 지역만이 경찰의 표적이 된다. 애크론 대학이 그 학교에 다니는 흑인 남학생들에게 보낸 이메일에서 보이듯이, 대학생이라는 지위도 그들에게 경찰 단속을 피할 특권을 부여하지는 않는다. 그렇기에, 한 흑인 상원 의원(여기선 버락 오바마를 의미)이 (다른 흑인 남성과) 유사하게 "잠재적 범죄자" 취급을 받는다.

마리화나를 합법화하는 것은 잠재적으로 흑인 남성 및 라틴계 남성에 대한 더 합법적인 경찰 단속으로 이어질 수 있다. 매우 가혹한 마약법을 줄이는 것이 양형에는 도움이 될 것이지만, 여전히 흑인과 라틴계 남성이 범죄자로 취급되는 방식을 바꾸지는 못한다. 이런 점에서, 이런 흑인과 라틴계 남성을 범죄화하는 전염병은 법적, 제도적인 문제일 뿐만 아니라 그만큼이나 사회적인 문제이기도 하다.

02

하위내용영역	배점	예상정답률
일반영어 A형 서술형	4점	40%

모범답안 Cognitive dissonance is holding (onto) contradictory values or beliefs at the same time. Next, the writer would recommend as a way of reaching understanding between faiths to look into the points of cognitive dissonance, where simultaneously-held ideas compete, in the given faith. Third the two words are "human culture".

채점기준 _Total 4pts

+ 1점 : 인지 부조화를 "holding (onto) contradictory values"라 정확히 서술하였다.

+ 2점 : 저자가 제안하는 서로 다른 종교에 대한 이해에 도달하는 가장 좋은 방법에 대해 "to look into the points of cognitive dissonance, where simultaneously-held ideas compete, in the given faith"라 정확히 서술하였다.

+ 1점 : 빈칸에 들어갈 두 단어를 "human culture"라 기입하였다. 이것 외에는 답이 될 수 없다.

한글 번역

중세 문화가 기사도와 기독교를 어떻게든 조화시키는 데 실패했던 것과 마찬가지로, 오늘날 세계는 자유와 평등을 조화시키는 데 실패하고 있다. 그러나 이것은 결함이 아니다. 그 모순은 모든 인간 문화에서 떼려야 뗄 수 없는 부분이다. 사실 이것은 문화의 엔진으로서, 우리 종의 창의성과 활력의 근원이기도 하다. 서로 충돌하는 두 음이 동시에 연주되면서 음악 작품을 앞으로 밀고 나아가듯이, 우리의 생각과 아이디어와 가치의 불협화음은 우리로 하여금 생각하고, 재평가하고, 비판하게 만든다. 일관성은 따분한 사고의 놀이터다.

만일 긴장과 분쟁과 해결 불가능한 딜레마가 모든 문화의 묘미라면, 어떤 문화에 속한 인간이든 누구나 상반되는 신념을 지닐 것이며 서로 상충하는 가치에 의해 분열될 것이다. 이것은 모든 문화에 공통되는 핵심적 측면이기 때문에, 별도의 이름까지 있다. "인지 부조화"다. 인지 부조화는 흔히 인간 정신의 실패로 여겨진다. 하지만 사실 그것은 핵심 자산이다. 만일 사람들에게 모순되는 신념과 가치를 품을 능력이 없었다면, 인간의 문화 자체를 건설하고 유지하기가 불가능 했을 것이다.

예컨대 기독교인이 근처 모스크에 참배하러 가는 무슬림을 정말로 이해하고 싶다면, 모든 무슬림들이 소중하게 여기는 순수한 가치들이 무엇인지 찾아볼 필요가 없다. 그보다는 무슬림 문화에서 가장 극심한 딜레마의 현장을 찾아봐야 한다. 규칙이 서로 충돌하고 규범이 서로 난투를 벌이는 지점 말이다. 무슬림들이 두 가지 지상명제 사이에서 흔들리고 있는 지점이야말로 당신이 그들을 가장 잘 이해할 수 있는 지점이다.

03

하위내용영역	배점	예상정답률
일반영어 B형 서술형	4점	55%

모범답안 The word is "algorithm". Second, the writer of the passage might call the steps as an algorithm.

채점기준 _Total 4pts

+ 2점 : 빈칸에 들어갈 단어를 "algorithm"이라 답하였다. 이것 외에는 답이 될 수 없다.

+ 2점 : 저자가 "자판기에 가서 커피를 주문하는 어떤 사람이 행하는 일련의 과정을 무엇이라 부르겠느냐"는 질문에 답을 "algorithm"이라 하였다. 이것 외에는 답이 될 수 없다.

한글 번역

알고리즘은 계산을 하고 문제를 풀고 결정을 내리는 데 사용할 수 있는 일련의 체계적인 단계들이다. 알고리즘은 특정한 계산이 아니라 계산할 때 따라오는 체계성이다. 예를 들어 당신이 두 수의 평균을 구하고 싶다면 간단한 알고리즘을 사용할 수 있다. 그 알고리즘은 이렇게 명령한다. "1단계 : 두 수를 더하라. 2단계 : 그 합을 2로 나눠라." 이 알고리즘에 4와 8을 입력하면 6이 나온다. 117과 231을 입력하면 174가 나온다.

더 복잡한 예로는 요리 레시피가 있다. 예컨대 채소 수프를 만드는 알고리즘을 이렇게 명령할 것이다.

1. 기름 반 컵을 냄비에 넣고 달군다.
2. 양파 네 개를 잘게 다진다.
3. 황금빛을 띨 때까지 양파를 볶는다.
4. 감자 세 개를 큼직하게 썰어서 냄비에 넣는다.
5. 양배추를 채 썰어 냄비에 넣는다.

대략 이런 식이다. 당신은 같은 알고리즘을 수십 번씩 실행할 수 있고, 매번 사용하는 채소를 조금씩 달리해 약간 다른 수프를 만들 수 있다. 하지만 알고리즘 자체는 그대로이다.

레시피만으로 수프가 만들어질 수는 없다. 레시피를 읽고 정해진 일군의 단계들을 행할 사람이 필요하다. 하지만 사람 대신 이 알고리즘을 자동으로 실행할 기계를 만들 수도 있다. 그러면 그 기계에 물, 전기, 채소를 넣기만 하면 기계가 알아서 수프를 만들 것이다. 우리 주변에 수프 만드는 기계는 드물지만 음료수 자판기는 흔하다. 그런 자판기들에는 대개 동전 넣는 구멍, 컵이 나오는 곳, 몇 줄로 배열된 버튼들이 있다. 첫째 줄에는 커피, 차, 코코아를 위한 버튼들이 있다. 둘째 줄에는 무설탕, 설탕 한 스푼, 설탕 두 스푼이라고 표시된 버튼들이 있다. 셋째 줄에는 우유, 두유, 선택하지 않음이라고 적힌 버튼들이 있다. 그 기계로 다가가 구멍에 동전을 넣고 '차', '설탕 한 스푼', '우유' 버튼을 차례로 누르면, 기계가 입력된 단계들을 따라 작동하기 시작한다. 티백을 컵에 떨어뜨리고, 뜨거운 물을 붓고, 설탕 한 스푼과 우유를 첨가한 뒤 탁! 소리와 함께 맛있는 차가 나온다. 이것이 알고리즘이다.

04

하위내용영역	배점	예상정답률
일반영어 B형 서술형	4점	35%

모범답안 Happiness has a "glass ceiling", which is composed of psychological and biological components, preventing people from reaching supreme happiness. For psychological, happiness relies on our expectations rather than on objective situations. (Though objective conditions can be improved all the time, our expectations may proportionally expand and remain out of reach.) In regards to biological, our happiness is based on our biochemistry (physiology) rather than our social, economic, and political condition. Happiness has been defined by philosophers such as John Stuart Mill as pleasure without pain, with no good or evil beyond that. This was controversial in its time but now is "scientific orthodoxy", with the source of unhappiness being identified as bodily sensations.

채점기준 _Total 4pts

ⓐ Topic sentence

+ 1점 : "Happiness has a "glass ceiling", which is composed of psychological and biological components components, preventing people from reaching supreme happiness."

ⓑ Summary

+ 3점 : "For psychological, happiness relies on our expectations rather than on objective situations. In regards to biological, our happiness is based on our biochemistry(physiology) rather than our social, economic, and political condition. Happiness has been defined by philosophers such as John Stuart Mill as pleasure without pain, with no good or evil beyond that. This was controversial in its time but now is "scientific orthodoxy", with the source of unhappiness being identified as bodily sensations."

▷ 글에 언급된 세 명의 철학자 가운데 "한 사람의 행복에 대한 정의"를 정확하게 서술하였으면 1점을 준다.

감점 ♥

• 글이 너무 짧았다(4줄 이하). −1pt
• 글이 너무 길었다(8줄 이상). −0.5pt
• 본문에 나오는 연속된 6단어 이상을 사용하였다. −0.5pt

한글 번역

마치 전례 없는 성과에도 불구하고 알 수 없는 유리 천장에 부딪혀 행복이 그 이상으로 올라가지 못하는 것 같다. 우리가 모든 사람에게 무상으로 음식을 제공하고 존재하는 모든 질병을 치료하고 세계 평화를 이룬다 해도, 그 유리 천장이 깨진다는 보장은 없다. 진정한 행복을 획득하는 것이 노화와 죽음을 극복하는 것보다 쉽지는 않을 듯하다. 두 개의 튼튼한 기둥이 행복의 유리 천장을 떠받치고 있는데, 하나는 심리적인 것이고 다른 하나는 생물학적인 것이다. 심리적 수준에서 보면, 행복은 객관적 조건보다 기대치에 달려 있다. 우리는 평화와 번영을 누릴 때 만족하지 않는다. 실제와 기대가 일치할 때 만족한다. 나쁜 소식은, 조건이 나아질수록 기대가 부풀어 오른다는 것이다. 최근 몇십 년 동안 인류가 겪은 것처럼 조건이 크게 좋아지면, 만족도가 높아지는 것이 아니라 기대치가 높아진다. 이 문제를 해결하지 못한다면, 우리는 앞으로도 성취하면 할수록 불만이 커질 것이다.

생물학적 수준에서 보면, 기대와 행복을 결정하는 것은 경제적·사회적·정치적 상황이 아니라 우리의 생화학적 조건이다. 에피쿠로스에 따르면, 우리는 불쾌한 감각에서 벗어나 유쾌한 감각을 느낄 때 행복하다. 제레미 벤담도 비슷한 주장을 했다. 그는 자연이 인간을 쾌락과 고통이라는 두 주인에게 맡겨 그들로 하여금 인간의 모든 행동, 말, 생각을 결정하게 했다고 말한다. 벤담의 후계자인 존 스튜어트 밀은 행복이란 고통 없이 쾌락을 느끼는 상태일 뿐이고, 쾌락과 고통 외의 선악은 존재하지 않는다고 말했다. 선과 악을 다른 어떤 것(예를 들면 신의 말씀이나 국익)에서 연역하려고 시도하는 사람이 있다면 그는 당신을 속이고 있는 것이다. 어쩌면 자기 자신도 속이고 있을지 모른다.

에피쿠로스 시대에 이런 발언은 신성 모독이었다. 벤담과 밀의 시대에 이런 발언은 급진적인 체제 전복이었다. 하지만 21세기 초에는 과학적 정설이다. 생명 과학에 따르면, 행복과 고통은 단지 그 순간에 어떤 신체 감각이 우세한가의 문제이다. 우리는 외부 세계에서 일어나는 사건에 반응하는 것이 아니라 자기 몸에서 일어나는 감각에 반응할 뿐이다. 사람들은 실직해서, 이혼해서, 전쟁이 일어나서 고통스러운 것이 아니다. 사람들을 비참하게 만드는 유일한 것은 몸에서 일어나는 불쾌한 감각이다. 실직이 우울증을 유발할 수 있지만, 우울증 자체는 일종의 불쾌한 신체 감각이다. 우리는 수천 가지 이유로 화를 내지만, 화는 추상적 관념이 아니다. 화는 항상 열이나 긴장과 같은 감각을 통해 일어나고, 그런 감각이 화를 솟구치게 만든다. 우리가 "열불" 난다고 표현하는 데는 그럴 만한 이유가 있는 셈이다.

50 회 문제은행

📖 본책 p.434

01

하위내용영역	배점	예상정답률
일반영어 A형 기입형	2점	50%

모범답안 moral

채점기준

• 2점: 모범답안과 같다. 이것 외에는 답이 될 수 없다.
• 0점: 모범답안과 다르다.

한글 번역

자유 시장 자본주의의 대부 아담 스미스는 "부자와 권력자를 존경하고 심지어 거의 숭배하는 기질은 우리 인간의 도덕적 정서를 부패시키는 가장 크고 보편적인 원인"이라고 말한 적이 있다. 스미스는 스스로 조절하는 "보이지 않는 손"—시장이 스스로의 오류를 교정해나가는 내적인 경향성—을 옹호한 반면에, 도덕적인 삶이 시장의 효과적인 경계나 통제 밖에 있다는 것을 날카롭게 인식했다. 스미스의 시대 이후 수세기에 걸쳐 경제 체제로서의 자본주의의 부도덕한 논리가 거침없이 다시 부각됐다.

이것은 특히 금융 부문의 경우였다. 최근 골드만 삭스를 "거대한 뱀파이어 오징어"로 묘사한 것은 19세기 월가를 "거대한 악마 물고기"로 맹비난했던 것을 상기시킨다. 당시 가장 악명 높은 월가 투기꾼 중 한 명인 제이 굴드는 "월가의 메피스토펠레"로 널리 알려져 있었다.

하지만 굴드와 월가는, 그때나 (현재의) 로이드 블랭크페인 시절에 이르기까지, 시장 경쟁의 철칙과 순익의 가차 없는 규율을 고수하고 있을 뿐이라고 주장해 왔는데, 그들은 항상 이 법칙을 통해 우리 모두에게 이득이 된다고 지적한다. 금융계가 자발적으로 도덕 규율을 적용하기를 기대하는 것은 소득없는 일이다. 도덕 규율은 금융계의 존재 이유에 너무나 이질적인 것이기 때문이다. 과거에, 골드만 삭스가 기소됐던 범죄와 유사하거나 더 큰 범죄를 저질러 고발당하거나 유죄로 판명된 기업들은 만일 도덕적 질문이 여전히 울려 퍼지는 (금융계) 바깥으로부터 엄격한 제약들이 부과되지 않는 한 우리가 최근에 목격하고 있는 방식으로 행동해 왔고 앞으로도 행동할 것이다.

02

하위내용영역	배점	예상정답률
일반영어 A형 기입형	2점	45%

모범답안 Overcome

채점기준

- **2점**: 모범답안과 같다. 소문자로 쓴 경우도 맞는 것으로 한다.
- **0점**: 모범답안과 다르다.

한글 번역

당신은 학교나 직장에 자주 늦나? 지각은 거의 우연이 아니다. 오히려, 당신의 학교나 직장에 대한 무의식적인 감정과 관련이 있을 가능성이 더 높다. 당신이 지루함을 느끼고 있을 수도 있는데, 지각은 시간을 낭비하는 것에 대한 당신의 저항의 표현 방법일 수 있다. 또는, 만약 당신이 형편없는 성취 때문에 불안감을 느낀다면, 지각은 불행한 상황에 대해 "아니오"라고 말하는 당신의 방식일 수 있다. 또 다른 한편으로는, 권위에 분개하는 것일 수도 있다. 당신은 규칙, 규정, 종, 시계, 그리고 신분증에 방해받지 않는 자유를 느끼고 싶어 한다. 이것들 중 어떤 것이라도 당신이 지각한 이유를 설명할 수 있다. 학교나 직장에 만성적인 지각에 대한 설명만큼이나 많은 알리바이가 있다. 하버드 의대의 수전 슈니더먼 교수는 몇 년 동안 이 문제를 연구해 왔고, 연구를 하는 과정에서 지각에 대한 몇 가지 창의적인 변명을 들었다: "저는 쓰레기를 버리러 나갔어요. (그런데) 문이 잠겼답니다. 문을 열어 줄 관리자를 찾는 데 한 시간이 걸렸습니다." "내 점성술사가 오늘 정오 전에 침대에서 일어나지 말라고 충고했어요." "어젯밤에 거실에 도배를 했는데 현관문을 찾을 수가 없어요." "동생이 홍역에 걸렸어요. 나는 오늘 아침 그의 신문을 배달해야 했어요." "눈송이가 제 시계 안으로 날아들어와 기계 장치의 속도를 늦췄습니다." 심리학자들은 찾은 지각을 극복하기 위해서 다음과 같이 조언한다. 지각이 사랑하는 사람들에게 상처를 줄 수 있는 바람직하지 않은 습관이라는 것을 인식하자; 삶의 방식을 바꾸려 노력하자; 하고 있는 활동을 매일 기록한 뒤, 어느 부분에서 시간을 절약할 수 있는지 파악하기 위해 그 기록을 분석하자; "꼭 해야 하는 일"과 "지금은 꼭 해야 하는 것은 아닌 일"로 과제를 나눠보자; 시간을 앞당겨 놓아라. 자신을 속여서 제 시간에 오도록 하자.

03

하위내용영역	배점	예상정답률
일반영어 A형 서술형	4점	35%

모범답안 Red hair and brown hair are examples of (=observable traits known as) "phenotypes". Second, approximately 2.5% of the differences in intelligence accounted for(=were influenced) by the key SNPs.

채점기준 _ Total 4pts

- **+2점**: 머리카락의 색깔은 무엇의 예인지에 대해 "phenotypes"라 답하였다. 이것 외에는 답이 될 수 없다.
- **+2점**: 과거에 행해졌던 GWAS에서, 핵심 SNPs가 인간의 지능에 어느 정도 영향을 미쳤는가에 대한 답을 "around 2.5%"라 답하였다. 이것 외에는 답이 될 수 없다.

한글 번역

부모로부터 자손에게 DNA가 전달되는 것이 유전의 생물학적 기초라는 것은 반박할 수 없는 사실이지만, 우리는 여전히 우리를 우리답게 만드는 특정한 유전자에 대해 상대적으로 거의 알지 못한다.

이런 상황은 전체 유전체 연관 분석(연구)—줄여서 GWAS라 불리는—을 통해 빠르게 변화하고 있다. 이러한 연구들은 사람들의 유전적 구성—즉 그들의 "유전자형"—의 차이를 찾는데, 이 유전자형은 "표현형"의 차이와 관련이 있다. 최근 학술지 〈Nature Genetics〉에 발표된 GWAS에서, 전 세계의 과학자 팀은, IQ 테스트로 측정되는 일반 지능과의 상관관계를 찾기 위해 78,308명의 DNA 염기 서열을 분석했다.

이 연구의 주요 목표는 지능 테스트 점수와 상당한 상관관계가 있는 단일 뉴클레오티드 다형성(SNP)이 무엇인지를 밝혀내는 것이었다. 신체의 대부분의 세포에서 발견되는 DNA는 뉴클레오타이드라고 불리는 네 개의 분자로 구성되어 있는데, 이것들은 유기염기로 불리며, 다음과 같다: 사이토신(C), 티민(T), 아데닌(A), 구아닌(G). 세포 내에서 DNA는 염색체라고 불리는 구조로 조직된다. 인간은 보통 23쌍의 염색체를 가지고 있으며, 각 염색체 쌍 중 하나는 각각의 부모로부터 물려받는다.

SNP는 사람마다 다를 수 있는 특정 염색체 영역의 뉴클레오티드이다. 예를 들어, 한 사람은 뉴클레오티드 삼중수소 TAC를 가지고 있는 반면, 다른 사람은 TCC를 가지고 있을 수 있으며, 이러한 변화는 지능과 같은 특성에서 사람들 사이의 차이에 기여할 수 있다.

분석된 1천 2백만 개 이상의 SNP 중 336개가 지능과 상당한 상관관계를 가지고 있었는데, 22개의 서로 다른 유전자가 연루되어 있었다. 그 (22개의) 유전자 가운데 한 개가 뉴런의 성장을 조절하는 것과 관련이 있고, 다른 한 개는 지적 장애와 뇌 기형과 관련이 있다. 모두 합치면 SNP는 지능에서 사람 간의 차이의 약 5%를 차지했는데, 이는 지능에 대한 그 이전의 GWAS에 비해 거의 두 배 증가한 수치이다.

04

하위내용영역	배점	예상정답률
일반영어 B형 서술형	4점	30%

모범답안 The meaning of the words in ⓐ is that Wilmington has won competitively in the sphere of industry but has become shabby in the process. Second, the implication is to ironically praise Wilmington for becoming "important" by the limited standard of industry while also describing New Castle as "poor", when in fact it is the more lovely, green and "agreeable" of the two (, therefore criticizing the thought that this kind of "progress" is best for cities).

채점기준   _ Total 4pts

+ 2점 : 밑줄 친 ⓐ의 의미를 "<u>Wilmington has won competitively in the sphere of industry</u> but <u>has become decayed in the process</u>"라 서술하였거나 유사하였다.

+ 2점 : 밑줄 친 ⓑ의 함축 의미를 "the implication is to ironically praise Wilmington for becoming "important" by the standard of industry while also describing New Castle as "poor", when in fact it is the more lovely, green and "agreeable" of the two"라 서술하였거나 유사하였다.

▷ "진보가 비껴간 New Castle이 (궁극적으로는) 운이 좋았고 반대로 진보가 이뤄졌던 Wilmington이 오히려 운이 좋지 않았다"라고 서술하였거나 유사하였으면 모두 맞는 답으로 한다.

한글 번역

델라웨어주의 뉴캐슬. 유럽 국가들이 누가 신대륙을 소유했는지를 놓고 다투던 17세기 전반 동안, 네덜란드인들과 스웨덴인들은 델라웨어 강에 10마일 떨어진 곳에 서로 경쟁적으로 마을을 세웠다. 얼마 지나지 않아, 영국인들은 그 두 곳을 점령하고 뉴캐슬과 윌밍턴이라는 새로운 이름을 지어 줬다.

한 세기 반 동안 두 마을은 빠르게 성장했지만, 점차 윌밍턴은 모든 이점을 얻었다. 필라델피아에 조금 더 가까웠기 때문에, 새로운 직물 공장이 문을 열었을 때, 그들은 뉴캐슬이 아닌 윌밍턴에 문을 열었다. 윌밍턴에는 강과 개울에서 나오는 수력 발전이 많았기 때문에 젊은 이레니 듀폰이 화약 공장 장소를 찾고 있을 때, 그는 뉴캐슬이 아닌 윌밍턴을 선택했다. 윌밍턴은 읍으로 그런 다음엔 도시가 됐는데, 델라웨어에서 가장 큰 또 하나의 중요하고 큰 도시가 됐다. 뉴캐슬은 윌밍턴을 번영시킨 고속도로와 수로가 지나지 않았고, 델라웨어 강에서 남쪽으로 10마일 떨어진 곳에서 잠들어 있었다. 이처럼 비슷한 역사를 가진 두 마을이 이 두 도시처럼 완전히 동떨어져 발전한 예는 없었을 것이다. 그리고 오늘날에는 이보다 더 다를 수 있는 두 장소가 없을 것이다. 고속도로와 주차장, 그리고 다른 모든 콘크리트 리본과 배지(훈장)를 가진 윌밍턴은 산업 전쟁의 지친 노장으로서 멍한 시선을 하고 있다. 사람들이 살고 쇼핑하던 거리들은 부서져 텅 비어 있다.

뉴캐슬은 진보(경제 발전)를 위해 자리를 양보해 줄 필요가 없었고, 따라서 17세기와 18세기의 집을 허물 이유가 전혀 없었다. 그래서 그 집들은 여전히 이곳에 있는데, 그 옛날의 모습 그대로 녹색의 마을 주변의 오래된 느릅나무 아래에 운치 있게 줄지어 서 있다. 뉴캐슬은 여전히 살기 좋은 곳이다. 뉴캐슬의 조용했던 과거(산업 혁명의 영향을 덜 받음)를 담고 있는 아름다운 건물들은 4,800명의 사람들이 살기에 적합한 평온한 환경을 만들어내고 있다. 뉴캐슬은 미국에서 가장 아름다운 도시일지 모르지만, 전혀 중요한 도시는 아니다. 진보가 그 도시를 지나쳐갔다.

가엾은 뉴캐슬. 행운의 윌밍턴.

05

하위내용영역	배점	예상정답률
일반영어 B형 서술형	4점	50%

모범답안 The words in ⓐ refer to health risks (such as cancer). Second, in the underlined ⓑ, the writer means that the people shout far too loud as if talking over traffic on a noisy roadway. Finally, if there were no phones on the Amtrak, the writer would work, read, or muse in peace.

채점기준 _____ _Total 4pts

⁺1점 : 밑줄 친 ⓐ가 가리키는 것을 "health risks" (or a health risk)"라 정확히 서술하였다. "cancer"라 했어도 맞는 것으로 한다.

⁺1.5점 : 밑줄 친 ⓑ가 의미하는 바를 "the people shout far too loud as if talking over traffic on a roadway"라 서술하였거나 유사하였다.

⁺1.5점 : Amtrak 열차를 탔을 때 핸드폰을 이용하는 사람이 없었다면 화자가 무엇을 했을지에 대해 "the writer would work, read, or muse in peace"라 서술하였거나 유사하였다.

한글 번역

1990년대 하이테크 붐이 한창일 때, 나는 샌프란시스코의 극장가에 있는 커피숍에서 많은 시간을 보냈다. 그곳은 관광의 중심지인 유니언 스퀘어 근처에 있었고, 나는 그곳에서 한 장면이 몇 번이고 반복해서 진행되는 것을 관찰했다. 엄마는 커피를 즐기고 있다. 아이들은 의자에 발이 매달려 머핀을 쪼아 먹고 있다. 그리고 테이블에서 약간 뒤로 물러난 아빠가 휴대폰으로 누군가와 대화를 하고 있다. 특히 기술을 사용하여, 우리는 인간 관심의 좁은 대역폭 내에서만 시사점을 논의한다. 건강상의 위험이 있나? 그것이 암을 유발할 수 있나? 휴대폰, 컴퓨터, 유전 공학, 그리고 많은 다른 새로운 개발에 관한 것이다.

나는 암의 중요성을 경시하지 않는다. 그러나 가장 있는 그대로의 실용주의적인 걱정을 넘어설 수 없는 논의로부터 빠진 것이 있다. 사실, 휴대폰의 문제들 중 일부는 전혀 물렁물렁하거나 추상적이지 않다. 만일 휴대폰을 들고 수다를 떨면서 모퉁이를 도는 자동차 운전자에 의해 부딪친 적이 있다면, 당신은 이것(물렁물렁하거나 추상적이지 않음)을 알 것이다. 물론 큰 문제는 소음이다. 방해 그 자체의 관점에서 보면, 휴대폰은 메가 앰프 자동차 스테레오와 정치 광고와 어깨를 나란히 한다. 하지만 (다른 것보다 더 안 좋은 점은) 휴대폰은 탈출하기가 더 어렵다는 점이다. 우리 모두 어떤 상황인지 알고 있다. 먼저, 새벽 5시 30분에 울리는 알람 시계와 같은 사랑스러운 삐 소리를 듣는다. 그런 뒤에 사람들은 휴대폰에 대고 마치 크로스 브롱스 고속화 도로를 가로지르며 이야기 하는 것처럼 큰소리친다. 이렇게 하는 것을 영화와 구기 경기, 식당과 공원에서 정기적으로 볼 수 있는 상황이 됐다. 휴대폰은 단순히 성가신 것 이상의 것을 나타낸다. 휴대폰은 경험에 근거한 사고방식을 가진 사람들이 파악할 수 없는 방식으로 삶에 영향을 미친다.

여행이 한 예이다. 토마스 칼라일은 한번은 앤서니 트롤롭에게 여행을 "가만히 앉아서 그의 생각을 정리하는" 시간으로 사용하라고 충고했다. 수세기 동안, 여행은 이 조용한 역할을 해왔다. 나는 암트랙(미국의 철도) 타는 것을 손꼽아 기다리곤 했는데, 그것은 거의 성스러운 안식처 같았다. 암트랙은 전화와 사무실의 방해 없이 일하거나 책을 읽거나 그냥 사색할 수 있는 귀중한 시간을 제공했었다. 하지만 이제 휴대폰이 나의 발목을 잡았다. 휴대폰은 암트랙을 수평 전화 부스로 바꾸어 놓았다. 최근 뉴욕 여행에서 아내와 나는 문자 그대로 사방에서 휴대전화와 그들의 사촌인 고성능 워크맨에게 포위당했다. 즐거움을 줬었던 여행이 이제 장시간의 골칫거리가 돼 버렸다.

📖 본책 p.442

01

하위내용영역	배점	예상정답률
일반영어 A형 기입형	2점	45%

모범답안 ⓐ frames　ⓑ conservatives

채점기준

- 2점: 모범답안과 같다.
- 1점: 둘 중 하나만 맞았다.
- 0점: 모범답안과 다르다.

한글 번역

사람들은 머릿속에 여러 개의 프레임을 가지고 다닌다. 우리는 단순히 이슈나 사건을 구성하는 한 가지 방법을 가지고 있지 않다. 레이코프는 미국에서 활동 중인 두 가지 메타 프레임 또는 문화적 테마를 강조하는데, 이 두 가지 프레임은 엄격한 아버지 대 양육자 부모라는 두 가지 경쟁적인 가족 은유로 구현된다. 그는 이러한 메타 프레임을 각각 보수적 사고와 자유주의적 사고의 근저로 본다. 하지만 레이코프는 우리가 머릿속에 이것들 중 하나만 가지고 다니는 것이 아니라 둘 다 가지고 다닌다는 것을 알 만큼 충분히 현명하다. 하나의 프레임이 훨씬 더 쉽게 촉발되고 습관적으로 사용될 수 있지만, 다른 프레임도 또한 우리의 문화유산의 일부이고 적절한 신호들이 주어지면 촉발되고 또한 사용될 수 있다는 것이다.

합법적 동성 결혼을 지지하는 진보주의자들과 동성 결혼을 반대하는 보수주의자들 사이의 프레임 대결에서, 성공적인 프레임 전략은 상대방의 세계관 속으로 들어가는 능력을 필요로 한다. 레이코프는 보수주의자들을 악마화하는 대신에 그들의 사고방식 속으로 들어가는 성공적인 노력을 한다. 그렇게 함으로써, 그는 유용한 경험 법칙을 보여준다. 즉, 메시지를 효과적으로 재구성하기 위해, 당신(자유주의자)은 당신이 동의하지 않는 프레임을 묘사할 수 있어야 하고, 그렇게 함으로써 그 프레임의 옹호자들(보수주의자)도 "네, 이것이 제가 믿는 것입니다"라고 말할 수 있게 해야 한다.

02

하위내용영역	배점	예상정답률
일반영어 A형 서술형	4점	50%

모범답안 The meaning of the underlined ⓐ is that the chances of Legacy admissions causing a problem are infinitesimally low. Second, the writer believes that "rational" decision making is to give preference to students whose parents contribute to the school's finances either through taxes or donations.

채점기준　　　　　　　　　　　　_Total 4pts

- +2점: 밑줄 친 ⓐ의 의미를 "the chances of Legacy admissions causing a problem are very low"라 서술하였거나 유사하였다.
- +2점: 저자가 "이성적인"것으로 간주한 것을 "to give preference to students whose parents contribute to the school's finances"라 서술하였거나 유사하였다.

한글 번역

부모들과 대학 지원자들 모두 안심하시길. 기여 입학은 지난주에 지구를 빗겨 간 소행성만큼만 당신에게 영향을 미칠 것 같다.

미국의 3,500개 대학 중, 오직 100개도 안 되는 ― 3퍼센트도 안 되는 ― 대학만이 자격 있는 지원자가 너무 많아서 그들 중에서 선택해야 한다. (또한) 이 한 줌밖에 안 되는 대학들에서, 기여 입학은 지원들 가운데서 극히 일부에 불과하다. 이 극소수의 기여 입학 가운데서, 모두가 합격이 되는 것도 아니며, 합격한 기여 입학생들 가운데 많은 경우엔 (기여 입학이 아니더라도) 어떤 식으로든 합격했었을 것이다.

하지만 비평가들은 이 아주 작은 비율조차도 불공평하다고 말한다. 즉, 그들은 말한다, 입학은 실력에 기초해야 한다고. 오케이, 그렇다면 실력이 뭔지 정의를 한번 해 보자. 쉬운 과목에서 A를 받은 것과 아주 어려운 과목에서 B를 받은 것 가운데 어떤 것이 실력이 더 좋은 것인가? 시험에 도가 튼 학생의 SAT 점수와 그 보다는 점수가 약간 낮은 시험 울렁증이 있는 실제로는 정말 똑똑한 학생 가운데 누가 더 실력이 있는가? 재능 있는 바순 연주자와 자원봉사를 대단히 인상적으로 한 학생 가운데서는?

인간은 단순히 실력으로만 순위를 매길 수는 없다. 친구들의 순위를 한번 매겨 보라. 가장 친한 친구, 아마도 쉬운 선택일 것이다. 하지만 47번과 48번, 혹은 입학처에서 꼭 해야 하는 것처럼 2,047번과 2,048번 중 어느 쪽이 더 실력이 있는 것일까: 가장 사려 깊고, 가장 재미있고, 가장 대화를 잘하는 사람, 가장 관대한 사람 가운데서? 그 어떠한 입학 결정이라도 합리적일 수 있다. 주립 대학교는 그 주내의 학생들을 우대해 주는데, 왜냐하면 그 학생들의 부모들이 내는 세금이 그 주립 대학을 지원하기 때문이다. 2010년도 기준으로, 졸업생들의 기부금은 70억 달러 이상으로 고등 교육(대학)에 제공했는데, 이것은 전체 기부의 1/4이 넘는다. 합리적으로 생각해서, 이 졸업생들의 자녀들에게 약간의 우대가 주어져야 하지 않을까?

03

하위내용영역	배점	예상정답률
일반영어 A형 서술형	4점	55%

모범답안 The two "Don'ts" are to not let the boss become surprised and not to underrate the boss. Second, the meaning of the underlined word is that if bosses are not protected against surprises. Third, the word is "boss".

채점기준 _Total 4pts

+ 1점: 두 개의 "Don'ts"가 "to not let the boss become surprised(0.5점) and not to underrate the boss(0.5점)"라 서술하였거나 유사하였다.

+ 2점: 밑줄 친 "otherwise"의 의미를 "if bosses are not protected against surprises"라 서술하였거나 유사하였다.

▷ "a situation where the underling(=subordinate) has allowed the boss to be caught unprepared"라 했어도 맞는 것으로 한다.

+ 1점: 빈칸에 들어갈 단어를 "boss"라 정확히 답하였다. 이것 외에는 답이 될 수 없다.

안 되는 게 몇 개 있다. 상사를 뜻밖의 상황에 노출시키지 마라. 뜻밖의 상황으로부터 상사를 보호하는 것은 부하 직원이 할 일이다. 심지어 즐거운 일(만일 그런 게 있다면)이라 할지라도. 조직 내에서 (상사가) 뜻밖의 상황에 노출되는 것은 그 조직을 책임지고 있는 상사에게는 굴욕인데, 보통 공개적인 굴욕이다. 서로 다른 상사들은 일어날 수 있는 뜻밖의 상황에 대한 서로 다른 경고를 원한다. 예를 들어 케네디 대통령은 약간의 뜻밖의 일이 일어날 가능성만 있더라도 상세한 보고를 요구한다. 하지만 모든 상사들은 뜻밖의 상황으로부터 보호받을 필요가 있다. 그렇지 않으면 그들은 부하 직원을 신뢰하지 않을 것인데, 여기엔 그럴 만한 충분한 이유가 있다.

상사를 과소평가하지 마라! 상사가 무식해 보일 수도 있다. 멍청해 보일지도 모른다. 그리고 외모가 항상 기만적인 것은 아니다. (즉, 그런 외모처럼 실제로 무식하고 바보일 경우도 없는 것은 아니라는 의미) 하지만 상사를 과대평가하는 것은 전혀 위험하지 않다. 그렇게 했을 때 발생될 수 있는 최악의 상황은 상사 본인이 우쭐해지는 정도이다. 하지만 만약 당신이 상사를 과소평가한다면, 그는 당신의 잔꾀를 간파할 것이고 (자신에게) 그렇게 한 것에 대해 격렬히 분개할 것이다. 또는 당신이 머리도 나쁘고 지식도 결핍되어 있다고 상사에게 전가한 바로 그것을 상사는 당신에게 전가하고, 당신을 무지하거나, 멍청하거나, 상상력이 부족하다고 여길 것이다.

04

하위내용영역	배점	예상정답률
일반영어 B형 서술형	4점	45%

모범답안 The underlined words mean that (the cost of computers was millions of dollars at a time before inflation had weakened the dollar, and that) the modern equivalent of that cost would be many times greater. Second, the greatest innovation implied by the writer is computer operating systems that were rewritten to handle hundreds of tasks at the same time (allowing for non-physical programming).

_Total 4pts

+ 2점 : 밑줄 친 부분이 의미하는 것을 "the modern equivalent of that cost would be many times greater"라 서술하였거나 유사하였다.

 ▷ "컴퓨터의 가격이 엄청 비쌌다"라고 서술하였어도 맞는 것으로 한다.

+ 2점 : 컴퓨터 공학에서 가장 큰 혁신이 "computer operating systems that were rewritten to handle hundreds of tasks at the same time"이라 서술하였거나 유사하였다.

한글 번역

1970년대 초반에 컴퓨터는 커다란 방 하나를 다 차지할 만큼 거대했다. 오늘날의 전자레인지만도 못한 메모리와 연산력을 가진 기계 한 대가 백만 달러를 넘었으며, 그것도 1970년대에 백만 달러였다. 그만큼 컴퓨터는 귀했고 접근을 허락받는 것이 쉽지 않았다. 설사 접근할 수 있다고 해도 빌려 쓰는 데 막대한 돈이 필요했다. 더욱이 프로그래밍 자체가 엄청나게 지루한 일이었다. 컴퓨터 프로그램이 카드에 구멍을 뚫어서 만들어지던 시절이라 코드의 모든 행은 천공기로 뚫은 구멍을 통해 표현됐다. 따라서 복잡한 프로그램의 경우에는 수백 장에서 수천 장의 카드 뭉치가 필요했다. 어쨌든 프로그램이 준비되면 프로그래머는 자신이 접근 권한을 갖고 있는 메인 컴퓨터로 가서 관리자에게 카드 뭉치를 넘기고 차례를 기다렸다. 그런데 컴퓨터가 한 번에 한 가지 일만 처리했기 때문에 순번에 따라 결과를 보기까지 몇 시간에서 며칠이 걸릴 수도 있었다. 만약 프로그램에 단 하나의 에러라도 발생한다면 설사 그것이 오타 수준에 불과할지라도 프로그래머는 카드를 돌려받아 모든 과정을 다시 시작해야 했다.

이런 환경에서 프로그래머가 되는 것은 극도로 어려운 일이다. 20대 초반에 전문가 수준에 이르는 것은 거의 불가능했다. 당시 이런 환경에 놓여져 있던 한 컴퓨터 과학자는 "카드로 프로그래밍을 하는 건 프로그래밍을 배우는 게 아니라 인내와 오류 찾기를 배우는 겁니다."라고 말했다.

1960년대 중반까지 프로그래밍 문제의 해법은 발견되지 않았다. 그러다가 컴퓨터가 한 번에 하나의 예약만 처리하지 않아도 될 만큼 발달하자, 컴퓨터 과학자들은 만약 운영 체계를 다시 만들어 낸다면 컴퓨터를 많은 사람들이 동시에 공유할 수도 있으리라는 것을 깨달았다. 그들은 컴퓨터가 한 번에 수백 개의 일을 처리할 수 있도록 만들 수도 있었다.

이는 프로그래머들이 관리자에게 수백 장의 카드를 넘길 필요가 없다는 것을 의미한다.

05

하위내용영역	배점	예상정답률
일반영어 B형 서술형	4점	50%

모범답안 Ecotourism has positive and negative effects locally in terms of the environment, development, and culture. First, it can generate money from and encourage care for the environment, yet the influx of tourists can degrade it as well. Second, it can create income for local people but also might limit their future prospects. Third, it may bring about empowerment and interest within local culture while at the same time has the risk of commodifying culture symbols and endangering the existing relations.

_Total 4pts

ⓐ Topic sentence

+ 1점 : "Ecotourism has positive and negative effects locally in terms of the environment, development, and culture"라 서술하였거나 유사하였다.

ⓑ Summary

+ 3점 : First, ① it can generate money from and encourage care for the environment, yet the influx of tourists can degrade it as well(1점). Second, ② it can create income for local people but also might limit their future prospects(1점). Third, ③ it may bring about empowerment and interest within local culture while at the same time has the risk of commodifying culture symbols and endangering the existing relations(1점).

생태 관광은 관광 산업의 중요한 분야이며, 유엔(UN)은 생태 관광이 세계 관광 수입의 25%를 차지할 것으로 추산하고 있다. 정확한 정의는 다양하지만, 유엔 식량 농업 기구는 생태 관광이란 용어를 "자연에 기반을 둔 지속 가능한 관광과 레크리에이션"으로 폭넓게 정의한다. 생태 관광은 자연환경 관리를 강조하며 관광 시설 제공에 지역 주민을 참여시키는 경우가 많지만 그것이 가져올 영향에 대해서는 찬성자와 반대자 모두 있다.

첫째, 생태 관광은 관광객들에게 방문하도록 장려하고, 그들이 머무는 동안 입장료, 할인, 면허와 같은 품목들에 지불하도록 함으로써 자연환경으로부터 돈을 창출한다. 지역 사회가 스스로를 돌볼 수 있는 방법으로 환경을 재구성하는 것은 지역민들로 하여금 환경을 돌보도록 권장한다. 그러나 반대론자들은 생태 관광객의 유입이 관광객들이 보게 되는 자연환경을 악화시킬 수 있다고 주장한다. 관광객들을 섬세한 생태계에 풀어놓는 것은 오염이라든가 예상치 못한 방법으로 환경에 영향을 미칠 수 있다 ― 코스타리카 국립공원에 대한 한 연구는 야생 원숭이들이 쓰레기를 먹고, 생태 관광객들의 존재에 익숙해지고, 그들이 남긴 음식과 쓰레기를 먹는다는 것을 발견했다.

또한, 지지자들은 관광객들을 수용하고 가이드 역할을 하는 데 지역 사람들을 참여시킴으로써 생태 관광이 지역 발전을 돕는다고 주장한다. 예를 들어, 우간다에서는 수백 명의 현지인들이 브윈디 임페네트러블 포레스트에서 경비원이나 현장 요원으로 일함으로써 수입을 보충한다. 많은 경우, 지역 사회는 참여자로서만 활동하기보다는 생태 관광 단체와 파트너로 활동한다. 그러나 생태 관광은 지역 사회의 발전 전망을 제한할 수도 있다. 일부 연구원들은 생태 관광이 "자연"을 보존하는 데 초점을 맞추는 것이 지역민들의 지속 가능한 발전과 빈곤에서 벗어날 수 있는 능력을 손상시킨다고 믿는다. 환경은 지역민들의 요구(즉, 경제 발전)보다 실제적으로 우선시된다. 마지막으로, 생태 관광은 지역 사회에 문화적 영향을 미칠 수 있다. 생태 관광객들은 종종 지역 문화를 경험할 수 있는 기회에 부분적으로 동기를 부여받는데, 이것은 그 문화에 긍정적이고 적극적인 영향을 미칠 수 있다. 의사 결정에 지역 사람들을 참여시키는 것은 그들을 관광에 대해 더 긍정적으로 만드는 경향이 있을 뿐만 아니라, 하나의 공동체로서 그들에게 힘을 실어준다. 그러나, 전통문화 상징이 방문객들에게 팔기 위한 상품으로 변모하는 것, 지역 사람들 사이의 기존 관계의 붕괴와 그리고 더 높은 범죄 발생과 같은 부정적인 영향도 존재한다.

52회 문제은행

📖 본책 p.449

01

하위내용영역	배점	예상정답률
일반영어 A형 기입형	2점	65%

모범답안 ⓐ emotional reasoning
ⓑ mind reading

채점기준

• 2점: 모범답안과 같다. 이것 외에는 답이 될 수 없다.
• 1점: 둘 중 하나만 맞았다.
• 0점: 모범답안과 다르다.

이런 속담이 있다. 정신은 훌륭한 하인이지만 형편없는 주인이라는 것이다. 만약 여러분이 자신에 대해, 관계에 대해, 또는 여러분의 삶에 대해 불안감을 느낀다면, 이 세 가지 사고 습관이 여러분의 정신을 지배하고 있을 수도 있다. 심리학자들은 이러한 독성 습관을 인지적 왜곡이라고 부르는데, 인지적 왜곡은 단지 "우리가 우리 자신에게 하는 거짓말"을 말하는 기술적인 방법일 뿐이다. 하지만 인지적 왜곡은 까다롭다. 왜냐하면 겉으로 보기에는 정확해 보이고, 더 중요한 것은, 그것들이 정확하다고 느끼기 때문이다. 그리고 바로 그것이 문제이다. 인지 왜곡은 우리를 어리석고, 지루하고, 부적절하고, 그렇지 않은 경우엔 불안하게 만든다. 감정적 추론은 "내가 질투를 느끼기 때문에, 네가 바람을 피운다는 것이 증명된다"거나 "내가 불안하기 때문에, 우리는 헤어질 것 같다"는 식으로 우리의 관계까지 확장될 때 가장 불안감을 느끼게 한다. 그런 생각들이 소용돌이치며 당신의 파트너가 전혀 예상하지 못한 싸움으로 변한다. 말할 필요도 없이, 감정적인 추론은 파트너들에게 특히 좌절감을 준다. 왜냐하면 직감 ― 심지어 부정확한 직감 ― 을 가지고 논쟁하는 것이 불가능하기 때문이다. 두 번째 독성 습관은 당신이 다른 사람들이 무엇을 생각하고 있는지 알고 있다고 가정하는 것이다. 당신의 불안감은 가상의 판단적 생각을 다른 사람들의 머리에 심어주고, 당신은 그것을 진심으로 믿게 되고, 이것이 결국 여러분을 더욱더 불안하게 만든다. 이것은 엄청난 악순환이다. 독심술은 다른 사람들이 당신을 판단하거나 거부한다고 생각하게 만든다. "나에게 답장을 보내지 않은 것을 보니, 그는 나를 증오함에 틀림없다." "상사가 나를 보고 싶어하는 것을 보니, 그녀는 몹시 화났음에 틀림없어." "내가 땀을 흘리고 있는 것을 모두가 보았으니, 날 괴상한 인간이라 생각할 거야."

또한, 개인화의 사고 오류는 모든 것을 당신에 관한 것으로 만든다. 배우자가 짜증이 난 것은, 당신이 한 짓 때문일 것이라 추측한다. 남자친구가 다른 여자를 본 것은, 당신이 그에게 부족하기 때문이라 생각한다. 당신의 친구가 짜증난 걸 보면, 당신은 그녀를 제대로 대접하지 못하고 있는 게 틀림없다고 생각한다. 개의치 않고, 개인화가 인도하는 어두운 골목이 그 무엇이든 간에, 개인화는 자책이라는 막다른 길에서 당신을 끝나게 만든다.

가령, 우리는 왜 몸에 좋을 것 없는 고칼로리 음식을 게걸스럽게 먹는 것일까? 오늘날의 풍요 사회는 비만이라는 악성 전염병으로 신음하고 있으며, 이 병은 개발 도상국으로도 빠르게 번져 나가는 중이다. 어째서 우리가 가장 달콤하고 기름기 많은 음식을 이렇게 탐하는 것일까에 대한 문제는 우리의 수렵 채집인 조상이 지녔던 식습관을 알기 전에는 혼란스럽게만 느껴진다. 조상들이 살던 초원과 숲에는 칼로리가 높은 달콤한 음식이 매우 드물었다. 전반적으로 먹을 것이 부족했던 시대이기도 했다.

02

하위내용영역	배점	예상정답률
일반영어 A형 기입형	2점	45%

모범답안 ⓐ hunter-gatherer (or forager)
ⓑ high-calorie

채점기준

- 2점: 모범답안과 같다. ⓐ에 pre-agricultural라 했으면 0.5점을 준다.
- 1점: 둘 중 하나만 맞았다.
- 0점: 모범답안과 다르다.

한글 번역

인간의 본성과 역사, 심리를 이해하려면 수렵 채집인 조상들의 머릿속으로 들어가는 수밖에 없다. 우리 종은 존속 기간의 거의 대부분을 수렵 채집인으로 살았다. 물론 지난 이백 년간 도시 노동자나 사무직 직원으로서 일용할 양식을 얻은 사피엔스의 숫자는 지속적으로 늘어났고, 이에 앞선 만 년 동안 대부분의 사피엔스는 농부와 목축인으로 살았다. 하지만 이 기간은 우리 조상들이 수렵과 채취를 한 수십만 년에 비하면 눈 깜짝할 새에 지나지 않는다.
오늘날 번성하는 진화 심리학에 따르면, 현대인의 사회적 심리적 특성 중 많은 부분이 이처럼 농경을 시작하기 전의 기나긴 시대에 형성됐다. 심지어 오늘날에도 이 분야 학자들은 우리의 뇌와 마음은 수렵 채집 생활에 적응해 있다고 주장한다. 식습관, 분쟁, 성적 특질 모두, 우리의 수렵 채집 정신이 후기 산업 사회의 환경과 그 대도시, 여객기, 전화, 컴퓨터와 상호 작용한 결과다. 이런 환경 덕분에 우리는 이전의 어떤 세대와 비교하더라도 물적 자원이 풍부해지고 수명도 길어졌지만, 이 환경은 또한 우리로 하여금 소외되고 우울하고 압박받는다고 느끼게 만들었다. 진화 심리학자들은 그 이유를 알려면 우리를 형성했던 수렵 채집 세계를 깊이 파고들어야 한다고, 우리는 무의식적으로는 아직도 그 속에 살고 있다고 주장한다.

03

하위내용영역	배점	예상정답률
일반영어 A형 서술형	4점	40%

모범답안 The types of investigation that have revealed short term effects of oil exposure are mortality estimation, clinical evaluation, and necropsy examination. Second, if the proposed study was successful, the rate of decline in Northern sea otters would decrease.

채점기준 _Total 4pts

+ 2점: 기름 유출에 의해 단기간에 나타나는 영향을 밝혀내는 조사의 방식이 "mortality estimation, clinical evaluation, and necropsy·examination" 임을 정확하게 서술하였다.
  ▷ 3개 중 2개만 서술했으면 1점; 1개는 0.5점을 준다.
+ 2점: 만일 제안된 연구가 성공적으로 실행된다면 수달에게 어떤 일이 일어날 것인지에 대해 "the rate of decline in Northern sea otters would decrease"라 서술하였거나 유사하였다.
  ▷ "수달의 수가 줄어들지 않을 것이다"라는 내용이 들어가 있으면 모두 맞는 것으로 한다.
  ▷ 다음과 같이 서술하였으면 1점을 준다.
    • "Scientists would gain a better understanding of the effects of hydrocarbon ingestion and exclosure on sea otters"
    • "Scientists would devise more effective means to protect sea otters from the effects of oil spills"

- "Scientists would better understand why some species of sea otters are more susceptible to the effects of exposure to oil than others"

한글 번역

특정 북방 해달의 개체수는 최근 감소하고 있다. 이러한 감소에 대한 제안된 원인은 복잡하며 다양한 생태학적 압력 또는 인위적 압력에 기인한다. 기름 유출과 같은 중대한 재해는 보통 해양과 해안 종에 갑작스럽게 극적인 영향을 미치는 것으로 널리 알려져 있다. 유출의 단기적 영향은 사망률 추정, 임상 평가 및 괴사 검사를 통해 평가된다. 이러한 비극의 장기적 영향은 문서화하기가 더 어려우며, 연구는 종종 인구 통계학적 모델링, 재생산 효율성의 추정 또는 시차적, 연령별 생존율에 국한된다. 최근의 몇몇 연구들은 많은 종들이 유출된 후에 기름과 관련된 장기적인 영향에 직면한다는 것을 웅변적으로 보여주었지만, 민감한 종들에서 기름에 의해 유발되는 치사적인 병리를 식별하는 생물학적 표지가 시급하다. 제안된 연구의 목표는 급성 또는 만성 탄화수소 피폭과 관련된 지속적인 병리학적 및 생리학적 손상을 나타내는 구체적이고 민감한 유전자 표지를 식별하는 것이다.

원유는 여러 방향족 및 지방족 탄화수소 성분을 가지고 있으며, 노출과 섭취의 독성 효과는 체내에서 다양하고 광범위할 수 있다. 이러한 상황에서 세포 수준에서 여러 생리적 과정을 나타내는 발현 유전자의 미묘한 변화에 대한 분자 연구는 특히 유용하다. 더 나아가서, 분자 조사에 필요한 샘플은 실험 대상 동물에게 최소한의 침습성이나 스트레스를 준다. 유전자 발현 기술은 연방 정부 목록에 등재된 놀아 기른 해달의 기름 노출의 장기적인 영향을 모니터링하는 방법을 제공할 수 있는 흥미로운 잠재력을 가지고 있다. 추가적인 이점은 이러한 방법들이 장기간에 걸쳐 개별 해달에게 해로운 영향을 미칠 수 있는 메커니즘을 설명할 수 있고, 따라서 기름 노출로부터 위험에 처한 취약한 개체와 모든 동물들을 치료하고 보호하기 위한 치료 및 예방 전략의 설계에 도움을 줄 수 있다는 점이다.

04

하위내용영역	배점	예상정답률
일반영어 A형 서술형	4점	45%

모범답안 The principle described is that the more people have sacrificed for it, the more committed they become to a belief or fantasy. Second, the word that best corresponds to the examples in the second paragraph is "stupidity".

채점기준 _Total 4pts

+ 2점 : "이러한 원칙"을 "the more people have sacrificed for it, the more committed they become to a belief or fantasy"라 서술하였거나 유사하였다.

+ 2점 : 두 번째 문단의 예시에 대해 첫 번째 문단에서 가장 적절하게 상응하는 한 단어를 "stupidity"라 서술하였다. 이것 외에는 답이 될 수 없다.

한글 번역

성직자들은 수천 년 전에 이 원리를 발견했다. 그것은 수많은 종교적 의식과 율법의 기초가 된다. 만약 여러분이 사람들이 신이나 국가와 같은 상상적 실체를 믿게 하고 싶다면, 여러분은 그들이 가치 있는 것을 희생하도록 만들어야 한다. 희생이 고통스러울수록 사람들은 상상 속의 수령자의 존재를 확신하게 된다. 제우스에게 값진 황소를 제물로 바치는 가난한 농부는 제우스가 정말로 존재한다고 확신하게 될 것이다. 그렇지 않으면 어떻게 그의 어리석음을 변명할 수 있겠는가? 그 농부는 이전의 모든 황소가 낭비되었다는 것을 인정하지 않기 위해 또 다른 황소들을 연속적으로 계속해서 희생시킬 것이다. 정확히 같은 이유로, 내가 이탈리아 국가의 영광을 위해 내 아이를, 혹은 공산주의 혁명에 내 다리를 희생했다면, 그것은 나를 열성적인 이탈리아 민족주의자나 열성적인 공산주의자로 바꿔 놓기에 충분하다. 이탈리아의 국가적 신화나 공산주의 선전 선동이 거짓이라면, 내 아이의 죽음이나 나 자신의 마비가 전혀 무의미하다는 것을 인정해야만 할 것이기 때문이다. 그런 것을 인정할 만한 배짱이 있는 사람은 거의 없다.

경제 분야에서도 같은 논리가 작용하고 있다. 1999년 스코틀랜드 정부는 새로운 국회 의사당을 세우기로 결정했다. 원래 계획에 따르면, 이 공사는 2년이 걸리고 4천만 파운드가 들어가기로 돼 있었다. 그러나 실제로는, 그것은 5년이 걸렸고 4억 파운드가 들었다. 건설업자들은 예상치 못한 어려움과 비용에 직면할 때마다 스코틀랜드 정부에 가서 더 많은 시간과 돈을 요구했다. 이런 일이 일어날 때마다 정부는 스스로에게 이렇게 말했다 : "음, 우리는 이미 4천만 파운드를 이 일에 투자했고 만약 우리가 지금 멈추고 반쯤 만들어진 뼈대만 남게 된다면 우리는 완전히 신용을 잃을 것이다. 4천만 파운드를 더 승인합시다." 6개월 후, 같은 일이 일어났는데, 그 때는 미완성 건물로 끝나는 것을 피해야 한다는 압박감이 훨씬 더 컸다. 그리고 그로부터 6개월 후, 그 이야기는 반복되었고, 실제 비용이 원래 추정치의 10배가 될 때까지 계속됐다. 정부만이 이 함정에 빠지는 것은 아니다. 기업체들은 종종 수백만 달러의 돈을 실패한 사업에 잠식당한다. 한편, 사적 개인들은 제대로 기능하지 않는 결혼과 앞이 보이지 않는 일에 매달린다.

05

하위내용영역	배점	예상정답률
일반영어 B형 서술형	4점	60%

모범답안 The things threatening the "amateur spirit" are professionals and bureaucrats. Next, the bureaucratic fallacy is to avoid any innovation or fresh path forward.

채점기준

+ 2점: 아마추어 정신을 위협하는 것이 "professionals (1점)" and "bureaucrats(1점)"이라 서술하였다.

+ 2점: 관료주의적 오류를 "to avoid any innovation" 이나 "to avoid fresh path forward", 또는 "not to do anything for the first time"이라 서술하였다.

한글 번역

진정한 지도자란 적절하고 본질적인 의미에서 아마추어 이다. 아마추어(라틴어로 연인이라는 뜻을 가진 'amator' 와 사랑한다는 뜻의 'amo', 'amare'에서 파생되었다.)는 어떤 일이 좋아서 하는 사람이다. 그가 일을 추진하는 것은 돈을 벌기 위해서, 군중을 기쁘게 하기 위해서, 또는 직업인 권위, 승진과 노년기의 정년 퇴직을 보장받기 위해서가 아니라 일 자체를 좋아하기 때문이다. 그가 그 일을 하지 않고는 견딜 수 없다면 그 이유는 외부의 강요 때문이 아니라 그가 지니고 있는 아마추어의 참신한 미래에 대한 비전 때문인 것이다.

자신들이 가지고 있는 힘과 권위로 아마추어 정신을 위협하는 두 가지의 새로운 유형은 전문가와 관료들이다. 이 양자는 미국의 부와 발전의 부산물이다. 그러나 이들은 미국 지도자들의 특별한 자질과 이상을 가늠하는 아마추어 정신을 위축시키고 있다.

첫째, 전문가들의 문제: 전문직은 우리가 알고 있듯이 현대 사회가 빚어낸 현상이다. "전문직"이란 단어가 영어에 최초로 등장했을 때는 성직자들의 서약을 의미했다. 아마추어 정신을 저해하는 두 번째 부류는 "관료주의자"들이다. 이들도 역시 현대의 특징적인 현상이다. 전문직이 전문화된 지식과 기술의 부산물인 듯이 관료주의는 기업 규모의 확대 추세와 정부 활동의 급격한 증가로 인해 생겨났다. 관료주의자들의 목표는 매사를 일정한 궤도에 고정시키고 자신들은 승직의 가도에서 최대한의 연금을 받고 정년 퇴직할 때까지 자리를 지키는 것이다. 우리를 지배하는 관료주의자들은 관료주의적 오류의 지배를 받는다. 이것은 어느 프랑스 공무원의 책상 위에 있는 "무슨 일이든지 맨 먼저 시도하지 말 것"이라는 표어에 가장 잘 표현돼 있다. 우리 정부에서 위대한 일은 살아 있는 아마추어 정신―그 말의 원래적 의미에서―을 유지할 수 있는 능력에 달려 있다.

53회 문제은행

📖 본책 p.458

01

하위내용영역	배점	예상정답률
일반영어 A형 기입형	2점	45%

모범답안 scientists

채점기준

• 2점: 모범답안과 같다. 이것 외에는 답이 될 수 없다.
• 0점: 모범답안과 다르다.

02

하위내용영역	배점	예상정답률
일반영어 A형 서술형	4점	50%

모범답안 The underlined "this view" is that achievement requires strong innate talent. Second, the writer references Ericsson's study to disprove the talent argument by showing that time devoted to practice actually yielded high achievement, not innate talent.

채점기준 _Total 4pts

+ 2점: 밑줄 친 "this view"가 가리키는 것을 "achievement requires strong innate talent"라 서술하였거나 유사하였다.

  ▷ "성취(성공)에 있어 타고난 자질(재능)이 중요하다"는 의미가 들어가 있으면 모두 맞는 것으로 한다.

  ▷ "성취(성공)에 있어 타고난 자질이 준비(노력, 연습) 보다 더 필요하다고 했어도 2점 준다.

+ 2점: 에릭슨의 연구를 언급함으로써 글쓴이가 말하려고 하는 입장이 "to disprove the talent argument by showing that time devoted to practice actually yielded high achievement, not innate talent"라 서술하였거나 유사하였다.

  ▷ "성공(성취)을 위해서는 (남들보다 더 많은 시간을 들인) 연습(준비)이 타고난 재능보다 더 중요하다"고 답하였으면 2점을 준다.

03

하위내용영역	배점	예상정답률
일반영어 B형 서술형	4점	45%

모범답안 The "diploma mills" are universities operated with the goal to award degrees to many with very little effort required. Second, the implied meaning of the underlined words is that Shanna the dog was suited for recreation management through her experience being a watchdog, and the writer ironically criticizes the absurdity of this selection.

채점기준   _Total 4pts

+ 2점 : "학위 공장"이 의미하는 것을 "universities operated with the goal to award degrees to many with very little effort required"라 서술하였거나 유사하였다.

+ 2점 : 밑줄 친 ⓑ의 함축 의미를 "Shanna the dog was suited for recreation management through her experience being a watchdog(1점) and the writer ironically criticizes the absurdity of this selection (approval/placement)(1점)"라 서술하였거나 유사하였다.

04

하위내용영역	배점	예상정답률
일반영어 B형 서술형	5점	40%

모범답안 The function of the Russian Federation's flag was to show the new, independent government and its cultural identity. On the other hand, the display of the Mexican flag was to show protest against a proposition and solidarity with Mexican immigrants. The "more protestors" are people concerned about illegal immigrants and their families, and marched to show opposition to Proposition 187.

채점기준   _Total 4pts

+ 2점 : 러시아 연방의 깃발과 멕시코 깃발이 상징적 기능을 "The function of the Russian Federation's flag was to show the new, independent government and its cultural identity(1점). On the other hand, the display of the Mexican flag was to show protest against a proposition and solidarity (support for) with Mexican immigrants(1점)"라 서술하였거나 유사하였다.

+ 1점 : "more protestors"가 가리키는 것이 "people in opposition to a proposition"이라 서술하였거나 유사하였다.

+ 1점 : 그들이 행진한 이유를 "to show opposition to Proposition 187"이라 서술하였거나 유사하였다.

05

하위내용영역	배점	예상정답률
혼합형(일반영어+문학) 서술형	4점	40%

모범답안 LSD is described as improving matters by increasing awareness, expanding consciousness and making the user love everyone. However, it is not a "perfect pill" because it only lasts for 8 hours and the user still had problems itching, smelling, burping and disliking his roommate's music while using it. Then, the moral is that pursuing the chemicals to achieve love or peace among human beings is a hazardous course and humans should not rely on pills to create peace or happiness(love).

채점기준   _Total 4pts

+ 1점 : LSD가 어떻게 상황을 증진시켰는지에 대해 "by increasing awareness, expanding consciousness and making the user love everyone"이라 서술하였다.

+ 1점 : LSD가 왜 완벽한 약이 아닌지에 대해 (단점을) 다음과 같이 서술하였다.

"it is not a "perfect pill" because it only lasts for 8 hours and the user still had problems itching, smelling, burping and liking his roommate's music while using it."

+ 2점 : 글의 교훈을 다음과 같이 서술하였거나 유사하였다.

"pursuing the chemicals to achieve love or peace among human beings is a hazardous course and humans should not rely on pills to create peace or happiness(love)."

54회 문제은행

본책 p.466

01

하위내용영역	배점	예상정답률
일반영어 A형 기입형	2점	45%

모범답안 ⓐ thoughts ⓑ arbitrary

채점기준

• 2점 : 모범답안과 같다. ⓐ에 ideas도 맞는 것으로 한다.
• 1점 : 둘 중 하나만 맞았다.
• 0점 : 모범답안과 다르다.

어휘

alleviate 완화하다
bristle at ~에 발끈하다
cliché 상투적인 문구
corrosion 부식(작용)
derivation (단어의) 어원(origin); 파생
euphemism 완곡어구
grapple 고심하다
insidious 모르는 사이에 진행되는; 음험한, 교활한
legislate (법적으로) 금지하다; 법률을 제정하다
oblivious 망각된; 의식하지 못하는
opaque 불분명한, 불투명한
orthodoxy 통설
render 묘사(표현)하다; 우리말 번역하다; (어떤 상태가 되도록) 만들다, 주다
vigilance 경계

한편에서는 언어가 교활하게 태도를 형성하고, 언어의 미묘한 공격에 대한 경계심은 편견을 없애기 위해서 필요하다고 말한다. 다른 이들은 언어를 법률로 금지하는 것에 대해 최상의 것으로 본다 해도 언어의 명료함과 표현력을 파괴하는 것이고, 최악에는 기자들이 사건과 의견을 전달하는 방식을 바꾸면서 사상을 통제하는 것이라 생각해 발끈한다. 이 두 가지 주장은 모두 언어와 또 언어가 어떻게 (우리 인간의) 사고와 태도와 연관되는지에 대해 추정을 세운다. 그러한 연관은 1946년 조지 오웰의 글, "정치학과 영어"에서 처음 제기됐으며, 이 글은 완곡어구, 상투적인 문구, 모호한 글이 통설을 강화하고 옹호될 수 없는 것을 옹호하는 데 사용될 수 있다고 주장한다. 우리는 오웰의 시대보다 언어와 사고를 더 잘 이해하고, 우리의 발견은 P.C. 즉, "정치적 올바름"이란 논란에 관한 통찰을 제공한다. 첫째, 말은 사고가 아니다. 앞의 이론이 언어가 사고를 결정한다고 주장하지만 어떠한 인지 과학자도 그 주장을 믿지 않는다. 사람들은 새 단어를 만들어 내고 바른 말을 찾아 고심하고, 다른 언어에서 우리말 번역을 하고 P.C.의 용어를 조롱하고 방어한다. 만약 말로 표현되는 생각이 그 말 자체와 같다면 이 중 어느 것도 가능하지 않을 것이다. 이는 우리가 두뇌 프로그래밍이 아닌 스타일 메뉴얼에 관해 논의하고 있음을 상기시켜 언어에 관한 양측의 불안감을 덜어낸다.

둘째, 말은 임의적이다. "오리"라는 단어는 오리처럼 생기지도, 걷거나 울지도 않지만 우리는 오리라는 소리와 뜻 간의 임의적인 연상을 기억하고 있으므로 그것이 오리를 뜻한다는 것을 안다. 어떤 단어들은 더 작은 요소로부터 만들어지고 그들의 의미는 그 요소들이 어떻게 배열됐는지(예 : 식기세척기는 식기를 세척한다)가 분석되면서 구별된다. 하지만 합성어는 불분명해지고 사람들은 합성어 형성 과정의 흐름을 의식하지 못하며 임의적인 상징으로 기억한다. (누가 "breakfast"를 "단식을 멈추다"로 생각하겠는가?)

02

하위내용영역	배점	예상정답률
일반영어 A형 기입형	2점	55%

모범답안 ⓐ mean ⓑ median

채점기준

• 2점 : 모범답안과 같다.

• 0점 : 모범답안과 다르다.

어휘

central tendency 중심 집중 경향
impassive 냉정한
invoke 이유를 들다
median 중앙값
mendacity 허위, 거짓
retort 반박하다
stretch the truth 진실을 왜곡하다

한글 번역

세 종류의 허위가 있다. 뒤의 순서로 갈수록 더 악한데, 거짓말, 벼락 맞을 거짓말, 그리고 통계 자료이다. 숫자로 진실을 왜곡하는 대표적인 예를 생각해 보자. 통계 자료는 "평균"의 다른 척도들을 인정한다. 산술 평균은 전반적인 평균에 대한 우리의 일반적인 개념이다. 즉, 항목들을 모두 더해서 항목의 수로 나누는 값이다. (할로윈을 대비해 다섯 명의 아이를 위해 수집된 100개의 사탕은 공평한 세상에서는 각자에게 20개씩 할당될 것이다.) 중심 집중 경향의 또 다른 척도인 중앙값은 중간 지점을 의미한다. 다섯 명의 아이들을 키 순서로 줄 세운다면 중간 값의 아이는 앞의 두 명(평균 몫의 사탕을 챙길 때 불리할 아이들)보다 키가 크고 뒤의 두 명보다 키가 작을 것이다. 영향력 있는 정치가는 우쭐거리며 말할지도 모른다, "시민 평균 수입은 매년 40,000불이다." 반대편의 지도자는 "하지만 우리 시민의 절반이 연 평균 25,000불보다 적게 번다."라며 반박할 수 있다. 둘 다 맞는 말을 하지만 둘 중 어느 누구도 냉정한 객관도를 지닌 수치를 인용하지 않았다. 전자는 산술 평균을 적용한 것이고 후자는 중앙값을 적용한 것이다.

이러한 경우에 산술 평균값이 중간값보다 높다. 왜냐하면 산술 평균을 측정할 때 한 명의 백만장자는 수백 명의 가난한 사람들보다 영향력이 크지만 중앙값을 계산할 때 그는 하나의 항목에 지나지 않는다.

03

하위내용영역	배점	예상정답률
일반영어 A형 서술형	4점	45%

모범답안 Ubiquitous computing is coming into our lives, with more computers being distributed and available throughout our lives. Ideally, these will be invisible and help us with mundane tasks. While this brings about concerns regarding accessibility for all and lack of privacy, they will also bring greater convenience and connectivity.

채점기준 _Total 4pts

+ 2점 : 글의 topic sentence "Ubiquitous computing is coming into our lives, with more computers being distributed and available throughout our lives"를 명확하게 서술하였거나 유사하였다.

+ 2점 : 글의 major supporting details 즉, "Ideally, these will be invisible and help us with mundane tasks. While this brings about concerns regarding accessibility for all and lack of privacy, they will also bring greater convenience and connectivity."를 명확하게 서술하였거나 유사하였다.

  ▷ 2개 중 2개 모두를 정확하게 요약한 경우 2점, 1개만 요약한 경우 1점, 요약하지 못한 경우 0점을 준다.

감점 ✪
- 본문에 나오는 연속되는 6단어 이상을 사용하였다. −0.5pt
- 문단을 두 개나 그 이상으로 구성하였다. −0.5pt
- 문법이나 영어 표현을 합쳐 3개 이상 오류가 있다. −0.5pt

어 휘

a host of 다수의
drive a wedge ~의 사이를 틀어지게 하다
embedded in ~에 내장되어 있는
help out with ~를 도와주다
in this regard 이런 점에서
legitimate 타당한; 이유 있는
prime mover 원동력, 장본인
without access to ~을 이용할 수 없는

한글 번역

우리는 "유비쿼터스 컴퓨팅"이라고 알려진 제3의 물결 시대에 들어가려고 한다. 컴퓨터는 대중과 사적 공간 도처에 퍼지게 될 것이고 일상의 물건들, 옷부터 의자, 커피 컵부터 케이크까지 침투될 것이다. 컴퓨터만의 컴퓨팅 능력으로 이 "똑똑한" 것들은 사람들의 삶 속 흔해빠진 일거리들을 덜어주고 많은 까다로운 업무들을 도와줄 것이다. 컴퓨터가 점점 더 흔해지고 시각적으로는 덜 명백해지면 두 가지의 즉각적인 질문이 제기된다. 우선, 컴퓨터에 대한 접근성이 떨어지는 "정보 최하층 계급"이 생기게 될 것인가? 두 번째로, 컴퓨터가 우리의 사생활을 침해할 것인가?

"유비쿼터스 컴퓨팅"의 목적은 기술이 보이지 않게 만들고 컴퓨터를 일상 생활 속 물체에 침투시켜서 그 물체들을 더 스마트하게 만드는 것이다. 하지만 이 목적이 사람들을 기술에 대한 통제력을 덜 사용하게 함으로써 더 바보로 만들 것인가? 내 생각엔 컴퓨터는 사람들을 더 바보로 만들지 않을 것이고 모두가 덜 흔해빠진 일들에 대하여 더 스마트해질 동등한 기회를 얻어야 한다고 생각한다. 이러한 관점에서 새로운 유비쿼터스 컴퓨터가 모두에게 동등하게 이용 가능하지는 않을 것이라는 타당한 우려가 있을 수 있다. 따라서 고도기술은 "가진 자"와 "못 가진 자" 사이에 쐐기를 박을 수 있다. 하지만 최신식 기술의 원동력은 기술 그 자체가 아니라 (우리 인간들이 만들어내는) 동의, 즉 인터넷이다. 컴퓨터가 인터넷상에서 서로 소통하는 방식에 대하여 동의하는 것은 정보 교류와 기술비용 절감에 있어 상당한 이점을 갖는다. 유비쿼터스 컴퓨팅은 우리의 삶을 더 편리하게 만들겠지만, 사생활을 침해하기도 할 것이다. 예를 들어 신문 구독과 같은 사적인 행동이 전 세계에 있는 다른 컴퓨터라든가 그것의 주인에게 공유될지도 모른다.

04

하위내용영역	배점	예상정답률
일반영어 A형 서술형	4점	45%

모범답안 The word is "love". Second, the all factors are as follows : (the mastery of) learning theory, (the mastery of) learning practice, and putting the mastery of the art above everything else.

채점기준 _Total 4pts

+ 2점 : 빈칸에 들어갈 단어를 "love"라 서술하였다. 이것 외에는 답이 될 수 없다.

+ 2점 : "The factors are as follows : learning theory, learning practice, and putting the mastery of the art above everything else"

▷ 3개 중 2개만 맞았으면 1점; 그 외는 0점을 준다.

어휘

by no means 결코 ~이 아닌
could it be that ~인 것인가
craving 열망   deep-seated 뿌리깊은
have no right to do(=of doing) ~을 요구할(~할) 권리가 없다
hold true 유효하다

한글 번역

기술을 배우는 과정은 편리하게 두 파트로 나뉜다. 하나는 이론의 정복이고 또 다른 하나는 실전의 정복이다. 내가 의술을 배우고 싶다면 나는 우선 인체에 대한 사실과 다양한 질병에 관한 사실을 알아야 한다. 내가 이러한 이론적 지식을 갖추었다고 해도, 나는 결코 의술에서 유능한 것이 아니다. 많은 양의 연습을 거치고 이론적 지식의 결과와 실전의 결과가 하나—어떤 예술의 정복이라도 그 본질이 되는 직관—로 합쳐지고 나서야 의술의 마스터가 될 수 있다. 하지만 이론과 실전을 배우는 것을 제쳐두고 어떤 예술이든지 마스터가 되기 위해 필요한 세 번째 필수 요소가 있다. 즉, 기술의 정복이 궁극적 목표여야 하고; 세상에서 기술보다 더 중요한 것은 없어야 한다. 음악, 의학, 목공 그리고 사랑도 마찬가지다.
그리고 여기 우리 문화 속 사람들이 명백한 실패에도 불구하고 왜 이 사랑을 배우려고 하지 않는지에 대한 정답이 있다. 사랑에 대한 뿌리깊은 갈망은 있지만 모든 것들—성공, 특권, 돈, 권력—이 사랑보다 중요하게 여겨진다. 우리 에너지의 대부분이 그러한 목표를 달성하는 법을 배우기 위해 사용되고, 사랑을 배우는 데는 어떤 에너지도 쓰지 않는다. 오직 저런 것들만이 돈 혹은 특권을 얻을 수 있어서 배울 만한 가치가 있는 것으로 여겨지는 것이고, 정신에만 도움이 되고 현대적 의미에서는 쓸모없는 사랑은 우리의 에너지를 쏟을 필요가 없는 사치품인가?

05

하위내용영역	배점	예상정답률
일반영어 A형 서술형	4점	55%

모범답안 The writer argues that the Great Depression was produced by government mismanagement, not by inherent instability of a private free-enterprise economy. Second, the two words are "government intervention".

채점기준   _Total 4pts

+ 2점 : "(The writer argues that) the Great Depression was produced by government mismanagement, not by inherent instability of a private free-enterprise economy."

+ 2점 : 빈칸에 들어갈 말을 "government intervention" 이라 답하였다.

어휘

bust 불황   catastrophe 재앙
comparable 비슷한
free-enterprise economy 자유기업경제
impediment to ~에 대한 방해
incentive to ~에 대한 혜택
ineptly 서투르게   inequitable 불공평한
intervention 개입
keep on an even keel ~을 안정된 상태로 유지하다
misleading (사실을) 호도하는
potent 강한   rallying call 슬로건
regulatory commission 규제 위원회
step in ~에 개입하다

한글 번역

"완전 고용"과 "경제 성장"은 지난 수십 년간 경제 문제에서 정부가 많은 개입을 하게 만든 주요한 핑계거리였다. 사적 자유기업경제는 본질적으로 불안정하다고 한다. 사적 자유기업경제 자체에 맡겨두면 호황과 불황의 순환을 되풀이하는 경향이 있다는 것이다. 정부는 그러므로 개입하여 경기를 안정된 상태로 유지해줘야 한다. 이러한 주장은 특히나 1930년대 경제 대공황 도중과 이후에 강력했고 미국의 뉴딜정책과 다른 형태의 비슷한 정부 개입 확대를 가져온 주요 원인이었다.
더욱이 최근에는 "경제 성장"이 더 인기 있는 랠리콜이 되어가고 있다. 이러한 주장은 완전히 오해의 소지가 있다. 사실은 실업률이 심각했던 다른 시기처럼 대공황도 자유기업경제의 내적 불안정성보다는 정부의 잘못된 경영 때문에 발생했다. 정부가 설립한 미국 연방 준비 제도는 재정 정책에 대한 책임을 맡아 왔다. 1930년과 1931년 연방 준비 제도는 이러한 책임을 너무 어설프게 행사하여 적절한 수준의 경제 위축이었을 뻔한 상황을 대재앙으로 만들어 버렸다. 오늘날 비슷하게 정부의 방안은 미국의 경제 성장에 주요 장애물이 되고 있다. 관세, 국제 무역에 대한 다른 제약, 과도한 세금 부담, 복잡하고 불공평한 세금 구조, 규제 위원회, 정부가 가격이나 임금을 정하는 것, 그리고 그 밖의 많은 규제들이 개인에게 자원을 오용하고 엉뚱하게 이용하도록 특혜를 주고 새로운 예금의 투자를 왜곡한다. 우리가 경제 안정과 경제 성장을 위해 당장 필요한 것은 정부 개입의 축소이다.

55 회 문제은행

📖 본책 p.474

평등고용추진위원회는 아이오와주 북부 지역에 있는 미국 연방지방법원에 유전자 검사를 상대로 지난주 최초의 소송을 제기했다. 벌링턴 노턴 산타페 철도 회사가 동의 없이 직원들의 유전자 검사를 시행해서 고발당한 것이다. 적어도 한 명의 직원이 유전자 검사에 동의하지 않으면 해고당할 것이라는 협박을 받았다고 그 기관은 (그 회사를) 고발하였다. 많은 전문가들은 잠재적 유전적 차별의 유일한 해결책은 그것을 명시적으로 금지하는 새로운 연방법이라고 믿는다.

01

하위내용영역	배점	예상정답률
일반영어 A형 기입형	2점	50%

모범답안 ⓐ discrimination ⓑ mapping

채점기준

- 2점: 모범답안과 같다.
- 1점: 둘 중 하나만 맞았다.
- 0점: 모범답안과 다르다.

어휘

compile 편집하다, 엮다　　consortium 협력단
dismissal 해고　　　　　　policy 보험증권
predisposed to ~할 성향이 있는
U.S. District Court 미국 연방지방법원

한글 번역

인간 유전자 지도는 의학 분야에 새로운 시대를 열기도 하지만 동시에 잠재적인 차별의 새로운 영역을 열고 있다. 새로운 유전자 연구는 개인의 평생에 걸친 암, 심장병 그리고 다른 병의 발병 위험을 확인할 수 있게 해준다. (하지만) 전문가들은 이러한 정보가 보험, 고용, 혹은 승진의 차별에 사용될 수 있다고 우려하고 있다. 기업의 소유주들과 보험업자들은 유전학적인 예측을 통해 만성 질환의 위험이 있는 노동자나 보험 가입을 원하는 사람들을 미리 확인하고 거부할 수 있기 때문에 수백만 달러를 아낄 수 있다. 따라서, 유전적 차별은 인종적, 민족적, 성적 차별과 마찬가지로 다른 종류의 차별의 대열에 합류할 수 있다. 유전적 차별은 최초로 완벽한 인간 유전자 지도와 염기서열이 발표되면서 관심을 끌고 있다. 사실상 동일한 두 가지 버전이 국제 공공 컨소시엄과 사기업에 의해 각각 편집되었다. 의학논문잡지인 네이처는 공공 협력단의 연구를 실었고, 사이언스 저널은 메릴랜드주 록빌의 셀레나 지노믹스라는 회사가 만든 서열을 발표했다. 유전적 차별에 대한 두려움은 이미 사람들이 인간 유전자 지도가 가져올 의학 혁명을 바라보는 시선에 영향을 미치고 있다.

02

하위내용영역	배점	예상정답률
일반영어 A형 서술형	4점	40%

모범답안 It means the doctor's wish to protect the narrator from the depressing truth of his illness. Second, the word is "cancer".

채점기준

- 4점: 모범답안과 같거나 유사하다.
- 2점: 둘 중 하나만 맞았다.
- 0점: 모범답안과 다르다.

어휘

abdominal 복부의
asbestos 석면(불연재, 단열재로 쓰이던 잿빛 물질)
bibliographic search program 문헌 검색 프로그램
brutally 잔인하게　　　　　chastity 순결
chemotherapist 화학 요법 치료사
diplomacy 사교술, 책략
make a beeline for ~로 곧장 가다
mesothelioma 중피종　　　revive 소생하다

한글 번역

나는 내가 복부 중피종이라는 석면 노출과 주로 관련된 희귀하지만 치명적인 암을 가지고 있다는 사실을 알게 되었다. 수술 후 깨어났을 때, 화학 요법 치료사와 의사에게 내가 제일 먼저 물어본 것은 "중피종에 관련한 가장 최고의 학문적 문헌이 어떤 것인가요?"였다. 그녀는 약간의 책략을 발휘해 의학 문헌은 읽을 가치가 있는 것이 하나도 없다고 답변했다. 물론, 지식인에게 책들을 멀리하라고 하는 것은, 가장 섹시한 영장류인 호모 사피엔스에게 순결을 강요하는 것과 다를 바가 없다. 내가 걸을 수 있게 되자마자 하버드 의학도서관으로 곧장 가서 문헌 검색 프로그램에 중피종을 검색해 봤다. 한 시간 뒤, 북부 중피종에 관한 최근의 문헌들로 둘러싸인 나는 왜 그 의사가 내게 그런 인간적인 조언을 해주었는지 단번에 알아차렸다. 그 문헌은 더 이상 잔인할 수 없을 만큼 분명했다 : 중피종은 발견 후에 평균적으로 8개월밖에 살 수 없는 불치병이었다. 선무당이 사람 잡는다는 말이 있다면, 나는 아주 제대로 된 예를 만난 것이다. 태도는 암 투병에서 확실히 중요하다.

한글 번역

미국의 엘리트 사립 대학교의 입학 지원이 급격하게 증가하는 현상은 불확실한 경기와 18세 인구 풀의 성장 결여를 고려해볼 때 놀랍게 보일 수 있다. 하지만 이는 미국 고등교육에 과도한 투자를 보여주는 것일 따름이다. 과거에 학사 학위는 부유한 중상층 삶으로 갈 수 있는 티켓이었다. 대학 졸업자 수가 상대적으로 고소득 직업의 수보다 빠르게 증가하자 대학 졸업자들이 상대적으로 고소득 직업이라는 목적을 달성하지 못하고 있다. 이제 그냥 학위를 따는 것만으로는 불충분하고, 질이 좋은 학위를 받을 필요가 생겼다. 이런 이유로 높게 가치를 인정받는 학교의 지원자 수가 급상승하고 있다. 하지만 최고의 학교에 입학하는 비용이 그냥 괜찮은 학교에 입학하는 비용과 거의 차이가 없다는 사실이 수요를 더 늘리고 있다. 사실 엄청나게 많은 기부금을 받고 있어 그 돈으로 학생들을 지원할 수 있는 엘리트 학교는 실제적으로 (그저 그런 대학들보다 학비가) 더 싸다. 엘리트 학교의 합격률 감소의 또 다른 요인은 입학생을 의도적으로 늘리지 않으려 하는 그 대학들의 정책이다. 대부분의 명망 높은 학교는 입학을 희망하는 자격을 갖춘 학생의 수가 엄청 증가하는데도 30년도 더 된 이전의 학부생 수와 거의 동일하게 유지하고 있다.

03

하위내용영역	배점	예상정답률
일반영어 A형 서술형	4점	40%

모범답안 The factors are as follows : the sharp rise in admissions applications at the elite schools and the schools' policy of refusing to expand enrollment. Second, the word is "degree".

채점기준 _____ Total 4pts

+ 2점 : 입학 합격률이 떨어지는 요인을 "the sharp rise in admissions applications(1점) at the elite schools and the schools' policy of refusing to expand enrollment(1점)."라 서술하였다.

+ 2점 : 빈칸에 들어갈 단어를 "degree"라 답변하였다. 이것 외에는 답이 될 수 없다.

어휘

endowment 기부금   prosperous 번창한; 부유한

04

하위내용영역	배점	예상정답률
일반영어 A형 서술형	4점	50%

모범답안 The word is "moral". Second, the real dangers are as follows : fraud not punished by law in business; viciousness towards employees; atrocity towards wife and children; harshness towards competitors; fierceness in political conflicts.

채점기준 _____ Total 4pts

+ 2점 : 빈칸에 들어갈 단어를 "moral"이라 답하였다.

+ 2점 : 실제 도덕적 위험을 "the real dangers are as follows : fraud not punished by law in business; viciousness towards employees; atrocity towards wife and children; harshness towards competitors; fierceness in political conflicts"라 서술하였거나 유사하였다.

▷ 5개 중 2~3개를 서술한 경우 1점을 준다.

어휘

be tempted to ~하게끔 유혹 받다

bestow upon ~에게 봉헌(헌정)하다

do one's bit 자기 본분을 다하다

ferocity 잔인함; 흉포	infantile 어린애 같은
irreverence 불경, 불손	make-up (사람의) 기질
malevolence 악의	reverence 존중

sharp practice 교활한 행위, 사기

unadulterated 순수한; 완전한; 다른 것이 섞이지 않은

vacillating 동요하는, 흔들리는

한글 번역

당신이 반은 이성에 의해 흔들리고 반은 어린애 같은 어리석음에 흔들리는 동요하는 피조물이 되는 것을 허락하지 말라. 당신의 어린 시절을 통제했던 사람들의 기억을 향해 불손한 태도를 취하는 것을 두려워 말라. 당신이 약했고 어리석었기 때문에, 그때(당신이 어렸을 때) 그들은 강하고 지혜로워 보였을 것이다; 이제 당신은 약하지도 어리석지도 않으므로, 그들의 겉으로 보이는 힘과 지혜를 검증하고 당신이 습관의 힘으로부터 그들에게 부여하는 존경심을 그들이 받을 자격이 있는지 생각해보는 것이 당신의 일이다. 이 세상이 젊은이들에게 전통적으로 전수되는 도덕 교육을 통해 더 살만한 곳이 됐는지 스스로에게 진지하게 물어보라.

관습적으로 미덕을 지닌 사람의 기질에 얼마나 많은 순수한 미신이 들어가 있는지 고려해보라. 그리고 모든 종류의 가상적인 윤리적 위험은 믿을 수 없을 정도로 어리석은 금기에 의해 지켜지는 반면, 인간이 실생활에서 만나게 되는 진정한 윤리적 위험은 언급되지 않는 것에 대하여 생각해보라. 평균적인 인간이 빠지기 쉬운 진정 해로운 행동들은 무엇인가? 사기를 쳤지만 법적 처벌을 받지 않는 사업, 직원들을 심하게 닦달하기, 아내와 아이들을 향한 잔인함, 경쟁자들을 향한 악의, 정치적 갈등에서 일어나는 흉포함, 이런 것들이 존경할 만하고 존경받는 시민들이 흔히 벌이는 진정 해로운 죄악들이다. 이러한 죄악을 수단으로 인간은 그와 가장 가까운 관계에 있는 사람들을 고통에 빠뜨리고, 문명 사회를 파괴하는 데 자신의 본분을 다한다.

05

하위내용영역	배점	예상정답률
일반영어 A형 단답서술형	2점	60%

모범답안 The narrator is lying in bed in the dark. Second, the intruder is the narrator's wife

채점기준

• 2점: 모범답안과 같거나 유사하였다.

• 1점: 둘 중 하나만 맞았다.

• 0점: 모범답안과 다르다.

어휘

accretion 부착물, (시간이 지나서) 쌓이는 것

dissipate 흩뜨리다; 소멸되다

excavate 발굴하다, 파헤치다

go through ~를 살펴보다

scramble (재빨리) 움직이다, 뒤죽박죽으로 만들다

shield 막다	squeak 끼익 하는 소리

voluminous 아주 큰

한글 번역

문 모서리가 열리고 틈 사이로 불이 번쩍거린다. 멀리서 흐릿하게 보이는 형태가 방으로 들어오는데 어두운 실루엣이다. 그 형태는 빛으로 변하고 그는 바라본다 : 그녀다. 그 자신의 몸처럼 너무나 익숙한 모습. 긴장감은 천천히 불안 속에 소멸되기 시작한다. 마치 매듭이 머리부터 발끝까지 그의 존재를 묶고 있는 것 같다. 그는 숨을 참고 그녀가 방을 가로질러 움직이고 옷장 문을 열어두고 습관적인 끽 소리를 피하려고 신중하게 노력하는 모습을 본다. 문의 경첩에 기름칠을 해야만 해, 그가 생각한다. 손전등 빛을 막기 위해 몸의 뒤쪽을 침대 쪽으로 향한 채, 옷장 뒤편에 쌓여있던 오랜 옷들을 휘젓고, 큰 코트의 호주머니를 뒤진다. 그녀가 이미 항아리들 속과 책장에 있는 책들 뒤쪽과 온갖 잡동사니로 가득 찬 더러운 서랍 뒤쪽을 이미 헤집으면서 온 집안을 살펴봤을 것이라는 것을 그는 안다. 이런 일은 일 년에 한 번 가량 일어난다. 악령이 한밤중에 그녀를 찾아오고, 그녀는 자기 자신의 집을 침입한다. 일상에서 오랜 시간 동안 쌓여왔던 것들을 파헤치면서, 필사적으로 삶의 기초인 과거의 잔여물을 발견하기 원하면서 뭔가를 말해야 할 것 같은 느낌이 생기면 "물어볼 것이 많지" 그런 뒤 "별 거 아냐"라고 말할 것이다. 그것은 다름 아닌 아주 간단하고 만족스러운 것 : 담배이다.

56 회 문제은행

📖 본책 p.479

01

하위내용영역	배점	예상정답률
일반영어 A형 기입형	2점	55%

모범답안 ⓐ propaganda ⓑ power

채점기준

• 2점 : 모범답안과 같다.
• 1점 : 둘 중 하나만 맞았다.
• 0점 : 모범답안과 다르다.

어휘

accentuate 강조하다 adept at ~에 능숙한
agitation 불안, 동요 indoctrinate 세뇌하다
outright 전면적인, 노골적인 tyranny 폭압
stir 동요시키다

한글 번역

선전은 정보를 퍼뜨려 여론에 영향을 미치고 사람들의 신념을 조작하기 위해 쓰인다. 선전의 메시지는 주로 메시지를 보내는 사람의 이익을 위해 쓰이며, 그렇게 함으로써 그의 권력을 더 강화시킨다. 모든 선전은 설득을 위한 체계적인 노력이다. 선전가는 편파적인 메시지를 전달하며 일면의 좋은 점과 다른 면의 부정적인 점을 강조한다. 설득의 예술로써 선전은 수천 년 동안 이용돼 왔다.
기원전 5세기, 페리클래스가 그의 아테네인 친구들에게 스파르타의 폭압과 비교하며 아테네 도시의 장점을 설명해줄 때 (비록 그의 말의 대부분은 사실이었지만) 선전을 사용했다. 수 세기 후, 소련 혁명가 레닌은 교육받은 사람들을 세뇌시킬 수 있는 선전의 가치를 깨달았다. 그는 교육받지 못한 사람들에게는 선동이라는 또 다른 전술을 이용했다. 이 과정에서 복잡한 주장에 대한 필요성을 피하기 위해 슬로건, 이야기, 반쪽 진실, 노골적인 거짓말이 이용됐다. 1933년부터 1945년 독일의 나치 정부는 선전에 능숙했다. 권력을 얻기 위해 아돌프 히틀러는 그의 능력을 이용하여 각 청중에게 그들이 듣고 싶어 하는 말을 해줬다. 그는 사업가들에게 말할 때는 공산주의에 대한 두려움으로 동요시켰고 공장 노동자들에게는 사회주의의 가치를 설교했다. 자신이 속한 당이 정부의 통제력을 가지고 나서 그는 조셉 괴벨스를 대중 계몽과 선전 부처의 수장으로 임명했다. 괴벨스를 통해서 히틀러는 언론, 라디오, 극장, 영화, 음악, 문학의 통제력을 얻었다.

02

하위내용영역	배점	예상정답률
일반영어 A형 단답서술형	2점	60%

모범답안 ⓐ work ⓑ play

채점기준

• 2점 : 모범답안과 같다.
• 1점 : 둘 중 하나만 맞았다.
• 0점 : 모범답안과 다르다.

어휘

artistry 예술적 기교 compatible 양립될 수 있는
conducive to ~에 도움이 되는
set free of ~에 자유를 주다(give freedom to~)

한글 번역

놀이는 문화를 생성한다. 놀이는 인간 상상력을 자유롭게 하여 공유된 의미를 창조해낸다. 놀이는 그것이 없이는 사회가 존속할 수 없는, 인간 행동의 기본적인 분류이다. 요즘 회사는 업무 측면보다 놀기 측면에서 정의되고 있다. 모든 종류의 회사들은 그들의 조직 환경을 되살려서 조직 환경이, 문화적 교류의 핵심인, 창의성과 예술적 기교와 더 잘 양립할 수 있게 만들기 시작하고 있다. 많은 회사 간부들은 직원을 더 이상 "근로자들"이라고 부르지 않는 대신 "놀이자들"이라는 표현을 더 선호한다. 문화 공연과 생생한 경험의 마케팅에 대한 새로운 강조를 반영하여 업무 환경은 점점 놀이 환경으로 형태가 바뀌고 있다. 회사는 모든 종류의 장난스러운 혁신을 도입하여 예술적 창의성에 도움이 되는 편안한 분위기를 조성하고 있다. 야후는 명상 공간을 설치했다. 구글은 장난감, 비디오, 게임으로 가득 찬 "유머 방"을 갖고 있다.

03

하위내용영역	배점	예상정답률
일반영어 A형 서술형	4점	50%

모범답안 The story takes place in a fast food restaurant in Northern Manhattan. Second, the central conflict is between a customer and cashier over the terms of a coupon at McDonald's, which had the exception of giving less of a discount in the borough of Manhattan.

채점기준   _Total 4pts

+ 2점: 사건이 발생한 장소를 "in a fast food restaurant (McDonald) in Northern Manhattan"이라 서술하였다.

+ 2점: 갈등이 일어난 이유를 "the central conflict is between a customer and cashier over the terms of a coupon at McDonald's, which had the exception of giving less of a discount in the borough of Manhattan"이라 서술하였거나 유사하였다.

어휘

borough 자치구; 지역
emphatic 강한, 단호한
finality 최후
make one's case 주장하다

electrified 흥분한
fatigues 작업복
fine print 작은 글씨
queue (대기자의) 줄

한글 번역

맨해튼 북쪽의 매우 붐비는 패스트푸드 레스토랑 안에서 매우 긴 손님 줄 끝에 서서, 스물세 살 먹은 흑인 남성인 덱스터가 반짝거리는 맥도날드 카운터 너머 그의 주문을 침착하게 받으려는 도미니카인 점원과 언쟁을 벌이는 것을 나는 유심히 들었다. 흰 회색빛의 검정 작업복을 입고 에어 조던을 신은 덱스터는 자신의 줄을 지키며 오른쪽 손바닥에 형형색색의 쿠폰을 흔들고 있었다. 일요판 지역 신문의 삽입 광고에서 잘라낸 쿠폰은 "맨해튼 지역"을 제외한 뉴욕시(아주 작은 글씨로 그렇게 써 있었다) 모든 곳에서 99센트짜리 빅맥으로 교환할 수 있었다. 대신 맨해튼에서는 같은 쿠폰으로 빅맥을 1.39달러로 할인받아 살 수 있었다. 점원인 팸이 지역에 따른 차이를 여러 번 말하자 덱스터는 점점 짜증이 나기 시작했다. 그는 단호한 제스처로 팔짱을 꼈다가 풀었다. 그는 큰 소리로 한숨을 쉬고 반복했다. 쭉 뻗은 왼손에 1달러와 10센트짜리 동전을 꽉 쥐며 (10센트는 "세금"이라며 여러 번 말했다) 덱스터는 주장했다. "여기는 할렘이야" 단호한 태도를 보이며 흥분

하며 말했다. "맨해튼이 아니라고! 할렘을 말하는 거였다면, 할렘이었다면, 할렘이라고 썼어야지! 할렘은 맨해튼이 아니야! 그러니까 나는 1.1달러만 내고 빅맥을 사겠어."

04

하위내용영역	배점	예상정답률
일반영어 A형 서술형	4점	50%

모범답안 He was expected to stop by the post office and come meet his father on time. Second, as his father was disappointed, he came to realize how much his parents rely on him.

채점기준

• 4점: 모범답안과 같거나 유사하다.
• 2점: 둘 중 하나만 맞았다.
• 0점: 모범답안과 다르다.

어휘

entice 유혹하다
force one's way into 침범해 들어가다, 밀고 들어가다
glowing 벌겋게 달군
mask one's pain 고통을 감추다
reel (실, 전선 등을 감는) 얼레
self-employed 독자적으로 일하는
sit behind the wheel 차를 운전하다
whisk 재빨리 가져가다
wrapped up in ~에 몰두한

한글 번역

나는 그 곳에 얼어붙은 듯 서 있었다. 나의 발은 마치 땅에 박혀있는 듯이 너무 깊게 자리 잡아서 움직일 수 없는 것 같이 느껴졌다. 아버지는 화를 내며 내게 소리를 쳤고, 그 지나간 몇 분 동안이 나에게는 영원처럼 느껴졌다. 오늘까지도 나는 내 마음에 침입해 내 심장을 뚫어버린 그 말들을 여전히 기억한다. 아버지의 구릿빛으로 그을린 얼굴은 내 눈 앞에서 벌겋게 달군 뜨거운 석탄과 같이 바로 벌겋게 변해버렸다. 그는

"나는 너의 친구가 아니고, 아버지야. 나를 네 친구 대하 듯 하지 마라."고 소리쳤다. 나는 상처받았고, 내 두려움 과 실망감으로 고통을 가렸다. 근면하고 부지런하고 좀처럼 게으른 법이 없는 나의 아버지는 나에게 격분했다. 그는 항상 미소로 사람들을 맞이할 준비가 돼 있었다. 외모에 신경 쓰면서, 그는 항상 깔끔하게 가느다란 머리카락을 빗어 놓았다. 그는 옷을 잘 입었으며, 편한 신발을 신었다. 그러나 오늘은 그것이 문제가 되지 않았다. 그가 내가 학교에서 집으로 돌아오기를 기다리는 동안에, 나는 그의 인내를 바닥내버렸다. 그날 방과 후에, 나는 부모님의 차로 내 친구를 집에 데려다줬다. 시간은 휙 지나갔다. 집으로 갔을 때, 5시 이후였다. 너무 늦은 시간이었다. 아버지는 내가 무언가 중요한 것을 하길 요구했다. 열여섯 살에, 부모님의 차로 방과 후에 집으로 오는 것은 내 생각이 아니었는데, 자유로운 오후의 특권을 만끽하고 싶었기 때문이었다. 차를 운전하는 매혹에 빠져, 친구들에게 열중한 나머지 시간 개념을 잃어버리기는 매우 쉬웠다. 내가 기억하는 한, 나의 부모는 항상 자영업을 하셨다. 그들은 작은 소매상을 운영했고, 대부분 그 둘뿐이었다. 그곳은 낚시도구들, 옷, 기타 용품들, 스포츠 용품 그리고 편안한 신발들이 있는 재고가 풍부한 상점이었다. 일요일과 공휴일을 제외한 매일, 하루에 두세 번 우체국에 가는 것이 일상이었다. 상점의 선반에 채워져 있는 모든 것들이 거의 우체국을 통해 보내졌다. 아마도 아버지는 손님에게 주문한 상품이 오후엔 갖춰질 것이라고 약속했을지도 모른다. 아니면 아마도 그는 낚시 얼레를 고치기 위한 특정 부품을 필요로 했을지도 모른다. 이유야 어쨌든 간에, 아버지는 우체국에 가고, 상품을 가지러 가고, 그것을 다시 상점으로 가지고 오기 위해 나에게 의존했었다. 그가 나에게 소리를 질렀던 그 전날까지는, 나는 이 간단한 일이 얼마나 중요한 일이며, 그들이 얼마나 나를 필요로 하는지에 대해서 깨닫지 못했었다.

05

하위내용영역	배점	예상정답률
일반영어 A형 서술형	4점	50%

모범답안 The teacher is trying to teach essay writing while the students are distracted with mobile electronic devices : cell phones and laptops. Second the two words are "cell phone".

+ 2점 : 교사는 "is trying to teach essay"; 학생들은 "are distracted with mobile electronic devices : cell phones and laptops"라 서술하였거나 유사하였다.

+ 2점 : 빈칸에 들어갈 단어를 "cell phone"이라 답하였다. 이것 외에는 답이 될 수 없다.

어휘

come to the forefront 세상의 주목을 받다
confiscate 몰수, 압수하다
dazzle 눈이 부시게 하다
legitimate cause 타당한 대의명분
metal detector 금속 탐지기
no hint of ~의 조짐이 없다
onus 책임
patch A through to B A를 B와 연결하다
Regents exam 리젠트 시험(졸업 및 대학 진학을 위해 필요한 졸업장 취득 시험)
scribble 갈겨쓰다   strike down 폐지하다

한글 번역

당신은 뉴욕시의 공립 학교 교사이다. 지금은 9월이고 당신은 에세이의 구조에 대해 강의를 하고 있다. 당신의 학생들은 수업을 이수하고 리젠트 시험을 통과하기 위해서 이 정보를 알 필요가 있다. 그리고 물론 당신도 언젠가 당신의 유능한 제자들이 전국의 영어 교수들을 눈이 부시게 하고 놀라게 만들 것을 희망한다. 당신은 등 돌려 칠판에 논제의 정의를 적는다.
그것은 약 15초 정도 걸린다. 당신은 25명의 학생의 그들의 노트에 그 개념을 갈겨쓰는 것을 보게 되길 기대하고 학생들을 향해 돌아선다. 대신, 당신은 나타난 기술의 부산물들을 보았다. 호세는 이어폰을 키워냈다. 마리아의 엄지손가락들은 양방향으로 싹텄다. 최근 중국으로부터 온 만큉은 그의 팔목에 연결된 휴대전화로 문자를 날리고 있다. 그리고 크리스티나는 그녀의 무릎에 포켓 PC를 두고 지뢰 찾기를 하는 듯 보였다. 그 학기가 끝날 때 쯤이면, 몇몇이 수업을 이수하지 못할 것이다. 몇몇은 절대 리젠트 시험을 통과하지 못할 것이다. 우리가 모두 알고 있듯이, 많은 수가 학교를 중퇴할 것이다. 그리고 나는 자부심 하나 없이 이것이 교사의 잘못이 아니라고 말할 수 있다. 우리 학교를 성가시게 해 온 다른 문제들만큼, 실패의 책임은 교실에서 우리의 주의를 산만하게 하는 것들이 져야 하는데, 그것이 구체적으로 휴대전화이다.

전자기기들이 공립 학교에서 수년간 금지되어 왔음에도 불구하고, 문제는 지난 달 조엘 클라인 교육감이 학교에서 금속 탐지기의 무작위 배치를 발표했을 때 주목을 받았다. 결과는 800개 이상의 휴대전화가 압수되었다는 사실이다. 안전상의 이유로 휴대전화에 의지한다고 말한 학생들과 그들의 부모들은 분노했다. 심지어 규정이 폐지되어야 한다고 주장하는 소송에 관한 이야기도 들려왔다. 그러나 뉴욕시의 전 공립 학교 교사로서, 나는 휴대전화가 교실 안에 있어서는 안 된다고 생각한다. 휴대전화를 가진 학생들은 공부에는 흥미가 없고, 사교 생활에만 더 신경 쓰는 집중력이 짧은 아이들이다. 부모들은 휴대전화를 비상 상황에서 자신의 아이들과 연락 수단으로 생각한다. 나는 그 학부모들에게 몇 가지 질문이 있다. 첫째, 당신의 아이와 진짜 즉각적인 연락을 필요로 하는 마지막 순간이 언제였는가? 대부분의 경우에, 병원 또는 경찰이 더 긴급할 듯하다. 둘째, 교무실에 연락하거나, 교무실을 통해 당신의 자녀에게 연결되는 것만으로도 충분히 빠르지 않은가?

그리고 셋째, 당신은 왜 아이들이 진짜 학교에 휴대전화를 가져가길 원하는지 아는가? 왜냐하면, 그들이 원하는 나이키 신발이나 로카웨어 브랜드 옷의 신상품처럼 휴대전화는 지위의 상징이기 때문이다. 왜냐하면 교사가 말하는 동안 휴대전화가 울릴 때, 모두가 웃기 때문이다. 왜냐하면 휴대전화로 비디오 게임을 하는 것은 그들을 멋져 보이게 하기 때문이다.

왜냐하면 옆 교실에 있는 친구에게 문자를 보내는 것이 중심 문장에 대해 배우는 것보다 더 재미있기 때문이다. 그들 휴대폰에 방금 다운로드받은 새로운 Three 6 Mafia 노래를 듣는 것도 마찬가지이다. 그리고 학생들이 사물함에 휴대전화를 보관할 수 있다고 말하는 것은 말도 안 된다. 만약 휴대전화를 가지고 있다면 그들은 휴대전화를 교실로 가지고 올 것이다. 학부모들이 맡아야 하는 타당한 대의들이 있다. 학급 인원 과밀에 대항해 집결하라. 억압적이고 문화적으로 편견이 있는 리젠트 시험에 맞서 싸워라. 그러나 이 휴대전화 문제와 관련해서는 당신이 잘못되었다. 이번 경우에는, 당신은 해결책이 아닌, 문제의 일부분이다.

57 회 문제은행

📖 본책 p.486

01

하위내용영역	배점	예상정답률
일반영어 A형 기입형	2점	40%

모범답안 ⓐ attractive ⓑ exchange

채점기준

- 2점: 모범답안과 같거나 유사하다.
- 1점: 둘 중 하나만 맞았다.
- 0점: 모범답안과 다르다.

어 휘

appetite for ~에 대한 욕구(=craving)
coyness 수줍어함
desirable 가치 있는; 바람직한; 성적 매력이 있는
domesticity 가정생활   on installment 할부로
overt 명시적인, 공공연한   standpoint 견지, 관점

한글 번역

우리의 전체 문화는 사고 싶은 욕구, 상호 호의적인 교환에 대한 개념에 기반을 둔다. 현대인의 행복은 가게 창문을 바라보고 현금으로든 할부로든 살 수 있는 모든 것을 살 때 오는 기쁨에 있다. 현대인은 사람을 볼 때도 비슷한 방식을 적용한다. 남자에겐 매력적인 여성이, 여자에겐 매력적인 남성이 뒤따르는 상품인 것이다. "매력적이다"라는 말은 성격 시장에서 유명하고 사람들이 갈망하는 자질의 훌륭한 패키지를 말한다. 개인을 구체적으로 매력적으로 만드는 것은 그 시대의 신체적일 뿐만 아니라 정신적인 유행에 달려 있다. 20대 동안 술 마시고 담배 피고 터프하고 섹시한 여자는 매력적이었다. 오늘날 유행은 가정적이고 더 수줍어할 것을 요구한다. 19세기 후반 그리고 20세기 초반에는 남자는 공격적이고 야망이 있어야 했다. 오늘날 남자는 매력적인 "패키지"가 되기 위해서는 사회적이고 인내심이 많아야 한다. 어쨌든 사랑에 빠지는 감정은 누군가 물물 교환할 가능성이 있는 범위 안에 있는 인간 상품에 관해서만 발전한다. 나는 팔리기 위해 나왔다. 상대방은 사회적 가치의 관점에서 보았을 때 가치 있는 것이야 할 뿐 아니라 동시에 나의 명시적이고 숨겨진 자산과 가능성을 고려했을 때 (그 상대방은)

나를 원해야만 한다. 두 사람이 자신의 교환 가치의 한계를 따져보면서 시장에 나온 최고의 상대를 발견했다고 느낄 때 사랑에 빠진다. 종종 부동산을 매입할 때, 발전 가능한 숨어있는 잠재력은 흥정에서 중요한 역할을 한다. 한마디로 시장 지향성이 우세한 문화에서 인간의 사랑 관계는 상품을 지배하는 물물 교환의 패턴과 똑같다.

02

하위내용영역	배점	예상정답률
일반영어 A형 단답서술형	4점	55%

모범답안 The word is "uniforms". Second, the title is "The Pros and Cons of a Mandatory Uniform Policy".

채점기준

- 4점 : 모범답안과 같거나 유사하다.
- 2점 : 둘 중 하나만 맞았다.
- 0점 : 모범답안과 다르다.

어휘

attire 옷   bandana 두건
baggy 헐렁한   bode well for 좋은 징조이다
bolster ~을 복돋우다; 강화(개선)하다
catalyst for ~의 촉매제; 기폭제
drastic 과감한   dress code 복장 규정
fear over ~에 대한 걱정   inadvertently 우연히
regimented (규율이) 엄격한 stifle 질식시키다
stride 성큼성큼 걷다

한글 번역

그 지역에서 교복을 도입하자는 주장의 촉매제는 아이들이 의도치 않게 잘못 고른 색상의 스카프나 모자를 써서 지역 폭력배 사이 경쟁 의식을 불러일으키지 않을까 하는 부모님의 우려다. 그 지역은 십 년도 더 전에 모자, 두건, 배기바지 등 깽패와 관련된 복장을 금지하는 복장 규정을 채택했다. 하지만 많은 사람들은 지역이 좀 더 극적인 접근을 취해야 한다고 생각했다. 바오 로가 프랭클린 중학교에 다니는 두 자녀가 있었을 때 그녀는 학교에 교복제를 도입하자는 노력을 하는 구성원 중 한 명이었다. 그녀는 현재 지역 초등학교에 다니는 아이가 있고 교복에 대해 여전히 열광적이다. "오늘날 아이를 약물 사용과

폭력으로부터 보호하는 한계선이 거의 없으므로 우리가 아이들에게 한계선을 마련해 수 있다면 좋을 것이다"라고 그녀가 말했다. 학교장들에 따르면 통일감은 학교에 다니지 않는 사람들을 발견하기 쉬우므로 안전성을 강화할 수 있다고 한다. 하지만 이 학군의 학생 대다수는 부모님과 선생님처럼 낙관적으로 바라보지 않는다. 나이를 더 먹을수록 교복을 점점 더 싫어하는 것 같다. 이것은 고등학교까지 교복 의무제를 확장시키자는 얘기에 대한 좋지 않은 징조이다. "우리가 꼭 감옥에 있는 것 같아요"라고 프랭클린 학교 7학년 헥터 곤잘레스가 말했다. "고상한 옷을 입으면 교복을 입을 필요가 없어요" 마찬가지로 8학년인 알리시아 누네즈가 엄격한 복장은 그녀의 창의성을 질식시킨다며 불평을 한다. "당신은 학교에 교육을 받으러 오는 거지, 누군가로부터 어떻게 복장을 입으라고 강요받기 위하여 오는 것이 아니다", 초콜릿 갈색 티셔츠와 청바지를 입은 14살 소녀가 캠퍼스를 가로질러 가며 말했다.

03

하위내용영역	배점	예상정답률
일반영어 A형 단답서술형	2점	50%

모범답안 The more painful the truth to be conveyed, the softer your delivery needs to be.

채점기준

- 2점 : 모범답안과 같거나 유사하다.
- 0점 : 모범답안과 다르다.

어휘

brutal 잔인한, 인정사정없는
gory detail 참혹한 장면에 대한 자세한 묘사
in a panic 공황 상태로

한때 남자친구는 나의 의견을 물었고, 답변을 주었을 때, 내가 영화 〈제리 맥과이어〉에 나오는 약혼녀를 상기시킨다고 그는 말했다. 제리는 그녀가 "인정사정없는 진실"에서 "인정사정없음"이라는 용어를 사용했다고 말했다. 이 비유는 나의 시선을 사로잡았는데 그 이유는 이 영화에서 이러한 "인정사정없는" 표현이 결국 파혼을 야기했기 때문이다. 관계에 있어 정직함은 중대한 요인이다. 그러나 잔인한 진실은 그렇지 않을 수도 있다. 나는 이러한 교훈을 나의 가장 소중한 친구 중 한 명으로부터 배웠다. 나는 관계에서 실수한 것을 깨닫고 공황 상태로 친구에게 조언을 구했다. 내가 참혹한 세부적인 뒷이야기를 모두 마치자, 친구는 "너는 내가 너를 아끼는 친구로서 널 위로하기를 원하니 아니면 솔직하게 말하기를 바라니?" 라고 물었다. 친구는 내가 들어야 하는 것, 즉 본질적으로 "켈리, 너 완전 바보처럼 행동했어"를 전달하기 위해 완벽한 질문을 한 것이다. 나는 이제 내가 사랑하는 이들에게 앞에 제시되었던 상황과 유사한 사실을 전달해야 할 때 "벨벳 장갑을 낀 쇠주먹(냉혹한 내용을 가능하면 부드럽게 전달)" 방법을 사용한다. 그러나 이 방법이 상대방의 충격을 완화할 것이라는 확신이 100% 들지 않으면 나에게는 또 하나의 준비된 비밀 무기가 있다.

04

하위내용영역	배점	예상정답률
일반영어 B형 서술형	4점	30%

모범답안 Coca-Cola was invented by pharmacist John Styth Pemberton first as a nerve tonic and stimulant along with the help of accountant Frank Robinson. Originally intended as a headache cure, by chance it was discovered that mixing with charged water made an enjoyable and stimulating drink, becoming the drink we know today.

채점기준

+ 2점: 글의 topic sentence "Coca-Cola was invented by pharmacist John Styth Pemberton first as a nerve tonic and stimulant along with the help of accountant Frank Robinson"을 명확하게 서술하였거나 유사하였다.

+ 2점: 글의 major supporting details 즉, "Originally intended as a headache cure, by chance it was discovered that mixing with charged water made an enjoyable and stimulating drink, becoming the drink we know today"를 명확하게 서술하였거나 유사하였다.

감점 ♡

• 본문에 나오는 연속되는 6단어 이상을 사용하였다. −0.5pt
• 문단을 두 개나 그 이상으로 구성하였다. −0.5pt
• 문법이나 영어 표현을 합쳐 3개 이상 오류가 있다. −0.5pt

어휘

a batch of ~한 처분　　a pinch of 약간의
audit 이해하다; 분석하다; 회계감사를 하다
cavalry 기사, 기갑 부대 cf. cavalier (기사도 정신을 가진) 신사; 무신경한
charged water 소다수　　concoction 혼합물
dollop 소량　　　　　　　end product 최종 산물
factotum 막일꾼, 직원　　fizzy (음료가) 거품이 나는
flowing 흐르는 듯한; 미끈한 oar 노
overindulgence 지나친 방임
perk up 생기가 돌다; 정신을 차리다
sniffing 코를 훌쩍이는, 킁킁거리며 냄새를 맡는
soda fountains 소다수 판매점
swish 휘두르다, 움직이다, (획획) 휘젓다
temple 관자놀이
testimonially ~을 기려서(=in honor of)
throb 욱신거리다, 지끈거리다　　troop 병력, 무리
unveil 발표하다, 제막식을 하다

코카콜라를 발명한 사람은 애틀랜타에서 태어나지 않았지만, 그의 장례식 날 이 도시에 있는 모든 약국이 (그를) 기려서 문을 닫았다. 그는 존 스타이스 펨버튼으로, 애틀랜타와 80마일 정도 떨어져 있는 조지아주 녹스빌에서 1833년에 태어났다. 의사로도 알려진 그는 약사로서 남북 전쟁 때 조 휠러 장군 밑에서 기병 중대를 지휘했다. 그는 1869년에 애틀랜타에 정착했고 특허 자격을 받은 Triplex Liver Pills(간 약)과 Globe of Flower Cough Syrup(감기 시럽)과 같은 약을 제조하기 시작했다. 1885년 그는 French Wine Cola라고 불리는 이상적 신경 및 강장 촉진제라는 상표를 등록했고, 몇 달 후 펨버튼 화학 공장을 차리고 프랑크 M. 로빈슨이라는 회계 장부 담당자를 채용했다. 프랑크는 계수에 밝은 두뇌를 지녔을 뿐만 아니라 킁킁거리기만 해도 시럽에 사용된 구성요소를 구분할 수 있는 탁월한 후각을 지녔다.

1886년에 — 현재의 코카콜라 임원들이 즐겨 말하는 코난 도일이 셜록 홈즈를 공개하고, 프랑스가 자유의 여신상의 제막식을 한 바로 그 해 — 펨버튼은 코카콜라라 불리는 시럽을 공개했다. 이것은 그의 French Wine Cola를 변형한 것이었다. 그는 이 제품에서 와인을 제거하고 소량의 카페인을 투입했다. 그리고 최종 생산물의 맛이 끔찍하자 콜라 나무 열매 추출물과 다른 몇 가지의 오일을 첨가해 그의 뒷마당에 있는 삼각 솥에 넣어 섞고, 노를 가지고 저었다. 그는 이것을 중고 맥주 병에 담아 소수 판매점에 배달했고, 로빈슨은 지금까지도 사용되고 있는 코카콜라 상표를 그의 유려한 회계 장부 담당자의 글씨로 고안해냈다. 펨버튼은 자신의 혼합물을 가벼운 음료라기보다 두통 치료제로 간주했다. 특히 과음으로 인해 지끈거리는 관자놀이에 시달리는 사람을 위한 것으로서, 1886년 말 어느 아침 지난 밤 과음한 한 환자가 애틀랜타 약국에 들러 소량의 코카콜라를 요구했다.
약사들은 관례상 한 컵의 물에 티스푼 한 숟갈 양에 해당되는 시럽을 넣어야 하지만, 당시 근무하던 직원이 몇 걸음 떨어진 정수기로 가기에는 너무 게을렀다. 대신에, 그는 더 가까운, 소다수에 시럽을 섞었다. 고객은 곧바로 정신을 차렸고 최고의 코카콜라는 탄산이 있는 것이라는 소문이 빠르게 퍼졌다.

05

하위내용영역	배점	예상정답률
일반영어 B형 서술형	4점	50%

모범답안 Dumping waste causes the bacteria population to explode, which consumes oxygen that ends up killing other organisms. Second the word is "harmful".

채점기준

- 4점 : 모범답안과 같거나 유사하다.
- 2점 : 둘 중 하나만 맞았다.
- 0점 : 모범답안과 다르다.

어휘

acid 산
anaerobic 혐기성의, 무산소성의
botulism 보툴리눔 식중독(썩은 소시지·통조림 고기에서 일어나는 식중독)
crisp 아삭아삭한   dead organism 사체
decompose 분해하다   inhibit 금지하다; 억제하다
sewage 하수, 오물
suffocate 질식사하다, 숨이 막히다

한글 번역

한 스푼의 요거트나 아삭아삭한 피클을 삼킨다면, 당신은 지금 박테리아의 활동에 의해 맛이 첨가된 음식을 섭취하고 있는 것이다. 박테리아는 산을 생산해내는데, 이 산이 음식에 신맛을 부여한다. 특정 박테리아는 당신의 소화 기관에 자연적으로 거주하고 있고 당신이 건강할 수 있도록 도와준다. E.coli와 L. acidophilus라는 두 종류의 박테리아는 다른 해로울 수 있는 박테리아의 활동을 제지하는 물질을 방출한다. 몇몇의 다른 종류는 특정 종류의 비타민을 생산해낸다. 많은 박테리아들은 분해자로서의 역할을 하는데 이는 사체의 조직을 분해하는 유기체와 같은 것이다. 이런 분해의 분해 과정은 박테리아가 사체의 조직을 먹이로 사용면서 발생한다. 어떤 박테리아는 물속에 있는 하수나 다른 쓰레기를 분해하기도 한다. 이런 면에서 박테리아는 호수나 개천의 소량의 오염이라도 막을 수 있도록 돕는다. 분해자 없이 지구는 사체와 그들의 찌꺼기로 뒤덮일 것이다. 많은 박테리아가 도움을 주는 반면, 몇몇은 해롭다. 예를 들어 박테리아는 쓰레기를 분해하면서 우리를 돕는다. 그러나 사람들이 호수나 강가에 대량의 쓰레기를 버리면 박테리아들은 다량의 음식을 공급받게 된다. 먹이가 넘치게 되면 박테리아도 자라고 번식하기에 자칫하면 그 수가 폭발적으로 늘어날 수 있다. 거대한 수의 박테리아는 물속에 용해되어 있는 산소를 고갈시킬 것이다. 그럼 결과적으로 물속에 사는 물고기나 다른 유기체들이 질식할 수 있다. 박테리아는 분해, 부패, 그리고 중독을 통해 다량의 음식 손실을 야기할 수 있다. 박테리아는 음식에서 자라면서 음식을 부패시킨다. 박테리아가 자라면서, 음식의 냄새와 맛을 바꿀 수 있다. 때때로 박테리아는 독소라는 독을 생산해낸다. 제대로 통조림 가공이 되지 않은 음식에서 식중독의 한 유형인 보툴리눔 식중독이 종종 발생한다. 보툴리눔 식중독을 발생시키는 혐기성균은 냄새가 없거나 특이한 맛을 가진 독소를 생성해내기에 쉽게 감지되지 않는다.
보툴리눔 식중독은 치명적일 수 있다. 이것은 마비 그리고 심지어 죽음까지 야기할 수 있다.

58회 문제은행

📖 본책 p.493

01

하위내용영역	배점	예상정답률
일반영어 A형 기입형	2점	45%

모범답안 ⓐ rhetoric ⓑ violence

채점기준

- 2점: 모범답안과 같거나 유사하다.
- 1점: 둘 중 하나만 맞았다.
- 0점: 모범답안과 다르다.

어휘

blogosphere 블로그 세상   condemn 규탄하다
disseminate (정보, 지식 등을) 퍼뜨리다
ethno-nationalism 종족 민주주의
gain ground 더 강력해지다, 성공하다
in the wake of ~에 뒤따라
intolerant 편협한, 너그럽지 못한
manifesto 성명서
perpetrate 자행하다   plot 음모
preclude 못하게 하다, 불가능하게 하다
rhetoric 수사(법); 미사여구
separatist 분리주의자
staple 일용할 양식; 주식; 주요한
trans-Atlantic 대서양을 횡단하는
vituperate 혹평하다

한글 번역

유럽 경찰 조직의 테러에 대한 최근 보고에 따르면 유럽 전역의 테러리스트의 행동과 음모가 종족 민주주의와 분리주의자에 의해 자행되고 있다고 한다. 그러나 이슬람 테러에의 초점은 다른 정치적 집단으로부터의 위험을 효과적으로 평가하는 것을 불가능하게 한다. 비록 최근 역사에서 노르웨이에서 있었던 끔찍한 공격이 이 정도 규모의 우파의 최초 행동이었지만, 편협한 미사여구를 대서양을 초월하는 블로그 세계에 퍼뜨리는 사이버 행동주의에 상당한 증가가 일어났다. 더 문제는 이 미사여구가 지난 20년 동안 유럽 주류 정치계에서 점점 더 강력해졌다는 것이다. 1980년대 당시 주변부 정치인이었던 프랑스 국민 전선당 장마리 르펜은 이슬람화의 위험에 대해

혹평한 자들 중 한 명이다. "내부의 적이자 외부의 적"으로서의 이슬람은 오늘날 유럽 정치 담론의 일용할 양식이다. 지난 6개월 동안, 안젤라 메르켈, 니콜라 사르코지, 그리고 데이빗 카메론은 다문화주의를 비난했는데, 다문화주의가 자신들 각자의 나라에 "이민자를 통합"—즉, 이슬람을 동화시키는 것을 의미하는—시키는 데 실패한 모델이라는 것이다. 노르웨이에서 발생한 공격들은 그런 미사여구의 최초의 폭력적인 우리말 번역이다. 하지만, 살인이 일어난 뒤에 다른 극우파의 멤버들은 그들 자신을 브레이비크의 행동과 선언의 폭력적인 성격으로부터 거리를 뒀다. 그들의 공격 직후, (극우파인) 스웨덴 방위 연맹의 대변인인 이삭 나이그렌은 다음과 같이 썼다. "비록 그 테러리스트가 나처럼 반이슬람주의자 반다문화주의자이지만, 나는 그 사람과 공통점이 정말 없다. 난 폭력을 지지하지 않는다."
하지만, 합법적인 생각과 위법적인 폭력 사이의 구별은 순진해 빠졌을 뿐 아니라 위험하다. 모든 반이슬람주의 미사여구는 "우리 대 저들"이라는 사고방식을 유럽 사회에 강화시킴으로써 무슬림과 무슬림이 아닌 사람들 모두에게 해를 끼치는데, 이런 태도는 결국 폭력을 낳을 수 있고 낳을 것이다.

02

하위내용영역	배점	예상정답률
일반영어 A형 서술형	4점	40%

모범답안 The two words are "cultural exchange". Second, the title is "Dubious Summer Visa Program Denounced".

채점기준

- 4점: 모범답안과 같거나 유사하다.
- 2점: 둘 중 하나만 맞았다.
- 0점: 모범답안과 다르다.

어휘

deduction 삭감, 공제   defiantly 반항적으로
dubious 좋다고 할 수 없는 rally 집회
underpaid 제대로 급여를 못 받는
walk off 화가 나서 떠나 버리다

<한글 번역>

주먹을 흔들고 반항적으로 많은 언어로 소리를 지르는 수백 명의 외국인 학생들이 허쉬 초콜릿을 포장하는 공장에서의 그들의 일들을 버리고 떠났으며, 문화 교류를 위한다고 했던 여름 프로그램이 그들을 제대로 급여를 못 받는 노동자로 전락시켰다고 말했다. 중국, 나이지리아, 루마니아, 우크라이나로부터 학생들은 2달의 근무 기간을 주고 여행을 할 수 있도록 해주는 오래된 주 설립 여름 비자 프로그램을 통해 미국에 왔다. 그들은 영어를 연습하고 돈을 벌고 미국에서의 삶이 어떤지 배우기를 기대했다고 말한다. 어떤 면에서 그렇긴 했다. 약 400명의 외국인 학생들은 무거운 박스를 들어올리고 빠르게 돌아가는 생산 라인에서 리즈스의 사탕, 킷캣, 아몬드 조이들을 포장하는 상황에 처해졌다. 그리고 그중 많은 학생들이 야간 근무를 했다. 프로그램과 관련된 수수료와 임대료로 급여가 공제되고 난 뒤 학생들은 거대한 공장 앞 집회에서 많은 이들이 비자를 얻기 위해 고국에서 들인 비용을 커버할 만큼 돈을 벌고 있지 못하다고 말했다. 미국 사회에서 그들의 경험은 그들이 기대했던 것과 매우 달랐다. 그들에 따르면 문화적 교류는 없었다고 한다. 그저 일, 더 빨리 일, 일만 했다고 한다. 수년 동안 여름 비자 프로그램은 머나먼 나라에서 온 대학생들에게 미국 일상생활에 들어가고 오랜 친구를 사귈 수 있는 기회를 성공적으로 제공해 왔다. 하지만 최근 몇 년 동안 프로그램은 저임금과 예상치 못한 열악한 근무 환경으로 학생들의 불만을 야기시키고 있다.

03

하위내용영역	배점	예상정답률
일반영어 A형 서술형	4점	40%

모범답안 The word is "instinctive". Second, repetition connects regular nursing with human face.

（채점기준）

- 4점 : 모범답안과 같거나 유사하다.
- 2점 : 둘 중 하나만 맞았다.
- 0점 : 모범답안과 다르다.

<어 휘>

antecedent 선조, 선행 사건
contentment 만족감
forehead 이마   human connection 인맥
memory apparatus 기억 장치
solemnly 진지하게, 장엄하게

<한글 번역>

아기가 왜 웃는지는 유아기에 사람에 대한 애착을 형성할 때의 초기 단계를 이해하는 데 있어 중요한 요소가 된다. 먼저 미소가 가지고 있는 이런 반응에 선행 조건이 있다는 점을 기억하자. 심지어 초기 몇 주 안에서도 수유하는 도중이나 수유가 끝나고 난 후의 만족감은 약간의 만족스러운 미소 속에서 입을 이완하도록 한다. 만족을 나타내는 초기 미소는 본능적인 반응이고 아직까지 사람의 얼굴에 대한 반응은 아닌 것이다. 그렇다면 아기가 젖을 먹는 과정을 계속 관찰해 보자. 아기가 딱히 졸리지 않다면 엄마의 얼굴에 그의 눈을 진지하게 고정한다. 우리는 아기가 자신 앞에 놓인 얼굴 전체를 인식하지 않고 얼굴의 상단 부분인 눈과 이마에만 주목한다는 점을 실험을 통해 알게 됐다. 수유의 경험과 그것과 동반되는 사람의 얼굴의 반복을 통해서 수유와 사람 얼굴 사이의 연상 관계가 형성될 것이다. 더 나아가자면, 수유로부터 오는 즐거움, 혹은 만족감이 사람의 얼굴과 연관될 것이다. 이 즐거운 경험의 반복은 점진적으로 사람의 얼굴의 이미지를 기억 장치 표면에 그려낸다. 그리고 기억의 가장 기본적인 틀이 형성된다. 심상이 확고하게 자리 잡으면 사람의 얼굴의 시각적 모습이 인식된다. 다시 말해, 사람의 얼굴에 대한 시야는 심상을 불러일으키고 이 심상이 "기억"되는 것이다. 이제부터가 전환점이다. 이 기억은 단순히 모습만을 기반으로 한 기억이 아닌 보살핌을 통해 형성된 모습과 만족의 모두에서부터 오는 것이다. 이제는 사람의 얼굴에 대한 아기의 반응이 기쁨의 반응이라고 여겨진다. 아기는 사람의 얼굴과 마주하게 될 때 웃는다. 본능적인 반응으로 출발하여 돌봄에 대한 만족의 표현이 된 작은 미소는, 이제 가끔씩 보이는데 더 많은 얼굴을 접할수록, 마치 얼굴이 만족과 행복의 감정을 불러일으키기라도 하듯이 미소의 빈도수는 더 강화된다. 아기는 인생 최초로 인간적 관계를 맺은 셈이다.

04

하위내용영역	배점	예상정답률
일반영어 A형 서술형	4점	45%

모범답안 The main idea is the feminist movement of the 1960s freed women to express themselves and to pursue their own choices in life. Second, by the underlined part, the writer means that women could raise their expectations for themselves and no longer be limited to the house (i.e., marriage and family).

채점기준　　　　　　　　　　　　　　_Total 4pts

+ 2점 : 글의 요지를 "the feminist movement of the 1960s freed women to express themselves and to pursue their own choices in life"라 서술하였거나 유사하였다.

+ 2점 : 밑줄 친 부분의 의미를 "women could raise their expectations for themselves and no longer be limited to the house"라 서술하였거나 유사하였다.

어휘

attic 다락방	blare 요란하게 울리다
chauffeur 기사를 하다	chocking 숨막혀 하는
coerce into ~하도록 강요하다.	
defuse 뇌관을 제거하다; 완화시키다	
delusion 망상	denigrate 폄하하다(=belittle)
divinely ordained 신이 정한	
eat at ~을 갉아먹다; ~을 계속 괴롭히다	
hypochondria 심기증	neurosurgeon 신경외과 의사
potter 도예가	self-expression 자기 표현
self-fulfillment 자기 실현	whoop 와 하는 함성

한글 번역

어머니의 장례식을 마치고 60년대 "Punch and Judy" 프로그램이 방영하기 시작된 지 얼마 되지 않아 여성 운동이 수면 위로 떠올랐다. 사람들은 사실상 나라 전체에 퍼진 안도의 함성을 들을 수 있었다. 첫 번째이자 가장 중요한 메시지는 무언가를 해야 할 의무도 없고, 할 필요도 없고, 다른 선택권이 있다는 것인데, 그것이 결혼에 대한 반대이든, 요리에 대한 반대이든, 아기를 가져야 하는 운명에 대한 반대이든지간에, 이것은 할 필요가 없고, 강요당하지 않고, 가구에서 빛이 날 때까지 닦는 것이 아니며, 가정에서 벗어나 의미 있는 것을 찾는 것이었다.

뜨거운 베이킹 쟁반 위에 놓여진 쿠키를 잡으며 앞치마 속에서 숨막혀 하는 여성들에게 이 페미니스트 바람은 얼마나 상쾌한 공기를 가져왔는가! 여성들은 이제 그녀의 아이들, 마치 엄마가 그들의 시중인 듯 마냥 그들의 테니스 라켓, 피아노 수업, 각종 리그와 스케이트 대회 그리고 연습 날짜 등을 챙겨주는 것을 필요로 하는 아이들이 그녀의 생기를 빨아먹고, 꿈을 앗아가고 밝은 미래를 갉아먹는 대상으로 볼 수 있었다. 항상 주기만 하고 절대 받지 않는 것은 신이 정한 것이 아니라는 사실을 깨달았다. 그녀는 단순히 누군가의 부인이거나 엄마만은 아니었다. 그녀는 자신의 욕망을 내쉬었고 자신의 분노를 표출했으며, 갑자기 모든 것이 변했다. 미국 전체의 의식이라는 것이 자신의 옥상을 (더 위로) 들어올리고 집 밖으로 탈출했다. 여성들은 자신들이 한때 미친 듯이 날뛰었고, 나무도 타보고, 이스탄불에 가기 위해 계획도 세워보고, 오토바이를 타거나 대학원에 가려 했던 것을 기억했다. 그들은 수업을 듣고, 가라테도 배우고, 자연이 의도한 대로 그들의 체모를 길렀다. 여성들은 문화 속에서 편하되는 자신들의 이미지와 잡지나 책, 영화와 아동들의 읽을거리, 광고판 등에서의 그들을 향한 지적 능력과 용맹에 대한 모욕을 인식하기 시작했다. 모욕에 대해 보게 된 것은 이 모욕의 힘을 약화시켰다. 다락방에 있는 광녀는 온갖 망상, 우울증, 심기증을 버리고 신경외과 의사나 도공이 되기 위한 계획을 세웠다. 1960년대 후반에 이르러서 만약 한 여성이 베개 위에 자신의 머리를 대면, 그녀는 다시 삶과 사랑에 빠져, 악단의 연주, 자유의 도래, 되찾은 권위－자기 표현－자기만족－새로 깨어난 지적 능력에 대한 희망을 들을 수 있을 것이다.

05

하위내용영역	배점	예상정답률
일반영어 A형 서술형	4점	50%

모범답안 Campus is the ideal place for freshmen to start. Second, the word is "campus".

채점기준　　　　　　　　　　　　　　_Total 4pts

+ 2점 : 글의 요지를 "Campus is the ideal place (for freshmen) to start"라 서술하였거나 유사하였다.

+ 2점 : 빈칸에 들어갈 단어를 "campus"라 답하였다. 이것 외에는 답이 될 수 없다.

aplenty 풍부한, 많이
check against ~에 대한 억제책
communal living 공동체적 생활
exacerbate 악화시키다, 화나게 하다
live off ~에 의지해서 살다
residence hall 기숙사
self-management 자가 관리
upperclassman 상급생

한글 번역

대학교 기숙사 생활은 시야를 넓히고, 소중한 생활 기술을 습득하고, 자기 자신에 대해 배울 수 있는 매우 훌륭한 방법이다. 이것은 대학 교육의 목표와 완벽하게 일치한다. 기숙사 생활은 또한 필요하면 부를 수 있는 학교 기숙사 조언가와 같은 자원 주변에 학생들을 위치시킨다. 그리고 사실상 그들의 인생 중 처음으로 학생들은 스스로 자신들이 필요한 모든 것의 균형을 맞추려고 배워가는 과정에 놓여 있기에 많은 도움이 필요할 것이다. 오늘날 많은 학생들은 학문적으로 많은 지식과 준비를 갖추고 있지만 그들의 삶은 부모님이나 코치, 지도 상담가, 그리고 다른 이들에 의해 계획됐기에 자가 관리의 경험은 전혀 가지고 있지 않다. 물론 기숙사 생활은 많은 방해 요소도 도사리지만, 학생들이 자기 훈련을 연습해 볼 수 있는 비교적 안전한 장을 마련한다.

많은 대학생들이 학업으로 인해 압도되고 스트레스가 쌓이거나 불안과 우울증과 같은 혼란을 겪는 시기에 다양한 배경을 가지고 있는 모르는 사람과 함께 생활하는 것 ― 내가 선택한 사람과 방을 공유하는 것이 아닌 ― 은 대학 기숙사 생활의 또 하나의 이점이다. 앞서 제시한 문제들을 수반하고 악화시키는 "고립"에 대한 하나의 방어책이기도 하다. 기숙사 생활은 1학년들에게 특히 중요한데 그 이유는 그들이 주변을 잘 파악할 수 있도록 위치시키기 때문이다. 기숙사 생활은 다방면에서 학생들을 자유롭게 ― 예를 들어 어디서 다음 식사를 해야 하는지와 같은 고민 ― 하는 동시에 도서관과 같은 중요한 자원 근처에 머무를 수 있게 한다. 이미 알고 있는 친구와 가족의 네트워크 (바로 옆 주변도 배제하게 되는 상황)에 집중하게 하는 휴대폰의 효과를 줄이기 위해 아마도 집단 생활의 경험은 이전보다 현대에 더 필수적일 것이다. 캠퍼스 바깥에 사는 것은 상급생들에게 남겨진 선택권이라고 보면 될 것이다.

59회 문제은행

📖 본책 p.501

01

하위내용영역	배점	예상정답률
일반영어 B형 서술형	4점	45%

모범답안 The rich and poor show different behaviors, which could be misunderstood that the poor are the nicer of the two. One study revealed that the poor are more "contextually-focused" and sensitive to those around them while the rich are "self-focused" because the poor see external forces as responsible for their circumstances while the rich attribute this to their own efforts.

채점기준 _Total 4pts

+ 2점: 글의 topic sentence "The rich and poor show different behaviors, which could be misunderstood that the poor are the nicer of the two"를 명확하게 서술하였거나 유사하였다.

+ 2점: 글의 major supporting details 즉, "One study revealed that the poor are more "contextually-focused" and sensitive to those around them while the rich are "self-focused" because the poor see external forces as responsible for their circumstances while the rich attribute this to their own efforts"를 명확하게 서술하였거나 유사하였다.

감점 ▾

• 본문에 나오는 연속되는 6단어 이상을 사용하였다. −0.5pt
• 문단을 두 개나 그 이상으로 구성하였다. −0.5pt
• 문법이나 영어 표현을 합쳐 3개 이상 오류가 있다. −0.5pt

어휘

a furry of 수많은   altruism 이타심
disengage 자유롭게 하다, 해방하다
doodle 낙서하다
leave some room for doubt 약간의 의심의 여지를 남기다
mixed 의견이 갈리다
no matter how you look at 여러모로 보아
purportedly 소문에 의하면
ran ~라고 쓰여 있다

한글 번역

부자들이 가난한 사람들만큼 친절하지 않다고 보여주는 한 연구를 인용하는 수많은 기사들이 인터넷상에 불쑥 나타나고 있다. "부자들은 다르다 : 좋은 의미가 아니라"가 헤드라인을 장식한다. 연구자 중 한 명인 대커 켈트너는 "하층 계급의 사람들은 여러모로 보아, 더 높은 공감 능력, 친사회적 행동, 연민을 보여준다"고 MSNBC에 말했다. "미국 보수 정치운동인 티파티의 영웅 아인 랜드의 말을 인용하겠다. '이타심의 도덕성이야말로 인간이 거부해야 할 것이다'"라고 그가 언급했다.

그러나 연구는 약간의 의심의 여지를 남긴다. 한 연구자의 말에 의하면, "소득과 이타적인 행동에 대한 연구는 항상 조금씩 의견이 갈린다." 우선, (Michael Kraus, Paul Piff and Mr. Keltner에 의해 행해진) 켈트너 연구는 가난한 사람은 더 "상황 중심적"이며, 주변 사람들에게 더욱 민감함을 의미하는 "타인 지향적"이라고 이론을 제시한다. 반면, 부유한 사람은 "자기 중심적"이다. 연구에 의하면 그 이유는 가난한 사람들은 더욱 타인(직장 상사, 정부 정책 등)에게 의존적인 반면, 부자의 삶은 개인의 통제나 영향력 훨씬 아래에 있기 때문이다.

두 그룹은 또한 현재 상황을 다르게 간주한다. 가난한 사람은 그들이 외부적 요인에 의해서 가난하다고 믿는 반면, 부유한 사람은 자신의 노력으로 인해 부유하다고 믿는다. 하나의 예에 의하면, 연구는 사회적 배경이 다른 두 사람을 비디오 테이프에 녹화했고, 상류 계층의 사람은 핸드폰을 확인하거나 설문지를 끄적거리는 것과 같이 비언어적으로 덜 참여적으로 보이는 반면, 하층 계층의 사람은 사교적인 눈맞춤, 끄덕임과 웃음을 더 드러낸다는 것을 발견했다.

02

하위내용영역	배점	예상정답률
일반영어 A형 서술형	4점	45%

모범답안   Chinese art collectors are becoming more active in art auctions due to new wealth and a reaction to decades of repression. The enjoyment and collection of Western as well as Asian art wasn't allowed during the Mao years, and, now, the public display of art auctions allow the Chinese to prize art and develop taste and expertise.

채점기준   _Total 4pts

+ 2점 : 글의 topic sentence "Chinese art collectors are becoming more active in art auctions due to new wealth and a reaction to decades of repression"를 명확하게 서술하였거나 유사하였다.

+ 2점 : 글의 major supporting details 즉, "The enjoyment and collection of Western as well as Asian art wasn't allowed during the Mao years, and, now, the public display of art auctions allow the Chinese to prize art and develop taste and expertise"를 명확하게 서술하였거나 유사하였다.

감점 ▽
• 본문에 나오는 연속되는 6단어 이상을 사용하였다. −0.5pt
• 문단을 두 개나 그 이상으로 구성하였다. −0.5pt
• 문법이나 영어 표현을 합쳐 3개 이상 오류가 있다. −0.5pt

어휘

big-ticket 비싼, 고가의   didactic 교훈적인
disparage 깔보다, 얕보다   expertise 전문적 식견
frivolous 경솔한, 보잘것없는
nascent 초기의   surge 급증

한글 번역

경매 전문회사가 가을 판매를 준비함에 따라, 중국인 수집가들이 고가의 예술품에 그들의 패를 올리기에 경매 시장에 주요한 원동력이 될 것으로 보인다. 중국의 경제 활성화와 더불어, 예술품 수집가들은 아시아뿐만 아니라 서양 예술에 증가하는 관심을 보여주면서 시장에서 점차 영향력 있는 세력이 돼 왔다. 중국의 (예술품) 수집은 최근의 부의 반영일 뿐만 아니라, 중국이 문화를 부인했던, 억압적인 마오쩌둥(Mao) 시대의 반작용이기도 하다. 예술을 감상하는 것은, 교훈적인 목적을 제외하고는 하찮은 행위로 경시했던 중국인들에게, 평범한 미적 즐거움을 추구하고, 역사적인 산물을 되찾고, 현재의 풍요를 과시하는 자유가 해방돼 왔다. 이러한 구매 경향은 어떠한 점에서 잃어버린 시간을 보상하기 위한 노력이다. 50~60년 동안 중국에서는 어떠한 것도 일어나지 않았다. 기나긴 휴지 기간이었다. 지난 250년은 치욕의 세월이었다. 중국인들은 이제 예술을 칭송하고, 다시 되찾아야 한다는 의무감을 느낀다. 이러한 역사로 인해, 특히 경매와 관련된 공개 전시와 같은 중국인들의 예술품 구매는 아직은 초기적 현상 단계이다. 중국인 수집가는 이제 막 예술적인 시각과 (예술에 대한) 전문 지식을 발달시키기 시작했다.

03

하위내용영역	배점	예상정답률
일반영어 A형 서술형	4점	50%

모범답안 The word is "protective". Second, it means that spoiled children (are given too many things and) are overprotected by their parents. Like a spoiled child, an automobile is overprotected. (or, Like a spoiled child, who is overprotected by her/his parents, an automobile is overprotected.)

채점기준

- 4점 : 모범답안과 같다.
- 2점 : 둘 중 하나만 맞았다.
- 0점 : 모범답안과 다르다.

어 휘

civilized 문명화된
fender 자동차나 자전거의 흙받기
rust 녹   stiff 뻣뻣한
undercoat 밑칠용 페인트를 칠하다
waxed paper 왁스를 입힌 종이

한글 번역

내가 어떤 기분이냐에 따라 미국에서 우리가 보호 덮개를 어떻게 보호하는지에 대해 생각할 때 성가실 때도 있고, 우스울 때도 있고 교양 있다고 느껴질 때도 있다. 장보기를 마치고 집에 돌아와 짐을 풀 때 음식을 포장하는 보호 포장재나 장식 포장재가 겹겹이 싸여 있는 것을 보면 좋지 않은 인상을 받는다. 우리가 구매하는 것 중에 적어도 2번 이상 포장되어 있지 않은 제품은 찾아보기 어렵고, 계산대 직원은 그중 몇몇을 모아 또 하나의 작은 비닐봉지에 물건을 담는다. 이렇게 모여진 작은 비닐봉지 묶음들은 또 다시 모여 거대한 봉지에 담긴다. 만약 당신이 여러 작은 봉지가 담긴 몇몇의 큰 봉지들을 가지고 있다면 그들은 당신이 가지고 있는 모든 것을 담을 수 있도록 박스를 제공할 것이다. 우리가 구매하는 많은 것은 사실상 보호 포장을 전혀 필요로 하지 않는다. 오렌지 껍질은 그것 자체로 충분히 오렌지를 보호하지만 우리는 자연이 준 것에 만족하지 않는다. 우리는 10개의 오렌지를 비닐봉지나 망에 넣고, 그 묶음 봉지를 다시 한 번 종이 백에 담는다. 종이 백 안, 비닐봉지 안, 그리고 껍질 안에 놓인 오렌지는 아마도 자신이 어디에 있을지 궁금할 것이다. 쿠키나 크래커 박스에는 쿠키 옆에 종종 왁스를 입힌 종이가 있는데, 종이 상자 박스가 그 쿠키들과 왁스 종이를 담고 있고 포장용 장식이 그 종이 상자를 또 싸고 있다. 여기서 필요한 것은 단단한 장식용 왁스 종이인 듯하다. 우리는 자가용도 믿을 수 없을 정도의 보호 층으로 포장해 왔다. 우리는 튀는 먼지로부터 우리를 보호하기 위해 자동차 바퀴 위에 펜더를 설치한다. 그 후 우리는 펜더를 보호하기 위해 자동차 앞, 뒤로 범퍼를 장착한다. 우리는 여기서 범퍼가 녹슬지 않도록 하기 위해 범퍼위에 크롬을 입히고 펜더를 밑칠해 펜더도 먼지로부터 보호받을 수 있도록 한다. 자동차의 금속을 보호하기 위해 우리는 그 위에 페인트칠을 하고 페인트를 보호하기 위해 왁스를 바른다. 그리고 우리는 모든 것을 보호하기 위해 차고를 설치한다. 이것이 만약 어린 아이였다면, 이 아이는 버릇없어질 것이 틀림없다.

04

하위내용영역	배점	예상정답률
일반영어 A형 서술형	4점	50%

모범답안 First, gerontogens are substances and activities that can accelerate the aging process. Second, most of the variation in the human life span is influenced by such environmental factors as accidents, injuries, and exposure to substances, not by genes.

채점기준 _ Total 4pts

+ 2점: 제로토젠을 "substances and activities that can speed up the aging process"라 서술하였다.
  ▷ "factors that can accelerate the aging process"라 답을 했어도 2점을 준다.
+ 2점: 쌍둥이 연구가 말하려는 요지가 "인간의 노화 작용을 가속화시키는 것은 타고난 유전자가 아니라 환경적 요인"이라고 서술하였다.
  ▷ 모범답안과 내용은 유사하나 "genes"와 "environmental factors"란 핵심어가 빠져 있으면 각각 0.5점 감점한다.

감점 ☑ 본문에 있는 내용을 8단어 이상 그대로 사용하였다. −0.5pt

어휘

arsenic 비소   benzene 벤젠
beta-amyloid 아밀로이드 베타 단백질
chemotherapy 화학 요법
cocktail 혼합제   frailty 허약함, 노쇠함
lag behind ~보다 뒤처지다
mental decline 정신 쇠약   telomere 말단 소립

한글 번역

왜 우리의 신체는 다른 속도로 늙어갈까? 왜 어떤 사람은 나이 70에 마라톤을 뛸 수 있고 어떤 사람은 지팡이를 쓸 수밖에 없을까? "제론토젠"(노화를 촉진시키는 환경 물질을 포함한 요인)에 대한 더 많은 연구가 필요하다. 가능한 제로토젠으로는 지하수의 비소, 산업용 배기가스의 벤젠, 햇빛의 자외선, 담배의 4000가지의 화학물 혼합제가 있다. 과도한 칼로리 섭취나 심리적 스트레스를 받는 것과 같은 활동도 포함될 수 있다. 이러한 요인들에 집중한다면 노체의 분자 변화를 연구하거나 장수와 관련된 유전자를 찾는 것과 같은 더 인기 있는 접근법을 보완할 수 있을 것이다. 당장 내일 과학자들이 안티에이징 약을 개발했다고 하더라도 사람들은 약을 수십 년 동안 복용해야 할 것이다. 건강한 사람들에게 오랫동안 약을 먹이는 것은 도전적이고 부작용은 항상 있기 마련이다. 만약 우리가 노화에 영향을 미치는 환경적 요인을 발견한다면 그것은 우리가 오늘날 바로 사용할 수 있는 지식이다.

쌍둥이 연구는 인간 수명의 변화의 오직 25%만이 유전자의 영향을 받는다는 사실을 밝혀냈다. 나머지 75%는 분명 사건, 부상, 노화 촉진 물질에 대한 노출을 포함한 다른 요인일 것이다. 환경 요인이 노화를 촉진한다는 생각이 한동안 있어 왔지만 제로토젠에 대한 연구는 노화 연구의 다른 분야에 비해 뒤처지고 있다. 많은 종류의 화학 요법과 안티-HIV 약들이 노쇠함과 정신 쇠약과 같은 노화의 시작을 가속화할 수 있다는 사실이 밝혀지자 과학자들은 환경 물질에 대한 관심을 더욱 높였다.

제로토젠에 대한 탐구는 어느 정도 생물학적 연령을 측정하는 더 나은 방법에 대한 탐구이다. 다양한 방법이 있긴 하지만 각자 나름대로 불완전하다. 연구자들은 뇌를 조사해서 알츠하이머병과 연관된 아밀로이드 베타 단백질의 레벨을 측정할 수도 있다. 하지만 이 레벨이 신체의 다른 부위의 노화를 반영해주지는 않는다. 또한, 말단 소립(시간에 따라 쇠약해지는 DNA 끝의 보호 캡)을 측정해 볼 수도 있다. 하지만 측정하는 방법이 어렵고 비용이 많이 들며 말단 소립의 길이는 같은 나이이더라도 사람마다 선천적으로 다르다.

05

하위내용영역	배점	예상정답률
일반영어 B형 서술형	4점	50%

모범답안 First, the Mountain Resort Utility shows the biggest reduction in revenue (with 24 percent decline). Second, this utility is more susceptible to revenue shocks because the dramatic reduction in revenue comes to pass when some customers, who are high-volume water users paying a premium for their extra expenses, reduces their water use.

채점기준   _Total 4pts

+ 2점 : 세수가 가장 많이 줄어든 곳이 "the Mountain Resort Utility"라 서술하였다.

+ 2점 : the Mountain Resort Utility가 세수 충격에 더 민감한 이유가 "물을 과다하게 많이 써서 추가로 비용을 더 냈던 소비자가 물 소비를 줄였기 때문"이라 서술하였다.

▷ "high-volume water"를 사용한 사람이 누구인지 언급이 없으면 1점 감점; 과다 사용한 것에 "a premium"(할증료)을 지불하는 사람이 누구인지 언급이 없으면 1점 감점한다.

어휘

by no means 결코 ~가 아니다
curtail 삭감하다
from a standpoint ~의 관점에서
infrastructure 기반시설
pay a premium 할증료를 내다
prolonged 장기간의
remarkably 현저하게   revenue 수입
whopping 큰

한글 번역

가격 책정은 물 사용과 같은 행동 조성에 효과적인 도구이다. 급수 시설은 가격 책정의 효과를 알기 때문에 고객의 물 절약을 위한 수도 요금을 채택했다. "절약 요금"이라 불리는 이 요금은 형태는 다양하지만 공통적으로 고객의 물 사용량이 증가하면 갤런당 가격을 높게 된다. 전국의 급수 시설들은 물 사용 감소량을 들먹이면서 가격 책정의 힘을 증명할 수 있다. 이는 절약 관점에서 좋은 소식이지만 예기치 못한 수입 감소를 가져오기도 한다.

수도사업자가 장기적인 가뭄과 낙후된 시설로 난관에 봉착했기 때문에 좀 더 신뢰성 있는 수입에 대한 요구가 그 어느 때보다도 중요하다. 불행하게도 이 요구는 절약을 급수 시설의 반갑지 않은 의붓자식으로 만들 수 있다.

물 수입 변동 측정 및 완화 기구는 북미 지역의 급수 시설 3곳으로부터 회계 자료를 받아 가격 책정이 어떻게 고객의 사용 패턴과 반응하여 수입 안정성과 불안정성을 야기하는지 조사했다.

예를 들어, 만약 3곳의 고객들이 물 사용량을 15%만큼 절약했다면 물 수입에서 일어나는 변화는 결과적으로 전혀 같지 않았다. 남동 해안 시설의 요금은 단지 7%의 수입 감소를 보여줬으므로 꽤 성공적이었다. 산악 휴양지 시설은 반면 24%의 매우 높은 수입 감소를 보여줬다. 산악 휴양지의 고객 대부분은 매달 만 갤런보다 적게 사용하지만 14%의 고객층은 2만 5천 갤런 이상의 물을 쓴다. 놀랍게도 이들은 한 달 평균 7만 3천 백 갤런의 물을 사용한다. 할증료를 내는 대량구매 고객들이 사용량을 줄이게 되면 결과적으로 수입에서 큰 폭이 감소하게 된다.

한글 번역

대다수의 최고경영자들도 물론 포함해 관리자들에게는 대체로 우두머리로 섬기는 상사가 있다. 이 상사만큼이나 관리자의 실적과 성공에 중요한 사람은 별로 없다. 그런데도 경영 서적과 경영 교과 과정에는 부하를 다루는 방법에 관한 충고는 풍부하지만 상사를 다루는 일에 언급이나마 한 것은 많지 않다. 관리자로서 상사를 다루는 일이 얼마나 중요한가를 깨닫기는커녕, 상사를 다룰 수 있다는 가능성 자체를 믿는 사람조차 거의 없는 듯하다. 관리자들은 상사의 일에 투덜대지만 상사가 남자이건 여자이건 그를 다루려고 애쓰지도 않는다.

하지만 상사를 다루는 일은 꽤 간단하다 ― 사실 부하를 다루는 일보다 대체로 훨씬 더 간단하다. 상사를 될 수 있는 대로 유능하게 하고 공을 세우게 하는 것은 부하의 임무이자 부하 자신에게 이롭다. 아직도 자기 자신의 성공을 위한 최선의 처방은 결국 성공의 길을 걷고 있는 상사 밑에서 일을 하는 것이다. 따라서 첫째 준수 사항은 1년에 적어도 한 번은 상사에게 가서 "당신의 일을 돕기 위해 저나 저의 직원이 무엇을 해드릴까요? 우리가 하는 일 중 당신에게 방해가 되고 당신의 생활을 더 어렵게 만드는 것이 있다면 무엇입니까?"라고 묻는 것이다. 이것은 너무나 당연한 사실처럼 들린다. 하지만 이런 명백한 사실을 그대로 실천하는 일은 좀처럼 없다. 왜냐하면 유능한 중역들까지도 관리자를 50년 전의 정의인 부하들의 일에 대해 책임이 있는 사람이라고 그릇된 정의를 내리고, 그렇기 때문에 관리자들에게 상사의 실적과 유무능에 대한 책임이 있다고 알아차리지 못하는 경향이 있기 때문이다. 그러나 올바른 정의의 관리자란 자기 자신의 실적에 영향을 주는 모든 사람의 실적에 대해 책임이 있는 사람을 말한다. 관리자의 실적에 영향을 주는 첫 번째 사람이 상사이며 따라서 상사의 실적을 관리자가 제일 먼저 책임을 져야 하는 것이다.

05

하위내용영역	배점	예상정답률
일반영어 B형 서술형	4점	45%

모범답안 Whites' representation is highest in the recruitment stage. Second, it is because whites can overcome the Hiring Barriers. In other words, whites meet educational requirements and physical fitness requirements as opposed to other ethnic/racial minorities.

채점기준
_ Total 4pts

+ **1점** : 지원 단계에서 가장 많이 대표된 것이 백인 (whites)이라 서술하였다. White나 Caucasian이라 답을 해도 맞는 것으로 한다.

+ **3점** : 백인이 고용 단계에서 가장 많은 이유가 "교육적 자격 요건과 건강적 자격 요건"을 충족하는 경우가 많았기 때문이라 서술하였다.

▷ 백인이 고용 단계에서 가장 많은 이유가 "교육적 자격 요건과 건강적 자격 요건"을 충족하는 경우가 많았기 때문이라 서술하였고 동시에 "lack of awareness" "lack of interest" "failure to qualify"도 영향을 미쳤다라고 서술하였으면 3점을 준다.

▷ 위와 같이 서술하지 않고 "lack of awareness", "lack of interest", "failure to qualify"라고만 서술하였으면 1점만 준다.

어휘

be traced to ~로 거슬러 올라가다
benchmark 기준
count towards (장차 이루기 원하는 일의 일부로) 포함되다 (가산되다)
demographics 인구 통계(자료)
fall off (양·수가) 줄다, (질이) 떨어지다
fall short of ~에 미치지 못하다
law enforcement 법 집행
outreach (지역 주민에 대한 기관의 적극적인) 봉사(원조·지원) 활동
sergeant 병장, 경사
target population 표적인구

한글 번역

다양성을 증가시키려는 노력에도 불구하고, 많은 법 집행 기관에서 인종/민족적 소수 집단 그리고 여성의 대표성은 노동 인구 기준점에 한참 못 미치고, 이런 것이 그들의 공동체의 인구 통계 지표를 반영하지 못하는 결과로 나타난다.

인력에서의 다양성을 성취하는 데 장애가 되는 것들이 경력 주기의 다양한 지점에서 나타날 수 있다―신입 모집 단계, 고용 단계, 승진 단계 등에서 그렇다. 도표는 어떻게 장애물들이 그들 스스로 경찰 부서에서 나타나고 있는지 보여준다. 이 부서에서, 백인은 그 지역 노동력 풀에서 그들의 대표성에 있어 증가된 비율로 지원하고 고용되고 승진된다.

인종과 성비에 따른 경찰 부서 X의 구성 비율(퍼센트)					
	백인	히스패닉계	아시안/태평양 제도민	흑인	여성
지역 노동력 풀 인구	50	30	10	10	50
지원자	60	20	10	10	30
취직한 경찰관	65	20	5	10	20
경사 이상	70	20	5	5	10

고용 장애물의 첫 번째 지표는 그 직업에 지원하는 여성과 인종/민족적 소수 집단의 불충분한 숫자에 있다. 법 집행 분야에서 이 문제는 하나 또는 세 가지의 요소의 결합으로 거슬러 올라간다. 즉, 그것들은 표적인구가 불균형적으로 잘 알지 못하고, 자격이 안 되고, 무관심하다는 데 있다. 이러한 인식의 부족은 외부의 활동과 행사의 결여를 나타낸다; 즉, 인구 통계 자료에 따르면 충분한 자격이 있는 여성과 인종/민족적 소수 집단 후보자를 찾을 수 있는 지역에서도 충분한 신입 모집이 없다. 관심 부족과 자격 미달은 더 복잡한 문제다.

대부분의 법 집행 기관에서는 다양한 필수 요구 사항을 갖고 있다. 건강, 교육, 그리고 다른 사회 경제적 통계들은 몇몇 필수 요구 사항들이 여성과 인종/민족적 소수 집단에게 장애물이 된다는 걸 보여준다. 대부분의 법 집행 기관들은 지원자들에게 고등학교 졸업장 또는 검정고시 자격증을 요구한다.

그러나, 전국 고등학교에서 흑인과 히스패닉계의 졸업률은 백인보다 거의 20%가 낮다. 결과적으로, 인종/민족적 소수 집단의 인력풀에서 교육적 요구 사항을 충족시킬 가능성이 더욱 낮아지는 것이다.

건강과 의료적 요구 사항을 충족시키는 것 또한 높은 비만율로 고통을 겪는 흑인과 히스패닉계에게 장애물을 나타낸다. 예를 들면 LA 카운티 내에서 흑인 아이들이 21.6%, 그리고 히스패닉계 아이들이 27.4%인 것에 비교하면, 히스패닉계가 아닌 백인 아이들의 비만율은 2007년에 12.8%였다. LA 경찰서의 아시안 고용 목표에 포함되는 태평양 제도민들은 학령인구의 아이들 가운데 비만율이 가장 높은데, 무려 비만율이 35%에 육박한다.

06

하위내용영역	배점	예상정답률
일반영어 B형 서술형	4점	45%

모범답안 There are two reasons why New Guineans have come to be smarter than Westerners. First, they are genetically superior to Westerners. Second, they are superior in escaping the devastating developmental disadvantages under which most children in Western societies now grow up.

채점기준 _Total 4pts

+ 2점 : "There are two reasons why New Guineans have come to be smarter than Westerners"를 명확하게 서술하였거나 이와 유사하였다.

+ 2점 : "First, they are genetically superior to Westerners(1점). Second, they are superior in escaping the devastating develomental disadvantages under which most children in Westerne societies now grow up(1점)."

감점 🔽

• 본문에 나오는 연속되는 6단어 이상을 사용하였다. −0.5pt
• 문단을 두 개나 그 이상으로 구성하였다. −0.5pt
• 문법이나 영어 표현을 합쳐 3개 이상 오류가 있다. −0.5pt

어휘

chronic 만성적인   epidemic diseases 전염병
infectious (특히 공기를 통해) 전염되는
irreversible (이전 상태로) 되돌릴 수 없는
judiciary 법관, 사법부
mental stunting 정신적 발달 저해
New Guinean 뉴기니인
smallpox 천연두   tribal warfare 부족 전쟁

한글 번역

유럽인들은 인구 밀도가 높고 중앙 집권적 정치 체제, 경찰력, 사법 제도 등이 갖춰진 사회에서 수천 년 살아왔다. 그와 같은 사회에서는 조밀한 인구 속에 널리 퍼지는 천연두와 같은 유행병이 역사상 주된 사망 원인이었으면, 상대적으로 살인은 드문 편이고 전쟁도 늘 있는 일이라기보다는 예외적인 경우에 가까웠다. 그래서 치명적인 전염병을 피할 수 있었던 유럽인들 대부분은 다른 잠재적 사망 원인들로부터도 무사히 벗어나서 자신의 유전자를 후손에게 전달했다. 오늘날 서구에서 사산되지 않고 태어난 신생아들은 자신의 지능이나 유전자와는 상관없이 치명적인 전염병으로 죽는 일도 거의 없고 대부분 무사히 성장해 자식을 낳는다. 그와는 대조적으로 뉴기니인들의 사회는 인구 조밀성 유행병이 진화할 수 있을 만큼 인구 밀도가 높지 않았다. 그 대신 전통적인 뉴기니인들을 살인, 만성적인 부족 간 전쟁, 각종 사고, 먹거리 조달 등의 어려움으로 높은 사망률을 견뎌내야 했다.

이와 같은 전통적 뉴기니 사회에서는 지능이 낮은 사람들보다 높은 사람들이 사망률의 각종 원인을 무사히 피하기가 쉽다. 그러나 전통적 유럽 사회에서 유행병이 기인한 사망률은 지능과는 거의 관계가 없었고 그 대신 체내의 세부적인 화학 작용에 따르는 유전적 저항력이 중요했다. 예를 들어 B형이나 O형의 혈액형을 가진 사람들은 A형의 혈액형을 가진 사람들에 비하여 천연두에 대한 저항력이 더 강하다. 다시 말해, 지능과 관련된 유전자를 촉진시키는 자연 선택은 뉴기니에서 훨씬 더 가혹했던 반면, 인구가 조밀하고 정치적으로 복잡한 사회에서는 체내 화학 작용을 위한 자연 선택이 더 우세했다고 볼 수 있다.

이러한 유전적 이유 외에도, 또 다른 이유가 있다. 현대 유럽과 미국의 어린이들은 텔레비전, 라디오, 영화 등을 수동적으로 즐기면서 많은 시간을 보낸다. 미국 가정의 평균적인 텔레비전 시청 시간은 하루 일곱 시간 정도이다. 반면에 전통적 뉴기니 어린이들에겐 그와 같은 수동적 오락을 즐길 기회가 사실상 전무하며 그 대신 그들은 다른 어린이들이나 어른들과 대화를 나누거나 함께 노는 등 어떤 능동적인 일을 하면서 깨어있는 시간의 거의 대부분을 보낸다. 아동 발달에 대한 거의 모든 연구는 정신적 발달을 촉진시키는 데는 어린 시절의 자극과 활동이 중요하는 것을 역설한다. 또한 어린 시절에 자극이 부족할 경우에는 정신적 발달이 돌이킬 수 없을 만큼 크게 저해될 수도 있는 것을 강조한다. 이런 영향이 뉴기니인 들의 정신적 기능을 평균적으로 더 우세하게 만들어 주는 비유전적 요소인 셈이다.

유희태 일반영어
❹ 문제은행
모범답안

초판 1쇄	2014년 4월 14일	
2판 1쇄	2016년 6월 15일	
3판 1쇄	2019년 2월 20일	
2쇄	2019년 5월 10일	
3쇄	2019년 7월 10일	
4판 1쇄	2020년 10월 23일	
2쇄	2021년 7월 30일	
3쇄	2022년 4월 15일	
5판 1쇄	2023년 1월 10일	

저자와의
협의하에
인지생략

저자 유희태 **발행인** 박 용 **발행처** (주)박문각출판
표지디자인 박문각 디자인팀
등록 2015. 4. 29. 제2015-000104호
주소 06654 서울시 서초구 효령로 283 서경 B/D
팩스 (02)584-2927
전화 교재 문의 (02)6466-7202 동영상 문의 (02)6466-7201

ISBN 979-11-6704-885-1

유희태 일반영어

❹ 문제은행

PMG 박문각

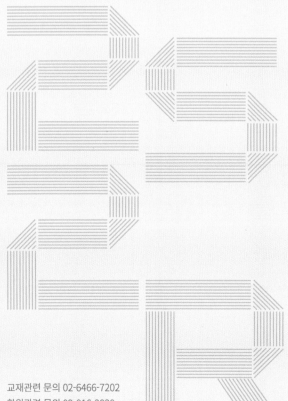

교재관련 문의 02-6466-7202
학원관련 문의 02-816-2030
온라인강의 문의 02-6466-7201

www.pmg.co.kr

13370

ISBN 979-11-6704-885-1